A Companion to the Literature and
Culture of the American West

Blackwell Companions to Literature and Culture

This series offers comprehensive, newly written surveys of key periods and movements and certain major authors, in English literary culture and history. Extensive volumes provide new perspectives and positions on contexts and on canonical and post-canonical texts, orientating the beginning student in new fields of study and providing the experienced undergraduate and new graduate with current and new directions, as pioneered and developed by leading scholars in the field.

Published Recently

A COMPANION TO

THE LITERATURE AND CULTURE OF THE AMERICAN WEST

EDITED BY

NICOLAS S. WITSCHI

⊛WILEY-BLACKWELL

A John Wiley & Sons, Ltd., Publication

This edition first published 2011
© 2011 Blackwell Publishing Ltd

Blackwell Publishing was acquired by John Wiley & Sons in February 2007. Blackwell's publishing program has been merged with Wiley's global Scientific, Technical, and Medical business to form Wiley-Blackwell.

Registered Office
John Wiley & Sons Ltd, The Atrium, Southern Gate, Chichester, West Sussex, PO19 8SQ, United Kingdom

Editorial Offices
350 Main Street, Malden, MA 02148-5020, USA
9600 Garsington Road, Oxford, OX4 2DQ, UK
The Atrium, Southern Gate, Chichester, West Sussex, PO19 8SQ, UK

For details of our global editorial offices, for customer services, and for information about how to apply for permission to reuse the copyright material in this book please see our website at www.wiley.com/wiley-blackwell.

The right of Nicolas S. Witschi to be identified as the author of the editorial material in this work has been asserted in accordance with the UK Copyright, Designs and Patents Act 1988.

Library of Congress Cataloging-in-Publication Data

A companion to the literature and culture of the American west / edited by Nicolas S. Witschi.
    p. cm. – (Blackwell companions to literature and culture)
  Includes bibliographical references and index.
  ISBN 978-1-4051-8733-6 (hardback)
  1. American literature–History and criticism.   2. West (U.S.)–In literature.   3. West (U.S.)–In mass media.   4. West (U.S.)–In art. I. Witschi, Nicolas S., 1966–
  PS169.W4C66 2011
  700'.45878–dc22

                                          2011000566

A catalogue record for this book is available from the British Library.

This book is published in the following electronic formats: ePDFs ISBN 9781444396577; Wiley Online Library ISBN 9781444396591; ePub ISBN 9781444396584

Set in 11 on 13 pt Garamond 3 by Toppan Best-set Premedia Limited
Printed and bound in Malaysia by Vivar Printing Sdn Bhd

1   2011

Contents

Notes on Contributors

Chadwick Allen is Associate Professor of English at The Ohio State University. The author of *Blood Narrative: Indigenous Identity in American Indian and Maori Literary and Activist Texts* (2002), he also writes about Indians in popular westerns.

Nina Baym is Swanlund Chair and Center for Advanced Study Professor of English Emerita at the University of Illinois. She is General Editor of the Norton Anthology of American Literature, and has published widely on American literary topics, especially on women writers. Her most recent book is *Women Writers of the American West, 1833–1927* (2011).

Peter J. Blodgett is the H. Russell Smith Foundation Curator of Western American History at the Huntington Library. Since joining the Huntington's staff in 1985 he has spoken and written widely on various aspects of the history of the American West and is the author of *Land of Golden Dreams: California in the Gold Rush Decade 1848–1858* (1999).

Neil Campbell is Professor of American Studies and Research Manager at the University of Derby, UK. He has published widely in American studies, including the book *American Cultural Studies* (with Alasdair Kean) and articles and chapters on John Sayles, Terrence Malick, Robert Frank, J.B. Jackson, and many others. His major research project is an interdisciplinary trilogy on the contemporary American West: *The Cultures of the American New West* (2000), *The Rhizomatic West* (2008), and *Post-Western* (forthcoming).

Krista Comer is Associate Professor of English at Rice University in Houston, Texas. Her books include *Landscapes of the New West* (1999) and *Surfer Girls in the New World Order* (2010). She is completing a memoir.

Nancy Cook teaches courses in western American studies at the University of Montana, Missoula. Her publications include essays on ranching, on Montana writers, and on authenticity in western American writing.

Corey K. Creekmur is an Associate Professor of English and Film Studies at the University of Iowa, where he also directs the Institute for Cinema and Culture. He is currently completing a book, *Cattle Queens and Lonesome Cowboys: Gender and Sexuality in the Western*, and has published numerous essays on American and South Asian popular culture.

Hal Crimmel teaches at Weber State University, in Ogden, Utah. He is the author of *Dinosaur: Four Seasons on the Green and Yampa Rivers* (2007) and co-editor of *Teaching About Place: Learning from the Land* (2008).

Brian W. Dippie, Professor Emeritus of History at the University of Victoria, BC, has published extensively on western American art. His most recent books are *The 100 Best Illustrated Letters of Charles M. Russell* (2008) and *Crossroads: Desert Caballeros Western Museum* (2010).

John L. Escobedo teaches at the University of Colorado at Boulder. His literary field of study includes US Latino/a literature and Chicano/a literature with a specialty in hybrid cultural productions and mestizo/a racial identities. He is currently completing his first book, *Dangerous Crossroads: Unraveling the Mestizo/a Conundrum.*

David Fenimore directs the undergraduate program in English at the University of Nevada, Reno. He writes on western American culture and moonlights as a Chautauqua performer, portraying, among other characters, Woody Guthrie and Zane Grey.

Audrey Goodman is Associate Professor of English at Georgia State University. She is the author of *Translating Southwestern Landscapes* (2002) and *Atomic Homelands* (2010).

Cathryn Halverson is an Assistant Professor in American Literature and Culture at the University of Copenhagen, Denmark, and the author of *Maverick Autobiographies: Women Writers and the American West* (2004). She is completing a book entitled *Playing House in the American West: Western Women's Literary Autobiography, 1840–1980.*

Eric Heyne is Professor of English at the University of Alaska Fairbanks, editor of *Desert, Garden, Margin, Range: Literature on the American Frontier*, and has published in *Extrapolation, Narrative, Western American Literature*, and elsewhere.

Hsuan L. Hsu, an Assistant Professor of English at UC Davis, is author of *Geography and the Production of Space in Nineteenth-Century American Literature* (2010) and editor of Sui Sin Far's *Mrs. Spring Fragrance* (Broadview, forthcoming).

Alex Hunt is Associate Professor of US literature at West Texas A&M University. He is editor and co-editor, respectively, of *The Geographical Imagination of Annie Proulx* (2008) and *Postcolonial Green* (2010). He has also published numerous articles on the American West with attention to postcolonialism, literary cartography, ethnicity, and the environment.

Michael K. Johnson teaches at the University of Maine-Farmington. He is author of *Black Masculinity and the Frontier Myth in American Literature* (2002) and has published in *Western American Literature* and *African American Review*.

Susan Kollin is Professor of American Literature at Montana State University, where she also teaches in the programs in American studies and gender and women's studies. Her essays have appeared in *American Literary History*, *Contemporary Literature*, and *Modern Fiction Studies*. She also edited *Postwestern Cultures: Literature, Theory, Space* (2007).

Nathaniel Lewis is the author of *Unsettling the Literary West* (2003) and co-editor, with William Handley, of *True West: Authenticity and the American West* (2004). He currently chairs the English department at St. Michael's College in Vermont.

Bonney MacDonald is Professor of English and Department Chair of English, Philosophy, and Modern Languages at West Texas A & M University. She has published *Henry James's Italian Hours* (1990) and essays and articles on writers such as William Dean Howells, Mark Twain, Hamlin Garland, John Muir, Frederick Jackson Turner, Gretel Ehrlich, William Kittredge, and Wallace Stegner. She is currently at work on a book on Turner and modern theories of mobility.

Susan Naramore Maher has published widely on the literature of the Great Plains and of the American and Canadian West. With Thomas P. Lynch, she is co-editor of a forthcoming collection, *Artifacts and Illuminations: Critical Essays on Loren Eisely* (2011). She is currently completing a book-length study entitled *Deep Maps: The Literary Cartography of the Great Plains*. Dr. Maher is Dean of the College of Liberal Arts at the University of Minnesota Duluth.

Barbara Barney Nelson teaches at Sul Ross State University in Alpine, Texas. She has published extensively about the rural West, including *The Wild and the Domestic* (2000) and *God's Country or Devil's Playground* (2002).

Tara Penry is Associate Professor of English at Boise State University, where she teaches nineteenth-century and western American literature, and where she has edited or co-edited the BSU Western Writers series since 2000. Her essays on nineteenth-century California periodicals have appeared in *Western American Literature* and *American Literary Realism*. She has also published on American sentimental literature, western and otherwise.

Karen E. Ramirez is the Associate Director of the Sewall Residential Academic Program at the University of Colorado, Boulder, where she teaches courses on Native American literature, women's literature, and the American West.

Gary Scharnhorst is Distinguished Professor of English at the University of New Mexico, editor or author of over thirty-five books, editor of the journal *American Literary Realism*, and editor in alternating years of the research annual *American Literary Scholarship*.

Jefferson D. Slagle is a member of the English faculty at Brigham Young University-Idaho. He is the author of articles on authenticity in the western dime novel and the construction of authenticity in the West. His current project examines the interplay between western performance and character representation in text westerns.

Stephen Tatum is a Professor of English and Director of the Environmental Humanities graduate program at the University of Utah. His most recent book is *In the Remington Moment* (2010).

Kathleen Washburn is an Assistant Professor of American and Native American literature at the University of New Mexico. Her work focuses on configurations of indigenous modernity in nineteenth- and twentieth-century literature and culture.

Edward Watts is Professor of English at Michigan State University. His books include *An American Colony: Regionalism and the Roots of Midwestern Culture* (2002) and *In this Remote Country: Colonial French Culture in the Anglo-American Imagination, 1780–1860* (2006).

O. Alan Weltzien is a Professor of English at the University of Montana Western, in Dillon, MT, where he teaches a range of courses in Montana, western American, and American literatures as well as courses in nonfiction and nature and environmental writing. He has authored, edited, or co-edited five books, and published dozens of articles. He is currently working on a book about the Pacific Northwest's volcanoes.

Nicolas S. Witschi is the author of *Traces of Gold: California's Natural Resources and the Claim to Realism in Western American Literature* (2002), of a Western Writers series monograph on *Alonzo "Old Block" Delano* (2006), and of articles and essays on Mary Austin, John Muir, Sinclair Lewis, and Henry James. At present he is Associate Professor and Associate Chair in the Department of English at Western Michigan University.

Gioia Woods was 2010 President of the Western Literature Association, author of the Western Writers series monograph *Gary Nabhan*, and co-author of *Western Subjects: Autobiographical Writing in the North American West* (2004). She is Associate Professor of Humanities in the Department of Comparative Cultural Studies at Northern Arizona University.

Daniel Worden is Assistant Professor in the Department of English at the University of Colorado at Colorado Springs. His work on representations of the American West from dime novel westerns to HBO's *Deadwood* has appeared in *Arizona Quarterly*, *The Canadian Review of American Studies*, and the anthology *Violence, the Arts, and Willa Cather*.

Part I
Introduction

1

Imagining the West

Nicolas S. Witschi

At the first meeting of a class I recently taught on western American literature, I asked my students to come to the next session prepared to share one interesting fact, impression, or idea that they could find out about the American West, something they did not already know. I did not specify a particular research method or source, and I left the definition of "American West" entirely up to them. Having learned through our initial conversations that very few of the students in this class could claim any real familiarity with the region other than the vague sense that "west" meant a direction on a map that indicated a region of the nation other than their own, my goal was simply to see what a group of students from the upper Midwest would come up with, to gauge their first impressions or, at the very least, learn the dominant clichés and assumptions with which they may have come into the class. Not surprisingly, the overwhelmingly favorite research method for this assignment was the online search engine. What was slightly surprising, however, at least to me, was the fact that not a single student brought in a piece of information about any time period other than the mid- to late nineteenth century. We heard about famous gunfighters, about notorious frontier cattle towns, even about some women of ill repute with hearts of gold. To be sure, not all of the mini-reports presented genre clichés – there were reports on the city of Seattle's rebuilding after an 1889 fire and about travelers' experiences on the overland trail, mostly from the California Gold Rush and afterward. A few students brought in information about such conflicts as the Modoc War and Custer's defeat at Little Bighorn, while one student presented information about the establishment of Yellowstone National Park. In short, what my students found when they went looking for the American West was by and large the late nineteenth-century West of popular culture and national mythology.

A Companion to the Literature and Culture of the American West, First Edition. Edited by Nicolas S. Witschi.

Although it would be easy to attribute the outcome of this admittedly brief, impression-based assignment to my students' rather limited understanding of the American West, the ostensible root causes are in fact much more complex. If the kinds of information that predominate in the results of a Google search are any indicator, then my students are not alone when, as a phrase, the "American West" evokes for them a preponderance of images, ideas, and historical artifacts from the post-Civil War, pre-twentieth-century period, the so-called "Old West." Which is to say, the typical results of a typical search-engine query actually reinforce, by virtue of their higher ranking through popularity, the kinds of ideas and impressions one might be seeking to move beyond. Of course, one must almost certainly first have a sense that there is a potential "beyond" to move toward when it comes to locating a powerful mythos within a larger framework of cultural production and history. This very well could mean that many of my students, upon finding the "Old West," were confident that they had found the West as it is more broadly understood. Such an assumption would not be entirely wrong, but as residents, artists, and scholars of the West have long recognized, it does not even come close to being entirely correct either; the West of myth is merely one extraordinarily powerful, overdetermined facet of a much more complex and, hence, much more interesting array of regionally specific cultural productions. My students had certainly heard about issues related to immigration along the borders of the Southwest, and they knew quite a lot about the popular music scenes in Los Angeles and Seattle. But in their minds, these phenomena were not part of something called "the American West," at least not at the start of our class. Bridging these different aspects of the geographically western portions of the United States thus posed both a problem and an opportunity, the very same challenges faced by a *Companion* such as this one.

On the one hand, as noted above the American West is a place. Its outlines are roughly demarcated in the east by the line of aridity indicated by the 98th meridian and in the west by the Pacific Ocean, while its northern and southern reaches are defined by the nation's borders with Canada and Mexico. Of course, the exact outer boundaries of this place have long been debated and contested, so much so that the American West is often rightly described as a dynamic region of ever-shifting demographic, geographic, and cultural indicators. It is, nevertheless, a place most people would say they recognize when they look at a map of the United States: those portions generally found on the left side. On the other hand, the American West is also an extremely powerful idea, one that has evolved over several centuries in the imaginations of countless people both in the US and abroad, an idea (re)produced in books, movies, paintings, and the like. It is an idea that shimmers with abstractions such as frontier, opportunity, honor, individualism, and justice, and it is often (but not always, to be sure) recognized by visual cues such as the cowboy hat, the horse, vast stretches of open rangeland rimmed by snowy peaks or desert mesas, and the handgun. It is an idea very much alive in a bumper sticker, widely popular in recent years, that asks, "Where Are You Now, John Wayne? America Needs You." This plaintive appeal for redemptive heroism (or perhaps retributive vigilantism) hardly concerns itself with anything even remotely specific to a regional geography; it is the idea that matters.

Of course, in the interaction of place and idea there are many more numbers than two, many more encounters and experiences than can be catalogued in a binary opposition between one region and one idea. In the matter of migration and settlement, for example, the American West has, to be sure, most commonly been imagined as a promised land for westward-moving pioneers. "Westward the course of Empire takes it way" declared Ireland's Bishop Berkeley in a 1726 poem entitled "Verses on the Prospect of Planting Arts and Learning in America," a sentiment that inspired more than a few generations of mostly Anglo-Europeans in their pursuit of conquest or, as some have put it, of new places to live and work. One admiring group in 1866 even named the town for a new university in California after the bishop. However, equally compelling are the patterns of movement prompted by the idea of Gold Mountain, the legendary icon that drew travelers from China to the shores of California and British Columbia and propelled them not westward but eastward across the continent. So too have immigrants from Japan and other parts of Asia crossed the Pacific Ocean in a movement that is distinctly anti-Hesperian in its orientation. Just as significantly, the promise of El Norte has for several centuries drawn people on a northbound trajectory, starting with the Spanish conquistadors who ranged from Mexico as far as central Kansas in search of Quivira. While such golden legends were never realized, the hope for greater economic certainty was and remains to this day an important motivation, though certainly not the only one, for people seeking to move northward into the so-called West. And when we also consider, as we should, the settlement patterns of Native Americans, for whom movement was not and is not a matter of immigration so much as fundamentally one of maintaining a rich tradition of local habitation, rural or otherwise, we might just begin to appreciate the full complexity of the patterns of exchange and cultural contact that have flowed across the continent, often along border-defying lines.

One particularly noteworthy demographic feature of the American West is the pace at which people moving from all directions – north, south, east, and west alike – are converging in the region's urban centers. In 1990, US Census data demonstrated that 86 percent of the West's population could be found in an urbanized environment, in contrast to only 75 percent of the population east of the Mississippi River (Riebsame et al. 1997: 55). Since then, this trend has only increased (see Abbott 2008), with demographic shifts and cultural crossings rapidly eliminating – or at least redefining – borders on all sides. This pattern contrasts sharply with the popular impression of the American West as a largely rural space populated by ranchers, cowboys, and the occasional outdoorsman. To be sure, vast stretches of land do remain sparsely populated in the extreme, giving the overall region a population density that is still lower than, for example, that of the Northeast. But the growth of western urban culture betokens a multiplicity that is not easily understood, or explained away, by a critical or historical focus on a single direction of travel or a single idea about a place. As the population of the American West continues to shift and diversify in not only urban but also suburban and rural settings, the region's cultural productions will no doubt continue to evolve such bold, new, and engaging forms as those that range from cowboy poetry to surf punk music to Chicano vampire fiction.

Sometimes the artists working with these evolving forms seek to engage ideas about the West as much as they strive to communicate something about themselves and the communities that sustain them, and sometimes they do not. That is, many producers of culture living in the West experience the tensions posed by the many variations of the idea of the West quite keenly. In such cases, one is never simply from the West or writing simply about "the West"; one is always working around popular ideas encountered both within and beyond the region. However, often enough the question of such ideas being a factor in a particular element of the literature and culture of the American West is irrelevant. Simply put, just as the West's patterns of migration give the lie to binary assumptions about what is and is not "western," so too does the work of many artists and writers argue for there being more numbers than two when adding up histories, genres, and forms. Is the Brooklyn-born son of Russian Jewish immigrants who while living in Oregon writes a fable about a baseball team called the New York Knights a western author? Is his novel? What about the poems rendered in Chinese characters on the walls of an immigration detention center in the middle of San Francisco Bay? Or how might one assess the western aspects of things like Seattle's grunge sound, or gangsta rap and hair metal from Los Angeles, or narco corridos from the borderlands? Judging by the kinds of assessments offered by recent scholarship and which are very much evident throughout this *Companion*, these things certainly are western American, even if they do little, if anything, to address the familiar mythos of the dominant narrative. Recent studies in the field have focused on such topics as women writers in the new urban West, the questions and problems associated with claims to authenticity that are both literary and identity-based, nature writing's relationship to ideologies of the real, the landscapes of waste created by the military-industrial complex, and the longstanding multicultural and multi-ethnic character of the West's diverse populations. And while a certain disciplinary contradiction has resulted from an academic and political call for recognizing distinctive, uniquely regional voices in the midst of theoretical and equally political claims about the inadequacy or undesirability of such, the essays found in this *Companion* should provide for the possibility of extending inquiry into just about every direction that might suggest itself when looking at the American West.

To that end, the essays in this book are arranged into three distinct but overlapping sections. The chapters in the first section that follows this introduction describe and interpret the American West chiefly through an orientation that is historical. Whether concerned with a strictly literary history or with narratives that are more broadly cultural, the chapters in "Regions and Histories" focus on the production of specific centers of expression that have been variously based on geography, on identity, and on a combination of the two. Topics in this section include early exploration narratives; the role of periodical publication in the fostering of a culture of literacy; and the mostly textual productions that characterize a number of generally recognized regions such as the Southwest, Alaska, Montana, and the Great Plains, as well as the texts emblematic of and/or often used to understand the West's various population, demographic, and ethnic groups. It is in this section that the desire to honor distinctive voices, to recognize the collective communities around which artists and critics alike tend to group people, is perhaps most prevalent, even as the concluding chapters on class, postcolonial perspectives, and suburban spaces begin to break down those lines.

Although it is also focused on identifying and analyzing specific histories of expression, the next section, "Varieties and Forms," attempts to look more specifically at how a wide array of genres have proven useful in imagining the West. The creators and purveyors of some of the West's most widely known iconography in both painting and literary realism are examined, as are the popular poetry and folk songs that are all too often overlooked in academic work. The accomplishments of autobiography and of domestically themed writing are also analyzed, as are the forms and genres perhaps most frequently invoked in understanding how the western US became the American West: environmentally sensitive literature and criticism, film, and, when considering the urban West, detective fiction. If the goal of the previous set of chapters can be thought of as providing analyses of what has been said of and in the West and where it has been said, then this next section is more intent on the ways of seeing, imagining, and (re)producing the West that have proven historically and culturally significant.

The final section offers even closer interpretations of specific histories, genres, and texts that highlight, with more sustained readings, a number of the persistent questions about the evolving nature of western American identity, movement, representation, performance, and iconography. Topics in this "Issues, Themes, Case Studies" section include the cross-marketing of *The Lone Ranger* radio programs; the annual performance of the *Ramona* pageant in California; Buffalo Bill's *Wild West*; the identification of place; and efforts to represent and understand such recent western phenomena as the growth of a nuclear weapons industry and the perduring prominence of Las Vegas.

Taken as a whole, the chapters in this *Companion* pose important questions about what counts as a valuable or useful text; how such texts contribute to the articulation of regional, communal, and individual identity; and what the social, cultural, or historical ramifications are for imagining the West, one's self, and oneself in the West in certain ways. Placing their various answers into dialogue with each other, the chapters that follow suggest ways of historicizing and theorizing cultural work both within historically determined or accepted divisions and across them. Ultimately, the chapters in each of these three sections do resist easy categorization, the arrangement into discrete sections being perhaps just another attempt to corral an inherent borderlessness. Yet, whether interested in a historical approach, a genre-based approach, or a case-study approach, each of the chapters that follow conveys something of the vital nature of the American West. In so doing, they each in their own ways reaffirm the value of regional studies in an age of globalization and trans-hemispheric studies.

For all the theorizing about the breakdown of borders and regional distinctions – and such work is quite valid and necessary, to be sure – we still find people living in and producing regionally distinctive cultures, erecting dividing lines, establishing ways of identifying equally through separation and combination. This process is as evident among those who would advocate a Virginian-like return to what they perceive as a once dominant Anglo-Saxon monoculture as it is among those who see endless hybridity and post-national, post-racial identities across the West. It thus falls to the study of regions to understand the products that arise in the interaction between places and ideas, bearing in mind that there will always be more than one or two of each in play.

References and Further Reading

Abbott, Carl. (2008). *How Cities Won the West: Four Centuries of Urban Change in Western North America*. Albuquerque: University of New Mexico Press.

Allmendinger, Blake. (1998). *Ten Most Wanted: The New Western Literature*. New York: Routledge.

Allmendinger, Blake. (2005). *Imagining the African American West*. Lincoln: University of Nebraska Press.

Aranda, José F. (2003). *When We Arrive: A New Literary History of Mexican America*. Tucson: University of Arizona Press.

Beck, John. (2009). *Dirty Wars: Landscape, Power, and Waste in Western American Literature*. Lincoln: University of Nebraska Press.

Berkhofer, Robert F. (1978). *The White Man's Indian: Images of the American Indian from Columbus to the Present*. New York: Knopf.

Campbell, Neil. (2000). *The Cultures of the American New West*. Edinburgh: Edinburgh University Press.

Comer, Krista. (1999). *Landscapes of the New West: Gender and Geography in Contemporary Women's Writing*. Chapel Hill: University of North Carolina Press.

Comer, Krista. (2010). *Surfer Girls in the New World Order*. Durham, NC: Duke University Press.

Cook-Lynn, Elizabeth. (1996). *Why I Can't Read Wallace Stegner and Other Essays: A Tribal Voice*. Madison: University of Wisconsin Press.

Deloria, Philip Joseph. (1998). *Playing Indian*. New Haven: Yale University Press.

Deverell, William Francis, ed. (2004). *A Companion to the American West*. Malden, MA: Blackwell.

Dorst, John Darwin. (1999). *Looking West*. Philadelphia: University of Pennsylvania Press.

Findlay, John M. (1992). *Magic Lands: Western Cityscapes and American Culture after 1940*. Berkeley: University of California Press.

Handley, William R., and Nathaniel Lewis, eds. (2004). *True West: Authenticity and the American West*. Lincoln: University of Nebraska Press.

Huang, Yunte. (2008). *Transpacific Imaginations: History, Literature, Counterpoetics*. Cambridge, MA: Harvard University Press.

Hyde, Anne Farrar. (1990). *An American Vision: Far Western Landscape and National Culture, 1820–1920*. New York: New York University Press.

Johnson, Michael K. (2002). *Black Masculinity and the Frontier Myth in American Literature*. Norman: University of Oklahoma Press.

Karell, Linda K. (2002). *Writing Together, Writing Apart: Collaboration in Western American Literature*. Lincoln: University of Nebraska Press.

Kollin, Susan, ed. (2007). *Postwestern Cultures: Literature, Theory, Space*. Lincoln: University of Nebraska Press.

Kolodny, Annette. (1975). *The Lay of the Land: Metaphor as Experience and History in American Life and Letters*. Chapel Hill: University of North Carolina Press.

Lamar, Howard Roberts, ed. (1998). *The New Encyclopedia of the American West*. New Haven: Yale University Press.

LeMenager, Stephanie. (2004). *Manifest and Other Destinies: Territorial Fictions of the Nineteenth-Century United States*. Lincoln: University of Nebraska Press.

Lewis, Nathaniel. (2003). *Unsettling the Literary West: Authenticity and Authorship*. Lincoln: University of Nebraska Press.

Limerick, Patricia Nelson. (1987). *The Legacy of Conquest: The Unbroken Past of the American West*. New York: Norton.

Limerick, Patricia Nelson. (2000). *Something in the Soil: Legacies and Reckonings in the New West*. New York: W.W. Norton.

Lye, Colleen. (2005). *America's Asia: Racial Form and American Literature, 1893–1945*. Princeton, NJ: Princeton University Press.

Matsumoto, Valerie J., and Blake Allmend-inger, eds. (1999). *Over the Edge: Remapping the American West*. Berkeley: University of California Press.

Milner, Clyde A., Carol A. O'Connor, and Martha A. Sandweiss, eds. (1994). *The Oxford History of the American West*. New York: Oxford University Press.

Mitchell, Lee Clark. (1996). *Westerns: Making the Man in Fiction and Film*. Chicago: University of Chicago Press.

Morin, Karen M. (2008). *Frontiers of Femininity: A New Historical Geography of the Nineteenth-Century American West*. Syracuse, NY: Syracuse University Press.

Murdoch, David Hamilton. (2001). *The American West: The Invention of a Myth*. Reno: University of Nevada Press.

Noriega, Chon A. (2000). *Shot in America: Television, the State, and the Rise of Chicano Cinema*. Minneapolis: University of Minnesota Press.

Owens, Louis. (1992). *Other Destinies: Understanding the American Indian Novel*. Norman: University of Oklahoma Press.

Pfister, Joel. (2004). *Individuality Incorporated: Indians and the Multicultural Modern*. Durham: Duke University Press.

Riebsame, William E., et al., eds. (1997). *Atlas of the New West: Portrait of a Changing Region*. New York: W.W. Norton.

Robbins, William G. (1994). *Colony and Empire: The Capitalist Transformation of the American West*. Lawrence: University Press of Kansas.

Robinson, Forrest G. (1993). *Having It Both Ways: Self-Subversion in Western Popular Classics*. Albuquerque: University of New Mexico Press.

Robinson, Forrest G., ed. (1998). *The New Western History: The Territory Ahead*. Tucson: University of Arizona Press.

Rothman, Hal. (1998). *Devil's Bargains: Tourism in the Twentieth-Century American West*. Lawrence: University Press of Kansas.

Slotkin, Richard. (1992). *Gunfighter Nation: The Myth of the Frontier in Twentieth-Century America*. New York: HarperPerennial.

Smith, Henry Nash. (1950). *Virgin Land: The American West as Symbol and Myth*. Cambridge, MA: Harvard University Press.

Solnit, Rebecca. (1994). *Savage Dreams: A Journey into the Hidden Wars of the American West*. San Francisco: Sierra Club Books.

Solnit, Rebecca. (2003). *River of Shadows: Eadweard Muybridge and the Technological Wild West*. New York: Viking.

Takaki, Ronald T. (1987). *From Different Shores: Perspectives on Race and Ethnicity in America*. New York: Oxford University Press.

Taylor, Quintard. (1998). *In Search of the Racial Frontier: African Americans in the American West, 1528–1990*. New York: Norton.

Tompkins, Jane P. (1992). *West of Everything: The Inner Life of Westerns*. New York: Oxford University Press.

Trachtenberg, Alan. (2004). *Shades of Hiawatha: Staging Indians, Making Americans, 1880–1930*. New York: Hill & Wang.

Truettner, William H., and Nancy K. Anderson, eds. (1991). *The West as America: Reinterpreting Images of the Frontier, 1820–1920*. Washington: Published for the National Museum of American Art by the Smithsonian Institution Press.

Weaver, Jace, Craig S. Womack, and Robert Allen Warrior. (2006). *American Indian Literary Nationalism*. Albuquerque: University of New Mexico Press.

Western Literature Association, ed. (1987). *A Literary History of the American West*. Fort Worth: Texas Christian University Press.

Western Literature Association, ed. (1997). *Updating the Literary West*. Fort Worth: Texas Christian University Press.

White, Richard. (1991). *"It's Your Misfortune and None of My Own": A History of the American West.* Norman: University of Oklahoma Press.

Witschi, Nicolas S. (2002). *Traces of Gold: California's Natural Resources and the Claim to* *Realism in Western American Literature.* Tuscaloosa: University of Alabama Press.

Womack, Craig S. (1999). *Red on Red: Native American Literary Separatism.* Minneapolis: University of Minnesota Press.

Part II

Regions and Histories

2

Exploration, Trading, Trapping, Travel, and Early Fiction, 1780–1850

Edward Watts

Introduction

The first Anglo-Americans who traveled to the West had certainly read *Gulliver's Travels* and *Robinson Crusoe*; they had also likely read the narratives produced by Captain James Cook's fellow sailors, Mungo Park's memoirs of Africa, and the writings of Daniel Boone and John Filson. When they published their stories and observations of their experiences in the West, then, they wrote aware of the long-established generic conventions of travel writing and the longstanding abuse of the genre as a source of speculation, satire, and self-promotion. Even as their subject was new, the West – along with every other "Terra Nullius" on eighteenth-century maps – had already been imaginatively filled with exotic places, peoples, and adventures. As we turn to these texts, we might read as early nineteenth-century readers would have: from a skeptical but still curious vantage.

In fact, the first "American" narrative of western travel was *Journey to the Unknown Parts of America in the Years 1786 & 1787* (1788) by "Alonso Decalves," better known as John Trumbull of the famous New England literary family. At the other end period, the opening chapters of Edgar Allen Poe's "Journal of Julius Rodman" (1840) foretell a thrilling narrative of Western adventure, prior to Poe's abandoning of the hoax before its implied climax. Both Trumbull and Poe – neither of whom had been west – openly broached the space between "travelers and travel liars," in the terms of Percy Adams. However, from the start, the subject was a point of contention. The botanist Thomas Nuttall, who traveled up the Arkansas River in 1819, acceded the linkage of his science and his style:

A Companion to the Literature and Culture of the American West, First Edition. Edited by Nicolas S. Witschi.
© 2011 Blackwell Publishing Ltd. Published 2011 by Blackwell Publishing Ltd.

> To those who vaguely peruse the narratives of travelers for pastime or transitory amuse-
> ment, the present volume is by no means addressed. It is no part of the author's ambition
> to study the gratification of so fastidious a taste as that, which but too generally governs
> the readers of the present day; a taste, which has no criterion but passing fashion, which
> spurns at every thing that possesses not the charm of novelty, and the luxury of embel-
> lishment. We live no longer in an age that tolerates the plain "unvarnished tale." (p. v)

Nuttall's admission of his anachronistic style can be extended to other data-based
accounts, many written as official accounts of expeditions sponsored by the government. Nonetheless, such an approach to description relies upon an imported frame of
reference; following the Bartrams in the eighteenth century, Nuttall's imposition of
Latin names and Linnaean hierarchies informs his organization of western materials,
bringing the region's raw materials into categories of knowledge established
elsewhere.

Nuttall was correct in noting, however, that most readers preferred their tales
varnished, and revised, ghost-written, and interpreted or "translated" western narratives soon became the order of the day. This can be seen in the publication of materials
from Lewis and Clark's famous expedition. The captains' journals themselves were
published only a century after their return, and are a compendium of encyclopedic
data. However, well aware that the early nineteenth-century reader demanded greater
narrative coherence, Thomas Jefferson arranged for Philadelphia men of letters Paul
Allen and Nicholas Biddle to produce the authoritative account in 1814, largely to
counter a number of less reliable texts by other members of the expedition. The literary exploration of the American West begins in the varnishing of these accounts,
following the model of the development of British fiction a century sooner.

During the eighteenth century, travelers' narratives – a staple of European print
culture from its origins – became one of the many non-fiction genres out of which
developed British fiction. Authors such as Swift and Defoe relied upon their readers'
familiarity with conventions they would borrow, reshape, corrupt, and, ultimately,
transform into the modern novel. In the texts discussed below, then, those with the
most deliberately *literary* qualities merit the most significant discussion. Straightforward
accounts are invaluable for their documentary materials, but less so in terms of their
role in the beginnings of a distinctly Western literature. It is in the transmutation of
the facts of an exploring expedition, a trading venture, a personal adventure, or a
military conflict into an interesting and compelling narrative – non-fictional or fictional – that the stirrings of a place-specific tradition of imaginative writing can be
traced.

However, the process of moving from fact to narrative, especially with regard to
western materials, was often shaped by forces antithetical to the development
of western voices. In particular, the appropriation of western materials to serve less
local eastern, or national, concerns represented an act of rhetorical colonization that
stunted the development of an unfettered local literature. Like every site of conquest,
colonization, and settlement, the West was compelled to subordinate its identity to

larger agendas of the Empire or Nation by means of careful patterns of misrepresentation, exoticization, and trivialization which were imposed, patterns that discouraged
accurate self-exploration and self-expression. At the same time, of course, even the
most authentic of western voices that emerged displaced indigenous voices and often
narrated their erasure, elimination, and annihilation. The most distinctly western
voices, then, emerge from that tension between the pressure to blend the region into
larger, East-based national ambitions and the fact that conquest meant violating the
republic's ideals.

As such, I focus on sets of texts that address these tensions as a vitalizing force in
the emergence of a distinctly western literary voice. Each section below places conventional voices against lesser-known voices, ones whose contrarian nature compelled
their exclusion from the triumphalist narrative that dominated most twentieth-century western cultural historiography and from the emergent canon of "western"
writing." A triumphalist narrative is intrinsically East-based and westward-moving.
Hector St. John de Crevecoeur promised in 1782 that the East's ambitions regarding
the West would complete "the great circle" of civilization's westward progress, a
promise bookended, of course, by John O'Sullivan's 1845 boast of the nation's Manifest
Destiny: the West was primarily a place to end European and eastern stories, and only
secondarily a place with stories of its own.

Yet western literature begins in such romantic, eastern texts in that western subjects and materials are cast before the reader's imagination. But it also begins in stories
written in response to them, often in texts deliberately intertextual, narratives that
openly challenge convention. In the play between narrative and counter-narrative,
trends emerge that inform western writing even into the early twenty-first century.
Even before the Treaty of Guadalupe Hidalgo, even before Sutter's Mill, the patterns
are in place that make western literature the site of never-ending debates concerning
conquest and race, gender and settlement, colonization and empire, and propaganda
and literary expression. For each of the following sections, dozens of texts exist
between and among those getting the closest scrutiny. In sum, I mean to suggest a
new reading strategy that should help readers coming to the literature of the American
West both to reread the texts they know and to discover those they have yet to
discover.

Part One. Explorers: Lewis and Clark's Ghostwriters, and Edwin James

The actual journals of the captains – the day-to-day log of events, embellished inconsistently with commentary and information – were the source materials upon which
Biddle (and Allen to a far lesser extent) generated the 1814 narrative referred to by
virtually every other westward-travelling writer for the next fifty years. Nonetheless,
a number of texts from other explorers were published in their rather raw journal-
based condition: the journals of Zebulon Pike, Alexander Mackenzie, and David

Thompson are fact-based catalogues: distance traveled, animals eaten, subordinates disciplined, landmarks noted. More extensive entries usually describe interactions with Indians – especially those resisting or impeding their progress – wherein the authors engage a proto-ethnology. However, the authors rarely impose subjective commentary: more like Joseph Priestley in his account of Cook's voyage, they strive for a model of Enlightenment-era empirical detachment.

Biddle's "varnished" 1814 edition, ultimately, would be far more influential for later explorers and almost equally compelling to the historians celebrating the expedition's bicentennial. Biddle's extrapolations upon the captains' logs might be seen in his comment concerning the French workers hired to work for the expedition in St. Charles, Missouri:

> The inhabitants … unite all the careless gayety, and the amiable hospitality of the best times of France: yet, like most of the countrymen in America, they are but ill-qualified for the rude life of a frontier; not that they are without talent, for they possess much natural genius and vivacity; nor that they are destitute of enterprise, for their hunting excursions are long, laborious, and hazardous: but their exertions are all desultory; their industry is without system, and without perseverance. (I.38–9)

Yet, time and again, the Frenchmen rescue the expedition. More generally, two generations of travelers and traders in the West noted the ubiquity and, often, superiority of Frenchmen on both the Oregon and Santa Fe trails. Moreover, the wealth of St. Louis-based trading families such as the Choteaus and the Sublettes – noted in dozens of texts – speaks to the ability of the Catholic French to meet the standard of the implied Protestant work ethic against which the captains measured them.

However, Biddle's goal is to clear the West of meaningful resistance to Anglo-American colonization and settlement. The fact that Frenchmen (and Alexander Mackenzie) had already been down the Columbia to the Pacific would have diminished the expedition's meaning. But if, like the Indians, the French existed only as nomads, unsuited to the continent's potential, they, like the Indians, become part of pre-history; and history could then begin with the expedition. Indians in the *History* are viewed as removable transients. A band of Pawnees strikes the chord:

> Still further to the westward, are several tribes, who wander and hunt on the sources of the river Platte and thence to the Rock Mountains. These tribes, of which little is known than the names and population … they are the most warlike of western Indians; they never yield in battle; they never spare their enemies; and the retaliation of this barbarity has almost extinguished the nation. (I.73–4)

A self-extinguishing tribe absolves the Anglos from any implication in genocide: they are doing it themselves, emptying the land, preparing it for the coming of, first, the captains, and then the colonists. Even before that, they are only wanderers and hunters, never owning the land. The theme of the liminality of the Indians runs through the *History*, and their French kinsmen come to share their fate.

Biddle's narrative introduces many of what would become standard elements of western narratives by which the Anglos gain ownership of the land. For example, on first sighting the Missouri Breaks, Biddle's describes Lewis's moment of sublime transportation: "The scene it presented was singularly beautiful, since without any of the wild irregular sublimity of the lower falls, it combines all the regular elegances which the fancy of a painter would select to form a beautiful waterfall" (I.344). Following up the falls, he finds an abundance of game, just waiting for him and Clark. The absence of the Indian, and the waiting fecundity of the West, make the captains feel the land is theirs in more than the legal terms of the Louisiana Purchase. On the whole, Biddle peppers the *History* with dozens of such episodes; in sum, the story of the expedition becomes a story of how the West is simply waiting for the East to come and take rightful possession of it.

Other expeditions told less varnished tales, especially when actual participants did the writing. Today, Edwin James is best known as John Tanner's interpreter for his 1830 *Narrative*. In that role, James did little to "varnish" Tanner's raw account of thirty years as an Ojibwa. A decade earlier, James served as science officer in Stephen Long's 1819–20 expedition up the Missouri. James published his account in 1823 before his posting to Sault Ste. Marie, where he worked with Schoolcraft and Tanner. Unlike Zebulon Pike's equally ambivalent narrative of his own expeditions, James's *Account* combines the best elements of the scientific perspective demanded by Nuttall and the "varnishing" demanded by North Atlantic readers. This can be seen in his treatment of the many Frenchmen surrounding the expedition. James's usual tone is fairly objective, noting important differences between Anglo and French ways, tacitly noting the French presence on equal footing with the Anglos. One incident, however, distinguishes James from Biddle most directly.

Among the Omaha, James describes how an Anglo trader, following the French model, had married a chief's daughter to gain a trade monopoly. However, unlike the Anglos in most of these narratives, this trader marries a white woman in St. Louis as well. Moreover, he demands his mixed-race children be raised among the whites, in violation of the longstanding French model wherein the children stayed in their mothers' tribes. James records the Omaha woman's articulate claim to her own children:

> Is my child a dog, that I should sell him for merchandise? You cannot drive me away; you may beat me, it is true, and otherwise abuse me, but I will still remain. When you married me, you promised to treat me kindly, as long as I should be faithful to you; that I have been so no one can deny. Ours was not a marriage contracted for a season; it was to terminate only with our lives. (I.248)

James Hall rewrote this incident in the short story "The New Moon" in 1834, and reproduced this speech verbatim (footnoting James). More directly, Long and his officers support the Omaha woman and send the trader downriver, a decision James views as just. In this case, James observes a richly diverse West: French, Omaha,

Anglo, and other presences coexist in the *Account*, and James never endeavors the sort of erasure that characterized Biddle's story. In fact his insistence on objective observation precludes the interposition of such speculative romantic constructions.

At the same time, James's *Account* remains anecdotal, and always recurs to his primary role as science officer. There is no master-narrative: in different places, he makes different observations and intervenes with stories such as the Omaha squaw only when it is necessary. Moreover, at times, James turns the text over to other members of the expedition. For example, Captain James Sibley is allowed to discuss US–Osage relations to critique the non-enforcement of an 1806 treaty:

> These facts concerning the Osage treaty are stated merely to show that we have not dealt fairly with the Osages and to infer from them, that unless immediate steps are taken to recover the confidence and respect which those Indians once had in the United States, the inevitable consequence will be their decided and active hostility against the settlement of the Missouri, and those back of the Lead Mines. (II.248)

In other words, James allows Sibley to characterize US policy as a hindrance rather than a boon to settlement, inverting the usual triumphalist narrative. This intervention represents James's method more generally: the book, like its subject, is admirably polyglot and amorphous. Much more than Biddle's *History*, James's *Account* tells a western story.

Part Two. Trappers and Traders: Kit Carson and James Pattie

All Kit Carson did was enlist with John C. Fremont in the young colonel's first two western expeditions. Long a guide on the Sante Fe Trail, Carson impressed Fremont with his embodiment of frontier virtues. On the expeditions, Carson served above and beyond the call of duty, though in his own dictated "autobiography" he diminished his role; yet Fremont's 1846 published account of the expedition and Carson's heroic doings on it made him a celebrity. Almost immediately, Carson's story was appropriated, distorted, and remolded in knock-off publications emanating from eastern publishers to shape, articulate, and embody a version of the West wholly different from that described by Fremont or experienced by Carson.

The most notorious was Charles Averill's *Kit Carson: Prince of the Gold Hunters* (1849). Here, Carson becomes an Indian-hating renegade whose actions – like those of the heroes of Robert Montgomery Bird and other Jacksonian and antebellum sensationalists – are justified by a teleological subtext: the extermination of the Indian is a component of Manifest Destiny, and "Kit" is only doing God's work. This fictional "Kit" also appears in novels by Emerson Bennett, Charles Webber, James Dallam, David Coyner, and Lewis Garrard, many of which also appropriate the "Hater" formula. Averill's Kit goes places the real Kit had never been and does things the real Kit had not, and never would. Carson himself repudiated the book and sought to "burn the damn thing." However, as one critic notes, "The image of the Indian Slayer, despite its untruthfulness, thereafter would stick to his heels like glue."[1] The image of the Indian Hater/Slayer – featured in over fifty narratives in the antebellum era – also inoculated the East from the crimes of conquest, and was based on actual eastern Haters such as Lewis Wetzel, Tom Quick, and John Moredock. The white frontiersman who could out-savage the savage, as it were, assured a white superiority and destiny, even at the atavistic level of individual combat.

Yet the Hater, like the Indian he exterminated, was doomed to vanish as "civilization" came west. In every story, Haters and their like keep moving west, clearing paths for settlement, embodying the stage version of frontier history first articulated by Crevecoeur as "New-made Indians": "Thus are our first steps trodden, thus are our first trees felled by the most vicious of our people; and thus the path is opened for the arrival of a second and better class, the true American free-holders" (pp. 53–4). Eastern readers could vicariously tremble as their avatars – the embodiments of the latent savage lurking within every civilized man – killed the Indians – safe that in the next chapter "Time will efface these stains." The frontiersmen either learn "subordination," or keep moving west. Averill's depiction of Carson as a Hater, safely a thousand miles west of the settlements, then, is part of the colonization of the West, in many ways a gesture more aggressive than Fremont's expedition. By portraying him as semi-savage transitional other, books like Averill's wrote Carson out of regional history and into national history.

Carson would speak for himself. However, like other marginal and intercultural figures such as Mary Jemison, John Tanner, and Black Hawk, he did so through the mediating, "varnishing" voice of an interpreter/ghost writer, purportedly Dr. De Witt Porter, though the manuscript signed by Carson in Taos in 1856 passed through many hands. Be that as it may, the voice that emerges from Carson's *Autobiography* is refreshingly unadorned and direct – no sign of the jingoism of Averill or the pathology of Bird. While Carson certainly implicates himself in acts of conquest and colonization, he writes as a common man. In fact, his behavior is more typically that of a Frenchman: he marries two Indian women and winters in their tribes; often with his in-laws; many of his strikes against Indians have to do with stealing horses and other livestock; and he moves among hostile and friendly tribes at will.

In short, the unlettered Kit depicts himself as an intercultural figure whose story complicates the simple-minded fictions of writers like Averill. However, Carson had already been appropriated and misrepresented to serve national needs for an Indian-killing superman, and his *Autobiography* was largely forgotten. However, other guides and traders on the Santa Fe Trail (many of whom are mentioned in the *Autobiography*) corroborated Carson's story of the trail as a peculiar mixing ground of Indian, Mexican, Spanish, French, and Anglo cultures. Just as important, western trade had been advertised as a way to gain wealth, and many of the narratives produced by Carson's former associates – like his own – tell a story of financial failure rather than one of easy money. While Zenas Leonard, Thomas James, and James P. Beckwourth evoke the Carson narrative of the unlettered guide and trapper, Josiah Gregg, Alexander Ross, and Ross Cox give the trader's perspective. Somewhere between these class-based divisions is James Ohio Pattie's *Personal Narrative*, edited by Timothy Flint in 1831.

While Flint's triumphalist novels *The Shoshonee Valley* and *Francis Berrian* borrow heavily from Pattie's story, he left Pattie's narrative relatively unmarred: "My influence upon the narrative regards orthography, and punctuation." However, he noted that, "Circumstances of suffering, which in many similar narratives have been given in downright plainness of detail, I have been impelled to leave to the reader's imagination, as too revolting to be recorded" (p. iv). A former missionary, Flint's squeamishness signals a reluctance to reveal just how dire life on the frontier was, for fear of slowing the manifest progress of filling the continent. Flint's minor interpositions notwithstanding, Pattie's narrative retains a darkness and an ambiguity that, more than Carson's *Autobiography*, complicate the idea of the West as a Terra Nullius awaiting the arrival of the Anglo-American. Pattie's West is violent, complicated, and, in the end, a place to leave rather than a place to stay.

Traveling west with his father – a hero in the war of 1812 – the young Pattie is immediately disabused of his romantic notions. One scene juxtaposes them efficiently: "From this spot, we saw one of the most beautiful landscapes that ever spread out to the eye. ... Here the sun rose, and set, as unobscured from the sight, as on the wastes of oceans. Here we used the last of our salt, and as for bread, we had seen none, since we had left the Pawnee village" (p. 29). The threat of starvation, despite the sublime beauty of the western landscape, introduces a tone of irony and disappointment. Like Tanner's, Pattie's story becomes a constant quest for food and safety. Money and various ventures come and go as he finally makes his way through the desert Southwest to San Diego, where he becomes a captive of the Spanish, and the last third of the book resembles Cormac McCarthy's *All the Pretty Horses*. Even before his captivity, though, Pattie records an inhospitable desert West:

> We attempted to chew tobacco. It would raise no moisture. We took our bullets in our mouths and moved them round to create moisture, to relieve our parched throats. We had travelled but a bit further before our tongues had become so dry and swollen, that we could hardly speak so as to be understood. In this extremity of nature, we should, perhaps, have sunk voluntarily had not the relief been still in view on the sides of the snow-covered mountains. We resorted to one expedient to moisten our lips, tongue, and throat, disgusting to relate and still more disgusting to adopt. (p. 159)

In drinking their urine in the Arizona desert Pattie and his friends fear that, as Crevecoeur had warned, they were losing what made them "civilized." But their choice to do so overcomes such niceties and they survive, only to be captured in San Diego.

In the end, back in Ohio, Pattie juxtaposes his preconceived romantic notions of the West with the facts of his lived experience:

> I have had too much of real incident and affliction to be a dealer in romance; and yet I should do injustice to my feelings if I closed this journal without a record of my

sensations on reaching home. … But the present reality is all as much changed as my heart … I look for the deep grove, so faithfully remaining in my memory, and the stream that murmured through it. The woods are leveled by the axe. (p. 252)

The deforestation of Ohio foreshadows the destruction of western nature by the forces of civilization in Pattie's dark narrative. A frontiersman, Pattie mourns for the openness of the West but, at the same time, cannot equate the image of the unspoiled West with the horrors of his time spent there. Nonetheless, Pattie's story of the trail, the silver mines, Mexican jails, near-starvation, and finally return is compelling and makes for a far more interesting read than the formulaic assumptions of more conventional texts, even Carson's.

Part Three. Travelers and Tourists: Francis Parkman and John Wyeth

In the summer of 1846, Harvard undergraduates Francis Parkman and his kinsman Quincy Shaw decided to have an adventure. Had they read their Harvard predecessor John B. Wyeth's *Oregon; Or a Short History of a Long Journey* (1833), they may have chosen a different venture. Parkman's story of his adventure, best known as *The Oregon Trail* (1849), however, seems to have erased every other belletristic account of the West. However, this is the richest and most unmined vein of western writing from the pre-Mexican War era. Overshadowed by Parkman are less self-indulgent books by Edwin Bryant, George Kendall, Thomas Farnham, George Catlin, George Ruxton, and, most overlooked, Matthew Field. Washington Irving's three western books – *Tour of the Prairie*, *Astoria*, and *Captain Bonneville* – also fall into this category, though his empire-building tone resembles Cooper, Parkman, and Biddle, Of these, though, Wyeth's stands in the most intriguing contrast with Parkman's.

Now known as much for his magisterial histories of the French and Indian war, Parkman first achieved fame for *The Oregon Trail*. Like many of these travelers (including Bryant and Field), Parkman thought the dry air of the West would clear up his effeminizing ill health. On the journey, he repeatedly pushes himself to the point of sickness to prove to himself (and to his more masculine companions) that being privileged and sheltered did not make him any less of a man. Parkman and Quincy engage a French guide, Henry Chatillon. Through Chatillon, Parkman learns to engage with the West in ways Irving and other, more aristocratic, travelers do not. Parkman's illnesses, ironically, expose him to a diversity of western populations since he becomes dependent on them as his care-givers. Yet even the best Frenchman – Chatillon – is best suited to subordination:

His manly face was a perfect mirror of uprightness, simplicity, and kindness of heart; he had, moreover, a keen perception of character, and a tact which would preserve him from flagrant error in any society. Henry had not the restless energy of an

Anglo-American. He was content to take things as he found them; and his chief fault arose from an excess of easy generosity, impelling him to give away too profusely ever to thrive in the world. (p. 49)

Decidedly, Henry is not "in the world," by which Parkman means the cosmopolitan world of the north Atlantic. Safe in the prehistoric West, Henry is a figure from an earlier time, the anachronism that links the Indian of the distant past to the thoroughly modern perspective to which Parkman aspires. Likewise, western nature is described if in a museum, with a quiet reverence that is posed in direct opposition to the urban setting he had left in the summer: "Here society is reduced to its original elements, the whole fabric of art and conventionality is struck rudely to pieces, and men find themselves suddenly brought back to the wants and resources of their original natures" (p. 106). For all his love of the West, Parkman is ultimately an adventure tourist. Like Hemingway's expedition in Africa a generation later, the wild setting exists to test his lingering atavism in the context of professionalism and urbanization, forces distancing nineteenth-century middle- and upper-class men from the usual sites of masculine achievement. Parkman ultimately travels west to learn about himself more than to learn about the West.

Like Parkman, Wyeth traveled west with his male relatives to test himself but, unlike their genteel Cambridge neighbors the Parkmans, the Wyeths, led by John's uncle, Nathaniel, viewed the West as a means of enrichment. His cousin has invented – or so he thinks – an amphibious wagon that should travel as easily on western waters as on prairies. Spurred by the propaganda of Hall J. Kelley, or so young John Wyeth claims, they embark for the West with not only one of these wagons but also the blacksmithing equipment necessary to manufacture more, as they figure other westerners will immediately crave their own. Writing retrospectively, after the venture's inevitable failure, Wyeth reflects on the role reading had played in their illusions:

> Yet the Captain of this Oregon Expedition seemed to say: All this availeth me nothing so long as I read in books in which I find that only going about four thousand miles over land from the shore of our Atlantic to the shore of the Pacific, after we have entrapped and killed the beavers and otters, we shall be able, after building vessels for the purpose, to carry our most valuable peltry to China and Cochin China, our seal-skins to Japan, and our superfluous grains to various Asiatic ports and lumber to the Spanish settlements on the Pacific, and to become rich by underworking and underselling the people of Hindostan; and to crown all, to extend far and wide the traffic in oil by killing tame whales on the spot, instead sailing round the stormy region of Cape Horn. (pp. 7–8)

Wyeth's prophetic linkage of global capitalism and imperialism with the books that fuel such enterprises represents a sophistication born of his own disastrous time in the West. Soon after leaving St. Louis, they are compelled to jettison, first, the manufacturing equipment and then the non-functioning amphibious wagon no one wanted to buy anyway. As the expedition nears the Rockies, now as a group of ordinary trappers, they are forced by hunger to submit to the discipline of a French group led by the Sublette family. Finally, John and some others split from Nathaniel and head back east.

The others seem to disdain John, and finally abandon him in St. Louis. Now broke and alone, he is forced to rely on his wits to get back to Boston. Unlike Parkman, whose adventures were always buffered by the fact that he had the resources to extract himself from them at will, Wyeth's masculinity is more genuinely tested. Like the mission itself, of course, it fails. Among the western traders, he realizes his comic inadequacy; once, in the settlements, he is arrested for not paying debts, and escapes by hiding in manure piles. However, he works his way to New Orleans as a fireman on a steamship and, in New Orleans, works as a gravedigger in the wake of the yellow fever plague of 1832. Appalled by New Orleans' physical and moral squalor, he leaves finally for Boston. Wyeth's *Oregon* is only eighty pages long and, in fact, he never gets to Oregon; however, in many ways it is more telling of the West as it was than as it had been reported in glowing accounts to be. In the end, Wyeth's *Oregon* reads as a mini-picaresque story, the adventures so haphazard as to border onto the territory of Laurence Sterne or Hugh Henry Brackenridge.

Wyeth's use of the phrase "A Short History" in his subtitle as well reminds us that "History," "Tales," and "Adventures" were employed interchangeably as fiction slowly grew apart from other forms of narrative in dozens of stories. In his "Concluding Remarks," Wyeth again reviews the literary sources of his fiasco but turns to an essay by William Snelling about the near-extinction of the fur trade east of the Rockies by 1830. From this, Wyeth extrapolates on the contradictory nature of the Americanization of the West as indicative of national circumstances more generally:

> Lewis and Clark, and some other travelers speak of friendly Indians, – of their kindness and hospitality and expatiate on their amiable disposition and relate instances of it. Yet, after all, this Indian friendship is very like the affection of the negroes in the Southern States for their masters and mistresses, and for their children – the offspring merely of fear. There can be no friendship where there is a disparity of condition ... What right have we to fit out armed expeditions, and enter the long occupied country of the natives, to destroy their game, not for subsistence, but for their skins? (p. 84)

Wyeth's diatribe essentially calls into question the larger goals of Manifest Destiny and *translatio imperii* on a global scale as well. More like a late twentieth-century New West historian, Wyeth views the American West with profound ambivalence. While his uncle would stay in the West, and feature in narratives by Ross, Cox, and others, John would remain in Boston, and the family would learn to paint.

Part Four. Fiction: James Fenimore Cooper and William Snelling

Like his friend John Wyeth, William Snelling wrote in the context of a vision of the Golden West deeply entrenched in the national imaginary. To be precise, James

Fenimore Cooper's *The Prairie* (1827) is the first sustained American fiction set entirely west of the Mississippi; in fact, 500 miles west along the Platt in what is now western Nebraska. Of all the western texts I have reviewed, *The Prairie* is the only one entirely devoid of the French populations so ubiquitous from New Orleans to Oregon. Cooper's omission is telling. Even while Biddle's captains needed to subordinate the French, they at least conceded their presence and utility. Cooper's sweeping act of erasure is telegraphed in his opening paragraph in reference to the Louisiana Purchase:

> It gave us sole command of a great thoroughfare of the interior, and placed the countless tribes of savages, who lay along our borders, entirely within our controul; it reconciled conflicting rights, and quieted national distrusts; it opened a thousand avenues to the inland trade, and to the waters of the Pacific; and, if ever time or necessity shall require a peaceful division of this vast empire, it assures us a neighbor that will possess our language, our religion, our institutions, and it is also hoped, our sense of political justice. (p. 9)

The novel places a nonagenarian Natty Bummpo (aka Leatherstocking or Hawkeye) in the Far West as a coda to his career in New York to conclude the Leatherstocking series, a favorite target of Mark Twain for its contrived plots and unrealistic melodrama. Natty considers himself a refugee from a greedy eastern nation: "Such hills and hunting grounds I have seen stripped of the gifts of the Lord; without remorse or shame! I tarried till the oaths of my hounds were deafened by the blows of the choppers, and then I came west, in search of quiet" (p. 75). The West is, then, important as an outlet, as a safety valve for the East, not for its own qualities. Cooper transposes his usual litany of Shakespearean types: the effeminate comic relief, the young upper-class white male, the young middle-class white male, the socially disruptive white frontier folk, and the white and non-white damsels in distress. In other words the setting becomes irrelevant as the usual Cooperian narrative of conflict and resolution plays itself out, the story always of the coming of stability and order through the marriage of the two elite whites, a formula endlessly repeated in less readable fictions by Flint.

Subsequently, borrowing liberally from Edwin James (just as British novelist Frederick Marryat would from George Kendall), Cooper restages the events of *The Last of the Mohicans*, substituting the good Pawnees for the good Mohicans and the bad Sioux for the bad Mingoes. Again, the western setting is really an eastern stage for working out national anxieties about westward expansion, racial conflict, social mobility, and liberal democracy, all of which Cooper feared. In the end, Natty dies, the bad whites learn their place, and the happy couples function as stand-ins for the nation's safe replication of the proper version of itself into the virgin soil of the West. While Cooper was deeply critical of the market forces driving much westward expansion, his hope is that West becomes a place for the realization of higher goals. The Pawnee's eulogy of Natty – "When the voice of Wahcondah called him, he was ready to answer. Go my children: remember the just chiefs of the pale-faces, and clear your own tracks from briars" (p. 386) – distinguishes just from unjust whites, and so reflects Cooper's hope that "just chiefs" achieve in West what had failed to be achieved in Andrew Jackson's East.

Cooper's stage is always national, allegorical, and, finally transcendent. Purged of French and Metis presence and the century of fur trade history, his western Nebraska is a true Terra Nullius. William Snelling knew better. Raised in his father's eponymous fort on the northern Red River before a career as a Boston journalist, Snelling knew the early nineteenth-century West was far more complicated. He collected his stories in 1830 as *Tales of the Old Northwest*, though the book immediately vanished in Cooper's America. In the stories, interracial couples are not punished, sexuality is considered a normal part of life, and whites often behave as savagely as Indian. In his preface he identifies his intertextual mission:

> No man can learn much of the character of the aborigines of North America unless by personal observation. The Indian tales, novel, etc., which teem from the press and circulating libraries, in which the savages are dragged from their graves to be scalped anew, are proofs of the assertion. … If the works alluded to may be considered a criterion, it seems to be the commonly received opinion that the aborigines are all heroes; that they are all insensible of fear, and strangers to weakness. (p. 3)

Snelling's implicit goal, then, is to rehumanize the rhetorical Indian in American writing. His Indians are at turns noble and selfish, faithful and unreliable, loving and vicious, wise and foolish, "as in civilized nations and about in the same proportion to their numbers" (p. 4). He also implicitly attacks Cooper for his Indians' constant articulation of aphorisms. Snelling reminds his readers that "In truth, nothing is more flat and commonplace than their common conversation. They speak with as little circumlocution, and as directly to the point as any people" (p. 5). Cooper's erasure of the Indians had made such scrupulous attention pointless; by contrast, Snelling's attention implies a future for Indians and so eastern readers should become familiar with Indians as they are, not as they have been (mis-)represented.

Snelling's West is best represented in the collection's novella, "The Bois Brule." It centers on the fur trade war between the Hudson's Bay Company and the Northwest Fur Company prior to their amalgamation. This conflict is noted in dozens of texts that address the early decades of the century. Its hero is Metis, Scottish, and Sioux, and capable of moving freely among white and Indian settlements. In the end, there are ignorant and violent Indians and whites, corrupt and honest French and Anglos. In the end, the conflict is resolved by the merger, a resolution in which there is no clear moral victor, no larger story moving toward a millennial outcome. In fact, Snelling's use of the short story format – not unlike James's and Pattie's episodic narratives – in the end best reflects the lack of coherence or unity Snelling finds in his western subject. By deliberately confronting the image of the Indian in his preface, in fact, Snelling is disputing the Cooperian image of the West more generally. By insisting on its messiness, Snelling insists on realistic representation and rejects the romantic speculation that yoked western subject and peoples eastern ambitions and ideologies.

Conclusion

Traditionally, "realism" in American writing traveled from west to east. Caroline Kirkland's *A New Home – Who'll Follow* (1838), describing life in the Michigan frontier of the 1830s, usually marks the beginning of that transition. However, *A New Home*'s generic categorization has often been smudged: the similarities between Mary Clavers – the narrator – and Caroline Kirkland – the author – are overwhelming to the extent that her biographers have referenced it as source material, as have historians of southeastern Michigan. Unlike Cooper, Kirkland resists the urge to frame frontier experience in larger narrative of teleological destinarianism. Her frontier is messy, multicultural, and fraught with both moral ambiguity and abandoned failures and grudging successes; irony is her most consistent mode of expression. While Snelling's realism pre-dates Kirkland's, each wrote from personal experience and transmuted that experience into fictions detached from the master-narratives of romantic nationalism or Manifest Destiny.

In both, realistic fiction emerges from an authorial urge to strip the misrepresentation of the "west" from the image that had been established for it in the national imaginary. As such, Kirkland and Snelling, like many of the authors discussed above, worked from a life-writing basis and worked toward a new kind of fiction more suited to the West itself. In essence, in challenging the place in the imperial archive given it in the East-based American public sphere, writers such as James, Pattie, Wyeth, and Snelling create a space for the exploration of other forms of western self-expression otherwise foreclosed by East-based writers such as Biddle, Averill, Parkman, or Cooper. A generation later, Mark Twain and Bret Harte would continue the process of creating realistic fictions whose relation to non-fiction often seems deliberately difficult to parse. While realism in American literature may not have begun in the localization of western materials, the ongoing quest for more accurate and place-specific means of writing about the West and westerners certainly contributed to the process.

The published literary history of virtually every Anglophone settlement colony begins with an apology of sorts. To paraphrase, "For a long time, the settlers were too concerned with the material progress to indulge in literary expression." Few actual westerners published much in the period in question, Moreover, James, Pattie, Wyeth, and Snelling wrote when they had returned east: none remained a westerner. Their conflict with the more conventional sources, then, was ultimately a conflict within American writing more generally. Would the local be assimilated and erased in a monolithic nation? Or would they contribute to a diverse collection of communities in a suppler model of nationhood? Obviously, these issues transcend the literary, but the literary conflict, in this case, epitomizes the cultural conflicts to come.

NOTE

1   Marc S. Simmons, "Kit and the Indians," in   *Indian Fighter or Indian Killer?* (Boulder: Uni-
    R.C. Gordon-McCutcheon, ed., *Kit Carson:*   versity of Colorado Press, 1996), pp. 73–90.

REFERENCES AND FURTHER READING

Non-Fiction (some lengthy titles have been abbreviated)

Biddle, Nicholas, ed. (1814). *History of the Expedition Under the Commend of Captains Lewis and Clarke.* 3 vols. Philadelphia: Biddle.

Bonner, T.D. (1965). *The Life and Adventures of James P. Beckwourth. (1856).* Repr. Minneapolis: Ross & Haines.

Brackenridge, Henry Marie. (1811). *Views of Louisiana, Together with a Journal of a Voyage Up the Missouri River, in 1811.* Pittsburgh: Cramer.

Bradbury, John. (1817). *Travels to the Interior of America in the Year 1809, 1810, and 1811.* Liverpool: Smith & Colway.

Bryant, Edwin. (1848). *What I Saw in California.* New York: Appleton.

Carson, Christopher. (1935). *Kit Carson's Autobiography,* ed. Milo Milton Quaife. Chicago: Lakeside. [Edited version: *The Life and Adventures of Kit Carson: The Nestor of the Rocky Mountains, from Facts Narrated by Himself.* (1858), ed. Dr. De Witt C. Peters. New York: Putnam.]

Catlin, George. (1844). *Letters and Notes on the Manners, Customs, and Conditions of the North American Indians.* Philadelphia: Carey & Lea.

Cox, Ross. (1957). *The Columbia River (1831).* Repr. ed. Edgar I. Stewart and Jane R. Stewart. Norman: University of Nebraska Press.

Crevecoeur, H. St. John de (Michel Guillaume). (1997). *Letters from an American Farmer,* ed. Susan Manning. New York: Oxford.

Cutts, James Madison. (1847). *Conquest of California and Northern Mexico in the Years 1846 and 1847.* Philadelphia: Carey & Hart.

Farnham, Thomas J. (1843). *Travels in the Great Western Plains.* New York: Greeley.

Field, Matthew C. (1957). *Prairie and Mountain Sketches (1843),* ed. Kate L. Gregg and John

Francis McDermott. Norman: University of Oklahoma Press.

Fremont, John Charles. (1970). *The Expeditions of John Charles Fremont. (1846),* ed. Donald Jackson and Mary Lee Spence. 3 vols. Urbana: University of Illinois Press.

Gregg, Josiah. (1844). *Commerce of the Prairies: or The Journal of a Santa Fe Trader.* 2 vols. New York: Langley.

Hall, Kelley J. (1932). *Kelley on Oregon: A Collection of Five of his Published Works,* ed. Fred Wilbur Powell. Princeton, NJ: Princeton University Press.

Hines, Rev. Gustavus. (1851). *Life on the Plains of the Pacific.* Buffalo: Derby.

Irving, John T. (1835). *Indian Sketches; Taken During an Expedition to the Pawnee Tribe.* Philadelphia: Carey & Lea.

Irving, Washington. (1835). *A Tour of the Prairies.* Philadelphia: Carey, Lea & Blanchard.

Irving, Washington. (1836). *Astoria, or Anecdotes of an Enterprise Beyond the Rocky Mountains.* Philadelphia: Carey, Lea, & Blanchard.

Irving, Washington. (1850). *The Adventures of Captain Bonneville, USA, in the Rocky Mountains and Far West.* Rev. edn. Philadelphia: Carey, Lea & Blanchard.

James, Edwin. (1823). *Account of an Expedition from Pittsburgh to the Rocky Mountains.* 2 vols. Philadelphia: Carey & Lea.

James, Gen. Thomas. (1966). *Three Years Among the Indians and Mexicans,* ed. Milo Milton Quaife. New York: Citadel.

Kendall, George Wilkins. (1844). *Narrative of the Texas Santa Fe Expedition.* 2 vols. New York: Harper & Brothers.

Leonard, Zenas. (1839). *Narrative of the Adventures of Zenas Leonard.* Clearfield, PA: Moore.

Mackenzie, Alexander. (1931). *Voyages from Montreal on the River St. Laurence through the*

Continent of North America to the Frozen and Pacific Oceans in the Years 1789 and 1793 (1801), ed. Milo Milton Quaife. Chicago: Lakeside.

Marcy, Randolph B. (1859). *The Prairie Traveler: A Handbook for Overland Expeditions*. New York: Harper & Brothers.

Nuttall, Thomas. (1821). *A Journal of Travels into the Arkansas Territory during the Year 1819*. Philadelphia: Palmer.

Parkman, Francis, Jr. (1849). *The California and Oregon Trail: Being Sketches of Prairie and Rocky Mountain Life*. New York: Putnam.

Pattie, James O. (1831). *The Personal Narrative of James O. Pattie of Kentucky*, ed. Timothy Flint. Cincinnati: Flint.

Pike, Zebulon. (1810). *An Account of Expeditions to the Sources of the Mississippi and through the Western Parts of Louisiana*. Philadelphia: Conrad.

Ross, Alexander. (1849). *Adventures of the First Settlers on the Oregon or Columbia River*. London: Smith, Elder.

Ruxton, George. (1848). *Adventures in the Rocky Mountains and Mexico*. New York: Harper and Brothers.

Tanner, John. (1830). *A Narrative of the Adventures of John Tanner (US Interpreter at the Sault Ste. Marie) during Thirty Years Residence among the Indians in the Interior of North America*, ed. Edwin James. New York: Blanchard.

Thompson, David. *Narrative, 1784–1812*. (1962), ed. Richard Glover. Publications of the Champlain Society. Toronto.

Wyeth, John B. (1833). *Oregon; A Short History of a Long Journey*. Cambridge, MA: Wyrth.

Fiction

Averill, Charles. (1849). *Kit Carson: Prince of the Gold Hunters*. Boston: G.H. Williams.

Bennett, Emerson. (1847). *The Bandits of the Osage*. Cincinnati: Robinson & Jones.

Bennett, Emerson. (1848). *The Prairie Flower, or, Adventures in the Far West*. Cincinnati: Stratton.

Bennett, Emerson. (1849). *Lena Leoti, or, Adventures in the Far West*. Cincinnati: Stratton.

Bennett, Emerson. (1852). *Viola, or, Adventures in the Far Southwest*. Philadelphia: Peterson.

Cooper, James Fenimore. (1827). *The Prairie*. Philadelphia, Carey & Lea.

Coyner, David H. (1847). *The Lost Trappers: A Collection of Scenes and Events in the Rocky Mountains*. New York: Hurst.

Dallam, James. (1848). *The Deaf Spy: A Tale Founded Upon Incidents in the History of Texas*. Baltimore: Taylor.

Decalves, Alonso [John Trumbull]. (1788). *Journey to the Unknown Part of America in the Years 1786 & 1787*. Keene, NH: Trumbull.

Flint, Timothy. (1830). *The Shoshonee Valley; a Romance*. Cincinnati: Flint.

Flint, Timothy. (1834). *Francis Berrian, or The Mexican Patriot*. Philadelphia: Key & Biddle.

Garrard, Lewis Hector. (1850). *Wah-To-Yah and the Taos Trail*. Cincinnati: Derby.

Hall, James. *Tales of the Border*. (1835). Philadelphia: H. Hall.

Irving, John T. (1837). *The Hunters of the Prairies; or The Hawk Chief*. New York: Hueston.

Marryat, Frederick. (1843). *Narrative of the travels and adventures of Monsieur Violet in California, Sonora, & western Texas, written by Captain Marryat*. RNCB Edition sanctioned by the author. Leipzig: Tauchnitz.

Poe, Edgar Allen. (1840). The Journal of Julius Rodman. *Burton's Gentleman's Magazine*, 6 (January–May). http://www.eapoe.org/works/TALES/rodmn1.htm.

Robb, John S. (1847). *Kaam; or The Daylight: A Tale of the Rocky Mountains*. Boston: Star Spangled.

Snelling, William Joseph. (1936). *Tales of the Old Northwest (1830)*. Minneapolis: University of Minnesota Press.

Webber, Charles W. (1848). *Old Hicks the Guide; or, Adventures in the Camanche Country in Search of a Gold Mine*. New York: Harper & Brothers.

Webber, Charles W. (1853). *Tales of the Southern Border*. New York: Harper & Brothers.

3

Worlds of Wonder and Ambition: Gold Rush California and the Culture of Mining Bonanzas in the North American West

Peter J. Blodgett

"Boys, I believe I have found a gold mine!" With those words, an obscure carpenter and mechanic from New Jersey named James W. Marshall launched one of the most astounding series of events in American history. Marshall's startling discovery on the morning of January 24, 1848 in the tailrace of an unfinished sawmill on the American River perhaps forty miles east of present-day Sacramento would rapidly transform the isolated Mexican province of Alta California into "El Dorado," the land of instant riches and vast fortunes, and propel it into the center of a furor of global proportions. So powerfully alluring did this vision of El Dorado prove that the search continued long after California's great boom subsided, stretching across the whole of western North America and spanning more than half a century. While mining as an industry became an economic mainstay of the region during the nineteenth century, the repeated rushes for riches that began with the California Gold Rush unleashed powerful cultural and social influences as well.

Before the great California rush reached its second anniversary, it was clear that the wealth of El Dorado would galvanize economic enterprises of all kinds. As gold production vaulted upward, from $250,000 in 1848 to more than $10 million in 1849 to beyond $40 million in 1850, and the number of miners increased tenfold in the same period, many astute men and women saw endless opportunities for profit from the combination of vast amounts of ready money and enormous demand for nearly every commodity and service imaginable. Many entrepreneurs gravitated to the mining camps and towns to meet the demands of the miners themselves for shirts and blankets, flour and beans, shovels, and long toms, not to mention the perennial threesome of wine, women, and song. Frank Marryat, commenting upon the mining business in his account, *Mountains and Molehills*, noted that "the diggings will be

A Companion to the Literature and Culture of the American West, First Edition. Edited by Nicolas S. Witschi.
© 2011 Blackwell Publishing Ltd. Published 2011 by Blackwell Publishing Ltd.

replenished by new comers, and high prices, whether for potatoes or trowsers, will still ... be maintained in a fair proportion to the yield of gold; ... for it is an extraordinary fact that, let the diggings fall off as they will, the miners will still require *bread* and *breeches*, and will find the money to pay for them" (p. 376). Other business people found that flush times in California meant good prospects in many other undertakings as well.

California's booming cities, for instance, contained fast-growing populations that comprised large markets in themselves as well as way stations for supplies and equipment funneled on to the mining country. Merchants like Collis Huntington, his eventual partner Mark Hopkins, and other aspiring entrepreneurs, in their struggle for success, cultivated a detailed appreciation of the possibilities for any merchandise. Mark Hopkins, writing home to his brother Moses in New York on July 30, 1850, found his commerce remarkably lively, reporting that "In New York the great trouble is to find sale for goods – Here it is the reverse, our greatest trouble is in buying goods. They sell themselves and there is hardly any goods that are wanted in this country. ... You would be astonished to see the loaded waggons that daily go out of this town bound for all parts of the country."[1]

Other business ventures responded to other needs common at a time of explosive population growth. While her physician husband pursued his medical practice, Mary Jane Megquier had set up her boarding house only months after their June 1849 arrival in San Francisco from Maine. By the summer of 1850, with the boarding house running full tilt, she found herself swamped by the chores it demanded, as she described them in a June 30 letter to her daughter Angeline in Maine:

> I should like to give you an account of my work if I could do it justice. ... I get up and make the coffee then I make the biscuit, then I fry the potatoes then broil three pounds of steak, and as much liver ... at eight the bell rings and they are eating until nine. I do not sit until they are nearly all done. ... I bake six loaves of bread ... then four pies, or a pudding, then we have lamb ... beef and pork, baked, turnips, beets, potatoes, radishes, sallad, and that everlasting soup ... and I have cooked every mouthful that has been eaten. ... I make six beds every day and do the washing and ironing ... and when I dance all night I am obliged to trot all day and if I had not the constitution of six horses I should [have] been dead long ago.

The cost of Megquier's success, in terms of the exhausting physical toil it required, demonstrated that, even at the height of the gold fever, few could win a golden reward in California without great effort.

Outside of the cities, the possibilities of exploiting California's fertile landscapes to feed the state's booming population attracted the attention of newcomers and longtime residents alike. Jesse Smart, a farmer and nurseryman from Maine who emigrated to California in 1852, found its climate and its rich soils exceptionally promising. Convinced that the Golden State offered opportunities far surpassing those of home, he wrote confidently to his son on October 31, 1852, urging him to "sell the Frye lot for what you can get in ready pay you had better sell your own for my word for it you will never work on it after you see California, its beauties, its health, its productions. ... The nursery business on a large scale will occupy all our efforts for the future 10,000 a year may be done at it."

With so many calculations of this sort underway in so many households, in California, across the United States, and around the globe during the 1850s, it is no surprise that speculations of all kinds became the constant practice of many who had become intrigued by the Golden State's possibilities. Despite such frequent obstacles as crushingly high interest rates and an alarmingly erratic boom-and-bust business cycle that characterized its economy, California's magnetic attraction to fortune hunters remained too powerful for many to resist. Ernest Seyd, an English commentator pondering the possibilities of the Golden State in his 1858 volume, *California and its Resources: A Work for the Merchant, the Capitalist, and the Emigrant*, admitted the terrible losses suffered by English and Continental investors during ill-considered investment booms in quartz mining or other ventures during the early years of the Gold Rush. Nonetheless, in light of California's "extraordinary natural advantages, her combined unparalleled mineral and agricultural resources ... and the present prosperous state of things," he argued that "there is not a country on the face of the globe more highly endowed with all the elements of prosperity, richer in precious metals, [or] richer in agricultural and other prospects, than California" (p. 20). To Seyd and like-minded observers, the golden dream of California was hardly a dream at all but rather a matter of applying good sense and cold hard cash to the opportunities that abounded.

As prognosticators and pamphleteers spun out their own golden visions, the unquenchable demand from the mining counties year after year for a fantastic array of goods also spawned an immense import trade. The port of San Francisco mushroomed into a bustling commercial hub only months after the gold discovery, with hundreds of ships arriving and departing each year well into the 1850s. In the autumn of 1854, for example, the customs ledger kept to record activity in the port noted the arrival of many vessels, large and small, hailing from Great Britain, Denmark, Holland, Germany, France, Sweden, and Chile as well as the United States. Aboard those well-traveled merchantmen were kegs of paint and casks of porter, pigs of iron and pigs of flesh and blood, bags of rice and cases of cigars, barrels of vinegar and barrels of molasses, baskets of champagne, boxes of dried oysters, coal by the ton, oranges by the tens of thousands, nails, rope, bricks, shawls, squashes, bananas, and tea. The markets for which such disparate products were intended thus reached far beyond the necessities required for mere survival in the gold fields. They clearly appealed to those who possessed the discretionary income to indulge personal tastes for luxury as well as to business enterprises that would deal in goods that represented sophistication, dissipation, and leisure to their consumers. At the same time, many of these commodities would fuel an urbanizing, industrialized society fully engaged in replicating many of the characteristics of similar societies in the Atlantic world and its global network of colonial outposts.

In such a setting, therefore, the dream of an imperial California seemed nearly at hand. Contemplating the astounding pace of California's evolution just in the few years since 1848, it became a commonplace for observers to speak in tones of reverence and wonder. William Van Voorhies, delivering the Admission Day anniversary oration to the Society of California Pioneers in September 1853, contrasted the California of his day with that of just a few years ago: "But now, how changed! The busy hum of active industry, like the tones of 'applauding thunder,' rings from the mountain top to the bosom of the valleys; cities and villages, as if by magic, spring up; mountain fastnesses are penetrated and subdued," while the world itself had become the back-yard of the Golden State, where "harbors whiten with the sails of a world-wide com-merce; the remote West grasps the hand of the remote East, and Brother Jonathan the 'Independent' familiarly exchanges with John the Chinaman, clocks for silks, teas and chessboards; while Hail Columbia is sung under the walls of Nankin, and Yankee Doodle whistled at the gates of Japan" (p. 5).

The dizzying rapidity with which such changes occurred seemed most evident to observers in the Golden State as they watched the seemingly overnight transformation of tiny villages and desolate mining camps into flourishing towns and cities. In many ways, San Francisco exemplified the process of nearly instant urbanization, especially in the startling pace and stunning consequences of such growth. One forty-niner, Orval Comstock, writing home to his parents on June 5, 1849, described the boom town in progress:

> On ascending a hill on the road from the landing we caught a view of the town beauti-fully situated in the valley below. Many of the houses are about as substantial as the usual board & cloth tents at a *Camp Meeting*. Stores, Groceries, Eatinghouses, & gambling shops are generally nothing more than temporary tents. ... I said that San Francisco was a miniature world & it may be called so for every nation that has any knowledge of the *Gold Mines* is represented here.

Already by then the gateway to El Dorado for the vast majority of the gold seekers and the goods that sustained them, San Francisco was in the midst of an astounding expansion that saw its population increase thirtyfold or more in only two years, from 1,000 or less in 1848 to approximately 30,000 in 1850. The ever-observant Mrs. Megquier, writing home from San Francisco to friends and family in the spring and summer of 1850, described in an April 19 letter some of the amenities beginning to appear for those who could afford them: "We are getting ahead of any thing on the other side in the way of improvements. We have soft water carried through the streets every day, for which you only have to pay a dollar and a half, a barrel, We have three daily papers put into our door handle every morning. ... We have concerts from Henri Herz, the pianist which are well attended at six dollars single ticket." By the spring of 1853, after the couple had gone home to Maine and then returned to California, she could write on April 8 with great enth-usiasm that

I have seen so much of things a little more exciting I fear I shall never feel perfectly satisfied with their quiet ways again [at home in Maine]. Here you can step out of your house and see the whole world spread out before you in every shape and form. Your ears are filled with the most delightful music, your eyes are dazzeled with every thing that is beautiful the streets are crowded the whole city is in the streets.

Such comforts and diversions, as Mrs. Megquier noted, meant improvements to not only the physical but also the social and cultural lot of the Argonauts very early in the great rush. With substantial and growing populations of well-to-do city dwellers came cravings for concerts, plays, balls, and dinner parties. Theaters and auditoriums appeared during the 1850s to meet the demand, hosting itinerant theatrical companies, minstrel troupes, orchestras, and a host of other entertainers from acrobats to aerialists. At San Francisco's Adelphi Theatre on May 26, 1852, for instance, "The Alleghanians" in their "Second Grand Concert in California" offered the public a "Grand Musical Soiree" consisting of duets, quartets, and solos with chorus. The Sacramento Theatre on May 23, 1855 could advertise the "Immense Attraction" of the "Chinese Dramatic Company" who would present "the Truly Wonderful Tragedy Of 'The Mountain Wizard'" followed by "The Great Rebellion" (while offering the public an assurance that "there shall be nothing of a vulgar nature in the performances, so that all may witness them with interest.") In 1856, Sacramento's Forrest Theater could offer the "Grand Complimentary Testimonial to Mr. Jas. Stark" playing the role of Sir John Falstaff in Shakespeare's *The Merry Wives of Windsor* accompanied by a "sailor's hornpipe" and a "Fancy Dance" performed by Miss Louisa Graves and "La Petite Susan Robinson," respectively, with the play "The Iron Chest or, The Mysterious Murder" to open the evening's festivities.

While many residents of San Francisco or Sacramento might applaud such performances as symbols of the increasing sophistication and cultivation present in their communities, no Gold Rush city or town could afford to jettison the more rough-and-tumble entertainments wanted by other Argonauts. Forty-niner physician Charles Ross Parke, during a visit to Sacramento in the fall of 1850, wrote disparagingly in his diary on September 6 that

if the good old saintly people of the States could only look in on these gambling dens for a minute or two, I know they would feel like calling home all *foreign* missionaries and turning them loose on this God-forsaken people. ... At every table, there is a man dealing Monte and surrounded by a crowd, some betting and some looking on. At the far end of the hall is a bar, where all fashionable drinks are dealt out for *one dollar* a drink. There is also a good band of music to enliven the crowd. ... At times those little tables are literally covered with buckskin bags filled with gold dust. Thousands and thousands of dollars changing hands every hour from morning until late in the night.

Although never rivaling the remarkable development of San Francisco, the biggest boomtowns such as Sacramento and Stockton certainly followed most of the patterns set by their coastal cousin during the 1850s. Upon his first acquaintance with

Sacramento, Dr. Israel Lord caustically portrayed its combination of thriving business activity and moral disintegration caused by the boomtown mentality, writing in his diary on November 26, 1850 that

> when business is lively, and three or four steamers and twice as many other vessels are unloading every day, the levee is a tangled mass of men and rogues and Mexicans and Chinese and Chileans and Kanakas and horses and mules and asses and oxen and drays and lumber and flour and potatoes and molasses and brandy and pickles and oysters and yams and cabbages and books and furniture and almost everything that one could think of – except honesty and religion. These articles not being in demand here are not thrown into market.

Especially at the height of the great excitement during the early 1850s, similar accounts were written about Stockton or Marysville or any one of several dozen other camps scattered throughout the mining districts.

Even as California's wealth steadily increased and many of its towns and cities flourished during the decade following gold discovery, its importance to the development of the trans-Mississippi West grew deeper and stronger as well. With the exhaustion of the placer deposits during the early 1850s and the subsequent focus upon more expensive and complex mining techniques, many experienced miners were left at a loose end. By the middle of the decade, they were crowded out of an industry that now emphasized saving labor (and the costs such labor entailed) with increasingly expensive and sophisticated equipment. This lure of finding another El Dorado, however, had already set many men to hunting for mineral wealth elsewhere in the West. As bonanzas or even rumors of bonanzas circulated, these "old Californians," as some described them, became an important reservoir of talent and expertise. Many first rushed north in 1858 to the Fraser River in modern-day British Columbia, a boom that quickly turned mostly to bust. The discovery a year later of incredibly rich deposits of silver ore to the east in Nevada Territory in what became known as the "Comstock Lode" ignited the first great post-California boom.

Californians armed with money, industrial plant, and entrepreneurial energy thus helped launch the great era of mining bonanzas over the quarter-century after 1860 that proved so critical to the development and settlement of the mountain West. Other California entrepreneurs threw their initiative behind other endeavors. Perhaps the grandest of them all was to be the Central Pacific Railroad, organized by Sacramento merchant Collis P. Huntington, his business partner Mark Hopkins, and their associates Charles Crocker and Leland Stanford. Inaugurated in 1862 as the western half of the first transcontinental railroad, the Central Pacific capitalized upon the long-standing agitation in California for a railroad stretching from the eastern United States to the Pacific. In a December 8, 1865 letter to his brother Solon back home in Oneonta, New York, Huntington assured him that "in relation to the Central Pacific Railroad stock that you hold, I can only answer that I think it very good," due to the fact that its route, "on an allmost direct line to the great Silver Mines of Washoe,

Rease River & Humbolt," would put the road in a perfect position to "do nearly all the business between California and the State of Nevada, the territory of Utah and Idaho, and is now doing the business of three of the best mining counties in California … if you do not want the money for say two years, I would not part with [the stock]."

With California's financial and industrial resources playing such a crucial role in powering the growth of a widening region, many of the patterns of California's own evolution took root in the soil of such far-flung locations as Nevada's Washoe or gulches below the peaks of the Colorado Rockies during following decades. Less than a year after the initial discoveries of precious metals along what would become known as the Comstock Lode, Virginia City, Nevada in 1860 had sprung into existence with stunning speed, sprouting everything from drugstores, bakeries, and blacksmiths to assayers, surveyors, and dozens of saloons. Observers such as Massachusetts newspaper editor Samuel Bowles, in his 1865 travel narrative *Across the Continent: A Summer's Journey to the Rocky Mountains*, could marvel that "California, mature at eleven, plants a colony [Nevada] in 1859–1860, which ripens into a new state in 1864" and write with astonishment of silver mining boom town Austin, Nevada, that "not a tree nor a flower nor a grass plot does the whole town boast, – not one; but it has the best French restaurant I have met since New York, a daily newspaper and the boot-blacks and barbers and baths are luxurious and aristocratic to the continental degree" (pp. 141, 142). Even once abandoned camps, monuments to thwarted ambitions and dreams, could be recalled to life by the electrifying touch of new-found wealth, as Leadville, Colorado took shape in 1879 out of the ashes of the earlier excitement of California Gulch. With 15,000 people clinging to its rocks and ridges in search of fortunes in silver, the town could well afford to support the hundreds of businesses (including scores of saloons) devoted to satiating every need or desire. And every mining bonanza, no matter how brief or lengthy, had its gaudy collection of speculators, who traded in everything from real estate to mining stocks; as Ernest Ingersoll wrote of Leadville in his 1879 *Scribner's* essay, "The Camp of the Carbonates: Ups and Downs in Leadville," "you meet persons of every grade and calling, and no matter what their position or occupation, their whole conversation is of mining … not only your banker, but your baker and grocer and the man who saws your wood has some cash interest in the silver diggings" (pp. 819–20).

However quickly they might bound from a humble collection of miners' shanties to an aspiring city, boom towns from Sacramento to Virginia City to Leadville thus rarely failed to acquire not only the trappings of the wild and wooly mining camp but also many of the physical and cultural amenities of the Victorian community. As John Loomis described it in an 1879 pamphlet entitled *Leadville Colorado: The Most Wonderful Mining Camp in the World*, "the heavy rumbling of immense freight teams, the rattle of express wagons, the clatter of horsemen, the hurrying tramp of the pedestrians, the familiar cries of the news-boy and boot-black, the braying of donkeys and the ear-piercing screeches of a dozen steam whistles, combine to startle the dullest imagination and fill the mind of the stranger with astonishment" (p. 16), portraying an instant city that had acquired everything from schools, newspapers, and waterworks to butchers, bakers, confectioners, jewelers, tailors, and booksellers. Hotels, theaters, and an opera house offered genteel amusements while lawyers, doctors, merchants, and bankers provided the solid foundations of commerce and finance so necessary for the entrepreneurial capitalism that underlay so many of these mining rushes.

Wherever and whenever they sprang up, however, and no matter how grand their ambitions, the instant cities produced by the uncontrolled and uncontrollable growth characteristic of these rushes for riches often paid a disastrous price for the unrestrained gusto with which they grew. In the early days of the California gold mania, for example, flimsy construction, shoddy building materials, and a dismaying tendency on the part of many inhabitants to be careless with open flames condemned communities large and small to fiery obliteration. San Francisco itself repeatedly suffered from devastating blazes in 1849, 1850, and 1851, setting loose forces of destruction that Frank Marryat in *Mountains and Molehills* captured after one conflagration in agonizing detail:

> No conception can be formed of the grandeur of the scene: for at one time the burning district was covered by one vast sheet of flame that extended half a mile in length. ... the shouts of the excited populace – the crash of falling timbers – the yells of the burnt and injured ... maddened horses released from burning livery-stables plunging through the streets ... as the swaying crowd, forced back by the flames, tramples all before it. (p. 188)

Other towns and cities, particularly low-lying Sacramento and Stockton, fell prey to the overwhelming power of swollen streams and rivers, fed by winter rainfalls or spring snowmelts in the mountains. Merchant Stephen Davis, arriving in Stockton on December 19, 1852, described in his diary the wilderness of water all around him:

> Ferrys were established across the principal streets which were now foaming cataracts, and unsafe to cross, or traverse with carriages. ... For miles around a vast sheet of water presents itself to view, with a fleet of houses, some apparently at anchor and some in motion, while boats are out in every direction stemming the flood, rescuing families from their aquatic situations, and also picking up goods that are floating in [every] direction.

Mrs. Megquier, writing home two years earlier about the disastrous floods that had swept into Sacramento in the winter of 1850, reported that the city

> has been entirely under water. those that had two story buildings could still transact business in the second story, those that had not, fled to the shipping, and the highlands, but an immense number of cattle and horses were drowned, they intend to levy the city at an expense of five million, quite a sum for the states but nothing for Cal.

Commenting further upon the imperishable optimism of California city pioneers in pursuing their vision no matter what the cost, she added that every spot that is not overflown, they are now building cities upon, lots two or three hundred miles up the river have in [a] week gone from nothing, to thousands, every one of them at the head of steamboat navigation, steamboats are running now where in two months time they cannot get a canoe but they do not stay one moment to consider.

Such devastating encounters with Nature's irresistible forces or the calamitous consequences of human negligence further demonstrated the essential ephemerality of the camps and towns that leapt into existence in the wake of successful "diggings" but that could be extinguished just as abruptly whenever the treasure beneath the earth seemed exhausted. Finely balanced on the knife edge between prosperity and desolation, therefore, every mining boom struggled to find its way to permanence, usually with a notable lack of success. Rare indeed was the localized mining excitement in the Far West that could duplicate the enduring impact exerted by the discoveries of 1848 upon California, revealing as they did over time amounts of precious minerals unprecedented in size and scope. Unrelenting optimism, of course, remained the coin of the realm for every mining bonanza from the first stirrings on the Comstock Lode in 1859 through the following half-century; nowhere would it become a more characteristic outlook on all fronts than in the California that unfolded in the wake of the Gold Rush decade.

Mary Jane Megquier's slightly bemused description of the fervent optimism represented by those who set to work immediately rebuilding drowned towns and cities thus aptly reflected the seductive appeal to so many Californians of a belief in the Golden State's great possibilities. Although the vast majority of those who attempted to earn their golden reward from the mines had failed to do more than pay their expenses, many of the Argonauts still found aspects of life in California too tempting to abandon easily. Intoxicated by the wonders of its climate, the beauties of its landscapes, or the richness of its natural resources, various gold seekers found new employment for their talents and their energies. John S. Hittell, in an 1869 address to the Society of California Pioneers on the anniversary of Admission Day, recounted his vision of what California had offered and would offer to the Argonauts who had put aside their restless ways to stay on the Pacific Coast:

> She gave to all a cherished home, a sunny and genial sky, a fertile soil, a delightful landscape, a clime suited to the development of every energy, the companionship of the most intelligent and enterprising people, and a site suited for the great city and for the concentration of the commerce of a wealthy coast. ... California will occupy in the hemisphere of the Pacific, as a focus of intellectual culture, a position similar to that long held by Attica in the basin of the Mediterranean. (pp. 16, 20–1)

Other writers, echoing some of Hittell's sentiments, put the matter in more concrete terms, appealing with specific details to those in the growing American middle class who had an interest in relocating permanently to better their circumstances or in traveling for recreation and leisure. Describing his purpose in writing his 1873 guidebook, *California for Travelers and Settlers*, Charles Nordhoff wrote that "I would like to induce Americans, when they contemplate a journey for health, pleasure, or instruction, or all three, to think ... particularly of California, which has so many delights in store for the tourist and so many attractions for the farmer or settler looking for a mild and healthful climate and a productive country" (p. 11). Discussing the wonders of its agriculture in greater detail, he affirmed that

> very few suspect that the Californians have the best of us, and that, so far from living in a kind of rude exile, they enjoy, in fact, the finest climate, the most fertile soil, the loveliest skies, the mildest winters, the most healthful region, in the whole United States. ... it is, in fact, the best part of the American continent, either for health or for profitable and pleasant living in any industrious pursuit" (pp. 118–19)

During the same years, through the late 1860s and early 1870s, such assertions in guidebooks such as *California for Travelers and Settlers* were only bolstered by the rapidly evolving art of photography. As photographic processes became more sophisticated and more portable, photographers were able to venture further afield from the studio to produce images which in turn could be more easily reproduced and distributed to a wider audience. Thus, greater numbers of people were exposed to a greater variety of California views. Stereographs, a pair of photographs taken of the same subject by a special double-lensed camera and mounted side by side upon stiff board stock, became all the rage. Placed a precise distance apart, these paired images created a remarkably vivid three-dimensional effect when seen through a viewer equipped with two lenses and an adjustable holder for the stereograph that allowed the user to move the image closer or further away depending upon one's eyesight.

Publishers such as Lawrence & Houseworth, their successor Thomas Houseworth & Co., or Bradley & Rulofson collected tens of thousands of stereographs and reproduced them as quickly as possible for a fast-growing market. The images thus distributed could inform, entertain, or intrigue the user, much as the Gold Rush-era pictorial letter sheets had done a generation earlier and postcards would do throughout the twentieth century. Now, however, although exotic subjects such as Chinese residents in full traditional regalia would appear because of their continuing sales appeal, many other more mundane images would commonly fill the catalogs and sample books such as Houseworth & Co.'s 1872 *Pacific Coast Scenery*. Many photographs would highlight the continued development of San Francisco into a great city, as marked by three- and four-story stone office buildings, grand wide boulevards, and majestic civic structures. Others would stress the ease and comfort in which one could make the journey to California from points east on the luxuriously equipped trains of the Central Pacific and the Union Pacific railroads on their linked transcontinental route, during which the passenger could enjoy the use of sleeping compartments, dining rooms, and parlors. And, still other images would promote a vision of a bucolic California countryside demarcated by tidy and prosperous towns and striking scenic vistas, knitted together by the epitome of industrial progress, the railroad.

By the 1880s, then, forty years after gold discovery, California's advantages were the stuff of legend, promoted around the world to attract tourists, investors, and especially immigrants. The railroads that served the western United States collaborated with local authorities and the state government to produce pamphlets and brochures to champion the proposition that California could be "Cornucopia of the World," a veritable paradise whose staggering natural abundance was matched only by the equally staggering amounts of land available for the taking, with "a climate for health & wealth, without Cyclones or Blizzards" (in the words of one 1883 brochure). Here, the boosters of California argued, was opportunity on an unparalleled scale "for immigrants desiring to secure lands at cheap rates, on which to make happy and prosperous homes." For the immigrants of the 1880s, like the Argonauts of 1849, here was El Dorado in all its glory, where they might reach for dreams once thought permanently out of their grasp.

Many of the Argonauts who had stayed on in the Golden State joined the cheering for California's glorious future, celebrating the remarkable transformation that had already taken place in the land they had once known. Alonzo Delano, in an 1868 pamphlet entitled *The Central Pacific Railroad or, '49 and '69*, wrote wonderingly about the comparison between California past and present:

> Six months upon the Plains, nineteen years ago, and California only a wilderness. What is it now? The Californian has only to cast his eye over our land, and see its growing cities, its beautiful towns, its immense commerce with the whole world, its magnificent homes, its manufactories, its railroads, and its overflowing abundance of the comforts and luxuries of life, the produce of its rich soil through the energies of our people. To an old pioneer, whose memory of his early trials is still fresh, these changes seem like the enchantment of the magician's wand. (p. 4)

As vigorously as they might applaud such spectacular progress, however, many of the gold seekers also shared a desire to ensure that their contributions to California's history would be remembered. With the passage of the years and the natural thinning of their ranks due to the deaths of fellow pioneers, former Argonauts began to organize celebrations of the monumental events in which they had participated. The model for them all was the Society of California Pioneers, founded in 1850 with the express intent "to collect and preserve information connected with the early settlement and conquest of the country, and to perpetuate the memory of those whose sagacity, enterprise, and love of independence induced them to settle in the wilderness and become the germ of a new state." Later, in the 1870s and 1880s, came other, more narrowly focused groups such as the Society of First Steamship Pioneers, the Territorial Pioneers of California, the Associated Pioneers of Territorial Days of California, the New England Associated California Pioneers, the Society of California Pioneers of New England, and the Western Association of California Pioneers. In their meetings and their memorials, they would commemorate the particular roles their members played (in the words of one publication from the Associated Pioneers of Territorial

Days) in helping "to *lick* … our splendid territory into shape, and soon after … erecting her into a vast and sovereign State" and would reminisce about the many challenges and hardships they endured while involved in what they only later realized was "the grand work of civilization."

Their reminiscences of times past grew more important to many of these pioneers as the years since "the days of '49" passed by, leaving fewer and fewer behind who had lived through those extraordinary circumstances. To John S. Ellis, presiding over the thirteenth annual meeting and dinner of the Associated Pioneers of the Territorial Days of California in New York City on January 9, 1888, these reunions had a special meaning. In his published remarks, he asserted that such gatherings allowed each pioneer, "after ascending the ladder of life, and getting more than half way down the other side," to look back "upon passages of his life, wherein he has a fair reason to be satisfied with his motives, his achievements, and the commendation of his friends and fellow citizens, if he has done anything worthy of such notice" and to gather around him "those who participated at the same period with him in stirring times" (p. 6).

In striking contrast to such elaborate mechanisms for recalling memories of times past in the California gold fields, later participants in later mining booms seemed to devote little or no energy to memorializing their stories in similar ways. While every survivor of the Comstock Lode or the scramble to Leadville or any other bonanza undoubtedly carried away a personal storehouse of memories, even the pioneers did not seem inclined to commemorate the events. In part, perhaps, this circumstance may have reflected the fact that many excitements burned themselves out in just a few years or even months, which meant that those who took part spent far less time in the Washoe or the Colorado Rockies or the Coeur d'Alene than had their predecessors in California. For them, the associations with Nevada or Idaho or Montana were far more attenuated than the ties that many of the Argonauts had felt with California. Moreover, while unchecked optimism about instant wealth for anyone still ran rampant at the beginning of each new rush, the intractable geology of later bonanza sites usually could only be overcome with the capital- and technologically intensive methods of hard-rock underground mining. Transformed under such conditions into industrial wage labor, the miners who populated the booms that followed gold discovery in California usually lacked the freedom from restraint and the independence in seeking a personal fortune that had been so thoroughly celebrated during and after the Gold Rush. For many of them, the El Dorado pursued by the California gold seekers lay impossibly out of reach and generated no fond memories of their experiences in the world of mining.

Contemporary accounts and reminiscences, whenever and however they were captured, reflected the grasp that many participants had of the significance of these events. Even as those who took part in different mining booms strove to record or recollect what they had experienced, however, other individuals began to put pen to paper in efforts to make sense of the bonanza west. In the 1860s and 1870s, for example, authors such as Bret Harte or Mark Twain found that the world of the California or

Nevada mining camps revealed much about the men and women who inhabited it. Both found in its primitive conditions and backwoods characters rich sources of humor about the miner and the life he led. Twain, in particular, discovered innumerable opportunities to satirize the pretensions and the ambitions of the get-rich-quick miner in his day on Nevada's Comstock Lode in his celebrated 1872 travelogue, *Roughing It*. At the same time, writing of his travels in the California gold country more than twenty years after its boom times, he conveyed a sense of the fascinating allure already exercised by that receding era: "They were rough in those times! They fairly reveled in gold, whisky, fights and fandangoes, and were unspeakably happy. ... It was a wild, free, disorderly, grotesque society! *Men* – only swarming hosts of stalwart men – nothing juvenile, nothing feminine, visible anywhere!" (p. 391). Harte, by contrast, in such stories as "The Luck of Roaring Camp" or "The Outcasts of Poker Flats," portrayed a world that might be filled with boisterous adventure but that usually possessed a rough-hewn sentimentality as well, tinged with nobility and pathos. Harte's Gold Rush characters often demonstrated that unexpected strengths and weaknesses might be found in the search for gold.

While Harte and Twain, like the Argonauts themselves, might concentrate upon the fate of the individuals caught up in the mining mania, other works appeared in the same years that devoted much attention to understanding the theoretical and practical dimensions of the mining industry whose growth followed so quickly in the wake of each new strike. Public agencies such as the California Geological Survey, the Geological Exploration of the 40th Parallel, and the United States Department of the Treasury's Commissioner of Mining Statistics were only some of the organizations whose missions in part or in whole were influenced by the bonanza mentality of these decades. Weighty compilations of facts and figures to document "the condition of the mining industry" aspired, in the words of the United States Mining Commissioner Rossiter Raymond in 1874, to reflect "the endeavors of the Government to assist at once the general welfare and the special prosperity of mining and the metallurgical arts by the diffusion of correct information" (p. 1). Similar reports, such as Samuel F. Emmons' *Abstract of a Report upon the Geology and Mining Industry of Leadville Colorado* (1882), flowed from the presses of the Government Printing Office in Washington, DC and those of state and territorial agencies year after year, illuminating an entire industry not only for its practitioners but also for those eager to profit from investments and speculations of all kinds. Even writers outside the realm of science, intent upon rendering a portrait of a boom town at its height, often would salute the role of the learned specialist, as Ingersoll did when he acknowledged that "one of the most important men in [Leadville] is the assayer ... the grimy worker and his rude laboratory become the center of the miner's hopes, and he [the miner] hangs over the process in silent expectancy while the mysterious investigation goes on" (p. 818).

Grappling as they did to understand the scientific realities that literally underlay each successive mining boom, the geologists and professional mining engineers who conducted the studies and gathered the data created what could be described as a literature of exploration and discovery that eventually spanned much of the Far West. As those labors unfolded, the societies established in response to the California Gold Rush and its successors attracted considerable study as well. Many writers, of course, echoed the full-throated approbation of the Golden State expressed by John Hittell in his *The Resources of California,* "I write of a land of wonders … I write of her while she still offers a wide field for the adventurous the enterprising and the young, who have life before them, and wish to commence it where they may have the freest career, in full sight of the greatest rewards for success and with the fewest chances of failure" (pp. iii, iv–v). Similar applause could be heard about the settings of other sensational mining strikes such as Leadville's silver mines, where, as George Dresher asserted in his 1881 account, *A Description of Colorado, Leadville, and the Sovereign Consolidated Silver Mines,* "the result of all this increase of population and prodigious mining production and profit is to make Leadville the liveliest town the world can show to-day … Leadville by lamp-light fairly 'booms' with excitement and life" (p. 80).

Other authors at work in the closing decades of the nineteenth century, however, found other subjects of equally compelling interest for them. In portraying the events that unfolded during the years from the American conquest of California through the frenzy of the Gold Rush, writers such as Helen Hunt Jackson in her celebrated 1884 novel *Ramona* imagined the pre-conquest days through an increasingly romantic sensibility, rhapsodizing about what had been lost in the transformation of Mexican California following gold discovery. María Amparo Ruiz de Burton, by contrast, the child of a well-established Baja California land-owning family, took a more complicated view of these events, reflecting her own personal circumstances. Linked by blood to various important Californio families, she also possessed connections to the new Yankee society through her husband, Colonel Henry S. Burton, an American army officer she had married after the Mexican–American War. Sharply critical of the premises on which the Land Commission Act of 1851 had been established and of the commission's operations, her 1885 novel *The Squatter and the Don* offered a stinging indictment of the resulting impoverishment and dispossession of many Californios. She also decried the ongoing concentration of wealth and power in California that she saw during the decades after the Civil War.

In this appraisal of California society, María Ruiz de Burton launched salvos reminiscent of other critics, most particularly the San Francisco newspaperman Henry George. George's writings, especially his most prominent work, *Progress and Poverty,* approached the unfolding nature of the American economy from a similarly critical perspective. For George, events in California particularly influenced his perspective as seen in the case of California's land titles. In his 1871 pamphlet *Our Land and Land Policy, National and State,* he concurred with the Californios who had so vocally if futilely opposed the proceedings of the Land Commission and decried the extravagant concentration of land ownership in a few hands. Had the Mexican land grants been confirmed and then incorporated by government purchase into the public domain, George argued, a realm of successful yeoman farmers would have brought California even greater prosperity and success, rather than instituting what he considered a regime of land monopolists, creating "the blight that has fallen upon California, stunting her growth and mocking her golden promise" (p. 25).

Two other interpreters of California's transformation in the Gold Rush decade, Charles Howard Shinn and Josiah Royce, even found that experience instructive for pondering the nature of contemporary American society. Shinn, a California newspaperman, had spent much time during the 1870s in the old mining camps talking with surviving pioneers. From these encounters, he grew fascinated with the ways and means by which the miners had conducted their affairs, even in the absence of other forms of government. Evaluating their successes and failures in an 1885 volume entitled *Mining Camps: A Study in American Frontier Government* (begun as a thesis at Johns Hopkins University), Shinn regarded the experience of the miners as indicative of certain common American traits, reaching back even beyond the colonization of North America to the roots of democracy that could be found in English and German folk cultures. Shinn noted when the miners' experiments with self-government fell short, especially in dealing with outsiders: "Sometimes, however, the Americans were unjust and overbearing, or were at least careless and indifferent to the rights of others." On the whole, however, Shinn concluded that "when youth and energy from older communities of the Atlantic States, and adventurers from every land under the sun, joined in the famous gold-rush of 1849, – the marvel of marvels is, that mob-law and failure of justice were so infrequent, that society was so well and so swiftly organized" (pp. 212, 231).

Royce, a California-born professor of philosophy at Harvard University, published his work, *California: From the Conquest in 1846 to the Second Vigilance Committee in 1856*, in 1886, a year after Shinn's book had appeared. Intrigued, like Shinn, by what the events in California meant for his country as a whole, Royce had chosen to describe his work with the subtitle, "A Study of American Character." Unlike Shinn, Royce discovered within the era far more deeply entwined roots of violence and disorder. In the wholesale abandonment of their duties to help maintain civil society, Royce found, the best men among the forty-niners and their peers aggravated the tensions that had begun to fracture what little social order existed in this frenzied era. Thus empowered by the dereliction of the best, the worst in any community could seize the day, especially in dealing with the foreigners who had come to the mines. Toward them, Royce wrote, "ours were the crime of a community, consisting largely of honest but cruelly bigoted men, who encouraged the ruffians of their own nation to ill-treat the wonders of another, to the frequent destruction of peace and good order. We were favored of heaven with the instinct of organization; and so here we organized brutality and, so to speak, asked God's blessing upon it" (p. 363).

In contrast to such wide-ranging and often sophisticated efforts undertaken by these and other observers to make sense of the California Gold Rush experience, writers who chose to follow the trail of subsequent mining rushes frequently produced works of significantly lesser weight. Beyond the literature oriented to the science of geological discovery and exploration, many authors found these settings ripe with the potential for humor, sometimes liberally spiced with irony. While Mark Twain sharpened his craft on the Comstock Lode, for instance, his peers Dan De Quille (newspaperman William Wright of the *Territorial Enterprise*) and J. Ross Browne, traveler and sometime public servant, produced their own satires and burlesques of this fabulous environment. Others, such as Ernest Ingersoll and George Dresher in their investigations of Leadville, delved into the passions that brought these mining booms to life, the astounding events that accompanied their rise to maturity, and the remarkable communities that took root as a result. Mary Hallock Foote, a well-known illustrator and budding author, applied her own experiences in Leadville at its zenith with her husband, mining engineer Arthur D. Foote, to explore some of the same issues in her 1883 novel, *The Led-Horse Claim: A Romance of a Mining Camp*, in which she wrote that "no disheartening combination of bad weather, worse roads, and worst accommodations at the journey's end, could deter the pioneers from bearing a city into the unfriendliest spot where such exotic growth every flourished" (p. 10). In *The Led-Horse Claim* and subsequently in *John Bodewin's Testimony* (1886) and *The Last Assembly Ball* (1889), Foote depicted that alien and often inhospitable world with a kind of poetry that few others found in it.

Perhaps most frequently of all, of course, many writers such as John Loomis in his breathless celebratory brochure, *Leadville Colorado*, played their part by helping to generate a promotional literature of substantial dimensions. Filled with paeans to progress achieved and possibilities soon to be realized, that literature could also furnish, as Loomis did, details on "the mining laws, how to stake a claim, wages paid to laborers and mechanics, and everything you need to know" (if your intentions included carving out a prosperous future in the Mountain West). Born of the pecuniary ambitions of the author or the mine owner or the investors or the speculators, the great bulk of these volumes had no more pretensions to literary excellence than insuring that they could attract the attention of aspiring capitalists. With titles sometimes as direct as B.C. Keeler's 1880 guidebook, *Where to Go to Become Rich*, such works possessed a considerable clarity of purpose (whatever other qualities they might lack). Drawing upon the earlier tradition of the emigrant's guide to the overland trails and the lands of milk and honey that were Oregon and California and bearing a close kinship to the evolving guide books intended for the traveler on the new transcontinental railroad, these exercises in boosterism became, in the aggregate, a noteworthy purveyor of persuasive imagery about the Far West. In doing so, they exerted significant influence upon popular conceptions of "the Wild West" that would become deeply embedded in American culture throughout the twentieth century and, with little change, into the twenty-first.

NOTE

1 Those quotations which are not followed by page numbers have been taken from original letters housed in the Manuscripts Department of the Huntington Library, San Marino, CA.

REFERENCES AND FURTHER READING

Associated Pioneers of the Territorial Days of California. (1888). *Thirteenth Annual Meeting and Dinner*. New York: Associated Pioneers of the Territorial Days of California.

Blodgett, Peter J. (1999). *Land of Golden Dreams: California in the Gold Rush Decade, 1848–1858*. San Marino, CA: Huntington Library Press.

Bowles, Samuel. (1865). *Across the Continent: A Summer's Journey to the Rocky Mountains, the Mormons and the Pacific States, with Speaker Colfax*. Springfield, MA: S. Bowles & Co.; New York: Hurd & Houghton.

Browne, J. Ross. (1869). *Resources of the Pacific Slope: A Statistical and Descriptive Summary of the Mines and Minerals, Climate, Topography, Agriculture, Commerce, Manufactures, and Miscellaneous Productions, of the States and Territories West of the Rocky Mountains*. New York: D. Appleton & Co.

Browne, J. Ross. (1959). *A Peep at the Washoe and Washoe Revisited*. Balboa Island, CA: Paisano Press.

California Immigration Commission. (1883). *California, Cornucopia of the World: Room for Millions ...* Chicago: Rand, McNally & Co.

De Quille, Dan. (1947). *The Big Bonanza: An Authentic Account of the Discovery, History, and Working of the World-renowned Comstock Lode of Nevada ... (1876)*. Repr. New York: Alfred A. Knopf.

Delano, Alonzo. (1868). *The Central Pacific Railroad, or '49 and '69*. San Francisco: White & Bauer.

Dresher, George B. (1881). *A Description of Colorado, Leadville, and the Sovereign Consolidated Silver Mines: an Historical, Statistical and Official Review of America's Greatest Mining Centre*. Philadelphia: G.W. Arms & Co.

Emmons, Samuel Franklin. (1882). *Abstract of a Report upon the Geology and Mining Industry of Leadville, Colorado*. Washington: Government Printing Office.

Foote, Mary Hallock. (1883). *The Led-Horse Claim: A Romance of a Mining Camp*. Boston: J.R. Osgood & Co.

Foote, Mary Hallock. (1886). *John Bodewin's Testimony*. Boston: Ticknor & Co.

Foote, Mary Hallock. (1889). *The Last Assembly Ball, and the Fate of a Voice*. Boston and New York: Houghton Mifflin & Co.

George, Henry. (1871). *Our Land and Land Policy, National and State*. San Francisco: White & Bauer.

Goodman, David M. (1966). *A Western Panorama, 1849–1875: The Travels, Writings, and Influence of J. Ross Browne on the Pacific Coast, and in Texas, Nevada, Arizona and Baja California, as the First Mining Commissioner and Minister to China*. Glendale, CA: Arthur H. Clark Co.

Greever, William S. (1990). *Bonanza West: The Story of the Western Mining Rushes 1848–1900 {1963}*. Repr. Boise: University of Idaho Press.

Gutiérrez, Ramón A. and Richard J. Orsi, eds. (1998). *Contested Eden: California before the Gold Rush*. Berkeley: University of California Press in association with the California Historical Society.

Harte, Bret. (1872). *The Luck of Roaring Camp, and Other Sketches*. Boston: J.R. Osgood & Co.

Hittell, John S. (1861). *Mining in the Pacific States of North America*. San Francisco: H.H. Bancroft & Co.

Hittell, John S. (1874). *The Resources of California: Comprising the Society, Climate, Salubrity, Scenery, Commerce and Industry of the State*. 6th edn., rewritten. San Francisco: A. Roman & Co.; New York: W.J. Widdleton.

Holliday, J.S. (1981). *The World Rushed In: The California Gold Rush Experience*. New York: Simon & Schuster.

Holliday, J.S. (1999). *Rush for Riches: Gold Fever and the Making of California*. Oakland: Oakland Museum of California; Berkeley: University of California Press.

Ingersoll, Ernest. (1879). The Camp of the Carbonates: Ups and Downs in Leadville. *Scribner's Monthly*, 18/6 (Oct.), 801–24.

Jackson, Helen Hunt. (1884). *Ramona: A Story*. Boston: Roberts Bros.

Johnson, Susan L. (2000). *Roaring Camp: The Social World of the California Gold Rush*. New York: W.W. Norton.

Kaufman, Polly Welts, ed. (1994). *Apron Full of Gold: The Letters of Mary Jane Megquier from San*

Francisco, 1849–1856. 2nd edn. Albuquerque: University of New Mexico Press.

King, T. Butler. (1850). *California the Wonder of the Age: A Book for Everyone Going to or Having an Interest in That Gold Region.* New York: William Gowans.

Kowalewski, Michael, ed. (1997). *Gold Rush: A Literary Exploration.* Berkeley: Heyday Books in conjunction with the California Council for the Humanities.

Levy, JoAnne. (1990). *They Saw the Elephant: Women in the California Gold Rush.* Hamden, CT: Archon Books.

Loomis, John Lewis. (1879). *Leadville, Colorado: The Most Wonderful Mining Camp in the World.* Colorado Springs: Gazette Publishing Co.

Lotchin, Roger. (1974). *San Francisco, 1846–1856: From Hamlet to City.* New York: Oxford University Press.

Mann, Ralph. (1982). *After the Gold Rush: Society in Grass Valley and Nevada City, California, 1849–1870.* Stanford, CA: Stanford University Press.

Marryat, Frank. (1855). *Mountains and Molehills, or Recollections of a Burnt Journal.* New York: Harper & Bros.

Nordhoff, Charles. (1973). *California: For Health, Pleasure and Residence. A Book for Travelers and Settlers (1873).* Repr. Berkeley: Ten Speed Press.

Owens, Kenneth N., ed. (2002). *Riches For All: The California Gold Rush and the World.* Lincoln: University of Nebraska Press.

Paul, Rodman. (1947). *California Gold: The Beginning of Mining in the Far West.* Cambridge, MA: Harvard University Press.

Paul, Rodman, ed. (1966). *The California Gold Discovery: Sources, Documents, Accounts, and Memoirs Relating to the Discovery of Gold at Sutter's Mill.* Georgetown, CA: Talisman Press.

Paul, Rodman. (2001). *Mining Frontiers of the American West, 1848–1880.* Rev. expanded edn. by Elliott West. Albuquerque: University of New Mexico Press.

Peterson, Richard H. (1991). *Bonanza Rich: Lifestyles of the Western Mining Entrepreneurs.* Boise: University of Idaho Press.

Points of Interest. California Views, 1860–1870, the Lawrence & Houseworth albums. (2002). Foreword Gary F. Kurutz, introd. Peter E. Palmquist. Berkeley: Berkeley Hills Books; San Francisco: Society of California Pioneers.

Rawls, James J. and Richard J. Orsi, eds. (1999). *A Golden State: Mining and Economic Development in Gold Rush California.* Berkeley: Published for the California Historical Society by the University of California Press.

Raymond, Rossiter W. (1874). *Mining Industry of the States and Territories of the Rocky Mountains: Including Descriptions of Quartz, Placer and Hydraulic Mining; Amalgamation; Concentration; Smelting; etc.* New York: J.B. Ford & Co.

Richardson, Albert. (1867). *Beyond the Mississippi: From the Great River to the Great Ocean. Life and Adventure on the Prairie, Mountains and Pacific Coast … 1857–1867.* Hartford, CT: American Publishing Co.; New York: Bliss & Co.

Roberts, Brian. (2000). *American Alchemy: The California Gold Rush and Middle-Class Culture.* Chapel Hill: University of North Carolina Press.

Rohrbough, Malcolm J. (1997). *Days of Gold: The California Gold Rush and the American Nation.* Berkeley: University of California Press.

Royce, Josiah. (1886). *California: From the Conquest in 1846 to the Second Vigilance Committee in San Francisco. A Study of American Character.* Boston: Houghton Mifflin.

Ruiz de Burton, María Amparo. (1992). *The Squatter and the Don,* ed. and introd. Rosaura Sánchez and Beatrice Pita. Houston: Arte Público Press.

Seyd, Ernest. (1858). *California and its Resources: A Work for the Merchant, the Capitalist and the Emigrant.* London: Trübner.

Shinn, Charles Howard. (1885). *Mining Camps: A Study in American Frontier Government.* New York: Scribners.

Smith, Duane A. (1992). *Rocky Mountain West: Colorado, Wyoming & Montana, 1859–1915.* Albuquerque: University of New Mexico Press.

Smith, Michael L. (1987). *Pacific Visions: California Scientists and the Environment, 1850–1915.* New Haven: Yale University Press.

Society of California Pioneers. (1869). *Nineteenth Anniversary of the Corporate Society of California Pioneers. Oration: by Hon. John S. Hittel.* San Francisco: Society of California Pioneers.

Starr, Kevin and Richard J. Orsi, eds. (2000). *Rooted in Barbarous Soil: People, Culture, and Community in Gold Rush California.* Berkeley: Published for the California Historical Society by the University of California Press.

Thomas Houseworth & Co. (1872). *Pacific Coast Scenery*. San Francisco: Thomas Houseworth & Co.

Twain, Mark. (1993). *Roughing It (1872)*. Repr. Berkeley: University of California Press.

United States Department of the Treasury. (1868). *Report of J. Ross Browne on the Mineral Resources of the States and Territories West of the Rocky Mountains*. Washington: Government Printing Office.

Van Voorhies, William. (1853). *Oration before the Society of California pioneers, at their celebration of the anniversary of the admission of the state of California into the Union*. San Francisco: C. Bartlett.

Vaught, David. (2007). *After the Gold Rush: Tarnished Dreams in the Sacramento Valley*. Baltimore: Johns Hopkins University Press.

Wyman, Mark. (1979). *Hard Rock Epic: Western Miners and the Industrial Revolution, 1860–1910*. Berkeley: University of California Press.

4

The Literate West of Nineteenth-Century Periodicals

Tara Penry

Asked to picture a western scene, most literate Americans in the nineteenth century, as today, would describe an outdoor landscape, with or without people in it. Few would conjure up a picture of a young woman writing by lamplight at her home, a girl searching her father's pockets for a book from the circulating library, a married couple reading letters in their one-room cabin, or a printer leaning over his typecase. Yet these images, if not *uniquely* western, belonged to the nineteenth-century West as much as did sublime mountainscapes, buckskinned hunters, or battle scenes between Plains Indians and the US army. In the popular imagination, literacy was crucial to *eastern* settlement – allowing colonists to organize themselves with documents like the Mayflower Compact, the Declaration of Independence, and the US Constitution – but unimportant to a region of armed conflict, oral negotiation, lynchings, and squatters' rights.

Contrary to popular associations of the West with nature and action, and the East with culture and literacy, when Frenchman Alexis de Tocqueville toured America in 1831–2, he reported "an astonishing circulation of letters and newspapers among these savage woods" of Kentucky and Tennessee (qtd. in Kielbowicz 1989: 64). As journalism historian Richard Kielbowicz points out, Tocqueville was traveling *with* the mail in a stagecoach on the major western roads, so settlements farther from the main roads would not have been visible to him. Nonetheless, a large number of scattered archival materials and a growing number of scholarly studies testify to the range and significance of literacy for western settlers during the nineteenth century. By the latter half of the century, the widespread distribution of newspapers, cheap novels, Sunday school books, and other printed materials meant that "the information world

A Companion to the Literature and Culture of the American West, First Edition. Edited by Nicolas S. Witschi.
© 2011 Blackwell Publishing Ltd. Published 2011 by Blackwell Publishing Ltd.

of most 'ordinary' Americans" – including westerners – "centered on print" (Pawley 2001: 1).

This essay pays particular attention to the role that western periodicals played in representing oral vernacular and literacy as simultaneously western. Newspapers and magazines published in the West help to dismantle binary myths of a literate East and preliterate West by demonstrating the westward spread of US print culture. Yet when western periodicals published dialect sketches and poems or local color fiction with dialect-speaking characters, they risked undermining their predominant representation of the West as a literate space. This essay argues that the context for dialect literature gives it a meaning in western periodicals that differs somewhat from its meaning in the East (where it was more abundant). Even in their use of dialect materials, western periodicals belie the coupling of orality with the West and literacy with the East, restoring to view instead a complex social landscape.

We must make clear before proceeding that this essay does not attempt a *social* history of western literacy. We will not, for example, chart the regional demographics of the "illiterate" people counted by the US Census in the late nineteenth century, even though Barbara Cloud indicates that such analysis shows at least some western states and territories to be relatively more literate than the general US population (Cloud 1992: 13). We will not dredge up debates about "common" or public schooling as the movement spread through the West (better supported in some states than in others). We will not analyze the circulation records of public libraries to determine how many and which members of particular communities used the library, as Christine Pawley does for Osage, Iowa. All of these approaches would shed a different angle of light on some truth behind the myth of western preliteracy. But the questions of this essay are fundamentally *literary* more than they are historical.

Ultimately, this essay asks why an industry of western literacy – the periodical industry – published local color and dialect literature which has helped to support the myth of the literate East and preliterate West for nineteenth- and twentieth-century readers. The first two sections of the essay provide some history to enable us to approach that question. Part one analyzes US Census data about national periodical production, surveys histories and bibliographies of nineteenth-century periodicals, and samples selected journals to show that literacy was significant to many aspects of western life. Part two examines the mission statements and the ideas of community proffered by selected periodicals from three western places and moments, comparing these western periodicals' aspirations to broader themes in American book history and finding them entirely consistent with national discourses – not regionally exceptional. Based on the reach of literacy into many western lives and the mission of periodical editors to emphasize their region's full, literate participation in the national life, part three asks why some western periodicals published local color and dialect works, when such works would seem to undermine their claims to literacy and regional progress. After reading closely a sample periodical from East and West, we will find that local color fiction potentially carried different messages about region and literacy depending on its site of publication.

Periodicals in the Nineteenth-Century West

When most literary histories comment on the financial success and cultural influence of periodicals in the nineteenth-century United States, they tend to limit their examples to New York City blockbusters such as the *Harper's* family of magazines, *Scribner's* and *Century*, or other northeastern peers. According to US Census data, however, the most rapid industry growth occurred in the western states, from Ohio to California. We can illustrate this point with a few statistics. Between 1860 and 1870, New York publishers increased their state's periodical production by about 60 percent; in the same period, the western states of Illinois, Iowa, Michigan, and California increased theirs by nearly 100 percent. Meanwhile (with considerable resources devoted on both sides to the Civil War), southern and New England states made smaller gains (Groves 2007: 226–7). To sift the data yet another way, the census-takers of 1840 found approximately the same number of periodicals (just over thirty) in Michigan, Louisiana, and New Hampshire; four decades later, New Hampshire published 87, Louisiana 112, and Michigan 464. In a period when the New England state doubled and the southern state quadrupled its periodical output, the western state increased its production by a factor of fourteen. In keeping with these regional trends, by 1840 Ohio produced more periodicals than Massachusetts, and by 1880 Illinois ranked second in production only to New York State. By that point, western states were producing more than half of the nation's newspapers and magazines (Groves 2007: 226–7). While New York led the nation in book and periodical production for most of the nineteenth century and deserves the attention of literary historians, the rapid growth of western periodicals during the settlement phase of successive frontiers shows us that the West did not concede all literary honors to New York. Literate settlers quickly established presses to meet a variety of needs for local readers.

If western periodicals were numerous, they were also diverse in their interests, representing by the end of the nineteenth century nearly every aspect of the economic and social life of regional settlers. As historian Frank Luther Mott shows in his *History of American Magazines*, western periodicals catered to many audiences, including homemakers, members of religious groups, and professionals in fields ranging from medicine and law to agriculture and education. While a large majority of western newspapers and magazines were founded by English-speaking Euro-Americans, the last decades of the century witnessed increasing numbers of newspapers founded by foreign immigrants in their native languages and by African Americans who had migrated from southern to western states (Miller 1987: xi; Potter 1993: 82–90, 98–101). Both trends would continue into the twentieth century. Native American newspapers also increased in number around the turn of the century, most of them in English; the earliest Native journals in the nineteenth-century West were, with a few exceptions, operated and edited by white missionaries or others in association with Native schools and other assimilation efforts (Littlefield and Parins 1984: 425–8). The sheer variety of periodicals founded in western states and territories during the nineteenth century suggests that literacy was embedded in western experience for women and men, for speakers of most of the region's non-native languages, and for most professions and economic activities. Only the unassimilated oral cultures of Native tribes seem unrepresented in the region's periodicals by the end of the nineteenth century.

Historians provide us with further insights into why periodicals appeared so profusely in the development of successive American frontiers. Richard Clement explains that American settlements from colonial times had required printers to produce newspapers, law books, almanacs, and school books for local markets; until about 1840 in the eastern states and later in the West, poor roads and slow transportation technologies meant that local printers could distribute such high-demand printed materials most efficiently (2003: 15–22). Later in the century, rural publishers managed for the most part to hold their own against urban competitors in the newspaper business in part thanks to a postal rate structure that allowed publishers to distribute newspapers most cheaply in the federal mail at the shortest distances (Kielbowicz 1989: 43, 63, 84, 182). Newspapers and magazines – not always easy to distinguish from each other – offered a combination of practical and symbolic benefits to a community. A town with a newspaper had a competitive edge over neighboring towns in luring new immigrants and investors, and a newspaper could attract attention for political candidates or businesses (especially bookstores and print shops) closely associated with the proprietor. Periodicals also provided "an aura of stability and an identity [for a new western community]. A town with a newspaper was a real town, just like the ones residents had left behind" (Cloud 1992: 5).

With faster industrial presses and improved transportation technologies in the middle decades of the nineteenth century, book production became more centralized in New York, but periodicals remained dispersed. When the 1870 US Census separated book publishing from newspaper publishing in its survey of national industries, it found only forty firms in ten states producing books, but over a thousand firms in thirty-eight states and territories (of forty-five surveyed) printing newspapers (Casper et al. 2007: 14). The 1880 Census found newspapers originating in 80 percent of the nation's counties (Kaestle and Radway 2009: 29). At that point, 91 percent of counties in the nation's four westernmost states (Oregon, California, Nevada, and Colorado) had at least one newspaper – though western territories posted much smaller numbers (Cloud 1992: 7). Newspapers had outpaced population growth since 1850 in both the states *and* the territories of the Far West (Cloud 1992: 6). Cheaper to produce and distribute than books, periodicals allowed western readers access to various kinds of social and professional communities.

If historians of print and journalism help us to understand the scope and motives of western periodical printing, the contents of western periodicals show some of the ways that periodicals mediated important social relationships. First, western periodicals tended to reflect the voice and views of their proprietors. In keeping with the nation's history of partisan journalism, western newspapers did not aim to deliver objective news; rather, they staked out clear positions on matters of local interest.

Thus the *Alta California* (San Francisco, 1849–91) praised controversial "vigilance committees," or citizen lynch mobs, for maintaining order when elected officials failed in the summer and fall of 1856, and the *Seattle Republican* (1894–1917) worked to raise the profile and respect of African Americans in the Northwest by combining essays on race progress with photographs of the paper's well-dressed black proprietor seated with white community leaders, among other symbolic images of racial prosperity and integration. In Portland, Oregon, activist Abigail Scott Duniway supported women's suffrage in the pages of her weekly *New Northwest* (1871–87), in competition with her brother Harvey Scott, chief editor of the anti-suffrage *Portland Oregonian* (Shein 2002: 17–19). In the West, as in other parts of the country, newspapers helped to define and give voice to political interest groups within a city or region.

Some periodicals also offered practical support to people already living in the West. Aside from the professional journals that appeared in major western cities and the missionary journals that illustrated the progress of western Christian missions to eastern donors, some "general" magazines – ranging in content from news and advice to humor and poetry – made themselves practically useful to readers through their correspondence columns. One of the most successful of these magazines was *The Prairie Farmer* of Chicago, in print continuously since its founding as the *Union Agriculturalist* in 1840. It offered one of the better correspondence columns, featuring informed and specific answers to readers from various parts of the country. In a sample issue from 1884, the *Farmer* answered questions about plant cultivation and poultry disease for readers in Mississippi, Iowa, and Texas ("Answers to Correspondents," Jan. 5, 1884). When the editor could not answer a question – about the diet of southwestern cowboys – it was referred to knowledgeable readers, creating a community of advice and information drawing on readers' expertise. Between the informative columns on midwestern stock and crop cultivation and the correspondence column, readers could find information essential to their financial decisions in *The Prairie Farmer*, as well as homemaking tips and a humor column for family entertainment.

While the internal evidence of periodicals does not help us understand the social affiliations or economic information sources of westerners (or other Americans) with low levels of literacy, the sheer number and variety of western periodicals, along with the correspondence columns of some like *The Prairie Farmer*, suggest that literacy supported and enhanced the lives of western settlers in social, professional, economic, and other ways. If the existence of western periodicals begins to make the West look more domesticated – less "western" – a closer look at the missions of some "general" western periodicals shows that even as they celebrated their regions, western editors did not characterize themselves as exceptional in literary terms. They hoped to publish the best *quality* of writing in their area, but they did not seek to create regionally distinctive literary genres. As the next section will explore, western periodicals expressed missions and ideas of community that were consistent with national trends. As various ideas of the public sphere dominated American thought and various rhetorical trends passed through the national periodical culture, western presses expressed those dominant ideas and trends as much as periodicals in other parts of the country.

In part three, then, we will explore what local color and dialect fiction may have meant to westerners in light of editors' evident preference to promote their region's literacy and to participate in national discourses of civilization and progress. Before we consider the entry of so-called "regional" fiction into western magazines, let us hear first how three western periodicals articulated their missions and ideas of the public sphere.

The Unexceptional West

From Cincinnati in the 1830s to California in the 1850s and Minnesota in the 1880s, western periodicals reflected major American conceptions of literary community and the public sphere. To understand western editors' relation to mainstream national discourses, this section samples three general magazines representing discrete moments in western literary development. Each magazine was more successful than many others like it, meeting or exceeding the four-year benchmark that Frank Luther Mott established as the "liberal estimate" of an average lifespan for a mid-century magazine (Mott 1938–57: III.5). The *Western Monthly Magazine* of Cincinnati (1833–6), *Hutchings' California Magazine* of San Francisco (1856–61), and the *Northwest Magazine* of St. Paul (1883–1903) participated fully in national trends and discourses identified by scholars, while at the same time communicating a western regional identity.

For the generation after the Revolution, according to media historian John Nerone, "both newspapers and books were considered key to the successful functioning of a public sphere that would produce a national culture, both political and literary" (2007: 231). Some western general magazines joined this effort, as well. The *Western Monthly* of Cincinnati offered itself as just such a forum for creating a "public sphere" of reader-citizens. Editor James Hall and his partners envisioned the magazine as a "neutral ground" where political combatants could meet "as under a flag of truce" to pursue the common goal of "learned and useful discussion" ("To the Reader," Jan. 1833: 2). Essays from knowledgeable contributors were expected to "enlighten and enlarge the public mind," as poems and stories would "inculcate kind and generous sentiments, and pour the oil of peace upon the troubled billows of dissension." The magazine served the *"national honor"* as well as the cause of western "education, literature, and refinement" by encouraging highly literate westerners to share their knowledge and taste in a forum that would help the country replace British books with products of native intellect ("American Literature," Apr. 1833: 188; "On the Formation of National Character," Feb. 1833: 354). With a vision of "authorship and public service" that was "typical of [their] generation" (Watts 2009: p. viii), Hall and his friends saw their western magazine as a tool for developing citizens and community in both region and nation.

Around mid-century, American literary culture encouraged more sentimental communities than civic ones. The emotional language and familiar (even clichéd) imagery of sentimental discourse helped to disseminate middle-class values such as domesticity and piety to wide national audiences, including readers in the West. Founded seven

years after the California Gold Rush by a forty-niner turned publisher, *Hutchings'*
California Magazine nostalgically celebrated the "common brotherhood" and "sympathy" of California miners (July 1857: 1) and cautioned readers against losing their
middle-class moorings in articles such as "A Homeless Nation," a reprint that criticized the American taste for travel because of its threat to "the sentiment of home"
(Jan. 1857: 321). An original article in a later volume applied the same theme to
California with the warning, "No State can rise to its proper magnitude and gain its
proper efficiency without the aid of mothers and children. No State can long exist
without the at once controlling and impelling influences of the hearthstone" ("The
Moral Power of the Family Hearthstone," Nov. 1858: 233). To encourage marriage
and domesticity, *Hutchings'* printed poems about loved ones at home and a flirtatious
exchange between "Sister May," a female reader who confessed to warm and sisterly
feelings for the sentimental miners featured in the magazine, and "Frank," a miner
who responded to Sister May by inviting her on a virtual visit to his lonely cabin.
The magazine also idealized mining partnership as a sentimental bond that helped
miners maintain domestic affections in the absence of women (Penry 2004: 330–51).
For western emigrants – especially men – suffering from loneliness and social disori-
entation, *Hutchings'* promoted the speedy establishment of middle-class institutions
in the sentimental language widely visible in Anglo-American publications of the
1850s.

Textual communities grew more complex in the last two decades of the nineteenth
century, when, according to book historians Carl F. Kaestle and Janice Radway,
American print culture grew paradoxically more consolidated and more diverse
(2009: 2). With the arrival of national brands and national advertising, syndication,
cheaper methods of reproducing colors and photographs, and other changes (Kaestle
and Radway 2009: 8–15), American periodicals, like other commercial products, had
access to larger markets and potentially larger profits than ever. Striking a balance
between Kaestle and Radway's forces of consolidation and "local" diversification, as
though demonstrating both impulses of the age, was the *Northwest Magazine* of
St. Paul. A general magazine devoted in early years to "literature, agriculture, and
western progress" and later to "western interests and progress," the *Northwest* drew its
regional identity from its corporate sponsor, the Northern Pacific Railroad. It offered
lengthy profiles of towns along the NPRR line and clipped news, humor, and advertisements whose origins ranged from the *Portland Oregonian* and *Butte [Montana]*
Bystander to the *Crookston [Minnesota] Times*. As a digest of news and wit from the
Northern Pacific territory, the magazine served to consolidate a "northwestern" region
from the Great Lakes to the Puget Sound with a common pioneer history, bourgeois
politics, and faith in upward mobility. Both a regional and a national consolidator,
the *Northwest* saw the nation reorienting itself westward in the transcontinental railroad era. It figured St. Paul as the new "hub of the universe" (after Boston), roughly
midway between Boston at 1,500 miles and Portland, Oregon, at 1,800 (Apr. 1885:
9). Hand in hand with this national sense of value were informed regional features
ranging from headline articles like "The Wheat Trade of Duluth" (Feb. 1885) to

reports on mining in the Klondike and reader letters about tradesmen wanted in particular settlements. For its western readers, the *Northwest* illuminated the micro-climates and subcultures of the northern West at the same time that it consolidated them into a broader region with a common theme of progress.

For the *Western Monthly Magazine*, *Hutchings' California Magazine*, and the *Northwest Magazine*, regional identity did not rely on breaking with national trends and discourses to create something "new" in literature, but on promoting local authors, meeting the needs of local readers, and covering local subjects. Even the needs of local readers, as editors James Hall, James Hutchings, and Eugene Smalley imagined them, were consistent with needs identified by publishers elsewhere in the nation for citizen formation, sympathetic companionship, and simultaneous participation in the national marketplace and in the local economy where any new fortune would first be made. When we seek to understand nineteenth-century western literature and culture from the perspective of the region's general magazines, we must be willing to do away with our expectation that the West is somehow exceptional – a region of "bear-killers and catamount-catchers," as one Tennessee editor put it in 1835 (Blair 1953: 16), or cowboys and sharpshooters, or sublime and untroubled landscapes. Instead, early western magazines show us a West where regional and national identities were bound closely together by literate conventions, and where literary discourses traveled well.

Local Color Literature in its Periodical Context

Among the literary travelers were stories and sketches in a genre we have come to call local color. Sketches and stories making prominent use of dialect, regional character types, and exotic rural settings enjoyed popularity after the Civil War in middle-class literary periodicals. As such tales became a staple of magazines in New York and Boston, local color fiction and other genres of dialect writing also appeared in western periodicals. The most literary form of dialect prose, the local color tale typically had a clear narrative perspective, either a sympathetic insider to the regional culture, an outsider mocking its provincialism, or perhaps a combination of the two (i.e., an outsider converted to sympathy). Regardless of the particular narrative stance and tone, the genre was consistent in its anthropological view of regional cultures as somehow distinct, set apart both geographically and culturally from modernity. Most interesting to the local colorist, as to the early anthropologists who also began working in the nineteenth century, were the folkways and languages of premodern communities – the human islands that had not yet crumbled into a cultural mainstream where technology seemed to be bringing people into closer contact and making them more alike. Local color stories and sketches seemed to preserve regional distinctions that were dying out, or – like some other dialect pieces – to hold up the uncouth for the amusement of the civilized.

Characteristic of the local color genre was a binary relationship between an implicitly literate reader and a preliterate or oral regional subject. The early work of one of the best-known local colorists, Bret Harte, illustrates the paradigmatic relationship between literate outsiders and oral, subliterate, or extraliterate regional insiders in this genre. After explicating the relations between region and literacy in a handful of Harte's early stories, this section will compare the contents of selected eastern and western periodicals to consider the different meanings for such fictions suggested by different regional environments.

Although the local color movement can be traced back to the Hudson River village tales of Washington Irving in the 1820s, dialect stories and sketches in this genre began to appear more frequently in American periodicals after California writer Bret Harte captured the national imagination with his exotic Gold Rush tales and poems between 1868 and 1871. As the editor of a San Francisco literary monthly, Harte published nine stories and several poems set in fictional mining camps of the mid-1850s. The stories were celebrated in the East, and Harte's dialect poem about race prejudice in a poker game, "Plain Language from Truthful James," was widely reprinted in newspapers from Providence, Rhode Island, to Selma, Alabama, making Harte a national celebrity (Scharnhorst 1995: 41–2; 2000: 51–3). Removed from their original periodical context, Harte's tales of this period seem to minimize literacy as a fact of western life; read *within* the context of their original periodical volumes, however, Harte's local color works help to affirm the advanced literacy of a certain class of Californians who would be reading the *Overland Monthly* in 1868. As paradigmatic local color texts, Harte's early stories provide the same kind of upper-class affirmation for western readers that the genre provided in eastern periodicals; implied relationships between region and class, however, did not transfer from West to East or vice versa.

Harte's first six *Overland* stories are fairly representative of the local color genre in that they make literacy seem insignificant to life in post-Gold Rush California. In "The Luck of Roaring Camp," a group of miners adopts a baby whose Indian mother dies giving birth to him in their camp. "The Outcasts of Poker Flat" follows the fate of three characters ejected from a mining community on the eve of a snowstorm. A miner of inscrutable motives tries to bribe a rural court on behalf of his partner, a highway robber, in "Tennessee's Partner." In three stories with prominent female characters, an admirable ex-saloon girl nurses a former client when he becomes incapable of caring for himself ("Miggles"), a schoolteacher spurns a miner as a lover when she learns he has fathered a child ("The Idyl of Red Gulch"), and a married woman prepares to leave her husband for an attractive gambler, who instead urges the husband to "quit the country" with his wife ("Brown of Calaveras"). Of these stories, all of the last three make at least a brief display of a character's education or literacy, but the teacher in the "Idyl," the wife in "Brown," and the stagecoach passengers in "Miggles" are all outsiders on a brief sojourn; none of these literates stays long in Bret Harte Country.

When literacy might be expected to play a pivotal role in the plots of these stories – as in the production of a birth certificate to prove paternity or the arrival of a learned judge with lawbooks to try a case – Harte characterizes Gold Country as preliterate or extraliterate, functioning on oral testimony and action. Thus the word of a mother is sufficient to establish paternity in "The Idyl of Red Gulch," and in the absence of written law, the case against Tennessee is tried "as fairly as was consistent with a judge and jury who felt themselves to some extent obliged to justify, in their verdict, the previous irregularities of arrest and indictment" (Harte 2001: 51). When Brown of Calaveras confesses to gambler Jack Hamlin that he loves his wife but fears that she loves someone else, Hamlin burns the woman's written summons and leaves town; although the man is foolish, his oral confession and trust prove stronger than the woman's literate appeal. Though some of Harte's outsiders display their advanced literacy by lacing conversation with quotations, for the most part his characters are defined and conflicts settled with spoken language and acts of body and nature, as when a flood washes out a valley or a stagecoach carries someone out of town.

This is not to say that Harte's Gold Country is bereft of written text or literate characters; rather, indigenous literacies in the *Overland* stories amuse *more* literate narrators and readers with their quaint ingenuity and their proximity to oral culture. Frequent targets of Harte's narrative wit are the provincial newspaper editors like those of the *Red Dog Clarion* or the *Wingdam Chronicle* whose "vigorous English" and cliché-ridden misjudgments of character render them easy targets for satire (Harte 2001: 54, 72–3). More complex are the unaffected literacies of characters like Tom Simson in "The Outcasts of Poker Flat" or Miggles. When Simson recites Homer to help others forget their hunger and danger in "The Outcasts of Poker Flat," the well-read narrator observes that the boy has "forgotten the words" of Pope's translation and therefore renders the story "in the current vernacular of Sandy Bar" (p. 34). But the choice of a Homeric poem reminds the educated reader that European literary history originated with oral recitations like those of California campfires. Similarly, in "Miggles," although the heroine's "conversation was never elegant [and] rarely grammatical," her selfless habit of reading aloud to her paralyzed companion from the newspapers that cover her cabin walls comes off as a superior use of her small stock of literacy than the Judge's genteel quotations from Shakespeare (pp. 43, 47, 41). Whether Harte's characters seem better or worse for their flawed literacies, it is easy to conclude from his fiction that California society is more primitive, closer to the oral phase of civilization, than the advanced, literate society of narrators and readers who travel freely.

Like many of the local color and dialect sketches published in western periodicals, Harte's *Overland* stories claim to describe only the region's past, making no pretension to characterize its present. Of the six stories considered here, five take place some ten to eighteen years prior to their date of publication. The narrator dates "The Luck," "Outcasts," and "Tennessee's Partner" explicitly to 1850 (pp. 16, 27) and 1854 (p. 49). References to other events date "Miggles" to about 1859 (p. 45) and "Brown of Calaveras" to some time before 1857 (p. 72). Only "The Idyl of Red Gulch" goes undated. In the *Overland* and other western periodicals, local color and dialect fiction answered the curiosity of modern, literate westerners for stories of their pioneer past, which, if only a decade or two distant in time, they could imagine across the epic gulf from literacy back to orality.

Literate westerners did have a concept of vernacular diversity within the contemporary region, which they represented not so much in local color fiction (with its outsider-narrator interpreting subliterate "folk") as in less polished dialect pieces that seemed to belong to the regional present. The genre of the dialect sketch or anecdote was treated in many ways unlike local color fiction in western periodicals: it did not carry the name of an author, but was printed as something overheard, passed along, or submitted in a letter from a semiliterate or foreign reader; it was likely to appear in a designated "Humor" column or among short, unauthored, amusing clips rather than among the magazine's original and more substantial articles; it had no narrator offering interpretation of its meaning, like the Bret Harte narrators who speculate about the moral nature of mining roughs. Instead, dialect sketches might stand alone or be structured as narrative jokes (i.e., "A long-waisted man, with the nose of a fox and an eye full of speculation, walked up to a second-hand clothier, in Buffalo, the other day, and said: ..."). Thus, in the January 1884 issues of *The Prairie Farmer*, among malapropisms, puns, and a dialogue satirizing overeducated college women, the "Humorous" column included two jokes using dialect to caricature Jewish characters ("'A Leedle Mistakes'" and "Sharper than a Razor," the latter quoted in the last sentence). St. Paul's *Northwest Magazine* ran a letter from "R. Fingerson Kanoot, Esq." in its "Western Humor" column, beginning, "Yentlemen: Ay greet yous fallers" (Jan. 1893: 13). Unlike past-tense local color sketches, these pieces represented ethnic figures of the modern West who were not keeping up with the higher level of English literacy that magazine readers found represented in the rest of the magazine.

When western local color fiction appeared in the eastern press, on the other hand, there was no indication of a modern, literate class of westerners set apart from the preliterate pioneers, nor a hint that humorous, contemporary dialect sketches were in any way different from the dialect of the local colorist's nostalgic past. All regional and dialect pieces became "local color" together, and past became indistinguishable from present. In the *Atlantic Monthly*, for example, Mark Twain's "Old Times on the Mississippi" shared traits of both the western local color sketch and contemporary dialect humor, with the effect of confusing "old times" with some sort of timeless western character. In the June 1875 installment, Twain praised the "unfettered and entirely independent" nature of riverboat pilots "in those days," but gave witness to a persistent exoticism in his own character when he used dialect, however sparingly ("It 'gravels' me, to this day, to put my will in the weak shape of a request, instead of launching it in the crisp language of an order") and when he hinted at a distrust of law and written language left over from "old" and "free" times ("So here was ... an absolute monarch who was absolute in sober truth and not by a fiction of words") (p. 721). Clearly the values and vernacular language forged in "old times" persisted in the modern character of the author Mark Twain.

A comparative reading of contemporary issues of the *Overland* and the *Atlantic* will help to distinguish the implied relations between region and literacy that surrounded local color fiction in eastern and western periodicals. When "The Luck of Roaring Camp" appeared in the San Francisco monthly in August 1868, both the *Overland* and the *Atlantic* relied heavily on genteel essays and romances, *not* dialect prose. Among twelve prose articles in the *Atlantic* for August 1868 and thirteen for the *Overland*, only Harte's "The Luck of Roaring Camp" used characters' vernacular speech as a significant part of the story. In the *Atlantic*, a serial romance from Normandy combined French phrases with French-accented English dialogue, and a minor character in another tale spoke briefly in an Irish brogue, but in the *Atlantic*, as in the *Overland*, the stories and essays were more or less uniform in their genteel voices and in the focus on a mood or idea over idiosyncrasies of language. While eastern periodicals were dabbling in regional tales using vernacular dialogue – like Rebecca Harding Davis's "Life in the Iron Mills," published in the April 1861 *Atlantic* – such tales had not yet in 1868 become essential fare of literary magazines.

By the summer of 1875, when the *Atlantic* was serializing Twain's *Old Times on the Mississippi*, dialect fiction had become a more prominent fixture in eastern literary periodicals. Four of nine prose articles in the June *Atlantic* used dialect or vernacular language to provide local color about an American region, including Twain's Mississippi, the antebellum South, Pennsylvania oil country, and an Adirondack mining district. A slave autobiography was rendered entirely in thick dialect, purportedly an oral history delivered verbatim to a literate frame narrator. Opposed to this transliteration of vernacular speech was an international novel by Henry James whose June installment began with the exchange of a letter between literate American travelers in Europe (p. 644). Teetering between these extremes of orality and literacy was the Adirondack mining romance whose hero's ungrammatical speech – "Them few black holes over there in the hill is all I have to show" (p. 700) – fades to propriety when Benjamin Jacques gives up on mining and becomes a hermit. Then his New England roots begin to show themselves: he is an impeccable housekeeper, he reads a copy of Milton given to him by an old love, and he has composed poems in his head, which two visitors record during a night at his cabin (p. 702). The more we learn of his literate history, the more his grammar improves: " 'I know a little,' " he tells the young travelers, " 'of the great world in which you live, and of literary men and fame; my grandfather was a writer for the press in France' " (p. 702). Neither a Jamesean literate nor a regional vernacular type, Jacques is a New England exile whose early literacy, like his love, was cut short. Together, the articles in the June 1875 *Atlantic* consolidate myriad American voices and experiences into a national whole, with dialect speech identifying regional and ethnic variations from literate New England and her traveling sons.

The *Overland* for June 1875, on the other hand, still favored the genteel diction of 1868. As the *Atlantic* and other eastern literary magazines with national aspirations added local color stories with prominent use of dialect to represent regional and ethnic diversity, the San Francisco magazine asserted its upper-class and literate status by maintaining an eclectic combination of articles only educated people would enjoy. The eleven prose articles (excluding book reviews) in the *Overland* for June 1875 included a history of mathematics and essays on subjects ranging from Shakespeare to California birds, and just one tale that depended significantly on vernacular diction. Joaquin Miller's "In a California Eden" featured the dialect speech of Missouri emigrants as well as the occasional vernacular expressions of a narrator influenced by both the colloquial Twain and the poetic Harte. Although Miller is less clear than Harte about the date of his story – making it unclear how far back in time his "California Eden" existed – he still makes Hartean distinctions between the relatively literate narrator and the "hairy, half-savage, unread Missourians" he describes. At the outset of Miller's story, the miners reject a candidate for public office because he has " 'too much book-larnin,' " and a character who cannot write his name is considered a camp poet (*Overland*, June 1875: 552, 550). Compared to John Muir's essay in the same issue about a Sierra storm or Frances Fuller Victor's story set in a San Francisco lodging house, Miller's poetic and subliterate "Eden" clearly belongs to the humorous local color school of Bret Harte, adding an entertaining view of the past for readers who possess considerably more "book-larnin" than the characters.

In the context of their eastern or western periodicals, then, local color and dialect pieces suggest different relations between the region and literacy. Since western periodicals assume literacy for their western audience, dialect narratives in this context make sense typically as some combination of history, humor, and description of a social class below the implied reader. Western periodicals show their region as a space occupied by multiple social classes speaking a variety of dialects over time. In eastern periodicals with national aspirations such as the *Atlantic Monthly, Harper's Monthly Magazine*, and *The Century Illustrated Magazine*, local color fiction and dialect sketches are, for a start, more abundant. With a local color sketch from one region juxtaposed against a dialect story from three others, these pieces in the nationalizing eastern magazines stand as metonyms for the regions they describe, equating regions with vernacular dialects and orality, and the New England–New York axis with advanced literacy and travel. Rather than subdividing regions into classes, the nationalist eastern magazines equate region *with* class, lumping westerners, southerners, and rurals into an oral, vernacular class distant from the literate reader – while general western periodicals use linguistic markers more sparingly to distinguish *between* regional classes.

From the *Western Monthly Magazine* in the old Northwest of 1830s Cincinnati to the *Seattle Republican* in the new Northwest of the 1890s, the western periodicals examined for this study insisted on literacy and a national, upper-class sensibility in the developing West. While their dialect pieces sometimes looked like contemporary work published in eastern magazines, as Nancy Glazener has observed, "Different periodicals invite different ways of being read" (1997: 189). Likewise, in the case of local color and dialect fiction, different periodicals also provided different meanings for the same genre. By the time local color fiction became a staple of northeastern literary periodicals in the 1870s, the West had become a fantasy landscape for dime novels and story papers, then for Buffalo Bill's Wild West shows in the 1880s. Even as a second or third generation of western periodicals urged civilization, the polite and impolite eastern press discovered the profitability of a timeless West, not yet grown out (and never to grow out) of its pioneer roughness. For eastern editors from Henry Mills Alden at *Harper's Monthly Magazine* to Richard Kyle Fox at the *National Police Gazette*, an illustrated weekly specializing in crime news and lingerie-clad actresses, the West was a violent, vernacular region. For their contemporary, Eugene Smalley at the *Northwest Magazine* of St. Paul, the West was a resource to be opened by human effort, and its pioneer history made for good fiction, as its multiethnic present made for good humor. In short, while eastern periodicals froze the West into a timeless myth that sold well, western periodicals throughout the century gained the most from selling the West itself – the land, not the legend. Representations of regional literacy, not an exotic vernacular, promoted local investment, and an orientation toward the present and future promised more to western editors than a mythologized past.

REFERENCES AND FURTHER READING

Blair, W. (1953). Traditions in Southern Humor. *American Quarterly*, 5, 132–42. Repr. in W. Blair & H.L. Hill. (1993). *Essays on American Humor: Blair through the Ages* (pp. 15–24). Madison: University of Wisconsin Press.

Brodhead, R.H. (1993). *Cultures of Letters: Scenes of Reading and Writing in Nineteenth-Century America*. Chicago: University of Chicago Press.

Casper, S.E., J.D. Groves, S.W. Nissenbaum, and M. Winship, eds. (2007). *A History of the Book in America, vol. 3: The Industrial Book, 1840–1880*. Chapel Hill: University of North Carolina Press.

Clement, R.W. (2003). *Books on the Frontier: Print Culture in the American West, 1763–1875*. Washington, DC and Hanover, NH: Library of Congress and University Press of New England.

Cloud, B. (1992). *The Business of Newspapers on the Western Frontier*. Reno: University of Nevada Press.

Duin, E.C. (1952). Settlers' Periodical: Eugene Smalley and the Northwest Magazine. *Minnesota History*, 33, 29–34.

Glazener, N. (1997). *Reading for Realism: The History of a U.S. Literary Institution, 1850–1910*. Durham, NC: Duke University Press.

Groves, J.D. (2007). Introduction to Periodicals and Serial Publication. In S.E. Casper et al., eds., *A History of the Book in America, vol. 3: The Industrial Book, 1840–1880*, pp. 224–30, 454–5. Chapel Hill: University of North Carolina Press.

Harte, B. (2001). *The Luck of Roaring Camp and Other Writings*, ed. G. Scharnhorst. New York: Penguin.

Huntley-Smith, J.A. (2005). "Such is Change in California": James Mason Hutchings and the Print Metropolis, 1854–1862. *Proceedings of the American Antiquarian Society*, 114, 35–85.

Hutchings' California Magazine. San Francisco. 1856–61.

Kaestle, C.F., and J.A. Radway, eds. (2009). *A History of the Book in America, vol. 4: Print in Motion – The Expansion of Publishing and Reading in the United States, 1880–1940*. Chapel Hill: University of North Carolina Press.

Kielbowicz, R.B. (1989). *News in the Mail: The Press, Post Office, and Public Information, 1700–1860s*. New York: Greenwood Press.

Littlefield, D.F., Jr., and J.W. Parins (1984). *American Indian and Alaska Native Newspapers and Periodicals, 1826–1924*. Westport, CT: Greenwood Press.

Miller, S.M., ed. (1987). *The Ethnic Press in the United States: A Historical Analysis and Handbook*. New York: Greenwood Press.

Mott, F.L. (1938–57). *A History of American Magazines*. 5 vols. Cambridge, MA: Harvard University Press, Belknap.

Nerone, J. (2007). Newspapers and the Public Sphere. In S.E. Casper et al., eds., *A History of the Book in America, vol. 3: The Industrial Book, 1840–1880*, pp. 230–48, 455–8. Chapel Hill: University of North Carolina Press.

Northwest Magazine. Also *The Illustrated Northwest Magazine*. (1883–1903). St. Paul.

Overland Monthly. (1868–1875). San Francisco.

Pawley, C. (2001). *Reading on the Middle Border: The Culture of Print in Late-Nineteenth-Century Osage, Iowa*. Amherst: University of Massachusetts Press.

Penry, T. (2004). Manly Domesticity on the Gold Rush Frontier: Recovering California's Honest Miner. *Western American Literature*, 38, 330–51.

Potter, V.R. (1993). *A Reference Guide to Afro-American Publications and Editors, 1827–1946*. Ames: Iowa State University Press.

The Prairie Farmer. Chicago. 1840–present. Jan. 1884 issues. Project Gutenberg. http://www.gutenberg.org/.

Scharnhorst, G. (1995). *Bret Harte: A Bibliography*. Lanham, MD: The Scarecrow Press.

Scharnhorst, G. (2000). *Bret Harte: Opening the American Literary West*. Norman: University of Oklahoma Press.

Shein, D. (2002). *Abigail Scott Duniway*. Boise State University Western Writers 151. Boise: Boise State University.

Watts, E., ed. (2009). Introduction. *"The Indian Hater" and Other Stories*, by James Hall. Kent, OH: Kent State University Press. (pp. vii–xxvii).

The Western Monthly Magazine. (1833–6). Cincinnati.

5

A History of American Women's Western Books, 1833–1928

Nina Baym

Thanks to historical and literary scholarship undertaken from the 1970s onward, we are beginning to recognize how much writing American women published about the West. Sandra Myres, Darlis Miller, Susan Armitage, and others have excavated accounts by frontier army wives and overland trailers – some in manuscript, some published. Victoria Lamont has looked for women's cowboy novels. Many scholars have worked to establish Willa Cather's identity as a western as well as modernist writer. Mary Austin's desert sketches and Mary Hallock Foote's stories about displaced female gentility in the crude West have entered the canon. But there is much, much more. Compiling and pursuing information from bibliographies, literary and cultural histories, biographical dictionaries, and similar sources, I've found more than 328 women publishing western-themed books by 1928; the total number of books exceeds 630. These books assume an interested audience, and do not worry about transgressing into male territory. Once again it turns out that where women were supposed to have been silent, they were not. What they were supposed not to have done, they did.

Among women for whom I could find biographical information, some two-thirds were professionals of some sort, either writing for a living or publishing on behalf of various causes: journalists, editors, teachers, community activists, clubwomen, local historians, novelists. Their books include memoirs, novels, short story collections, histories, biographies, reportage, descriptive sketches, textbooks, poetry volumes, works for young people, political and social polemics, travel books, and more. The books were published by major houses on the East Coast, by regional western publishers, and by local printers. Writing about the West as they knew it, as they thought they knew it, or as they wanted it to be known, women contributed both to their own western identity and to the identity of the West.

A Companion to the Literature and Culture of the American West, First Edition. Edited by Nicolas S. Witschi.
© 2011 Blackwell Publishing Ltd. Published 2011 by Blackwell Publishing Ltd.

The proportion of white, Anglo-descended, and apparently heterosexual women in this group is, as one might expect, overwhelming – only eighteen of 630, or just under 3 percent, are ethnically "minority" women. The white women's four intermeshing subjects are, first and foremost, the many wests themselves, the particular features of landscape and history differentiating one section of the west from another while still enclosing these within an idea of the West itself. Second: political or social views about the western present and future. Third: belief that transforming the Old West into the New – the purpose of westering – required male–female cooperation. Women were needed to settle and develop territory, to make "the desert blossom as the rose," as the biblical mantra had it. A passage from Sarah Pratt Carr's *The Iron Way* of 1907, a book about railroad building, puts it succinctly when a railroad executive proposes a toast. He recognizes women in general (represented with a capital W) and also Sally B., wife of a shiftless prospector, who deals with his frequent absences by owning and managing a hotel for railroad personnel:

> You ask what Woman has to do with the Pacific Railroad? Everything! Doesn't Woman make the home? Don't home make the nation? Doesn't Uncle Sam protect his nation? And doesn't he need this railroad to do it? ... Could you *build* this railroad without woman? Where under the canopy would it get to without Sally B.? Where would be your banquets, your square meals three times a day? ... What are you building your railroad for, anyway. ... The supreme reason, – you are building this railroad to carry women, to found homes in the great West. (pp. 186–7)

Fourth is the question what women themselves derived from this transaction. Ideas of a particularly western female type centered in her ability to overcome challenges – Sally B., for example, runs her hotel because her prospecting husband is usually away and seldom successful. The result is a mental and physical development denied to non-western women, who have no choice but to exploit their weakness and, in most ways, trudge at the rear of the historical procession. In western books the woman protagonist stands for what the West allowed women to become, what all women might become: hardy, capable, physically active, and – because she doesn't have to resort to female tricks and wiles – honest and forthright. This female type had emerged in American writing soon after the Revolution as a sign of women's access to freedom and opportunity. In its western version, the type made the West itself into the truest expression of the thoroughly American spirit.

Although nineteenth-century women are conventionally imagined to be more pious than men, these books understand Manifest Destiny as history not theology. Anglo-Saxons (the term is in regular use by the 1830s) who, back in Europe, had been overrun by Gallic and Roman invaders now had their turn. They headed West, crossing the Atlantic and then the prairies. Often this view of historical inevitability assumed that Saxons were more energetic, enterprising, innovative, and forward-looking than those they were displacing on the continent. But in the past they had been displaced, and in the future they would be displaced again – by century's end it's often supposed that the Chinese will eventually dominate the US. Anglo-Saxon traits did not make people better ethically, but simply better equipped for the current contest. White women enjoyed being on history's winning side.

The small number of minority women did not unite in opposition to this Anglo-Saxon declaration. They saw that this group movement was succeeding. Their own identities did not overlap. Sui Sin Far is interested in immigrant and usually merchant-class Chinese. María Amparo Ruiz de Burton and María Sacramenta Lopez de Cummings from southern California, and Adina De Zavala from Texas, insist on their pure Castilian – as opposed to Native American – legacies. Native women affiliate with their local groups – these are Yurok (Lucy Thompson), Okanogan (Mourning Dove), Sioux (Zitkala-Ša and Marie McLaughlin), Northern Piute (Sarah Winnemucca), Creek (S. Alice Callahan), Cherokee (Mabel Washbourne Anderson, Rachel Eaton, Margaret Ross, Narcissa Whitman), and Choctaw (Muriel Wright). The Indian women who published usually accepted some kind of assimilation as at least inevitable. Three of five African American women – Maud Cuney-Hare from Texas, Emma S. Ray from Washington, and Delilah Beasley from California – accepted Manifest Destiny but revised it to include at its end point the full acceptance of black people into the US citizenry. (The other two are Josie Briggs Hall, who wrote to help black Texans succeed in life, and Bernice Love Wiggins, an exponent of black Texas "folk.")

The only two books from the 1830s are both by Mary Austin Holley, and both called *Notes on Texas* (1833, 1836). Their themes prefigure women's western work – they are place-specific; they proudly connect a family – the Austin family – with a regional enterprise; they have a public purpose, in this case to attract settlers to Austin property and thus, quite literally, to sell Texas. Written for women as much as or more than for men, they show women acting to advance a territorial and family agenda while developing female capacities.

Living in Kentucky at the time, Holley aimed her books at potential emigrants from the South. In the 1833 book, she uses the familiar letter format and a flowery rhetoric to stress her female identity: "I am charmed with this beautiful country. Its mountains, its prairies, its forests, and its rivers, all have their charms for me. Hence it is, I suppose, that what you may regard dry geographical details, affect my mind with much of the inspiration of poetry" (pp. 78–9). Women readers get advice on clothing, kitchen implements, and other household needs. Speaking to both men and women, Holley assures readers that the Mexican government – in 1833 Texas was a Mexican province – is both benign and remote. Advising settlers to keep out of politics, she assumes they are coming for personal reasons – to improve their life circumstances – and have no interest in Mexican affairs.

The 1836 version, published during the Texas Revolution, abandons the letter format and introduces a nationalist, racially charged ideology. Mexicans are now contemptible yet dangerous:

The justice and benevolence of Providence will forbid that that delightful and now civilized region should again become a howling wilderness, trod only by savages, or that it should again be desolated by the ignorance and superstition, the tyranny and anarchy, the rapine and violence of Mexican misrule. The Anglo-Saxon American race are destined to be forever the proprietors of this land of promise and fulfillment. Their laws will govern it, their learning will enlighten it, their enterprise will improve it, their flocks alone will range its boundless pastures. (p. 298)

In 1836 she says that adversity makes women strong. The Texas frontier produces "a hardihood and courage which is truly surprising" in women; they

have been known to perform exploits, which the effeminate men of populous cities might tremble at. ... It is not uncommon for ladies to mount their mustangs and hunt with their husbands, and with them to camp out for days. ... All visiting is done on horseback, and they will go fifty miles to a ball with their silk dresses ... in their saddle-bags. ... Hardy, vigorous constitution, free spirits, and spontaneous gaiety are thus induced. (p. 145)

For the 1840s I've also found just two western books, one by Jane Cazneau, a New York journalist who advocated expansion in the *New York Magazine and Democratic Review*, the other by Massachusetts historian and educator Emma Willard. Cazneau promoted Texas settlement and invested in Texas territory. Her 1845 *Texas and her Presidents* said the US should annex Texas because both were Anglo-Saxon republics. Willard's *Last Leaves of American History* is a hastily written appendix to her US school history, adding the Texas Revolution and the discovery of gold in California. The conservative Willard reached beyond her school audience, admonishing the forty-niners to remain true to New England ideals:

many of our ablest and most enterprising citizens are now on the wing, of whom numbers are intending to settle in that salubrious clime. God grant that nobler views than the mere love of gold, accompany them thither. May they feel, with a deep sense of responsibility, that they are going to lay the foundations of a new and an important state. Let them look back for an example to their forefathers. ... Let their faces be sternly set against anarchy, the source, and too often the destroyer of free governments. TO THIS END, LET THEM UPHOLD LAW, FOUND SCHOOLS, OBSERVE THE SABBATH, AND MAINTAIN PURE CHRISTIANITY. (p. 230)

Among thirteen books from the 1850s, I'll mention only the five from 1856, in which Utah, Kansas, and California join Texas as western places. *The Mormons at Home* by Cornelia Ferris, wife of a Utah territorial judge, merged Utah politics with overland travel. Cornelia's claim that Mormon women were not demoralized drudges told eastern readers that Utah women would not rise up against the LDS hierarchy. By including Utah as an episode in an overland narrative, she masks her husband's political failure – he'd been prevented from holding a single sitting in his federal court and resigned after six months – publishing like many women to defend or celebrate a male relative. (Best-known of such women is Elizabeth Bacon Custer.) As if to underscore Ferris's point, the Mormon poet Eliza Snow published her *Poems, Religious, Historical, and Political* in Liverpool and London. These cities were centers of immigration recruitment to Utah, and the book appealed to potential emigrants.

The 1856 books about Kansas are Hannah Ropes's *Six Months in Kansas* and Sara Robinson's *Kansas: Its Interior and Exterior Life*. The importance of Boston as a venue for Kansas-themed literature involves Boston's significance as a hub for recruiting and arming settlers in Kansas. Ropes's sojourn, living with a son outside Lawrence, lasted only six months, as her title indicates. The threat of border hostilities and, even more, endemic disease in unsanitary emigrant living quarters discouraged her. Robinson, whose husband became Kansas' first elected governor, stayed on and called for more immigrants to outnumber the Missourians. All pioneer writing involves this kind of doubling: "normal" pioneering, whatever that might have been, is always troubled by the presence of others – from Indians to Mexicans to Missourians to Mormons to ranchers (from the homesteading perspective) to homesteaders (from the ranching perspective), somebody always wants "your" land.

Also in 1856, Eliza Lee Farnham chimed in from the Far West with *California, In-Doors and Out; or, How we Farm, Mine, and Live Generally in the Golden State*. The book describes her life as an independent female farmer, touting the superiority of agriculture to mining for human virtue as well as economic reward, and urges respectable women to immigrate and outnumber the state's numerous fallen women. All five 1850s books use personal testimony to comment on the larger project of western settlement.

The output of the 1860s included four dime novels published by Beadle in New York City: two by Metta Victor (*The Gold Hunters*, 1863; *The Two Hunters; or, the Canon Camp, a Romance of the Santa Fe Trail*, 1865); one by Frances Victor (*Alicia Newcome, or, the Land Claim, a Tale of the Upper Missouri*, 1862); and one by Ann Sophia Stephens (*Esther: A Story of the Oregon Trail*, 1862). Appearing under their authors' own names, these books show that, at least in the early years, dime novels were not a wholly masculine (or boyish) genre. Miriam Colt added her anguished hard-luck story, *Went to Kansas*, to accounts of Kansas failure. The family is lured to Kansas by false advertising: community amenities (a mill, houses) don't exist; there is in fact no community. Their garden is continually raided by Indians and after only two months they start back home. But on the homeward trek, both her husband and son get sick and die; disease, once again, is the great killer. Kansas emerges as central to the westernizing saga – site of several kinds of border violence and a place where farmers usually fail. They are still failing in Kansas books of the 1910s and 1920s.

Ten of twenty-two books from the 1870s include Frances Fuller Victor's 1870 history of the Pacific Northwest, *The River of the West*. Using her dime-novel narrative skills, Victor takes the life of one man – Meek, who began as a trapper and ended as an Oregon legislator – as emblematic. In 1872 she published a booster-like guide to Oregon and Washington (San Francisco: J.H. Carmony), updated with new interests in business entrepreneurship and tourism in 1891 as *Atlantis Arisen* (Philadelphia:

J.B. Lippincott). In 1877, she collected previously published work in *The New Penelope and Other Stories and Poems*.

In 1871 Fanny Kelly's *My Captivity Among the Sioux Indians*, took the well-worn form of a captivity narrative. Kelly wanted a financial reward from Congress for, supposedly, having alerted the frontier army to Indian plans; historians have been unable to corroborate many of her facts. But memoirs, after all, are essentially another form of fiction. Still in the 1870s: two anti-Mormon books by apostates, both published in Hartford (a center of anti-Mormon sentiment), contributed to debates about Utah statehood by focusing on polygamy. One is Fanny Stenhouse's 1874 *Tell it All; the Story of a Life's Experience in Mormonism; an Autobiography*; the other is Eliza Young's 1875 *Wife No. 19, or The Story of A Life in Bondage, Being a Complete Exposé of Mormonism, and Revealing the Sorrows, Sacrifices, and Sufferings of Women in Polygamy*. T.B. Stenhouse, Fanny's apostate husband, had published *The Rocky Mountain Saints* in 1873; she redirected his arguments by adding much more anti-polygamy detail. For her the great Wasatch Range is an imprisoning barrier, and she welcomes the railroad, not only for its commercial possibilities (her husband's perspective) but also as way out of Utah. Eliza Young, one of Brigham Young's later wives, had a successful post-Utah career lecturing. She expanded her lectures through this book about life in Salt Lake City as a plural wife.

The completion of the transcontinental railroad in 1869 increased western tourism and led to books by and about tourists. Many were shaped by the itineraries of excursion companies (the Raymond Excursions out of New England were the most popular), with set stops at Denver, Salt Lake City, and California. The much-read political commentator Grace Greenwood (pen-name for Sarah Lippincott), wrote *New Life in New Lands* from a moralistic New England perspective; mining and polygamy were deplorable but Colorado was wonderful for rest and recuperation: "I find Colorado women everywhere, on mountain or plain, in town or ranch, singularly courageous and cheery, and I think that the cause in great part lies in their excellent health" (p. 63). She lauded Greeley as

> a really wonderful place. Established on a purely agricultural basis, with an inexhaustible capital of intelligence, energy, economy, and industry, it has thriven steadily, constantly, with no wild leaps of speculation, or fever-heats of ambition and greed. With an orderly and virtuous population, it has had to pass through none of the dark and dire and tempestuous scenes of pioneer life, such as are found in mountain mining towns. (pp. 38–9)

Caroline Churchill's 1877 *Over the Purple Hills*, reminiscences about stage coach travel in California, where this Denver-based pro-suffrage author traveled to sell subscriptions to her feminist journal, *The Colorado Antelope*. Miriam Leslie, an editor and wife of the media mogul Frank Leslie, traveled West in a private railroad car, met many distinguished statesmen, and published a book about it in 1877, *California: A Pleasure Trip from Gotham to the Golden Gate*. The book caters to reader appetites for celebrities and luxury. Helen Hunt Jackson's essay collection *Bits of Travel at Home* shows none of the sympathy for Native Americans that animates *Ramona* six years later. Jackson's 1878 *Nelly's Silver Mine*, is a didactic book about Colorado for young people, teaching that true wealth lies within, and – perhaps inconsistently – that an eastern education is a much surer route to success than western prospecting. Jane W. Bruner's 1877 melodramatic *Free Prisoners: A Story of California Life*, uses the Gold Rush as a narrative device to bring together an unlikely cast of characters. Set in San Francisco, Sacramento, and Grass Valley, it reports that mining has changed Grass Valley from a once beautiful place "into a scene of confusion and desolation" (p. 23).

Around 1880 the number of books published becomes too great for complete summary, so I'll select one year from each decade to represent the various kinds of literary production. Across the decades, the books register changing conditions in the West, literary movements, and – especially after World War I – a decisive modernization of women's identity across the nation with more psychology, more sex, and more independence than one found in earlier books. This process leaves out more than 75 percent of the authors and books, only hinting at how much there is to be studied, analyzed, and understood in connection with the history of the book, with women's writing, and with women authors.

For the 1880s, my year of choice is 1884, with eleven books about Texas, Utah, California, Colorado, and Nebraska. Amelia Barr's Texas novel, *The Hallam Succession*, is about English settlers (Barr herself had emigrated from England), representing Yorkshiremen as "sturdy, shrewd and stalwart ... a handsome race, the finest specimens extant of the pure Anglo-Saxon" (p. 3) and thus particularly well suited to be Texans, enjoying the "healthy, happy life of the prairies ... the joy of encamping in forests, and seeing the sun rise between the leaves" (p. 159). Reminiscences by Mary S. Helms, an early Texas settler who'd long since moved to Indiana, were published as *Scraps of Early Texas History* in Austin. The Texas *Clarendon News* had solicited her reminiscences of the early days; with her first husband, a surveyor, she was a founder of Matagorda, and often accompanied him on his searches for new town sites. She writes about the so-called "runaway scrape" when fear of the Mexicans induced a panic among early settlers. She attributes the Anglo-Saxon triumph to racial superiority. "Anglo-Americans," she writes,

> are hardy and enduring beyond all other races. Endowed with an incredible and inexhaustible energy, they never turn back or yield to reverse however severe or crushing. On the other hand, the modern Mexicans are, as it were, the debris of several inferior and degraded races; American and Indian crossed and mixed, and even the old Spanish blood was mixed with the Moorish and demoralized by a long course of indolence and political corruption; both physically and mentally they are the very antithesis of the Anglo-Americans.
>
> They are as weak as he is strong; they run where he fights; they starve in the midst of abundance, while he knows how to pluck wealth and prosperity from rocks and sterile plains. (*Scraps*, pp. 52–3)

Two works by Mormon women, published in Salt Lake City, addressed a Utah audience. The Mormons, having gone to what was a Mexican territory, found Utah annexed to the US and directly on the route of the forty-niners, thus in constant contact with the country they thought they had left. Augusta Crocheron, plural wife and poet (a small volume of her poems appeared in 1881), brought out *Representative Women of Deseret: A Book of Biographical Sketches*, a gathering of celebratory biographies and autobiographies. Hannah Tapfield King's ambitious *An Epic Poem. A Synopsis of the Rise of the Church of Jesus Christ of Latter-Day Saints, from the birth of the prophet Joseph Smith to the arrival on the spot which the prophet Brigham Young pronounced to be the site of the future Salt Lake City*, was – as its title indicates – a history of Mormonism and of Joseph Smith, making the point that his very lack of education (what the eastern scholars all laughed at) fitted him to receive a direct communication from God.

Helen Hunt Jackson's *Ramona* was a sensationally popular best-seller, sentimentalizing the settled Native Americans around San Diego who were farmers, and – what the author seems not to have anticipated – launching both a wave of nostalgia for glamorous Spanish California and a lucrative tourist industry connected with missions and padres. A very different type of California novel, Maud Howe Elliott's *San Rosario Ranch*, is about wealthy ranchers and Gold Rush tycoons; like many San Francisco and northern California books, it showcased the social sophistication of successful Californians. A third California work is Mallie Stafford's *"The March of Empire" through Three Decades, Embracing Sketches of California History*, which blends a gold-driven history of Manifest Destiny (gold being "the powerful lever that moves the civilized world," p. 67), with the story of her husband's repeated failures in one Sierra mining milieu after another. Alice Polk Hill, a Denver journalist, traveled around Colorado to interview old-timers for *Tales of the Colorado Pioneers*, hoping to preserve their stories in local history. Frances Fulton, having decided not to settle in Nebraska herself, surveyed homesteading opportunities in the northern part of the state on her way home in *To and Through Nebraska, by a Pennsylvania Girl*.

For the 1890s my year of choice is 1895. The ten books include Josephine White Bates' *Bunch-Grass Stories*; Emma Pow Bauder's *Ruth and Marie*; Ina Coolbrith's *Songs from the Golden Gate*; Mary Stewart Daggett's *Mariposilla*; Gertrude Atherton's *A Whirl Asunder*; Mary Hallock Foote's *Coeur d'Alene*; Molly Moore Davis's *Under the Man-Fig*; Josephine Spencer's, *The Senator from Utah, and Other Tales of the Wasatch*: Clara Spalding Brown's *Life at Shut-In Valley, and other Pacific Coast Tales*; and Janie Chase Michaels' *A Natural Progression: A Story of Phoenix, Arizona*. Most of these books were published by prominent houses, a sign of the popularity of Western books with eastern audiences.

Josephine White Bates had published a couple of novels set in the Pacific Northwest before *Bunch-Grass Stories,* among whose eight tales six are set in various parts of the West, mostly Washington and Oregon. Two involve people who went West in the sixties to avoid the Civil War – another slant on westward emigration; others are about failed miners and railroad building. Bauder's *Ruth and Marie* is a San Francisco reform novel merging melodrama with sermonizing about temperance, labor, women's property, and women's suffrage. *Songs from the Golden Gate* is the only book of poetry that Ina Coolbrith – a nurturer of literary talent and an editor of the *Overland Monthly* – published in her lifetime; except for the invocation to "California," the title does not indicate a western focus but, on the contrary, goes to show that California women can publish poems on traditional subjects in traditional meters. "California" imagines the state speaking and – a switch from the normal disapproval of mining – celebrating the Gold Rush because it will make her known to the world. Having sat alone for many years listening only to birds, panthers, and "the savage tongue / Of my brown savage children" (p. 4), now she hears "the sharp clang of steel, that came to drain / The mountain's golden vein. ... 'now,' I said, 'I shall be known! / I shall not sit alone; / But reach my hands unto my sister lands!" (p. 5).

In *Mariposilla*, Daggett, a social leader in early Pasadena, wrote a latter-day seduction novel. The beautiful Mexican victim, naively supposing herself to be the social equal of an Anglo male, comes to the usual sad end. The prolific Atherton's short *A Whirl Asunder*, set in Marin County, displays her fondness for emotional contests, as a California heroine clashes with an English peer. She tells him that the forty-niners' "savage spirit, that instinct to trample to a goal over anything or anybody, that intolerance of restraint ... still lingers in the very atmosphere, and is quick in the blood of many of the present generation," giving more distinct "individuality to the women than to the men" (p. 53).

Coeur d'Alene is Foote's take on the miners' strike; although then an Idaho resident, she was several hundred miles south of the region and relied on newspapers for information in a novel where miners are misled by outside agitators. Davis, the best-known Texas fiction writer of her time, set her novel on the Brazos River, and identified the state with southern culture, geography, and history (but a later book, *The Wire-Cutters* of 1899, makes Texas a western state). Spencer's *Senator from Utah* is an unusual Utah book because its secular situations involve tourism, strikes, and other non-Mormon subjects, as if to show that Utah – on the verge of statehood – was no longer an enclave. *Life at Shut-in Valley* is journalist Clara Spalding Brown's only published book (she'd lived in and reported on Tombstone until 1882 but then moved to California). Ten of its twelve stories are set in coastal or inland southern California; the other two take place in Arizona. Several stories show refined young women who have gone West to escape poverty or failed courtships but have lost neither inner strength nor virtue, which are manifested externally in the clarity of their gaze and the erectness of their posture. Janie Chase Michaels – whose book's publication in Bangor may indicate a Maine origin – also writes about Arizona; her view of the city of Phoenix is of a promising, interesting, socially and culturally variegated town, in short a place entering into modernity as its population swells with incoming easterners.

Among sixteen books in 1902 is Atherton's *The Splendid Idle Forties*, a republication of stories about pre-Anglo California appearing first in 1894 as *Before the Gringo Came*. In her numerous California historical works Atherton managed to suture romantic fascination with pre-annexation California to a strong sense of Saxon superiority. Journalist Nellie Blessig-Eyster, a Quaker reformer originally from Maryland, published *A Chinese Quaker*, a novelized biography of a Chinese youth she had befriended. This is one of many San Francisco books featuring the Chinese, ranging from gothic representations of Chinatown to sentimental depictions of Chinese children ripe for conversion to American and Christian ways. Eva Emery Dye, who wrote history and fiction about the Pacific Northwest, published *The Conquest: The True Story of Lewis and Clark* for the centennial celebration. Naming Lewis and Clark as first in the unstoppable westward march that now continues across the Pacific, she makes Sacagawea a Victorian princess: "Heroine of the great expedition. ... Madonna of her race, she had led the way to a new time. To the hands of this girl, not yet eighteen, had been intrusted the key that unlocked the road to Asia. ... Across North America a Shoshone Indian Princess touched hands with Jefferson, opening her country" (p. 290).

In Mary Hallock Foote's somewhat melodramatic Idaho novel, *The Desert and the Sown*, a young man with an absent father and brought up by his stylish mother discovers his father in the low-class guide who is taking a group into the snowy mountains. The novel combines Foote's descriptive elegance with her class consciousness; she writes for example of "those bare high plains escarped with basalt bluffs that open every fifty miles or so to let a road crawl down to some little rope-ferry supported by sheep-herders, ditch contractors, miners, emigrants, ranchmen, all the wild industries of a country in the dawn of enterprise" (p. 190). Eleanor Gates, with *The Poor Little Rich Girl* still ahead of her, published the quasi-autobiographical *The Biography of a Prairie Girl*. Set in South Dakota near the Yankton Sioux reservation, it follows the little girl until she leaves the prairie for school. Her mother looks to the future when "Every quarter-section will hold a house, and there will be chimneys in sight in every direction. Churches and better schools will follow. ... The frontier will have moved far to the west"; but she tells her daughter that "One woman in a family is enough to sacrifice to the suffering and drudgery of frontier life. ... So I want you to go East, to go where the sweetest and best influences can reach you. The prairie has given you health. It has never given you happiness. ... Ah! Those who are born and bridge on the edge of things give more than the work of their hands to the country's building" (p. 286).

Sarah Raymond Herndon's *Days on the Road: Crossing the Plains in 1865* republished an overland diary serialized twenty years earlier. Elizabeth Higgins, a journalist for the *Omaha Bee* and Chicago newspapers, published her populist Nebraska novel, *Out of the West*, in which soil, climate, and railroad fees cooperate to defeat the farmers. Told from the perspective of a male newcomer – converted to the cause by a young woman lecturer from Colorado – it also inventories small-town life with particular attention to mothers who want to find husbands for their daughters and daughters who want to find lives for themselves. The male perspective on women's lives, from the perspective of a woman author, complicates the telling. Agnes Laut, a Canadian émigrée long settled in the United States, contributed *The Story of the Trapper* to a series heroicizing various vanishing masculine types from the Old West.

Alice MacGowan's *The Last Word* begins and ends in west Texas, contrasting the open plains to the crowded city where the heroine goes to make her way as a journalist. Pauline Bradford Mackie's novel for young women, *The Story of Kate*, is an Alcott-like tale of three rural California friends who go to San Francisco and, discovering who they are, make three different life choices. Easterner Frances McElrath's fairy tale of female entrapment and redemption, *The Rustler: A Tale of Love and War in Wyoming*, features a schoolteacher visiting her brother's ranch for the summer. Attracted to the lower-class foreman, she foolishly flirts with him. Her rejection turns him into a criminal; within days, it seems, he becomes a successful rustler. He kidnaps her and keeps her under guard for an entire year, but in the hidden town where he reigns supreme she turns to good works, nursing the sick and educating the rustlers' children. His violent death, with events loosely based on the Johnson County range war of 1892, frees her; but she breaks her engagement to an easterner in favor of continuing her career of good works. Mary MacLane's confessional autobiography of boredom and anomie, *The Story of Mary MacLane*, is set in a banal Butte, Montana, that shows no traces of any colorful mining past. Emma Merserau Newton's *Veil of Solana* is a zesty first-person narration about southern California; a young woman has gone to San Luis Obispo – "Such a whimsical old town! Modern American shops jostle antique Spanish abodes, and Chinese hovels bask in the radiance of electric streetlamps" (p. 21) – to find a veil mentioned in her grandfather's papers. This starting point leads to a recital of early California stories and legends: suppression of the Indians by the padres, secularization, mountain men, gold discovery, Fremont.

Mary M. North's *A Prairie Schooner: A Romance of the Plains of Kansas* is a circumstantially descriptive novel about early settling.

> As soon as the "town" was laid out, the tide of immigration set in, and when this story opens, there were a few general stores, on a small scale, a blacksmith shop, which was a crying necessity, as there were always horses to be shod – those belonging to the Government, or those of people on the "trail," and wagons to be repaired. To this embryo town came also a physician, and with the first settlers, there were two lawyers. There were a few houses which were entitled to the name, a number of shanties, and "dugouts" of settlers who had come west to try their fortunes, and get rich, as they fondly hoped, by raising cattle or some other method which might present itself. There was also a boarding-house for those who were without a home. (p. 21)

The protagonist grows up a "fine type of a happy, healthy western girl ... a fearless horsewoman, and many a time had helped her father herd the cattle" (pp. 48–9). Evelyn Raymond's girls' book, *Jessica Trent: Her Life on a Ranch*, is set in southern California. Like other girls' books in this era, as well as those by this particular author, this is a quite literate performance. In this story, the 11-year-old protagonist becomes de facto manager of a big ranch after her father dies. Many characters converge in a fantasy of the West as a place where the tired, hungry, and poor gentlepeople of the earth can flourish as beet farmers, ostrich raisers, coalminers. A character says: "This big West is like a romance, a fairy tale; not the least of its marvels to find a little girl like you riding alone on such a steed up such a desolate Canyon, yet not in the least afraid" (pp. 14–15). Florence Kimball Russel's *Born to the Blue* is an army novel for boys, construing the frontier army as a training ground for virtuous manhood. It begins in Sioux territory and takes the protagonist from boyhood there, on to a "little four-company post in Arizona, sixty miles from anywhere – a post that has long since been abandoned, and which with little difficulty resolved itself into the surrounding miles of alkali prairie, broken only by the gray of sage-brush and giant cactus" (p. 156). The book preaches peaceful virtues, but keeping Indians in line is the army's mission, and eventually an Indian has to be killed to demonstrate manhood – an act that is rationalized by making it a rescue.

Nineteen books from 1915 include the first volume in Elizabeth Abel's eventual three-volume study of the slaveholding Indians: *American Indian as Slaveholder and Secessionist*; Ada Woodcock Anderson's densely factual novel about the interconnections of Washington State and Alaska in *Rim of the Desert*; Cherokee author Mabel Washbourne Anderson's biography of her grandfather's cousin, *Life of General Stand Watie*; Nettie Barker's brief *Kansas Women in Literature*; three novels by B.M. Bower (the most prolific western writer by far, with forty novels published by 1928 and an eventual total of sixty-eight novels all set in the West): *Jean of the Lazy A* (New York: A.L. Burt); *The Flying U's Last Stand*, and *The Phantom Herd* (both published in Boston by Little, Brown and reissued by Grosset and Dunlap). In Bowers' romantic and action-filled novels, threats of violence were usually neutralized by cowboy cleverness. *The Flying U's Last Stand* is about the breakup of the big Wyoming ranches in the face of homesteading; a group of Wyoming cowboys (already familiar to readers from other Bower novels) seek to delay historical inevitability by becoming homesteaders themselves. The other two – one featuring a heroine, the other a hero – are about how movies are appropriating and adapting western ranch themes (thereby providing work for unemployed cowboys) as the ranches themselves go under. Willa Cather published *The Song of the Lark* – the second of her three early books about strong women. Thea Kronberg from "Moonstone, Colorado" must leave the provincial West to succeed in opera, but her cosmopolitan art is indelibly shaped by Colorado and the desert Southwest. In *The Story of the Marking of the Santa Fe Trail* (Topeka: Crane), Almira Cordry celebrated the marking of the trail across Kansas to Santa Fe with a geographical tour, marker by marker, across the state. Another Kansan, Anna Arnold, a teacher and school administrator, published *A History of Kansas* – the second of her two widely used texts – claiming that knowledge of "the difficulties that have been met and conquered in building the State" will "create in the minds of the boys and girls a greater respect for the sturdy qualities of the pioneers … give them a wholesome sense of the great cost at which the ease and comfort of to-day have been purchased," and "stimulate in them a desire to live up to the past" (p. 5). Mary Hallock Foote's *The Valley Road* is set in the Sierra foothills where mining interests prevent idealistic engineers from constructing the dams that the region needs for agriculture. Harrie (*sic*) Forbes self-published the third edition of her guide to *California Missions* in Los

Angeles in connection with the marketing of the "Camino Real," a route supposedly established by Junipero Serra, which she was marking with mission bell replicas she'd designed and manufactured in the California Bell Company founded by her and her husband. Effie Price Gladding's *Across the Continent by the Lincoln Highway* appeared the year after this road officially opened, signaling a new form of western travel and a new kind of travel book, wherein motoring tourists could imagine themselves crossing the plains like pioneers a half-century earlier.

Mary Jane Hayden's brief memoir of the Pacific Northwest, *Pioneer Days*, complains about diverse aspects of the overland journey and pioneer life. She remembers the Civil War army with dismay:

> It was well known about New York that we had mines on this coast, and plenty of a certain class who had not the means to take so long and expensive a journey either by land or water were ready to enlist in order to get here, when they would desert and go to the mines, where they could ply their trade (which was gambling and stealing). ... In less than a week after the arrival of the 14th Infantry ... it was drinking, gambling, fighting, house breaking and several citizens beaten nearly to death. (p. 53)

Alice Polk Hill's second book, *Colorado Pioneers in Picture and Story*, was illustrated with photographs of people and buildings, more about businessmen – the second generation of Colorado settlers – than miners. Caroline Lockhart published her fourth novel, *The Man From the Bitter Roots*, about mining in Idaho; the book is notable for its satirical nastiness. Honoré Willsie published her first novel, *Still Jim*, about a civil engineer from the East who works first in the Pacific Northwest and then Arizona. Elizabeth M. Page's *Camp and Tepee* is a tribute to Reformed Church missionary work among Comanche, Apache, Cheyenne, Arapahoe, Winnebago, and Omaha mostly in Oklahoma but also in New Mexico and Nebraska.

Elinore Stewart's *Letters on an Elk Hunt* is her second collection of sketches about settlers and tourists in southern Wyoming. In Kathleen Norris's *Julia Page*, Julia – daughter of a working girl from San Francisco's mission district who'd married and divorced a salesman – matures into the faultless, gorgeous victim of bad romantic choices (a typical formula for female romance). Julia unwisely flirts with a married man, takes up with an unstable Jewish lad who kills himself, and marries an insanely jealous physician. Like the seven other California novels Norris published before 1928, the story is about bad marriages; the setting, which shows that women's lives are much the same whether lived on the East or West Coast, marks the entrance of the West into modernity.

Among the eleven books from 1926 are Bess Streeter Aldrich's collection of linked stories about an ordinary, middle-class, small-town Nebraska family, *The Cutters*; Sarah Bixby-Smith's engaging family memoir of childhood in southern California, *Adobe Days*; Ethel Dorrance's *The Rim O' The Range*, whose protagonist lives with her uncle on a border ranch, the Arizonomex, during dire times when drought and falling prices bring trouble throughout the West:

cow and sheepmen were in trouble, many of them unable to provide gasoline for the high-priced limousines they had bought with the tremendous profits made at the beginning of the World War period. Their heavy losses, potential or real, had foundation in three years' protraction of an unprecedented drouth. ... Always have stockmen been large borrowers of money, and from them in the past most regional bankers had waxed fat. But this time, loans on both cattle and sheep had been made at the peak of valuation, and now that prices had tumbled and freights had risen beyond endurance they were finding their bargains bad. (pp. 41–2)

Forrestine Hooker's *Just George* is a story for boys, set like Russel's in Arizona (Hooker, daughter of an army captain, had grown up in southwestern army posts and married a rancher). George, a slum child rescued by a ranch foreman, eventually goes to West Point. Agnes Laut publicized *The Enchanted Trails of Glacier Park*. Mae Van Norman Long's theosophically inflected *The Canyon of the Stars* describes a southern California of languorous climate, floral profusion, starry nights, and mission architecture. The protagonist, from Michigan, is lonely and despairing at the story's outset but is invigorated by the arrival of two wonderfully handsome men, each representing a different kind of southern California agriculture: a commercial gardener and a rancher. The unearthly beauty of the setting symbolizes an idyllic future for all mankind; southern California is as close as you can get to heaven without actually going there: "starlight nights articulate with mockingbirds and thrush ... golden days, looking off toward the Simi Hills and the rose-flushed mountains, followed by lavender twilights" (p. 69).

Aileen Nusbaum's *Zuni Indian Tales* and Elsie Clews Parsons' *Tewa Tales* retell Indian stories. *Zuni Indian Tales* narrates sixteen traditional Zuni stories for children as though Indian stories were always already childlike because Indians are childlike people. The scholarly *Tewa Tales* carefully transcribes informants' oral tales but also thinks of Indians as childlike in their preference for myth over history: "In what we call history the Pueblo Indians are very little interested; emergence myth and prehistoric migration myth are *their history*, fully satisfying their sense of the historic" (p. 2). Mary Katrine Sedgwick's *Acoma, The Sky City: A Study in Pueblo-Indian History and Civilization* fleshes out two quick visits to that pueblo with anthropological findings about other pueblos, and hopes that some day the Acomans will be more welcoming to snoopy scholars and tourists than they are now. Emma Ray's *Twice Sold, Twice Ransomed: Autobiography of Mr. and Mrs. L.P. Ray* is the life story of two African American evangelists who went from St. Louis to Seattle; its picture of life in Seattle, with dope addicts, derelicts, prostitutes, and the backrush of failure from the Alaskan mines, is unique.

Alice Dolan Shipman's self-published *Taming the Big Bend: A History of the Extreme Western Portion of Texas from Fort Clark to El Paso* narrates the settlement and domestication of west Texas by white people late in the state's history; a biography of her father, cattleman and Texas ranger Pat Dolan, forms part of the story. He's an ideal of western manhood, believing that none should be posers, that life should be unaffected, democratic, that a man's past should count for nothing. This was a new land. If a newcomer was the son of a titled father, he did not parade the fact. ... If a man's past had been a bit too colorful, that was overlooked. ... Probably the westerners were a bit rough from society's viewpoint, but those who are capable of judging true values will appreciate their magnificent souls. To those whose ideal is of form, scale, and glitter, the westerner, like the West, will have no appeal. (p. vi)

The book has outlaws, Indian fights, and Mexican bandits, and brings in an occasional frontier heroine like Alice Stillwell Henderson, who experienced "adventure and desperate encounters ... as a part of her daily life" (p. 103). It ends by conceding that the Old West is gone:

Today, in Marfa and Alpine, luncheons, dinner parties, receptions, bridge clubs, federated literary club meetings, swimming parties, and dances are much the same as in any other town. Though we still have our old time barbecue and rodeo about once a year, the real "Old West" is only a memory. But even today in this unostentatious land, where people are not loud spoken but say what they mean and let it go at that, it matters not if you hail fresh from a throne, if you don't "measure up" to requirements you go unnoticed. ... Altogether, the Big Bend is tame and will remain so unless our neighbors across the river have another revolution. (p. 170)

This last aside brings in the menacing Mexicans again as the all-purpose villains of southwestern white mythology.

Among productive women – novelists in the main – who didn't publish in the years I have summarized are Mary Austin, Geraldine Bonner (a San Francisco historical novelist), Kate Boyles (a South Dakota novelist), Margaret Hill McCarter (author of intensely anti-Indian historical novels about Kansas), Vingie E. Roe (who set heroic women characters in novels from Oregon to Arizona), and Marah Ellis Ryan (whose quest for non-Anglo spirituality recurred in pro-Indian books set from Montana to New Mexico). My sample has included only one of eleven Native writers, one of five African American writers (three of them Texans), none of the three Hispanics – two Texans and a Californian, and doesn't include Sui Sin Far's only book. For those interested in the development of a female print culture, in women's literary and political writing, and in the West – or wests – itself or themselves – there is much, much more.

REFERENCES AND FURTHER READING

Abel, Elizabeth. (1915). *American Indian as Slaveholder and Secessionist*. Cleveland: Arthur H. Clark.

Aldrich, Bess Streeter. (1926). *The Cutters*. New York: D. Appleton.

Anderson, Ada Woodcock. (1915). *Rim of the Desert*. New York: A.L. Burt.

Anderson, Mabel Washbourne. (1915). *Life of General Stand Watie*. Pryor, OK: Mayes County Republican.

Arnold, Anna. (1915). *A History of Kansas*. Topeka: State of Kansas.

Atherton, Gertrude. (1895). *A Whirl Asunder*. New York: Frederick A. Stokes.

Atherton, Gertrude. (1902). *The Splendid Idle Forties*. New York: Macmillan.

Barker, Nettie. (1915). *Kansas Women in Literature*. Kansas City: S.I. Mesereaull & Son.

Barr, Amelia. (1884). *The Hallam Succession*. New York: Philips & Hunt.

Bates, Josephine White. (1895). *Bunch-Grass Stories*. Philadelphia: Lippincott.

Bauder, Emma Pow. (1895). *Ruth and Marie: A Fascinating Story of the Nineteenth Century*. Chicago: American Bible House.

Bixby-Smith, Sarah. (1926). *Adobe Days*. Cedar Rapids, IA: Torch.

Blessig-Eyster, Nellie. (1902). *A Chinese Quaker*. New York: Fleming H. Revell.

Bower, B.M. (1915). *The Flying U's Last Stand*. Boston: Little, Brown.

Bower, B.M. (1915). *Jean of the Lazy A*. New York: A.L. Burt.

Bower, B.M. (1915). *The Phantom Herd*. Boston: Little, Brown.

Brown, Clara Spalding. (1895). *Life at Shut-In Valley, and other Pacific Coast Tales*. Franklin, OH: Editor Publishing.

Bruner, Jane W. (1877). *Free Prisoners: A Story of California Life*. Philadelphia: Claxton, Remsen & Haffelfinger.

Carr, Sarah Pratt. (1907). *The Iron Way*. Chicago: A.C. McClurg.

Cather, Willa. (1915). *The Song of the Lark*. Boston: Houghton Mifflin.

Cazneau, Jane. (1845). *Texas and her Presidents*. New York: E. Winchester.

Churchill, Caroline. (1877). *Over the Purple Hills*. Chicago: Hazlitt & Reed.

Colt, Miriam. (1862). *Went to Kansas*. Watertown, NY: L. Ingals.

Coolbrith, Ina. (1895). *Songs from the Golden Gate*. Boston: Houghton Mifflin.

Cordry, Almira. (1915). *The Story of the Marking of the Santa Fe Trail*. Topeka: Crane.

Crocheron, Augusta. (1884). *Representative Women of Deseret: A Book of Biographical Sketches*. J.C. Graham.

Daggett, Mary Stewart. (1895). *Mariposilla*. Chicago: Rand McNally.

Davis, Molly Moore. (1895). *Under the Man-Fig*. Boston: Houghton Mifflin.

Dorrance, Ethel. (1926). *The Rim O' The Range*. New York: Chelsea House.

Dye, Eva Emery. (1902). *The Conquest: The True Story of Lewis and Clark*. Chicago: A.C. McClurg.

Elliott, Maud Howe. (1884). *San Rosario Ranch*. Boston: Roberts Brothers.

Farnham, Eliza Lee. (1856). *California, In-Doors and Out; or, How we Farm, Mine, and Live Generally in the Golden State*. New York: Dix, Edwards.

Ferris, Cornelia. (1856). *The Mormons at Home*. New York: Dix & Edwards.

Foote, Mary Hallock. (1895). *Coeur d'Alene*. Boston: Houghton Mifflin.

Foote, Mary Hallock. (1902). *The Desert and the Sown*. Boston: Houghton Mifflin.

Foote, Mary Hallock. (1915). *The Valley Road*. Boston: Houghton Mifflin.

Fulton, Frances. (1884). *To and Through Nebraska, by a Pennsylvania Girl*. Lincoln: Journal Company.

Gates, Eleanor. (1902). *The Biography of a Prairie Girl*. New York: Century.

Gladding, Effie Price. (1915). *Across the Continent by the Lincoln Highway*. New York: Brentano's.

Greenwood, Grace. (1873). *New Life in New Lands*. New York: J.B. Ford.

Hayden, Mary Jane. (1915). *Pioneer Days*. San Jose, CA: Murgotten.

Helms, Mary S. (1884). *Scraps of Early Texas History*. Austin, TX: Warner.

Herndon's Sarah Raymond. (1902). *Days on the Road: Crossing the Plains in 1865*. New York: Burr.

Higgins, Elizabeth. (1902). *Out of the West*. New York: Harper.

Hill, Alice Polk. (1884). *Tales of the Colorado Pioneers*. Denver: Pierson & Gardner.

Hill, Alice Polk. (1915). *Colorado Pioneers in Picture and Story*. Denver: Brock-Haffner.

Holley, Mary Austin. (1833). *Notes on Texas*. Baltimore: Armstrong & Plaskitt.

Holley, Mary Austin. (1836). *Notes on Texas*. Lexington, KY: J. Clarke.

Hooker, Forrestine. (1926). *Just George*. Garden City: Doubleday, Page.

Jackson, Helen Hunt. (1878). *Bits of Travel at Home*. Boston: Roberts Brothers.

Jackson, Helen Hunt. (1878). *Nelly's Silver Mine.* Boston: Roberts Brothers.

Jackson, Helen Hunt. (1884). *Ramona.* Boston: Roberts Brothers.

Kelly, Fanny. (1871). *My Captivity Among the Sioux Indians.* Hartford: Mutual Publishing.

King, Hannah Tapfield. (1884). *An Epic Poem. A Synopsis of the Rise of the Church of Jesus Christ of Latter-Day Saints, from the birth of the prophet Joseph Smith to the arrival on the spot which the prophet Brigham Young pronounced to be the site of the future Salt Lake City.* Juvenile Instructor Office.

Laut, Agnes. (1902). *The Story of the Trapper.* New York: Appleton.

Laut, Agnes. (1926). *The Enchanted Trails of Glacier Park.* New York: Robert M. McBride.

Leslie, Miriam. (1877). *California: A Pleasure Trip from Gotham to the Golden Gate.* New York: Carleton.

Lockhart, Caroline. (1915). *The Man From the Bitter Roots.* New York: A.L. Burt.

Long, Mae Van Norman. (1926). *The Canyon of the Stars.* Hollywood: David Graham Fisher.

MacGowan, Alice. (1902). *The Last Word.* Boston: L.C. Page.

Mackie, Pauline Bradford. (1902). *The Story of Kate.* Boston: L.C. Page.

MacLane, Mary. (1902). *The Story of Mary MacLane.* Chicago: Herbert H. Stone.

McElrath, Frances. (1902). *The Rustler: A Tale of Love and War in Wyoming.* New York: Funk & Wagnells.

Michaels, Janie Chase. (1895). *A Natural Progression: A Story of Phoenix, Arizona.* Bangor: Charles B. Glass.

Newton, Emma Merserau. (1902). *Veil of Solana.* New York: Frank F. Lovell.

Norris, Kathleen. (1915). *Julia Page.* Garden City: Doubleday, Page.

North, Mary M. (1902). *A Prairie Schooner: A Romance of the Plains of Kansas.* Washington, DC: Neale.

Nusbaum, Aileen. (1926). *Zuni Indian Tales.* New York: Putnam.

Page, Elizabeth M. (1915). *Camp and Tepee.* New York: Fleming H. Revell.

Parsons, Elsie Clews *Tewa Tales.* New York: American Folk-lore Society.

Ray, Emma. (1926). *Twice Sold, Twice Ransomed: Autobiography of Mr. and Mrs. L.P. Ray.* Chicago: Free Methodist Publishing House.

Raymond, Evelyn. (1902). *Jessica Trent: Her Life on a Ranch.* Racine: Whitman.

Robinson, Sara. (1856). *Kansas: Its Interior and Exterior Life.* Boston: Crosby, Nichols.

Ropes, Hannah. (1856). *Six Months in Kansas.* Boston: John P. Jewett.

Russel, Florence Kimball. (1902). *Born to the Blue.* Boston: L.C. Page.

Sedgwick, Mary Katrine. (1926). *Acoma, The Sky City: A Study in Pueblo-Indian History and Civilization.* Cambridge, MA: Harvard University Press.

Shipman, Alice Dolan. (1926). Taming the Big Bend: A History of the Extreme Western Portion of Texas from Fort Clark to El Paso. Self-published.

Snow, Eliza. (1856). *Poems, Religious, Historical, and Political.* Liverpool: P.D. Richards; London: Latter-Day Saints' Book Depot.

Spencer, Josephine. (1895). *The Senator from Utah, and Other Tales of the Wasatch.* Salt Lake City: George G. Cannon.

Stafford, Mallie. (1884). *"The March of Empire" through Three Decades, Embracing Sketches of California History.* San Francisco: Geo Spaulding.

Stenhouse, Fanny. (1874). Tell it All; the Story of a Life's Experience in Mormonism; an Autobiography. A.D. Worthington.

Stephens, Ann Sophia. (1862). *Esther: A Story of the Oregon Trail.* Beadle: New York.

Stewart, Elinore. (1915). *Letters on an Elk Hunt.* Boston: Houghton Mifflin.

Victor, Frances. (1862). *Alicia Newcome, or, the Land Claim, a Tale of the Upper Missouri.* Beadle: New York.

Victor, Frances Fuller. (1870). *The River of the West.* Hartford: R.W. Bliss.

Victor, Frances Fuller. (1877). *The New Penelope and Other Stories and Poems.* San Francisco: A.L. Bancroft.

Victor, Frances Fuller. (1891). *Atlantis Arisen* [San Francisco: J.H. Carmony, 1872]. Philadelphia: J.B. Lippincott.

Victor, Metta. (1863). *The Gold Hunters.* Beadle: New York.

Victor, Metta. (1865). *The Two Hunters; or, the Canon Camp, a Romance of the Santa Fe Trail.* Beadle: New York.

Willard, Emma. (1849). *Last Leaves of American History*. New York: Putnam.

Willsie, Honoré. (1915). *Still Jim*. New York: Frederick A. Stokes.

Young, Eliza. (1875). *Wife No. 19, or The Story of A Life in Bondage, Being a Complete Exposé of Mormonism, and Revealing the Sorrows, Sacrifices, and Sufferings of Women in Polygamy*. Dustin, Gilman, by subscription.

6

Literary Cultures of the American Southwest

Daniel Worden

The American Southwest complicates many of the common notions about "the region" in American literary history. Regional writing in America is often considered to be hostile to modernity, nostalgic for small-town life, and detached from the literary experimentations central to modernism and postmodernism. The American Southwest, in contrast, connotes both ancient and radically contemporary cultures, and southwestern writers are central to modern American literary history. New scholarship on literary regionalism emphasizes the region's constitutive role in American culture. Literary critic Hsuan Hsu has argued that the region in literature, which often "serves as a focus of nostalgia and a privileged site of geographical feeling," should not be characterized as a stable, isolated, and local entity, immune to the pressures of modernity (Hsu 2005: 36). Instead, Hsu posits that the region is key to literary history, for regionalism not only creates a sense of regional culture but also "occurs in relation to larger-scale phenomena such as migrant flows, transportational networks, and international commerce" (Hsu 2005: 37). Moreover, as Judith Fetterley and Marjorie Pryse propose, late nineteenth- and early twentieth-century "regionalism marks that point where the region becomes mobilized as a tool for critique of hierarchies based on gender as well as race, class, age, and economic resources" (Fetterley 2003: 14). The Southwest was a product of imaginative construction, imperial conquest, and fantasy long before its annexation to the United States in the nineteenth century, and its literature often critiques conventional narratives of conquest that reinforce social hierarchies. As a region in literature, the Southwest resonates as an alternative to conventional histories of the United States, and early proponents of the Southwest, such as Frank Hamilton Cushing and Charles Lummis, down to contemporary writers such as Cormac McCarthy and Leslie Marmon Silko have emphasized the

A Companion to the Literature and Culture of the American West, First Edition. Edited by Nicolas S. Witschi.

Southwest's unique position as a region that demands recognition of the United States' relatively recent role in a complicated nexus of conquest, settlement, colonialism, and development that spans millennia.

For all of the above reasons, the Southwest broadens the historical and cultural scope of western American literature. While modernism and postmodernism are often equated with urban centers like New York and Los Angeles, the diversity of genres, styles, and meanings employed by writers to represent the Southwest evidences the importance of the region to literary aesthetics. In fact, the Southwest is a central site for writers to experiment with new formal strategies, rethink history, and come to terms with contemporary American culture. In an essay on landscape in American literature, fiction writer Annie Proulx characterizes contemporary American culture as growing increasingly distant from nature and the landscape, in part because of the automobile and the highway system:

> On a long journey, the landmarks we look for and at are motels, signs, eateries, gas stations. The larger landscape is simply amorphous background. This fading view produces novels where streets, feeling, body language, contemporary manners, interiors, clothes, and consumer products are the salient features of a place. (Proulx 2008: 18)

Proulx's interest in shifting attention back to the landscape resonates as the goal of much southwestern literature, which, even if it does not spend much time describing the landscape, often critiques modern life and its excesses. As historian Robert L. Dorman argues, regionalism in the early twentieth century advocated a similar rejection of hollow modernity and a new conception of life amidst the land:

> the region, it was hoped, would provide the physical framework for the creation of new kinds of cities, small-scale, planned, delimited, and existing in balance with wilderness and a restored and rejuvenated rural economy. (Dorman 1993: pp. xii–xiii)

The interest in locality and nature, so often evidence of the backwardness and nostalgia of regionalism, can now be seen "as marking a significant stage in the unfolding history of conservationism, preservationism, urban planning, and environmentalism" (Dorman 1993: p. xiii).

The significance of the Southwest to twentieth-century literature can perhaps be best illustrated by two literary texts that treat the Southwest in quite different ways. In 1930 Ansel Adams and Mary Austin published a collaborative photobook, *Taos Pueblo*, which contained an ethnographic essay on Taos by Austin and photographs by Adams. In her essay, Austin reflects on the allure of Taos to the Anglo tourist:

> Always, for the most casual visitor at Taos, there is the appeal of strangeness; the dark people, the alien dress, the great house-heaps intricately blocked in squares of shadow and sunlight on tawny earthen walls. There is the charm of aloofness: the absence of clamor, the soft voices, the motionless figures high on the flat roofs, secure in the

impersonal privacy of the blanket … And in not one attitude anywhere a clue, a suggestion as to what it is all about. Everywhere peace, impenetrable timelessness of peace, as though the pueblo and all it contains were shut in a glassy fourth dimension, near and at the same time inaccessibly remote. (Austin 1996: 237–8)

In this passage, Austin employs many common tropes about the Southwest and its Native American population. Traveling to Taos Pueblo gives the tourist access to a world outside of modernity, a culture alien to fast-paced urban life, that is nonetheless familiar and relaxing. The paradox at the conclusion of Austin's paragraph, "near and at the same time inaccessibly remote," is one employed quite often in treatments of the Southwest and Native American culture. Taos is cast as incredibly therapeutic for the modern tourist, for it evidences a lifestyle closer to natural rhythms. Yet it is also captivatingly exotic, distant from and untranslatable into the tourist's own language and worldview. This understanding of Taos Pueblo is part of what Marianna Torgovnick describes as "the primitive," which "has been an influential and powerful concept, capable of referring both to societies 'out there' and to subordinate groups within the West" (Torgovnick 1990: 20). As literary critic Leah Dilworth writes, the primitivist conception of the Native American as radically different from Austin and her fellow Anglo travelers casts cultures like that of Taos Pueblo as models of an authentic connection to nature and society: "Although Austin's longing for authentic ways of being, for experience, was undoubtedly genuine, her identification of authenticity as other and primitive was problematic and ultimately precluded personal (and cultural) transformation" (Dilworth 1996: 209). Austin's characterization of Taos Pueblo as primitive assumes that it is isolated from history and impermeable to modern understanding. For Austin and other writers of southwestern literature, this distance from modernity is precisely the promise of the Southwest; living in and writing about the region and its Native American inhabitants demands that the writer rethink modern assumptions about life, time, and space.

While Austin treats Taos Pueblo as an isolated, primitive utopia, Hunter S. Thompson writes about a very different part of the American Southwest in *Fear and Loathing in Las Vegas* (1971). Ostensibly in Las Vegas to report on the Mint 400 Race, Thompson's alter ego, Raoul Duke, along with his attorney, Dr. Gonzo, turn their trip into a drug-fueled quest for the American Dream. As Duke and Gonzo arrive at the Desert Inn to see Debbie Reynolds in concert, Thompson's narration contrasts the glamour associated with Las Vegas with its tacky reality:

This was Bob Hope's turf. Frank Sinatra's. Spiro Agnew's. The lobby fairly reeked of high-grade formica and plastic palm trees – it was clearly a high-class refuge for Big Spenders … the moment we got inside we lost control. The tension had been too great. Debbie Reynolds was yukking across the stage in a silver Afro wig … to the tune of "Sergeant Pepper," from the golden trumpet of Harry James.

"Jesus creeping shit!" said my attorney. "We've wandered into a time capsule!" (Thompson 1998: 44)

Las Vegas, like Austin's Taos Pueblo, is immune to history, a "time capsule." The isolation from history here, though, registers as tacky, pathetic, and ultimately dystopic. Debbie Reynolds jumbles signifiers of the 1960s counterculture – the afro, the Beatles – into a middle-class performance for all of the Las Vegas tourists drawn to the casinos because of their classy connotations and plastic luxury. As Duke meditates later in their journey, Las Vegas comes to represent the death of the American Dream. Looking out the window and thinking about his life in San Francisco during the 1960s, Duke thinks about "that sense of inevitable victory over the forces of Old and Evil" that he had, that feeling of "riding the crest of a high and beautiful wave" (Thompson 1998: 68). In Las Vegas, Duke realizes that he has found its endpoint: "So now, less than five years later, you can go up on a steep hill in Las Vegas and look West, and with the right kind of eyes you can almost *see* the high-water mark – that place where the wave finally broke and rolled back" (Thompson 1998: 68). Thompson's countercultural hopes are thwarted by the Southwest, and in particular by Las Vegas, which represents middle-class consumerism, the appropriation of countercultural styles by mainstream America, and conservative politics. Rather than being removed and isolated from mainstream America, Las Vegas is the embodiment of late twentieth-century American culture, and Thompson's Raoul Duke is a western hero disappointed by the modern, urban Southwest.

While both Austin and Thompson frame the Southwest as a land out of time, their views of the region's timelessness complicate any easy assessment of the region as out of step with modernity. In fact, representations of the Southwest cast the region in an explicit relationship to modernity, as its foil or evidence of its omnipresence. The Southwest is a vast region, and its literature seizes upon that vastness in a variety of ways. A fruitful way to approach this region – and to understand its importance as a region to literary history – is to focus on the many different literary cultures that have thrived there. By focusing less on individual writers and more on the literary communities, forms, methods, concepts, and devices used at different historical moments to represent the Southwest, one can begin to understand how it has been imagined to represent both an idealized frontier and its undoing.

The Southwest and Regionalism

The Southwest exceeds territorial boundaries and borders. As the Texas writer J. Frank Dobie remarks in his *Guide to the Life and Literature of the Southwest*,

> The term Southwest is variable because the boundaries of the Southwest are themselves fluid, expanding and contracting according to the point of view from which the Southwest is viewed and according to whatever common denominator is taken for defining it ... The principal areas of the Southwest are, to have done with air-minded reservations, Arizona, New Mexico, most of Texas, some of Oklahoma, and anything else north, south, east, or west that anybody wants to bring in. (Dobie 1952: 13–14)

As Dobie points out, the Southwest has no precise limits, in no small part owing to the fact that it is not a region contained within the borders of the United States. Because it was acquired by the United States in large part following the signing of the Treaty of Guadalupe Hidalgo in 1848, the Southwest blends into northern Mexico both historically and culturally.

The Southwest's inherent transnational quality can be traced to two literary cultures that precede the Mexican–American War: Native American and Spanish. The many Native American cultures in the Southwest – including the Pueblo communities, Navajo, Apache, Ute, Sioux, and many others – have unique oral traditions, accessible to the modern scholar through a history of translation, transcription, and ethnographic projects. While many translations of Native American songs, stories, and ceremonies bear the traces of their translator and his or her historical moment, it is nonetheless important to consider Native American stories like the Kochinnenako, or Yellow Woman, tales as a rich literary tradition that spans centuries. The modern scholar accesses these stories through layers of exploitation, misrepresentation, and primitivist projection, yet they are nonetheless central to the history of the Southwest, its people, and its literature. As Leslie Marmon Silko writes in her essay "Language and Literature from a Pueblo Indian Perspective,"

> Within the clans there are stories that identify the clan. One moves, then, from the idea of one's identity as a tribal person into clan identity, then to one's identity as a member of an extended family ... Anthropologists and ethnologists have, for a long time, differentiated the types of stories the Pueblos tell. They tended to elevate the old, sacred, and traditional stories and to brush aside family stories, the family's account of itself. But in Pueblo culture, these family stories are given equal recognition. There is no definite, preset pattern for the way one will hear the stories of one's own family, but it is a very critical part of one's childhood, and the storytelling continues throughout one's life. (Silko 1997: 51–2)

Silko's account of storytelling emphasizes the interconnectedness of individuals, families, clans, and nature through narrative. Understanding Native American storytelling entails recognition of the ways in which language, story, and culture interact with, shape, and are shaped by the environment.

The first published accounts of the Southwest were the many travelogues and journals published by Spanish explorers and missionaries. The best-known account of the Southwest from the period of Spanish exploration is Álvar Núñez Cabeza de Vaca's *La Relación* (1542), an account of the explorer's perilous journey from Spain to the Gulf Coast and, eventually, Mexico City. Other Spanish accounts of the Southwest include Gaspar Pérez de Villagrá's *Historia de la Nueva México* (1610), a verse history that chronicles Juan de Oñate's colonizing expeditions in the Southwest. This history of Spanish exploration, missionary activity, and colonialism has had a lasting impact on southwestern literature. In a territory under often violent European control, the peoples of the Southwest both adapted to and reacted against the intrusions of European colonialism and Catholicism. The Southwest has a complex history as a site of exchange between indigenous cultures in ancient sites like Chaco Canyon, a Spanish territory, a region of resistance during, for example, the Pueblo Revolt of 1680, a part of independent Mexico, and an acquired United States Territory following the Mexican–American War. This history figures prominently in modern literature, and writers frequently invoke it to represent the Southwest as a region that is radically different than the rest of the United States.

Both Native American and Spanish cultures are very much alive in the many reservations, churches, and ceremonies of the present-day Southwest. These traditions still carry the promise of regionalism in the United States as an alternative to dominant, nation-centered narratives of Manifest Destiny. Owing to the legacy of conquest, the Southwest is a region powerfully charged in literature with both the promise of rich cultural contact and the disastrous consequences of modernity. For example, in John Nichols's *The Milagro Beanfield War* (1974), the US acquisition of the Southwest, Spanish Catholicism, and indigenous resistance are all evident in the struggle between the fictional Milagro, New Mexico's Chicano residents, and the Anglo resort developer Ladd Devine. Smokey the Bear, in Nichols' fictional New Mexican locale,

> is a symbol of the United States Forest Service. And for almost a hundred years the United States Forest Service had been the greatest landholder in Chamisa County, although most of the land it held had once not so very long ago belonged to the people of Milagro ... the poor people of Milagro tended to look upon Smokey the Bear as a kind of ursine Daddy Warbucks, Adolf Hitler, colonialist Uncle Sam, and Ladd Devine all rolled into one. (Nichols 2000: 192–3)

Smokey the Bear connotes US conquest and economic exploitation to the longtime residents of Milagro. The narrator goes on to describe how the US Forest Service commissions the local artist Snuffy LeDoux to carve Smokey the Bear statues out of wood, in the hopes that tourists will purchase them as souvenirs. Instead, the "Smokey the Bear santos," as the local residents call them, serve an entirely different purpose:

> No tourist ever wound up with a little wooden Smokey. Because as soon as they went on sale, people from town began stealing them off the counter ... People were treating those pudgy, diminutive Floresta statues the way one might treat a voodoo doll. In short, they kicked the little Smokeys around their houses; they poured kerosene on the little Smokeys and lit them; they hammered nails into the little Smokeys; and in a great many other imaginative and bestial ways they desecrated Snuffy Ledoux's carvings in hopes of either destroying the United States Forest Service or at least driving that Forest Service away from Chamisa County, and, in particular, away from Milagro. (Nichols 2000: 193)

The "Smokey the Bear santos" are designed as souvenirs yet are appropriated by the locals as symbols of economic and territorial exploitation. This form of symbolic resistance conflates the legacy of Spanish colonialism, through Ledoux's "santo" wood-carving style, the long history of indigenous resistance to imperial conquest, and the tourist economy now so significant to much of the Southwest.

Nature Writing

The southwestern landscape has inspired countless meditations, and many of them fall into the genre of nature writing. Non-fiction accounts of the landscape that focus on the desert – its mesas, valleys, rivers, cacti, and wildlife – appeared throughout the twentieth century. An early example of the genre, John C. Van Dyke's *The Desert* (1901), details a heavily fictionalized trip that the Rutgers College librarian and art critic took to the Southwest by train, although he claimed to have traveled on horseback and by foot. The book values the vacant, open spaces of the southwestern desert, an image that recurs throughout much writing about the region. This emphasis on vacancy leaves Van Dyke free to project his own ideas onto the landscape, making the region function as a site of self-exploration and discovery for the tourist:

> Nature never designed more fascinating country to ride over than these plains and mesas lying up and back from the desert basin. You may be alone without necessarily being lonesome. And everyone rides here with the feeling that he is the first one that ever broke into this unknown land, that he is the original discoverer; and that this new world belongs to him by right of original exploration and conquest. (Van Dyke 1999: 200)

In this passage, Van Dyke relives the experience of conquest. One discovers oneself as one discovers the seemingly uncharted, unknown landscape. In contrast, Charles Lummis chose to live in the region and write essays and stories about the desert that take into account the cultures that existed prior to white settlement. However, as Audrey Goodman argues about Charles Lummis's *Some Strange Corners of Our Country* (1892), the book was designed to "provide guidance and accurate illustration for the 500,000 rail passengers and tens of thousands of automobile parties that traversed the region each year" (Goodman 2002: 33). One of the functions of early twentieth-century nature writing about the Southwest was to interest urban tourists in the region, and the success of these endeavors can be measured by the vast tourist industry there, from early twentieth-century Indian expeditions, hunting trips, and Harvey Houses to contemporary folk art markets, ski resorts, and retirement communities.

Nature writing about the Southwest continued throughout the twentieth century and includes such important works as Mary Austin's *The Land of Little Rain* (1903), Roy Bedichek's *Adventures with a Texas Naturalist* (1947), and Joseph Wood Krutch's *The Desert Year* (1952). Edward Abbey's *Desert Solitaire: A Season in the Wilderness* (1968), a memoir about the author's years as park ranger in Arches National Monument in southeastern Utah, uses the genre of nature writing to express a more radical environmentalist politics. Hostile to land developers, callous tourists, and the exploitation of the Southwest by mining interests, Abbey's writings feature noble, often violent, environmentalists engaged in heroic struggles against greedy capitalists, most notably in *The Monkey Wrench Gang* (1975). In *Desert Solitaire*, Abbey reflects on the desert's meaning:

Time and the winds will sooner or later bury the Seven Cities of Cibola – Phoenix, Tucson, Albuquerque, all of them – under dunes of glowing sand, over which blue-eyed Navajo Bedouin will herd their sheep and horses, following the river in winter, the mountains in summer, and sometimes striking off across the desert toward the red canyons of Utah where great waterfalls plunge over silt-filled, ancient, mysterious dams. (Abbey 1990: 127)

Abbey fantasizes in this passage about the eventual ruin of urban developments in the Southwest and the return to a nomadic life more in tune with the rhythms of the land. This radical vision is, of course, bound up in a utopian vision of Native American life, an idealization of the solitary, masculine hero, and hostility toward modernity. Nonetheless, Abbey's emphasis on the desert as a sublime force, indifferent and hostile to real-estate developments and user-friendly national parks, demands that the reader pay attention to the desert itself, a landscape often misrepresented as a kind of waste-land or a picturesque tourist destination.

Less focused on militant environmentalism, Terry Tempest Williams also writes about her personal relationship to the southwestern landscape. In her collection of essays and stories *Red: Passion and Patience in the Desert* (2001), Williams ruminates on the American Redrock Wilderness's centrality to everyday life:

This country's wisdom still resides in its populace, in the pragmatic and generous spirits of everyday citizens who have not forgotten their kinship with nature. They are individuals who will forever hold the standard of the wild high, knowing in their hearts that natural engagement is not an interlude but a daily practice, a commitment each generation must renew in the name of the land. (Williams 2001: 70)

Unlike Abbey, Williams finds a sense of community in the desert not only among humans but also between humans and the land. This almost spiritual connection to the desert signifies a key component of nature writing. Being in touch with nature, for Williams, gives the subject a sense of belonging.

Descriptions of the southwestern landscape are also common in novels, short stories, and poems. For example, in Willa Cather's 1927 novel *Death Comes for the Archbishop* the main character, Jean Latour, arrives in New Mexico on horseback after a long and taxing journey. When he sees the desert, the narrator describes his reaction:

This mesa plain had an appearance of great antiquity, and of incompleteness; as if, with all the materials for world-making assembled, the Creator had desisted, gone away and left everything on the point of being brought together, on the eve of being arranged into mountain, plain, plateau. The country was still waiting to be made into a landscape. (Cather 1990a: 94–5)

This passage casts the Southwest as incomplete, a site of great possibility yet open to further development, work, and interpretation. On the one hand, Cather engages in familiar primitivism by casting the Southwest as a land untouched by civilization, ripe for colonization. On the other, the Southwest challenges the viewer to engage with the land, to participate in the environment rather than keeping one's distance as an impartial observer. Texts like Cather's *Death Comes for the Archbishop* and Van Dyke's *The Desert* often wrongly depict the desert as void of culture, yet they also challenge readers to become aware of their own role as readers, consumers, tourists, and possibly conservators of the land. Contemporary nature writing implores readers to question their treatment of the Southwest as a place to buy exotic goods, a site of untouched yet paradoxically accessible nature, and a zone of urban and suburban development. As Edward Abbey asks of tourists in *Desert Solitaire*, "Yes sir, yes madam, I entreat you, get out of those motorized wheelchairs, get off your foam rubber backsides, stand up straight like men! like women! like human beings! and walk – *walk* – WALK upon our sweet and blessed land!" (Abbey 1990: 233).

Southwestern Modernism

One of the major literary cultures in the Southwest emerged in the 1910s as writers and artists, predominantly from the Northeast, settled in Taos and Santa Fe, New Mexico. Mabel Dodge Luhan, a New York bohemian, moved to Taos in 1919, and Mary Austin, whose literary reputation had been made by *The Land of Little Rain* (1903), moved from California to Santa Fe in 1924. These two writers fostered an incredibly vibrant and productive modernist arts community in New Mexico and attracted writers such as Willa Cather and D.H. Lawrence, painters such as Marsden Hartley and Georgia O'Keeffe, and photographers such as Ansel Adams and Paul Strand to the Southwest. Many of them created major works about the region and some, like O'Keeffe, eventually settled in New Mexico.

Like modernist movements in New York, Paris, and London, modernism in New Mexico was documented in a "little magazine," *Laughing Horse* (1922–39), edited and printed by Spud Johnson. *Laughing Horse* printed short works by Austin, Lawrence, and Luhan, as well as other local writers like the poets Witter Bynner and Alice Corbin Henderson. Often parodic in editorial tone, the magazine nonetheless articulated a modernist aesthetic, as Sharyn Rohlfsen Udall claims: "Beneath the verbal horseplay, however, there were serious efforts to upset the literary status quo and replace it with fresher voices. Along with other little magazine like the *Dial* and *Poetry*, [*Laughing Horse*] launched a lively assault on the leftover standards of the Victorians, especially in literature" (Udall 1994: 105). Spud Johnson's *Laughing Horse* provided a central vehicle for the formation of a modernist aesthetic in the Southwest.

Many writers were drawn to New Mexico for its Pueblo Indian culture. Frank Applegate's *Indian Stories from the Pueblos* (1929), for example, is a collection of trickster stories. Many of these stories make light of Anglos who travel to New Mexico to get in touch with some kind of primitive truth. In the story "The Artists and the Snakes," two painters from Europe travel to Hopi Pueblo to paint dances and ceremonies. The snake chief at Hopi gives the artists a small house to stay in, but he has forgotten that he has stowed away snakes in the house's floorboards for his ceremonies. After a fire is lit in the house's stove, the snakes awaken and frighten the artists, who quickly flee to Santa Fe. Applegate's story concludes with an explanation:

> Now in this situation of the two artists the Indians saw nothing amusing. They only saw that their sacred snakes had been jeopardized and thought that these men were more in sympathy with the culture of the Hopis than were the general run of white people they had known and had considerably suspended themselves from the rafters to avoid stepping on and injuring the sacred snakes. (Applegate 1994: 41)

This comic story juxtaposes the artists' unfamiliarity with southwestern wildlife against the Hopi valuation of nature, mocking the naive appropriation of Native American culture by Anglo artists. While southwestern modernists were often enthralled by Pueblo culture, writers like Applegate also parodied those who came to the region as tourists, hoping for a brief encounter with primitive truth and beauty.

In the 1920s, Mary Austin published a number of works about Native American storytelling and song, and Austin's *The American Rhythm* (1923) is one of the most significant early attempts to treat Native American storytelling in the terms of "high" literature. In her extensive introduction, Austin makes a strong case not only for the historical value of Native American verse but also its significance as a model for avant-garde poetic experimentation:

> In the best Amerindian poetry the object is absorbed into the singer and is seldom seen except as a link in the chain, completing the circle of interest between the object and his own breast ... Thus the poetry becomes the means by which men and their occasions are rewoven from time to time with the Allness; and who is there to tell me that this, in art, is not the essence of modernity? (Austin 2007: 57)

According to Austin, Native American song reconciles the singer with the landscape, creating a spiritual unity. While her claims about Native American song are often primitivist, her emphasis on poetics nonetheless made a case for the aesthetic – rather than the ethnographic – significance of Native American culture.

Willa Cather wrote three novels that take place in the Southwest, *The Song of the Lark* (1915), *The Professor's House* (1925), and the aforementioned *Death Comes for the Archbishop*. All of these texts treat the Southwest as a site of regeneration. In *The Professor's House*, Tom Outland and his friend discover ancient Pueblo ruins. Tom decides that these ruins should become a national park, and he travels to Washington, DC, only to be rebuffed by government bureaucrats. He returns to New Mexico to discover that his partner, Roddy, has sold ancient potsherds at the site to a European antiquities collector. Angered by this, Tom explains the importance of these artifacts:

I never thought of selling them, because they weren't mine to sell – nor yours! They belonged to this country, to the State, and to all the people. They belonged to boys like you and me, that have no other ancestors to inherit from. (Cather 1990b: 219)

In *The Professor's House,* ancient artifacts from the Southwest pose the possibility of a system of value more eternal, more inclusive, than the modern marketplace. Tom's artifacts have the value of art, a worth that is not reducible to money, and ancient Pueblo ruins provide all Americans with a universal heritage. As in *The Professor's House*, the Southwest was a place that seemed at odds with modern commerce and, therefore, a place of older, more universal values, a key concept to many modernist writers, like Cather, who were suspicious of consumer culture and located transcendent value in art.

In her book about Mabel Dodge Luhan's home, Lois Rudnick argues for the importance of the Southwest as a site for modernism, in part because artists projected on New Mexico "an essential, noncontingent, and transhistorical truth that would substitute for the anxiety of temporality and subjectivity" (Rudnick 1996: 5). Treatments of these modernist writers and artists often discuss the problematic politics of locating universal truth and unchanging human nature in Native American culture. In her treatment of D.H. Lawrence's writings, Marianne Torgovnick comments that, for Lawrence, "New Mexico is vital and active, but it is defined as a force from 'the outside world' acting on an 'I' firmly boundaried as an observer" (Torgovnick 1998: 57). While much of the writing produced by modernists in the Southwest engages in primitivism, there nonetheless did develop a sincere interest in making Native American culture central to a reimagined American culture. Part of an intensely regionalist movement, the Southwest modernists found the region to hold out a promise of a life apart from the homogenizing, consumerist culture of urban centers. The notion that an authentic artistic life involves a rejection of modernity and a return to nature was quite powerful, and one sees the persistence of this idea in works such as Jack Kerouac's *On the Road* (1957), Jane Rule's *Desert of the Heart* (1964), Barbara Kingsolver's *The Bean Trees* (1988), and Jon Krakauer's *Into the Wild* (1996), all works in which the Southwest comes to signify the possibility of authentic experience and self-realization.

The major works of the Southwest modernists are diverse in form; Mary Austin, for example, wrote novels, autobiographies, short stories, poetry, and literary criticism. The consistent theme of their literary work, though, tends to be the regenerative encounter between the individual – usually a white individual from an urban location – with the Southwest. Mary Austin's *Land of Journey's Ending* (1924) and Mabel Dodge Luhan's *Edge of Taos Desert: An Escape to Reality* (1937) are both autobiographical accounts of their lives and self-discovery in New Mexico. Another important New Mexico figure, Edith Warner, lived at Otowi Crossing, near Los Alamos, where she ran a restaurant and boarding house frequented by scientists such as Robert Oppenheimer. Warner's life is documented in a number of texts, including the collection *In the Shadow of Los Alamos: Selected Writings of Edith Warner*, edited by Patrick

Burns, Peggy Pond Church's history *The House at Otowi Bridge: The Story of Edith Warner and Los Alamos* (1960), and Frank Waters' novel *The Woman at Otowi Crossing* (1966). Other notable works of southwestern modernism include Alice Corbin Henderson's *Red Earth: Poems of New Mexico* (1920), Oliver La Farge's novel *Laughing Boy*, which won the Pulitzer Prize in 1930, and D.H. Lawrence's novel *The Plumed Serpent* (1926), as well as his collection of essays *Mornings in Mexico* (1927), both of which were inspired by his travels in the Southwest. Southwestern modernists also experimented with the boundaries between visual and literary culture. *Laughing Horse's* use of woodcuts and reproduction of paintings, Mary Austin's collaboration with Ansel Adams on *Taos Pueblo*, the inclusion of Native American art in both Frank Applegate's *Indian Stories from the Pueblos* and Elsie Clews Parsons' edited anthropological volume *American Indian Life* (1922) all evidence the importance of painting and photography to the experimental modernism that developed in New Mexico during the 1920s and 1930s. Iconic images such as Georgia O'Keeffe's painting *Cow's Skull with Calico Roses* (1931) and Ansel Adams' photograph *Moonrise, Hernandez, New Mexico* (1941) have helped to shape the meaning of the Southwest, and these images are complemented by a vibrant literary culture that tried, in Mary Austin's words, to produce texts that articulated "American experience shaped by the American environment" (Austin 2007: 42).

History, Identity, and Politics

Native American and Chicano writers from the late twentieth century both continued the work begun by the modernists and offered correctives to their sometimes misguided, primitivist politics. There is a history of Native American, Chicano, and Mexican writing about the Southwest, including works such as Walter Dyk's autobiography *Son of Old Man Hat* (1938), Lynn Riggs' play *Green Grow the Lilacs* (1931), adapted into the Rodgers and Hammerstein musical *Oklahoma!* (1943), Americo Paredes' *George Washington Gomez: A Mexicotexan Novel*, written from 1936 to 1940 but not published until 1990, and Mariano Azuela's stark novel about the Mexican Revolution, *Los de Abajo* (1915, translated as *The Underdogs*) originally serialized in the El Paso, Texas, newspaper *El Paso del Norte*. After World War II, southwestern literature focuses less on the utopian promises of the region for personal renewal and spiritual truth than on the harsh realities one encounters in places like Gallup and Albuquerque. Through grittier, less romanticized representations of southwestern life, Native American and Chicano writers dramatize the importance of the "legacy of conquest" to the modern-day Southwest as well as the difficulties of preserving one's ancestral culture in the face of modernity.

Leslie Marmon Silko's *Ceremony* (1977), for example, centers on Tayo, a veteran of World War II who has returned to his native Laguna Pueblo. Tayo is of mixed ethnicity, and he therefore feels like an outcast at home on the reservation and in white culture. The novel details Tayo's recovery of Laguna and Navajo traditions, emphasizing, as Silko does throughout her work, the need to adapt Native American traditions to the present day. As the medicine man Betonie remarks, "after the white people came, elements in this world began to shift; and it became necessary to create new ceremonies" (Silko 1986: 126). Ultimately, Tayo finds that storytelling allows him to connect his traumatic experiences in the Philippines during World War II with his life on the reservation, and the novel emphasizes this connection when Tayo stumbles upon an abandoned uranium mine in New Mexico, "the point of convergence, where the fate of all living things, and even the earth, had been laid" (Silko 1986: 246). The Southwest connects Tayo's own Native American identity to his experiences in World War II and the destructive potential of nuclear warfare.

Leslie Marmon Silko has written a number of works that address the politics of contemporary southwestern identity, including *Storyteller* (1981) and *The Almanac of the Dead* (1991). Silko is but one figure in one of the most vibrant literary cultures in contemporary southwestern literature, Native American literature. Other notable texts include Joy Harjo's *How We Became Human: New and Selected Poems* (2002), N. Scott Momaday's *The Way to Rainy Mountain* (1969), Simon Ortiz's *From Sand Creek: Rising in this Heart which is Our America* (1981), and Frank Waters' *The Man who Killed Deer* (1942).

Chicano poet Tino Villanueva's *Scene from the Movie Giant* (1993) meditates on the poet's first viewing of George Stevens' classic 1956 film, adapted from Edna Ferber's 1952 novel *Giant* about a ranching family, the Benedicts, in west Texas and their struggles with a nouveau riche oilman, Jett Rink. One of *Giant*'s climactic moments occurs when the Benedict patriarch, Bick, gets into a violent confrontation with a racist cook in a roadside diner after the cook, Sarge, insults Bick's Latina daughter-in-law and his grandson and then refuses to serve a poor Latino family that happens to have entered the restaurant during the men's argument. Villanueva's poem focuses on this scene and its effect on him as an adolescent moviegoer. In this passage, Villanueva writes about his reactions to *Giant* as he leaves the movie theater in 1956:

> The fiery art of film
> had sent my head buzzing – :
> I arose in penumbra, vexed at the unwinding
> course of truth and was now lost in my steps
> eyes struggling with unnatural chasms of light.
> I walked home for a long time
> and in my mind   I regarded
> the tall screen bearing down on me –
> I was drifting away
> from its outburst, yet its measure of violence,
> like an indictment from Sarge,
> did not fade.
>
> (Villanueva 1993: 41)

Villanueva meditates on the power of popular western films to shape identity, and the poem describes the experience of watching the film as traumatic and vertiginous. *Scene from the Movie Giant* exposes the ways in which western film, even when supporting a message of racial equality, relies on racial hierarchies. As Rafael Pérez-Torres claims, Villanueva "responds directly to the voicelessness imposed upon the mestizo by the film" by writing from a Chicano perspective (Pérez-Torres 1998: 156).

The "Recovering the U.S. Hispanic Literary Heritage" series at Arte Público Press has published and recovered many works of Chicano literature since its inception in 1992. Major works in this series include Cecilio García-Camarillo's *Selected Poetry* (2000), Jovita González' *Dew on the Thorn* (1997), and Miguel Antonio Otero's *The Real Billy the Kid* (1936), to name a few. Other notable works of Chicano literature include Rudolfo Anaya's *Bless Me, Ultima* (1972), Ana Castillo's *So Far From God* (1993), Sandra Cisneros' *Woman Hollering Creek and Other Stories* (1991), and José Antonio Villareal's *Pocho* (1959).

The Native American and Chicana/o literary traditions portray a Southwest quite different from the land of untouched, primitive truth often found in writings by the southwestern modernists. Attuned to the "legacy of conquest" in the American West and aware of the differences in lifestyle, privilege, and mobility afforded to well-heeled tourists versus those who have lived and struggled for generations in the region, these literary traditions provide a necessary counterpoint to much of the frontier mythology associated with the Southwest.

Rewriting the Western

As Tino Villanueva does in *Scene from the Movie Giant*, late twentieth-century writers have often rewritten and critiqued the vision of the Southwest, often dramatized in the western genre as an exotic location for the pursuit of either primitivist truth or heroic adventure. One of the reasons for this metafictive trend is the increasing sense that the regional and the local are receding in the face of globalization. Rather than shifting away from the western genre, though, contemporary writers have returned to it and made it relevant within the context of globalization. By complicating the conventional narratives, tropes, and images associated with the Southwest, writers such as Cormac McCarthy and Larry McMurtry have returned to the genre, critiquing the form's biases while, at the same time, reinforcing the power of popular westerns to allegorize the contemporary moment.

Writers of popular westerns in the early twentieth century often set their works in the Southwest, and the setting itself often serves as a major character in these texts. For example, Zane Grey's *The Riders of the Purple Sage* (1912) takes places in southern Utah, and the landscape is vividly and sensually described as an extension of its central characters' emotions. In this passage, Venters, one of the novel's two masculine heroes, realizes that he is in love during a storm: "No more did he listen to the rush and roar of the thunder-storm. For with the touch of clinging hands and the throbbing bosom he grew conscious of an inward storm ... A storm in his breast – a storm of real love" (Grey 2002: 154). As Jane Tompkins remarks about the western, these types of connections between a character and the landscape heighten the emotional charge of the narrative by turning hardship "into the most desirable of human endeavors: action that totally saturates the present moment, totally absorbs the body and mind, and directs one's life to the service of an unquestioned goal" (Tompkins 1992: 12). Grey's novel turns emotion into compulsion and glorifies violence as a natural extension of those heartfelt sentiments. Along with Zane Grey, a number of cowboy memoirs were published in the late nineteenth and early twentieth centuries such as Andy Adams's *Log of a Cowboy* (1903), Nat Love's *The Life and Adventures of Nat Love* (1907), and Charles Siringo's *A Texas Cowboy* (1886). Other westerns set in the Southwest include Mollie Evelyn Moore Davis' *The Wire-Cutters* (1899), other novels by Zane Grey such as *Heritage of the Desert* (1910) and *The Rainbow Trail* (1915), as well as many of the works of Max Brand, such as *Destry Rides Again* (1930), and Louis L'Amour, perhaps most notably *Hondo* (1953). These texts, like *The Riders of the Purple Sage*, focus on a western hero who struggles to bring justice to the frontier.

Another notable western, Walter Van Tilburg Clark's *The Ox-Bow Incident* (1940), is set in Nevada and foregrounds the racial tensions that often underlie western stories about heroic, noble cowboys and vicious outlaws. *The Ox-Bow Incident* depicts the lynching of a man wrongfully accused of cattle rustling, and the novel addresses the ways in which frontier "justice" was often employed as a way of violently reinforcing racial and class divisions. Following Clark, writers in the late twentieth century continually returned to the western genre to rewrite its central tropes and images. One of the most prolific writers of western fiction, Larry McMurtry, has published a number of works of historical and contemporary fiction, such as *Lonesome Dove* (1985), *The Last Picture Show* (1966), and *Terms of Endearment* (1975), that both share in western genre conventions and complicate their associations with heroism, nationalism, and regenerative violence.

While McMurtry writes novels that pay close attention to historical detail, Ishmael Reed's *Yellow Back Radio Broke-Down* (1969) parodies western genre conventions. Reed's novel is part of a tradition of African American writing about the Southwest, including Ralph Ellison's essays about growing up in Oklahoma in *Going to the Territory* (1986) and Sutton E. Griggs' political novel *Imperium in Imperio* (1899). The novel begins with the introduction of its hero, the Loop Garoo Kid, who is

> a cowboy so bad he made a working posse of spells phone in sick. A bullwhacker so unfeeling he left the print of winged mice on hides of crawling women. A desperado so ornery he made the Pope cry and the most powerful of cattlemen shed his head to the Executioner's swine. (Reed 2000: 9)

The novel goes on to include a traveling circus, voodoo spells, a Native American who travels by helicopter, and a group of "neo-social realist" bandits. Reed's novel mocks the racism implied in many western genre narratives by featuring an overtly racist villain, a Chinese servant, and numerous references to violence against Native Americans and African Americans. Gunfights, torture, and executions are common-place in the text, pointing to the brutality that underlies this cherished genre. *Yellow Back Radio Broke-Down* is a postmodern pastiche of the western, foregrounding the genre's mutability and its adaptability to contemporary literary styles.

Cormac McCarthy's widely renowned *All the Pretty Horses* (1992), the first volume in his Border trilogy, also dramatizes the persistence of western mythology in the modern Southwest, but in a less parodic fashion. Set after World War II, the novel's two central characters, John Grady Cole and Lacey Rawlins, leave their west Texas home to live as cowboys in Mexico. The novel opens with the funeral of John Grady Cole's grandfather, and the teenager quickly learns afterwards that his family plans to sell their ranch land. Frustrated by the ubiquity of cars and railroads in west Texas, Cole and Rawlins reenact the western trope of journeying into the wilderness, only this time their travels take them south to Mexico, not west. At the novel's conclusion, after returning from Mexico, John Grady Cole rides off into the sunset, but he does so without a clear sense of purpose. As he says to Rawlins when he asks "where is your country?," "I don't know where it is. I don't know what happens to country" (McCarthy 1992: 299). John Grady Cole recognizes the obsoles-cence of his imagined cowboy life yet pursues it nonetheless. Accordingly, *All the Pretty Horses* both mourns the passing of the Wild West and dramatizes its persist-ence as an ideal way of life. McCarthy's other southwestern novels include the two subsequent novels in the Border trilogy, *The Crossing* (1994) and *Cities of the Plain* (1998), *Blood Meridian, or, the Evening Redness in the West* (1985), and *No Country for Old Men* (2005).

Rewriting the western genre remains a vibrant site of experimentation for south-western literature. Other works that adapt, challenge, and rearrange the genre include William S. Burroughs's surreal *The Place of Dead Roads* (1983), Brian Evenson's apoca-lyptically violent *Altmann's Tongue* (1994), Percival Everett's historical novel *God's Country* (2003), Oakley Hall's playful retelling of the *Tombstone*, Arizona story *Warlock* (1958), Tony Hillerman's detective stories, such as *Skinwalkers* (1986) and *A Thief of Time* (1988), Jonathan Lethem's rewriting of the John Ford film *The Searchers* as *Girl in Landscape* (1998), Michael Ondaatje's experimental *The Collected Works of Billy the Kid* (1970), and Jane Rule's lesbian romance *Desert of the Heart* (1964).

The Literary Southwest

There is a long history of literary culture in the American Southwest, and the region continues to serve as a site of literary production and experimentation. Increasingly urban and suburban, yet still rural in many ways, the Southwest continues to adapt and change while retaining its distinct history and cultural traditions. The region signifies both modernity and tradition, familiarity and exoticism. Literature has done much to construct our vision of the American Southwest, and it continues to complicate our received notions about the region and the lives that are lived among its vast deserts, tall mesas, deep canyons, and modern cities.

REFERENCES AND FURTHER READING

Abbey, Edward. (1990). *Desert Solitaire: A Season in the Wilderness* [1968]. New York: Touchstone.

Applegate, Frank. (1994). *Indian Stories from the Pueblos* [1929]. Carlisle, MA: Applewood.

Austin, Mary. (1996). Excerpts from *Taos Pueblo* [1930]. In Esther F. Lanigan (ed.). *The Mary Austin Reader* (pp. 236–40). Tucson: University of Arizona Press.

Austin, Mary. (2007). *The American Rhythm: Studies and Reexpressions of Amerindian Songs* [1923]. Santa Fe: Sunstone Press.

Cather, Willa. (1990a). *Death Comes for the Archbishop* [1927]. New York: Vintage.

Cather, Willa. (1990b). *The Professor's House* [1925]. New York: Vintage.

Dilworth, Leah. (1996). *Imagining Indians in the Southwest: Persistent Visions of a Primitive Past*. Washington, DC: Smithsonian Institution Press.

Dobie, J. Frank. (1952). *Guide to the Life and Literature of the Southwest*. Rev. edn. Dallas: Southern Methodist University Press.

Dorman, Robert L. (1993). *The Revolt of the Provinces: The Regionalist Movement in America, 1920–1945*. Chapel Hill: University of North Carolina Press.

Dunaway, David King, and Sara Spurgeon, eds. (2003). *Writing the Southwest* [1995]. Albuquerque: University of New Mexico Press.

Fetterley, Judith, and Marjorie Pryse. (2003). *Writing Out of Place: Regionalism, Women, and American Literary Culture*. Champaign: University of Illinois Press.

Goodman, Audrey. (2002). *Translating Southwestern Landscapes: The Making of an Anglo Literary Region*. Tucson: University of Arizona Press.

Grey, Zane. (2002). *The Riders of the Purple Sage* [1912]. New York: Modern Library.

Hsu, Hsuan L. (2005). Literature and Regional Production. *American Literary History*, 17/1, 36–69.

McCarthy, Cormac. (1992). *All the Pretty Horses*. New York: Vintage.

Nichols, John. (2000). *The Milagro Beanfield War* [1974]. New York: Owl.

Pérez-Torres, Rafael. (1998). Chicano Ethnicity, Cultural Hybridity, and the Mestizo Voice. *American Literature*, 70/1, 153–76.

Proulx, Annie. (2008). Dangerous Ground: Landscape in American Fiction. In Timothy R. Mahoney and Wendy J. Katz, eds., *Regionalism and the Humanities* (pp. 6–25). Lincoln: University of Nebraska Press.

Reed, Ishmael. (2000). *Yellow Back Radio Broke-Down* [1969]. Normal, IL: Dalkey Archive Press.

Rudnick, Lois. (1996). *Utopian Vistas: The Mabel Dodge Luhan House and the American Counterculture*. Albuquerque: University of New Mexico Press.

Silko, Leslie Marmon. (1986). *Ceremony* [1977]. New York: Penguin.

Silko, Leslie Marmon. (1997). *Yellow Woman and a Beauty of Spirit: Essays on Native American Life Today*. New York: Touchstone.

Thompson, Hunter S. (1998). *Fear and Loathing in Las Vegas: A Savage Journey to the Heart of the American Dream* [1971]. New York: Vintage.

Tompkins, Jane. (1992). *West of Everything: The Inner Life of Westerns*. New York: Oxford University Press.

Torgovnick, Marianna. (1990). *Gone Primitive: Savage Intellects, Modern Lives*. Chicago: University of Chicago Press.

Torgovnick, Marianna. (1998). *Primitive Passions: Men, Women, and the Quest for Ecstasy*. Chicago: University of Chicago Press.

Udall, Sharyn Rohlfsen. (1994). *Spud Johnson and Laughing Horse*. Albuquerque: University of New Mexico Press.

Van Dyke, John C. (1999). *The Desert: Further Studies in Natural Appearances* [1901]. Baltimore: Johns Hopkins University Press.

Villanueva, Tino. (1993). *Scene from the Movie Giant*. Willimantic, CT: Curbstone Press.

Williams, Terry Tempest. (2001). *Red: Passion and Patience in the Desert*. New York: Pantheon.

7

Literary Cartography of the Great Plains

Susan Naramore Maher

The Plains as a Contact Zone

Along the Interstate 80 corridor in central Nebraska sits John Raimondi's once con-troversial artwork, *Erma's Desire*, part of a bicentennial sculpture project in the 1970s that brought modern art to the masses. A series of steel spears or lightning bolt-like cages, Erma's reclined body sinks into the grassy landscape, while abstract arms and legs point suggestively across many dimensions, vertical and horizontal. Writer John Janovy, Jr. interprets Erma's geography in this way: "The combination of points and directions, emphases and bases, settings and an infinite number of ephemeral contexts, from which finally emerges the luxury of a new idea, a single message – these things say *Erma's Desire* to me" (1981: 5). A solid, fixed presence, Erma also paradoxically aligns herself with mobility, with the freedom of the road and of the day. Her station-ary figure has become an ironic icon of the interstate, a goddess figure of restlessness and unsettled energy. Erma's very complexity engages the imagination and forces one to grasp the matrices of land and sky that frame her, the human intelligence that forged her. She exists in relation to the Plains geometry (see Figure 7.1).

I begin my essay with *Erma's Desire*, a familiar landmark for travelers east and west across the Great Plains, because this sculpture's multiple axes have become a trope for me of the literary culture that I study. One should not study Great Plains literature without considering the landscape that defines it, in all of its real and imagined dimensions. Literary scholars of the Great Plains agree upon one thing: the land is primary, is "fact," in Robert Thacker's assessment. The Great Plains of North America cover nearly 1.4 million square miles of land extending from northern Mexico

A Companion to the Literature and Culture of the American West, First Edition. Edited by
Nicolas S. Witschi.
© 2011 Blackwell Publishing Ltd. Published 2011 by Blackwell Publishing Ltd.

Figure 7.1 John Raimondi, *Erma's Desire*. Photo: John Janovy Jr. Reproduced by permission

to the Canadian provinces of Manitoba, Saskatchewan, and Alberta. The east-to-west horizontal plane reaches from the Rocky Mountain spine to watersheds that empty in the Gulf of Mexico or Hudson Bay. In years of extreme drought, the Plains stretch even farther. It is fluid landscape, never settling into firm borders or fixed horizons. The transitions from tall to short grasses, from farm to ranch country, from lower prairies to mile-high plains make one appreciate the variegated complexity of the expansive grasslands biome. David J. Wishart, geographer and editor of *Encyclopedia of the Great Plains*, notes that "vast distances, the flowing grasslands, the sparse population, the enveloping horizons, and the dominating sky ... convey a sense of expansiveness, even emptiness," what he calls one of the "defining" characteristics of Plains country. The Plains are huge and overwhelming, demanding an astute eye, keen attention to "skyscape," and an appreciation of openness (Wishart 2004: p. xiv).

Too often in popular accounts, though, the Plains – as a landscape and a people – are reduced to fly-over country, flattened to a horizontal nothingness, and presented as boilerplate: spare, empty, and existential. As John T. Price points out, in this region "the land is often seen as flat and uninteresting, its future already written in the furrows and pastures it has become," as if all possibility has been halted (2004: 24). However, Diane Quantic argues that the seemingly "featureless" Plains landscape can often obscure the depths of "emotional power," of personal and communal memory written into the land (1995: 168). Price notes as well the many "familiar tensions" connected to the grasslands: "migration and entrenchment, wildness and domesticity, presence and absence, body and earth" (2004: 24). These are complex relationships. "In modern society," Yi-Fu Tuan explains, "the relation between mobility and a sense of place can be very complicated." Modernity often works to "deny" or "forget," to lessen what Tuan calls "the burden of awareness" (Tuan 1977: 182, 203). Brief surface mapping, dismissive and scornful of Plains realities, erases the enormous variance of topographic realities, cultural nuances, ecological matrices, and climatic extremities that define the history of life on the grasslands and inform Plains writing.

Moreover, Plains literature is necessarily transnational, cross-sectional, and inter-cultural; it exists in a contact zone of the imagination (Pratt 1992: 4). Encompassing Mexico, the United States, and Canada, its Native cultural narratives reach back thousands of years, reminding us that literary production predates European contact. As Dan Flores asserts, "At the time of contact between Europe and the Americas, at least 350 generations (probably more) of men and women had been living in and transforming North America across a time span of well over a hundred centuries" (2001: 189). Contact itself generated important literary documents from the Plains. Elliott West has contended that "the consequences of that first contact came so fast and ran so deep that they made for a material and imaginative revolution." Once the Plains became "a system of users and used and as perceived living space," West continues, it "became a different place" (1998: 33). Writers from the period of contact forward have attempted to define, to represent this space in literary docu-ments. These authors have provided translations and interpretations of the enormous grassland region and its diverse communities of Native and non-Native people in the continent's core.

The published journals, reports, and narratives of expeditions, surveyors, and trave-lers generated deep interest in the Plains through the nineteenth century. Whether presented as fertile park and garden or sterile desert and wasteland, the Plains entered literary narrative and the public's imagination. Among the most influential were the accounts of Meriwether Lewis and William Clark (1804–6), Zebulon Pike (1804), and Stephen Long (1820). American novelist James Fenimore Cooper, who had never traveled to the Plains, transformed such accounts into fiction when he published *The Prairie* (1827), the aging Natty Bumppo's farthest venture west in Cooper's series. Other American writers, like Washington Irving (*A Tour of the Prairies*, 1835) and Francis Parkman (*The Oregon Trail*, 1849), would transpose their experiences on the Plains into memorable narrative. As Frances W. Kaye discerns, "[i]ncreasing numbers of men and women, professional and amateur writers, traveled west and recorded their experiences" (2004: 469). With the advent of magazine and newspaper culture after the Civil War, the Plains fed into popular culture. Even those who had traversed the Plains to make a living – men like Kit Carson, James Butler Hickok, and William Cody – became dime novel heroes, their exploits exaggerated or made up, writ large over the center of the continent. Cody became so entangled with the Plains topography he gained a nickname grounded in hoof and grass: Buffalo Bill. Easterner Owen Wister would transform his travels to the Dakotas and Nebraska into the quintessential western novel, *The Virginian* (1902), changing the landscape of the literary West and establishing an indelible icon: the cowboy. Popular adventure fiction privileged movement across space and masculine imperatives. Contemporaneously, literary works that transformed the Plains to home place flourished as well. Wister's genius is the dialogic relationship in his novel between a cowboy hero and a school-teacher heroine, Molly Wood, between movement and settlement. He bridges modes of writing the Plains.

At the turn of the twentieth century, modern American and Canadian literature owed much to the sons and daughters of the homesteading era and their descendants, people who lived formative years on the Plains and witnessed enormous transformation. The reorganization of the Plains economically, culturally, politically, and physically took only a few generations, spanning the railroad and aeronautical eras. Foremost in this modern literary history are Willa Cather, Hamlin Garland, William Inge, Frederick Manfred, John G. Neihardt, Tillie Olsen, Katherine Anne Porter, O.E. Rölvaag, Mari Sandoz, Ross Sinclair, Wallace Stegner, and Laura Ingalls Wilder. In their stories, the undeveloped land frequently beckons, a geography of hope, and individuals respond with desire and imagination. Susan J. Rosowoski astutely states that "[a] radical experience of emptiness or lack is the wellspring of desire" in much western writing (1999: 60). But hard, back-breaking work and difficult conditions challenge the migrants' dreams. The experience of the Dust Bowl, the Dirty Thirties, clouds literary writings from the Plains. As John Steinbeck (*The Grapes of Wrath*, 1939) and Tillie Olsen (*Yonnondio*, 1934; 1974) present in their fiction, the catastrophe of the Dust Bowl unleashed forces destructive of the land, of the social fabric of communities, and of the individual psyche. They expose social and racial divisions, defying the optimism of earlier settlers. Historian Donald Worster reminds us that to live on the Plains means "running along the thin edge of disaster" (1982: 234). This thin environmental edge is mirrored in the fragile traditions of civility, justice, and tolerance.

Literature from the Dust Bowl forward often bears witness to the unraveling of people's lives. Writing in 1931, historian Walter Prescott Webb noted that the Great Plains marked "an institutional *fault*": "At this *fault* the ways of life and of living changed. Practically every institution that was carried across it was either broken and remade or else greatly altered" (1981: 8). Contemporary Plains writers, like Jonis Agee, Julene Bair, Sharon Butala, Ron Hansen, Linda Hasselstrom, Lois Hudson, Margaret Laurence, Larry McMurtry, Wright Morris, Kathleen Norris, Dan O'Brien, and Larry Woiwode, examine white settlement from a troubled later-century perspective. Their ambivalent perspectives cast doubt on material development, cultural homogenization, and sustainability, as family farms and ranches collapse and the environment turns toxic. Diane Quantic remarks that the heirs of white settlement face the same "Great Plains facts" as their ancestors: this is land "where the threat of change is the only constant" (1997: 726). Extreme weather, isolation, and economic vulnerability – the pressing contingencies of a hardscrabble country – continue to press upon the fortunes of individuals and communities. In such conditions, the more imaginative children often turn away from their parents' dreams. This generational shift, this rejection of westering and imperial mythologies, marks much Great Plains literature published since the 1960s.

Plains stories of migration, displacement, and emplacement cross ethnic and racial experiences, adding variant and contrary notes to regional storytelling. The exodusters, freed slaves and their descendants, share part of this literary company as migrants to the Plains in search of land and work. If former cowboy Nat Love helped establish western outlaw icons like Jesse James and Billy the Kid in his popular autobiography, it was as much fiction as fact (*The Life and Adventures of Nat Love, Better Known in the Cattle Country as Deadwood Dick*, 1907). Love embraced the adventure tale paradigm, the celebration of masculine movement in space. African American writers also contributed to the literature of place, of homes lost and found. Fiction writer and film-maker Oscar Micheaux wrote four agrarian novels, including *The Conquest: The Story of a Negro Pioneer* (1913) and *The Homesteader* (1917), which dramatize the contributions of African American settlers on the Plains. Following in his groundbreaking steps came Oklahoma writer Ralph Ellison and Kansas writers Langston Hughes, Gwendolyn Brooks, and Gordon Parks. Micheaux, a Renaissance man, was dexterous across media – a writer, screenplay writer, director of silent films and "talkies," and producer. Ellison, Hughes, Brooks, and Parks were equally adept at crossing genre boundaries. Hughes, for instance, wrote poems, plays, short stories, nonfiction, novels, and children's books. Their contributions to American arts would help document the flight from the farms and smaller towns and cities to the opportunities of urban, cosmopolitan centers like Chicago, Los Angeles, New York, and Paris.

At the same time, Native American writers from the Plains – Louise Erdrich, Joy Harjo, Linda Hogan, Thomas King, Emma LaRoche, N. Scott Momaday, D'Arcy McNickle, and James Welch among them – present complex fictional stories, nonfiction essays, and poems that trace the tragedy of genocide and relocation as well as document the triumph of survival and the endurance of oral and spiritual traditions in Native communities. Their literary works offer alternative readings of Great Plains history and culture, challenge and revise the European American myths of pioneering and conquest, and articulate an aesthetic with the deepest connection to the grasslands. Moreover, in Chicano/a works like Tomás Rivera's 1971 story of migration ... *y no se lo tragó la tierra* (... *And the Earth Did Not Devour Him*), Gloria Anzaldúa's multi-generic exploration, *Borderlands/La Frontera: The New Mestiza* (1987), and Norma Elia Cantú's *Canícula: Snapshots of a Girlhood en la Frontera* (1995), political, cultural, familial, and racial boundaries prove painful and transfiguring. These writers help define the cultural borderlands that extend onto the Plains and navigate the "temporal geographies" of this space where worlds disappear and change is constant (Brady 2002: 5). Migrations mark many incoming directions, many origins, and many exits from a place of nurturance. When one examines Plains literary production across cultures and ethnicities, one is struck with the point and counterpoint, the interaction and resistance, the opposition and confluence – in other words, the rich paradoxical soil of this literary region.

Rhizomes, Folds, and Deep Maps

Surveying Plains literary history establishes the difficulty of staking out, identifying, and translating this region's many literary idiolects. Historian Peggy Pascoe suggests one useful metaphor: viewing the West (which includes the Great Plains) as a "cultural crossroads" (1991: 46). Literary expression on the Great Plains emerges from exchanges across centuries, across cultures, across ecological boundaries, across gender, and across a continent. Pascoe decries the old frontier mythology as "a one-way thruway for white settlers" (1991: 45). Pascoe's argument suggests that interpretive strategies that build from geographical or cartographical metaphor open up rather than reduce readings of Plains literature and provide a different platform on which to create this literature.

In recent years, a number of writers and scholars have explored Plains literature geographically, from William Least Heat-Moon's idea of deep mapping in his exploration of Chase County, Kansas in *PrairyErth* to Neil Campbell's stratagem of the rhizome and the fold, perfect metaphors for grasslands literature. A rhizome, as geographers Karen Moss and Karen Falconer-Al Hindi explain, "is a complex, underground root system comprised of nodes and internodes that spread horizontally" (2008: 12). Because the nodes and internodes grow at varying speeds, new plants can emerge unpredictably, at different intervals, and they are difficult to destroy. To think rhizomatically, Moss and Falconer-Al Hindi assert, means that "[ideas] are introduced, discussed, picked up, transferred, engaged, rejected, contested, reworked, transformed, and reintroduced again" (2008: 12). In Campbell's reading, the rhizome represents "a complex space of migratory, hybrid cultures that extends both within and without the region" (Campbell 2008: 35). As a root system, it is comfortable in the ecological contact zones, the crossroads, of a biome. As a metaphor, it provides guidance across vexed, complicated literary terrain. Folds, as well, break down barriers and present "a world full of curves and textures, folding and unfolding so that the inside and the outside become inseparable and interconnected" (Campbell 2008: 36). To imagine the Plains as folded, "inflected," and amorphous – as a number of twentieth- and twenty-first-century Plains writers do – allows one to write the Plains as "following connections, trails, traces, pathways, and echoes," to see the land "transmotionally" (Campbell 2008: 37). Modern Plains writers, then, engage in a dialogic of roots and routes, stasis and movement, location and dislocation (Stanford Friedman 1998: 151).

Rhizomatic, transmotional territory is William Least Heat-Moon's preferred literary landscape. In *PrairyErth (a deep map)* (1991), Heat-Moon presents the Jeffersonian grid, the survey system of the West, as an imposed abstraction that ignores the contours and landmarks of a place, a method steeped in conquest and imperialism that disconnects people and towns from nature. His deep map steps off the grid and enters into a place, "where the splendid lies within the plain cover" (p. 28). Cartographic thinking brings him into a reimagined place. Heat-Moon's idiosyncratic version of Chase County has proved highly influential in Plains writing, particularly since his subtitle has established an environmental genre: the deep map (Roorda 2001: 259).

He follows many routes, not to discover an original source of culture or life on the Plains, but to celebrate and mourn the many historical passages, cultural inventions, singular adaptations, and epic losses marked upon the grasslands. He imaginatively examines many people, dead and living, Native and non-Native, working-class and privileged, dreamers, drifters, and demagogues. Chase County, Kansas, also "contains the bulk of the Flint Hills, which hold the nation's largest remaining stretches of tallgrass prairie, an ecological community which once predominated across the mid-continent" (Roorda 2001: 258). Here one can tap into what Canadian writer Don Gayton has called "tallgrass dreams," intimations of an ancient biome now existing in fragments and isolated "fossil" islands (1996: 99). In a land that has undergone enormous transformation through eons of time, Heat-Moon puts together a county compendium that is inexhaustible. Chase County, Kansas, exists in a state of becoming, and the literary artist's job is to present the movement of time and space, not to capture it or force stasis but to process change, ephemera, and life's transient energy.

Heat-Moon discerns the many axes of history and experience, the many ways that space informs time and time directs the physical world of the Plains. To understand Chase County, Kansas, one has to see multiple landscapes and perceive the interplay of horizontal and vertical dimensions. From the start of his journey, Heat-Moon notices that the horizontal surface conceals; "most prairie life," he comments, "is *within* the place" (p. 28). The Flint Hills' stark conditions also wear away at physical structures, whether natural or human-made. If concealment is one facet of the prairie's story, erosion and erasure is another. White settlement began in the nineteenth century, but vestiges from that time are scarce in the Flint Hills. "No place is emptier than the one where someone has been," Heat-Moon muses, "and will not return to" (p. 547). In such abandoned, forgotten corners of the Plains, no memories have established meaning or a sense of place.

Memory is essential material for the literary artist, and in spare country it takes on enormous weight. As he traverses the mapped quadrangles of Chase County, as he breaks through shallow borders and artificial boundaries, Heat-Moon memorializes and catalogues natural and human histories. Through somatic contact with the grasslands, his walking body retraces older passages, ancient routes. He walks the stories: "Whenever we enter the land, sooner or later we pick up the scent of our own histories, and when we begin to travel vertically, we end up following road maps in the marrow of our bones and in the thump of our blood" (p. 273). Along the way, Heat-Moon's steps capture the tidal movements of Permian Seas, the thunderous migrations of bison, the seasonal pathways of Native people, and the rutted roadways of the US army and the white settlers. Eroded trails, finished and unfinished railway lines, gridded county roads, waterways, ancient flyways, and animal perambulations compete in his imagination, herald infinite stories, and lay out a new map of discovery and memory, a deep map of the Plains.

Heat-Moon's stratigraphic storytelling suggests a way of writing and reading the Plains that connects older writers with a postmodern method. Heat-Moon's obsessions – writing the landscape, delving vertically and horizontally, preserving multiple histories, privileging memory – suggest a regional praxis that connects writers from Willa Cather forward. His deep map interweaves elemental, spiritual, affective, and intellectual materials; it engages memory, dream, and instinct to achieve embodiment and dimensionality. Heat-Moon uses all of his creative resources to "touch on and explore what is on and under [the] landscape, literally and metaphorically" (Wall 2008: 70). In this way, *PrairyErth* is a touchstone loosely organizing and bespeaking a long, complex, multi-tongued literary heritage thousands of years old.

Cather and Fictional Cartography

Examining the deep-map metaphor from a wide angle, one can discern something of the deep mapper stirring in many Plains writers. In fiction, nonfiction, poetry, drama, and filmmaking, representations of the Plains often work cartographically. Cather's brilliant oeuvre, for instance, is deeply biological and topographical, "edging [us] toward a virtual science of place, embodiment, and human nature" (Love 2003: 6–7). Problems of space organize many of her narratives: buying land on the divide as opposed to the river bottoms (*O, Pioneers!*); translating one's life from Bohemia or Virginia to the prairies (*My Ántonia*); revising one's view of Plains life from a farmhouse in France (*One of Ours*); journeying to the American Southwest to tend one's flock (*Death Comes for the Archbishop*) – the list could go on. Moving and routing across space – "unrelenting, incessant, and psychic mobility across spatial, historical, and imaginative planes of existence" – define her stories, as Joseph Urgo has argued (1995: 5). Roots, however, counter migration in her narrative. In Glen Love's assessment, Cather's fiction is "engrossed with the human need to find one's place, literally and figuratively" (2003: 11). Love speaks to the "lived sensations of the body in place" that bring her characters close to an intensely realized, somatic attunement with the landscape (2003: 11). As one of the formative non-Native writers from the Plains, Cather early establishes the quintessence of the cartographical imagination.

Mapping the experience of "roots, routes, and intercultural encounter" is at the heart of Plains literature and is particularly defining of Cather's work (Stanford Friedman 1998: 151). *My Ántonia*, her most celebrated Plains novel, illuminates her cartographical methods lucidly. Roots – the homing instinct – stand in creative tension with routes – the moving impulse – and the act of memory provides a way of mapping the multiple human desires in play with the landscape. Formative memories clarify Jim Burden's vision of Black Hawk and the surrounding country and preserve the ephemeral human lives dependent on the earth's uncertain gifts. There are any number of character types, visions, and motivations among the men and women in the novel. Cather views their lives as fragile and mortal; while they may be participating in the experiment of homesteading over the long haul, the world they are building is as ephemeral as they are. Just as little remains of the passions, needs, and dramas of long-gone souls, so too will the future erase the present landscapes, Jim's and Ántonia's included. Jim's memories serve as a stay against loss and change. What gives his narrative gravitas is the multidimensional world he recreates and negotiates, the present time blurring into the past, landscapes conflating upon landscapes. Memory becomes a possession, in Jim's closing words, that encompasses "the precious, the incommunicable past" (p. 244).

From the start, this displaced orphan reaches into *terra incognita*. He befriends Ántonia, despite linguistic and cultural separation, crossing class and gender differences (even racial, if one considers nineteenth-century racial concepts). His initial act of empathy, reaching out to this strange, foreign girl, matches the openness of the landscape, a space with "no fences, no creeks or trees, no hills or fields," a space with no boundaries (p. 54). In landscape that leaves one feeling "erased, blotted out," new rules of engagement apply, and young Jim finds this liberating. Underneath, above, and within the kinetic landscape, Jim perceives energy: "I felt motion in the landscape," he recalls, "in the fresh, easy-blowing morning wind, and in the earth itself, as if the shaggy grass were a sort of loose hide, and underneath it herds of buffalo were galloping, galloping ..." (p. 58). This primeval world rapidly closes, however, as homesteaders settle and transform the Plains, and towns like Black Hawk organize and monitor economic and social realities. While Ántonia remains on the land, a signifier of Jim's past, she too will become a shadow, her home a vestige of a bygone age. Time and space, on the Plains, seemingly conspire to return lived worlds to the barest elements: wind, grass, and sky.

Across her career, Cather ponders the meaning of time and space for her characters and for herself. She invents geographies that are multifaceted and in process. Alexandra Bergson, whose hapless father transports his family across the Atlantic to homestead on difficult, unyielding land, wrests control of the land around her and attempts to build some permanence on her farm, to plan for its heirs. But life on the Plains defies these desires, and it is a much humbled Alexandra who must release her grip and mastery, who must allow the *genius loci* to carry her into an uncertain future. Many Cather protagonists puzzle over the outlines of their existence, and those who map most deeply – the Archbishop, Cécile Auclair, Anton Rosicky among her finest cartographers – live humbly and gratefully in peace upon the land. A cartographic reading of Cather's Plains and frontier fiction (which includes her great Canadian novel, *Shadows on the Rock*) underscores the significance of the deep-map metaphor across generic and generational treatments of the Plains. Her geographic imagination reaches all the way to the present, an intertextual presence in much contemporary Plains fiction.

Nonfiction Mappings of the Plains

Walter Prescott Webb's nonfiction masterwork, *The Great Plains* (1931), is a signature effort in writing the Plains. From opening chapters that examine the "Physical Basis of the Great Plains" and "The Plains Indians" to his closing chapters on "The Literature of the Great Plains and About the Great Plains" and "Mysteries of the Great

Plains," Webb begins to build the base of environmental deep-map writing. His work, contemporary with Cather's, examines many of the facets that Heat-Moon interweaves in dialogic form sixty years later: geology, Native American Plains culture, modern economic theory, transnationalism, political and legal structures, literary and spiritual responses to the Plains, building on and fencing in the Plains. Always a lucid writer, Webb constructs a comprehensive study of the landscape, and introduces environmental and social concerns. His study is the wellspring of Plains nonfiction, and Heat-Moon's *PrairyErth*, in its scope and thick description, owes much to Webb's scholarship. What Webb had not discovered, however, was how to imaginatively transform this information into art, into a new kind of narrative or literary cartography.

Loren Eiseley, in experimental essays written during the 1940s and 1950s, developed a form that could provide a cross-sectional weaving of story that collapsed time and space. In these "concealed" essays, Eiseley sought a method that would allow him to map multiple entries into the Plains landscape, that would conjoin his poetic, spiritual insights with intellectual inquiry (Christianson 1971: p. xi). Paleontological fieldwork with the famed South Party of 1933 brought him to western Nebraska for a short six months (Christianson 1990: 129). His scientific journeys from the Platte River north to the Pine Ridge – the borderlands of Nebraska, Wyoming, and South Dakota – provoked his creativity, and Eiseley began initial drafting of essays and poems in his field notebooks for later publication. Somatic contact with wind, water, grass, rock, and sky – his physical encounters on and literally delving into the land – provided him with an entry into the Plainscape and an opening up of a literary form. Like Cather, his cartographic vision underlies later Plains deep maps.

Two of Eiseley's most celebrated concealed essays, "The Slit" and "The Flow of the River" (in *The Immense Journey*), spring from somatic contact with grasslands. Discovering a slit in the earth, Eiseley enters into a place where time collapses. It is as if the Plains open up to him, revealing secrets from "deep, deep below" (p. 4). Unexpectedly, the skull of an early mammal, "embedded in the solid sandstone," grins back at him (p. 4). The encounter brings the scientist face to face with the past, but in this dark place time becomes cyclical, not linear. Eiseley entertains the idea that the fossil and his living body are one and the same: "I would never again excavate a fossil under conditions which led to so vivid an impression that I was already one myself" (p. 5). This insight, that the living contain evolutionary deep maps, reveals a connection both profound and unsettling. The hand that chinks away at sandstone "has been fin and scaly reptile foot and furry paw" (p. 6). This hand will someday join the eons of dead, and perhaps the human species will cease to be as well. Eiseley's resonant encounter defines the slit as both womb and grave. Here the imagination births multiple stories and layered connections. Here, too, however, whispers death. If the routes of our lives share common ground, so too will our inevitable deaths.

In Eiseley's essays, routes are privileged. Life is a contingent thing and habitation an experimental venture that leads as often to failure as it does to success. Connecting his fossil skull to "present-day prairie dogs and chipmunks," he notes the environment "peculiarly open to exploitation," the ecological setting "crowded" with "a varied assemblage of our early relatives" (p. 9). The grasslands served, and continue to serve, as a living laboratory in which species struggle for resources and long-term survival. Some life forms perfect their grasslands lives for a time; others retreat or die out. The destiny of primates and early humans would be played out in grasslands, a history that leads to Eiseley's hand tapping stone away from the "shabby pseudo-rat" (p. 10). He experiences vividly this immense journey, acted out in a short morning beneath the high Plains. "I had come a long way down since morning," Eiseley comments. "I had projected myself across a dimension I was not fitted to traverse in the flesh" (p. 11). Easing himself back to the surface, he looks around "carefully in a sudden anxiety" (p. 11). What if his horse, left to graze, had turned into Mesohippus? What if the earth, which had been his home, had slipped away? Eiseley's awareness of passage, transience, and mutability destabilizes the local reality that humans, "[like] the wistaria on the garden wall," are "rooted in [their] particular century" (p. 11). Eiseley's literary cartography preserves what it can, but he is always alert to absences, unconformities, and mysteries.

"The Flow of the River" adds spiritual dimensions to his map of the Plains, for "[if] there is magic on this planet, it is contained in water" (p. 15). Shifting from the rugged terrain of the Wildcat Hills in western Nebraska in "The Slit," Eiseley enters fluid space, the Platte River. Once more, he psychically and physically merges into the medium. The river's movement, its watery energy, contains "whole eons, the eons that mountains and deserts know" (p. 16). The river "reaches everywhere; it touches the past and prepares the future; it moves under the poles and wanders thinly in the heights of air" (p. 16). Water enters all living forms; it chisels the earth's foundations and carries their materials to new geographies. Part of a watershed, the Platte River connects Eiseley to many places at once: the mountains, the Plains, and the oceans. Alone in the river shallows, Eiseley's body touches "the immense body of the continent itself, flowing like the river was flowing, grain by grain, mountain by mountain, down to the sea" (p. 19). Eiseley is somatically connected to deep histories, both natural and human, that span the age of ancient reptiles and mammals to the recent history "that has buried the broken axles of prairie schooners and the mired bones of mammoth" (p. 19). The "mother element" – water – suggests to Eiseley the complexity of any landscape and the body's embedment in that landscape. "I *was* water," he famously declares, but he is also the composite of life's history (p. 19).

Science provides Eiseley with theories and accumulated data that reveal deeper connections extending out into the universe and focusing tightly on atomic and nucleic structures. Armed with modern science, Eiseley "[develops] an acute ear for the sound of the surf on Cretaceous beaches where now the wheat of Kansas rolls" (p. 21). The deep-map essay that Eiseley invents, the concealed essay, evolves out of the new sciences of geology, evolutionary biology, and astrophysics. But it also augments science with woven fabrics from dreams, intimations, and the divine. Creating narrative that could interlace so many threads of histories, so many shades of time and scale, Loren Eiseley reshaped Plains essay writing and helped guide American nonfiction writing of place into new and expansive literary territory.

Poetic Mappings of Plains Space

Nonfiction deep-map writing, as I have asserted elsewhere, is a signature "multigenerational project" of Plains writers (2001: 10). But cartographic imagination extends across genres, and Plains poets delineate "Prairie Time" in lyrics that compress and distill time and space, that suggest connections subtle and profound. Explaining "Prairie Time," Texas writer Matt White notes "the countless eons when prairie grasses held sway before they were met by the advancing crush of civilization" (2006: 3). In bending to "Prairie Time," writers "attempt to reclaim that lost world through the fruits of imagination and intellectual understanding" (2006: 3). Like Eiseley, White also underscores mystery and "lost remnants ... forgotten and overlooked, as sometimes happens along railroad rights-of-way, in cemeteries, and on rocky outcroppings" (2006: 7). Plains poets bring their distinct sensibilities to this deep mapping of place, to this reclamation of "Prairie Time."

John G. Neihardt elevated Plains poetry with ambitious verses that culminated in a five-part epic, *A Cycle of the West* (1949), published separately as *The Song of Hugh Glass* (1915), *The Song of Three Friends* (1919), *The Song of the Indian Wars* (1925), *The Song of the Messiah* (1935), and *The Song of Jed Smith* (1941). As Vine Deloria, Jr. notes, Neihardt's works concentrate on "the exploration of the High Plains and western mountains and a profound universal mysticism that found unique expression in the various religions of mankind" (1984: 2). While Neihardt examines larger questions of history and the vast cosmos, William Stafford focuses his efforts on the minutiae, the small, telling details of lived space on the Plains. Poet Ted Kooser argues that Kansas-born Stafford is the Plains' most celebrated poet, "who continued to write tellingly and movingly about life on the Plains even after he moved to Oregon" (1994: 489). Moreover, Kooser, an eminent Plains poet himself, asserts that this region's poetry "follows these general parameters: it is descriptive, anecdotal, noncelebratory, and generally accepting of circumstances" (1994: 489). Neihardt and Stafford provide two foundations of Plains poetry – epic and lyric – but this essay focuses on one year – 1994 – during which two significant volumes of poetry appeared: Ted Kooser's *Weather Central* and Joy Harjo's *The Woman Who Fell from the Sky*. Written during a decade of prolific, profound deep-map writing, these titles bridge the northern and southern Plains, attend to particular inflections of place, and present poetic visions that leap temporally and spatially.

Weather Central, one of Kooser's most acclaimed volumes, turns a keen eye toward the land and the traces of multiple histories in the land. In Jo McDougall's words, he documents the "crossroads of time, place, and eternity" (p. 413). While his farm in Garland, Nebraska, provides the poet with a temporary anchor, he looks out for details in the natural and human-made worlds that speak to the ephemeral and loss: a deer's foreleg in "A Finding," the detritus of floods in "An Elegy," an old beer bottle in "A Heart of Gold," or the vestiges of the County Poor Farm in "Site." Kooser, like the anthropologist Eiseley, perceives beauty in discarded things, even if they are portents, reminders that all dies in the mortal world. A snakeskin, examined, is "a dusty tunnel echoing" ("Snakeskin," l. 3), but the motion of scales and muscles maintains its presence, just as an old lace glove mimics a goodbye wave, or a moving train off in the distance suggests time's passage: "All it knows is behind it already / Nothing it knows is ahead" (ll. 15–16). In terse lines, Kooser connects life and death, motion and stillness, light and dark, not so much as polarities but as shared dimensions of existence, intersected coordinates on a corporal map.

His lines also reverberate cycles and celebrate the ageless rituals of animal life. Kooser's Plains sensibility knocks the human out of the center and places it within the larger nexus of the biome, the flora and fauna, the soil and water and rock that bear life. He witnesses flies hatching, hundreds emerging "into the first / warm day of the year" ("A Hatch of Flies," ll. 4–5). Their actions display the same mixture of intelligence, organization, aggression, and sexual desire that humans enact, but in the briefest of moments. Birth, procreation, and death: the stark outline of nature's paradigm. Elsewhere in *Weather Central*, ants, brown recluse spiders, fireflies, ducks, cows, and mice join Kooser's passing show. The wild of the Plains resides both within and outside the poet's body. His somatic contact with wind, sky, and grass connects him to Plains truths. If the human, in the scheme of things, is diminished, it still exerts influence on the environment, often to the biome's distress. In his poems "Lincoln, Nebraska" and "City Limits," Kooser extends his cartographic vision to settlement and its aftermath, to nanosecond history in the geologic scale. Beneath the railroads and roadways of urban space lies a deeper layer, "[a] clump of prairie grass," the suggestion of the Pawnee or the lingering of a bison essence ("Lincoln, Nebraska," l. 18). These vestiges speak to the ruptures in history, the dissonance between ancient grasslands and ways and modernity's impudence and cruelty. The city represents recent cultural implantation, but Kooser discerns decay and creeping chaos in this nascent Plains experiment:

> city nested on ledges
> runny with lime; old rail-head
> with lice in its wings
> and a broken beak, its eggs
> all gone to vinegar.
>
> (ll. 6–10)

This "dirty town in rain," with its "tin cans … toppled shopping carts," and other thrown-away objects, appears part of a wounded empire (ll. 26–8).

Kooser is more explicit about contact history in "City Limits." On the west edge of town – unnamed, to represent any Plains town – he peers west and contemplates frontier mythology, its contradictions and its horrors. Horace Greeley's "Go West, young man" must be read alongside the costs of westering myths, "the cattle dying, the children sick, the limits / always ahead like a wall of black mountains" (ll. 8–9). The expansive Plains landscape, the "nowhere" that white Americans once hungered for, ends in topocide: "Generations spilled out," Kooser laments, "and we settled for limits: strung fence wire, drew plat maps / with streets squared to the polestar" (ll. 12–14). At the city limits, he sees the ugliest aspects of this history, of nature scarred and Native people run off, stolen from, and murdered. In grabbing it all, in settling in and "[signing] on the line at the bank" (l. 34), European Americans tied themselves to a heartless bargain. While Kooser's larger vision in *Weather Central* lingers primarily on nature's cycles and daily routines, his rare poems of outrage in this volume remind us all the more loudly of conquest's underbelly.

Native writers critically view the settlement landscape that Kooser limns, perceiving it as colonized, hegemonic space (Hussain 2000: 41). Native poets like Joy Harjo remap Plains space, connect it to an ancient Native mythos, and set coordinates that are global and cosmic. In *The Woman Who Fell from the Sky*, Harjo magnifies the millennia of Native voices that first gave voice to the Plains and remind us of the deepest literary foundation: Native oral traditions. Her lyrics help address the urgent question that Elizabeth Cook-Lynn posited: "Who gets to tell the stories?" (1993: 64). Skeptical of the "new American storytellers of the Plains," Cook-Lynn specifically targets Heat-Moon's *PrairyErth* and Kathleen Norris's *Dakota: A Spiritual Geography*, books that spiral around the first-person "I," that are "seduced into the modern examination of the Self" (1993: 64). Harjo begins her collection with "Reconciliation: A Prayer," acknowledging the plurality of her vision in an intonation "Oh sun, moon, stars, our other relatives peering at us from the inside of god's house walk with us as we climb into the next century naked but for the stories we have of each other" (II.1). Her cartographic traditions pre-date European contact and follow a different set of "cultural verities" (Belyea 1999: 179).

Born on the southern Plains of Oklahoma of Muscogee Creek background, Harjo seeks in her many landscapes reawakenings and love, spiritual antidotes to broken country, ruptured history, economic injustice, and racism. Azfar Hussain calls hers an "anticolonial geographical imagination" (2000: 52). Harjo's poetic mapping also depends upon the primacy of communal, tribal memory, and her talents serve the many voices, stories, and places of Native people. Harjo explains, "I feel strongly that I have a responsibility to all the sources I am: to all past and future ancestors, to my home country, to all places that I touch down on and that are myself, to all voices, all women, all of my tribe, all people, all earth, and beyond that to all beginnings and endings" (qtd. Hussain 2000: 29). Harjo also honors the earth as primal, spiritual home place. Reconnecting to the land and returning to natural rhythms and cycles provide a significant healing gesture in "[grappling] with the alienation, anger, and (at times) hopelessness of living within modern civilization" (Bryson 2002: 170). Her poems serve to recover "a perspective that is mindful of both *place* and *space*" (Bryson 2002: 170).

The poems in this collection are deeply cartographical. Harjo presents multiple geographies, a plethora of landscapes, including imagined ones from the deep past or from the future. Among the places her poems mark are "the icy parking lot of the Safeway" ("The Woman Who Fell From the Sky," VI.1), Jay, Oklahoma ("The

Naming"), Oakland, California ("A Postcolonial Tale"), Lake Superior ("Northern Lights"), Chicago ("Letter From the End of the Twentieth Century"), Albuquerque, New Mexico ("Witness"), Brooklyn, New York ("The Place the Musician Became a Bear"), and Pisa, Italy ("The Field of Miracles"). Often in her poems cosmic, mythic dimensions enter into everyday places; stories millennia old fold into the quotidian. Harjo's vision is rhizomatic and resistant, the nodes and internodes birthing new worlds that pop up in unexpected places. She seeks the routes and roots of many histories and people to counter nothingness, the modern world's plague.

In response to hegemonic space, Harjo enters into geography that is rhizomatic and folded, where space blurs in multiplicity. In "Fishing," she refigures the river and the act of fishing in cosmic terms. An everyday activity reverberates with "symbology" and archetypal passage, bridges eons of warriors, and establishes communication among animal life, cicadas, fish, and people. The river bank is "soft earth made of fossils and ashes," the vestiges of other times supporting the present (II.3). Walking the banks in her imagination, Harjo illuminates this point in Oklahoma, this gateway through space and time. She sees that "[the] leap between the sacred and profane is as thin as fishing line, and is part of the mystery on this river of life, as is the way our people continue to make warriors in the strangest of times" (IV.1). Her friend, Muscogee poet Louis Oliver, has died, a man for whom fishing "was holy communion" (V.2). Memory and imagination reclaim his essence and connect her people to their land and history upon this land. "The right place on the river" resonates with connections, "collapses temporal boundaries" (Bryson 2002: 181).

Repeatedly Harjo honors the lost, the wounded, and the dead – those who have lived and died in the modern "drought" world of forgotten stories ("The Flood," XIX.3). She weaves in family tales from the Oklahoma Plains – stories ranging from cosmogony to sharecropping, from tornadoes to the monstrous, mythic tie snake that lurks in rivers and lakes. Her landscapes are urban and rural, blasted and regenerative, distressed and deeply affiliative. She begins her poems in the vast cosmos ("The Creation Story") and ends at the microscopic kitchen table, where "[p]erhaps the world will end … while we are laughing and crying, eating the last sweet bite" ("Perhaps the World Ends Here," XI.1). Azfar Hussain insightfully comments that the kitchen table "constitutes a site of language, a site in which love stories, dreams, nightmares, laughters, cries, frustrations, triumphs, and defeats all coalesce to account for the history of the past and the present" (2000: 53). Though written across the modern landscape, Harjo's Plains cartography returns us to the oldest Plains stories, the earliest understandings of place. She and other Plains Native writers have energized writing from this region and are guiding its literary production into the twenty-first century.

Plains writers across communities increasingly recognize the uniqueness of the region's environment, the necessity of redressing injustice, the mixed repercussions of settlement, and the need to heal the wounds of a complex, at times violent, history. Writing that is imaginatively cartographic binds Plains writers as a group and guides them into art that seeks, if imperfectly, the deeper truths of place. In this way, Great

Plains writers reflect the larger trajectory of western American literature in the twenty-first century. As Richard W. Etulain notes, these literary efforts "depict a complex American West, filled with a variety of enduring and swiftly changing cultures. Of late, we have begun to tell far more complex stories about the West. These complicated narratives allow us to hear the voices of many westerners and to view rapid changes over time within and without the region" (2000: 7).

REFERENCES AND FURTHER READING

Belyea, Barbara. (1999). Mapping the Marias: The Interface of Native and Scientific Cartographies. *Great Plains Quarterly*, 17, 165–84.

Brady, Mary Pat. (2002). *Extinct Lands, Temporal Geographies: Chicana Literature and the Urgency of Space*. Durham, NC: Duke University Press.

Bryson, J. Scott. (2002). Finding the Way Back: Place and Space in the Ecological Poetry of Joy Harjo. *MELUS*, 27, 169–96.

Campbell, Neil. (2008). *The Rhizomatic West: Representing the American West in a Transnational, Global, Media Age*. Lincoln: University of Nebraska Press.

Cather, Willa. (2003). *My Ántonia* [1918], ed. Joseph R. Urgo. Peterborough: Broadview.

Christianson, Gale E. (1971). Introduction. In *The Night Country* by Loren Eiseley, pp. vii–xiii. Lincoln: University of Nebraska Press.

Christianson, Gale E. (1990). *The Fox at the Wood's Edge: A Biography of Loren Eiseley*. Lincoln: University of Nebraska Press.

Cook-Lynn, Elizabeth. (1993). Who Gets to Tell Our Stories? *Wicazo Sa Review*, 9, 60–4.

Deloria, Jr., Vine. (1984). Introduction. In John Gneisenau Neihardt and Vine Deloria, Jr., eds., *A Sender of Words: Essays in Memory of John G. Neihardt*, pp. 1–4. Salt Lake City: Howe Brothers.

Eiseley, Loren. (1959). *The Immense Journey: An Imaginative Naturalist Explores the Mysteries of Man and Nature* [1968]. New York: Vintage.

Etulain, Richard W. (2000). Western Stories for the Next Generation. *Western Historical Quarterly*, 31, 5–23.

Flores, Dan. (2001). *The Natural West: Environmental History in the Great Plains and Rocky Mountains*. Norman: University of Oklahoma Press.

Gayton, Don. (1996). Tallgrass Deam. In *Landscapes of the Interior: Re-Explorations of Nature and the Human Spirit*, pp. 95–107. Gabriola Island, BC: New Society.

Harjo, Joy. (1994). *The Woman Who Fell From the Sky*. New York: Norton.

Heat-Moon, William Least. (1991). *PrairyErth*. Boston: Houghton Mifflin.

Hussain, Azfar. (2000). Joy Harjo and her Poetics as Praxis: A "Postcolonial" Political Economy of the Body, Land, Labor, and Language. *Wicazo Sa Review*, 15, 27–61.

Janovy, Jr., John. (1981). *Back in Keith County*. Lincoln: University of Nebraska Press.

Kaye, Frances W. (2004). Literary Traditions. In David J. Wishart, ed., *Encyclopedia of the Great Plains*, pp. 469–73. Lincoln: University of Nebraska Press.

Kooser, Ted. (1994). *Weather Central*. Pittsburgh: University of Pittsburgh Press.

Kooser, Ted. (2004). Poetry. In David J. Wishart, ed., *Encyclopedia of the Great Plains*, p. 489. Lincoln: University of Nebraska Press.

Love, Glen. (2003). Nature and Human Nature: Interdisciplinary Convergences on Cather's Blue Mesa. *Cather Studies*, 5, 1–27.

McDougall, Jo. (2005). Of Time, Place, and Eternity: Ted Kooser at the Crossroads. *The Midwest Quarterly*, 46, 410–13.

Moss, Pamela, and Karen Falconer-Al Hindi, eds. (2008). An Introduction: Feminisms, Geographies, Knowledges. In *Feminisms in Geography: Rethinking Space, Place, and Knowledges*, pp. 1–27. Lanham: Rowman & Littlefield.

Naramore Maher, Susan. (2001). Deep Mapping the Great Plains: Surveying the Literary Cartography of Place. *Western American Literature*, 36, 4–24.

Pascoe, Peggy. (1991). Western Women at the Cultural Crossroads. In Patricia Nelson Limerick, Clyde A. Milner II, and Charles E.

Rankin, eds., *Trails: Toward a New Western History*, pp. 40–58. Lawrence: University of Kansas Press.

Pratt, Mary Louise. (1992). *Imperial Eyes*. London: Routledge.

Price, John T. (2004). *Not Just Any Land: A Personal and Literary Journey into the American Grasslands*. Lincoln: University of Nebraska Press.

Quantic, Diane Dufva. (1995). *The Nature of the Place: A Study of Great Plains Fiction*. Lincoln: University of Nebraska Press.

Quantic, Diane Dufva. (1997). Contemporary Fiction of the Great Plains. In *Updating the Literary West*, pp. 720–7. Fort Worth: Texas Christian University Press.

Roorda, Randall. (2001). Deep Maps in Eco-Literature. *Michigan Quarterly Review*, 60, 257–72.

Rosowski, Susan J. (1999). *Birthing a Nation: Gender, Creativity, and the West in American Literature*. Lincoln: University of Nebraska Press.

Stanford Friedman, Susan. (1998). *Mappings: Feminism and the Cultural Geographies of Encounter*. Princeton, NJ: Princeton University Press.

Thacker, Robert. (1989). *The Great Prairie Fact and Literary Imagination*. Albuquerque: University of New Mexico Press.

Tuan, Yi-Fu. (1977). *Space and Place: The Perspective of Experience*. Minneapolis: University of Minnesota Press.

Urgo, Joseph R. (1995). *Willa Cather and the Myth of American Migration*. Urbana: University of Illinois Press.

Wall, Eamonn. (2008). Walking: Tim Robinson's *Stones of Aran*. *New Hibernian Review*, 12, 66–79.

Webb, Walter Prescott. (1981). *The Great Plains* [1931]. Lincoln: University of Nebraska Press.

West, Elliott. (1998). *The Contested Plains: Indians, Goldseekers, and the Rush to Colorado*. Lawrence: University of Kansas Press.

White, Matt. (2006). *Prairie Time: A Blackland Portrait*. College Station: Texas A & M University Press.

Wishart, David J., ed. (2004). The Great Plains Region. In *Encyclopedia of the Great Plains*, pp. xiii–xviii. Lincoln: University of Nebraska Press.

Worster, Donald. (1982). *Dust Bowl: The Southern Plains in the 1930s*. New York: Oxford University Press.

8

The Literary Northern Rockies as *The Last Best Place*

O. Alan Weltzien

In a July 1992 issue of *U.S. News & World Report*, a one-page feature with the cutesy title, "Don't Fence Them Out," surveyed the "Intermountain Literary Renaissance," speculating about the growth of the Rockies as a distinct literary region. One of the shaded sidebars endemic to such pieces teased with its provocative title, "Places Where There Are Too Many Writers," listing three places: Albuquerque, NM, Portland, OR, and "All of Montana." The ironic shift from city to an entire state gives the nod to Montana's preeminent literary reputation in the later twentieth century. Lois Welch has recently argued that Montana literature thrives under a condition of "post-colonial double-consciousness": "Montana regularly serves the country as a kind of cultural Timbuktu, an inland antipode, a repository of exotic escapes from 'real' … metropolitan life" (Welch 2009: 220), As Brady Harrison remarks in his introduction to *All Our Stories Are Here*, "Montana boasts such a long and diverse literary tradition that the bookshelf looks, the closer one investigates, more and more like a well-stocked library" (Harrison 2009: p. x). The *U.S. News & World Report* article conferred a *Good Housekeeping* seal of approval upon several facts, particularly the excellent reputation of the University of Montana's MFA program in creative writing – what Lois Welch has dubbed "a remote but sparky nexus" (Welch 2009: 221) – and the publication of Montana's state literature anthology, immodestly and memorably titled *The Last Best Place* (Kittredge and Smith 1988).

This review essay chronicles the back story that led to such features as the MFA program and state literature anthology. It then surveys some of the range of writers, with national or international reputations, who have called Montana home, particularly since Montana's literary renaissance of the 1970s. In the final section, it reviews

A Companion to the Literature and Culture of the American West, First Edition. Edited by Nicolas S. Witschi.

the prominent critical books or collections published since *The Last Best Place.* The number of titles published within the past decade testifies that the rate of literary production and excellence in this section of the American West shows no signs of slowing down. Any survey of Montana area literature proposes, implicitly and explicitly, varying answers to questions like the following: (1) How does the Montana region provide a shorthand of the American West? (2) How does Montana recapitulate or revise (white) frontier experience in other regions of the country? (3) How does the region's literature criticize and subvert the West homogenized and packaged by Hollywood, dime novels, and their contemporary, popular cultural descendants? and (4) How does the regional literature mediate between the local and the national? How does it bridge the contrary claims of being exceptional and being universal? Montana writers addressed in this panorama treat these questions and, by the twentieth century's final decades, collectively define a regional literature with some claims to distinction.

Two towering literary figures from the first half of the last century, H.G. Merriam and Joseph Kinsey Howard, explain, as much as anyone, the genesis of UM Missoula's MFA program and Montana's famous literary anthology, respectively. Merriam, arriving in Missoula in 1919 to chair the English Department (at "Montana State College"), started teaching classes in regional literature and creative writing almost immediately. Within his first year he founded a literary magazine, subsequently known as *The Frontier* (and later *Midland*), which was published for nineteen years (1920–39). (see Ginny Merriam 1999) During part of that time, Merriam had Montanan Grace Stone Coates as an associate editor: her poetry and novels have been republished in recent years. *The Frontier* provided a publication venue and voice for many writers of the region. A decade after his arrival, a bachelor's degree program in creative writing was established in Missoula – only the second one in the nation, in fact. In the 1930s and 1940s, Merriam hosted summer writing conferences in Missoula, which again promoted regional literary identity and self-confidence. In a commemorative article written for *The Missoulian* (April 21, 1999), granddaughter Ginny Merriam quotes William Kittredge, unofficial dean of Montana letters, stating "If it hadn't been for him, Montana wouldn't have been a literary state."

Only a dozen years after Merriam's 1954 retirement, the University of Montana established its MFA program, and, under Richard Hugo (1964), Earl Ganz (1966), and William Kittredge (1969) among many, it quickly gained a high reputation, one it has not relinquished in the past forty years. It routinely ranks very high in national MFA program surveys. In recent decades, it has proven extremely difficult to gain admission into this program, particularly for Montanans.

J.K. Howard, a working journalist (*Great Falls Tribune*) rather than an academic historian, not only wrote one of the most influential books about Montana, *Montana: High, Wide, and Handsome* (1943); he also published the first state literary anthology, *Montana Margins* (1946), an ambitious survey of over 500 pages divided into ten topics. This survey inspired an editorial board of seven who, forty years later, assembled *The Last Best Place.* This big book grew out of a retreat in 1984 sponsored by the Montana Committee for the Humanities (since renamed Humanities Montana).[1] The board eventually constructed an anthology in eight sections that runs to 1,158 pages and weighs about five pounds. Kittredge and writer Annick Smith served as general editors. Reminiscing about their work a decade later, historian William L. Lang asserted, "We discovered a literature that denied Montana's exceptionalism, yet confirmed the place as special." His conclusion suggests Montana as a metonym for a larger literary region: "we are more like the world we have drawn from than not. Our uncommonness and its legacy are particularistic and are vested precisely in the way we have described and explained our lives in this landscape" (Lang 1996: 185, 187). Published for Montana's state centennial (1989), it sold out of its initial print run within weeks; to date, it has sold over 60,000 copies, and has thus set a gold standard among western states literature anthologies. The board members concluded that, within a decade or so, a single-volume project would prove impossible, given the explosion of writing in the northern Rockies. The surviving members (five) also have publicly discussed (during a panel discussion at the 2008 Montana Festival of the Book) the myriad ways in which work on the book unlocked their own writing, as most of their own books have appeared since 1989.

By beginning with "Native American Stories and Myths," *The Last Best Place* honors, as any such anthology should, the region's indigenous stories first. This section was edited by the late James Welch, easily Montana's most famous Native American writer. Welch, who figured prominently in the 1970s Montana renaissance, was inspired by Montana's D'Arcy McNickle, who became a nationally known anthropologist and advocate for Native American peoples. McNickle published a remarkable first novel, *The Surrounded* (1936), *Runner in the Sun* (1954), a novel for young adults, and *Wind from an Enemy Sky* (1978), on which he worked for decades. Welch, of mixed Blackfeet-Gros Ventre heritage, began as a poet in Missoula, working under Richard Hugo, and after *Riding the Earthboy 40* (1971), an initial book of poetry, he switched to fiction, producing five remarkable novels and a book of nonfiction before his death in 2003. Two of these novels, *Fools Crow* (1986) and *The Heartsong of Charging Elk* (2000), set in the late nineteenth century, represent profound works of historical imagination. Welch's first and second novels, *Winter in the Blood* (1974) and *The Death of Jim Loney* (1979), signified a prominent new voice in Native American writing. These novels, spare and taut and dark, explore their protagonists' search for some stable identity in worlds that mostly subvert such stability, and in that process Welch blends existential crises with traditions of tribal homing plots. As with many contemporary Native American writers, he explores the minefield of being a "breed," or mixed race identity. Welch was knighted (Chevalier de l'ordre des arts et des lettres) by the French government in 1995.

Welch's successor is Debra Magpie Earling, a Salish-Kootenai writer who has been part of the UM Missoula MFA faculty for many years. She worked a long time on *Perma Red* (2002), a prize-winning novel set in Montana's Mission Valley, also the Flathead Reservation, in the 1940s. *Perma Red* traces a tangled love story that reveals a range of white–Native entanglements and sharply focuses the racist realities and economic inequalities of reservation life. But Earling's prose continually charges her landscapes with spiritual values, as though they redeem the typically sordid human stories enacted upon or within them. The Mission Valley signifies her main character, and to that extent *Perma Red* represents another contribution to Montana's rich literature of place (Weltzien 2007–8: 184).

A group of earlier writers created the soil for the regional renaissance of one generation ago: a period during which several writers (including Welch) gained prominent voice for the first time.[2] Frank Bird Linderman, who reached Montana as a teenager in the 1880s, gained fame in old age for his reminiscences about his days as a trapper and guide. His most significant contribution, though, came through his literary transcriptions of the life stories of Plenty-coups (1930) and Pretty Shield (1932), chief and medicine woman, respectively, of the Crow tribe. Linderman's "as told to" writing is analogous to John Neihardt's work with Black Elk during the same period in Nebraska. Fourteen of Linderman's twenty-two books are still in print (Hatfield 2008: 46). Andrew Garcia lived among the Nez Perce and Flathead Indians, marrying several tribal women, before the tribes' final containment on reservations, and in old age he worked on a memoir, which wasn't published until twenty-four years after his death. Edited by Bennett H. Stein, *Tough Trip Through Paradise* (1967) gives the lie to romantic clichés about the old West, and particularly, Indians. Part of this memoir's popularity consists in its insider, first-person view that treats the ambivalences inherent in the title.

Another pioneering memoir of enduring literary value, Nannie T. Alderson's *A Bride Goes West* (1942), recounts the story of a 22-year-old Virginia belle who accompanied her husband to southeastern Montana, where he ranched for the rest of his life. Written in old age in "as told to" format (to interviewer Huntington Smith), it chronicles life in Montana's Tongue River country during the 1880s–1910s. Her memoir provides crucial snapshots (for example "The Last Buffalo"). Critic Julia Watson calls it "a book of wisdom inscribing both the transience and the intensity of the moment in a time of profound historical transition" (Watson 2003: 128). Among the literary voices recording the passing of the open range and the first decades of statehood, including Teddy Blue Abbott (*We Pointed Them North*, 1939) and Granville Stuart (*Forty Years on the Frontier*, 1925), Charles M. (Charley) Russell deserves mention. Russell remains not only Montana's most famous western artist and an enduring icon; he also gained fame as a storyteller, frequently scribbling on original postcards and drawings and writing humorous sketches using "Rawhide Rawlins" as his persona, following longstanding American traditions of vernacular humor.[3] Years after Russell's death, his Rawlins stories were published as *Trails Plowed Under* (1937).

Historically, Butte signifies Montana's most important city, and arguments can be made that the state's modern history is more significantly industrial than agricultural. Butte is the only city to merit its own section in *The Last Best Place* (Kittredge and Smith 1999: part IV). Butte and nearby Anaconda, for decades the centers of copper mining in the US, attracted a range of writers, three of whom reflect, in differing ways, Butte's international, audacious, wide-open reputation. Published when she was

21, Mary Maclane's *The Story of Mary Maclane* (1902) set a new high-water mark in women's autobiographical writing. The book became a bestseller, was translated into thirty-six languages, and was hailed by modernist writers as an exemplary tale. Its notoriety derives from both Maclane's sexual frankness and her excoriation of her native town – which she continued to identify with.

Barely a generation later, Dashiell Hammett began his literary career, and seminal contributions to American hard-boiled detective fiction, in Butte. Using his grim experiences as a Pinkerton Agency operative working occasionally out of Butte, he set his first novel, *Red Harvest* (1929), in Butte, as its famous opening declares:

> I first heard Personville called Poisonville by a red-haired mucker named Hickey Dewey in the Big Ship in Butte. He also called his shirt a shoit. I didn't think anything of what he had done to the city's name. Later I heard men who could manage their r's give it the same pronunciation. I still didn't see anything in it but the meaningless sort of humor that used to make richardsnary the thieves' word for dictionary. A few years later I went to Personville and learned better.

In the same period, Myron Brinig commemorated Butte in six of his eventual twenty-three novels. Arriving in Butte at age 3, Brining left in 1918 and never returned. Jewish and openly gay, Brinig in his best Butte novels – *Singermann* (1929) and *Wide Open Town* (1931) – captures its multiracial, multi-ethnic, full-throttle energy in a modernist prose that reflects those Roaring Twenties. Called by H.G. Merriam (in 1979) "the best native Montana novelist" (Ganz 1996: 27), Brinig has mostly disappeared from literary memory.

Until the past decade, Grace Stone Coates had also been forgotten, but, thanks largely to biographer Lee Rostad, Coates has resurfaced as an important Montana writer of the late 1920s and early 1930s – a contemporary of Brining in his Butte novels. As mentioned earlier, Coates worked for years with H.G. Merriam on *The Frontier*, and in 1931 she published a tightly wrought novel, *Black Cherries*. A linked set of stories narrated from the point of view of the youngest daughter in a large family, *Black Cherries* records a grim, late nineteenth-/early twentieth-century marriage, the father preoccupied with his deceased first wife. Coates shows herself a literary modernist, writing in a spare, symbolic style. Two books of poetry quickly followed, most of the poems recently republished as *Food of Gods and Starvelings* (2007). Wife of a Martindale, Montana grocer, Coates writes with some of the same compression as Emily Dickinson, many poems unflinchingly critiquing the battle of the sexes.

By the mid-twentieth century, then, Montana had already revealed a mixture of writers who treated the near or distant past with varying degrees of nostalgia or criticism. Some wrote out of a tradition of realistic or humorous reminiscence; others sustained an ambitiously modernist sensibility. By this period, northern Rockies literature was gaining significant momentum – and national critical and popular attention. I turn next to an arbitrary set of seven writers who collectively stamp Montana as a distinct literary region and who usher in the 1970s literary renaissance. This group is variably literary and popular, known or overlooked. Only one or two wrote close to Hollywood conventions of western dime novels; most critique, with varying irony, pop cultural conceptions and obsessions with the region as part of the so-called Old West. Several help create what William Bevis and Rick Newby have characterized as a tradition of "terse eloquence" (Newby 2003: p. xi).

In many respects, A.B. Guthrie, Jr. stands as supreme historical novelist of the region, one whose sextology (1947–82) provided Montanans – and all readers – their preferred version of the white past in this region. In many cases, readers overlook the sometimes trenchant criticism implicit in his story, particularly in the first two novels, considered the best. Guthrie won a Pulitzer Prize for *The Way West* (1949), but it is the first, *The Big Sky* (1947), that constitutes Montana's ur-novel. In 1961, through an agreement struck between Guthrie and the state government, Montana adopted that title as its unofficial descriptor, one which has graced license plates for decades. In *The Big Sky* Guthrie inscribes the fur trapper era (1830s–40s) as a paradise lost – what Ken Egan, Jr. memorably describes as the "siren song of apocalypse" (Egan 2003: 9–19). Egan and other critics astutely critique the seductive lure of "she's all sp'iled," a mistaken, golden age myth that has influenced a quantity of literary production ever since. That "siren song of apocalypse" also proves an enduring theme in several subsequent writers, as Egan argues in *Hope and Dread in Montana Literature* (2003). The essential place of *The Big Sky* in modern Montana literature was marked, in 1997, by a memorable conference, "Fifty Years After *The Big Sky*," in Missoula. That conference, in turn, led to a volume of the same title (Farr and Bevis 2001). No other Montana novel has inspired such ongoing discussion, if not debate.

Guthrie proved one of a trio of writers, including Wallace Stegner and Bernard DeVoto, who changed the ways the West is understood: by rewriting the nineteenth or early twentieth centuries, they reshaped contemporary identity in crucial ways.

By the time Guthrie published *The Big Sky*, Mildred Walker, who lived for decades in Great Falls, had published several novels including what is considered her best, *Winter Wheat* (1944). With protagonist Ellen Webb, Walker foregrounds a young, female protagonist whose transition into adulthood is marked by a more complex, and realistic, appraisal of her parents' marriage. Walker sets *Winter Wheat* in eastern Montana, and through the character of Ellen's mother provides a realistic view of an old country emigrant, a woman who speaks English idiosyncratically but whose toughness matches the difficult climate for growing wheat. In *The Curlew's Cry* (1955), Walker provides a sort of twentieth-century Montana allegory, as the protagonist, Pamela Lacey, is forced to convert the family ranch into a dude operation in order to save it. Much contemporary regional literature plots the decline of traditional modes of work as well as the rise of a recreation-based economy. In a late novel, *If A Lion Could Talk* (1970), Walker in some respects rewrites Guthrie's *The Big Sky*: now, though, a missionary couple from Massachusetts in Blackfeet country are themselves permanently changed by their trials in Indian country.

Dorothy Johnson's journalistic career took her to New York City for fifteen years (1935–50) before returning to Montana, where she worked as a news editor on her hometown paper (Whitefish, MT) before teaching journalism at the University of Montana. Johnson led a remarkable career, one chronicled in a recent documentary film, *Gravel in Her Gut and Spit in Her Eye* (2004), written by Sue Hart. In her short stories placed in popular magazines, Johnson wrote closer to popular Western conventions than many of her colleagues. According to Hart, Johnson is one of very few Montana writers who thought Hollywood improved her fiction (Hart, pers. comm. 2000). Among her most famous stories are "The Hanging Tree" and "A Man Called Horse." Her most famous story, "The Man Who Shot Liberty Valance," became film director John Ford's last great western (1962), a Fordian allegory wherein rural lawyers replace sharpshooters, senators live a tough guy lie, and signed streets and political campaigns shove outlaws out of the way.

One example of a writer central to late nineteenth- and early twentieth-century Montanan history is Dan Cushman who, like Myron Brinig, has largely disappeared from regional memory. Like J.K. Howard, Cushman worked for *The Great Falls Tribune*. Like Johnson, Cushman wrote less critically about ground realities in the northern Rockies. He wrote dozens of novels, the most famous of which is *Stay Away, Joe* (1953), a novel about Montana reservation life that aroused some controversy: controversy exacerbated by the movie adaptation that starred Elvis Presley in the title role. In the *New York Times* (October 2, 2001), James Welch vetoed inclusion of any excerpt of *Stay Away, Joe* in *The Last Best Place* because of his perception of badly worn Indian stereotypes.

A neglected novelist of some distinction, Thomas Savage did not even rate mention in Montana's big anthology; nor did his wife, novelist Elizabeth Fitzgerald Savage. Savage, a Montana native, returned to Montana infrequently after age 22, yet eight of his thirteen novels are set in southwestern Montana or the Lemhi River valley in Idaho. Savage critiques popular western myths as incisively as any writer, which tendency might explain his obscurity. Yet he stands as a novelist of the recent past whose work ranks with the best of Guthrie, or Ivan Doig. In his best novels, *The Power of the Dog* (1967) and *I Heard My Sister Speak My Name* (1977; retitled *The Sheep Queen*, 2001), Savage condemns received, romantic notions about ranching dynasties and small-town life. Along the way, he excoriates parochial attitudes including rigid gender boundaries and local expressions of bigotry, hypocrisy, and that universal tendency towards naive self-congratulation. Savage was producing some of his best work during the 1970s literary renaissance, yet other writers were barely aware of his novels, though reviewers such as Jonathan Yardley (in *The Washington Post*) championed his career.

Of these writers, Johnson and Cushman link Montana with the popular Old West; Guthrie helps shape Montana's historical consciousness and literary self-identity; Walker writes realistic narratives showcasing women accommodating change rather than protesting it; and Savage criticizes patterns of self-aggrandizement implicit in the notion that a big sky produces or sustains big people. The next pair of writers set, as much as anyone, Montana's reputation for literary excellence as measured through Missoula's MFA program.

Before turning to them, however, mention must be made of Leslie Fiedler, the region's most famous literary critic in the mid-twentieth century, who served on the University of Montana faculty for twenty-three years (1941–64) before departing for SUNY-Buffalo. During this period, Fielder gained an audacious reputation as an original wild man in American literature, publishing several essay collections including *An End of Innocence* (1955), which includes "Montana, or the End of Jean-Jacques Rousseau," one of the most infamous essays about Montana. Fiedler's most famous study, *Love and Death in the American Novel* (1960), climaxed his Montana years and enhanced the region's intellectual repute.

Richard Hugo, a south Seattle native who studied at the University of Washington under Theodore Roethke, arrived in Missoula in 1964 having already published his first poetry collection, *A Run of Jacks* (1961). In the next eighteen years, until his untimely death from lung cancer (1982), Hugo became probably Montana's most famous poet and poetry teacher. His ten books and many new poems were collectively published as *Making Certain It Goes On* (1984), the title of which belongs to one of his last and best poems. Hugo's poetics celebrate the down and out and express a thoroughly democratic vision of poetry. In Hugo's world, as Steve Davenport claims, "a man's masculinity is always in question," but despite his commitment to a tough guy ethos, "It is ... the failure of his flight from sentiment, his self-imposed prohibition against melancholy that makes his poetry so powerful, so affecting, so human" (Davenport 2009: 200, 212). His narratives, evoking experiences of disjunction or abandonment (whether of Montana place, or other settings), helped further the careers of a generation of poets including Sandra Alcosser, Madeline DeFrees, Roger Dunsmore, Patricia Goedicke, Ed Lahey, Rick Newby, Robert Wrigley, and Paul Zarzyski. According to James Welch, "For Hugo ... failure *was* the last best place" (Bevis 1988: 1034). Hugo, a mesmerizing reader of his own work, was fond of placing particular poems in specific Montana locations (for example "Degrees of Gray in Philipsburg"). As William Bevis remarks, much Montana poetry in the late twentieth century "bears his stamp: the dense lines, the landscape like a pressure, the sense of loss" (Bevis 1988: 1034).

Another great teacher in the MFA program who changed Montana literature was Hugo's friend, William (Bill) Kittredge, who arrived in 1969. For years now the grand old man of Montana literature, Kittredge proved a generous teacher who, like Hugo, inspired many subsequent writers. His position in regional letters is marked by such honors as the Charles Frankel Prize (1994, President Clinton), the Robert Kirsch Lifetime Achievement Award (2007, *Los Angeles Times*), and the Distinguished Achievement Award (2008, Western Literature Association). Early in his career Kittredge wrote short fiction, then in middle age switched to nonfiction, and in recent years returned to fiction, publishing *The Willow Field* (2006), his first novel, at age 74. Kittredge provides probably his most detailed literary credo in *Taking Care: Thoughts on Storytelling and Belief* (1999). In that book, Scott Slovic, the editor of the Credo series, comments, "This vacillation between reverie and grief, reformist hope and guilt-ridden despair, defines the overarching tenor of Kittredge's writing"

(Kittredge 1999: 87). In some respects his first nonfiction collection, *Owning It All* (1987) represents his most important book, as he began exploring his own family's ranching story in Oregon's Warner Valley. In his subsequent memoir, *Hole in the Sky* (1992), Kittredge enlarges the portrait, an allegory of the exploitative development of the American West – his personal version of what Patricia Nelson Limerick memorably titled, in her foundational book of New Western history, *The Legacy of Conquest* (1987). Kittredge's environmentalism has influenced a newer generation of writers in the Big Sky.

James Welch's first two novels and William Kittredge's first short story collection (*The Van Gogh Field*) appeared during the 1970s, and Richard Hugo published the majority of his books during that decade. I turn now to five additional writers who launched their careers during this time and who variously critique Guthrie's golden age mythology in their inscriptions of Montana. Norman Maclean's story poses one of the oddest in American letters. The longtime University of Chicago English professor changed Montana literature, after his retirement, with the publication of *A River Runs Through It and Other Stories* (1976), an odd sandwich of two novellas with a short story in between. Maclean worked a decade or more on his second book, the highly acclaimed nonfiction *Young Men and Fire* (1992), published posthumously. His literary reputation rests upon just two books. In his first book, Maclean plays the fluid border between autobiographical nonfiction and fiction. The title novella, acclaimed as a perfectly constructed 104-page work, stands as both a treatise on fly fishing and a universal parable of a fatally troubled younger sibling. It changed the fly fishing industry in Montana, and Robert Redford's film adaptation (1991) has brought additional literary fame to Maclean – and tourist hordes to Montana in search of big trout.

Ivan Doig has proven himself, over the past three decades, one of the region's steadiest novelists. After earning a Ph.D. in history (1969, University of Washington) and publishing scores of historical articles, Doig published his memoir, *This House of Sky* (1977), for many readers still his best book. After a second nonfiction book and a novel (*The Sea Runners*, 1982), both set in the Pacific Northwest, Doig imaginatively returned home, writing what's become known as his Montana trilogy (or McCaskill trilogy) during the 1980s, the third novel, *Ride With Me, Mariah Montana* (1990), published in time for the state's centennial. Doig uses Montana as primary setting for his fiction. A meticulous researcher, Doig gets period details correct and publishes a new novel every three to four years, most recently, *The Eleventh Man* (2008). Critics regard Doig's historical novels (for example *Dancing at the Rascal Fair*, 1987, or *Prairie Nocturne*, 2003) as his best work. He enjoys both critical and popular success and has become the region's premier historical novelist. His fiction often spotlights a particular episode in Montana's history. For example, *Bucking the Sun* (1996) focuses upon the building of Fort Peck Dam in northeast Montana (1933–8).

Besides Welch, Maclean, and Doig, the careers of Rick DeMarinis, Tom McGuane, and James Crumley all accelerated during the 1970s. Each of these writers stretched Montana's territory. DeMarinis, like Doig, has published steadily and is equally at home in short and long fiction. Of his nine novels (as of 2010), *The Burning Women of Far Cry* (1986) stands as one of his best. DeMarinis may even be stronger in the short story, *Borrowed Hearts: New and Selected Stories* (1999), representing his most comprehensive collection to date. DeMarinis' fiction features zany characters and plots, and his absurdist comedy pushes regional literature in a direction away from realist representation or criticism.

Called by *The New York Times Book Review* "a writer of the first magnitude," Tom McGuane has, like DeMarinis, produced a shelf of high-quality fiction. McGuane has long run a 3,000-acre ranch in McLeod, Montana, where he and his wife continue to raise cutting horses. In addition to nine novels (1969–2002) and two short story collections, McGuane has written three nonfiction books devoted to outdoors life, fishing, and horses. In his *Books & Writers* column, "Tom McGuane on Ranching, Writing, and Rattlesnakes," Hal Herring discusses McGuane's influence "on a generation of readers who dreamed of Montana as a place of anarchic freedom, of fast rivers and trout, the prime example of the un-bounded life promised by the American West. That promise, and its illusory, deceptive reality, remains a hidden engine in most of his work" (Herring 2006). McGuane, a superb stylist, exposes, in his most representative novels (for example *Nobody's Angel*, 1981, or *Nothing But Blue Skies*, 1992), that "hidden engine" – a yawning gap between the promise of landscape and the shortcomings, if not self-destructive tendencies, of characters – in a style that is all his own.

James Crumley, more than any other regional writer, stamped his mark on the tradition of American hard-boiled crime fiction. Crumley developed a cult following and influenced a number of other area writers in suspense fiction, including Peter Bowen, Neil McMahon, and Jamie Harrison. A descendant of Dashiell Hammett and Raymond Chandler, Crumley wrote nine novels featuring detectives C.W. Sughrue and Milo Milodragovitch. His second and third novels, *The Wrong Case* (1975) and *The Last Good Kiss* (1978), introduce Milodragovitch and Sughrue, respectively, and are judged his best. For both, the Vietnam War era never ends, and both wrestle with a range of demons and addictions. Crumley and fellow suspense writer James Lee Burke, who boasts an enormous readership, are beloved figures in the Montana community of writers. In an apt summary of Crumley's signature, critic Patrick Anderson remarked "You read [Crumley] for his outlaw attitude, his rough poetry and his scenes, paragraphs, moments. You read him for the lawyer with 'a smile as innocent as the first martini'" (qtd. in Sullivan 2008).

Since the 1970s resurgence, a number of writers who happen to be women have joined the front ranks of regional literature (for example D.M. Earling, discussed earlier). Two, Mary Clearman Blew and Annick Smith, served on *The Last Best Place* editorial board. Three of the five I shall mention are products of the Missoula MFA program. The work of Mary Clearman Blew and Judy Blunt provides the best regional perspective on the acute pressures facing ranch daughters. Blew began writing short stories, publishing two collections (*Lambing Out*, 1977, and *Runaway*, 1989) before turning to memoir. Blew has moved easily between nonfiction and fiction, her recent novel, *Jackalope Dreams* (2008), winning a Western Heritage Award (2009). She has published three books of memoirs, two based upon her independent aunt, Imogene, who taught rural school in Washington State. Of all her books, *All But The Waltz* (1991) has received the highest acclaim. In his Afterword to the paperback edition of *Ten Tough Trips*, William W. Bevis calls *Waltz* "a pioneering work" that "raises crucial issues of feminism and postmodernism in the new West" (Bevis 2003: 209) For Bevis, Blew's "anti-narrative storytelling" represents an "open technique" that "sometime[s] answers patriarchal or rational or imperial control with open-ended, irrational, contradictory, and indeterminate forms" (Bevis 2003: 218, 219). Judy Blunt's memoir, *Breaking Clean* (2002), won a Whiting Award. Bevis regards it as the clear successor to Blew's *Waltz*, and sees both writers adapting "a terse, western male voice to their own purposes" – a voice that, in Blunt's case, is "bioregional," as it "reflects Hi-Line [northern Montana] realities" (Bevis 2003: 222). In both cases, the writers eventually flee their home places, as they preclude their emergence into adulthood as independent women.

Another Hi-Line Montana writer who emerged in the 1990s, Deirdre McNamer, has published four novels, three of which are set, in whole or in part, in her native region. McNamer, formerly a journalist with *The Missoulian* and for some years part of the MFA faculty (along with Earling and Blunt), memorably depicts the sparse Hi-Line in her first novel, *Rima in the Weeds* (1991), which Ken Egan, Jr. describes as "quirky, tender, and refreshingly humorous" (Egan 2003: 154). Egan links its protagonist, Margaret, into a tradition of resilient female characters that includes Mildred Walker's Ellen Webb, protagonist of *Winter Wheat*, and Mary Clearman Blew's Aunt Imogene: "hers will be a completed pilgrimage, not one truncated by violence and misunderstanding. Margaret provides yet another affecting symbol of western maturation, of finding a way toward canniness and empathy" (Egan 2003: 158).

Annick Smith has published two essay collections, *Homestead* (1995) and *In This We Are Native* (2001). And, since co-editing *Circle of Women: An Anthology of Contemporary Western Women Writers* (1994), Kim Barnes has published two memoirs and two novels. Her first memoir, *In The Wilderness* (1997), a Pulitzer Prize finalist, chronicles her childhood and young adulthood in central Idaho logging towns. In it and its successor, *Hungry For The World* (2001), Barnes eloquently demonstrates the cost of reaching a stable adult identity as a woman, since she had to negotiate between a patriarchal value system and a backwoods Christian fundamentalism, among other conflicting pressures. Writers such as Blew, Blunt, McNamer, Smith, and Barnes testify to the prominent places western women occupy in regional literature – a position confirmed by the recently published anthology, *Montana Women Writers* (Patterson 2006).

In addition to Native American literature, suspense or detective fiction, and Montana women's literature, the Treasure State has seen a number of nature or environmental writers gain prominence, some of whom have been mentioned in other contexts. Many of these writers complicate or dispute the blanket notion, endorsed by *The Big Sky*'s character Uncle Zeb Calloway, that "She's all gone. The whole shitaree." That faux lamentation of paradise lost is both questioned and, at times, echoed by some of the region's best environmental writers. Out of this diverse community, I shall cite only three.

David James Duncan, an Oregonian who moved to the Lolo-Missoula area many years ago, has written two novels (*The River Why*, 1983, and *The Brothers K*, 1992) and a couple of collections of nonfiction. Of the latter, *My Story as Told by Water* (2001) passionately testifies to Duncan's grassroots activism concerning rivers. In three sections, the second – *Activism* – is the longest, as it features eight essays including the book's longest: "A Prayer for the Salmon's Second Coming." His subtitle tips his hand and suggests his politics. *My Story* consists of *"confessions, Druidic rants, reflections, birdwatching, fish-stalkings, visions, songs and prayers refracting light, from living rivers, in the age of the industrial dark."*

Residing in Bozeman for many years now, David Quammen has developed an international reputation as a science writer and traveler to remote locales. Beginning as a novelist, he published several books of essays that collect many of his columns from *Outside* magazine, and he recently published a short biography, *The Reluctant Mr. Darwin* (2006). Quammen is best known, though, for two big books, *The Song of the Dodo: Island Biogeography in an Age of Extinctions* (1996) and *The Monster of God* (2003). The former constitutes a course in conservation biology. Quammen's interdisciplinarity, ability to camp out anywhere on the globe with field biologists with diverse specialties, and literary excellence together explain his reputation.

Probably Montana's best-known environmental writer, and a prominent voice in the past generation's literary scene, is Rick Bass, prolific writer of fiction and nonfiction. Bass has published over two dozen books, including four short story collections, two collections of novellas, a big novel (*Where The Sea Used To Be*, 1998), and many books of polemical essays. He recently published a memoir, *Why I Came West* (2008), which covers familiar environmentalist ground but also describes the personal toll after twenty or more years of local activism in the Yaak Valley Forest Council and the Montana Wilderness Association, for instance. Over the past fifteen years Bass has become famous – or infamous – for his relentless propagandizing on behalf of his beloved Yaak Valley, in Montana's far northwestern corner. He tirelessly advocates protecting that valley's last roadless areas. In fiction and nonfiction, Bass repeatedly evokes the Yaak, chronicling its range of flora and fauna as a unique intersection between the marine Pacific Northwest and the drier northern Rockies. Bass's newest short story collection, *The Lives of Rocks* (2006), again displays his extravagant talents in fiction. The memoir, though, suggests anew that the split between fiction and activism has become Bass's primary subject. His newest memoir, *The Wild Marsh* (2009), emphasizes his lyricism and mutes angry polemicism: it represents his *Walden*, and is organized by the oldest convention in natural history writing, the calendar year.

The Last Best Place is not the only work to symbolize Montana's literary coming of age. In the past twenty years, four works of literary criticism and four anthologies have confirmed the region's literary identity. Together, these books demonstrate the region taking its measure within larger currents in contemporary western American literature. They also suggest that the region's literary production continues to surge.

Glancing back thirteen years to his first edition, William W. Bevis judges *Ten Tough Trips* (1990) and *The Last Best Place* "companion volumes" (Bevis 2003: 209).

Taking his title from Andrew Garcia's *Tough Trip Through Paradise*, Bevis's study completed his own editorial work on the big state anthology and set Montana literature in the national literary limelight (cf. his subtitle, *Montana Writers and the West*). Divided into three chronological sections, *Ten Tough Trips* solidly surveys Montana's coming of age as a literary region. Bevis features ten writers: Guthrie, Garcia, Alderson, Linderman, McNickle, Welch, Hugo, Doig, Maclean, and, interestingly, Fenimore Cooper ("Cooper: Then and Now"). The new edition (2003) spotlights Blew and Blunt as representative Montana women writers of the 1990s. Brady Harrison calls *Ten Tough Trips* "the urtext of Montana literary scholarship," a study that "performs the best sort of public intellectual work" (Harrison 2009: p. xiv). Clearly, Bevis climaxes his study with the 1970s literary renaissance and one 1990s extension of it, and analyzes contemporary writers' revisionist definitions of Montana past and present. He concludes his original edition with a statement signifying Montana as metonym for the literary West:

> Montana – in the heart of the West, old and new, Indian and white. Its writers speak very well for the high plains and northern Rockies, that area of beaver, gold, cattle, and cold that to the whole world is "The West." We are connected to Afghanistan, to Arab cries, to Paris papers, even by the myth that we are not. The dream of Montana as a fresh start was the dream of an old world. (Bevis 2003: 207)

After Bevis's pioneering study, Rick Newby and Suzanne Hunger published a collection, *Writing Montana: Literature Under the Big Sky* (1996), which includes "twenty-seven essays by twenty-six of the state's leading historians, literary scholars, poets, fiction writers, and journalists," in the editors' words (1996: p. viii). This collection succeeds in showcasing subjects missed in *The Last Best Place* – "the writers of eastern Montana, Native American literature; Montana philosophers, genre fiction; folk literatures; and the works of the state's women writers" (1996: p. viii). Newby and Hunger above all wanted to celebrate the "contending voices" and "sheer cussedness" of the region's voices.

The year 2003 saw the publication of Ken Egan, Jr.'s critical study, *Hope and Dread in Montana Literature*, in some respects a successor to *Ten Tough Trips*. Egan develops an Hegelian dialectic which he calls apocalyptic tragedy and pragmatic comedy, and he uses it to reread Montana literary history. Egan developed his study to help explain two end-of-decade (and end-of-century) individuals or movements that rendered Montana notorious in the national press: Unabomber Ted Kaczynski and the Freemen of Montana. Egan sees Montana literature oscillating between a "tragic sensibility" (for example Guthrie) and "provisional hope" (for example Doig).

The past decade has seen four new collections of Montana literature published: *The New Montana Story* (Newby and Hunger 2003), *The Best of Montana's Short Fiction* (Kittredge and Jones 2004), *Montana Women Writers: A Geography of Hope* (Patterson, 2006), and *Poems Across the Big Sky* (Jaeger 2006). These anthologies can be seen as extensions of, revisions to, and commentaries about *The Last Best Place*. This review of Montana literature ends with the recently published *All Our Stories Are Here: Critical Perspectives on Montana Literature* (Harrison 2009), in turn an extension of Newby's and Hunger's critical anthology. In his introduction, Brady Harrison states that the diverse contributors "agree that Montanan literature merits far more critical consideration" and that its writers "share a determination to expand, complicate, and celebrate the study of Montana and western writing." He doubts "such a thing as a distinctly Montanan literature exists" and the collection critiques, more overtly than the three earlier critical studies, omissions from earlier conceptions of canon (for example *The Last Best Place*). (Harrison 2009: pp. xvi–xvii)

The spate of anthologies and critical collections suggests that, in the early twenty-first century, the literary "last best place" shows no sign of decreasing energy or quality since the 1970s regional renaissance. Quite the contrary.

NOTES

1   The state anthology's title was inspired by one of the late James Crumley's most critically praised suspense novels, *The Last Good Kiss* (1978).
2   For a current review of the Montana literary renaissance of the 1970s, see Brady Harrison's Introduction: Toward a Postpopulist Criticism, in Harrison 2009: p. xi.
3   This vernacular tradition of humor was memorably surveyed, in the mid-twentieth century, by Walter Blair in *Native American Humor* (1950). Russell, like Twain originally from Missouri, extends Blair's southwestern school of humor.

REFERENCES AND FURTHER READING

Bevis, William W. (1988). Words and Space. In William Kittredge and Annick Smith, eds., *The Last Best Place: A Montana Anthology*, pp. 1029–36. Helena: Montana Historical Society Press, distributed by University of Washington Press.

Bevis, William W. (1990). *Ten Tough Trips: Montana Writers and the West*. Norman: University of Oklahoma Press.

Bevis, William W. (2003). Afterword to the paperback edition of *Ten Tough Trips*, pp. 209–24. Norman: University of Oklahoma Press.

Davenport, Steve. (2009) Richard Hugo's Montana Poems: Blue Collars, Indians, and Tough Style. In Brady Harrison, ed., *All Our Stories Are Here: Critical Perspectives on Montana Literature*, pp. 199–216. Lincoln: University of Nebraska Press.

Egan Jr., Ken. (2003) *Hope and Dread in Montana Literature*. Reno: University of Nevada Press.

Farr, William E., and William W. Bevis, eds. (2001). *Fifty Years After* The Big Sky: *New Perspectives on the Fiction and Films of A.B. Guthrie, Jr.* Helena: Montana Historical Society Press.

Ganz, Earl. (1996). Brinig: The Truth Game. In Rick Newby and Suzanne Hunger, eds., *Literature Under The Big Sky*. Helena: Montana Center for the Book, distributed by Falcon Press.

Garcia, Andrew (1943, 1967). *Tough Trip Through Paradise*, ed. Bennett H. Stein, Boston: Houghton Mifflin.

Harrison, Brady, ed. (2009). *All Our Stories Are Here: Critical Perspectives on Montana Literature*. Lincoln: University of Nebraska Press.

Hart, Sue. Personal communication, 2000.

Herring, Hal. (2006). An Interview with Tom McGuane. *Books & Writers*, July 10. www.

newwest.net/main/article/an_interview_with_thomas_mcguane.

Hugo, Richard. (1984 [pbk 1991]). *Making Certain It Goes On: The Collected Poems of Richard Hugo*. New York: W.W. Norton.

Jaeger, Lowell, ed. (2006). *Poems Across the Big Sky*. Kalispell, MT: Many Voices Press.

Kittredge, William, and Allen Morris Jones, eds. (2004). *The Best of Montana's Short Fiction*. Guilford, CT: The Lyons Press.

Kittredge, William, and Annick Smith, eds. (1988). *The Last Best Place: A Montana Anthology*. Helena: Montana Historical Society Press, distributed by University of Washington Press.

Kittredge, William, and Annick Smith. (1999). *Taking Care: Thoughts on Storytelling and Belief*. Credo series. Minneapolis: Milkweed Editions.

Lang, William L. (1996). *True Hyperbole*. In Rick Newby and Suzanne Hunger, eds., *Literature Under the Big Sky*, pp. 184–8. Helena: Montana Center for the Book.

Linderman, Frank Bird. (2008). Learn a Trapper's and Hunter's Art. Introd. Sarah Waller Hatfield. *Montana: The Magazine of Western History*, 58/4, 42–61.

Merriam, Ginny. (1999). 83: H.G. Merriam. In *The 100 Most Influential Montanans of the Century, The Missoulian*. www.missoulian.com/specials/100montanans/list/083.

Newby, Rick, and Suzanne Hunger, eds. (1996), *Literature Under the Big Sky*. Helena: Montana Center for the Book, distributed by Falcon Press.

Newby, Rick, and Suzanne Hunger. (2003). *The New Montana Story*. Helena, MT: Riverbend Publishing.

Patterson, Caroline, ed. (2006). *Montana Women Writers: A Geography of Hope*. Helena, MT: Farcountry Press.

Russell, Charles M. (1937). *Trails Plowed Under*. New York: Doubleday.

Sullivan, Patricia. (2008). James Crumley Inspired a Generation of Crime Writers. *Washington Post*, Sept. 19.

Watson, Julia. (2003). Engendering Montana Lives: Women's Autobiographical Writing [1996]. In Rick Newby and Suzanne Hunger, eds., *The New Montana Story*, pp. 121–62. Helena, MT: Riverbend Publishing.

Welch, Lois (2009). Semicolonial Moments: The History and Influence of the University of Montana Creative Writing Program. In Brady Harrison, ed., *All Our Stories Are Here: Critical Perspectives on Montana Literature*, pp. 217–39. Lincoln: University of Nebraska Press.

Weltzien, O. Alan. (2007–8). High, Wide, and Greening: A Survey of Montana's Environmental Literature. *Drumlummon Views*, ed. Rick Newby, 1/3, 179–85.

Weltzien, O. Alan. (2008). Thomas Savage, Forgotten Novelist. *Montana: The Magazine of Western History*, 58/4, 22–41.

9
North by Northwest: The Last Frontier of Western Literature

Eric Heyne

Away up north and separated by a large hunk of Canada from the continental United States, Alaska is often thought of as an island of sorts. Its frequent depiction off the coast of Los Angeles on weather maps is a perversely apt expression of the general feeling that Alaska is a place apart, a mysterious hinterland, inhabited by its own uniquely large and wild fauna, and still magically in touch with the American dream of self-reliance, a Romantic rugged individualism that has elsewhere been exiled by technology and bureaucracy. Alaska is the exception that justifies American exceptionalism. How else explain the peculiar and powerful appeal of Sarah Palin except through the aura of Alaska? If she were governor of Nevada, say, would she ever have had a shot at ascending the national stage? And just as Palin is the strongest believer in her own myth, so many Alaskans are dedicated to the idea that they live in a place apart, a "last frontier" that, like Eden, one leaves only by going "Outside."

What makes Alaska different, though, is mostly a heightened sense of many qualities that are recognizably western. Among the many important characteristics it shares with other western states are: a transient population of mixed ethnicity immigrating into areas inhabited by threatened Native communities; economies driven by resource extraction and its characteristic boom-and-bust cycles; federal control of huge tracts of land gathering hordes of tourists in a few select locations; disdain of government interference coupled with massive dependence on government subsidy; and a self-image rooted in nostalgia for a nineteenth-century way of life that never really existed. There would be no denying that Alaska is western even if it didn't contain the westernmost point of the United States (which it does). The interesting question is, how did that western culture change in moving from the "high plains" to the "far north"? More specifically for our purposes, how does the literature of Alaska reflect both the

A Companion to the Literature and Culture of the American West, First Edition. Edited by Nicolas S. Witschi.

western-ness of this place and its northern-ness? Put yet another way, how do the people of Alaska reconcile their pride in being "the last frontier" with the cultural survivor guilt of being the last land standing – and what does the rest of America make of this conflict?

Robert Service, the poetic half (Jack London is the prose man) of the same-sex parents of Alaskan literature, found a lot of ways to talk about the peculiar status of "the last of the lands, and the first." He celebrated this paradox most exuberantly in "The Law of the Yukon," where the North waits for just the right men to "take to [her] bosom, and speak as a mother speaks": not those evil resource-extracting abusers who "rape my riches, and curse me and go away," but settlers who build "cities leaping to stature," leading her in turn to "pour the tide of [her] riches in the eager lap of the world" (with those "Strong" settlers presumably claiming a rightful share of those same "riches" somewhere in the journey from one lap to another). It's not rape as long as they stick around and build communities afterwards. Or, as an old bumper sticker has it, "Please, God, give us another Prudhoe Bay – we promise not to piss it away this time."

The tangled notion of loving a place to death – waxing poetic over its pristine beauty and unspoiled state while simultaneously celebrating the extraction of every paying resource – has found new complications recently with the Pebble Mine controversy in southwest Alaska. In one corner we have the noble tradition of hard-rock mining in Alaska and the promise of jobs for locals (including many Natives); in the other we have the equally profitable and historically significant commercial salmon-fishing industry (including many Native fishermen). Communities and families are split. A rich white man with a hunting lodge near the proposed mine site may have been secretly funding an advertising campaign arguing against the mine on behalf of traditional Yupik subsistence. The battle is as much over what Alaska should mean as it is over tangible things like jobs, toxic run-off, and fish counts. The past is a guide not only to what we can and should do, but what we can't and shouldn't. Forty or even twenty years ago there would have been no battle. The mine would have been built with only nominal opposition from "greenies," and any effects on the fishing would have been calculated afterwards. In fact, without that lone rich white guy fighting it, doing the right thing for the wrong reasons, this mine might already have been built. And maybe that would have been the best thing for the local community, as many people believe the Red Dog Mine has been for people in northwest Alaska. But for now the battle continues, at the ballot box, in the newspapers, and in the collective Alaskan imagination.

The Pebble Mine controversy is local, unlike the long-running battle over oil-drilling in the Arctic National Wildlife Refuge, which pits the majority of Alaskans (including many Democrats) against "Outside interests," groups like the Sierra Club and the Wilderness Society, along with the majority of voters in the other forty-nine states. Apparently many Americans want to preserve, not a place they will ever visit, but a particular image of Alaska as unspoiled, pristine. No one is going to suggest putting oil wells in the middle of the Tetons, but how many Americans would object to drilling in a large, flat, empty part of, say, Wyoming? There is something very precious in the image of untouched Alaska wilderness that many Americans living on the East Coast are apparently afraid of spoiling or losing. The last chance, the last frontier, the last blank spaces on the map, the last unnamed mountains and creeks, the last great land, "the last of the lands, and the first" – this is the mythopoetic burden facing Alaskan writers today, who are not all as comfortable shouldering that burden as Service and London were one hundred years ago.

The outstanding fact of Alaskan literature is that, until recently, very little of it was written by Alaskans. Native oral tradition extends back for millennia, of course, but written literature is a European innovation, and Europeans are still relatively new to Alaska. Moreover, the ones who do show up often don't stay long. Even Jack London was only in the North for thirteen months. Despite setting parts of several novels and dozens of short stories (including most of his most popular work) in the North, and thereby creating an indelible impression of Alaska in the minds of several generations of readers, he only passed through Alaska briefly on his way into and out of the Klondike. Service was a Scotsman by birth, a Canadian immigrant, whose Yukon Territory experiences have been ruthlessly appropriated by Americans, as can be seen in any number of Alaskan tourist venues where reciting Service poetry is summer stock. Perhaps the first famous tourist writer in Alaska, whose time in the North preceded that of London and Service but whose book (*Travels in Alaska*) was only published posthumously in 1915, John Muir saw a great deal of the Alaskan coast and pioneered the ecstatic response to wild nature that would be echoed by so many later visitors to places like Glacier Bay. But he never pretended to live in Alaska, and wasn't much interested in the parts of Alaska where people did live. Rex Beach, author of *The Spoilers* and other popular novels loosely based on historical events in Alaska, actually lived in Nome for a while during the boom days, and wrote out of a great deal of first-hand experience. Of course, that didn't prevent him from choosing California locations when he made film versions of *The Spoilers*, thereby helping inaugurate two parallel traditions: most of the famous books about Alaska are written by Outsiders, and most of the popular movies about Alaska are filmed Outside.

For one hundred years the location for such films was usually California (although nowadays it's more likely to be British Columbia or New Zealand). There has long been a special connection between California and Alaska, exemplified in the careers of Muir, London, and Beach. Seattle may have been the commercial gateway to Alaska, but California is the true anima to the animus of Alaska. One of the things that Muir so loved about Glacier Bay was that he saw it as a glimpse into the past of his beloved Yosemite and the doomed Hetch Hetchy. As he heads north in *Travels in Alaska*, he follows the course of the long, slow "Gold Rush" that began in central California in 1849 and worked its way north along the spine of the continent over the ensuing half-century. London explored the contrasts between California and Alaska through his two dog novels, *The Call of the Wild* and *White Fang*, with the two dogs' careers moving in opposite directions like passing trains headed north and south. The neglected London novel *Burning Daylight* is actually split between the North and northern California, the Klondike and the Valley of the Moon, with London's own preference shown in the final scene when the hero actually re-buries the gold he discovers on his California ranch in order to preserve his Eden. As much as movie versions of Nome may have tried to make Alaska look like just another part of the American West, London is right about there being important differences. As one heads northward out of the populous Canadian southlands on what used to be called "the Al-Can Highway," somewhere in northern BC or the southern Yukon there is a transition – no more horses to speak of, fewer hayfields or pastures, fewer fences, almost no windmills or silos or other signs of agriculture – and at some point the traveler realizes that he has passed from agriculture and ranching into a hunting and gathering landscape. The West becomes the North. Both have plenty of wide-open spaces, but the differences, though subtle, are profound. Sometimes it takes years of close observation to figure out those differences.

Rex Beach may only have spent a few years in Nome, but that's a lot compared to the residence of many other Outside writers who have set books in Alaska. There are enough novels by big-name visitors to fill a semester of Contemporary American Fiction, from Norman Mailer's *Why Are We in Vietnam?* and John Hawkes' *Adventures in the Alaska Skin Trade* to Ken Kesey's *Sailor Song*, Robert Olen Butler's *Sun Dogs*, T.C. Boyle's *Drop City*, and Michael Chabon's *The Yiddish Policemen's Union*. (Boyle's novel actually reverses the trajectory of London's *Burning Daylight*, as he moves his characters north from California to Alaska in search of a new Eden.) For the less highbrow there are Louis L'Amour's *Sitka* and James Michener's *Alaska*. And who knew that Gore Vidal's first novel, *Williwaw*, was set in the waters off Alaska, the same setting chosen decades later by Martin Cruz Smith for his novel *Polar Star*? More than a quarter-century ago John McPhee's *Coming into the Country* and Joe McGinniss' *Going to Extremes* provided, between them, a broad introduction to Alaska's people (admired by McPhee, despised by McGinniss) and its natural beauty (equally appreciated by both). More recently, John Krakauer's *Into the Wild* revisited the question of what Alaska means to the rest of the country, by exploring what it meant to one doomed idealist.

That list of books might be supplemented by any number of individual stories, poems, and essays written about Alaska by visiting writers. (One might start with essays and stories by Barry Lopez, or Leslie Marmon Silko's "Storyteller") One anthology, John A. Murray's *A Republic of Rivers: Three Centuries of Nature Writing from Alaska and the Yukon*, reaches back to include reports from some of the earliest European visitors, many of whom left their names on the landscape and wildlife, people like Steller, Cook, Vancouver, Mackenzie, von Kotzebue, Wrangell, and Dall. But most of the anthologies of Alaskan writing that have emerged over the last twenty years include a number of genuine sourdoughs, people who lived long enough in the state not only to qualify for their share of oil royalties through the annual Permanent Fund Dividend, but also to qualify for something less tangible: the right to speak as a resident. No one's quite sure how long it takes, exactly, but in a place where white people generally introduce themselves on public occasions by name and how long they've lived there, we have finally built up a respectable body of home-grown writing.

The boom-and-bust cycle of the Alaskan economy has responded to fluctuations in the price of gold, furs, salmon, crabs, and other resources, but it has been primarily shaped by three major events: the turn-of-the-century gold rushes, World War II at mid-century, and the pipeline boom in the 1970s. London, Service, and Beach depicted the early boom, and McPhee and McGinniss documented the craziness of pipeline construction, but the middle years were relatively quiet, and the literary output from those years is fairly sparse. Robert Marshall, one of the founders of the Wilderness Society and a US Forest Service employee who rose to the post of head of recreation management before dying at the age of 38, came north in 1929, ostensibly pursuing research on the tree line in the Brooks Range, but actually just looking for an excuse to explore one of the last remaining blank places on the map. He fell in love with the central Brooks Range and also with the people of its few isolated communities, and wrote two wonderful books about them. *Arctic Village*, first published in 1933, is a quasi-anthropological account of the small village of Wiseman, Alaska, in the southern slopes of the Brooks Range, near what would become the route of the Alyeska Pipeline decades later. Marshall dedicated the book "To the people of the Koyukuk who have made for themselves the happiest civilization of which I have knowledge," and shared his royalties with all the citizens of Wiseman. *Alaska Wilderness: Exploring the Central Brooks Range*, a posthumous collection of Marshall's journal entries, was first published in 1956 as a deliberately political act, designed to inspire preservation efforts on behalf of what became Gates of the Arctic National Park and Preserve.

Margaret Murie's memoir, *Two in the Far North*, was first published just one year later (1957), and became in subsequent editions an increasingly political book, arguing for the creation and continued preservation of what became the Arctic National Wildlife Refuge. Murie's Alaskan credentials were impeccable; she came north at the age of 5, traveled alone from Fairbanks to Valdez at the age of 9, was the first woman to graduate from the University of Alaska (then called the Alaska Agricultural College and School of Mines), married the very influential wildlife biologist Olaus Murie and traveled with him on his research, and continued to visit the state and advocate conservation until her death in 2003. Her other Alaskan book, *Island Between*, is a work of popular narrative anthropology that has not held up well against contemporary standards of ethnological practice. But her memoir is a thoroughly engaging account of traveling across Alaska by dogsled, horse-drawn sledge, steamboat, outboard, and eventually airplane, spanning most of the twentieth century, and inspiring readers with its cheerful optimism and evident affection for the people and animals of the North.

The work of Marshall and Murie has been kept alive by new editions, as their politics and prose have been freshly appreciated by new generations of tourists and conservationists. The woman who was sometimes called "Alaska's first novelist," however, has not been so lucky. Barrett Willoughby published several popular volumes of fiction and nonfiction in the 1920s and 1930s, but her romantic novels are entirely out of print. A 1994 biography by Nancy Ferrell has the potential to stir up some renewed interest, but for now Willoughby remains relatively unknown, despite the unique stature of being a successful mid-century woman novelist living in Alaska.

A fourth writer to emerge from the years before the pipeline boom, and the one who has achieved the highest literary reputation of any Alaskan writer, is the poet and memoirist John Haines. Haines first came to Alaska as a navy veteran shortly after the end of World War II, with the twin goals of getting closer to nature and improving his painting. But in the course of homesteading, learning to trap for furs, and honing the other skills necessary to survive in rural Alaska, Haines found his voice as a poet, and left painting for writing. His publishing career began slowly, with slim collections of short poems that for many readers perfectly evoke the landscape of interior Alaska. *Winter News* (1966) distilled the experiences of almost two decades into brief moments of quiet, elegiac insight that were thoroughly at odds with the long, loose lines and hip subject matter of much 1960s poetry. In recent years Haines' poetry has become more explicitly political, but looking back from this vantage one can see that the politics was there all along, grounded in the essentials of human existence, but no less crucial to Haines' overall vision than the precise descriptions of land and animals. *The Owl in the Mask of the Dreamer* (1993), including much of the poetry in Haines' earlier books and adding dozens of new and uncollected poems, won the William Stafford Memorial Poetry Award and brought Haines to the attention of a new generation of readers. *New Poems 1980–1988* also won important awards, and Haines continues to publish new poetry well into his eighties. Haines is also an influential prose writer, and the memoir *The Stars, the Snow, the Fire* (1989) is perhaps as widely read as his poetry.

The quiet of postwar Alaskan life gave way in the 1970s to the frenzied construction of "the Pipeline" from Prudhoe Bay to Valdez, made possible by almost equally frenzied political negotiations. The Alaska Native Claims Settlement Act (ANCSA), passed in 1971, was an ambitious attempt to replace the treaty/reservation system with a modern "corporate" approach to indigenous land claims. In 1980 President Carter signed the Alaska National Interest Lands Conservation Act (ANILCA), which doubled the size of the total US park and refuge systems and tripled its official wilderness area. These two pieces of legislation took the vast majority of Alaskan land out of a post-territorial limbo and parceled it out among the federal government, Native corporations, and the state, which received by far the smallest piece of the pie. Control of huge stretches of Alaska was now explicitly in the hands of either its original inhabitants or bureaucrats in offices thousands of miles away. The state was left wondering whether it wasn't still a kind of protectorate, and it didn't take long before a jurisdictional impasse ensued regarding fish and game management.

Between the passing of ANCSA and that of ANILCA, the 1976 "Molly Hootch decision" (*Tobeluk v. Lind*) mandated the establishment of high schools to serve Native students in up to 126 Alaskan villages. A huge chunk of the new oil money was invested by the state in school construction and staffing, and there was widespread

excitement about preserving and extending Native languages and traditional practices. For the first three-quarters of the twentieth century Alaskan schools were mostly
segregated, with local Native schools seldom continuing past the eighth grade. The
legacy of the powerful missionary Sheldon Jackson made itself felt throughout the
Alaskan territorial government, resulting in a vocational boarding school approach to
secondary education and a rigorous enforcement of assimilation that required Native
students to be punished for speaking their first languages. From 1947 to 1965 one
lone boarding school, in Sitka, served as the high school option for all Native students
across Alaska, while thousands of other Native children were sent to Bureau of Indian
Affairs boarding schools in Oregon and Oklahoma. Many indigenous languages and
dialects almost disappeared during this period. The new schools built after "Molly
Hootch" and the expansion of the University of Alaska system into rural sites across
Alaska laid the groundwork for a renaissance of Native literature that has built
momentum slowly but steadily over the last thirty years.

Indigenous peoples in Alaska include many distinct cultural groups, speaking more
than a dozen different languages and dialects. The commonly used term "Alaska
Native," like the term "Native American," is a political convenience that blurs a
wide range of differences in order to promote useful alliances. Preferred practice in
Alaska (as in the Lower 48) when talking about individual writers is to use more
specific cultural affiliations, including (but not limited to) Tlingits in southeast
Alaska, Yup'ik in southwest Alaska, Inupiak in northwest and northern Alaska, and
Dena'ina or Athabaskan in much of central Alaska. The cultural variations among
indigenous Alaskans are enormous, including everything from traditional foods and
food-gathering/hunting practices to language, clothing, kinship practices, and, nowadays, economic investment in different Native corporations. Because Christian
churches agreed early on to divide Alaska Natives up rather than compete for converts
(much as the Pope divided the Old and New Worlds between Spain and Portugal
along a particular longitude, thus ensuring that Brazil would end up speaking
Portuguese), there are also denominational differences strongly associated with geography and now deeply embedded in local traditions.

The previous generation of Alaska Native elders and many who are still alive today
grew up speaking only their traditional languages, and a great deal of both traditional
and original material has been gathered by ethnographers in recent years in collaboration with those elders. One of the most ambitious of such projects has been undertaken
by Tlingit writer Nora Marks Dauenhauer and her husband Richard (Dauenhauer and
Dauenhauer 1987). It was the first in an ongoing series of publications of Tlingit
stories in bilingual scholarly editions. (Both Dauenhauers are distinguished poets as
well.) Two other recent anthologies provide scholarly and entertaining versions of
traditional stories from two other large Native groups connected by language and
culture: *Our Voices: Native Stories of Alaska and the Yukon* (Ruppert and Bernet 2001)
is primarily Athabascan narrative, and *Words of the Real People: Alaska Native Literature
in Translation* (2007) collects stories originally told in Eskimo-Aleut languages. One
of the elders included in *Our Voices* whose versions of traditional stories have been

especially influential, both within and beyond his own community in south-central Alaska, is Peter Kalifornsky. *A Dena'ina Legacy – K'tl'egh'I Sukdu: The Collected Writings of Peter Kalifornsky*, published in 1991 just two years before his death, is another scholarly, bilingual edition that makes his work useful to both casual readers and scholars.

In addition to Nora Dauenhauer, perhaps the best Tlingit poet is Robert Davis, who recently added his wife's surname, Hoffman. Although he is doing more visual art than writing these days, and has published only one book of poetry, the 1986 *SoulCatcher*, Davis Hoffman's influence has been maintained through reprintings of his poems in a number of anthologies. "Saginaw Bay: I Keep Going Back," a powerful blend of personal and cultural history ranging in tone from anger to celebration and from humor to mystical peace, is especially resonant, and is a poem that readers will frequently go back to. Perhaps the most widely read Alaska Native poet is Athabascan Mary TallMountain, who was taken to California when she was a child, but who returned later in life to re-establish her personal and poetic roots in interior Alaska. Among a younger generation of Native poets the most promising is Joan Kane, who recently received a Whiting Writers' Award and has published her first collection, *The Cormorant Hunter's Wife* (2009). Her poem "The Relation" is a good example of how Kane's dense and toothy writing is always exploring boundaries – between ocean and shore, water and ice, human and animal, past and present, city and village, life and death.

Much of the best writing by Alaska Natives inhabits a cultural and literary space that might be called "autoethnography." Nora Dauenhauer uses that term to describe her mixed-genre collection *Life Woven with Song*, which includes drama and memoir as well as poetry. Beginning in the 1950s Emily Ivanoff Brown (Ticasuk) published a number of local stories from her Inupiaq community, beginning with *The Roots of Ticasuk: An Eskimo Woman's Story*. Loretta Outwater Cox has published two books based on a mixture of biography and traditional stories. *Winter Walk* recounts an epic journey on foot across Alaska in 1892, and is based on actual events in Cox's family history. *The Storyteller's Club* is framed as a group of Inupiaq women gathering regularly for tea and taking turns telling stories, which range from personal history to cultural history and mythology. Gwich'in Athabascan writer Velma Wallis began her career with two short novels based on traditional stories: *Two Old Women* and *Bird Girl and the Man Who Followed the Sun*. Her most recent book is a memoir, *Raising Ourselves*, which explores the profound challenges of growing up Native in rural Alaska in the middle of the twentieth century. Sidney Huntington's *Shadows on the Koyukuk* (written with journalist Jim Reardon) is perhaps the most widely read Native autobiography; it spans most of the twentieth century, moving in sprightly prose from Huntington's mixed-race childhood and variety of early jobs to some of the projects he took on in later life as an important Native leader. The subtitle of Huntington's book, *An Alaskan Native's Life Along the River*, is clearly echoed in the title of a more recent memoir, Jan Harper-Haines' *Cold River Spirits: The Legacy of an Athabaskan-Irish Family from Alaska's Yukon River*.

One of the best places to experience the variety of Alaska Native writing is via either of two mixed-genre and mixed-culture anthologies: *Raven Tells Stories*, edited by Joseph Bruchac with an introduction by James Ruppert; and an expanded version of a 1986 special issue of the *Alaska Quarterly Review*, published under the title *Alaska Native Writers, Storytellers, and Orators* (Spatz et al. 1999). And no discussion of Alaska Native literature would be complete without a mention of the only published work of fiction in a Native language, the 1990 novel *Elnguq*, written in Yup'ik by Anna Jacobson, and published in an English translation in 1997.

Much less noticeable than the political, economic, and social upheavals of the pipeline and its accompanying legislation, but perhaps just as influential in the long run for Alaskan writing, was the establishment of undergraduate and graduate creative writing programs, first in Fairbanks and later in Anchorage. Since the 1980s there has sprung up a corps of faculty and students (some of them even raised in Alaska) who are able to compete in quality if not always in sales with those famous Outside writers discussed earlier. Even within the historically mobile populations of the American West, Alaska's non-Native population is highly transient, and of course many students come to Alaska from elsewhere and go elsewhere when they graduate, so the residency period required to be an "Alaskan poet" is probably shorter than in other places, even other places in the highly transient West. However, John Morgan, Tom Sexton, and Peggy Shumaker have each put in their "twenty years" and more, and trained up another entire generation of poets behind them even while they were writing their own excellent poems. (Shumaker has also published a lyrical memoir, *Just Breathe Normally* [2008], that links the two halves of her life in Arizona and Alaska.) Jerah Chadwick taught and wrote in the Aleutians for twenty years, and although he has left Alaska, his poems are a moving legacy of life in one of the farthest corners of the state. Although he has only lived in the North for ten years, another professor, Derrick Burleson, has produced an impressive body of Alaskan poetry, including a series of poems addressing the issue of climate change in the North. Right now there are so many good poets working in Alaska that there's no room here to discuss them all. A good place to start would be an anthology such as *The Alaska Reader* (Hanley and Kremers 2005) or *Crosscurrents North* (Holleman and Coray 2008), both of which include prose as well as poetry and serve as handy cross-sections of contemporary Alaskan writing.

As I've been asserting throughout this essay, there are two ways to be an Alaskan writer – living there and writing about it. I listed above some of the many Outside authors who have published books set in Alaska, but I've also been taking for granted the fact that the Alaskan writers I've discussed have been writing *about* Alaska. Indeed, it turns out that there is relatively little writing by Alaskans that does *not* feature Alaska in some form, even if it's a fictionalized historical-fantasy version such as in Elyse Guttenberg's *Sunder, Eclipse, and Seed*, a post-apocalyptic future version like that in Michael Armstrong's *After the Zap*, or a far-future/alternative world version like in the graphic novel *Raven's Children* by Layla Marie Lawlor. One science fiction writer who has received a lot of critical attention recently, David Marusek, does not often write about a recognizably Alaskan landscape, and certainly most writers living in Alaska occasionally turn to other locales. But the literature associated most strongly with Alaska is, not surprisingly, set in Alaska.

Moreover, much of the best writing by Alaskans in the last thirty years is in the genre of nonfiction prose, or "creative nonfiction" to use the fashionable term. Such attempts to capture the "really real" Alaska resonate strongly with readers everywhere. Former journalist Dan O'Neill has written two books looking at Alaska's history – or three, if we extend Alaskan history back into the last ice age. *The Last Giant of Beringea* follows the life and career of geologist Dave Hopkins as a device to explore the pursuit of knowledge about the Bering Sea land bridge. *The Firecracker Boys* describes Project Chariot, a plan by Edward Teller and the Atomic Energy Commission in the late 1950s to use nuclear bombs to create a deep-water harbor in northwest Alaska. It seems incredible to us now that such a project could have come so close to fulfillment, but it was seen at the time as crucial to making the case for the peaceful use of atomic energy, and why should there be any more opposition to exploding nukes in rural Alaska than in rural Nevada or on an atoll in the south Pacific? *A Land Gone Lonesome* is O'Neill's most personal book, an exploration by canoe of empty stretches of Yukon River shoreline that were once busy with goldminers. In all three books O'Neill provides entertaining insight into aspects of Alaskan history (and prehistory) that have been often overlooked.

Another multi-book writer who has worked along the border between journalism and personal experience is Jennifer Brice. *The Last Settlers* is an account of two families who were among the last to take advantage of federal laws permitting homesteading on free land. A version of the Homestead Act endured in Alaska until the 1980s, but the two families profiled by Brice offer very different versions of the pioneer spirit. No book I know of addresses more directly the paradoxes of Alaska's place in the American Dream. Her second book, *Unlearning to Fly*, is a memoir of growing up in Fairbanks, with special attention to her complex relationship with the myth and reality of the Alaskan bush pilot.

Nick Jans and Sherry Simpson, both regular contributors to *Alaska Magazine*, have published collections of essays that penetrate the stereotypes about Alaska, turning them inside out to show both their enduring power and their profound limitations. In addition to the short essays making up Jans's several collections, he also wrote *The Grizzly Maze: Timoth Treadwell's Fatal Obsession with Alaskan Bears*, which makes a nice contrasting companion piece to the Werner Herzog film *Grizzly Man* and even to Krakauer's *Into the Wild*. Jans, like many Alaskans, has little patience for those who would romanticize the Alaskan experience to the point of recklessly endangering their lives. One of the essays in Simpson's most recent book, *The Accidental Explorer*, takes a similarly critical view of people like Timothy Treadwell and Christopher McCandless. Simpson's roots are in Juneau, but she spent many years in both Fairbanks and Anchorage, and her essays are set in locales ranging from far southeast to farthest north Alaska. Her sense of humor is exquisite, and by frequently directing it at herself she manages to avoid the melodramatic self-importance that too often creeps into personal-experience essays about Alaska.

One of the best and most controversial Alaskan writers is Richard Nelson, who as an anthropologist spent years studying Inupiak and Koyukon Athabaskan communities. His early scholarly work evolved into more creative endeavors, including the book and five-part video series entitled *Make Prayers to the Raven*. In 1989 he published *The Island Within*, a sort of cross between Thoreau's *Walden* and Faulkner's "The Bear," with a healthy dose of *Lame Deer, Seeker of Visions*. The book recounts a year's worth of visits to an island near his home in Sitka, some of those trips made for the purposes of hunting, and the hunting experiences always powerfully informed by what Nelson had learned from Native elders. The similarities to *Lame Deer* are what make Nelson relatively controversial: although he is generally careful about qualifying what he says regarding traditional Native beliefs, his position as a white outsider makes everything he says on the subject suspect for some readers. Given Nelson's enthusiasm for the natural world and willingness to express his views in strong language, perhaps another apt comparison would be to Canadian writer and activist Farley Mowat.

A different kind of controversy is engendered in three memoirs by Marybeth Holleman, Carolyn Kremers, and Eva Saulitis. Holleman's *The Heart of the Sound* describes events in the aftermath of the Exxon Valdez oil spill, among them her deepening romance with a spill recovery crusader. Kremers' *Place of the Pretend People* is, like Nelson's writing, deeply informed by traditional beliefs of the Native people among whom she lived (in her case Yup'ik people in southwest Alaska), and it also details a romance that takes place against a dramatic backdrop full of iconic Alaskan images. Saulitis' *Leaving Resurrection* intercuts events in her personal life with her work studying orcas in Prince William Sound. All three of these memoirs walk the same challenging line, it seems to me, in not merely setting their authors' lives against the backdrop of Alaska, but claiming that those lives and that place are inextricably intertwined. When an author can pull it off, it makes for powerful regionalist writing, maybe even the best kind of writing about place. But such an author always risks the sentimentalism of finding significance in one's life by mere association with dramatic events like the Exxon Valdez spill or charismatic megafauna like wolves and killer whales.

Besides memoir, the other genre in which Alaskan writers are currently very productive is detective fiction. Dana Stabenow is the most prolific, with her most popular series, the Kate Shugak mysteries, at fifteen volumes and counting. She also has several books in another detective series set in Alaska and three books in a science fiction series. Sue Henry is another writer with a popular detective series, at half a dozen books. Both Henry and Stabenow have connections to the creative writing program at the University of Alaska Anchorage, which has long been much more supportive of genre fiction than the older (and some would say stuffier) creative writing program at the University of Alaska Fairbanks. (In the interest of full disclosure, I should point out that I teach at UAF.) As mentioned above, those two programs between them have nurtured many of the best writers now living in Alaska. It will be interesting to watch what happens with those programs and their students as they go through changes such as Anchorage's shift to a low-residency program and Fairbanks' recent promotion of a professor who has published "genre fiction."

A relatively recent novel that is not afraid to take on controversial questions is Cindy Dyson's *And She Was* (2006). Dyson has Alaskan roots, although she has not lived there in some time, and in setting her first-person novel about a young blonde (her hair color is crucial) woman in Unalaska against the backdrop of 250 years of Aleut history, she engages some very big questions regarding who should be telling whose story. She makes it clear that her protagonist is an outsider, a highly flawed character who is drawn into some mysterious and unsettling aspects of Aleut history (which remain the subject of scholarly controversy) while wrestling with her own demons. And she creates some engaging and also highly flawed Aleut characters. For all its feminist and anti-racist themes, the novel does not preach, or neatly resolve difficult issues. Some readers will struggle with the decision by Dyson's sympathetic characters to respond to violence with violence, while other readers will balk at Dyson's enfolding of Aleut cultural struggles into the search for selfhood of one particular white woman.

The best novel so far written by an Alaskan, and certainly the one that has received the most critical attention, is Seth Kantner's *Ordinary Wolves*. This coming-of-age-in-the-bush story is honest and complex, and serves as a provocative introduction to many important issues about life in Alaska in the twenty-first century. Kantner's protagonist Cutuk is a white kid who lives a version of the traditional Native subsistence life, and must work through profound self-loathing due to his father's scorn for modern Western culture and the local Eskimo kids' scorn for a bush kid who can't play basketball and doesn't share their admiration for Western culture. The gritty, often horrifying, details of growing up in rural Alaska – drug and alcohol abuse, routine violence including rape and suicide – make up some of the most compelling passages of the book. And if this unflattering portrait of village life were not controversial enough, the fact that is presented from an inside-out white-kid perspective adds a turn of the screw. Another tricky issue that Kantner addresses head on is hunting, and in particular that touchstone of liberal sensibilities, the hunting of wolves, which we witness from the perspectives of both hunter and hunted. Cutuk's mentor is a skilled wolf hunter, and although Cutuk swears after his first snowmachine-powered kill that he will take no more wolves, at the end of the book he is still a hunter, still proud of his skills and determined to survive by shooting caribou and moose. Because Kantner's life parallels Cutuk's in many ways, *Ordinary Wolves* has frequently been taken for a *roman-à-clef* or even an autobiography, but Kantner recently published a memoir, *Shopping for Porcupine*, that should help readers distinguish author from character.

Besides Kantner there are two more double-genre-threat writers that should be included in the list of Alaska's best. John Straley, who served as Alaska State Writer from 2006 to 2008, has written six books in the Cecil Younger detective series, starting with *The Woman Who Married a Bear* in 1992. Cecil Younger is about as different from Stabenow's Kate Shugak as two Alaskan private detectives could be, and Straley is as focused on setting as Stabenow is on plot. Straley recently published a historical novel called *The Big Both Ways* that moves north from Washington to Alaska, and indeed all of his writing illustrates how southeast Alaska is metaphorically as well as geographically halfway between Seattle and Fairbanks. Straley's most recent book is a collection of poetry, *The Rising and the Rain*, the title of which reveals that his poetry, like his fiction, is rooted in a powerful sense of place.

Straley's successor as Alaska State Writer, current honoree Nancy Lord, has just published her fourth book of nonfiction, and has also published three short story collections. Each of the nonfiction books is very different from the others, but all four showcase her profound understanding of Alaskan life along with a deep humility in the face of the complexities of that life. *Beluga Days* is a compelling exploration of human interaction with one particularly charismatic species, but the perspective is never sentimental. (The chapter entitled "The Green Machine" is a painful depiction of the bureaucracy of environmental activism.) *Green Alaska* looks back at the 1899 Harriman expedition, exploring changes in Alaska over the succeeding hundred years and providing a fascinating portrait of nature writer John Burroughs alongside his western counterpart John Muir. *Fish Camp* and her newest book, *Rock, Water, Wild: An Alaskan Life*, are her most personal books, but even these memoirs are not particularly intimate, compared for instance to most of the memoirs I have discussed above. Lord's focus is always outward, on landscape, history, animals, cultures, and the web of human and nonhuman interaction; when she talks about herself, it is generally only to provide us with a sense of who our witness is and how her view might be shaping what we see. Among the many excellent stories in Lord's three fiction collections I'll mention only one, the title story of her book *Survival*, which gives us a female protagonist in a condensed version of the Christopher McCandless story several years *before* McCandless made himself famous by dying in Alaska.

Just as Alaska's place in the American imagination is secure, and is not likely to melt away even if the polar ice cap does, so at this point is Alaskan literature firmly established, and there is plenty of material waiting for scholars. To date there has only been one book-length scholarly treatment of Alaskan writing: Susan Kollin's *Nature's State: Imagining Alaska as the Last Frontier*. A highly readable piece of cultural criticism, this book is an excellent place to begin talking about what Alaska means in the American imagination. For a critic of Western literature, two essays may be of particular theoretical interest: Sherrill E. Grace's "Comparing Mythologies: Ideas of West and North" and Aron Senkpiel's "From the Wild West to the Far North: Literary Representations of North American's Last Frontier." Both essays by Canadian critics contrast the Canadian "northern" with the American western, but much of what they say about northern Canadian literature applies to Alaskan literature as well.

Grace contrasts the "meta-narrative" of the West, "the garden/playground of youth and individuality, of freedom and adventure or bountiful fertility," with the "meta-narrative" of the North, which is "inseparable from the terror of survival on the one hand, and the power of vision on the other" (1991: 254). The genre of the western grew up during the Romantic period, and is deeply infused with its characteristic optimism. True, the western came of age only after the frontier had been declared "closed," but the result is a built-in nostalgia, a longing for the days when the frontier was open-ended and anything was possible (for a white man with a gun and a horse, anyway). The "northern" was not born until after the Turner thesis, and is a child of the Naturalist period rather than the Romantic period. There never was an endless frontier off to the north (except in the hollow-world fantasies of Edgar Rice Burroughs). The north ends in a wall of ice. This is why *McTeague* has always seemed to me the most "northern" of all American westerns: Death Valley in that novel's final scene is reminiscent of Jack London's "White Silence," a blankness that will never be conquered by any pioneer spirit, a desert that can never be made to bloom by hardy settlers. The last section of that novel might as well be titled "Two in the Far West," with gold fever substituting for cabin fever.

If it is in the trope of the desert that West meets North, then the western and the northern are both built upon an essentially imaginative space. A desert is defined by its inhospitality to humans, and one of the eternal mysteries of the desert for newcomers who are simultaneously drawn to and repelled by it is the inexplicable fact that people do live there, and have always lived there. Large, intact communities of Native people survive in those places that Europeans never really wanted and so never got around to taking away, places such as Navajo country and most of rural Alaska. If the genre of the "northern" necessarily involves confronting terror and invoking visions, as Grace claims, then perhaps that genre must exist in tension with another way of writing about the North, a story that sees the ice not as a desert but as a refuge; not as a wall but as a passage. This is the direction that Alaskan literature is moving today, with the balance of literary power shifting from "the last frontier" towards "the center of the world" to which we "keep going back," as Robert Davis Hoffman puts it. In the end, once again, is our beginning.

REFERENCES AND FURTHER READING

Brice, Jennifer. (1998). *The Last Settlers*. Pittsburgh: Duquesne University Press.

Bruchac, Joseph, ed. (1991). *Raven Tells Stories: An Anthology of Alaska Native Writing*. Greenfield Center, NY: Greenfield Review.

Dauenhauer, Nora Marks, and Richard Dauenhauer, eds. (1987). *Haa Shuká, Our Ancestors: Tlingit Oral Narratives*. Seattle: University of Washington Press. http://www.ipl.org/div/natam/bin/browse.pl/B214.

Ferrell, Nancy. (1994). *Barrett Willoughby: Alaska's Forgotten Lady*. Fairbanks: University of Alaska Press.

Fienup-Riordan, Ann, and Lawrence D. Kaplan, eds. (2007). *Words of the Real People: Alaska Native Literature in Translation*. Fairbanks: University of Alaska Press.

Grace, Sherrill E. (1991). Comparing Mythologies: Ideas of West and North. In Robert Lecker, coordinating ed., *Borderlands: Essays in Canadian–American Relations*, pp. 243–62. Toronto: ECW Press.

Haines, John. (1992). *The Stars, the Snow, the Fire: Twenty-Five Years in the Alaska Wilderness* [1989]. New York: Simon & Schuster.

Haines, John. (1996). *The Owl in the Mask of the Dreamer: Collected Poems* [1993]. St. Paul, MN: Graywolf.

Hanley, Anne, and Carolyn Kremers, eds. (2005). *The Alaska Reader: Voices from the North*. Golden, CO: Fulcrum.

Holleman, Marybeth, and Anne Coray, eds. (2008). *Crosscurrents North: Alaskans on the Environment*. Fairbanks: University of Alaska Press.

Kantner, Seth. (2004). *Ordinary Wolves*. Minneapolis: Milkweed.

Kollin, Susan. (2001). *Nature's State: Imagining Alaska as the Last Frontier*. Chapel Hill: University of North Carolina Press.

Lord, Nancy. (2004). *Beluga Days: Tracking a White Whale's Truths*. Cambridge, MA: Counterpoint.

Marshall, Robert. (1991). *Arctic Village* [1933]. Fairbanks: University of Alaska Press.

Marshall, Robert. (2005). *Alaska Wilderness: Exploring the Central Brooks Range* [1956]. Berkeley: University of California Press.

McPhee, John. (1978). *Coming into the Country*. New York: Farrar, Straus & Giroux.

Murie, Margaret. (1962). *Two in the Far North*. New York: Knopf. [First published 1957; repr. in multiple expanded edns.]

Nelson, Richard. (1991). *The Island Within* [1989]. New York: Vintage.

O'Neill, Dan. (2007). *The Firecracker Boys: H-Bombs, Inupiat Eskimos, and the Roots of the Environmental Movement*. New York: Basic Books.

Ruppert, James, and John W. Bernet. (2001). *Our Voices: Native Stories of Alaska and the Yukon*. Lincoln: University of of Nebraska Press.

Senkpiel, Aron. (1992). From the Wild West to the Far North: Literary Representations of America's Last Frontier. In Eric Heyne, ed., *Desert, Garden, Margin, Range: Literature on the American Frontier*, pp. 133–42. New York: Twayne.

Straley, John. (1992). *The Woman who Married a Bear*. New York: Soho Press.

Spatz, Ronald, Patricia H. Partnow, and Jeane Breinig, eds. (1999). *Alaska Native Writers, Storytellers, and Orators: The Expanded Edition*. Anchorage: Alaska Review.

10
Chronotopes of the Asian American West

Hsuan L. Hsu

Although historically the largest concentration of Asian Americans has been in the western states, they have been written out of dominant narratives of the region. When they are represented, it is often through stereotypes such as the "Heathen Chinee," Charlie Chan, the "Yellow Peril," the model minority, or the laundrymen, prostitutes, and cooks that infuse western settings with "local color." If the frontiersman was represented as a boisterous, sociable, nationally representative personality, the Chinaman was, by contrast, essentially foreign and "inscrutable." This absence in the cultural imaginary reflects (and has enabled) the history of exploitation and exclusion inflicted upon Asian Americans, which included the coolie trade, Exclusion acts, lynchings, Chinese purges, discriminatory wages, prohibitions on testimony, internment, and housing discrimination. Whether or not they contain any truth with regard to other groups, frontier stereotypes such as freedom of movement, voluntary self-reinvention, individualism, and westwardness have seldom applied to Asian immigrants and their descendants.

Despite their cultural marginalization, however, Asian Americans have played crucial roles in the development of the US West. As Glen Mimura writes, "from the mid-nineteenth century until the Second World War, migrant labor from China, Japan, the Philippines, Korea, and India was fundamental to the plantation economy of Hawai'i, to building the railroads, and to the economic miracle of West Coast agricultural production" (2009: 1). For well over a century, Asian and Asian American authors have written from marginalized spaces whose very existence challenges familiar western myths. The spaces in which Asian American bodies appear – characterized by captivity, coerced mobility, extraterritorial violence, and cross-racial affiliation – are situated on the far side of the frontier myth of "regeneration through violence"

A Companion to the Literature and Culture of the American West, First Edition. Edited by Nicolas S. Witschi.
© 2011 Blackwell Publishing Ltd. Published 2011 by Blackwell Publishing Ltd.

(Slotkin 2000: 5). I will call these situations "chronotopes" of the Asian American West, drawing on Mikhail Bakhtin's term for the historically contingent "intrinsic connectedness of temporal and spatial relationships that are artistically represented in literature" (1981: 84). While the frontier is already a culturally valorized chronotope featuring open space, linear progression, and a regeneration of national ideals, my use of the term aims to highlight the racial specificity of chronotopic experience: different groups can experience the same space as open or constrained, liberating or paralyzing, public or agoraphobic. Without attempting a comprehensive survey, this chapter examines Asian American experiences of space that have been marginalized by master-narratives of frontier exceptionalism and westward expansion.

Captivity

Whereas the West is popularly associated with the suspension of law that led to conflicts between vigilante heroes and gangs of outlaws, Asian Americans in the region have been targeted by a series of laws restricting immigration and denying the positive protections of US citizenship. Perhaps the most glaring examples of Asian American narratives effaced by the frontier myth are those of institutionalized captivity in which subjects were detained not for breaking the law, but rather because the law construed them as excluded aliens or potential enemies. By contrast with frontier images of movement across a vast expanse, captivity writings focus on the slow passage of time as isolated subjects cope with their circumscribed environments.

During the Exclusion era, when western novels and films were propagating images of vast frontier lands, more than 175,000 Chinese immigrants were detained on Angel Island. The poems that detainees inscribed on the walls of their barracks between 1910 and 1940 represent San Francisco Bay not in terms of commerce, mobility, or natural beauty, but through "anti-pastoral" (see Bennett 2001) motifs that expose how nature was utilized for surveillance and control: "I wish to call to the earth, but the earth does not answer. / The trees are also gloomy outside the prison; a hundred birds cry mournfully. / Clouds and mists enshroud the mountain-side; a thousand animals, startled, flee" ("Imprisonment in the Wooden Building," in Lai et al. 1980: 140). Another piece, titled "Crude Poem Inspired by the Landscape," begins: "The ocean encircles a lone peak. / Rough terrain surrounds this prison. / There are few birds flying over the cold hills" (Lai et al. 1980: 128). The open expanses and rugged terrain that have made Angel Island a popular state park appeared to captives as natural extensions of their prison walls.

The War Relocation Authority's attempts to mask the horrors of internment with notions of "colonists" moving into a "pioneer community" in the "frontier" evokes the ironic distance between the mythical West and the experience of Japanese Americans (Streamas 2007: 175). "For internee 'pioneers,'" writes Heather Fryer, "there was no chance for the prosperity and independence that drove white settlers west – the Japanese had already made their hard-earned gains as successful immigrants" (2008: 85). Mitsuye Yamada critiques this situation by dedicating her collection of internment poems, *Camp Notes*, to "MY ISSEI PARENTS / TWICE PIONEERS (1975: n.p.). Miné Okubo's pictorial narrative, *Citizen 13660* (1946), graphically depicts the ironies of "pioneer" internment: one early image shows her family awkwardly trying on boots and broad-brimmed hats in response to instructions to "Bring work clothes suited to pioneer life" (p. 15). Familiar western topoi associated with leisure and open space, such as "[r]ace tracks and county fair grounds," were "changed overnight into assembly centers surrounded by military police and barbed wire" (p. 15). Okubo's tightly packed, claustrophobic drawings – in which numerous bodies are often crowded into the space of half a page – heighten the effect of confinement within spaces like the "whitewash[ed]" stables at Tanforan race track or the hastily constructed barracks at "Topaz, the Jewel of the desert" (p. 121).

The discomfort and the illnesses caused by western deserts, swamps, dust storms, and heat are common motifs in internment writings (see Girdner and Loftis 1969: 218; Limerick 2001: 201–13). Lawson Fusao Inada ironically juxtaposes the camps' idyllic names with their harsh terrains in "Concentration Constellation." The poem connects the sites of internment camps on a map of the western states, beginning with the "Golden State" and ending

> with *Amache*
> looming in the Colorado desert,
> *Heart Mountain* high in wide
> Wyoming, *Minidoka* on the moon
> of Idaho, then down to Utah's
> jewel of Topaz before finding
> yourself at northern California's
> frozen shore of *Tule Lake* ...

(ll. 28–35)

The constellation of "dark" locations resembles a "jagged scar" through the western states, "like the rusted wire / of a twisted and remembered fence" (ll. 38, 40–1). While these accounts of Angel Island and internment camps document situations whose social consequences extended far beyond the barracks, experiences of captivity were not unique to such exceptional locations. The following section will focus on more mundane experiences of constraint in the domestic lives of Asian immigrants.

Domesticity

Beginning with the gendered patterns of immigration and exclusion established in the nineteenth century, Asian American modes of domesticity have often deviated from the heteronormative ideal of the nuclear family. Commenting on the "bachelor communities" that resulted from restrictions on the immigration of Chinese women such as the 1875 Page Act, David Eng writes: "Physically, socially, and psychically isolated, these segregated bachelor communities might easily be thought of as 'queer' spaces institutionally barred from normative (hetero)sexual reproduction, nuclear family formations, and entitlements to community" (2001: 18). In his comprehensive historical study of such spaces, Nayan Shah similarly describes "several types of queer domesticity, such as multiple women and children living in a female-dominated household, the affiliation of vast communities of men in bunkhouses and opium dens, and common law marriages of Chinese men and fallen white women" (2001: 13). In turn, these deviant forms of domesticity made Chinese men available to perform traditionally feminized labor, working as cooks, laundrymen, and "domestics" to sustain white families. Despite different patterns of immigration, similar trends towards nonstandard kinship practices and domestic labor have developed among other Asian American immigrant groups.

The bachelor communities established in US Chinatowns by gendered exclusion laws led to widespread cases of domestic captivity. Smuggled slave girls were kept indoors to perform their work, or "rescued" and held in mission homes; though legally permitted to immigrate, merchants' wives customarily remained indoors as well. The romantic tales collected in Sui Sin Far's *Mrs. Spring Fragrance* (1912), which often feature women living in US Chinatowns, dramatize these states of domestic captivity. "The Sing Song Woman" begins with a Chinese actress "gaz[ing] up at the narrow strip of blue sky which could be seen through her window" (p. 125). In another story, a "cripple[d]" Chinese woman spends her days sitting at the window for hours "watching those who passed below and all that took place" (p. 102). Even middle-class wives are generally constrained within their homes, as we see when Far describes women leaning over their balconies to gossip while taking a break from their housework (p. 48). Although she describes the constrained spaces of Chinese domesticity in detail, Far does not directly critique genteel assumptions about "separate spheres": when Chung Kee's recently purchased wife (and "slave") is persuaded to bring her baby out to a baby show at the Presbyterian Mission school in "The Prize China Baby," both are struck and killed by a butcher's cart in the street (p. 117).

Male immigrants also performed housework, in part because the labor movement protested the hiring of Asian workers for industrial jobs. The opening episodes of Henry (Yoshitaka) Kiyama's *Four Immigrants Manga* (1931) depict four young Japanese men working as fashionable "schoolboy" servants in wealthy San Francisco households. Due to a series of comic accidents and cultural misunderstandings, they are repeatedly dismissed from these positions with the summary command: "GO HOME." While many of the dismissals result from misunderstandings (dismantling a stove in order to clean it, attempting to scrub the mistress while she is bathing), others highlight the awkwardness of western interiors for these new immigrants. For example, Frank observes: "I was impressed by American houses, but they use too much reinforced concrete. Bump into something 'n it *hurts* like crazy!!" (p. 35). Henry takes a fall on a slippery waxed floor, and has trouble when he's asked to feed a family's parrot. Ironically, these early scenes depict the most luxurious interiors in the series: later episodes show two of the immigrants, Frank and Charley, sharing a bed, while their friends enter arranged marriages and raise children in overcrowded homes.

Jade Snow Wong's *Fifth Chinese Daughter* (1945) – one of the earliest novels by an Asian American woman – presents a more hopeful picture of domestic service. The semi-autobiographical novel juxtaposes Jade Snow's coming of age with her achievement of independence from the "imprison[ing]" constraints of traditional Chinese gender roles (p. 110). Jade Snow grows up in a home located behind her father's overall factory, where "Home life and work life were … mixed together" (p. 4). Her domestic life is unpleasant: her father whips his children with cane switches economically drawn from rice sacks; her mother does piecework in the kitchen; and she performs dull household chores in exchange for money (p. 60). Initially, Jade Snow escapes this tedium vicariously, going with her mother and siblings to the movies, where "the attractions of Western life or jungle thrillers" enable them all to temporarily "forg[e]t who whey were, how hard they worked, or how pressing were their personal problems, as they share the excitement of six-shooters, posses, runaway stagecoaches, striking cobras, the unconquerable Tarzan, and organized apes" (p. 71). Ironically, it is by watching westerns, in which Chinese characters hardly ever appear, that this Chinese family living in the West "forgot who they were." Ultimately, Jade Snow escapes her household chores by doing housework for others: working in white households provides both "a solution to her money problem" and a privileged view "of the private lives of these American families" (p. 103). She subsequently pays her way through Mills College by working on the dean's household staff. While Jade Snow feels "accepted as an equal" at Mills, Wong's novel presents several details – such as the Orientalist décor of the dean's home (named "Kapiolani" as a reminder of Mills's missionary roots in Hawai'i) and an entirely Chinese kitchen staff ("some of them descendants of the first Chinese kitchen help who worked for the founders of the college") – that suggest that Wong has merely escaped into a different position as a domestic servant and culture broker (p. 158).

Housework is just one of many forms of affective labor – including nursing, "caregiving" (as depicted, for example, in Bharati Mukherjee's *Jasmine*), and sex work – disproportionately performed by Asian American and other racialized women. Heinz Insu Fenkl's autobiographical novel, *Memories of My Ghost Brother* (1996), depicts forms of affective labor situated at the threshold of imperial and "domestic" spaces in military "camptowns" that are often marginalized by both US and South Korean accounts of the Korean War. For displaced and impoverished women living in camptowns, both sex work and marriage to GIs involve costly affective labor. Under such conditions, kinship itself is subject to terrible calculations in which undesirable children are given up for adoption and even murdered in exchange for the social stability promised by marriage and "refuge migration" to the US (see Yuh 2005). "*I would learn that women – even seemingly devoted mothers – will traffic in children for the mythic promise of America. And they would all look back in regret from the shores of the Westward Land*" (Fenkl 1996: 232). Insu – the son of a military bride and her GI husband – learns of an older half-brother whom his "mother gave up for adoption as a precondition to marrying his father, who did not want to raise another man's child and who is ashamed even of his own mixed-race son." As Jodi Kim has argued (Kim 2008: 298), given the tremendous role of the more than 100,000 war brides who immigrated to the US from Korea in enabling the immigration of extended families, their affective labor and sacrificed children in the offshore bases of the US empire should be seen as constitutive factors in the history of Korean America.

Mobility

If Asian immigrants were constrained by barracks and domestic spaces, they were also, paradoxically, constrained by mobility. As Sau-Ling Wong has shown, Asian American literature's widespread depictions of movement tend to involve "subjugation, coercion, impossibility of fulfillment for self or community – in short, Necessity" (1993: 121). Wong provides an extended account of the historically specific situations – including the purges of Chinese settlements from western towns, the annexation of the Philippines, and refugee situations resulting from various foreign wars – that have imposed horizontal mobility while blocked vertical mobility for different Asian American groups. Instead of chronicling extravagant journeys of "home-seeking or home-founding," Asian American authors dramatize forms of real and metaphorical homelessness and displacement, conflating themes of mobility with "images of *immo*-bility" (1993: 122–3).

Among the earliest Asian immigrants to the US were Chinese laborers contracted to work on the transcontinental railroad from 1865 to 1869. David Eng has shown how two classic Chinese American novels – Maxine Hong Kingston's *China Men* (1977) and Frank Chin's *Donald Duk* (1991) – dramatize the erasure of these laborers from the historical record and the resulting crisis of Chinese American masculinity (Eng 2001: 35–103). While both these novels comment on the absence of Chinese Americans from the memorializing photographs of the Last Spike ceremony, Kingston provides an especially detailed account of the railroad's consequences for Chinese Americans' mobility: "While the [white] demons posed for photographs, the China Men dispersed. It was dangerous to stay. The Driving Out had begun" (p. 145). She then chronicles the wanderings of scattered railroad workers who traveled in all directions looking for work on smaller railroads, plantations, and factories. While the railroad enhanced the mobility of commodities and white Americans, its completion led to massive and widespread purges of Chinese throughout the western states. Kingston's narrator interweaves the most notorious of these incidents into a negative biography of her thinly documented ancestor Ah Goong:

> Good at hiding, disappearing – decades unaccounted for – he was not working in a mine when forty thousand chinamen were Driven Out of mining. He was not killed or kidnapped in the Los Angeles Massacre. ... He was lucky not to be in Colorado when the Denver demons burned all chinamen homes and businesses, nor in Rock Springs,

Wyoming, when the miner demons killed twenty-eight or fifty chinamen. … Ah Goong was running elsewhere during the Drivings Out of Tacoma, Seattle, Oregon City, Albania, and Marysville. The demons of Tacoma packed all its chinamen into boxcars and sent them to Portland, where they were run out of town. (p. 148)

In *The Buddha Bandits Down Highway 99*, a Beat-inspired project first performed in 1977 at California State University, Long Beach, Garrett Hongo, Alan Chong Lau, and Lawson Fusao Inada present a more hopeful picture of mobility. The collection – which presents each poet's responses to California's Route 99 – begins with Hongo invoking Whitman's "Starting from Paumanok" to insert California into both a national and geological narrative: "Starting in a long swale between the Sierras and the Coast Range, Starting from ancient tidepools of a Pleistocene sea …" (Hongo et al. 1978: n.p.). In "The Only Chinese Restaurant in Town, the Fragrance of Our History," Lau focuses on a more mundane relation to the 99, giving an account of his childhood in a small-town Chinese restaurant. "[B]eing up in the valley, 99 was more than a white line down some blacktop, it was a lifeline to the city where others of our kind thrived and prospered, at least in numbers – San Francisco" (Hongo et al. 1978: n.p.). Inada recalls the thriving folk culture of his native Fresno – "German, Italian, Russian, Greek, Portuguese, Okie, Basque, Armenian, etc." – as well as the nomination of Route 99 as the eastern boundary for the initial phase of Japanese Americans' wartime relocation. Whereas Lau represents the 99 as a "lifeline" connecting the Chinese throughout California to cultural and economic resources in San Francisco, Inada nostalgically views the highway as an equally vital lifeline for Fresno's heterogeneous working-class culture (which has since given way – also thanks to the highway – to commercial culture embodied by a new shopping mall).

Shawn Wong underscores the darker aspects of highway travel in *Homebase* (1979), an extended meditation on the forms of displacement experienced by generations of Chinese American men in the US West. Wong's narrator, Rainsford Chan, is named after a California town that no longer exists – the town his great-grandfather and other Chinese workers settled and were subsequently "driven out of" in the nineteenth century (p. 2). Nevertheless, Rainsford recalls that his father taught him to sing "Home on the Range" and indulged his interest in planes, trains, and automobiles as they traveled throughout the western states during his childhood; likewise, he imagines riding horses with his grandfather in the west (pp. 2, 52). Rainsford's own memories include iconic western landscapes such as Yosemite National Park and Mount Shasta as well as offshore stints in Guam and Hawai'i. Paradoxically, it is in these experiences of displacement and travel that Wong's narrator finds a "homebase" in the US, as he drives from town to town perceiving the ghosts of Chinese workers in the landscapes they laboriously transformed. "We are buried in every town," Wong writes. "My father is in every canyon I've journeyed into in the West" (pp. 96, 97).

Unlike Wong, the heroine of Bharati Mukherjee's *Jasmine* (1989) finds no ancestral roots in the land as she moves from Punjab to Florida, New York (where she works as an au pair), Iowa, and California. The narrator draws on frontier motifs in describing and rationalizing her series of self-reinventions (see Burkhart 2008). Leaving her disabled lover for her former employer, she observes, "It isn't guilt that I feel, it's relief. I realize I have already stopped thinking of myself as Jane. Adventure, risk, transformation: the frontier is pushing indoors through uncaulked windows" (p. 214). Yet even the western farm country of Iowa harbors "a way of life coming to an end" as finance capital, new immigrants (including Vietnamese and Hmong who have been displaced by a failed imperial war), and a new golf course revolutionize the landscape in ways that recall the (US-engineered) "Green Revolution" in the narrator's native Punjab (p. 204). Jasmine interprets her knack for leaving situations and lovers as freedom, but it is not without a melancholic undercurrent that may be traced to her early experiences of religious violence, rape, and murder. Escaping towards the "frontier," she is both the subject and object of regeneration through violence: "There are no harmless, compassionate ways to remake oneself. We murder who we were so we can rebirth ourselves in the images of dreams" (p. 25). Although Mukherjee's novel has been criticized for speaking for the position of a subaltern Indian peasant, it does draw critical connections between Punjab and the US West: "Doesn't the novel really say that the United States is just as dangerous, its educated and supposedly freer citizens just as irrational, fearful, and adrift as the people in the Punjab? Doesn't Mukherjee invite us to see Jasmine herself as a scarred and damaged survivor, incapable of the naïve and hopeful first love she offered her husband Prakash ... and deeply saddened by the compromises she makes[?]" (Chu 2000: 136).

The Circumpacific West

While his exceptionalist thesis about the individualistic, national character of the US frontier is well known, Frederick Jackson Turner elsewhere articulates a *trans-national* frontier thesis in which Pacific expansionism represents the logical extension of westward migration: "the demands for a vigorous foreign policy, for an interoceanic canal, for a revival of our power upon the seas, and for the extension of American influence to outlying islands and adjoining countries, are indications that the movement will continue" (1996: 219). As scholars have noted, Asian Americans have been situated on the geographical threshold between national, regional (western), and global aspects of capital accumulation and empire (see Eperjesi 2005; Huang 2008; Lowe 1996; Lye 2004; Palumbo-Liu 1999; Wilson and Dirlik 1995). Situating the US West (and particularly California) as a node within a larger Asia Pacific region – a region in which US naval power protects and imposes unequal circumpacific trade – makes visible both the centrality of Asians and Asian Americans to the "West" and the formative role played by offshore and "foreign" locations in the making of Asian American subjects. Whereas traditional immigrant narratives feature a developmental plot whose protagonist assimilates to national ideals, a focus on the Asia Pacific region draws attention to the "tense and tender ties" connecting the US with unevenly developed offshore spaces that sustain its economic and military dominance (Stoler 2006).

US-owned plantations began bringing Chinese, Japanese, Korean, and Filipino contract laborers to Hawai'i in the nineteenth century; by the 1920s, Asians comprised more than half of the territory's population (see Takaki 1983). Milton Murayama's *All I asking for is my body* (1975) analyzes the intersections of gender, race, and class on the "Frontier Mill Plantation" in Kahana. In an oft-cited commentary on the plantation's racial – and spatial – hierarchization of labor, Murayama writes: "It was a company town with identical company houses and outhouses, and it was set up like a pyramid. At the tip was Mr. Nelson, then the Portuguese, Spanish, and Nisei *lunas* in their nicer-looking homes, then the identical wooden frame houses of Japanese Camp, then the more run-down Filipino Camp" (p. 28). Living in a plantation town "cut off from the world," Murayama's narrator feels "like my childhood was chopped off clean" (p. 28). The remainder of the novel dramatizes how the plantation system brutalizes the body, pits Japanese and Filipino laborers against each other, and coerces the labor of Kiyo's family through an intricate system of debt, "filial piety," and family honor (p. 27). The novel concludes with Kiyo's compromised escape from the plantation: enlisting during World War II offers a way out of the plantation system, but this escape requires putting his own body on the line to defend the nation that had annexed Hawai'i as a colonial territory, and that was interning citizens of Japanese ancestry as potential traitors.

Along with Hawai'i, the US also claimed Cuba, Puerto Rico, the Philippines, and Guam as "unincorporated territories" in 1898. Although it is the least known of these overseas territories, Guam has played a particularly important role as a strategic naval base and refueling station for Pacific vessels. Craig Santos Perez's *from unincorporated territory* (2008) chronicles the subjection or "reducción" of Guam through "subduing, converting, and gathering natives" into various imperial projects as the island was colonized by Spain, the US, and Japan (p. 11). Incorporating native Chamorro words and fragmentary English phrases (and quotations), the collection of poems dramatizes both the cultural fragmentation wrought by "[t]he colonial school system of Guam" (p. 12) and the poet's own effort to create a postcolonial, heteroglossic voice adequate to the island's history. Fragmentary poems titled "from Tidelands," "from Aerial Roots," and "from Stations of Crossing" articulate a diasporic sense of identity rooted not in cultural essentialism but in natural phenomena (water, wind, light) and scattered scenes of colonial violence. The ironic title "from Stations of Crossing" alludes to the fact that the Chamorros were converted to Catholicism only to have their island serve as a "station of crossing" for successive maritime empires.

Colonial incursions have also displaced vast populations of war refugees, many of whom have immigrated to the US and other western nations. Kim Ronyoung's *Clay Walls* (1986) focuses on a Korean family living in exile in Los Angeles. The novel documents early Korean immigrants' economic and affective involvement in struggle against Japanese colonialism, as Haesu and her husband Chun open up their home to meetings of Korean patriots attempting to support the government-in-exile. Barred by the 1913 Alien Land Law from buying a home in the US (except through the proxy of a white family friend), Haesu arranges to buy a plot of land in northern Korea. While Haesu's hopes for the future rest on Korean independence, the nation's partition after World War II results in North Korea's seizure of her land in Qwaksan. As Haesu's dream of returning to Korea as a landowner is foreclosed, her children continue to struggle with racial discrimination in the US.

Whereas *Clay Walls* evokes the hope of exiled Korean nationalists working to liberate their homeland, lê thi diem thúy's *The Gangster We are All Looking For* (2003) focuses on the feelings of displacement, deracination, and loss that are integral to diasporic experiences. The novel commences with a series of relocations that destabilize the concept of home:

> Linda Vista, with its rows of yellow houses, is where we eventually washed to shore. Before Linda Vista, we lived in the Green Apartment on Thirtieth and Adams, in Normal Heights. Before the Green Apartment, we lived in the Red Apartment on Forty-ninth and Orange, in East San Diego. Before the Red Apartment we weren't a family like we are a family now. We were in separate places, waiting for each other. Ma was standing on a beach in Vietnam while Ba and I were in California … (p. 3)

The landscape of southern California is saturated with traces of loss incurred overseas. Even an idyllic billboard – one of the first things the narrator sees upon arriving in the US – is loaded with signs of violence and yearning:

> Above the palm trees were large block letters that looked like they were on fire: SUNNY SAN DIEGO. The man was lying on his stomach, his face buried in his folded arms. The woman was lying on her back … I looked through the triangle formed by the woman's tanned knee, calf, and thigh and saw the calm, sleeping waves of the ocean. My mother was out there somewhere. My father had said so. (p. 6)

Formally, the novel shuttles between California and Vietnam to show that, for the narrator's family, everyday life in California is haunted by the anticipation of Ma's arrival, the memory of a drowned brother, and Ba's traumatizing detention in a re-education camp after the war. Associated with both the Vietnamese homeland and with drowning, swimming pools, beaches, and images of water convey a diasporic sense of home and/as loss.

Juxtaposing transpacific migrants with South and Central American characters, Karen Tei Yamashita's novels situate Asian immigrants in hemispheric circuits of exchange and migration. In *Tropic of Orange* (1997), the freeway that enabled cultural nationalists like Hongo, Lau, Inada, and Shawn Wong to claim the US landscape is shown to be a means of transnational connectedness that makes Los Angeles "the second largest city of México" (p. 212). While the novel's multiracial ensemble cast highlights the diversity of Los Angeles' inhabitants, its geographical allegory – in which a magical orange brought to the US from Mexico drags the Tropic of Cancer northward along with it – indicates the material differences between Los Angeles and the foreign spaces and bodies that support its economy. Along with the present policing of the US–Mexico border, Yamashita's plot encompasses the entire history of colonial violence in the Americas and the racial division of labor in LA. The character of Manzanar Murakami – an eccentric former internee who conducts abstract symphonies on a freeway overpass – focalizes a prophetic vision of the differentiated geographies that intersect in and through the city's freeway system. By attending carefully to traffic patterns, he perceives "a complex grid of pattern, spatial discernment, body politic" (p. 56). Manzanar accesses the different stratifications that comprise the city's space: "the prehistoric grid of plant and fauna and human behavior … the historic grid of land usage and property, the great overlays of transport … patterns and connections by every conceivable definition from the distribution of wealth to race, from patterns of climate to the curious blueprint of the skies" (p. 57). Elsewhere, Yamashita describes a "larger" vision encroaching on Manzanar's mapping of LA's layers:

> the great Pacific stretching along its great rim [and] the names of places he had never seen, from the southernmost tip of Chile to the Galapagos, skirting the tiny waist of land at Panama, up Baja to Big Sur to Vancouver, around the Aleutians to the Bering Strait. From the North, that peaceful ocean swept from Vladivostok around the Japan Isles and the Korean Peninsula, to Shanghai, Taipei, Ho Chi Minh City, through a thousand islands of the Philippines, Malaysia, Indonesia, and Micronesia … (p. 171)

These locations – many of which have been sites of US military intervention – limn the transnational circulation of commodities, capital, and laborers in which LA plays a central, orchestrating role. By juxtaposing Asian American characters and transpacific settings with its allegory of NAFTA, *Tropic of Orange* invokes cross-racial and translocal affiliations between groups differently affected by Western imperialism. The next section will continue to consider explorations of cross-racial alliances in Asian American texts.

Cross-Racial Affiliations

Asian Americans are not the only group that has been excluded, exploited, and denigrated within the US West. Whether by analogy or through living in proximity with other racialized groups, Asian Americans have formed both real and imaginary alliances with African Americans, Chicanos, and Native Americans (see Hong 2006; C.J. Kim 1999; D. Kim 2005; Lee 2004; Raphael-Hernandez and Steen 2006). It is worth recalling that the institutionalization of Asian American studies occurred within the broader context of ethnic studies and anti-colonial student movements in California. But if cross-racial affiliations draw attention to common issues such as cultural marginalization, expropriation, housing discrimination, media stereotyping, and environmental injustice, they also risk leveling the historical specificities of racial formation. In dramatizing and critiquing different forms of cross-racial affiliation, Asian American writers explore possible forms of lateral assimilation with other groups that might short-circuit the hegemonic trajectory of assimilation toward whiteness. Emerging relations between racialized groups also transcend the associations with the past that dominant narratives often attribute to both "Asia" and the US West.

Like the offshore and imperial sites discussed above, Carlos Bulosan's *America is in the Heart* (1943, 1946) suggestively preludes its narrative of migrant farmers following seasonal work throughout the western US with a detailed account of the gradual expropriation of peasant farmers at the hands of banks, absentee landlords, and corporate farms following US annexation of the Philippines (see Hsu 2009). After migrating to the US, Bulosan's narrator is constantly on the move, traversing a dizzying array of towns and casual jobs: as Sau-ling Cynthia Wong observes, the novel presents "no blazed trail, only chaos, a senseless jumble of brutalities" (1993: 134). In the short story "As Long as the Grass Shall Grow" (1949), Bulosan draws a bitter analogy between displaced Filipino peasants and Native Americans. The protagonist – a young farm worker in a coastal town – develops a relationship with a white schoolteacher who decides to teach English to him and his co-workers. When the townspeople learn about these lessons, however, the protagonist is beaten up by white vigilantes upset at the prospect of a white woman meeting privately with Filipino men. When she leaves town after losing her job, Miss O'Reilly promises, "I will go on teaching people like you to understand things as long as the grass shall grow" (p. 51). This invocation of Andrew Jackson's cynical promise to the Choctaws and Cherokees (that they would possess new trans-Mississippi lands "as long as Grass grows or water runs") discredits Miss O'Reilly's authority as a teacher, while also associating expropriated Filipinos with displaced Native Americans (see Zinn 2003: 134). For both groups, the US government offered assimilative education and pastoral rhetoric as substitutes for land, natural resources, and self-determination.

Chitra Banerjee Divakaruni's "Yuba City Poems" (1997) sequence chronicles the history of Sikh settlers in California's Central Valley. "Yuba City Wedding" dramatizes one of the cross-racial marriages that occurred between the Sikh men who settled in the area and their Mexican American neighbors. While the older settlers tolerate "going out" with Mexican women, they deplore the implications that interracial marriage has for social reproduction: "*A Christian, a woman who speaks a different language, who eats pig's flesh and cow's and isn't even white-skinned. Unclean. How can she bring your children up as good Sikhs?*" (p. 99). The poem concludes with the wedding at the Iglesia Santa Maria (where the groom's Sikh friends also dance with Mexican women) and the subsequent news that Manuela is pregnant. Whereas the final poem in Divakurni's sequence features a young woman leaving the sexually conservative community under the influence of magazines, television, and fuchsia lipstick, "Yuba City Wedding" highlights an earlier instance of lateral assimilation in which Sikh men (particularly

before immigration restrictions on women were lifted in the 1940s) risked ostraciza-
tion to form families with women who, like themselves, "[were]*n't even white-skinned.*"
After experiencing the "black emptiness" of social expulsion on his wedding night,
the poem's speaker concludes by imagining himself (and the new form of social life
implicit in his marriage to Manuela) as and through their unborn child: "I open my
eyes in water and imagine what he sees. ... Ready, I lift my face and breathe in the
bright waiting air" (p. 101).

Just seventy miles from Yuba City is the town of Locke, settled by Chinese immigrants in 1915 and the only rural Chinese settlement that survived the "Driving Out."
In *Water Ghosts*, Shawna Yang Ryan dramatizes the lives of Locke's early settlers, which
revolved around the seasonal pear harvest, the gambling house, and the brothel. As
Ryan writes, the "cruelty of laws has twisted the place into a Wild West throwback,
where men outnumber the women twenty to one" (p. 65). The transnational and
transregional ties that underlie this apparently insular Chinese settlement become
visible when three mysterious women appear in town on a boat one day. First,
these women – recently arrived from China – bear witness to the trafficking of slave
women and the hardships borne by married couples separated by both geographical
distance and gendered exclusion laws. Yet when the women turn out to be "water
ghosts" attempting to rejoin the world of the living, the narrative begins to echo the
magical realism of Toni Morrison's *Beloved*. The novel's cross-regional and cross-racial
connections do not end with its debts to Morrison's formal and thematic treatments
of haunting: the brothel's mistress turns out to have learned her trade while traveling
with a multiracial burlesque show through the South; when the police raid the
Chinese gambling house, they do so in blackface. Finally, the fictionalized inundation
of Locke after the flooding Sacramento River bursts its levees (which had been built
largely by Chinese laborers in the nineteenth century) in the climactic scene of *Water
Ghosts* echoes not only the ending of Zora Neale Hurston's *Their Eyes Were Watching
God* and the Louisiana flood of 1927, but also the more recent tragedy of Hurricane
Katrina.

Focusing on the urban (and suburban) context of Los Angeles, Hisaye Yamamoto's
memoir, "A Fire in Fontana" (1985), presents a more skeptical treatment of identifications across racial lines. "A Fire" interrogates Hisaye's feelings of identification with
African Americans during the decades between World War II and the Watts uprisings
of 1965. The sketch begins with Hisaye's encounters with Jim Crow "on a bus going
back to the camp in Arizona where my father still lived": while these indicate possible
parallels between internment and segregation, Hisaye – who chats with her white
seatmate and uses the white washroom – is not actually subjected to the impositions
of Jim Crow. The "event" that connects her with blackness pertains not to her outward
experiences, but to "my inward self" (p. 150). Yamamoto then shifts the scene to Los
Angeles, where she worked for an African American newspaper that aimed to ally
itself with Japanese Americans returning to Little Tokyo/Bronzeville, which had been
settled by African Americans during the internment years. At the newspaper, a man
named Short asks Hisaye to publicize "get-out-or-else" threats against his family,

which had recently purchased a house in Fontana (p. 153). Hisaye's weak response to the report – a "calm impartial story" in "cautious journalese" – does not stop the family from being killed when their house burns down later that week (p. 154). The sketch concludes with Hisaye having moved to the whitewashed suburbs herself, married to "a pale husband" and watching the Watts uprisings on television. "Appalled" (a word that derives from pallor or whiteness) and "inwardly cowering," she nevertheless feels "an undercurrent of exultation" at the sight of "burning and looting" on the screen, as if the uprisings were a cathartic retribution for the Short family's murder (p. 157). As James Kyung-Jin Lee observes, "Hisaye's moment of articulating her now scripted racial consciousness emerges precisely when and where her own material existence gives her access to a zone of comfort and privilege, a space that Black bodies themselves cannot enter" (2004: 90–1). Hisaye's "gratifying" misreading of the sight of more black casualties and burned black residences on television highlights the difficulties inherent in affiliations across divergent histories and geographies of racialization (Yamamoto 2001: 157).

Whereas Yamamoto shows how identifications from afar can occlude material and geographical inequalities, Sesshu Foster's autobiographically informed poetry explores cross-racial affiliations forged on the basis of lived proximity. The speaker of *City Terrace Field Manual* (1996) is the son of a white man and a Japanese woman growing up in east Los Angeles. Abandoned by his father – who "is traveling around the / world like white men do" – the speaker records the brutal conditions endured by Chicanos and other exploited groups: "I was the Chinese / woman a floor below the street, bent over her machine / in the dusty half-dark. I was the only white guy on the / Mexican railroad crew, I was the breed who caught it / from three sides. I was the one always on the out. I was / the government worker piling slash after the logging / company had gone, knowing I was laid off when the job/ was done. ... I was the guy whose only call / came to sweep up at the factory, and I hurried to take it" (pp. 167, 85). While Foster does include several poems that expose the historical violence of Chinese purges, the War Relocation Authority, media stereotypes of Asians, and the Vietnam War, the prose poems primarily feature the speaker's Chicano friends and neighbors. By affiliating his poems with the neighborhood of east LA rather than any single ethnic group, Foster exposes the racially uneven distributions of housing, wealth, and resources precipitated by urban disinvestment.

The Asian American chronotopes explored in this essay reveal the heterogeneity of the US West – not just the racialized bodies and racializing spaces that are erased by dominant frontier mythologies, but also the commercial, migratory, and military connections between the West and various circumpacific locations. Both through proximity and analogy, spatialized Asian American experiences of forced displacement, migrant labor, domestic service, and sweatshop labor overlap with those of other racialized groups within and beyond the West. These intersections suggest that a comparative analysis of racialized chronotopes could produce a fuller understanding of the manifold spaces hidden within (and constitutively beyond) the US West.

REFERENCES AND FURTHER READING

Bakhtin, Mikhail. (1981). *The Dialogic Imagination: 4 Essays*, ed. Michael Holquist, trans. Caryl Emerson and Michael Holquist. Austin: University of Texas Press.

Bennett, Michael. (2001). Anti-Pastoralism, Frederick Douglass, and the Nature of Slavery. In Karla Armbruster and Kathleen Wallace, eds., *Beyond Nature Writing: Expanding the Boundaries of Ecocriticism*, pp. 195–210. Charlottesville: University of Virginia Press.

Bulosan, Carlos. (1943, 1946). *America is in the Heart*. New York: Harcourt, Brace.

Bulosan, Carlos. (1983). As Long as the Grass Shall Grow [1949]. In E. San Juan Jr., ed., *If You Want to Know What We Are: A Carlos Bulosan Reader*. Minneapolis: West End Press.

Burkhart, Matthew. (2008). Rewriting the West(ern): *Shane*, Jane, and Agricultural Change in Bharati Mukherjee's *Jasmine*. *Western American Literature*, 43/1 (Spring), 5–22.

Chin, Frank. (1991). *Donald Duk*. Minneapolis, MN: Coffee House Press.

Chu, Patricia P. (2000). *Assimilating Asians: Gendered Strategies of Authorship in Asian America*. Durham, NC: Duke University Press.

Divakaruni, Chitra Banerjee. (1997). *Leaving Yuba City: New and Selected Poems*. New York: Doubleday.

Eng, David. (2001). *Racial Castration: Managing Masculinity in Asian America*. Durham, NC: Duke University Press.

Eperjesi, John. (2005). *The Imperialist Imaginary: Visions of Asian and the Pacific in American Culture*. Hanover: University Press of New England.

Far, Sui Sin. (1912). *Mrs. Spring Fragrance*. Chicago: A.C. McClurg & Co.

Fenkl, Heinz Insu. (1996). *Memories of My Ghost Brother*. New York: Plume.

Foster, Sesshu. (1996). *City Terrace Field Manual*. New York: Kaya Press.

Fryer, Heather. (2008). Miné Okubos War: *Citizen 13660*'s Attack on Government Propaganda. In *Miné Okubo: Following Her Own Road*, pp. 82–98. Seattle: University of Washington Press.

Girdner, Audrie, and Anne Loftis. (1969). *The Great Betrayal: The Evacuation of the Japanese-Americans during World War II*. New York: Macmillan.

Hong, Grace Kyungwon. (2006). *The Ruptures of American Capital: Women of Color Feminism and the Culture of Immigrant Labor*. Minneapolis: University of Minnesota Press.

Hongo, Garrett, Alan Chong Lau, and Lawson Fusao Inada. (1978). *The Buddha Bandits Down Highway 99*. Mountain View, CA: Buddhahead Press.

Hsu, Hsuan L. (2009). New Regionalisms: Literature and Uneven Development. In John T. Matthews, ed., *A Companion to the Modern American Novel, 1900–1950*, pp. 218–39. Oxford: Blackwell.

Huang, Yunte. (2008). *Transpacific Imaginations: History, Literature, Counterpoetics*. Cambridge, MA: Harvard University Press.

Inada, Lawson Fusao. (1992). *Legends from Camp*. Minneapolis: Coffee House Press.

Kim, Claire Jean. (1999). The Racial Triangulation of Asian Americans. *Politics and Society*, 27/1 (March), 105–38.

Kim, Daniel. (2005). *Writing Manhood in Black and Yellow: Ralph Ellison, Frank Chin, and the Literary Politics of Identity*. Palo Alto, CA: Stanford University Press.

Kim, Jodi. (2008). I'm not Here, if This Doesn't Happen: The Korean War and Cold War Epistemologies in Susan Choi's *The Foreign Student* and Heinz Insu Fenkl's *Memories of My Ghost Brother*. *Journal of Asian American Studies*, 11/3 (Oct.), 279–302.

Kim, Willyce. (1972). *Eating Artichokes*. Oakland, CA: Women's Press Collective.

Kingston, Maxine Hong. (1989). *China Men* [1977]. New York: Vintage.

Kiyama, Henry (Yoshitaka). (1999). *The Four Immigrants Manga: A Japanese Experience in San Francisco, 1904–1924* [1931], trans. Frederik L. Schodt. Berkeley: Stone Bridge Press.

Lai, Him Mark, Genny Lim, and Judy Yung, eds. (1980). *Island: Poetry and History of Chinese Immigrants on Angel Island, 1910–1940*, pp. 138–46. Seattle: University of Washington Press.

160 *Hsuan L. Hsu*

Lau, Alan Chong. (1980). *Songs for Jadina.* Greenfield Center: Greenfield Review Press.

lê thi diem thúy. (2003). *The Gangster We Are All Looking For.* New York: Knopf.

Lee, James Kyung-Jin. (2004). *Urban Triage: Race and the Fictions of Multiculturalism.* Minneapolis: University of Minnesota Press.

Limerick, Patricia Nelson. (2001). *Something in the Soil: Legacies and Reckonings in the New West.* New York: Norton.

Lowe, Lisa. (1996). *Immigrant Acts: On Asian American Cultural Politics.* Durham, NC: Duke University Press.

Lye, Colleen. (2004). *America's Asia: Racial Form and American Literature, 1893–1945.* Princeton, NJ: Princeton University Press.

Mimura, Glen. (2009). *Ghostlife of Third Cinema: Asian American Film and Video.* Minneapolis: University of Minnesota Press.

Mukherjee, Bharati. (1989). *Jasmine.* New York: Ballantine.

Murayama, Milton. (1988). *All I asking for is my body* [1975]. Honolulu: University of Hawai'i Press.

Okubo, Miné. (1983). *Citizen 13660* [1946]. Seattle: University of Washington Press.

Palumbo-Liu, David. (1999). *Asian/American: Historical Crossings of a Racial Frontier.* Palo Alto, CA: Stanford University Press.

Raphael-Hernandez, Heike, and Shannon Steen, eds. (2006). *AfroAsian Encounters: Culture, History, Politics.* New York: New York University Press.

Ronyoung, Kim. (1986). *Clay Walls.* Sag Harbor, NY: Permanent Press.

Ryan, Shawna Yang. (2009). *Water Ghosts.* New York: Penguin.

Santos Perez, Craig. (2008). *from unincorporated territory.* San Francisco: University of San Francisco.

Shah, Nayan. (2001). *Contagious Divides: Epidemics and Race in San Francisco's Chinatown.* Berkeley: University of California Press.

Slotkin, Richard. (2000). *Regeneration through Violence: The Mythology of the American Frontier, 1600–1860.* Norman: University of Oklahoma Press.

Sohn, Stephen Hong. (2009). These Desert Places: Tourism, the American West, and the Afterlife of Regionalism in Julie Otsuka's *When the Emperor Was Divine. Modern Fiction Studies*, 55/1, 163–88.

Stoler, Ann Laura. (2006). Tense and Tender Ties: The Politics of Comparison in North American History and (Post) Colonial Studies. In Ann Laura Stoler, ed., *Haunted By Empire: Geographies of Intimacy in North American History*, pp. 23–67. Durham, NC: Duke University Press.

Streamas, John. (2007). Frontier Mythology, Children's Literature, and Japanese American Incarceration. In Susan Kollin, ed., *Postwestern Cultures: Literature, Theory, Space*, pp. 172–85. Lincoln: University of Nebraska Press.

Takaki, Tonald. (1983). *Pau Hana: Plantation Life and Labor in Hawaii, 1835–1920.* Honolulu: University of Hawai'i Press.

Turner, Frederick Jackson. (1996). The Problem of the West. In *The Frontier in American History*, pp. 205–21. New York: Dover.

Wilson, Rob, and Arif Dirlik, eds. (1995). *Asia/Pacific as a Space of Cultural Production.* Durham: Duke University Press.

Wong, Jade Snow. (1995). *Fifth Chinese Daughter* [1945]. Seattle: University of Washington Press.

Wong, Sau-ling Cynthia. (1993). *Reading Asian-American Literature: From Necessity to Extravagance.* Princeton, NJ: Princeton University Press.

Wong, Shawn. (1991). *Homebase* [1979]. New York: Penguin.

Yamada, Mitsuye. (1975). *Camp Notes and Other Poems.* San Lorenzo, CA: Shameless Hussy Press.

Yamamoto, Hisaye. (2001). A Fire in Fontana [1985]. In *Seventeen Syllables and Other Stories*, rev. edn., pp. 150–7. New Brunswick: Rutgers University Press.

Yamashita, Karen Tei. (1997). *Tropic of Orange.* Minneapolis: Coffee House Press.

Yuh, Ji-Yeon. (2005). Moved by War: Migration, Diaspora, and the Korean War. *Journal of Asian American Studies*, 8/3 (Oct.), 277–91.

Zinn, Howard. (2003). *A People's History of the United States, 1492–Present.* New York: Harper.

11
African American Literature and Culture and the American West

Michael K. Johnson

In a column published in the *Meagher County News* (May 25, 1955) entitled "My Mother Was a Slave," White Sulphur Springs, Montana, resident Rose Gordon narrates the story of a remarkable African American western pioneer, her mother Anna Gordon. "In the year of 1881," Gordon writes,

> a brown-skinned colored woman who bore the name of Mrs. Annie Gordon stood at the boat landing at Cairo, Illinois where the Ohio flows into the mighty Mississippi. Tears rolled down her cheeks and were falling on her baby boy whom she held in her arms. Her friends had gathered to bid her farewell. Her baggage and trunks had been loaded on the river steamer called the Katie. She sailed up the Mississippi River to Saint Louis and from there she began her journey up the Missouri River. (p. 2)

After three months of river travel, Anna joined her husband John Francis Gordon in Montana Territory. The Gordons made their way to a mining camp in Barker where John was employed as a cook, and where Rose was born in 1883. A lifelong resident of Montana, Rose Gordon grew up in White Sulphur Springs, where she assisted with her mother's catering business, and where she eventually owned and operated her own restaurant. Throughout her life, Gordon regularly submitted letters as well as articles of local history and biographical items like "My Mother Was a Slave" to the *Meagher County News*, to which she eventually contributed a regular column called "Rose's Recollections."

Drawn by jobs made available by a mining boom, Anna and John Gordon were just two of the many emancipated slaves who traveled from the former slave states of Kentucky or Missouri up the river into Montana Territory and beyond. From a

A Companion to the Literature and Culture of the American West, First Edition. Edited by Nicolas S. Witschi.
© 2011 Blackwell Publishing Ltd. Published 2011 by Blackwell Publishing Ltd.

territory-wide population of 346 individuals in 1880, continuing migration brought the total African American population in Montana to 1,523 by 1900 (Taylor 1998: 135). These African American pioneers settled in Butte, Great Falls, and Helena as well as in smaller communities such as White Sulphur Springs. For example, Irwin Smith, a talented blacksmith, preceded Anna Gordon on his own journey from a former slave state to seek greater freedom and prosperity in the newly opened western territory. Arriving in White Sulphur Springs in 1880, he operated a forge in the town for twenty years. "Buggies, wagons, riding plows, etc., crowd the way in front of Irwin Smith's blacksmith shop," reports the *Rocky Mountain Husbandman* in a one-sentence item published April 11, 1889, "while steady rings the hammer of the stalwart smith within." A pioneer settler in the Springs, the "stalwart smith" quite literally helped build the town into a prosperous turn-of-the-century resort.

From the earliest incursions into the Americas by Spanish explorers to the California Gold Rush and to the Oklahoma land rush, African Americans have been present at every frontier and have been active participants in transforming those frontier settlements into thriving communities. As did Montana, all the western mountain states and territories (as did the Plains states and the Pacific coast) saw rising black populations after the Civil War, with Idaho, Wyoming, Colorado, New Mexico, Arizona, Utah, and Nevada increasing "thirteen fold" between 1870 and 1920 (Katz 1996: 183).

That the stories of such vibrant and even larger-than-life historical figures as Anna and Rose Gordon and Irwin Smith remain largely invisible and untold may seem surprising, but the dominant mythologies surrounding western migration and settlement have until recently dampened investigation of the black West. However, as Peggy Riley observes, "The history of African Americans in the West, long marginalized, is emerging as a dynamic field … in part because of a growing recognition that blacks were active participants in the westward movement" (2003: 123). Recent publication of books such as Quintard Taylor's *In Search of the Racial Frontier* (1998), Matthew Whitaker's *Race Work: The Rise of Civil Rights in the Urban West* (2005), and the anthology *African American Women Confront the West* (Quintard and Moore 2003) provides evidence for Riley's claim that specialists in African American history are reinvigorating the study of the historical development of the American West.

If the *history* of African Americans in the West has become an emergent field of study, *literary* history is still lagging far behind. Even in the context of a spate of such recent publications as Noreen Groover Lape's *West of the Border: The Multicultural Literature of the Western American Frontiers* (2000) and Nathaniel Lewis' *Unsettling the Literary West: Authenticity and Authorship* (2003) that have worked to revise and expand the canon of western American literature to include the work of minority writers, these new anthologies of western literary criticism contain, as Eric Gardner observes, "at best, a radically limited sense of the black West" (2007: p. xxvii). Indeed, the lack of literary criticism related to the black West leads Gardner to comment, "The first step in this process may simply be recognizing that there *was* a black literary West, one that reached back well into the nineteenth century, and one that most scholars have ignored" (2007: p. xxvi). Certainly, individual articles on African American western writers have appeared in journals and anthologies, but only two book-length studies of the African American literary West have been published, my own *Black Masculinity and the Frontier Myth in American Literature* (2002) and Blake Allmendinger's *Imagining the African American West* (2005). Additionally, Daniel Moos' *Outside America: Race, Ethnicity, and the Role of the American West in National Belonging* (2005) includes important chapters on Oscar Micheaux's South Dakota memoirs and novels (and provides one of the most comprehensive overviews available of the whole of Micheaux's literary output) and on African American "self-published" western narratives (which includes discussions of the work of Micheaux, Nat Love, Thomas Detter, and Robert Ball Anderson).[1]

This paucity of critical literary and cultural studies work on the black West stands in direct contrast to the richness of the field of available texts depicting and imagining African American western experience, a field that includes such traditionally defined literary documents as memoirs and novels as well as other forms of literature such as letters, newspaper columns, and periodical writing in general. To the available field of documents, we might add depictions of African American western experience in such media as music, film, and television. To begin the task of understanding the African American West requires us to let go of the paradigms that limit our ability to strike out into new territory, it requires us to revise and expand the ways literary history has conceptualized the West as a field of study, and it requires us, most importantly, to reconsider a restricted notion of the literary text in order to be more open to the discovery of the full richness of the ways in which the African American West has been experienced, imagined, written, and represented. In the pages that follow, I hope to move in that direction by providing a sketch of some of the available textual material and by suggesting several interpretive frameworks for understanding these representations of the African American West.

In both memoirs and fiction, writers have documented the experiences of black western pioneers. The earliest account may be *The Life and Adventures of James P. Beckwourth* (1856), an as-told-to biography of the life of the famed trader, scout, and the discoverer of Beckwourth Pass through the Sierra Nevada mountains. Thomas Detter's *Nellie Brown, or, The Jealous Wife, with other sketches* (1871) was, as Daniel Moos points out, "the first book published by an African American in the American West" (2005: 90). Although the title story is set in Virginia, Detter's autobiographical sketches describe his experiences (and encounters with racism) living in Idaho. Mifflin Wistar Gibbs's *Shadow and Light* (1902) describes his journey to seek out "hidden opportunities in a new country" in Gold Rush California, where he arrived in 1850 (p. 37). *The New Man* (1895) is Henry Clay Bruce's account of his escape from Missouri slavery to freedom in Kansas. In *Black Frontiersman: The Memoirs of Henry O. Flipper* (1916), Flipper narrates his experiences with the 10th Cavalry while stationed in Oklahoma and Texas. Nat Love's *The Life and Adventures of Nat Love, Better Known in the Cattle Country as "Deadwood Dick"* (1907) is probably the best known and is one of the most written-about narratives of African American western experience. Love's photograph, posed with a saddle and rifle and wearing his cowboy clothes, has become the iconic image of the black cowboy. Oscar Micheaux features less gunslinging and more farming in his autobiographical novels *The Conquest* (1913) and *The Homesteader* (1917), which focus on his experiences homesteading in South Dakota. Taylor Gordon (brother of Rose Gordon) in his autobiography *Born to Be* (1929) tells of his childhood in turn-of-the-century Montana before turning to the story of his rise to fame as a spirituals singer in the 1920s. Robert Ball Anderson's *From Slavery to Affluence* (1927) is a memoir of homesteading in Nebraska. Era Bell Thompson focuses similarly on homesteading experiences (in North Dakota) in her autobiography *American Daughter* (1946).

Although memoir and autobiography have been the primary forms of African American western writing, fiction (particularly for contemporary writers) has also been an important mode for depicting black western experience. Sutton Griggs' novel *Imperium in Imperio* (1899) reimagines Texas as an all-black state within the larger United States. Pauline Hopkins' novel *Winona: A Tale of Negro Life in the South and the Southwest* (1902) adapts the tradition of the dime-novel western to tell a story of conflict between slavery and anti-slavery forces set on the Kansas–Missouri border. Additionally, numerous contemporary African American writers have depicted black experience in the historical West. Pearl Cleage's play *Flyin' West* (1995) takes place in turn-of-the-century Nicodemus, Kansas, one of the all-black towns established by the exodusters. Toni Morrison's novel *Paradise* (1998) focuses on an all-black town in Oklahoma. Percival Everett, who in novels such as *Watershed* (1996) and *Wounded* (2005) often writes about contemporary black western experience, visits the old West in his satirical novel *God's Country* (1994), a parody western that follows in the foot-steps of Ishmael Reed's story of the Loop Garoo Kid (the "HooDoo cowboy") in *Yellow Back Radio Broke-Down* (1969). David Anthony Durham's *Gabriel's Story* (2001) is a more serious take on the western genre, a violent coming-of-age story centered on title character Gabriel. Bruce Glasrud and Laurie Champion's *The African American West: A Century of Short Stories* (2000) collects a range of short fiction. We might observe as well recent fiction by white writers such as Paulette Jiles, who bases the story of one of the characters in her novel *The Color of Lightning* (2009) on her archival research into the life of Britt Johnson, a free black man who lived in Texas near the end of the Civil War.

While this is by no means a complete list of African American writing about the West, the richness of the material outlined here begs the question, why is the African American contribution to the literary West still mostly undiscovered territory? Some of the issues that have long plagued western history have also been problematic for literary history. As Matthew Whitaker writes in *Race Work*, his biography of Lincoln and Eleanor Ragsdale and their civil rights activism in Phoenix, Arizona, the dominant story of the West (influenced by historian Frederick Jackson Turner) has "posited that rugged Anglo American pioneers, fighting to subdue an ever-expanding western frontier, ushered in the taming of the wilderness, civilization, and a process of self-definition" (2005: 9). Within a vision of western history that has opposed "chivalrous white men" and "barbaric Indians," there has been literally no place for African Americans, who, as neither conquerors nor indigenous inhabitants of the West, fall outside the established categories (2005: 9). The challenge for the African American author has been to find a way to write his or her specific experiences of race and place into an existing narrative that has no vocabulary for articulating those experiences.

For example, in Rose Gordon's "My Mother Was a Slave," her description of her own birth demonstrates the difficulty of articulating her identity as a black westerner through the dominant conventions of frontier narratives: "I was born in this mining camp and claim the distinction of being the first white child born there. All the rest of the babies were Indian babies. I was delivered by an Indian woman." The story of Rose's individual life begins here, and she starts that story with the conventional "I was born" opening of the slave narrative, a connection to African American tradition and identity that is subsequently erased by her claim to being "the first white child born there," by which she seems to mean the first non-Indian born in what was formerly Indian territory. Born to a black former slave, delivered by an Indian midwife, and destined to grow up in a predominantly white community, Rose's sense of identity is more complicated than the vocabulary made available for her by existing narratives of western experience, and thus she falls back on the traditional racialized white/Indian opposition in her attempt to describe her place in the story of western settlement.

The Life and Adventures of James P. Beckwourth suggests another reason that such experience has gone relatively unnoticed. Biographer Thomas Bonner makes no mention of Beckwourth's race. Such erasures, intended perhaps to make the stories of black western heroes acceptable to white audiences, contribute to a dominant vision of the American West "as a region with few if any African Americans and virtually no black history" (Whitaker 2005: 9). Even for those African Americans who have told their stories without the filter of a white biographer, erasure of race is one of the dominant tropes of black western writing, and it is a troubling one that has contributed to the relative absence of consideration of the black West not only in dominant culture accounts of the American West but also in African American literary history.

As Houston Baker, Jr., has observed, "tales of pioneers enduring the hardship of the West for the promise of immense wealth are not the tales of black America," even though such tales of enduring frontier hardship for the promise of wealth (or at least a good steady income) are indeed the tales of African American individuals such as Oscar Micheaux, Nat Love, and Robert Ball Anderson (Baker 1972: 2). The mythic western narrative is a story of opportunity and conquest, of obstacles overcome, of rebirth and transformation. Those works by African American writers that follow those conventions sometimes do so at a cost – the erasure, or at least the understated depiction, of racial identity and difference. Such erasures (or seeming erasures) have also contributed to negative critical assessments of these books, which have often focused on their incorrect or inaccurate portrayals of racial relations. The "tales of pioneers" and the "tales of black America" are inevitably opposed to one another, and the individual narrative must fall on one side or the other of that opposition.

Thus, as the title of Joseph Young's *Black Novelist as White Racist: The Myth of Black Inferiority in the Novels of Oscar Micheaux* (1989) suggests, there is no potential for complexity in Micheaux's negotiation of early twentieth-century racial discourse. He is a black man who has completely accepted white dominant culture views of black identity, so much so that he has himself become a (black) "white racist." However, in considering the African American West, we will discover that oppositions of all sorts are difficult to maintain, and I would suggest as well that the work of African American western writers often contains complex (and even contradictory) representations of racial experience – even if criticism about that work has not always recognized that complexity. Between "the tales of pioneers" and the "tales of black Americans," there is an unexplored textual space still in need of explication. Following deconstructive reading practices, we might regard race as being placed under erasure, *sous rature*, in these texts, bracketed but not eradicated. Much work needs to be done in order to understand the strategies (and we might consider erasure not as a betrayal or a failure but as a representational *strategy*) that African American writers have used to adapt unfriendly and even hostile cultural narratives to articulate their own experiences.[2]

The Life and Adventures of Nat Love, which follows the mythic storyline of opportunity, conquest, rebirth, and transformation in telling Love's life history, provides a good example of the strategy of erasure. A former slave, Love leaves Tennessee in 1869 for Kansas, where he begins a career as a cowboy and becomes part of an integrated group of predominantly white cowboys: "as jolly a set of fellows as on[e] could find" (p. 41). After proving he knows how to ride a wild horse with the best of them, Love is accepted as an equal in the group, his membership further cemented by a fight with a group of Indians, during which "I unlimbered my artillery and after the first shot I lost all fear and fought like a veteran" (p. 42). Love presents his experiences as a model of perfect assimilation into white society. Within a vision of western history that has opposed "chivalrous white men" and "barbaric Indians," Love aligns himself with the "chivalrous white men," his own otherness seemingly erased by violent action against "barbaric Indians."

The Life and Adventures also tells the type of story that Quintard Taylor has referred to as the new myth of African American life in the West (one that has grown up to replace to the "old myth" of a West in which blacks were absent), the "stereotype of the black westerner as a solitary figure loosened from moorings of family, home, and community" (1998: 22). The solitary black westerner is such a popular stereotype that he has been a staple character in western films from the silents and early sound films to contemporary movies. The black westerner transcends race in part by separating himself from the black (eastern) community in order to become a member of a white (western) society. However, even a book that so neatly follows this "new myth" as does Love's narrative can at the same time undermine it. For the frontispiece of the book, Love has chosen a photograph of himself posing with his wife and daughter. The photograph tells a different story (of Love's continuing connection to the African American community, of the importance of family and home) than the narrative. The photograph suggests silently that in Love's life history there is another story about African American western experience, one that is not narrated but that he nonetheless chose to represent visually. Rather than a complete erasure of race, Love's identity in *Life and Adventures* exists between the textual absence of verbal racial markers and the photographic presence of the same.[3]

In terms of understanding more completely African American historical experience in the West, we also should be aware of the work of contemporary writers working within the genres of the traditional western or the historical novel. Writers such as Toni Morrison, Pearl Cleage, David Anthony Durham, and Percival Everett acknowledge in their novels the continuing presence of the racial prejudice and hatred in the West, telling stories of black experience in the West that articulate what earlier writers could not, or would not, tell. Morrison and Cleage in particular work to fill an important gap in the available literature – by telling the stories of black western women. In focusing on black communities, both Cleage's *Flyin' West* and Morrison's *Paradise* also take on the myth of the solitary westerner.

Percival Everett's *God's Country* includes the figure of the "lone black westerner" as part of its pastiche of the western genre. Ostensibly the story of a black cowboy and expert scout and tracker named Bubba, *God's Country* at times reads like a parody specifically of *The Life and Adventures of Nat Love*, and at other times as a commentary on the genre of the as-told-to biography that *The Life and Adventures of James P. Beckwourth* belongs to. Like Nat Love, Bubba is a heroic black cowboy who accomplishes impossible feats of daring with his fists and his gun. Like *The Life and Adventures of James P. Beckwourth*, the story of this particular African American scout is told by a white narrator, but while Beckwourth's biographer Thomas Bonner conceals his own authorial voice, Everett creates a white narrator, Curt Marder, whose consciousness – and whose conscious prejudice – is at the forefront of the story. The novel begins when Marder's house is burned down and his wife kidnapped by white outlaws. Marder hires the African American Bubba, a legendary tracker, to find his wife, which Bubba agrees to do for the price of half of Marder's homestead. That immediately after making the agreement Marder loses the whole homestead in a card game and never mentions that fact to Bubba says much about his character, or lack of it. The only thing Marder has going for him is his whiteness, and the only time that whiteness is much of an asset is when Bubba does something useful or heroic, for which Marder takes the credit.

Bubba fixes the broken wagon wheel on the stranded stagecoach, Bubba knocks General Custer cold with one punch, and Bubba guns down the fastest gunfighter in the West, but Marder mistakenly thinks he's telling his own story rather than Bubba's. The filtering consciousness of Marder's narration produces a disjunction between his response and Bubba's actions that contributes both to the humor of the tale and to its implicit critique of white narratives of westward migration. As we often have to look to the margins of historical accounts of the West in order to see the real presence of African Americans, so do we have to look to the margins of the story Marder tells to find out about Bubba.

Whereas Nat Love describes an American West where his race is unmarked and certainly is no hindrance to either his geographic or social mobility, Everett tells a story in which Bubba is constantly reminded of racial difference, and we have Marder's narration to keep his otherness as much at the forefront of the reader's consciousness as it is Marder's (p. 218). The white narrator brings to the story the continued existence of racial hatred in the integrated band of frontier companions that is absent from Nat Love's narrative. Still, in spite of Marder's lack of perception, we see enough of Bubba's story to realize that he doesn't enjoy the absolute freedom that Love claims. Bubba's awareness of racial difference shapes his behavior and choices throughout. He rides a mule rather than a horse because "Nobody ever wonders if a mule is stole" (p. 50). Contemporary African American narratives of western experience such as Everett's revise historical accounts such as those of Beckwourth and Love by making explicit the racial experience downplayed in those accounts.

However, it would be inaccurate to assume that only contemporary narratives call into question western myths. If some nineteenth- and early twentieth-century writers have adapted erasure as a strategy, other writers have taken the opposite approach, using their experiences of continuing racial prejudice in the American West to critique and contest the myth of an egalitarian and exceptional West. For example, Mifflin Wistar Gibbs in *Shadow and Light* goes to California seeking "hidden opportunities in a new country" (p. 37). What he finds is not opportunity but another set of limitations on black achievement. While life in California might be better for African Americans than in other parts of the country, still, "from every other point of view they were ostracized, assaulted without redress, disfranchised and denied their oath in a court of justice" (p. 46). Life in the West, it turns out, could be very much like life in the East.

Thus, we might make two observations about African American narratives of western experience. They often repeat the dominant myths of western history and tell stories of an exceptional West where the limitations of race can be transcended and the African American individual can find prosperity and equality. They also often tell the opposite story, of hopes for a new life crushed by the existence of unexceptional western prejudice. The first type of narrative follows white western conventions to the degree that it no longer seems to fit within the category of African American literature, especially in terms of the element of "social protest" against inequality that has been central to African American writing from fugitive slave narratives to the contemporary novels of Alice Walker and Toni Morrison. The second type of narrative calls into question the myth of western exceptionalism and thus has been marginalized as "unrepresentative" of western experience. Which story of African American experience in the West is the true one?

That is, perhaps, the wrong question to ask, as it assumes an opposition that is not supported by the available textual evidence, which suggests that African American western experience is sometimes paradoxical, and which suggests that both the myth of western exceptionalism and the revisionist critique of that myth each contain elements of truth. As Blake Allmendinger observes, "African Americans disagree about whether or not the West is a place of promise," so we may find that the West of Oscar Micheaux and Nat Love is not the same West as that of Henry O. Flipper (2005: p. xvii). The whole picture that emerges of African American life in the West is a complicated one, suggesting the existence of both prejudice and opportunity.

Even individual writers may be divided in their responses to the American West. While Oscar Micheaux's *The Homesteader*, for example, ostensibly tells a story of the solitary black westerner, Jean Baptiste, whose success depends on his willingness to leave the black East and become part of community of white homesteaders in South Dakota, the primary tension in the novel derives from Baptiste's efforts to both operate his farm and maintain his connection to Chicago's black community. The moorings of family, home, and community are not quite so loose as he first suspects, and he finds himself inexorably drawn back to a black community that he has presumably left behind. Era Bell Thompson finds herself similarly torn between her allegiance to the beautiful North Dakota prairie that she comes to love and the "land of my people" back "east," "the world of colored girls and boys as well as white, of colored stores and churches, of big city lights" (p. 159). One of the clever ways that both Micheaux and Thompson adapt western conventions to better reflect African American experience is to revise the West/East opposition in order to illustrate what W.E.B. Du Bois called the experience of "double consciousness," the internal conflict occasioned by trying to belong to two worlds, one white, one black. Torn between the opportunities available in the predominantly white society in the West and the sense of belonging to the African American community back East, black western writers sometimes externalize their internal division through narratives that emphasize movement from one place to another.

This core group of texts written in traditional literary forms provides an essential starting place for investigating the literary history of the black West, but if we confine ourselves to novels and memoirs, much of the richness of the black West will be lost. To come to a comprehensive understanding of the ways in which African Americans have imagined the West, we need an expanded notion of the text, one that includes not just the novel, the memoir, and the periodical, but also other media. As Blake Allmendinger observes, the literature about the African American western experience includes "futuristic fiction and historical novels, Westerns and mysteries, contemporary urban dramas and regional autobiographies, not to mention music and film" (2005: p. xvi). To even outline the full scope of representations of the black West in various media is clearly too large a task for one essay, but I would like to say a few words about the representation of African American western experience in television and cinema – especially as advances in technology, DVDs, online sites such as YouTube and Hulu, have made this archive more readily available for scholars.

African American actors have been included consistently in film casts from the earliest days of the Hollywood western, mostly in supporting roles, sometimes as cowboys, most often as cooks or servants, and, most especially, as comic relief (see Johnson 2005). Although most of these films are implicitly or explicitly racist in their portrayals, a full account of the way the African American West has been imagined should include as well a critical examination of dominant culture representations of black westerners. At the very least, these westerns provide a context for understanding how independently produced "race movies" (or black-audience films) respond to and revise western movie stereotypes.

Any discussion of the African American West on film should begin with novelist and filmmaker Oscar Micheaux, whose 1919 silent adaptation of his novel *The Homesteader* was the first full-length feature film produced by an African American. Micheaux broke similar ground with *The Exile* (1931), an adaptation of his first book *The Conquest*, in which he returned to the story of his homesteading experiences for the first African American full-length sound film. Additionally, his *The Symbol of the Unconquered* (1920), one of the few extant Micheaux silent films, returns to the South Dakota setting of *The Conquest* to tell the story of a heroic black homesteader who not only succeeds in his enterprises but also defeats a band of Ku Klux Klan members in the process.

From the 1920s through the 1940s segregated theaters were common, and an industry (in which Micheaux was a leading light) grew up making films for these African American audiences. In the late 1930s, there was even a series of remarkable black-cast "B" westerns, starring singer Herb Jeffries as cowboy Bob Blake. Several of these films are still extant and available, *Two-Gun Man From Harlem, Harlem Rides the Range*, and *The Bronze Buckaroo*.[4] Of particular importance to the scholars of the African American West on film is *The Tyler, Texas Black Film Collection*, a three-DVD boxed set of black-cast films from the 1930s and 1940s (available from Southern Methodist University). These films were originally shown in segregated movie theaters to black audiences in the region. The films themselves, which include both features and shorts, are fairly eclectic in genre as well as setting, but several films (*Midnight Shadow, Marching On, The Girl in Room 20*) do feature western settings (Texas, Oklahoma, and Arizona).

Although there has been some critical attention to African Americans in western film (see, for example, Loy, *Westerns and American Culture* [2001]), television series westerns are another source of representations of the black West that has not been sufficiently examined. The rise of the civil rights and black power movements in the 1960s and 1970s resulted in television programs of the period taking tentative steps toward exploring racial issues through western stories and settings. *The Rifleman* (ABC; 1959–63), starring Chuck Conners as Lucas McCain, was one of the first television westerns to feature an African American guest star (Sammy Davis, Jr.) in 1962.[5] Although John Ford's revisionist western film *The Man Who Shot Liberty Valance* (1962), which includes a black actor in a prominent role (Woody Strode as the character Pompie), has received more critical attention, the two episodes of *The Rifleman* featuring Davis are just as groundbreaking in their positive portrayal of a black westerner.

In the episode "The Most Amazing Man" (first aired November 26, 1962), Davis plays Wade Randall, "the most amazing man I ever met" (as Mark McCain writes in an essay for a school assignment). Randall arrives in North Fork with a reputation as a gunfighter, which (as Lucas McCain suspects) is unearned and untrue. Although the episode does not verbally raise the issue of race at any point in the narrative, and although there is no acknowledgment other than the obvious visual presence of Davis that Wade Randall is African American, I want to suggest that a reading strategy similar to the one applied to *The Life and Adventures of Nat Love*, one that acknowledges how such a visual presence may alter our interpretation of the verbal text, may be productive here as well.

Called out by the friend of a man Randall claims to have killed, he reveals the truth about his identity to Lucas: "My name: it's Orly Fudd. I work for the railroad, but as a cook. They call me Cookie. Every time I heard that name, it pained me something terrible. They don't let cooks wear guns, Mr. McCain, but I bought me one." The idea that cooks aren't allowed to have guns seems absurd, but that very absurdity points to the transparency of the episode's racial allegory, through which the episode addresses the contemporary issues that it can't address directly. As an epithet, "Cookie" doesn't have the sting ("it pained me something terrible") that the racial slur it replaces surely would. That Randall is relegated to the role of "cook" also suggests an intertextual connection to the history of African Americans in western films, where the dominant role has been that of the ranch or camp cook. As does Wade Randall himself, actor Sammy Davis, Jr. steps outside the traditional African American role as servant to play an important part, the guest star whose character's story is at the center of the episode.

In another episode, "Two Ounces of Tin" (February 19, 1962), Davis plays Tip Corey, a former member of the Buffalo Bill Wild West Show with expertise as a trick shooter – and, unlike the pretender Wade Randall, Davis in this role gets to show off some skills with a firearm. As with "The Most Amazing Man," the issue of race is raised only subtextually and obliquely. Corey has vowed to kill the sheriff of North Fork, whomever that might be, as revenge against the actions of a former sheriff of the town. Racial injustice in the past is a key plot point, although the racial element is not underscored. The former sheriff refused to intervene to stop a group of drunk white men from assaulting an Indian woman. When Corey's father tried to stop them, he, in turn, was killed by the gang. The sheriff neither prevented these deaths nor brought the killers to justice. "Two Ounces of Tin" could just as easily have been cast with a white actor playing Corey, but the decision to cast Davis in this part suggests a subtext that would not otherwise have been visible. The presence of African American actor Davis in the role of Corey suggests that Tip's vigilantism, his vow to see the badge of the sheriff of North Fork tossed in the dirt, is a response to a past injustice that is racial in nature.

Later western series such as *Gunsmoke* on CBS ("The Good Samaritans" in 1969, and "Jesse," 1973, featuring Brock Peters in the title role), NBC's *Bonanza* ("The Desperado" in 1971 featuring Louis Gossett, Jr.), and ABC's *Alias: Smith and Jones* ("The Bounty Hunter" in 1971, also guest-starring Louis Gossett, Jr.) make explicit the issue of racial injustice that remains a subtext in *The Rifleman*. All three of the episodes from the 1970s involve an African American character responding to or experiencing racially motivated violence. As in the world of cinematic westerns such as John Ford's *Sergeant Rutledge* (1960) (with Woody Strode as the title character, a cavalry soldier falsely accused of rape and murder), these television episodes respond to the civil rights movement in America by relocating contemporary questions of justice and equality to Old West settings.[6] To a large extent, *The Rifleman* episodes do so as well, but, appearing a decade earlier, they do so more covertly.

Developing an accurate picture of the African American literary West requires us to acknowledge the intellectual and aesthetic value of multiple types of documents and narratives, on the page and on the screen. Despite recent interest in acknowledging and documenting the history of the black West, "we still know woefully little about large areas of the African American past in this region" (Taylor 1998: 23). Some of the most interesting recovery work currently taking place in considering African American contributions to the literary West involves the study of periodical literature, particularly newspaper columns and letters, and I want to close by returning to a discussion of the evolving literary archive.

Of particular note in this regard is the recently published *Jennie Carter: A Black Journalist of the Early West* (edited by Eric Gardner). From 1867 to 1874, Jennie Carter contributed regularly to the San Francisco *Elevator*, a weekly black newspaper, publishing essays, sketches, and poems under the pennames "Ann J. Trask" and "Semper Fidelis." Witty and passionate, alternately arch and sentimental, Carter's columns are comparable to contemporaneous masters of the short sketch, Fannie Fern and Mark Twain. As editor Gardner notes in his introduction, "Jennie Carter's life and work call on us to begin to reexamine just what the 'literary West' and the 'black West' might mean," and such a reexamination hinges on an expanded notion of the literary, one that goes beyond traditional literary genres (2007: p. xxviii). "If we are to have a fuller sense of black women, black literature, and the black West," Gardner continues, "we need to use the archive more and to build that archive into something much more widely accessible" (2007: p. xxxi).

As a resource for expanding our available knowledge of the black literary West, black periodicals are largely untapped. Gayle Berardi and Thomas Segady observe that between 1880 and 1914, forty-three African American newspapers operated in the West, primarily in six states, Colorado, California, Montana, Utah, Washington, and Oregon (1998: 225). Nebraska, Oklahoma, and Kansas were also home to black-audience newspapers during this period, although the newspapers in those states are not listed in the Berardi and Segady accounting. In addition to the untapped archive of African American western writing extant in black-audience newspapers and periodicals, we need to be more attentive to locating the work of African American writers who published in white-owned western periodicals. To return to the opening of this chapter, Rose Gordon published throughout her life in her local newspaper. Although White Sulphur Springs had a small but thriving African American population at the turn of the century, by the middle of the twentieth century when Rose published most frequently in the *Meagher County News*, she and her brother Robert were the only remaining African American residents of the Springs. Nonetheless, Rose was able to find an audience for her "recollections" of life in the early days of the Springs, and by so doing she was able to tell the stories of some of Montana's black pioneers, not only those of her mother Anna but also others who lived in or passed through White Sulphur Springs.

As the very title of her article "My Mother Was a Slave" suggests, Gordon's writing is both consistent with other depictions of the black West and offers something new. As does Nat Love, Gordon tells a story in which western migration is a means of leaving behind an identity as a slave in order to experience a more fully realized humanity. Such self-realization is made possible by becoming an accepted member of a predominantly white western community (the band of cowboys for Nat Love, the community of White Sulphur Springs for Anna Gordon). However, the fact that Rose's story centers on a black female pioneer (and is narrated by that woman's daughter) makes "My Mother Was a Slave" quite a departure from most of the memoirs mentioned above. From the moment when Anna Gordon is described with tears "roll[ing] down her cheeks" and "falling on her baby boy whom she held in her arms," Rose signals that she is telling a very different sort of western story than that of the "solitary figure loosened from moorings of family, home, and community." "My Mother Was a Slave" is first and foremost a story of family and of making a home in a seemingly unlikely place – the pioneer town of White Sulphur Springs, Montana Territory.

In *Imagining the African American West*, Blake Allmendinger writes, "I came to realize that there is no such thing as a 'representative' African American western experience" (2005: p. xvi). Rather, "there are many different impressions of place, just as there are many different types of racial experience," an observation that is borne out by the diverse and often complicated responses to western experience found in the work of black writers and in the many different mediums and forms through which the African American west has been imagined (2005: p. xvi). The variety of historical experience combined with the variety of primary materials, much of which does not fit neatly within traditional paradigms, requires us as scholars to be open-minded and to continue to develop flexible methods for understanding and interpreting this expanded archive of the African American West.

NOTES

1   We might also note *African Americans on the Great Plains: An Anthology* (Glasrud and Braithwaite 2009).

2   The field of Oscar Micheaux criticism, especially criticism related to his films, has developed significantly. Recent work such as Bowser and Spence's *Writing Himself into History* (2000) and Patrick McGilligan's biography of Micheaux (2008) have recognized and effec-

tively explained the complexity of the racial portrayals in both his films and his novels.

3   See also Kenneth Speirs (2005) for a discussion of the visual imagery, including a series of pen-and-ink drawings, that illustrates *The Life and Adventures of Nat Love*.

4   For discussions of the Bob Blake black-cast westerns, see Allmendinger 2005, as well as Johnson 2005; see also Leyda 2002; Miller 2005.

5   The episodes of *The Rifleman* were preceded by
    an episode of *Zane Grey Theater*, an anthology
    series, called "The Mission" (CBS; Nov. 12,
    1959), also starring Sammy Davis, Jr., this
    time as a member of the 10th Calvary, the so-
    called Buffalo Soldiers. An episode of *Frontier
    Circus*, entitled "Coals of Fire" (CBS; Jan. 4,
    1962), also preceded *The Rifleman* episodes and
    featured the story of a former slave (played,
    once again, by Sammy Davis, Jr.).

6   We should note here the continuing tenacity
    of the myth of the solitary black westerner.
    With notable exceptions such as *Gunsmoke's*
    "The Good Samaritans" and the later seasons
    of *Daniel Boone* (which featured several recur-
    ring African American cast members; NBC,
    1964–70), most television shows feature a
    single black character whose story is primarily
    important for the response it elicits from the

central white characters of the series. The
repetition of the myth of the solitary black
westerner is typical in both television and film
in the era, with the exception of a series of
"blaxploitation" films including *100 Rifles*
(1969) and *Take a Hard Ride* (1975) (both starring Jim Brown), which are comparable in
their broadly populated depiction of an African
American West to the black-audience films of
the "race movie" era (see also director Mario
Van Peebles' 1993 film *Posse*). And not until
The Adventures of Briscoe County, Jr. (Fox; 1993)
do we get a television series western that
includes African American actors in frequent
and wide-ranging roles. More recently, the
HBO series *Deadwood* (2004–6) has been attentive to treating African American western
experience as part of its revisionist take on the
genre.

REFERENCES AND FURTHER READING

Allmendinger, Blake. (1993). Deadwood Dick: The Black Cowboy as Cultural Timber. *Journal of American Culture*, 16/4, 79–89.

Allmendinger, Blake. (1997). African Americans and the Popular West. In Dan Flores, ed., *Updating the Literary West*, pp. 916–20. Fort Worth: Western Literature Association, in association with Texas Christian University Press.

Allmendinger, Blake. (1998). *Ten Most Wanted: The New Western Literature*. New York: Routledge.

Allmendinger, Blake. (2005). *Imagining the African American West*. Lincoln: University of Nebraska Press.

Anderson, Robert Ball. (1988). *From Slavery to Affluence: Memoirs of Robert Anderson, Ex-Slave* [1927]. Steamboat Springs, CO: Steamboat Pilot Printer.

Baker, Houston A., Jr. (1972). *Long Black Song: Essays in Black American Literature and Culture*. Charlottesville: University Press of Virginia.

Berardi, Gayle K., and Thomas W. Segady. (1998). The Development of African American Newspapers in the American West, 1880–1914. In Monroe Lee Billington and Roger D. Hardaway, eds., *African Americans on the Western Frontier*, pp. 217–30. Niwot: University Press of Colorado.

Bowser, Pearl, and Louise Spence. (2000). *Writing Himself into History: Oscar Micheaux, his Silent Films, and his Audiences*. New Brunswick: Rutgers University Press.

Brown, Jayna. (2001). Black Patriarch on the Prairie: National Identity and Black Manhood in the Early Novels of Micheaux. In Pearl Bowser et al., eds., *Oscar Micheaux and his Circle: African-American Filmmaking and Race Cinema of the Silent Era*, pp. 132–46. Bloomington: Indiana University Press.

Bruce, H.C. (1996). *The New Man: Twenty-Nine Years a Slave, Twenty-Nine Years a Free Man* [1895]. Lincoln: University of Nebraska Press.

Cleage, Pearl. (1999). *Flyin' West and Other Plays*. New York: Theatre Communications Group.

Detter, Thomas. (1996). *Nellie Brown, or The Jealous Wife, with other sketches* [1871]. Lincoln: University of Nebraska Press.

Donner, Thomas D. (1972). *The Life and Adventures of James P. Beckwourth* [1856]. Lincoln: University of Nebraska Press.

Du Bois, William Edward Burghardt. (1989). *The Souls of Black Folk* [1903]. New York: Penguin.

Durham, David Anthony. (2002). *Gabriel's Story* [2001]. New York: Anchor Books.

Everett, Percival. (2003). *God's Country* [1994]. Boston: Beacon Press.

Everett, Percival. (2003). *Watershed* [1996]. Boston: Beacon Press.

Everett, Percival. (2005). *Wounded*. St. Paul: Graywolf Press.

The Exile. (1931). Dir. Oscar Micheaux. Perf. Eunice Brooks, Stanleigh Morrell.

Flipper, Henry O. (1997). *Black Frontiersman: The Memoirs of Henry O. Flipper, First Black Graduate of West Point* [1916], ed. Theodore D. Harris. Fort Worth: Texas Christian University Press.

Gardner, Eric. (2007). Introduction. In Eric Gardner, ed., *Jennie Carter: A Black Journalist of the Early West*, pp. vii–xxxiii. Jackson: University Press of Mississippi.

Gibbs, Mifflin Wistar. (1995). *Shadow and Light* [1902]. Lincoln: University of Nebraska Press.

Glasrud, Bruce A., and Charles A. Braithwaite. (2009). *African Americans on the Great Plains: An Anthology*. Lincoln: University of Nebraska Press.

Glasrud, Bruce A., and Laurie Champion. (2000). *The African American West: A Century of Short Stories*. Niwot: University Press of Colorado.

Gordon, Rose. (1955). My Mother Was a Slave. *Meagher County News* (White Sulphur Springs, Montana), May 25, 1955, 1+.

Gordon, Taylor. (1995). *Born to Be* [1929]. Lincoln: University of Nebraska Press.

Green, J. Ronald. (2000). *Straight Lick: The Cinema of Oscar Micheaux*. Bloomington: Indiana University Press.

Griggs, Sutton. (1899). *Imperium in Imperio*. Cincinnati: Editor Publishing Co.

Hopkins, Pauline. (1988). *Winona: A Tale of Negro Life in the South and the Southwest* [1902]. In *The Magazine Novels of Pauline Hopkins*, pp. 285–437. Schomburg Library of Nineteenth-Century Black Women Writers. New York: Oxford University Press.

Jiles, Pauline. (2009). *The Color of Lightning*. New York: William Morrow.

Johnson, Michael K. (2001). Migration, Masculinity, and Racial Identity in Taylor Gordon's *Born to Be*. In Scott E. Casper, ed., *Moving Stories: Migration and the American West*, pp. 119–41. Reno: University of Nevada Press.

Johnson, Michael K. (2002). *Black Masculinity and the Frontier Myth in American Literature*. Norman: University of Oklahoma Press.

Johnson, Michael K. (2004). "Try to Refrain from that Desire": Self-Control and Violent Passion in Oscar Micheaux's African American Western. *African American Review*, 38/3 (Fall), 361–77.

Johnson, Michael K. (2005). Cowboys, Cooks, and Comics: African American Characters in Westerns of the 1930s. *Quarterly Review of Film and Video*, 22/3, 225–35.

Johnson, Michael K. (2007). Looking for the Big Picture: Percival Everett's Western Fiction. *Western American Literature*, 42/1 (Spring), 26–53.

Katz, William Loren. (1996). *The Black West* {1987}. New York: Touchstone.

Lape, Noreen Groover. (2000). *West of the Border: The Multicultural Literature of the Western American Frontiers*. Athens: Ohio University Press.

Lewis, Nathaniel. (2003). *Unsettling the Literary West: Authenticity and Authorship*. Lincoln: University of Nebraska Press.

Leyda, Julia. (2002). Black Audience Westerns and the Politics of Cultural Identification in the 1930s. *Cinema Journal*, 42/1 (Fall), 46–70.

Love, Nat. (1995). *The Life and Adventures of Nat Love, Better Known in the Cattle Country as "Deadwood Dick"* [1907]. Lincoln: University of Nebraska Press.

Loy, R. Philip. (2001). *Westerns and American Culture, 1930–1955*. Jefferson, NC: McFarland & Co.

McGilligan, Patrick. (2008). *Oscar Micheaux: The Great and Only* [2007]. New York: Harper Perennial.

Micheaux, Oscar. (1994). *The Conquest: The Story of a Negro Pioneer* [1913]. Lincoln: University of Nebraska Press.

Micheaux, Oscar. (1994). *The Homesteader* [1917]. Lincoln: University of Nebraska Press.

Miller, Cynthia J. (2005). Tradition, Parody, and Adaptation: Jed Buell's Unconventional West. In Peter C. Rollins and John E. O'Connor, eds., *Hollywood's West: The American Frontier in Film, Television, and History*, pp. 65–80. Lexington: University Press of Kentucky.

Moos, Dan. (2005). *Outside America: Race, Ethnicity, and the Role of the American West in National Belonging*. Lebanon, NH: University Press of New England.

Morrison, Toni. (1998). *Paradise*. New York: Knopf.

Painter, Nell Irvin. (1986). *Exodusters: Black Migration to Kansas after Reconstruction* [1976]. New York: Norton.

Patterson, Martha H. (1998). "kin o' rough jestice fer a parson": Pauline Hopkins's *Winona* and the Politics of Reconstructing History. *African American Review*, 32/3 (Fall), 445–60.

Reed, Ishmael. (2000). *Yellow Back Radio Broke-Down* [1969]. McLean, IL: Dalkey Archive Press.

Riley, Glenda. (2003). African American Women in Western History: Past and Prospect. In Quintard Taylor and Shirley Ann Wilson Moore, eds., *African American Women Confront the West, 1600–2000*, pp. 22–7. Norman: University of Oklahoma Press.

Riley, Peggy. (2003). Women of the Great Falls African Methodist Episcopal Church, 1870–1910. In Quintard Taylor and Shirley Ann Wilson Moore, eds., *African American Women Confront the West, 1600–2000*, pp. 122–39. Norman: University of Oklahoma Press.

Scheckel, Susan. (2002). Home on the Train: Race and Mobility in the *Life and Adventures of Nat Love*. *American Literature*, 74/2 (June), 219–50.

Speirs, Kenneth. (2005). Writing Self (Effacingly): E-Race-D Presences in *The Life and Adventures of Nat Love*. *Western American Literature*, 40/3 (Fall), 301–20.

The Symbol of the Unconquered. (1920). Dir. Oscar Micheaux. Perf. Iris Hall, Walker Thompson, Lawrence Chenault.

Taylor, Quintard. (1998). *In Search of the Racial Frontier: African Americans in the American West, 1528–1990*. New York: Norton.

Taylor, Quintard, and Shirley Ann Wilson Moore, eds. (2003). *African American Women Confront the West, 1600–2000*. Norman: University of Oklahoma Press.

Thompson, Era Bell. (1986). *American Daughter* [1946]. St. Paul: Minnesota Historical Society Press.

VanEpps-Taylor, Betti Carol. (1999). *Oscar Micheaux, A Biography: Dakota Homesteader, Author, Pioneer Film Maker*. Rapid City: Dakota Press.

Whitaker, Matthew C. (2005). *Race Work: The Rise of Civil Rights in the Urban West*. Lincoln: University of Nebraska Press.

Young, Joseph A. (1989). *Black Novelist as White Racist: The Myth of Black Inferiority in the Novels of Oscar Micheaux*. Westport, CT: Greenwood Press.

12
Mythical Frontiers: Manifest Destiny, Aztlán, and the Cosmic Race

John L. Escobedo

In line with the objectives of this new *Companion* I would like to engage with, perhaps further complicate, some of the queries concerning the creation of the American West. The American ambition of settling the vast and opulent western frontier was made possible by the close proximity between two neighboring nations: Mexico and the United States. Mexico's inability to extensively populate its northern territories resulted in the foreseeable encroachment upon this geographical area by Americans to lay claim to the West. Whether viewed as the northern national boundary of Mexico or a western frontier for the US, the West was and remains what one made it, or simply how one perceived this great mythical frontier. After all, frontiers are socially constructed cultural symbols enacted to carry out historically specific political agendas that are usually veiled by national imaginaries: West as a mythical land of vastness and plentitude overflowing with the redemptive power of hopes and dreams. Legends are born in such places and new vibrant peoples are celebrated in the magical lure of frontier folklore. Unfortunately, frontiers inhabit a paradoxical existence that only commemorates the composition of these myths and legends at the expense of the existing inhabitants of these areas. In other words, one man's quest to settle the wild frontier represents another man's displacement and subsequent subjugation.

The Mexican–American War and the signing of the Treaty of Guadalupe Hidalgo (1848), which surrendered Mexico's northern territories (Texas, New Mexico, Colorado, Utah, Nevada, Arizona, California, and Wyoming), finally legitimized the existence of an American western frontier. As with all conquered territory, the American West has since burst at its seams by the force of the various, and oftentimes divergent, histories of its colonial past. This chapter is my attempt to sort through the multi-layered frontier narratives that have been imagined and claimed by the American

A Companion to the Literature and Culture of the American West, First Edition. Edited by Nicolas S. Witschi.

West, Chicano Southwest, and Mexico's El Norte (northern territory). The carto-graphic construction – whether physical or imaginary – of these three frontiers has always shown them closely intertwined with one another, endlessly converging and regenerating conflicting histories, traditions, and identities. The constant element, however, lies with the effective use and manipulation of the myth of origin. The refiguring of myths through a series of symbolic codifications dramatically transforms the historical narrative, political order, and national identity of the three aforemen-tioned temporal frontiers. As a critical tool of analysis, the myth of origin serves as a cultural sieve that sifts through the various historical movements that have utilized it to shape the political identity of this highly contested frontier space. The following pages of this study demonstrate the effectiveness of the myth of origin in Manifest Destiny as Americans expanded westward, the reconstruction of Aztlán during the Chicano/a civil rights movement, and the legendary tale of a future nation ruled by a hybrid civilization: the Cosmic Race.

My analysis of the malleable dimensions of this particular frontier unsettles any claim of a singular American western history by highlighting the multiple cultural movements inhabiting and thriving within this single geographical territory. A great point of departure leads this study to the mid-nineteenth-century popular movement of Manifest Destiny. Perhaps no other ideological movement in US history can be credited with such astronomical success: the ignition the Mexican–American War, the acquisition of over 500,000 square miles of new American territory, and the introduc-tion of a new US minority group – Mexican Americans – and their marginal existence as second-rate citizens under North American rule. Manifest Destiny proved to be a force to be reckoned with due to its support among high-ranking political officials and the strong support for this ideological doctrine among the working-class masses during the mid-nineteenth-century. As such, a review of this unconscionable, but effective, discourse is in order.

John O'Sullivan first coined the term Manifest Destiny in 1845 as editor of the *Democratic Review* with his political piece "Annexation" and later popularized the catchphrase in a subsequent article for the *New York Morning News* concerning the annexation of Texas and Oregon (Sampson 2003: 194). These territories, argued O'Sullivan, were essential to secure the future progress of American ideals: democratic liberty. In a single swoop, America's wings of freedom were destined to glide steadily across the American continent to graciously bestow the natural economic, political, and social liberties vital to the development of all human progress. Regrettably for Mexico, Texas was viewed as the gateway leading to the settlement of the West, which would inevitably lead to the Mexican–American War. Again, the general assumption among advocates of Manifest Destiny was that aggressive expansion from the Atlantic seaboard to the Pacific coast could only benefit the development and use of natural resources found throughout the West and, to a much smaller extent, improve the impoverished condition of the Mexican population that inhabited these underdevel-oped territories. As if this popular belief required further legitimacy, the appeal of Manifest Destiny was enhanced by the religious belief that Providence had specifically selected Americans and Christianity to impose democracy throughout the American hemisphere. This new crusade, argues Robert Sampson, represented a righteous mission for the American people to achieve the nation's "potential in all pursuits – religious, commercial, industrial, political, and artistic" (2003: 194). According to John O'Sullivan, this great American endeavor was destined to enlighten all by the "fulfillment of our manifest destiny to overspread the continent allotted by Providence for the free development of our yearly multiplying millions" (*Democratic Review*, June 1845, qtd. in Sampson 2003: 194). The lofty aspiration and notion of advancing a whole civilization through a clouded vision of democracy swept through the American imaginary with such force that it became a nationally recognized topic of discussion in all facets of American life.

Unfortunately, the uncanny appeal of Manifest Destiny relied on its ability to include while simultaneously excluding certain individuals from its democratic system on the basis of race, as Americans extended their national borders westward. Racial categorizations found a vital niche at the height of American expansion (1830s–1840s) that established a convenient hierarchical arrangement between Americans and Mexicans. At the top of this pecking order Anglo-Saxonism reigned supreme. If Manifest Destiny represented the democratic vision for the American continent, Anglo-Saxons were the "chosen people" destined to carry out this sacred mission. According to the logic of Manifest Destiny, racial lineage and pedigree determined the difference between civilized nations and barbaric tribes. Unlike the racially mixed populace of Mexico, Americans claimed a direct line to the Anglo-Saxon Germanic tribes of the European continent – the original settlers of England before the Norman Conquest. These tribes were thought of as racially pure and unmixed. Popular folklore claimed that the Anglo-Saxon trait of possessing pure bloodlines carried a biological inclination for higher moral codes and a natural inclination toward freedom and individual rights. Such naturally endowed qualities were the foundational elements of a free-enterprising Anglo-Saxon democracy that sustained the integrity of their political institutions. Due to this genetic blueprint, Anglo-Saxons were believed to be the founding fathers of democracy on European soil – an ambition Americans wished to emulate and carry forth throughout the American continent.

Embracing the Anglo-Saxon myth of origin proved to be extremely functional for a fledgling nation on the move. As a reference point of origin, it provided Americans with a useful narrative of great antiquity that influenced the construction of their own distinct identities based on past histories and myths – instantly rooting a genealogical tree bearing the fruit of democratic traditions. Americans could now claim a history imbued with cultural traditions of mythical proportions that fused perfectly with the expansionist goals of Manifest Destiny. After all, the progression of American democratic ideals throughout the New World resembled the legendary migration of their Saxon ancestors. The drafting of the Declaration of Independence and subsequent American Revolution, argues Reginald Horsman, followed "the same natural right under which "their Saxon ancestors had left the woods of northern Europe and settled in England" (1981: 22). That is to say, Americans considered their split from

England a necessary act to carry forth the democratic doctrine of their Saxon ancestors to the American continent. Ultimately, the successful independent movement against the British monarchy sealed the legitimacy of an American democratic spirit.

Although the founding fathers of the United States were ardent antiquarian scholars of the Anglo-Saxon branch, their interest did not lie with racial pedigrees but rather with the philosophical principles of Saxon democracy. It was not until the middle of the nineteenth century during the Mexican–American War that a sense of innate white racial superiority grew rampant among supporters of Anglo-Saxonism. Manifest Destiny simply became a rhetorical means to supply a racial identity to American democracy as the US extended its boundaries westward. The racial construction of a superior American race provided a united domestic front during a time of immense territorial growth that produced dramatic social changes in US race relations. American racial identity was not necessarily threatened by its own western expansion, but the introduction of a new minority Mexican class after the Mexican–American War and the sudden diversification of the American populace certainly raised concerns. Anglo-Saxonism conveniently settled the racial order throughout the western frontier. After all, the benefit of being a self-described superior race lies in the freedom to designate other races as inferior.

Nearly a century later, Chicano/a scholars began to deconstruct the racist doctrine behind Manifest Destiny, and actively questioned prominent American beliefs of a white superior race on North American soil. This political awakening resulted in the construction of new terms of self-identification within the Mexican community that affirmed and celebrated a distinct regional historiography that redefined Mexican representations within US historical narratives. For Chicano/as, the conclusion of the Mexican–American War did not represent a glorious achievement in US continental expansion, but rather a historical outcome of armed conflict that introduced a new geographical marker that restructured American racial categorizations: a border. The Rio Grande River that separated the US from Mexico was but one division among many that further antagonized American–Mexican relations across racial lines, religious backgrounds, and national languages. These differences quickly shifted the popular belief of an opulent western frontier to that of a conflict-laden border territory, which redefined the western designation of this frontier space to that of a "southwestern borderland."

As a popular catchphrase among Chicano/a scholars, the term acknowledged the Mexican historiography that is inherently tied to the American West. This southern regional idiom immediately supplied Chicano/a scholars with usable new histories, a familiar cultural heritage, and a distinct regional folklore, which questioned popularly held American beliefs that portrayed Mexicans as a barbaric, degenerate species in order to depict Americans as the redeeming champions of the western frontier. The maligned historical depiction of the Mexican community within the US resulted in the construction of a unique relationship between Chicano/as and the actual physical border region, an intimate bond that began to rehabilitate the image of the Mexican subject by celebrating the cultural heritage and regional folklore rooted in the southwestern borderlands. As a result, a new generation of scholars, artists, and activists began formulating innovative cultural forms that intersected, clashed, and reformulated the multilayered folklore produced within this highly contested border space. Out of this eclectic landscape arose the legendary tale of Aztlán: the Aztec myth of origin.

Conceptually, Aztlán supplied a historical direction for Chicano/a intellectual circles as well as a rising bohemian artistic class. In this respect, the Aztec myth of origin accomplished a crucial objective during the Chicano/a civil rights movement: it pointed back to Mexico both historically and culturally. This initial move provided Chicano/as with a deep historical pool to borrow from in order to tailor usable historical narratives, integrate iconic Mexican political figures to the Chicano/a movement, and utilize Mexico's rich folkloric traditions to establish many of the foundational political tenets in Chicano/a history, literature, and popular culture. Fundamental Chicano manifestos such as *El Plan Espiritual de Aztlán* reach back toward Mexico's official historical record and mythical folklore to forge a political culture for the Chicano/a community. In other words, the myth of Aztlán conveniently merged Mexico's history and folklore in a way that allowed Chicano/a scholars and artists alike to modify the Aztec myth of origin to match the political objectives of the Chicano/a civil rights movement. The historiography and cultural identity Aztlán supplied to the Chicano/a community warrants a historical overview to appreciate the political value it supplied to Chicano/a scholars, activists, and artists.

Appropriately enough, the Spanish Catholic Church conducted the initial research on the subject of Aztlán after the conquest of Mexico by the Spanish empire, which represents the first recovery project investigating the history of Aztlán. With the aid of indigenous Aztec converts, Catholic chroniclers began the daunting task of interviewing hundreds of Aztecs to record their native history. Aztlán proved to be an important historical reference point and concept since it represented their place of birth as a people. According to Martha Menchaca, the recorded interviews failed to locate Aztlán geographically, but "indicated to sixteenth-century cartographers that it was to the north of the Valley of Mexico" (2001: 21). Aztlán's bearing northward of Mexico makes sense and aligns with the great migration of the Chichimec people. The Chichimec are direct ancestors to many indigenous tribes found throughout Mexico, which included the Aztecs. Historians have generally agreed that a migration by the Chichimec did exist and is based on actual events: a southern migration that began somewhere in the US southwestern region and ended in central Mexico. Scholarly accounts of the great migration have centered on the religious beliefs of the Chichimec, specifically the mythical tale of their banishment from their homeland at the hands of their own deity Huitzilopochtli. At their deity's request, the Chichimec migrated southward for four epochs until they reached the Valley of Mexico. Once there, they were instructed to build a great city over the site where they spotted an eagle devouring a serpent upon a cactus sprouting from a rock. This location rests in the center of present-day Mexico City, ending the legendary southern migration of the Chichimec people that led to rise of the Aztec empire.

The simple belief of having a "homeland" is a critical ideological notion for any developing culture – whether spiritually oriented or politically driven. For the Chicano/a community, however, identifying a homeland within the US was more a necessity for cultural survival. Let us recall that the perception of the Mexican was that of a common criminal – a stereotype linked to their indigenous ancestry – that, coincidentally, justified the perpetual persecution of this community under North American rule. Again, these dominant beliefs and practices "obscured and misrepresented the collective histories, worldviews, and cultural practices of Mexicans and Mexican Americans" (Haas 1995: 167). Change, however, was in the air as Chicano/as began to organize politically during the Chicano/a civil rights movement. In the summer of 1969, 3,000 Chicano/as rallied around Rodolfo "Corky" Gonzalez and his political organization, Crusade for Justice, to attend the first National Chicano Liberation Youth Conference in Denver, Colorado. The historical significance of this conference is far-reaching. The conference itself brought national attention to the Chicano/a movement by attracting young activist from all over the United States – representing the first true national conference in Chicano/a history. The significant contribution of this national event lies in the intellectual exchange that shaped the political culture and identity of the Chicano/a community as a whole. This is the site where renowned Chicano poet Alberto Baltazar Urista, better known as Alurista, first recited the "Epic Poem of Aztlán" (July 6, 1969). The poem's reception at the conference was so enthusiastic that it was adopted as the preamble for *El Plan Espiritual de Aztlán*, the political manifesto for the Chicano/a movement.

Through this single poem, Chicano/as finally found a historical narrative that not only located their homeland, but also supplied a mythical tale of origin that celebrated their existence as a people within the United States. By appropriating and revising the Aztec myth of Aztlán, Alurista refigured much more than just a myth. The manipulation of Aztlán involved a series of pre-Columbian recodifications of Mexico's history that weaved together a distinct Chicano/a historical narrative. Alurista's new interpretation of Aztlán simply added an innovative twist to the great Chichimec migration: the epic return home. The Chicano/a revision basically begins where the Mexican version ends – a genius adaptation that follows the cyclical historical changes of the Chicano/a experience: Mexican (before the Mexican armed conflict with the US), Mexican American (after the Mexican–American War), and Chicano/a (Chicano/a civil rights movement). In true symbolic fashion, the 3,000 migrating Chicano/a activists who attended the conference in Denver, Colorado, embody Alurista's evocation of their ancestral return to Aztlán:

> [W]e, the Chicano inhabitants and civilizers of the northern land of Aztlán from whence came our forefathers, reclaiming the land of their birth and consecrating the determination of our people of the sun, *declare* that the call of our blood is our power, our responsibility, and our inevitable destiny [to] declare the independence of our mestizo nation. We are a bronze people with a bronze culture. Before the world, before all of North

America, before all our brothers in the bronze continent, we are a nation. We are a union
of free pueblos. We are Aztlán.

Chicano/as could now claim a history of mythical stature that is undeniably rooted
in the American Southwest. Although Aztlán links myth to history and ties history
to land as significant transitions in Chicano/a political thought and self-identification,
the historical dexterity of Aztlán proved, yet again, to be multifaceted by influencing
another major aspect of Chicano/a culture: their heritage.

As Luis Leal argues, *El Plan Espiritual de Aztlán* is important because it enabled
Chicano/as to recognize Aztlán as a Mexican territory lost to the United States after
the Mexican–American War – a historical event that marks the political displacement
of an entire Mexican community and subsequent future generations. More importantly, states Leal, the myth of Aztlán allowed the Chicano/a community to publicly
embrace their Pre-Columbian Aztec origins (1989: 11). By reclaiming these southwestern territories and their indigenous heritage, Chicano/as were attempting to assert
a legitimate cultural and political space within the United States. As such, Aztlán
provided Chicano/as with a malleable historical narrative to tailor a specific genealogy,
that highlighted a cultural heritage, that retrieved a pre-Columbian indigenous identity and folklore, and that began to construct a specific Chicano/a political identity.
This final aspect was extremely useful for Chicano/a scholars, activists, and artists who
sought to uncover their indigenous history that had been erased from the historical
narrative and national identity of the United States. This is a point that *El Plan
Espiritual de Aztlán* makes quite clear, "We are a bronze people with a bronze culture
… reclaiming the land of their birth and consecrating the determination of our people
of the sun." Whether it was the Aztecs or their Chichimec ancestors, an indigenous
heritage legitimized all claims to the land; after all, the Aztec myth of origin supplied
an antiquarian history within the United States that trumped the widely held belief
among Americans that Mexicans were foreign subjects of the western frontier. The
ability of the myth of origin to instantly produce usable historical narratives and
cultural identities captured the attention of notable Chicano/a artists and poets such
as Alurista, Luis Valdez, Lorna Dee Cervantes, and Gloria Anzaldúa. Claiming indigenous roots suddenly became a source of cultural pride among Chicano/as that began
to mend the derogatory image of this community.

Let us recall that Mexicans have historically personified the antithetical obstruction
to Manifest Destiny's quest to settle the West. Stereotypes depicting the racial inferiority of Mexico's indigenous population were abundant prior to Mexican armed
conflict with the US, but proliferated during and after the Mexican–American War.
Warfare literature, for instance, proved to be extremely innovative with its demoniza-
tion of bloodthirsty Mexican soldiers. George Lippard, in his widely distributed serial
Legends of Mexico, was quite prolific in this craft: "Again, hark! The howl of the jackal,
comes like a funeral knell over the waste. Hideous, prolonged, distant, that cry chills
your heart with dread, for it speaks of a loathsome beast, mangling with gray teeth
and fangs, the cold face of the battle dead" (1847: 14). Disturbingly effective in his

primordial description of the feasting Mexican jackal, Lippard evokes the age-old fable of the cannibalistic tendencies of barbaric Aztec tribes in order to embellish the piercing gray fangs that threaten American democracy. The sensationalized representation of the bloodthirsty Aztec proved to be a difficult image to shed.

Along with the monstrous Aztec descriptions that struck fear into the imagination of the American public during the Mexican–American War, Mexican inter-racial mixing was also widely believed to be the key source for their overall racial inferiority and barbaric disposition. Mexico's colonial conquest at the hands of the Spanish empire proved to be a favorite source among Americans to explain the crude character of the Mexican community. At the heart of this argument stood Mexico's heterogeneous population largely made up of an indigenous class, former African slave communities, and the Spanish populace – an abomination that was heightened by the cross-fertilization that took place between these races. Americans, on the other hand, were racially pure, had higher moral codes, were brave beyond measure in their defense of democracy, and were introducing civic institutions to develop the uncharted terrain of the western frontier. Mexicans, in general, could never measure up to these standards or accomplish such great deeds. In fact, Mexican society was in a downward spiral with each successive cross-racial union. This degenerative racial element formed the sovereign "tri-colored flag of Mexico, typifying the three predominant influences in that golden and bloody clime, Superstition, Ignorance, and Crime" (Lippard 1847: 22). In short, Mexico typified the demise of a civilized nation as a result of its own tainted national bloodlines.

It would take yet another national myth from Mexico to refute these negative views. The early twentieth-century political figure and scholar José Vasconcelos clearly recognized the racial tensions that existed between US and Mexico. Only a generation removed from the Mexican–American War, he believed that the political climate during this period "became, and continues to be, a conflict of Latinism against Anglo-Saxonism; a conflict of institutions, aims, and ideals" (1997: 10). Vasconcelos' recognition of existing institutional differences between Latinism and Anglo-Saxonism reminds us that any attempt to define a nation, or construct a national identity, on the basis of "aims" and "ideals" relies on predetermined notions of race – a conceptual relationship tailored to serve specific political agendas that legitimize the racial superiority of one nation over another. In other words, the political utility of merging race and nation is almost always intended to classify humans into racial categorizations that reify hierarchical orders of difference. In an attempt to balance the racial disparity between the feral Mexican and Saxon American, Vasconcelos published *La Raza Cósmica / The Cosmic Race* (1925).

The publication of *La Raza Cósmica* proved to be a major turning point in the construction of a Mexican national identity during the early twentieth century. The brilliance behind this groundbreaking text lies in Vasconcelos' appropriation and manipulation of the same racial formula that deemed Mexico an inferior nation. As previously stated, Americans truly believed that Mexico's deficiency as a nation rested on its adulterated national bloodlines that were irreversibly tainted by centuries of extensive inter-racial breeding: *mestizaje* (miscegenation). According to the pseudoscientific tenets of Anglo-Saxonism, Mexico's historical record of *mestizaje* led to the effacement of the best qualities found in the original white races. Vasconcelos' solution to challenge the racial hierarchical order of this doctrine was simply to reverse it: where Anglo-Saxonism saw racial degradation in Mexico's heterogeneous population, Vasconcelos observed the fusion of a superior "cosmic race," and where Anglo-Saxonism saw the demise of a Mexican nation, Vasconcelos witnessed the forging of a new dynamic national identity. The birth of the *cosmic race*, states Juan De Castro, "became a way for the three numerically dominant races living in the Americas – white, Amerindian, and black – to become incorporated into the same national project: they would commingle to form a new *mestizo* race, in which the constitutive qualities of each original race would contribute to and form a new and different whole" (2002: 19). Under Vasconcelos' theoretical discourse, *mestizaje* ceased to exist as a term that only defined racial miscegenation and began representing a broader political conceptualization that embraced Mexico's cultural hybridity. Moreover, the racial restructuring of the pseudoscientific principles underlying Anglo-Saxonism proved, at least in theory, that Mexico's indigenous class, former African slave communities, and the Spanish populace had and could contribute "good" qualities to humanity. In one broad sweep, Vasconcelos transformed what was once thought of as a degenerative biological characteristic of *mestizaje* into the cultural backbone of a new forging national body: the cosmic race. The popular reception of Vasconcelos' racial theory instantly installed *mestizaje* as a major cultural component of Mexico's national identity.

The national and international acclaim Vasconcelos received on publication of *La Raza Cósmica* rendered the text too tantalizing to be forgotten. Nearly half a century later, the concept of the cosmic race proved to be perfectly tailored to combat the same discriminatory views that persisted to haunt the Chicano/a community in the US under the southern Jim Crow law. However, it was Vasconcelos' successful national project on behalf of Mexico that intrigued and ultimately informed the political culture and thinking of Chicano/a intellectual circles. As the popular belief that the publication of *La Raza Cósmica* corresponded to a national plea throughout the Americas to question North American world dominance during the early twentieth century, the text's political philosophy quickly became associated with the political emergence of the Chicano/a civil rights movement of the 1960s and 1970s. With time Chicano/a activists, artists, and scholars managed to assemble an impressive array of work that transformed what was once Mexico's national myth into the political consciousness of a new Chicano/a subjectivity.

The attractive aspect of the cosmic race, like Aztlán, lies in that it not only connects the past to a shared collective memory, but also constructs a political identity for Chicano/as within the belly of the beast: the United States. For example, Guillermo Fuenfrios, in his essay "The Emergence of the New Chicano," describes the Chicano as "a pluralistic man, a universal man, combining the racial strains and cultures of the entire world in his own person." Fuenfrios goes so far as to suggest that

Vasconcelos "coined the term 'la raza cósmica' to describe him" (1972: 284). The pluralistic, universal, and multiracial elements of a *mestizo/a* subjectivity quickly became a celebrated cultural aspect of Chicano/a identity. Consider Fuenfrios' closing statement:

> For the Chicano, Indian forms and symbols are no affectation. They are in his blood, his religion, and his culture. ... Oh, Chicano: you are here at the crisis of man's existence on the earth, the legitimate heir to the culture of the entire community of man. Wandering Jew, exiled Arab, dispossessed Indian, Spanish bastard and American orphan, you have in your language all the cultures of Europe; in your blood the mystery and wisdom of Native America and the Orient and Africa – the "Cosmic Race." Find your voice and sing and you will save the world. (1972: 284)

Clearly, Chicano/a scholars, artists, and activists bought into Vasconcelos' *mestizo* imaginary to validate the existence of a new breed of people that crossed the frontiers of Europe, Native America, the Orient, and Africa. Fuenfrios' "New Chicano" interpretation and representation began to move away from a regional experience to a more expansive border-crossing account of the world's colonized people – a cultural similarity that became extremely useful for Chicano/a scholars a decade later.

If Guillermo Fuenfrios recognized the value of border-crossing as an essential characteristic of the New Chicano, Gloria Anzaldúa achieved its full potential through her publication of the *Borderlands / La Frontera: The New Mestiza* (1987). According to Anzaldúa, borders are designed to separate the civilized from the barbaric and distinguish the foreign and alien from the citizen. To maintain this balance, geographical boundaries were outlined to detain the "squint-eyed, the perverse, the queer, the troublesome, the mongrel, the mulato, the half-breed, the half dead; in short, those who cross over, pass over, or go through the confines of the 'normal' " (Anzaldúa 1987: 3). Her innovative breakthrough, however, reminds us of the porous and fluid nature of all borders, whether physically or socially constructed – a malleable quality she suggests can be used as a means to resist the restrictive disposition of these same borders. By learning to navigate through the permeable contours of the borderlands, border inhabitants begin to construct a new consciousness informed by the cultural exchanges taking place within the various borders "where two or more cultures edge each other, where people of different races occupy the same territory" (1987: 1) that ultimately results in the "new *mestiza* consciousness." Anzaldúa describes this mental state as:

> [A] conscious rupture with all oppressive traditions of all cultures and religions. She communicates that rapture, documents the struggle. She reinterprets history and, using new symbols, she shapes new myths. She adopts new perspectives toward the dark-skinned, women and queers. She strengthens her tolerance (and intolerance) for ambiguity. She is willing to share, to make herself vulnerable to foreign ways of seeing and

thinking. She surrenders all notions of safety, of the familiar. Deconstruct, construct. (1987: 82)

The multiple border transitions – whether physical, racial, gendered, or psychological – proved to be a perfect subversive tactic to resist the multiple fronts of hegemony. In time, Anzaldúa's new *mestiza* consciousness became a highly regarded academic methodology that is now officially recognized as border theory. The border subject's ability to speak and move within hegemonic centers of power has propelled border theory into the ranks of postcolonial theory and postmodernism.

Anzaldúa's immediate success can be attributed, in many ways, to the unorthodox structure of *Borderlands / La Frontera: The New Mestiza*. As the title suggests, the text stands as a compilation of poetry, autobiography, historical text, and creative writing that is articulated in a multilingual patois: English, Spanish, Spanglish, Tex-Mex, and Nahuatl. Although Anzaldúa tailors a truly unique theoretical approach toward the hybridity of the borderlands, she depends and harks back to the same indigenous past and inter-racial heritage that Vasconcelos formulated for Mexico during the early twentieth century. It should be no surprise, then, to find a link between Anzaldúa's new *mestiza* consciousness and Vasconcelos' cosmic race. Vasconcelos' influence on Anzaldúa is quite evident through her version of his written motto for the National University of Mexico, "For my race my spirit shall speak" with her own Chicana reinterpretation "For the women of my race my spirit shall speak" (Anzaldúa 1987: 77). Anzaldúa goes on to cite and interpret Vasconcelos' cosmic race as a theory of racial inclusion and views his theoretical formulation as the hybrid building blocks of an "alien consciousness presently in the making – a new *mestiza* consciousness, *una conciencia de mujer*. It is the consciousness of the borderlands" (1987: 77). The fusion of the cosmic race with the political emergence of the New Chicano and its influence in the development of the new *mestiza* consciousness exemplifies the cross-national exchanges, cultural blending, and intellectual borrowing that takes place within this multilayered border space.

The need for Chicano/as, as well as American patriots, to define, or at least start formulating, a national praxis to legitimize their contributions to the historical development of the United States has been the cardinal goal since their first encounter within this single, multifaceted geographical territory. Both parties have relentlessly tried to accomplish this objective by conceiving nationalist discourses informed by their own cultural origins, histories, and traditions. The myth of origin proved to be an effective rhetorical tool to accomplish these ends. As Americans merged the ideological doctrine of Manifest Destiny with the Anglo-Saxon myth of origin to lay claim to the West, Chicano/as formulated their own mythical homeland in Aztlán and created an indigenous national identity to reclaim the Chicano Southwest. Clearly, the ideological systems at work within both of these myths were meant to disparage the credibility of one another. Despite these tensions, both myths of origin have as much in common as they do differences.

The Anglo-Saxon myth of origin and Aztec myth of Aztlán were not only borrowed from other nations, but were also altered, sacrificing historical accuracy in order to support specific political agendas. As discussed earlier, Americans viewed the settlement of the western frontier as an extension of the legendary migration of their Saxon ancestors, a view that resulted in armed conflict, the annexation of half of Mexico's northern territories, and the subjugation of a new minority Mexican class in the United States – all of which was simply viewed as democracy's divine plan to civilize these uncharted lands. Aztlán, on the other hand, conveniently located a home of origin for Chicano/as within the US through the great migration of the Chichimec people. The significance of this mythical migration represents the epic return to their northern homeland: the southwestern borderlands. Chicano/a intellectual circles complemented this myth of origin with Vasconcelos' concept of the cosmic race to celebrate the political awakening of an entire community: the new Chicano/new *mestiza*. However, the adaptations to these myths of origin were carried out for the same strategic purpose: to lay claim to a single geographical space through the manipulation of socially constructed national symbols.

Now, considering all the major historical, cultural, and national alterations to Mexico's national myths, a question arises that needs to be asked, or at least pondered: what does Mexico have to say? After all, Mexico is the constant denominator underlying the national imaginaries of the American West and Chicano Southwest. Is Mexico to remain silent throughout this entire process? Surely, Mexico's intellectual circles and own cultural thinkers have their own interpretations of this frontier space that lies north of Mexico – a territory that is officially recognized as El Norte (the North) in the popular imagination the Mexican populace. Fortunately, Vasconcelos was a prolific writer who not only supplied an answer to my inquiry, but also posits some interesting thoughts concerning the true political functionality underwriting the cosmic race. Surprising revelations, I would argue, that impact the footing of foundational Chicano/a manifestos, literary works, and academic methodologies.

Although Vasconcelos describes, and to some extent can identify with, the Chicano experience, we must remember that the cosmic race was tailored in a particular period that served a specific political purpose. As Marilyn Grace Miller points out, late nineteenth-century and early twentieth-century Latin American intellectuals who utilized *mestizaje* as a cultural movement interpret a "colonial history that is marked by war and atrocity [to] paradoxically produce utopia" (2004: 14). Under Miller's analysis, Vasconcelos' cosmic race represents the type of discourse that discounts the brutality of Spanish colonialism by romanticizing the colonial violence of miscegenation. Latin America's political elite has historically used *mestizaje* as a rhetorical web to cloak its colonial tensions and racial differences, using pro-indigenous liberal discourses to maintain power during the rise of independence movements. In the cosmic race, Vasconcelos foresaw an opportunity to homogenize the Mexican population through selective miscegenation to erase the inferior species in order to do away with the indigenous class: "step by step, by voluntary extinction, the uglier stocks will give way to the more handsome" (Vasconcelos 1997: 32). Despite Vasconcelos' relative success in creating a national identity for Mexico, he would clearly dislike the national identity the Chicano/a movement is founded on.

Unlike Chicano/a intellectuals who searched for a usable indigenous past as a national point of departure, Vasconcelos focused his efforts on fabricating a credible future that excluded the indigenous class. The unforeseen paradoxical result of the cutting and pasting of Mexican national myths is the clear and obvious discrepancy between historical accuracy and political objectives. Chicano/as are basically revitalizing an indigenous history that Vasconcelos spent a lifetime trying to eradicate from the official historical narrative of Mexico. My investigation of Vasconcelos' racial theory attempts to demonstrate how Chicano/a appropriations of Mexico and assemblages of "indigenousness" are not only produced by dominant and hegemonic groups, but implicitly involve the illusory representations imposed by our own Chicano/a community. These strategies, states Sheila Marie Contreras, eerily resemble the mythification of indigenous history and primitivizing practices of early Western anthropologists, archeologists, and American modernist authors (2008: 165). It is here, within the cultural tradition of borrowing, altering, and reimagining the national myth of origin where I believe these interlocking narratives change the "way we think of cultural identity and its representation" and shed new light on the "examination of history, cultural identity, ethnicity, literature, and politics in relationship to each other" (Alarcón 1997: p. xvi).

In an effort to understand and find a place for these contradictory moments, José Aranda has argued that the contradictory impulses existing within our own communities, historical record, and scholarship provide the proper starting point to reassess the status and currency of Chicano/a studies (2003: 127) – an academic reassessment that should certainly include the American West and Latin American studies. If this dialectical currency gains value in the academic marketplace, scholars can begin to sort through and make sense of the historical, cultural, and literary ambiguities resulting from the multiple western, southwestern, and northern crossroads that clash within this single mythical frontier region. These investigations will not only revisit historical blind spots in our own fields of study, but also allow scholars to come to terms with the reality that academic paradigms must become adaptable to the spontaneous cultural combustions of their own object of study. The numerous interconnecting narratives that simultaneously construct and deconstruct this geographical landscape will undoubtedly raise new questions that will broaden our understanding of the American West, Chicano/a Southwest, and Mexico's El Norte. New inquiries, I argue, that need to include the place of Native Americans within this frontier space. What is their position within and response to these mythical tales of origin? And, more importantly, how do we interpret the colonial conquest of Native Americans under the ancestral homeland of Chicano/as: Mexico? These investigations and their potential answers are essential for scholars who are trying to construct the pedagogical framework in which to teach the history, culture, and literature of a continuously evolving American landscape that points in multiple directions at once.

References and Further Reading

Alarcón, Cooper Daniel. (1997). *The Aztec Palimpsest: Mexico in the Modern Imagination.* Tucson: University of Arizona Press.

Anaya, A. Rudolfo, and Francisco A. Lomelí. (1989). *Aztlán: Essays on the Chicano Homeland.* Albuquerque: University of New Mexico Press.

Anzaldúa, Gloria. (1987). *Borderlands / La Frontera: The New Mestiza.* San Francisco: Aunt Lute Books.

Aranda, José. (2003). *When We Arrive: A New Literary History of Mexican America.* Tucson: University of Arizona Press.

Contreras, Marie Sheila. (2008). *Bloodlines: Myth, Indigenism, and Chicana/o Literature.* Austin: University of Texas Press.

De Castro, Juan E. (2002). *Mestizo Nations: Culture, Race, and Conformity in Latin American Literature.* Tucson: University of Arizona Press.

Fuenfrios, Guillermo. (1972). The Emergence of the New Chicano. In Luis Valdez and Stan Steiner, eds., *Aztlán: An Anthology of Mexican American Literature.* New York: Knopf Press.

Haas, Lisbeth. (1967). *Conquest and Historical Identities in California: 1769–1936.* Berkeley: University of California Press.

Horsman, Reginald. (1981). *Race and Manifest Destiny: The Origins of American Racial Anglo-Saxonism.* Cambridge, MA: Harvard University Press.

Leal, Luis. (1989). In Search of Aztlán. In Rudolfo Anaya and Francisco Lomelí, eds., *Aztlán: Essays on the Chicano Homeland.* Albuquerque: University of New Mexico Press.

Lippard, George. (1847). *Legends of Mexico.* Philadelphia: T.B. Peterson.

Menchaca, Martha. (2001). *Recovering History, Constructing Race: The Indian, Black, and White Roots of Mexican Americans.* Texas: University of Texas Press.

Miller, Grace Marilyn. (2004). *Rise and Fall of the Cosmic Race.* Austin: University of Texas Press.

Sampson, Robert D. (2003). *John L. O'Sullivan and his Times.* Kent: Kent State University Press.

Stepan, Leys Nancy. (1991). *The Hour of Eugenics: Race, Gender, and Nation in Latin America.* Ithaca, NY: Cornell University Press.

Stephanson, Anders. (1995). *Manifest Destiny: American Expansionism and the Empire of Right.* New York: Hill & Wang.

Valdez, Luis, and Stan Steiner. (1972). *Aztlán: An Anthology of Mexican American Literature.* New York: Knopf.

Vasconcelos, José. (1997). *The Cosmic Race: A Bilingual Edition* [1st pub. in Spanish 1925; trans. into English 1979]. Baltimore: Johns Hopkins University Press.

13

Writing the Indigenous West

Kathleen Washburn

Joy Harjo's 2007 poem "The Path to the Milky Way Leads Through Los Angeles" highlights many of the complex and shifting relationships among Native American communities, models of indigenous literature, and critical paradigms of the American West. Citing the stomping grounds of Okmulgee in Muscogee (Creek) territory, the poem takes as its primary subject the sunny vistas and crowded streets of Los Angeles. At first glance, such attention to a sustaining homeland and an alienating metropolis on the western edge of the continent suggests a familiar opposition between long-standing indigenous traditions and the more recent phenomena of American urbanization and development. Indeed, the music of turtle shells and the dreamlike "song of human voices" (Harjo 2000: 45) stand in stark contrast to the "whine of civilization" and the rasping call of the crow as urban scavenger. If one persistent notion of the American West continues to be grounded in a national mythology of westward expansion, then Harjo's poem seems to offer an alternate perspective on this legacy of colonization as modernization.

At the same time, such rigid categories fail to account for the poem's playful reconfigurations of history, region, community, and identity. Even as Muscogee songs and ceremonial practices inflect Harjo's lyrical and lively vision, Los Angeles also offers new possibilities for indigenous expression and cultural production. This modern supercity serves not simply as the crossroads of Native ceremony and American consumer culture, but as a vital juncture on the title path to the Milky Way. The brilliant stars of the night sky and the glittering celebrities of Hollywood come together in uneasy confluence, so that somehow "the gods are easier to perceive here," even in "a city of the strange and getting stranger." By invoking a cosmic scale far grander than that of landscape or city streets, this poetic map also moves beyond

A Companion to the Literature and Culture of the American West, First Edition. Edited by Nicolas S. Witschi.
© 2011 Blackwell Publishing Ltd. Published 2011 by Blackwell Publishing Ltd.

familiar oppositions of the natural world and the built environment. In this respect, Okmulgee and Los Angeles may well be disparate as distinct locations, but they are not wholly incompatible or even disconnected in a broader web of American, global, and even galactic significance. The poem thus presents a new kind of star map, one that encompasses traditional forms of indigenous knowledge as well as an iconic American city mythologized alternately as a place to escape the past or as the supercity prototype of a globalized future. For Harjo, Los Angeles offers both the alluring "illusion of the marketplace" and the beautiful "starry road" of the heavens. The poem's search for the Milky Way in the detritus of the urban cityscape is embodied in the figure of the crow "finding gold in the trash of humans." Following the crow's example, the speaker resolves to "collect the shine of anything beautiful I can find." The resulting poetics of scavenging offers a new indigenous song, one that speaks to a world overlaid with a dizzying mix of signs and cultures.

Harjo's twenty-first-century poem resonates with important questions for Native American literature and studies of the American West in broader terms. Where does one locate the American West, both in various historical contexts and for a contemporary moment? In what ways do these histories overlap or diverge? How are Native American traditions and communities constructed and represented in such narratives of place and space? Which literary strategies are employed for such purposes, and who are the readers or consumers of such texts? Finally, what are the points of intersection between Native American literatures and broader constructions of a regional, national, or globalized American West? This discussion highlights key lines of inquiry and recent critical trends in the diverse and often conflicting categories of Native American literature and the literature of the American West. The American West continues to serve as a compelling category for literature and critical analysis. Intersecting with this protean field, the discipline of indigenous studies calls for reconsidering the subjects as well as the methodologies of literary analysis. In addition to unsettling and reconfiguring familiar critical categories, such attempts to "indigenize the academy" (Mihesuah et al. 2004: 4) also highlight the relationship between academic forms of knowledge and the lived experiences of Native people in regional, national, and global frameworks.

One familiar and still persistent narrative of the American West unfolds as a westward expansion and progression from the East as domestic base and center of historical memory. In this nationalist vision, Los Angeles functions as an iconic western location in overlapping ways, first as a place of natural wonders and exploitable resources; consider Mulholland's dream to bring water across the desert in order to build a tropical paradise by the ocean, as well as the legacy of that project in terms of the ongoing snare of property and water rights among urban and rural constituencies as well as county, state, national, and indigenous stakeholders. Another powerful imaginary of Los Angeles is that of a young city, a twentieth-century metropolis whose history begins not with Chumash traditions or even Alta California but with the Gold Rush, California statehood, and subsequent migrations to a place imagined and promoted as a golden land of plenty. In turn, the rich archive of Los Angeles literature often is reduced to narratives of arrival, displacement, and novelty. From the work of Helen Hunt Jackson and Raymond Chandler to John Fante and Pico Iyer, the city often is sifted through a mesh of comparisons, legible only in relation to elsewhere: the West as not-East, as invented, strange, or unfamiliar territory.

Here, too, Harjo's poem is instructive. First, the focus on Los Angeles in a collection entitled *A Map to the Next World* suggests significant points of intersection between Native American literature and the discourse of new worlds in terms of region as well as voice. In keeping with the rich literary history of this iconic California city as American utopia or dystopia, "The Path to the Milky Way Leads Through Los Angeles" hails the city as a place of extraordinary natural beauty as well as a center for mass culture, both a generative space and a dumping ground for the messy "trash of humans." Los Angeles serves as a repository for diverse territorial histories as well as the site for producing and disseminating ideas of the American West through literature, film, television, music, and other cultural forms. In this respect, the poem serves as an indictment of the American marketplace for selling lands (and souls), but also as an ode to the ongoing strains of Muscogee tradition. Harjo brings together the multilayered sounds of the city, Okmulgee as Muscogee homeland, and even the music of the spheres. Beyond a structure of point and counterpoint, the poem thus offers a new form of indigenous song that incorporates such discordant tones of the American West. Territorial boundaries may shift and change, but the voices of Okmulgee persist, even as far west as the Pacific.

Such a focus on Los Angeles as both visionary and "precarious" city also speaks to the complex histories of Native dislocation, mobility, and alliance in a cultural site better known for Hollywood mythmaking. In addition to its deep history as homeland for Tongva and Chumash communities, Los Angeles also served as a target city for Native relocation as federal policies sought to dismantle reservations in booming postwar America. Then as now, Los Angeles has the largest Native American population of any city in the country, followed not by Seattle or Albuquerque but New York. In fact, the majority of enrolled Muskogee Creek tribal members today not only live outside Okmulgee, but also beyond the borders of Oklahoma. Los Angeles and Okmulgee as sites of cultural production thus resonate in surprising ways, for both are linked to narratives of indigenous experience, cultural borderlands, and nation formation. In this respect, the federal relocation – or "termination" – policy for Native tribes dictates a rural-to-urban movement that echoes the "Okie" flight from the Dust Bowl to California in the 1930s. Though different in important ways, these twentieth-century migrations situate a present-day Los Angeles in relation to a deeper history of displacement in the American West.

Now mapped within the borders of the state of Oklahoma, Okmulgee signals indigenous persistence as well as the contested history of a complex region. As the capital of the Muscogee nation since the 1860s, Okmulgee marks land designated in succession as part of the Creek Confederacy, then Indian Territory, and later the state of Oklahoma. Huckleberry Finn famously ends his fictional escapades through a pre-Civil War American past by lighting out "for the Territory ahead of the rest" – a phrase that would signal Indian Territory for nineteenth-century readers. Whether fleeing the constraints of the "sivilizing" process or embracing an American mythology of self-making, many settlers likewise sought out available lands and affordable homestead opportunities created through the displacement and dispossession of Native communities. Today Okmulgee continues to signify ongoing Muscogee cultural and political traditions, including the annual Green Corn Ceremony, but also carries the residue of an imperial history often lauded in the discourse of the "Sooners" as pioneering American subjects. As many critics have noted, narratives of the American West as a project of nation-building frequently leave out stories of indigenous alliances, forced removals, and disputes over sovereignty so central to Native histories. A deeper history of Okmulgee and surrounding regions includes the vast geographical and cultural networks of the Mississippian Mound Builders as well as the political influence of the Creek Confederacy in resisting American and European expansion into indigenous lands throughout the eighteenth and nineteenth centuries.

Joy Harjo's poem moves between Los Angeles, Okmulgee, and even the Milky Way to map such visible and submerged points of correspondence in literary and cultural worldviews. In a similar vein, the broad rubric of Native American literature brings together a wide spectrum of distinct tribal literatures as well as interconnected stories of cultural change, adaptation, and continuity. Thus Harjo's body of work in various media (poetry, music, film) can be framed in relation to Muscogee storytelling traditions, Native American literature, and visions of the American West, as well as in relation to the varied cultural contexts of places including New Mexico, southern California, and Hawai'i, where she has lived and worked; her work also brings together influences as varied as jazz, experimental American poetry, and indigenous world music. Just as New Western history has opened up new possibilities for investigating the West as frontier, borderland, or postnational experiment, Native American literature offers potent challenges to critical models of the American West in terms of genre, literary history, and notions of print culture. In spatial terms, indigenous literature pressures a national narrative of westward expansion into wide-open spaces while also interrogating the effects of constructing or imagining such lands as environmental systems, tribal homelands, or even indigenized urban cityscapes.[1] Fundamental to an increasingly expansive archive of the American West, Native literatures call for reading practices that recognize the rich variety of tribal cultures as well as complex networks of regional and global exchange.

Cultural and Critical Sovereignty

The most significant critical development in Native American literary studies in recent years is an increased emphasis on indigenous cultural practices and perspectives as a vital foundation for reading Native texts. Following the model of indigenous studies as an interdisciplinary field and echoing similar developments in disciplines such as law and history, the turn to indigenous cultural forms as the basis for literary interpretation allows for the recuperation of modes of knowledge that previously have been marginalized or excluded from academic institutions. From oral traditions and material culture to kinship networks and treaty agreements, attending to such resources often calls for a departure from the theoretical underpinnings and discursive conventions of various academic disciplines. Vine Deloria Jr.'s influential (and controversial) critique of the imperial history of anthropology and the field's continued risks of cultural appropriation serves as a powerful example of how indigenous scholarship can expose the damaging effects of dominant discourses of "the Indian" as well as a pervasive disconnection between academic institutions and Native communities. From Taiaiake Alfred's *Peace, Power, Righteousness* and Linda Tuhiwai Smith's *Decolonizing Methodologies* to Devon Mihesuah and Angela Cavender Wilson's *Indigenizing the Academy*, indigenous studies scholars continue to argue for considering tribal cultural traditions in relation to the needs and ethics of Native communities rather than as objects of study visible only through European frameworks of thought and experience.

For literary studies, the critical turn toward tribal contexts and indigenous forms of knowledge affects research methodologies as well as reading practices for Native texts – and, arguably, for canonical American texts as well. First, such renewed attention to indigenous cultural forms seeks to recuperate modes of knowledge that previously have been marginalized in academic institutions, from songs and stories from oral traditions to texts that have fallen out of print. Second, accounting for indigenous cultural traditions calls for a recalibration of disciplinary histories and conventions, from the popularity of Indian captivity narratives in early American print culture to the genre of autobiography as grounded in the discourse of individuality and self-making. Thus rather than simply incorporating Native American texts and writers into established areas of study, an indigenous studies praxis seeks to draw upon Native discourses and worldviews for literary and cultural texts. Categories of realism, sentimental fiction, regionalism, or even postmodernism may apply to Native American literature, but such texts also are recognized as cultural productions linked to particular indigenous communities and tribal traditions. For instance, in the book-length study *Our Fire Survives the Storm*, Daniel Heath Justice charts a Cherokee literary history from its "deep roots" (Justice 2006: 2) to the present day. He brings together texts on Cherokee Removal by John Ross with works by John Oskison in the early twentieth century and contemporary voices such as Marilou Awiakta in order to trace common themes of kinship relations, political coherence, and experiments with language.

This shift in framing Native texts exposes the connections between dominant discourses of the West and the material effects of American expansion into Native homelands. For although Native lands, cultures, and communities are central to any imaginary of the American West, such complex relationships often have been elided entirely or restricted to narratives of "the Indian" as an impediment to Western expansion or as the savage foil to the iconic figures of settler or cowboy. Accounting for

Native literatures reshapes the textual archive of the American West and provides alternate narratives of land and community, while also opening up new possibilities for imagining Indians in literature.

The collection *Reasoning Together* by the Native Critics Collective (Womack et al. 2008) demonstrates the range of interpretive approaches that emerge from careful attention to tribal specificity and forms of Native cultural sovereignty. For instance, Lisa Brooks calls for a critical practice grounded in community histories and experiences. As she illustrates by connecting readings of the Haudenosaunee (Iroquois) creation story, appeals for "Indian" alliances by the seventeenth-century leader Mantonomi, and the varied publications of Mohegan teacher and missionary Samson Occum and Pequot writer William Apess, literary analysis can be attentive to the particularities of tribal history and cultural contexts while also charting a deep history of intertribal alliances and forms of intellectual exchange. In a similar vein, Phillip Carroll Morgan turns to an 1830 essay on Choctaw forms of storytelling by writer James L. McDonald as a guide to contemporary criticism that seeks to engage both oral and written texts in new forms. Daniel Heath Justice models literary analysis that "puts kinship principles into practice" (Justice 2008: 148) by reading tribal stories in relation to an ongoing tradition of indigenous literature. He writes: "The decolonization imperative in our literature both *reflects* the indigenous continuity of the past and present and *projects* that continuity into the future" (2008: 150). In each case, models of indigenous community include adaptive traditions and cultural transformations rather a vision of stories and relationships trapped in a prior time.

Penelope Myrtle Kelsey's recent book-length work expands upon such "tribal theory" (Kelsey 2008: 6) by taking up a range of Dakota fiction and nonfiction texts as an interconnected body of work. Kelsey calls for building stronger connections between forms of academic knowledge production and the needs and desires of indigenous communities; she also proposes the study of indigenous languages as vital to literary analysis. Through her readings of print translations of various forms of Dakota oral storytelling to autobiographies by Zitkala-Ša and Charles Eastman, Kelsey highlights the ways in which Dakota understandings of gender, community, and *tiyospaye* undergird a range of English-language texts. The focus on writers from the late nineteenth and early twentieth centuries is particularly useful, as such texts have enjoyed renewed critical attention in recent years in relation to Native, western, and American literature. Both Zitkala-Ša and Eastman were associated with the flagship Carlisle Indian Industrial School, worked in political advocacy, and wrote in multiple genres. Yet whereas many critics have situated texts by Native writers at the turn of the century in relation to the assimilation project of Indian boarding schools and the nostalgia of non-Native reading publics, Kelsey instead argues that these early twentieth-century texts give voice to Dakota worldviews in powerful ways. Rather than framing Eastman's text exclusively in terms of European/American conventions of the autobiography as genre, she notes that Eastman incorporates "several traditional forms of self-narration" (2008: 55), from key references to the journey of the warpath and attention to naming practices to reports of bravery. In this respect, the title *From the*

Deep Woods to Civilization may suggest a progress narrative of Americanization, but the text itself offers profound moments of literary resistance by writing Dakota cultural traditions into an English form. Only by attending to such "unique tribal knowledges, epistemology, and philosophy" (Kelsey 2008: 1) can readers appreciate the complexities of discursive strategies at work in such texts that negotiate between distinct worldviews.

Interestingly, Eastman has proven to be a popular figure in debates about representations of the American West. Gerald Vizenor describes him as a "conversionist" (Vizenor 1994: 155) who sought to promote the value of indigenous cultures at a time when the discourse of the "vanishing Indian" dominated popular culture as well as federal Indian policy. Vizenor thus defends Eastman's texts as resisting the markers of "simulated" Indian identity and thus enacting native "survivance" over "aesthetic victimry" (1994: 100). The 2007 Home Box Office production of *Bury My Heart at Wounded Knee* imported Eastman into the drama of the Indian wars, the quest for gold in the Black Hills, and the Ghost Dance movement linked to Paiute leader Wovoka. Eastman's first-person text recounts his experience at Pine Ridge Agency as a medical doctor who arrived at his new post just weeks before the massacre of Ghost Dancers on December 26, 1890. The made-for-television special draws upon this source material in order to position Eastman as the product of the boarding schools, a key architect of allotment policy (here using considerable poetic license), and eyewitness to the hyperbolic violence of federal troops against the Lakota. Like Dee Brown's popular collection of case studies in Indian history first published in 1970, the "television event" of *Bury My Heart at Wounded Knee* is designed to rewrite a triumphant narrative of winning the American West by documenting the abuses of federal Indian policy and the extreme violence of national expansion.

Despite the film's realist exposé mode, Eastman's role in the production is reduced to that of naive protégé whose faith in the United States government and American domestic order is shaken by his return to a home community. The character acts as a foil to that of Sitting Bull as traditional leader, one who fights against American encroachment on Native lands but who ultimately becomes corrupted by commerce and pride. And whereas Eastman's multiple publications repeatedly uphold the value and beauty of indigenous storytelling and cultural traditions, the HBO film presents this important writer as a tragic and alienated figure caught between two incongruent cultures. Such portrayals of both Sitting Bull and Charles Eastman are in keeping with what Louis Owens terms the "Chief Doom school of literature" (Owens 1998: 82), the popular and persistent association of Native cultures with (and only with) suffering and loss.

In contrast to such tragic spectacles, modes of Native critical and cultural sovereignty often emphasize the persistence and innovations of tradition for diverse communities. In contrast to the HBO film *Bury My Heart at Wounded Knee*, the 2008 PBS series *We Shall Remain* focuses on stories of cultural tradition and transformation in various historical settings. In turn, the final episode features the occupation of Wounded Knee from 1969 to 1971 by members of the American Indian Movement

(AIM), thus recognizing the deeper history of the 1890 massacre of Ghost Dancers while moving beyond a tragic frontier narrative of the American West at the close of the nineteenth century. Director Chris Eyre's choices in subject matter, script, and filmic style are open to debate, but his success as a key figure in new Native cinema marks a significant shift toward increased Native access to active and visible participation in such forms of cultural production. Eyre's series for a broad American audience reminds viewers that such technologies of representation have a complex history – the final installment includes film footage shot by AIM members – and also offers new possibilities for the field of Native American literature and culture. By linking the histories of varied communities in different historical periods, *We Shall Remain* emphasizes shared experiences of indigenous cultural transformation and persistence in the face of colonization. In a similar vein, the term "Native American" can indicate such connections among tribal communities, but also risks collapsing key cultural and linguistic differences in favor of an undifferentiated category of racial or ethnic identity; as a result, most critics are careful to cite specific tribal names, nations, and confederations (Muscogee, Diné, Iroquois) for literary texts and contexts.

Just as representations of the occupation of Wounded Knee in film and literature necessarily engage with a history of pan-tribal alliance and Native–federal conflict in the American West, Native critical sovereignty is constructed in contradistinction to standard paradigms of the West as wilderness or frontier space defined by exploration, settlement, and incorporation into a national domestic order. Thus Craig Womack's *Red on Red*, which calls for "literary separatism" to the extent of recognizing and privileging specific Creek contexts for Creek literature in many forms, necessarily engages with broader conventions of representing the American West. Womack dismisses S. Alice Callahan's 1891 novel *Wynema* as troubling or even insistently inauthentic for its representations of Creeks in Indian Territory living in "tipis" as well as the novel's reliance upon discourses of American progress and the civilizing project. He argues that Callahan cites the iconography of Plains cultures as a popular signal of Native presence rather than engaging with the vital traditions and relationships of Creek society at the close of the nineteenth century.

Some have criticized Womack's call for literary separatism as narrow or even essentializing in focus, but his study also extends to new readings of the "Queer Oklahomo Indian theory" (Womack 1999: 273) of Cherokee writer Lynn Riggs in plays such as *The Cherokee Night*. Womack argues that Riggs encodes complex ideas about gay and Native identity in dramas that may seem otherwise empty of Cherokee themes or reliant upon reductive stereotypes such as the "rather typical end-of-the-trail icon" (1999: 294). Notably, Riggs also wrote *Green Grow the Lilacs*, the play set in "Indian Territory, 1900" that serves as the basis for the popular Rodgers and Hammerstein musical *Oklahoma!* As the exclamatory title suggests, the Broadway (and Hollywood) musical production sings the praises of regional character through a colorful western tale of homesteading folk and closes with a chorus to impending American statehood. Thus even as Womack's "Red Stick" criticism privileges forms of Creek storytelling, he also registers the irony of Riggs' work as part of a broader national nostalgia for Indian Territory.

Whether focused on Native literary nationalism, forms of "intertribal rhetoric" (Roppolo 2008: 305) or what Tol Foster calls "relational regionalism" (Foster 2008: 268), the critical practices linked to sovereignty debates seek to account for tribally specific practices and worldviews and also to link the work of literary study with the needs and interests of indigenous communities.[2] Yet recognizing the "plurality of sovereign experiences" (Christie 2009: 217) does not imply that current Native literary criticism marks a complete departure from prior work in the field. The introduction to *Reasoning Together* addresses book-length studies in the field from 1986 to 1997; drawing attention to the rapid growth of Native literary criticism in recent decades, Womack builds on a deeper foundation of interrogating the territories and discourses of literature as a result of the rise of cultural studies, poststructuralist literary theory, gender studies, and pedagogical reform. By linking the growing visibility of Native literature with "seismic shifts in literature departments as well as in federal Indian policy," (Womack 2008: 5) *Reasoning Together* hails the connections between lived experiences of communities and developments in literary criticism. In turn, such a sustained critique of conventional academic disciplines and literary studies in particular stems from the longstanding and often stark disconnection between academic professionals and indigenous communities. Native people and cultures long have served as the subjects of Native American literature and thus the objects of academic study, but not necessarily as active participants in the creation and circulation of such discourses. Studies of the literature of the American West likewise continue to be reoriented with and through Native literatures as well as this call for an ethical critical praxis.

The American West as Indian Country

Philip Deloria's *Indians in Unexpected Places* surveys various modes of American discourse in the early twentieth century in order to investigate what he terms "the secret history of Indian modernity" (Deloria 2004: 224). From popular music and early Hollywood film to technology and sports, Deloria notes the persistent and often surprising presence of indigenous figures, languages, or traditions, thus refuting persistent narratives of Native vanishing in a modern age. For the literature of the American West, of course, depictions of Indians are anything but unexpected. The familiar story of the West as frontier or national proving ground has been told in endless variations. "Indians" serve as key figures in virtually every genre in this national mythology, from the early American bestselling genre of the Indian captivity narrative and the expedition journals of Lewis and Clark to twentieth-century dime novels and Hollywood westerns. Indeed, it is difficult to assess any period or genre of American literature without encountering representations of Native Americans or literary reflections about the history – and future – of indigenous communities. Yet such engagements with

Native forms have long been narrow and incomplete. Narratives of westward expansion as manifest destiny often feature stock characters such as hardy pioneers and stoic
cowboys, all set in heroic contest against an undifferentiated Indian foe, an antagonist
who is constructed as lacking recorded history, "civilized" culture, or even coherent
language systems. That Native Americans serving as colorful but only minor characters speaks to the insistent and repetitive discourse of constructing of the West as a
project of nation-building.

As critics across various disciplines have noted, what often is missing from the
influential narrative of westward expansion are the stories of the forced removal of
indigenous people, the destruction of tribal land holdings, and additional forms
of violence against Native communities, along with the continuity and reinvention of Native communities in sacred homelands and new tribal territories. In
response to the fresh insights of indigenous studies as well as discourse analysis across
disciplines, academic scholarship in literature and history have followed similar
though not corresponding trajectories. In new western history, texts such as Gordon
Sayre's *The Indian Chief as Tragic Hero* and Ned Blackhawk's *Violence Over the Land:
Indians and Empires in the Early American West* reimagine historical periods and subjects.
Sayre addresses the uses of Indian oratory in tribal contexts versus their appropriation
to European and American discourses of Indian nobility and vanishing, from the
Pueblo Revolt of 1680 to confederated tribes under Tecumsah; in a different vein,
Blackhawk investigates the roles of the Utes, Paiutes, and Shoshone communities of
the Great Basin in a regional study that corrects for the longstanding critical tendency
to focus on Plains tribes and Native people of the Southwest as representative Indians.
In tracing a borderlands history in relation to Spanish allies and American settlers,
Blackhawk necessarily touches upon the literary legacy of Mark Twain's depictions of
Utes in *Roughing It*. Such attention to emergent discourses of indigenous communities
and the American West is vital in terms of periodization, genre, and regional study.
For even as the national success of N. Scott Momaday's Pulitzer Prize-winning novel
The House Made of Dawn in 1968 marks an important watershed moment in Native
American literary history, such studies have a longstanding critical tendency to privi-
lege contemporary writing and attention from a broad American audience over a long
and rich heritage of Native writing and storytelling.

Native literatures also offer new possibilities for notions of the West as either an
era of pioneering individualism or as a distinct region that ties land to cultural formation. N. Scott Momaday's *The Way to Rainy Mountain* juxtaposes three voices in an
innovative text that incorporates prose, poetry, and image to represent a journey. The
conventional voice of historical narrative relates observations, dates, and figures as
means to render indigenous communities comprehensible: "They called themselves
Kwuda and later Tepda, both of which mean 'coming out.'" And later still they took
the name Gaigwu, a name which can be taken to indicate something of which the
two halves differ from each other in appearance" (Momaday 1969: 17). The distancing
effect of describing the Kiowa as "they" and the imprecision of the translation contrasts with the spoken rhythms of the tribal voice: "You know, everything had to

begin, and this is how it was: the Kiowas came out one by one into the world through a hollow log" (1969: 16). Yet beyond setting competing discourses against one another, Momaday includes a personal voice that refracts such forms of story through individual and family experience. In doing so, the text fractures the authority of the anthropological voice and multiplies through the resonance among related segments. In this way the meteor shower of 1848 is both a historical event recorded by observers and a story that becomes tribal memory. The Kiowa pasts of emergence into the fifth world and the journey to the Plains are present for a contemporary moment in the narrator's trip to visit his grandmother's grave. It is the stories that define the relationships between people and the land, and no single register is adequate to encompass such complexities.

In attending to Native presence in the American West, the turn of the century has received significant critical attention, particularly in the vein of cultural studies. Alan Trachtenberg's 2004 *Shades of Hiawatha* investigates the mutable figure of the Indian in relation to modern narratives of progress and the national assimilation of immigrants to a national domestic order. He argues that Longfellow's immensely popular poem "The Song of Hiawatha" connects this sentimental configuration for a lost aboriginal past with similar performance of imperial nostalgia through Buffalo Bill's Wild West shows, theatrical productions, and department store advertisements. Studies such as Joel Pfister's *Individuality Incorporated* (2004) and Lucy Maddox's *Citizen Indians* (2005) also turn to this period of dramatic social and cultural change in order to chart the interactions between Native American traditions of storytelling, discourses of racial difference, and the politics of citizenship in an era of federal reservation policy, the allotment of tribal lands, and the abrogation of treaties. In addition, Indian boarding schools continue to receive critical attention in relation to education policy, language heritage, and intertribal relationships. Brenda Child's 2000 *Boarding School Seasons* and Clifford Trafzer et al.'s 2006 collection *Boarding School Blues* investigate connections across region and community through off-reservation schools, and Amelia Katanski's 2007 *Learning to Write "Indian"* takes up Robert Warrior's call to investigate the relationship between boarding schools and Native literary production in English. Such attention to the distance among Native families and the role of literacy in a national order open up new ways to interrogate the continued presence of indigenous cultures and communities in an American century often defined against a frontier past. Thus Francis LaFlesche's 1900 memoir of boarding school, *The Middle Five,* rewrites the "boy book" genre of Huck Finn as an immersion in – not an escape from – the "sivilizing" process and the subsequent transformation of home into not-home.

Simon Ortiz also explores the legacies of a western past by interweaving visions of the 1864 Sand Creek massacre of peaceful Cheyenne and Arapaho with the experiences of a twentieth-century war veteran in the 1981 collection *from Sand Creek*. Here the violence from the United States cavalry of the West still is felt in the present day, and the Indian wars continue in different form. Sherman Alexie's *Reservation Blues* takes up similar themes in a dark and yet exuberant tale of an Indian blues band trying to make it big in the music business. Representatives of the ominously named Cavalry records include architect of the Indian wars General Philip Sheridan as well as General George Wright, a general who fought in the Seminole wars, the Mexican–American War, and the Civil War before slaughtering 800 Native horses in 1858 as part of the Yakima War. In this novel of extremes, the family losses for Spokane and Flathead characters recall the destructive power of such campaigns against Native communities, and the poverty of the reservation stands as one result of such cowboy-and-cavalry pasts.

In a more somber vision, Luci Tapahonso recalls the Long Walk of the Navajo under Kit Carson as a form of generational trauma that continues to reverberate for contemporary families. "In 1864" presents a scene of storytelling that lays bare the suffering of the forced march to Hwééldi or Fort Sumner and the pain of "leaving Dinetah, our home" (Tapahonso 1998: 9). The first-person mode of eyewitness brings home the immediacy of the event to the contemporary figures in the poem and to readers. And even as the poem acknowledges the prayers of the survivors as carrying through the generations, Tapahonso notes additional commonalities across time. She writes: "it was at Bosque Redondo the people learned to use flour and now / fry bread is considered to be the 'traditional' Navajo bread." Like fry bread, velvet shirts, and dark coffee, the materials of removal and trauma become adapted and reconstituted as "traditional." The poem ends with connections across generations and an insistent present tense: "It is always something to see – silver flashing in the sun / against dark velvet and black, black hair." Here Kit Carson as iconic cowboy is an agent of empire, and the American West intrudes upon Dinetah as displacement and trauma.

Such attention to movement across the land importantly revises the category of West as region and destination from elsewhere, usually east or south. Simon Ortiz addresses this alignment of westward movement with an alluring future in the poem "East of San Diego":

> I tell the bus driver
> but he doesn't hear,
> "Keep to the hills
> and avoid America
> if you can.
> I'm a fugitive
> from bad, futureless dreams
> in Southern California."

(Ortiz 1992: 111)

Ortiz frequently invokes methods of travel – buses, airports, the A-train, highways – in poems that mix movement with a keen sense of place. Whether a fugitive of a "futureless" California or a lost traveler in the "American labyrinths" of Los Angeles International airport, Ortiz repeatedly turns to the land of Acoma Pueblo as grounding and sustaining the people over time. In turn, such a poetic prayer rewrites early Indian boarding-school narratives of dislocation and separation from home communities. From Luther Standing Bear's account of being one of the first students at the flagship Carlisle Indian Industrial School to Zitkala-Ša's shuttling back and forth from boarding school to her mother's home in the Dakotas, such west-to-east trajectories reverse the national narrative of westward expansion and stage the American West as a place of increasing defamiliarization and dislocation. D'Arcy McNickle's *The Surrounded* begins with the return of the Salish protagonist to his Montana home after school in Portland and proceeds through a series of disorienting movements for Archilde among his mother's people, the church, and threatening figures of the law. Whereas his father came west from Spain to settle a ranch, Archilde turns to the mountains in an attempt to recover a Salish past and to evade the cloying sense of being surrounded, immobilized even in mobility.

Thus even as many writers and critics attend to an indigenous sense of place as a marker of community and counterpoint to an American narrative of conquering the "Wild West," others draw upon such contested territory in order to tease out the spaces of Native American literature. Consider James Welch, whose first novel *Winter in the Blood* follows a nameless character in his struggle to reconcile mixed racial heritage and the legacy of colonization in a bleak Montana landscape; the spare language, dark humor, and narrative ambiguity echo the protagonist's sense of marginalization and uncertainty. Welch's subsequent novel *Fools Crow* takes place more than a century earlier, recreating the specific cultural landscape of a Pikuni Blackfeet community immediately prior to the arrival of United States troops. Welch seeks to reimagine the popular materials of western frontier spaces by claiming Native characters as central to the scope of historical fiction and relegating settler culture to the narrative margins. In turn, his last novel *The Heartsong of Charging Elk* follows the title character from the Lakota Stronghold to London and France as a performer with Buffalo Bill's Wild West. This story of alienation and isolation, a kind of reverse captivity narrative, recalls Native histories of transnational exchange while also pressuring the boundaries of Native identity through the dilemma of a stateless protagonist unable to return home.

John Rollin Ridge's 1854 Gold Rush novel *The Life and Adventure of Joaquin Murieta, the Celebrated California Bandit* also poses questions about the parameters of Native American literature. Along with attention to the possibilities of contemporary literature, Native criticism has recuperated texts from earlier periods, from the bilingual Cherokee Phoenix to a litany of "firsts" in English (first novel, first tribalography, first Native film). Often heralded as the first Native American novel, *Joaquin Murieta* has a fascinating history as a novel based on actual events and written by a member of the prominent and controversial Ridge family only one generation after forced removal in the 1830s from southeastern Cherokee homelands to Indian Territory. Yet the novel includes only minimal references to Cherokee language or traditions, instead turning to the contested terrain of Gold Rush California for its tale of heroic resistance and class conflict. While some critics read this revision of Murieta legend as an allegory for Indian dispossession (and resistance), others situate the novel in terms of a literary and political history of the Latino (or Californio) presence in the Americas both before and after the Mexican–American War. In either case, the novel's deployment of hyperbolic violence and language redirects the sensationalism of popular literature toward the West's transnational and multicultural pasts. Ridge writes an outlaw tale in the vernacular of Wild West literature as the means to deconstruct the myth of rugged individualism and the self-made man in the context of a stratified racial order. Yet despite the indictment of Americans as agents of disorder in an imperial rush for gold, the novel's stereotypical portrayal of California Indians remains uncomfortably close to Twain's representations of "Injuns." Reclaiming Ridge for a canon of Native American literature highlights the pervasiveness of popular discourses of Native people – in this case the "civilized" Cherokee versus an image of benighted tribes of California – and reminds readers that the category of Native literature is necessarily broad and contested in multiple ways.

Scholars continue to weigh how literary texts negotiate the competing discourses of Indians as bit players in the American West and the American West as Indian Country. In addition to rewriting the silences of the western "savage" or the tragic tales of Indian vanishing, Native literature also refashions popular narratives of wide-open spaces available for reinventing national character. Sherman Alexie's short story "South by Southwest" stages a Bonnie and Clyde-style narrative of escape with a would-be Indian robber who only takes $1 from each "victim" and who recruits an uncertain white sidekick on his drive to the Grand Canyon in search of love and redemption. Alexie often takes aim at the popular icons of the American West. John Wayne is a frequent target, from the musical riff on Wayne's (fake) teeth in the film *Smoke Signals* (based on Alexie's short story "This Is What It Means to Say Phoenix, Arizona") to a surprising oral history by a 100-year-old Navajo woman in "Dear John Wayne." The latter story unfolds as a dialogue between an intrusive, uninformed, and skeptical anthropologist and the unflappable protagonist, who recounts a brief affair with Wayne during the filming of one of Ford's many westerns. Referring to the Hollywood icon by his given name of "Marion," Alexie's protagonist recalls her lover's desire for emotional intimacy and belonging, so much so that his obsessive love for the Native extra plagues the movie star until his death. Cross-dressing, weepy, and sentimental, the man behind the cowboy icon reveals the western narrative of reticent hyper-masculinity as both a national fantasy and a personal fiction. The humorless anthropologist becomes unnerved by the destabilization of the Wayne legend and the splitting of this figure into the offspring of this affair, the twins John and Marion. Though played for laughs, Alexie's spoof on white desires (John Wayne and anthropologist) for a Native Other locates Western adventuring and the authority of storytelling with an uncompromising elder woman.

As the controversy over Alexie's recent young adult novel *The Absolutely True Diary of a Part-Time Indian* indicates, the trickster dynamics of his postmodern humor are not always embraced as a model for contemporary Native literature. Yet as David Treuer notes in his provocative study *Native American Fiction*, productive criticism must account for literary form and language rather than focusing too narrowly on Native characters, themes, or notions of cultural identity. Treuer declares that Native literature as a distinctive category is a fiction and instead connects such writers to broader developments in American literature. By resisting an uncritical canonization of well-known figures such as Leslie Marmon Silko and Louise Erdrich, Treuer challenges critics to reexamine assumptions about indigenous storytelling, orality, and literary influence. In doing so, he calls for new directions in Native literary criticism and sparks debate about the foundations and possible future of indigenous literature in the Americas and beyond.

New Directions in Native Literary Criticism

In keeping with the foundations of Native literary criticism in the work of Paula Gunn Allen and Simon Ortiz, one key aspect of the rapidly growing field continues to be the recovery of indigenous texts, traditions, and forms of knowledge. Such acts of recuperation dovetail with an expansive view of text in literary studies more broadly, and the resulting inclusion of Native creation stories, songs, and oratory in anthologies of American literature (and world literature) reflects this renewed attention to cultural productions in various forms. The growing archive of oral and written Native literatures involves an expansive idea of textuality, one that may include ledger books, winter counts, dental imprints on birch bark, petroglyphs, and wampum. Unlike the project of "salvage ethnography" at the turn of the century, which sought to document Native cultures before their expected demise in the face of American modernity, such efforts consider continuities as well as discontinuities between forms of print culture and diverse tribal traditions. And whereas Gloria Bird and Joy Harjo declare English to be "the enemy's language" (Bird and Harjo 1998: 2), many writers and critics claim the language of the Americas as a tribalized language in its own right.

Interestingly, the multiplicity of contemporary Native literary forms encompasses a reemergence of tribal languages as well as "indigenized" English. Noenoe Silva's recovery of Hawai'ian language texts protesting annexation by the United States in the late nineteenth century usefully reconfigures any simple alignment between print culture and English for indigenous written literatures, and such a deeper history grounds contemporary works by young writers such as Brenda Nalani Macdougall or the critical manifestos of Haunani Kay-Trask. And whereas Tapahonso's poems and stories often move between Diné and English, with translation as a form of repetition, Diane Glancy's novel of the Trail of Tears *Pushing the Bear* goes even further by incorporating elements of the Cherokee syllabary from the 1840s. By providing a glossary at the end of the novel rather than line-by-line translations, Glancy challenges readers to register the Cherokee language as a linguistic presence throughout the narrative and a form of expression that cannot be reduced to an English equivalent. As Treuer might suggest, Glancy's use of multiple narrators can be connected to the formal experiments of modernist innovators like William Faulkner; at the same time, the disjunctions of language and point of view in the novel attest to the dislocations and cultural fragmentation of the Trail of Tears in very specific ways.

In this respect, Glancy's experiments in language as well as the mixed genres of poetry and prose echo the trajectory of Silko's successful and influential novel *Ceremony* in thematizing the integration of old and new traditions in a narrative that weaves together Laguna Pueblo stories and the novel form for a contemporary ceremony of healing and reconciliation for the veteran protagonist. Silko's American West includes Los Angeles as staging area for American troops headed to the Pacific in World War II as well as the distinctive landscape of high desert around Laguna Pueblo. Importantly, Silko's West is marked by the violence of colonization that extends not only to family relations and a racialized logic of blood quantum but also to uranium mining for use in the atomic bomb. The novel thus explores how the land becomes a source for massive destruction as well as for renewal and recreation. In turn, Louis Owens cites the interconnected narratives of sickness and healing, resource extraction and care for the land as a new model of Native story through "webs of identity" that conjoin Laguna Pueblo worldviews with American (or specifically western) discourses of land, nation, and racial formation.

As Lindsay Claire-Smith notes in her recent study on the rhetorics of environment in Native literature, the procedures to establish tribal entity in legal terms serve as one basis for *Watermelon Nights* by Greg Sarris. The situation of California tribes is particularly complex due to the extreme violence of Spanish and American colonizing projects, the cultural and territorial legacies of the rancheria system, and the disparity between state and federal recognition of various nations and confederated tribes. Sarris, of Pomo, Miwok, Filipino, and white heritage, explores themes of family, borders, and belonging throughout his work, often focusing on the conflicts and loyalties of multiple generations in the Santa Rosa area. As in his critical work *Keeping Slug Woman Alive*, Sarris traces the complexities of family history, personal identity, and community connections in a region that tends to erase indigenous heritage even as it cites or even celebrates a multicultural past. This is not to say that Sarris' fiction merely reflects or reenacts the political struggles for tribal recognition in contemporary California. Instead, his work reconfigures notions of Native identity beyond the more culturally visible forms of Plains traditions or southwestern cultural landscapes. In turn, his work's focus on the Santa Rosa area – a rural region not contained within the familiar opposition of urban centers in southern and northern California – brings an alternate West into focus even as it resonates with earlier representations of indigenous groups and transnational settler narratives in Alta California.

In a similar vein, new scholarship also investigates models of affiliation, alliance, and exchange within and beyond tribal discourses. Gender and sexuality studies offer a particularly rich area of study, and the growing field of indigenous feminism likewise interrogates the gender dynamics in various configurations of nation and tradition as well as the discourses of gender normativity and expression in Native literatures. In indigenous studies, Andrea Smith's influential study of gender, sexuality, and violence speaks to the ongoing legacy of colonial structures of power in women's lives; in a similar vein, Jennifer Denetdale critiques the ways in which rhetorical appeals to nation and tradition are used to perpetuate gender imbalance in tribal (Navajo) contexts. Critics in literature and cultural studies are beginning to investigate indigenous feminism in relation to specific textual archives as well as theories of gender, sexuality, and women of color in global contexts. In turn, a recent special issue of *GLQ* investigates intersections between queer theory and indigenous studies. Andrea Smith usefully positions the "subjectless critique" (Smith 2010: 42) of queer theory as one useful means to reconsider a critical reliance upon identity politics and static models of culture in indigenous studies. Such theories of "postidentity" (or even the posthuman) need not result in the colonization of indigenous studies by non-Native scholars or critical theories, but instead can provide new lenses of analysis for assessing historical and contemporary texts.

Additional contrapuntal forms of analysis take up formulations of the indigenous in the interrelated histories (literary and otherwise) of multiple Indian and non-Indian groups. For instance, echoing the trajectory of his *Monkey King in China*, Gerald Vizenor's haiku poetry draws upon Asian literary forms without jettisoning his longstanding interest in the locations and performances of "indian" selves. Instead, the resonance of Monkey King sagas with Coyote stories, or of transpacific Asian American literatures with indigenous histories of cultural exchange and adaptation, provide new sites of inquiry. After all, the category "Asian American" encompasses as many diverse spaces and forms as its counterpart in Native American literature; the artifice of such respective canons can be limiting as well as productive. Parallel with developments in what Françoise Lionnet terms *Minor Transnationalism*, such new directions of study investigate the interrelated constructions of ethnic and cultural forms in indigenous and Asian American, African American, or Chicano/Chicana (and Latin American) literatures as well as formations of Native texts and subjects in hemispheric studies. The growing scholarship on black Indians illustrates the richness of such literature across periods, and the urgency of such theories of community and belonging speaks in powerful ways to contemporary debates about tribal enrollment and the federal recognition of tribes such as the Cherokee or the Lumbee.

Leslie Marmon Silko's *Almanac of the Dead* (1992) takes up the deep histories and complex territory of indigenous narratives of the Americas before and after the formation of the United States. The long, intricate, and apocalyptic novel charts a world saturated with violence and brimming with revolutionary potential as the stories of dozens of characters converge in a kind of global uprising against the forces of environmental desecration, racism, and capitalism. In a section fittingly entitled "Prophecy," an indigenous-led army (a collective that grows as it advances northward) gathers south of the United States border to turn loose the rivers and take back the land for its original inhabitants. Silko stitches these songs together in an extended poem on the page, also a spoken proclamation. The character who quotes these songs is Lakota Wilson Weasel Tail – a Lakota "raised on a small, poor ranch forty miles from the Wounded Knee massacre" (Silko 1992: 713) – who gives up law for poetry and social activism (much like Silko herself). Weasel Tail exhorts his audience about the changes to come, quoting Pontiac, Wovoka, and the Ghost Dance songs to declare the continuity and claims of indigenous people:

> "The truth is the Ghost Dance did not end with the murder of Big Foot and one hundred and forty-four Ghost Dance worshipers at Wounded Knee. The Ghost Dance has never ended, it has continued, and the people have never stopped dancing; they may call it by other names, but when they dance, their hearts are reunited with the spirits of beloved ancestors and the loved ones recently lost in the struggle. Throughout the Americas, from Chile to Canada, the people have never stopped dancing; as the living dance, they are joined again with all our ancestors before them, who cry out, who demand justice, and who call the people to take back the Americas!" (Silko 1992: 724)

Here as in many contemporary Native American texts, the Ghost Dance functions as a metaphor for shared suffering as well as a common desire to regain lost territory – the "living dance" of survival and indigenous cultural expression in all its forms. Weasel Tail explains how the Ghost Dance has been misconstrued as a false belief in the ability to withstand bullets rather than the act of setting indigenous coalition into motion across generations. Silko's novel-as-almanac reconnects the stories and experiences of indigenous communities of the borderlands and redefines the American West in terms of such transnational connections to the land and to an indigenous future.

As the field of American literature continues to expand in terms of transnational or global forms of exchange, interdisciplinary methodologies, and textual subjects, studies of Native American literature offer an important balance to critical paradigms that privilege postnational frameworks of analysis, mixed forms, and increasingly expansive networks of influence and exchange. As Robert Warrior asserts, "the history of Native writing constitutes an intellectual tradition, a tradition that can and should inform the contemporary work of Native intellectuals" (Warrior 2005: p. xiii). Sean Kicummah Teuton takes up this call to trace the "intellectual trade routes" of literature and criticism by proposing "tribal realism" as a theoretical term and practice that brings together "Indian identity, tribal experience, and social transformation" (Teuton 2008: 12). Teuton rejects both "reductive essentialism" and "trickster inde-terminacy" (2008: 15) as critical extremes that cover over the nuances of intercon-nected movements in literature and culture, as in the "Red Power novel." In this model, literary texts are in conversation with social movements, not defined by eras of political change.

Tol Foster echoes this critical shift in calling for regional frameworks of analysis that may reveal literary connections or formations that may not be legible in a strictly tribal model of analysis. Such efforts do not necessarily elide tribal specificity in favor of external models of history and influence. For the American West in particular, an area shaped by notions of regional identity and global exchange, such theories can offer new ways of understanding literary strategies in relation to shifting cultural contexts. Rather than reducing Native literary criticism to a bounded repertoire of investigative forms, the opening up of theoretical approaches – sovereignty studies as well as comparative work – allows for multiple forms of analysis that make visible distinct and yet related formations of indigenous writing and community.

For example, Thomas King also notes how the pervasive influence of the cultural iconography of the American West extends beyond the borders of the territorial United States. In the novel *Green Grass, Running Water*, four ancient Indians travel across time and take various forms in a kind of storytelling quest. By disguising these indigenous women as the iconic figures of Robinson Crusoe, Hawkeye, Ishmael, and the Lone Ranger, King's novel sets loose the cultural markers of Indian history and literature of the Americas. In his exuberant postmodern world, Coyote and a Christian God (or dog) compete for storytelling rights, an old Hollywood western unites Indian characters as resisting spectators, and historical figures from the American West blur the lines between cowboys and Indians. King's satirical reappropriation of western iconography reminds readers of the fluidity of cultural forms and the inescapability of such colonial discourses in contemporary indigenous literature. In terms of critical models, Daniel Heath Justice places the work of Thomas King in terms of a specific history of Cherokee literature. King's work also may be framed in relation to western or American literature broadly speaking, to First Nations writing in Canada, and even at the crossroads between indigenous literature and postmodern experiments with form.

As scholars of indigenous studies have demonstrated so forcefully, sovereignty and nationalism continue to serve as foundational concepts for a field linked to the political realities of federal recognition for individual tribes, legal questions of governance and jurisdiction, and debates about cultural property and tribal membership. Yet in order to keep pace with the implications of a rich history of Native texts and cultural contexts, consumers and critics of Native American literature and culture also need to develop new ways of seeing, reading, and theorizing indigenous cultural production. As ideas of the American West are revised to account for local specificity and various forms of transnational exchange, questions about Native American languages, literatures, and communities persist. Just as the American West has come to signal a diverse landscape with multiple and overlapping communities and literatures, Native American literature is no longer restricted to the imposed boundaries of the present-day United States. Yet just as the increasingly expansive field of American studies seeks to account for national exceptionalism within and against broader categories of the Americas, related critical debates illustrate that the categories for defining indigenous communities and traditions vary according to context and purpose. Once defined in academic terms as a subset of American or even western literature, Native American literary studies now constitutes a vital and growing field that brings together a wide range of tribal literatures, pan-Indian texts, and even global traditions. In turn, such debates about cultural property, academic discourse, and the relationship between educational institutions and Native communities inflect debates about curricula for undergraduate and graduate students, standards for scholarship in various disciplines, forms of educational leadership, and the purpose and practices of a range of professional organizations.

NOTES

1 Harjo's association with Native Hawai'i
   adds another layer of complexity to her categorization as a Muscogee or Native American
   writer and also marks the shifting boundaries
   of the American West in political history and
   academic study.
2 The scope and applications of the critical
   term "sovereignty" have been debated at
   length, not only in relation to the term's

European etymology and history, but also with
regard to its usefulness in relation to Native
communities not recognized as sovereign
nations under the United States federal standards. Despite such limitations, the term nonetheless continues to signify indigenous
self-determination, cultural property, and the
continuation of tribal tradition.

REFERENCES AND FURTHER READING

Alexie, Sherman. (1994). This Is What It Means
to Say Phoenix, Arizona. In *The Lone Ranger
and Tonto Fistfight in Heaven*. New York:
HarperCollins.

Alexie, Sherman. (2001). Dear John Wayne. In *The
Toughest Indian in the World*, pp. 189–208. New
York: Grove Press.

Alexie, Sherman. (2001). South by Southwest. In
The Toughest Indian in the World, pp. 57–75. New
York: Grove Press.

Alexie, Sherman. (2005). *Reservation Blues*. New
York: Grove Press.

Alexie, Sherman. (2007). *The Absolutely True Diary
of a Part-Time Indian*. New York: Little, Brown.

Alfred, Taiaiake. (1999). *Peace, Power, Righteousness*.
Ontario: Oxford University Press.

Bird, Gloria, and Joy Harjo. (1998). *Reinventing the
Enemy's Language*. New York: W.W. Norton.

Blackhawk, Ned. (2006). *Violence Over the Land*.
Cambridge, MA: Harvard University Press.

Brown, Dee. (1970). *Bury My Heart at Wounded
Knee*. New York: Owl Books/Henry Holt & Co.

Child, Brenda J. (2000). *Boarding School Seasons*.
Lincoln: University of Nebraska Press.

Christie, Stuart. (2009). *Plural Sovereignties and
Contemporary Indigenous Literature*. New York:
Palgrave Macmillan.

Claire-Smith, Lindsey. (2008). *Indians, Environment,
and Identity on the Borders of American Literature*.
New York: Palgrave Macmillan.

Deloria, Philip. (2004). *Indians in Unexpected Places*.
Lawrence: University Press of Kansas.

Deloria, Jr., Vine. (1969). *Custer Died For Your Sins*.
Norman: University of Oklahoma Press, 1988.

Denetdale, Jennifer. (2007). *Reclaiming Diné
History*. Tucson: University of Arizona Press.

Eastman, Charles. (1916). *From the Deep Woods to
Civilization*. Mineola, NY: Dover Publications,
2003.

Eyre, Chris. (1998). *Smoke Signals*. Miramax Films,
United States.

Eyre, Chris. (2009). *We Shall Remain*. Public
Broadcasting Service, United States.

Foster, Tol. (2008). Of One Blood: An Argument
for Relations and Regionality in Native
American Literary Studies. In Craig S. Womack,
Daniel Heath Justice, and Christopher B.
Teuton, eds., *Reasoning Together*, pp. 265–302.
Norman: University of Oklahoma Press.

Glancy, Diane. (1998). *Pushing the Bear*. San Diego:
Harvest/Harcourt.

Harjo, Joy. (2000). The Path to the Milky Way
Leads Through Los Angeles. In *A Map to the
Next World*, p. 45. New York: W.W. Norton.

Justice, Daniel Heath. (2006). *Our Fire Survives the
Storm*. Minneapolis: University of Minnesota
Press.

Justice, Daniel Heath. (2008). "Go Away, Water!"
Kinship Criticism and the Decolonization
Imperative. In Craig S. Womack, Daniel Heath
Justice, and Christopher B. Teuton, eds.,
Reasoning Together, pp. 147–68. Norman:
University of Oklahoma Press.

Katanski, Amelia. (2007). *Learning to Write
"Indian"*. Norman: University of Oklahoma
Press.

Kay-Trask, Haunani. (1999). *From a Native
Daughter*. Honolulu: University of Hawaii Press.

Kelsey, Penelope Myrtle. (2008). *Tribal Theory in Native American Literature*. Lincoln: University of Nebraska Press.

King, Thomas. (1994). *Green Grass, Running Water*. New York: Bantam Books.

LaFlesche, Francis. (1900). *The Middle Five*. Lincoln: University of Nebraska Press, 1963.

Lionnet, Françoise, and Shu-mei Shi, eds. (2005). *Minor Transnationalism*. Durham: Duke University Press.

Maddox, Lucy. (2005). *Citizen Indians*. Ithaca, NY: Cornell University Press.

McNickle, D'Arcy. (1936). *The Surrounded*. Albuquerque: University of New Mexico Press, 1978.

Mihesuah, Devon, and Angela Cavender Wilson, eds. (2004). *Indigenizing the Academy*. New York: Bison Books.

Momaday, N. Scott. (1968). *The House Made of Dawn*. New York: HarperPerennial, 2010.

Momaday, N. Scott. (1969). *The Way to Rainy Mountain*. Albuquerque: University of New Mexico Press, 1976.

Morgan, Phillip Carroll. (2008). "Who Shall Gainsay Our Decision?" Choctaw Literary Criticism in 1830. In Craig S. Womack, Daniel Heath Justice, and Christopher B. Teuton, eds., *Reasoning Together*, pp. 126–46. Norman: University of Oklahoma Press.

Ortiz, Simon J. (1981). *from Sand Creek* Tucson: University of Arizona Press, 2000.

Ortiz, Simon J. (1992). East of San Diego. In *Woven Stone*, p. 111. Tucson: University of Arizona Press.

Owens, Louis. (1998). *Mixedblood Messages*. Norman: University of Oklahoma Press.

Pfister, Joel. (2004). *Individuality Incorporated*. Durham, NC: Duke University Press.

Ridge, John Rollin. (1854). *Life and Adventures of Joaquin Murieta*. Norman: University of Oklahoma Press, 1977.

Riggs, Lynn. (1936). *The Cherokee Night and Other Plays*. Norman: University of Oklahoma Press, 2003.

Roppolo, Kim. (2008). Samson Occom as Writing Instructor: The Search for an Intertribal Rhetoric. In Craig S. Womack, Daniel Heath Justice, and Christopher B. Teuton, eds., *Reasoning Together*, pp. 303–24. Norman: University of Oklahoma Press.

Sarris, Greg. (1993). *Keeping Slug Woman Alive*. Berkeley: University of California Press.

Sarris, Greg. (1999). *Watermelon Nights*. New York: Penguin Books.

Sayre, Gordon. (2005). *The Indian Chief as Tragic Hero*. Chapel Hill: University of North Carolina Press.

Silko, Leslie Marmon. (1977). *Ceremony*. New York: Penguin Books, 2006.

Silko, Leslie Marmon. (1992). *Almanac of the Dead*. New York: Penguin Books.

Silva, Noenoe K. (2004). *Aloha Betrayed*. Durham, NC: Duke University Press.

Simoneau, Yves. (2007). *Bury My Heart at Wounded Knee*. HBO Films, United States.

Smith, Andrea. (2010). Queer Theory and Native Studies: The Heteronormativity of Settler Colonialism. *GLQ*, 16/1–2, 42–68.

Smith, Linda Tuhiwai. (1999). *Decolonizing Methodologies*. London: Zed Books.

Standing Bear, Luther. (1928). *My People the Sioux*. Lincoln: University of Nebraska Press, 1975.

Tapahonso, Luci. (1998). In 1864. In *Sáanii Dahataal: The Women Are Singing*, pp. 7–10. Tucson: University of Arizona Press.

Teuton, Sean. (2008). The Callout: Writing American Indian Politics. In Craig S. Womack, Daniel Heath Justice, and Christopher B. Teuton. eds., *Reasoning Together*, pp. 105–25. Norman: University of Oklahoma Press.

Trachtenberg, Alan. (2004). *Shades of Hiawatha*. New York: Hill & Wang.

Trafzer, Clifford, Jean A. Keller, and Lorene Sisquoc, eds. (2006). *Boarding School Blues*. Lincoln: University of Nebraska Press.

Treuer, David. (2006). *Native American Fiction*. St. Paul, MN: Graywolf Press.

Twain, Mark. (1872). *Roughing It*. New York: Penguin Books, 1981.

Vizenor, Gerald. (1990). *Griever: An American Monkey King in China*. Minneapolis: University of Minnesota Press.

Vizenor, Gerald. (1994). *Shadow Distance*. Hanover: Wesleyan University Press/University Press of New England.

Warrior, Robert. (2005). *The People and the Word*. Minneapolis: University of Minnesota Press.

Welch, James. (1975). *Winter in the Blood*. New York: Bantam Books.

Welch, James. (1986). *Fools Crow*. New York: Viking Penguin.

Welch, James. (2001). *The Heartsong of Charging Elk*. New York: Anchor Books.

Womack, Craig S. (1999). *Red on Red*. Minneapolis: University of Minnesota Press.

Womack, Craig S. (2008). A Single Decade: Book-Length Native Literary Criticism between 1986 and 1997. In Craig S. Womack, Daniel Heath Justice, and Christopher B. Teuton, eds., *Reasoning Together*, pp. 3–105. Norman: University of Oklahoma Press.

Womack, Craig S., Daniel Heath Justice, and Christopher B. Teuton, eds. (2008). *Reasoning Together*. Norman: University of Oklahoma Press.

Zitkala-Ša. (1921). *American Indian Stories*. Lincoln: University of Nebraska Press, 1985.

14

Framing Class in the Rural West: Cowboys, Double-wides, and McMansions

Nancy Cook

Class and the Rural West

It is a truth universally acknowledged that the United States has been, and remains, a classed society. Writers taking on the American class system have focused primarily on urban manifestations of class difference. Such accounts tend to embrace distinctions between blue-collar and white-collar work, while their analyses of the markers of class feature education, dwellings, and consumer products. Paul Fussell's *Class* demonstrates this approach to status. This kind of work draws on a large field of data and examples in order to make the case that the US is a classed society, but such a national portrait goes awry when applied to the rural West.

The West, since Lewis and Clark's expedition, has been a complicated place of class stratification, conflict, and negotiation. What holds in the West's urban areas doesn't hold in rural areas, and those class differences, whether urban or rural, bear distinct markers as western rather than national. And while what happens in the rural West bears a resemblance to other rural social interactions, the markers of class combine differently.

Both the New Western history and American social history have opened up the West as a region where social class mattered and continues to matter, but very little work examines how social class functions within particular local cultures in the rural West. Moreover, in the New West, social relations and resettlement patterns have created a class structure that differs from the Old West. The cattle baron may persist in small numbers as well as in our imaginations, but in the New West he's just as likely to be a buffalo baron, and rather than having faithful retainers and drifters on his spread, now he has salaried employees with 401Ks and health insurance.

A Companion to the Literature and Culture of the American West, First Edition. Edited by Nicolas S. Witschi.
© 2011 Blackwell Publishing Ltd. Published 2011 by Blackwell Publishing Ltd.

In the New West, some legacies of the era of the open range remain, but in terms of both land use and social relations they are not always what one would expect. Furthermore, these legacies bear little resemblance to those of the southern plantation system, for the new economies of these regions have taken their development in a very different direction. Paul Fussell's markers may continue to ring true for Dallas, Los Angeles, and even Seattle, but they don't fit Phillips County, Montana or Fremont County, Wyoming. And when applied to places with rapid in-migration such as Gallatin County, Montana or Teton County, Wyoming, they simplify the complicated stratification that often aligns interests across traditionally configured class boundaries. Certainly in the New West, if not the Old, both the markers of class position and negotiations between classes differ between urban and rural West.

While the current trend in class analysis gives primacy to cultural rather than economic factors, scholars continue to debate the relative merits and difficulties associated with the way class difference is figured. For a study of the class in the US West, economic models remain useful. Using broadly historical models, and following one route that leads from Marx, one might make distinctions based on who owns and who does not own property. The agricultural West then, might seem more feudal than capitalist. But, in the twenty-first century, western agricultural producers have both non-monetary obligations to workers and community and are themselves pawns within a global commodity marketplace. What gets lost when class relationships are represented as fundamentally and rigidly hierarchical: lower, middle, upper? And how might one describe classes in relation to production?

"Working-class" according to Raymond Williams, describes a relation to production, but in the American West a rancher might be both upper-class and working-class simultaneously – nominally owning the land, but with the bank owning the cows and the rancher working at manual labor, with the surplus value of that labor going to pay down the bank loan. An attentiveness to the economics of class relations offers a turn away from class as a set of categories or rigid hierarchies, and toward a view of class as a process; dynamic, shifting, negotiating economic and demographic changes in the rural West.[1]

Class has been a challenging lens through which to read in the rural West for a few reasons. While the majority of cultural representations of the West are produced in and refer to urban centers – which in the New West is an oasis culture – we have, in some ways, more assiduously attached all the mythic baggage once associated with the Old West to those parts of the West that remain sparsely populated. Ads present unpeopled mountains as the site for escape from urbanity via SUV; architectural and lifestyle magazines show us some star or mogul's "ranch"; TV shows such as *Northern Exposure* offer an idealized version of life in a small community. Too often the West continues to be figured imaginatively, both for insiders and outsiders, as a classless space, where "rugged individualism" has triumphed over class division and demarcation.

Outside the region, the myth of the rugged individual suggests that location offers freedom from the constraints of contemporary capitalism and social stratification associated with urban life. Inside the region, this myth forestalls collective anger that might be directed to economic exploitation, keeps people from seeking public assistance or health insurance, and fuels the ranks of the supposedly independent self-employed. This essay claims that one can be of a class without necessarily identifying as a member of that class. In the rural West, insiders or old-timers, regardless of class position, might stand against either "rich" outsiders or "lazy" poor people, or both. In the early years of the twenty-first century, the rural West faces both rapid in-migration, from those who would change land use from production to consumption, and rapid out-migration, of young and old alike, seeking better-paying jobs and a more stable economy for fixed incomes.

The focus here will be on the northern Rockies, for the rural West represents far too many economies, population mixes, environments, and representational traditions to be considered as a whole. In addition, this region has been the focus of more research that touches on class issues than any other in the rural West. Geographers offer only a modest corrective. *The Atlas of the New West* hints at cross-class negotiations, and a few scholars look at the rural working classes.[2] Recent work informed by cultural studies focuses on wage and migrant labor, as well as the economic and social consequences of rapid population shifts in rural areas of the northern Rockies. These studies look at sites of rapid demographic and economic change, the often dramatic shift from productive land use to consumptive land use, in areas that have attracted people who earn their living elsewhere, but seek rural areas for solace and recreation. Although several articles promise analysis of class difference in the rural American West, few offer any sense of class difference as lived experience.

One such article, "'Sophisticated People Versus Rednecks': Economic Restructuring and Class Difference in America's West," insists on "the importance of constructing a human geography of white class difference" and offers a "theoretical framework for understanding the cultural politics of class and whiteness in the context of rural restructuring " (Jarosz and Lawson 2002: 8). As is common in such articles, the theoretical framework takes the bulk of the article, with only one page of case study involving a western place. The framework is provocative; the case study unilluminating.

Another article promises to examine "the consequences of contemporary forces of restructuring on communities" in the rural West in terms of "land use, family and class discourses" (Nelson 2001: 395). This author makes the case for the rural West as a classed society, and draws on the literature from British rural geography, with its attentiveness to class. This article includes selections from interviews conducted in three rural counties where rapid and extensive in-migration has occurred, yet it contains less than a page of quotations about changing class dynamics.

Many such articles set up the problem clearly, but either never get to the experiences of people in the studied communities or include a few quotations, but never analyze them. I see these as issues involving disciplinary research methods more than as failings of the individual authors. As a corrective, I'm suggesting that it would be more profitable to examine creative representations that either mythologize (what the

West could be) or examine (the way the West figures as lived experience) life in the rural American West. Looking at the ways contemporary TV shows, movies, and fiction use character, story, and conflict to put issues of social class in context while suggesting consequences and outcomes offers a means to view the complex ramifications of land use and population change in the twenty-first-century rural West.

Class, Cowboys, and Popular Culture

In an essay about photographer Dorothea Lange, Jonathan Raban invokes William Empson's *Some Versions of Pastoral* to describe social relations between rich and poor in the US West. Raban claims that "heroizing of simple cowboys, farmers, and miners in the western stories of Bret Harte, the movies of John Ford, and the art of Frederic Remington" among others, "might be read as pastorals in Empson's sense" (Raban 2009). Raban's invocation of Empson recalls the tendency within popular representations of the rural West for cultural producers to imagine both "a beautiful relation between the rich and the poor" (Empson 1974: 11) and to answer the musical question, "what do the simple folk do?"

Raban reminds us how useful Empson can be in thinking about distinctions between urban and rural, and about class. For Empson, the pastoral tradition is "based on a double attitude of the artist to the worker, of the complex man to the simple one ('I am in one way better, in another not so good')" (Empson 1974: 14). For a region more often represented than representing itself, Empson's formulation foregrounds the logic that favors mythic representations over realist ones, and forestalls any significant representation of negotiations, tensions, or conflict between classes.

In the twentieth century the pastoral position was abundantly represented in American popular culture. Beginning in the1940s, and continuing into the 1970s, US television producers fell in love with the rich and noble rancher. Rather than the rapacious cattle baron, ranchers on television in shows such as *Sky King* (on network television, 1951–66), *Bonanza* (prime-time television, 1959–73), *The Big Valley* (prime-time television, 1965–9), and *The Virginian* (prime-time television, 1962–71), reoriented popular perceptions about the landed gentry of the American West. Most of these shows endured much longer through syndication, both in the US and worldwide. While all but *Sky King* were set in the western past, they appealed to viewers with their contemporary ethical and moral frameworks, and frequently cast charismatic young male stars.

In each of these shows, the landed family has a feudal relationship to those affiliated with the ranch, as well as those in nearby communities. Ben Cartwright (*Bonanza*), Victoria Barkley (*The Big Valley*), and Judge Garth (*The Virginian*, seasons 1–4) were tough-minded paternalists, sometimes at loggerheads with weak-willed or greedy town folks but always victorious due to their more worldly, wealthy perspective. Neither examples of the idle rich, nor speculators, nor primarily investors, these stalwart heads of families lived in large, comfortable homes, dressed well but sensibly, and were productive members of their societies; oligarchs who brought order, fairness, and law to the developing rural West. From the 1950s into the 1980s, ranchers were portrayed in film and television as rich, successful, and unaccustomed to physical labor. Viewers never saw them build a fence, never saw them sweat, but the narratives revealed that ruling an otherwise unruly land was very much like a contact sport.

Those of us who grew up in the rural West during this period were no doubt influenced by these images. Town kids (and their parents) tended to think of ranchers as wealthy, and, in terms of assets, many were; but few ranchers lived in the opulent surroundings of their TV peers, and I never met a rancher with the unsullied attire or soft hands of Ben Cartwright. Moreover, however asset-rich, most ranchers lived on borrowed money, and many of the supposed "rich" kids had fewer toys and older clothes than the average town kid because their parents weren't comfortable using operating loans to buy bikes.

Sky King presented a gentleman rancher who used his leisure time and twin-engine airplane to fight crime. Although horses occasionally appeared in episodes, the focus was not on ranch life, but on adventure. Presumably Sky didn't need to worry about day-to-day ranching (that's what his ranch manager was for) so he spent nearly all of his time rescuing people, mostly his exceedingly unlucky niece, Penny, or apprehending criminals. *Sky King* was unusual in that the show celebrated Sky's ownership of a twin-engine airplane, a vehicle associated with significant wealth. The show also offered a dizzying combination of icons from both Old and New Wests: horses and hitching posts, abandoned mines, and six-guns, alongside cars, jet aircraft, and bombs. There was never any doubt that the rancher was wealthy; the only issue was how that wealth served the larger community.

While many of the serial films and "B" westerns represented ranchers bathed in the same benevolent light, from the 1950s forward, Hollywood films worked to tell a version of western history where the rancher was more often portrayed as villainous land baron. Now, two distinct landowning classes – the bad land baron and the good homesteader – struggled to define what was being represented as a new civilization in a rigid two-class culture. Unlike the traditional working-class/ruling-class divisions, these westerns exploit a conflict between two competing theories of property ownership: empire-building versus self-sufficiency.

Into this dynamic, filmmakers began to introduce a character of indeterminate class origin: the gunslinger or cowboy. Among the best-known films following this formula is *Shane* (1953). The villain is a cattleman whose cowhands spend more time harassing the settlers than tending to ranch work. The settlers have families rather than employees, and viewers see them performing the hard labor of homesteading. In *Shane* and other films like it, settlers sweat while cattlemen spend more time at the saloon than on the ranch. But however righteous a group of laboring agriculturists might be, their skills with axe and shovel can't protect them from rapacious cattle barons, and they need the help of the rugged individualist who happens along. While the attitude toward the rancher differs in *Bonanza* and *Shane*, the representations aren't that far apart. In Hollywood, ranchers have leisure time to work off of the ranch for good or ill, as they have the means to hire employees who either tirelessly keep ranch and household going (Hop Sing: the cook, nurse, and houseman in *Bonanza*) or harass settlers and kill them and their livestock.

The revisionist period in Westerns offered wider screens, bloodier battles, and a larger cast of characters, but, for the most part, the formula never changed. One thinks of *Once Upon a Time in the West* (1968), *Missouri Breaks* (1976), *Tom Horn* (1980), *Heaven's Gate* (1980), and *Silverado* (1985). Other films take up a version of the story, that include issues of race – *Posse* (1993) – or gender – *The Ballad of Little Jo* (1993). In lionizing the yeoman farmer or homesteader the drama in many western movies came at the expense of the Indian. The cavalry came to the rescue more times to save the landed, and powerful (*Heaven's Gate*) than they did the isolated homesteader, though they come to help out the fools who homesteaded in Monument Valley (*The Searchers*, 1956). When homesteaders served corporate interest, as they did the land-grant railroads, they could expect to be protected. But when westerns took up race as an issue, whether with African Americans or Native Americans, race trumped class even though most of these films take the conflict over land as their subject.

In the popular culture industry, one can alter the identity of the bad guy, but simplistic class relations are emplotted in the action. In Hollywood westerns class warfare appears literally as warfare in *Heaven's Gate*, for example. Most of the films that represent class in the rural, ranching West cast landowners as either greedy elites who imagine themselves both as having a right to the land and as above the rule of law, or as tough-minded but ultimately benevolent paternalists, taking care of both the livestock and humans in their charge.

One thing all of these Hollywood land barons had in common was the ubiquitous cowboy hat. Cowboy attire provides an iconography rich in cultural associations and short on historical ones. Historically wage laborers, cowboys have been near the bottom of the economic scale, but have always had status above their economic rank. According to William W. Savage, Jr., "The work was undeniably dirty and hard. To portray it accurately is to bore the spectator, which explains why the cowboy hero is a histrionic fabrication" (Savage 1979: 37–8). Savage explains that cowboys' economic rank did not matter, because "to the casual viewer their economic circumstances are less important than the fact that they appear to control their own destinies, which is something that large numbers of Americans feel increasingly powerless to do" (1979: 32). The cowboy's indeterminate social position allows him to act as a pivot in class negotiations throughout popular culture. One thinks of Bud (John Travolta) in *Urban Cowboy* (1980), a wage laborer on an oil rig, who is exempted from the boundaries of his class position when out at Gilley's, the cowboy bar. Bud, dressed in his cowboy duds, can pick up women from all classes, and has a heated affair with an oil heiress.

The cowboy can either move up the rungs of social hierarchy or down, as is the case in many popular romances, where the young heir disguises his riches through his cowboy persona and thus assures himself that the girl loves him and not his money. And just as often, the cowboy can play his "aw shucks" role without having to acknowledge his significant assets, as with Tom Booker (Robert Redford) in *The Horse Whisperer* (1998). Although, as Savage claims, "the cowboy hero has always been a commodity," as an icon in popular culture, he has allowed us to maintain the fiction of a class-blind western society (Savage 1979: 109).

Trailer Trash and RV Elites

Housing offers one lens through which to examine class difference as experienced in the rural West. Many small cities in the West have "green" subsidized housing – apartments and condos sporting solar panels, high "R" value insulation, and low-flow toilets. On the other hand, western Indian reservations have been pocked with notoriously sub-standard and toxic HUD dwellings, vivifying the term "death trap." But by and large, most westerners outside cities and large towns simply make do. While the trophy ranch often includes a log mansion straight out of *Bonanza*, much housing in the rural West consists of first-generation houses falling into decrepitude, or double-wide trailers. Those new ugly subdivisions one sees just off the interstate miles from any town are a function of economic limitations rather than aesthetic sensibilities, for rural westerners tend to choose convenience over beauty and privacy. Subdivisions in the middle of nowhere suggest a dearth of choices, both for the occupant and the subdivider.

An analysis of mobile housing – the now ubiquitous mobile home and its more transient cousin, the RV – in historical, geographical, and social contexts reveals hierarchies within each "community," while at the same time it shows us how classed the rural American West really is.[3] "Trailers" have often been sites of contestation, revealing the sometimes contradictory interface between economic and regulatory issues in the New West. A look at mobile housing, which represents a spectrum from the vacationer's RVs and camping trailers to mobile homes and manufactured housing, can be used as a case study, showing the continued power of a Turnerian fantasy of self-reliance, independence, innovation, and movement as freedom, as well as how this mythology has been manipulated to serve class interests.

For the traveler in a $750,000 RV "land yacht," or even its $70,000 poor relation, the desire to be footloose and fancy free is both powerful and positive. Yet for the service industry worker struggling to find and maintain affordable housing, the supposed mobility of the mobile home signifies shiftlessness, transience, and a rejection of a commitment to community and its values. In this context, even the noblest efforts to curb sprawl, to protect open space, and to restore environmental health tend to come at the expense of underclasses. The trailerite is the foot soldier in the new West's continued class war.

The travel trailer got its big push with the beginning of auto camping, a pleasure for the well-heeled technophile, men such as Ford, Firestone, and Edison. Quickly, the travel trailer was adapted for longer-term use. As housing for seasonal workers, the travel trailer still has a place in the West. The shepherd moves her trailer a couple of times a week during the summer forage season when she's working with the sheep. The seasonal Park Service worker, the agricultural worker, or contract laborer for the government (a fire crew member, say) may live out of a camper or small travel trailer for the season. Rightly or not, we assume these workers have a more fixed home to return to when their seasonal work is completed.

While the average American moves several times over a lifetime, the presumption remains that we move from one site-built dwelling to another. Despite evidence to the contrary, as a culture we imagine the travel trailer, the RV, or the camper as vacation shelter, not as a home. Indeed, for those who have driven any western scenic route in any summer between 1970 and 2010, the behemoth RV has been ubiquitous. For travelers who can pay mortgage-sized totals at the gas pump, the RV promises one can be truly "at home" in the outback West. One need not leave any comforts behind. The life of the temporary vagabond has no relation to what it's like to live in one of these vehicles once the tires have rotted and the registration has expired, and one is stuck in a wage-labor economy.

While the trailer and the RV might be seen as a fulfillment of a Turnerian fantasy for an always "westering" group of self-reliant Americans, as homes these dwellings don't often appear in representations of the contemporary West. Current emphases on both the wilderness West and the urban West have left the mobile home and its smaller counterparts hidden on the outskirts of western American studies. The trailer, originally designed to provide short-term housing, heralded both the technology of mass production and the fantasy of better geography through engineering. And, in many cases, at least some of that promise was fulfilled. Yet even as temporary housing the mobile home reminds its inhabitants that it is not a home.

Oilfield workers in Wyoming, as described by Alexandra Fuller in her book, *The Legend of Colton H. Bryant*, typically share such temporary housing, barracks-style:

> The midsummer heat seemed to be breeding with itself to create baby pockets of heat that crawled under the skin and got behind the eyes. They were predicting a high of ninety today, which was nothing, in the scheme of a national heatwave, but without air-conditioning and with all those bodies piled next to one another, the rented double-wide trailer felt downright soupy … The rest of the boys were lined up on the sofa, watching television. "Pinedale has got to be the boringest freakingest place in the entire nation," said one of them. "Nothing to do."
> "No one to do it with," complained another. (Fuller 2008: 91–2)

Neither at home nor at work, lodgers in these accommodations live in limbo. Away from their home territory and their social network, these men struggle to match their regular recreational pursuits with both the limited time between shifts and their dislocation. Drive to any mountain resort in the interior West and you will find the route dotted with disheveled mobile housing. Typically, these residents are service workers for the resort nearby. As land values increase so does displacement, and their commute to work lengthens. Hunkered down on a windswept plain outside of town, alone and battered by the elements, the mobile home represents the isolation, and even despair, of rural wage labor.

Some planners and sociologists have suggested "mobile homes may be the last genuine communities in America. ... The sociability of park life ... results from the physical organization: a relatively small number of households live in close proximity, share common facilities, and keep an eye out for each other. ... Social cohesiveness ... often results from the homogeneity of the residents" (Wallis 1997: 188). While this may be true within a given trailer park community, in many small towns in the West the perception is often of a loose confederation of habitual losers and the down-and-out. Until recently in most states, and still in some, trailer park space renters are legally defined as transient lodgers, not as tenants. Trailer parks are often on "the other side of the tracks." Historically, towns and cities have denied permits for mobile home developments in traditional middle-class neighborhoods.

In places such as Santa Fe, New Mexico, mobile housing doesn't conform to the city's strict zoning that demands an adobe look, so trailers occupy spaces adjacent to state government buildings and in areas zoned for light industrial businesses. No place for kids to ride their bikes, but they have those "million-dollar" views, across the six-lane road. In Whitehall, Montana, a huddle of mobile homes lies between the railroad tracks and the fairgrounds, set off from the downtown and its residences. Most cities and towns refuse permits for new parks, and conventional loans are hard to come by as land prices have escalated. A used mobile home sold without a space has little value. While land values appreciate, mobile homes depreciate, like cars.

In many western spaces where there has been an influx of the upper middle class and wealthy, the wrong side of the tracks affords views, but not the community amenities of million-dollar houses. The isolation can be spatial, economic, and ideological. "As used by the media, the terms 'white trash' and 'trailer trash' often have similar meanings, whether or not the individuals in question actually live in trailers" (Kendall 2005: 158). With fewer trailer parks receiving permits, their number dwindles as land values escalate. For many residents of western trailer parks, the "mobility" implied by their form of housing is a cruel joke. If they own their mobile home, there are few options for moving, and many residents only rent these places. The only real mobility is downward. From the distinctive trailer-park alignment of dwellings to the vernacular site-built add-on, usually a porch, an entryway, or a storage shed, to the fantasy of mobility that the RV parked in the drive asserts, all over the rural and small-town West one sees the paradox of stasis and mobility, of individuality and conformity. As one drives the West or wanders the back streets of small towns, one sees how residents have modified and propped up the aged mobile home that continues to provide shelter long past its spoil date.

Perception, however, often can be at odds with statistics. Manufactured home industry sources claim, for example, that in 1998, 22.7 percent of all new single-family housing starts were "manufactured homes." They also claim that manufactured homes cost 20–50 percent less than site-built homes. In the New West, one in six people live in a manufactured home. In the Las Vegas of the late 1990s, one in three new homes arrived by truck. In four Nevada counties, mobile homes make up over half the housing stock, and in some towns nearly 80 percent. In the resort and destination West, most service workers commute long distances from affordable housing outposts to the hotels, ski areas, and parks.

Spurred by unregulated sprawl, many communities, both large and small in the West, have initiated restrictive zoning in order to save open space and tidy up the look of their towns and counties. As a consequence, ghettoized subdivisions for manufactured homes have sprung up where land values have not skyrocketed. Unable to afford pricy lots or rejected by tony subdivisions, buyers flock to new developments without restrictive covenants that welcome manufactured homes; these soon acquire the bedraggled, scattershot look of the unplanned communities they sought to supplant. Without policies for things like weed abatement and livestock, such subdivisions soon are marked by their healthy stands of noxious knapweed, which provide a sharp contrast to the denuded horse paddock that has replaced the back yard. These affordable lots come with a view of clear cuts instead of snow-capped peaks, as well as the sights, smells, and sounds of the interstate freeway they adjoin. Frontage, miles from the nearest off ramp, is affordable land. Meanwhile, closer to town, new subdivisions contribute to sprawl, while enforcing a housing hierarchy. In order to "protect" property values, covenants might allow a manufactured home, but will turn away the single- or even traditional double-wide mobile home. Residents get tangled up in a confusion of issues and definitions of fixed versus mobile, of "square feet," or "poured foundations," as they seek to establish their community *bona fides.*

These housing distinctions become troubling for everybody. No one wants the neighborhood or even the "view shed" cluttered with blown-out hulks of abandoned trailers. Once mobile homes can no longer be occupied, where do they go? It costs several thousand dollars to move most mobile homes. They are often composed of a wide range of toxic materials, so they can't be burned like trash. In Edwards, Colorado, near Vail, trailer park residents were forced to destroy all of the homes that had depreciated significantly. Under the terms of their negotiated settlement with the condo developers who evicted them, if any signs remained of the park or trailers they would receive no severance payment. Older mobiles are routinely turned away from many parks, for they ruin the look. Many of the trailer park residents in Edwards relocated to more trailer-friendly towns, many a two-hour commute from their service-work jobs at the ski resort.

While often as rooted as other members of the community, mobile home residents constantly deal with the perception that they are transient. But site-built property owners, no matter how many times they move, are presumed by their neighbors to become as invested in the community as they are in the land. Newcomers often work zealously to enact policies and laws that will protect their adopted place, but in so doing they often inadvertently set up increasingly rigid hierarchies in their communities. Wage earners who commute two hours a day to their service-sector jobs often haven't the time or money to eradicate weeds, beautify their homes, or haul dead vehicles to the dump. They can't afford to board a horse, so they keep it out back.

They might have a chicken or two that disturbs the peace and quiet sought by those in flight from urbanity. They move out of town to avoid the higher taxes that come with new roads, fire stations, and schools. The conflicts between newcomers and old-timers, between haves and have-nots, escalate with the influx of residents with money and ideas about life in "the last best places" of the American West.

McMansions and Double-wides

Many of the analyses of social relations in the New West focus on insiders versus outsiders, subsuming class distinctions to relocation patterns. The editors of *The Atlas of the New West* consider changes in income patterns, but do so mostly under the banner of the "Aspenization of small Western towns" where there has been an influx of "amenity migrants" (Riebsame et al. 1997: 12–13). The editors point out some of the consequences of this migration: the most visible migrants bring to smaller communities a "seemingly unlimited mass of capital in search of real estate: second, third, and fourth homes seldom used, large ranches not ranched" (1997: 97). While the service economy workers struggle to find affordable housing far away from their workplaces, these "ghost houses" owned by elites loom empty for all but a few weeks of the year. "A common complaint echoes through the New West: only newcomers can afford to live there" (1997: 102–3).

The myth of a classless West has been perpetuated in literature. It offers, however, a fruitful place for examination of the ways social class functions in the contemporary rural West. In the twentieth century, we can look back to *The Virginian* for such distinctions, but here I will survey only thirty or so years, and I'll focus on literature set in Montana. I'm interested in the ways the observations that prompted the geographers of *The Atlas of the New West* to map things such as jet service to cities and towns, retirement hot spots, espresso bars, Orvis shops, and "ghost houses" figure in literary representations of the New West. And it is in the literary representations that one finds the richest and most complex renderings of the experience of social class.

Representations of the traditional working classes more commonly consider urban places, with only a few writers offering rural working-class characters.[4] Perhaps the most vivid representations of rural poverty and "hard knocks" occur in memoirs such as those from Ivan Doig, Mary Clearman Blew, and Judy Blunt. Cyra McFadden's *Rain or Shine* considers the middle class, and, although not set in Montana, William Kittredge's *Hole in the Sky* confronts the ruling class head-on.

Working-class characters in novels set in the West are often are subject to forces created and manipulated by unseen or caricatured rich people, or by economic forces beyond their control, as in Larry Watson's novels. While much work by Native American writers offers vivid portrayals of poverty, discussion of social class is often forestalled by discussion of race. In the detective genre we see more inter-class conflict, but it generally takes place in town. With the exception of romance novels and a few works I will discuss, fiction offers little interaction between rural social classes. And it's no wonder. How does one make distinctions between different kinds of property: the hardscrabble ranch cobbled together from failed homesteads, the heavily mort-gaged ranch with an annual operating debt, and the, free-and-clear ranch with abun-dant water?

Since the 1970s, Thomas McGuane has been writing about conflicts between New West and Old, rich outsiders versus the cash-poor local property owners. McGuane has complicated this story over time, but his characters remain clearly divided by values and disposable income. Often, McGuane pits an affable but damaged local against rich recreationists with extravagant second homes. Usually McGuane's char-acters cause trouble, or get into it, when they aren't actively working on the land.

Reviewers have called McGuane "a great chronicler of the vanishing West," who has "a nostalgia for a less self-indulgent culture, one in which people kept to their (preferably stoic) codes."[5] For the most part, McGuane creates cardboard-cutout baddies whose most redeeming quality is their trophy wives who are sassy enough to have an affair with the typical McGuane protagonist. These relationships usually do not bridge the gulf between working and upper classes; rather, they negotiate between a high-assets class (ranchers) and a high-income class (interlopers with portfolios, not calluses). Legacy issues recur in McGuane's books, and if a protagonist can't hang on to the ranch, he can at least hang on to the Old West values that supposedly go with ranching culture – an admiration for hard work outdoors, respect for animals and the humans who appreciate them, and an ability to abide the harsh conditions of rural Montana. In McGuane's world, women add interest to the plot, reveal character traits in men, then either move on or take a back seat in the narrative. McGuane borrows the markers of rednecks for his characters, so while they might own land, they func-tion as working-class within the conflict. They are caught up in a process that works to displace them, either from the land or from their livelihood.

Some of the most interesting manipulations of western class dynamics occur in contemporary romance novels. These novels are about husbandry, animal and human, and as such the plot works to yoke two characters together who must, in the course of the book, work out all the impediments to their eventual marriage. Contemporary romance novels need to evoke enough of the actual world to reel their readers in, so they work a delicate balance of familiarity and fantasy, and in many books this makes for some interesting class negotiations. Tami Hoag's *Dark Paradise* stands as a frilly twin to any of the McGuane novels of the 1980s and early 1990s. In Hoag, the rich and arrogant interloper buys up ranch land as fast as he can intimidate the owner into selling out. He will meet his match in the feisty heroine who will show that she is no one's trophy wife when they meet; she is a distant cousin to the temptresses in McGuane's novels. Hoag plays with class markers, largely to appeal to a broad audi-ence, to provide happy endings at different strata of the class system, and to preserve the fundamentally conservative nature of the genre. Hoag lines up class with insider/outsider distinctions, but only to create an opportunity for her heroine to move from outsider to insider. Hoag works to make distinctions between new wealth and old assets, between exploitation of the working classes and protection of them, and the novel turns on misapprehensions and confusions about status.

In the novel, Mary Lee, a Californian running from a failed relationship, will meet and mate with J.D., a fourth-generation Montana rancher. J.D. faces displacement from Bryce, the Hollywood mogul who is buying up all of fictional New Eden, Montana. Bryce collects land, celebrities, young vulnerable women, exotic animals, and drugs: a perfect caricature of the trophy ranch buyer. J.D., the last rancher to hold out, is a sticker who lives modestly to serve his family legacy, his faithful retainers, his livestock, and the land ethic. Hoag makes J.D. a descendant of southern rebels gone West and gives him a redneck veneer that disguises his Virginian-like inner man. In the course of the novel, J.D. must learn that not all newcomers are bad, for some, like Mary Lee, will stick. Mary Lee must learn that all that glitters is not gold, that under the redneck lies an earthy gentleman, and that she can love the ranching life without a trip to town for an espresso.

In McGuane's novels, the insider/outsider barrier trumps any class affinities the characters might share. In Hoag, characters work to break down the insider/outsider distinctions to line up affinities based on sexual attraction and shared class background. And since romance novels often are about "husbandry," J.D. and Mary Lee will go on to produce a hybrid child, an insider with outsider grandparents and a sensibility shared not only with other fifth-generation landowners, but also the token Native Americans sprinkled into the text.

Several short stories by Montana writers attempt a deeper look at the classed experiences of a single character. These stories reveal the often complex negotiations between classes, eschewing simple binaries. Deirdre McNamer's story "Virgin Everything" provides the perspective of an outsider; an "amenity migrant," while Maile Meloy's "Ranch Girl" plumbs the intricacies of class relations among insiders in a small ranching community. Each resists simple alignment of insider/outsider with plebian/elite.

In "Virgin Everything," McNamer offers a glimpse into the life of Elise Lavender, who comes to Montana "by way of Tuscaloosa, Briarcliff, Manhattan, and Santa Barbara" (p. 13). With husband Dave, Elise moved to Montana to start a family. They chose a suitably scenic location, a ranchette about twenty miles outside of town within view of the Gallatin Range. When they prove unable to produce a baby, Elise becomes a realtor who specializes in expensive properties, selling the fantasy of a private retreat from the world of commerce into an aesthetically composed vision where recreation takes the place of work. Although the fantasy dissipates for Elise and Dave, Elise sells the fantasy to others, and Dave "goes native," to become a large-animal vet, maybe keep a few horses, and drink beer with the locals.

When prospective buyers balk at a closing, Elise creates stories that make Montana more than a place to retreat, briefly, from the life they lead, and into a place where life occurs: in salvific nature to be sure, but also a life much like Mary Lee's at the end of *Dark Paradise*. In the fantasy Elise creates two lovebirds who are "not giving up their professional lives. They will do their work from here. They will fly where they need to fly. They will email and voice mail and fax" (p. 14). In spite of her stories, Elise knows that for these buyers, Montana will never be home. As a sideline to her real estate business, she "relaxes" other people's homes. "Elise and her helpers would make sure the family's Montana retreat was warm, that a Christmas tree was up and decorated. ... The house now looked invitingly tousled; convincingly lived in" (p. 15).

Elise tries to do this in her own home too, but while the artifacts imply a robust social life, her Montana is one without society. She has clients rather than friends. The few children who come to the door on Halloween are strangers, occupying a distantly lower-class position, and frighten her into retreat behind locked doors and closed blinds. Her attempt to import a friend from New York for a visit only serves to heighten her sense of alienation. At the story's end McNamer leaves her amenity migrant Elise gazing out her picture window, imagining a family: her visiting friend Lily, husband Dave, and their fictitious child turning away from her, walking away in the snow. The alienation is complete. Elise is a newcomer to be sure, but McNamer suggests that it is, in part, class distinction and a fantasy of refuge that makes her miserable. Montana remains a scene, a picture through a window, and not a place for making a home, a community.

Maile Meloy's "Ranch Girl," narrated in the second person by the daughter of a ranch foreman, offers a complementary version of Montana life, one that draws insistently on class negotiations within a world that is relentlessly social. The attention to class begins with the first sentence: "If you're white, and you're not rich or poor but somewhere in the middle, it's hard to have worse luck than to be born a girl on a ranch" (p. 249). For the foreman's daughter, no place, not even home, offers retreat from the markers of class distinction. The substandard foreman's house, "with walls made of particleboard, one bathroom (no tub)" is no place to indulge in the rituals of a teenage girl (p. 249). Her mother has fled to town for an office job; her father comes home to a beer and falls asleep in his chair. She spends time at the ranch owner's house, where the daughter, Carla, has her own bathroom, but the girls pursue different tracks; Carla will go to the state university and marry a boy whose family owns "most of central Montana." And although the narrator excels in school, and her teachers encourage her to leave:

> You could get scholarships they say. But you know, as soon as they suggest it, that if you went to one of those schools, you'd still be a ranch girl – not the Texas kind, who are debutantes and just happen to have a ranch in the family, and not the horse-farm kind, who ride English. Horse people are different, because horses are elegant and clean. Cows are mucusy, muddy, shitty, slobbery things, and it takes another kind of person to live with them. (p. 252)

The narrator works to make her grades fall and lowers her sights to the small college in Dillon, where the boy she likes will go. Fitting into her designated class position rankles. At college, her professor accuses her of plagiarism because her first paper is readable. Class distinctions run deep. Although the narrator was called to her dying sweetheart's bedside after a car accident, she reads in his obituary that he was engaged to a slutty doctor's daughter, which he wasn't. The doctor's influence extends to the obit section. In ranch communities, people of different class status live intimately together: they see each other regularly, they talk, and they lie to each other.

For both McNamer and Meloy, social class defines and delimits the range of social relations and occupations, and these limitations are specifically gendered in their stories. While McGuane's characters rage and duke it out over women and ethics, and Hoag's characters work out class differences in bed, the women in McNamer's and Meloy's stories fantasize or resign themselves to a New West that preserves, even enforces, class distinctionLiterature and literary readings of social phenomena reveal the manifestations of the ways that social class plays out differently in the rural West. While   looking at the economics, statistics, and demographics of life in the rural West can provide facts about class difference, income disparity, and migration patterns, they fail to explain or consider the consequences for the people and communities in the outback West. Neither simply a repository for Old West mythology nor an outcome of new money, the rural West as portrayed in literature comes closest to showing what it's like to grow up as the daughter of a "rich" rancher who wears hand-me-down jeans, whose family never takes a vacation, and who goes to the same high school as the field hand's son.

What the literature does that none of the statistics do is to reveal the emptiness of having the amenities without a community; buying a dream ranch and having no one to go riding with. It situates the West as an important site for more complicated understandings of the way social class works in the United States. The field is ready for new readings that allow class to figure in the matrices of influences that determine the contours of new western terrain. In the rural West, a "cowboy" could be a multi-millionaire, or a guy who doesn't have ten bucks in his pocket. The markers of social class are not straightforward. This complexity is likely true in other places, and if we think harder about the ways social class is represented in the West, we may be moving toward a richer analysis of class in general.

NOTES

1 For a discussion of recent conversations about class as an analytical category, see Day 2001. For Day's characterization of Raymond Williams' analysis of the language of class distinction, see pp. 8–9.

2 Until the 1990s, much of the research published about class and rural places looked at rural poverty, rural economies outside the US, and within the US they looked at the South and at wage laborers in resource-based industries in the West: mining, logging, and agriculture.

3 I will refer to mobile homes and double-wides, forms of manufactured housing "largely assembled in factories and then transported to sites of use." In terms of marketing, these differ from the travel trailer, portable housing meant to be towed behind a vehicle on a journey.

Travel trailers are one subset of the recreational vehicle, or RV, which include motorhomes, converted buses, campervans, and campers. Mobility is a key feature of RVs and travel trailers, while for mobile homes, the key feature is their manufacture in factories rather than on site. In lived experience, however, these distinctions begin to collapse (see Wikipedia: "Manufactured Housing," "Recreational Vehicle," and "Travel trailer").

4   The only collected work on social class in the American West that includes a strong offering on the rural West can be found in *Western American Literature*, 40/4 (2006), a special issue on "Working-Class Literature of the American West."

5   See reviews of *The Cadence of Grass* in the Orlando *Sentinel* and *Publishers Weekly*.

REFERENCES AND FURTHER READING

Brooks, David. (2000). *Bobos in Paradise*. New York: Simon & Schuster.

Day, Gary. (2001). *Class*. London and New York: Routledge.

Empson, William. (1974). *Some Versions of Pastoral* [1935]. New York: New Directions.

Fuller, Alexandra. (2008). *The Legend of Colton H. Bryant*. New York: The Penguin Press.

Fussell, Paul. (1983). *Class*. New York: Ballantine.

Gibson-Graham, J.K., Stephen Resnick, and Richard D. Wolff, eds. (2000). *Class and its Others*. Minneapolis: University of Minnesota Press.

Hoag, Tami. (1994). *Dark Paradise*. New York: Bantam.

Jarosz, Lucy, and Victoria Lawson. (2002). "Sophisticated People Versus Rednecks": Economic Restructuring and Class Difference in the American West. *Antipode*, 34/1, 8–27.

Kendall, Diana. (2005). *Framing Class: Media Representations of Wealth and Poverty in America*. Lanham, MD: Rowman & Littlefield.

McNamer, Deirdre. (2003). Virgin Everything. In Rick Newby, ed., *The New Montana Story*, pp. 13–24. Helena, MT: Riverbend Publishing.

Meloy, Maile. (2004) Ranch Girl [2002]. In William Kittredge and Allen Morris Jones, eds., pp. 249–55. *The Best of Montana's Short Fiction*. Guilford, CT: The Lyons Press.

Nelson, Peter B. (2001). Rural Restructuring in the American West: Land Use, Family and Class Discourses. *Journal of Rural Studies*, 17, 395–407.

Raban, Jonathan. (2009). American Pastoral. *The New York Review of Books*, 56, 18. www.nybooks.com/articles/23373.

Riebsame, William E. et al., eds. (1997). *Atlas of the New West*. New York: W.W. Norton.

Savage, William W., Jr. (1979). *The Cowboy Hero: His Image in American History and Culture*. Norman: University of Oklahoma Press.

Wallis, Allan D. (1997). *Wheel Estate: The Rise and Decline of Mobile Homes* [1991]. Baltimore: Johns Hopkins University Press.

Zweig, Michael. (2000). *The Working Class Majority: America's Best Kept Secret*. Ithaca, NY: ILR/Cornell University Press.

15
Postcolonial West

Alex Hunt

In that Empire, the Art of Cartography attained such Perfection that the map of a single Province occupied the entirety of a City, and the map of the Empire, the entirety of a Province. In time, those Unconscionable Maps no longer satisfied, and the Cartographers Guilds struck a Map of the Empire whose size was that of the Empire, and which coincided point for point with it. The following Generations, who were not so fond of the Study of Cartography as their Forebears had been, saw that that vast Map was Useless, and not without some Pitilessness was it, that they delivered it up to the Inclemencies of Sun and Winters. In the Deserts of the West, still today, there are Tattered Ruins of that Map, inhabited by Animals and Beggars; in all the Land there is no other Relic of the Disciplines of Geography. (*Suarez Miranda, Viajes de varones prudentes, Libro IV, Cap. XLV, Lerida, 1658*, in Borges 1998: 325)

Borges' fragment on cartography and empire is a suggestive parable of colonial and postcolonial America: while the populace may have forsworn the map, forgetting its history and the parameters of its dominion, the power of that map continues. The populace still lives, in a sense, within that map of empire that is the size of the empire, within lines of township and range, interstate flows of commerce and trade, suburban lawns. But at the fringes of things, "in the Deserts of the West," the map in its tatters remains visible, and the history of empire is not forgotten. In this space, the territory has not absorbed the map, the map has not disappeared in a transparent illusion. Here "Animals and Beggars" dwell in the interstices of empire and outlands, nation and globe, nature and culture – a place of multiple ongoing histories that give the lie to the perfection of the imperial cartographic project.

Maps are one of the many literary tropes shared by postcolonial and western American writers and scholars, one that constitutes a fitting start, as a map suggests

A Companion to the Literature and Culture of the American West, First Edition. Edited by Nicolas S. Witschi.

a space, both imaginary and real, where we might question the parameters of our disciplinary project. This essay makes an argument for the importance of postcolonial theory to western American literary and cultural studies. This project is vital both as it seeks justice for dwellers within US territories – those desert inhabitants of the ruins of the map – and as it has the potential to critique ongoing US foreign policy – other ruins, other deserts. After all, today's US neocolonial oil wars pick up where manifest destiny left off – Richard Slotkin could write another volume – as some continue to use language of the Indian wars to describe conflict in Afghanistan and Iraq. Robert Kaplan in *Imperial Grunts*, for a blatant example, describes the US Indian wars of the nineteenth century in heroic terms before pointing out the ways in which the military is once again building an American empire, this time on a global scale. Kaplan finds it charming that soldiers refer to hostile regions of Iraq and Afghanistan as "Injun Country" and explains that they name their attack helicopters Apaches as a tribute:

> "Welcome to Injun country" was the refrain I heard from troops from Colombia to the Philippines, including Afghanistan and Iraq. To be sure, the problem for the American military was less fundamentalism than anarchy. The War on Terrorism was really about taming the frontier. But the fascination with Indian County was never meant as a slight against Native North Americans. Rather, the reverse. The fact that radio call signs often employed Indian names was but one indication of the troops' reverence for them. (Kaplan 2005: 4)

Kaplan goes on to consider the role of representation in colonial process, noting that "Remington, more than Francis Parkman, was the Kipling of early American imperialism, turning it from fact into heroic myth." That such men might be accused of racism is inappropriate, according to Kaplan, since both men understood that "'the white man's burden' meant only the righteous responsibility to advance the boundaries of free society and good government into zones of sheer chaos, a mission not unlike that of the post-Cold War humanitarian interventionists" (2005: 10) – presumably including Bush II, Cheney, and cabinet, America's ministers of preemptive humanitarianism.

Such triumphalist views are nothing new, and are at the basis of western American literature's most popular form – the genre western. We can cite earlier progenitors, but Owen Wister's *The Virginian* is generally recognized as the first western, and Wister's relationship with Frederick Jackson Turner and Theodore Roosevelt, whose work commemorates the western frontier and opens the way to global imperialism, makes Wister's novel resonate all the more strongly with American historiography and empire. *The Virginian* reads like a trope of Turner's 1893 essay "The Significance of the Frontier in American History," perpetuating a Romantic, if elegiac, picture of the region and its mythic history. Both works justify ideologically the presence of a settler culture as heroic, the new and rightful heir to the American West, and in some sense natural or indigenous. This literature is heavily invested in historical authenticity, but often of a kind that Renato Rosaldo termed "imperialist nostalgia," an expression of sadness over the destruction that is one's own doing (1989: 69–70). What Wister rather ruefully admits is a "colonial romance" (p. xlvii) gives rise to a genre concerned with territorial power and steeped in violence (empire-building, in short) but light on implications – at least overtly[1] –but it is no coincidence that Wister dedicated his novel to his Yale buddy Theodore Roosevelt, that great white hunter of the western frontier who, at this period as twenty-sixth president, was happily engaged in the extension of US imperial power into the Pacific with his corollary to the Monroe Doctrine. This western American triumvirate forms the basis for the traditional "canon" (a questionable term, as arguably the literature of the American West has never had a legitimately canonical status) that runs from Wister to A.B. Guthrie to Wallace Stegner to Edward Abbey to Cormac McCarthy.[2]

Critique of the western American triumphalist view is nothing new either, as Helen Hunt Jackson's and Sarah Winnemucca Hopkins' writings attest. Relatively recently, the project of the New Western historians was to force a reconsideration of the history of the American West as a history of conquest. Yet interestingly, certain forms of western exceptionalism have survived this revisionist history unscathed. Kaplan certainly has no trouble embracing the conquest model of American history as a civilizing force. And after all, it is the very cachet of "westernness" itself that gave the revisionists their popular appeal. As I see it, the continuing work of western American literary and cultural scholars, then, is to further a critique of US imperialism in its own territories and abroad, employing postcolonial theory to decolonize US rhetoric and territories, to put US western literatures in dialogue with other postcolonial literatures, to take regionalism, with its defense of indigenous peoples, local cultures, threatened places and environments, and marginalized lives, transnational – in other words, to compare deserts.

Postcolonialism is crucial in lending a critical vocabulary to the American West, a landscape that is a mosaic of overlapping histories, cultural identities, and degrees of power, self-determination, adaption, and hybridity. But postcolonial theory is also vital because it puts the American West in a particular global context. Reversing a long tradition of western exceptionalism, postcolonialism holds a mirror to the American West that forces the recognition that it is, more than a regional or national tradition, part of a global literature of colonization, indeed a literature of the Age of Imperialism. The postcolonial West is a space crisscrossed, torn, and stitched with contested borders and microfrontiers. US postcolonial studies is by no means geographically limited to the western US, but in studying the western regions, postcoloniality commands attention: US history is shorter out west, whereas Spanish, Mexican, and indigenous history is vibrant; the arid lands are more resistant to the terraforming of progress west of the 100th meridian; and of course in the West indigenous peoples continue to reside on and struggle for reservation lands to an extent greater and more visible than those further east. Out west, the nation, like Borges' map of the empire, is a bit tattered at the edges. Postcolonial theory offers a means to a further reckoning and reconciliation of an ongoing colonialist history, creates a methodology for reading a multiethnic regional literary tradition, and provides a necessary bridge from region to world. Postcolonial theory has been demonstrably useful in approaches to western American literature, a regionally defined field, in which the boundaries of the region and the field in our globalized moment pose healthy questions about the project.[3] Scholars of western American literature have long championed and attempted to create – with mixed success – a pluralistic "big tent" approach to including without (mis)appropriating Native American, Chicano, and other historically marginalized literary traditions, studying the literary and cultural production of diverse writers of the American West and its edges and borderlands, broadly defined.[4]

Consider, for example, the work of Simon Ortiz. For my purposes here, I do not seek to categorize him as primarily a western American writer, nor to make him a representative figure for what western American literature should be. Rather, in considering the topic "Postcolonial West," I am drawn to Ortiz because he is a Native American writer whose work engages issues of colonialism and postcolonial theory. Ortiz's work reminds one of Arnold Krupat's 1993 argument concerning postcolonialism and Native America:

> contemporary Native American literatures cannot quite be classed among the postcolonial literatures of the world for the simple reason that there is not yet a "post-" to the colonial status of Native Americans. Call it domestic imperialism or internal colonialism; in either case, a considerable number of Native people exist in conditions of politically sustained subalternity. (1996: 30)

The fact that more recent scholars tend to define postcolonialism less as a historical stage than as the study of the circumstances of colonial experience more broadly defined does not detract from Krupat's substantive point: Native Americans exist in a space of ongoing colonization, a point Ortiz makes unambiguously. Ortiz's vision is also noteworthy for its politics of inclusivity even as it defends the integrity of Acoma culture and identity. His writing therefore enables us to make useful comparisons to other postcolonial literatures of the American West, whether Hispanic/Chicano traditions, other literatures of migration and diaspora, or Euro-American "settler" narratives.

Simon Ortiz, as a member of the Acoma nation, or Aacqumeh hanoh, establishes throughout his book of poetry *Fight Back: For the Sake of the People, For the Sake of the Land* (1980; updated and republished, 1992), the necessary connection between a people and a landscape, for it is this connection that provides Acoma identity. The poems in the collection are primarily narrative, blending personal and Acoma history, moving between English and Acoma language to "map" the Acoma landscape. But at the outset of the collection's central piece, "Our Homeland, A National Sacrifice Area" – a lengthy poem interspersed with discourses in prose – he describes this relationship as increasingly troubled; while Ortiz had been in the mountains, "being with Srhakaiya," a mountain "west of Aacqu," he feels "sick" with "a sense of otherness," which he describes as "an electric current coursing in ghost waves through me" (p. 337). The "otherness" which Ortiz goes on to diagnose through the rest of "Our Homeland" is caused by a rift in the relationship between self and place, and is thus a threat to identity. This rift is the result of a long history of colonial waves that have dispossessed and threatened Acoma people. In particular, Ortiz's suggestion is that of radioactive contamination of the region's water and lifeblood; this narrative is eminently one of environmental racism and environmental justice, both of which figure predominantly as regionalist subjects. More generally, Ortiz's feeling of "otherness" comes as a function of his dissociation from a landscape expropriated and damaged by corporate exploitation – specifically, the capitalist forces of US empire. In this sense, the Acoma Pueblo landscape is now double for Ortiz, as he is aware of both the indigenous and the colonial layers that inhabit and shape the land. Just as the landscape is two, so is Ortiz himself both Acoma (as he has been raised) and "Indian" (as constructed though American culture), a colonized subject. As a younger man, as he tells it in "The First Hard Core," he is unable to articulate a response to the racist Texan "Herb," who demands to know why New Mexico indigenous people don't have proper Indian names like Sitting Bull (p. 307). Ortiz's voicelessness resonates with Gayatri Spivak's famous pronouncement that "the subaltern cannot speak" (p. 308); with Ortiz's ability to gain a public voice comes a clear sense that he feels a responsibility to speak for Acoma and other peoples voiceless against or unconscious of the effects of colonialism upon them. Ortiz's ability derives from the relative integrity of Acoma culture, language, and grounding in place, yet even as an adult more secure in his identity, the catastrophic changes wrought on the land are powerful enough to create in him a sense of "electric current" and "ghost waves." The land retains its powerful hold.

The construction and oppression of the other is in no small degree the function of language, both in the sense of different languages (English vs. Acoma) and in the sense of discursive power (who is more powerfully positioned as speaker). The image of the stoic silent Indian, Ortiz asserts, is "mostly crap": "Lots of times / we were just plain scared / and we kept our mouths shut" (p. 327). Ortiz relates his own birth into the sound of Acoma language being spoken, and its fundamental importance in "sustaining" his writing, even as he grew up with English and Spanish, learning English in school. He relates also, as seemingly all Native American writers do, stories of the suppression of native languages by American schools, part of a program of assimilation and indigenous cultural fragmentation (pp. 4–5). He characterizes US colonization of the New Mexico pueblos as a function of language:

> They were so shrewd, talkative, even helpful, and so friendly they didn't look like thieves. As the Mericano stole unto the land, claiming it, the people didn't even feel like anything was being taken away from them. And they even blamed themselves and began to feel it was their fault. They couldn't or didn't speak English or write; that's why it turned out so badly for them they decided. (p. 347)

Language as colonial tool against "others" the indigenous people who are colonized not only territorially, but through psychological conditioning, thus blaming themselves for their victimization.

In terms of his own writerly use of language, Ortiz considers the problem of translating Acoma into English as one of "objectifying" Acoma language (p. 5). By this he clearly means the loss of nuance and cultural specificity when translating from any language into another, but also the sense of moving from the dynamic forms of oral tradition to the translated written form of English, from something alive to a linguistic object. Surprisingly, however, Ortiz states that his role as a writer and storyteller is "to demystify language" (p. 3). His statement implies that his fundamental goal is not narration, exposition, or invocation but rather abrogation, a rejection of standard discourse that contains mystifications, whether "realist" or "romantic," in favor of a language self-reflexive and analytical: giving people the tools to understand how language shapes their sense of the world and their place in it. Ortiz can be seen as writing what Deleuze and Guattari describe as a "minor" language that deterritorializes, shifting the relationship between language, world, and identity. Consider the word "Mericano," for example, a not-quite-Spanish term for "Anglo-American," one that suggests "outsider." In "What I Mean," Agee, a young Acoma man who was always in trouble in school for "talking Indian / (you couldn't do that) / and making English sound like Indian (you couldn't do that either.)," becomes a labor organizer when working in the uranium mines, where he speaks to fellow workers "in English that sounded Okie and Mexican and Indian" (pp. 327–8). Agee dies at 19, but his story, Ortiz writes, sounds like "the language of our struggle / just sounds and reads like an Indian, / Okie, Cajun, Black, Mexican hero story" (pp. 328–9). To my ear, the Ortiz's language, like Agee's, "mak[es] English sound like Indian" and moreover reaches for a language "demystified," stripped of affect and pretense in a political plain style, and thus seeks community and consensus across lines of ethnicity.

The role of language in constructing and confining the colonized others, as we see in Ortiz, resonates with much of western American history, contemporary cultural politics, and literature. After all, the American West is "home" to hundreds of indigenous languages, colonial languages, Spanish as well as English, and immigrant languages from Basque to Hmong to Somali. Gloria Anzaldúa's 1987 tour de force *Borderlands/La Frontera* is a resonant example of the contested language of the "third country" which she calls her own, where there exist many languages between Spanish and English, "a patois, a forked tongue" (p. 55). Such borderlands languages must be affirmed, Anzaldúa insists: "I will no longer be made to feel ashamed of existing. I will have my voice: Indian, Spanish, white. I will have my serpent's tongue – my woman's voice, my sexual voice, my poet's voice. I will overcome the tradition of silence" (p. 59). Maxine Hong Kingston's *Woman Warrior* (1976) is the memoir of the discovery of a voice between Chinese tradition and English America, a reminder of earlier immigrant waves, diasporas of American empire-building, the labor of colonization. In these heterogeneous cultural and linguistic spaces of hybridity, what Edward Soja (drawing on Homi Bhabha) has termed "thirdspace," is a postcolonial geography, a postcolonial West, of what Ortiz ironically refers to as "the west after all, barren and undeveloped, with only a few red men and jackrabbits on it" (p. 354). Yet it is also, for Ortiz as for Anzaldúa and others, a space of possibility.

A major preoccupation of western American literature is place, which might take the form of exploration and discovery, claiming place, or with or with "becoming native" to the place. Such an attempt may take many forms, from Wister's imperialistic cartography of a West that is brought under domesticated control to far more progressive attempts on the part of nature writers like Barry Lopez, who seek reconciliation with Native Americans and attempt to honor indigenous epistemologies. In "Our Homeland, A National Sacrifice Area" Ortiz makes an indigenous claim to place and culture, but also engages other western American tropes of writing place. "Our Homeland" is structured as a walk from the mountain Srhakaiya back to the community of Deetseyamah – "The North Door" – also known as Grants, New Mexico. Defining place is crucial to Ortiz's identity as Acoma and to the critique enacted in the poem which exemplifies a cartographic function of language. One way Ortiz achieves his literary cartography is to assert indigenous place by reinserting Acoma place names in opposition to a geography of imperialism and capitalism associated with the science of cartography and military-industrial power. Ortiz writes, "U.S. and New Mexico maps do not know the Aacquemeh honoh's name for the local community. It is Deetseyamah–The North Door" (p. 337). Ortiz makes it certain at the outset that an indigenous geography underlies and pre-dates the geography of official place names: "Looking northward, too, from Aacqu, one can see Kaweshtima–Snowed Peak–a dark blue misted mother mountain. Those Aacqumeh names do not appear anywhere except in the people's hearts and souls and history and oral tradition and in their love. But you will find the easy labels: Mt. Taylor, Elevation 11,950 ft., and Acoma: The Sky City" (p. 338). A key aspect of the postcolonial remapping of the landscape involves translation from Acoma and transcription of oral tradition. In Ortiz's examples, the English place names like McCartys and Taylor, which commemorate Euro-American settlers and politicians, sought to replace and erase the Acoma names. Ortiz reapplies Acoma place names and provides English translations. These names emphasize landscape description and direction and suggest the connection between an indigenous people's sense of identity as connected to landscape through oral tradition. The fact that Ortiz provides these translations is edifying for a non-Acoma readership. It seems even rather diplomatic, especially when contrasted with the one American ostensible (mis)translation of Acoma to English as "Sky City" – the term in Acoma actually describes the mesa rock on which the main pueblo sits.

The science of cartography is crucial for colonial processes and settler nations, for through cartography (indigenous) territory is defined as wilderness and then controlled, epistemologically, through the grid and through place-naming. Ortiz realizes the physical presence of imperialist cartography literally inscribed in the land: "I found a marker, / its head stamped / with an official seal and number / … The markers are brass / set in concrete" (p. 347). In narrating the history of Spanish and US colonization, Ortiz notes that Acoma lands were coveted because they were well watered:

The railroads were the first large industrial users of the water belonging to the land and people. They found it easy enough to get; they simply took it. The railroads had been given grants of land by the US government and they got right of way through Indian land. Choice Aacqumeh lands which were the flatlands along the Rio de San Jose were taken as a right of way. (p. 343)

Ortiz is keenly aware of the power of nationalist myth in this process. For although "to cast away Indians was easy enough," the US "even [had] something called Manifest Destiny which ordained the US with a religious mission. There was no need for conspiracy to seal and defraud; rather there was a national goal to fulfill and godly purpose to be done" (p. 349). Ortiz clearly shows, as well, the mechanism through which this works – romanticizing and dehumanizing indigenous peoples – enables the colonist to envision the land as wilderness in need of redemption through his development.

Therefore, along with land taken for purposes of development, Ortiz is critical of federally created parks which are meant to preserve wild lands and archeological sites for the public but which from his perspective silence native peoples by enshrining an archeological colonialist view of natives as archaic and extinct. Such a constrained representation of indigenous peoples in historical time and geographical space exemplifies the phenomenon theorized by Kevin Bruyneel, who begins by asserting that US colonial relations with Native Americans "seek to justify the coherence of repressive spatial boundaries by invoking temporal boundaries, characterizing indigenous people as too far behind the times to be active agents within the territorial, legal, and/or political space of modern life" (2007: 7). Postcolonial theory, writes Bruyneel, drawing on Homi Bhabha's work, is useful because it enables us "to uncover and theorize the active cultural and political life occurring in the interstitial, in-between, neither-nor locations that we commonly refer to as boundaries" (2007: p. xviii). Bruyneel describes a nation that seeks to define indigenous peoples narrowly "in space and time" – by the reservation and the historical museum, we might say – thereby limiting their ability to "define their own identity and develop economically and politically on their own terms" (2007: p. xvii). This critique by Bruyneel and Ortiz also recalls Spivak's attention to state institutions which act as "screen-allegories" for the "broader narratives of imperialism" (Spivak 1988: 291). For while these institutions may provide valuable information, Spivak warns, "in the long run [they] cohere with the work of imperialistic subject-constitution, mingling epistemic violence with the advancement of learning and civilization" (1988; 295). And it is just such a minefield that Ortiz, as an Acoma individual, must traverse as a child learning English in US schools and in claiming the writer's public – published – voice.

Bracketed by a discussion of Acoma oral tradition concerning the people's origins in a country to the northwest, Ortiz criticizes Mesa Verde National Park, in particular, as the epitome of friendly, polite, and helpful federal bureaucracy, a fine example "Americanhood." Yet this park is sinister, protecting "monuments, or ruins / as they are called ... by the latest technology / in preserving antiquity" (p. 339). Ortiz also recounts the history of "Esther," a naturally preserved corpse, "a child, born / from a woman 1000 years ago" who was kept on display by the park until "some Indian people / demanded her freedom. Government bureaucrats / said Indians were insensitive / to U.S. heritage" (p. 339). Ortiz concludes his ironic presentation of this issue, which represents nationalism through historical and scientific presentation, with the comment, "See Museum For More Information." Ortiz is responding to a binary tendency, strong in western American Turnernian frontier ideology, to think in terms of civilization and wilderness, with indigenous people both dehumanized and romanticized through their association with the savage wild. Ortiz here diagnoses the US colonial view of the Southwest as exotic space, a phenomenon consistent with the nineteenth-century view of the West as "passage to India" and consistent with Edward Said's critique of "orientalism" (Said 1979: 12) an exoticization of this "manifestly different … world" and its non-western other. Orientalism is, as Said defines it, political and powerful, but exists in a manner "distributed" through "aesthetic, scholarly, economic" and other texts (1979: 12); such treatments of the American West are institutionalized, again, in such spaces as Mesa Verde as well as in art and literature, familiar from texts such as Willa Cather's *Death Comes for the Archbishop* (1927) and Barbara Kingsolver's *Animal Dreams* (1990).

While much "settler" literature of the American West can be seen as reenacting on some level imaginative acts of exploration, discovery, and colonization, the possibility for an anti-colonial "rediscovery" – as Barry Lopez termed it – can be particularly powerful as it consciously invokes and revokes imperialist claims.[5] In *Savage Dreams*, for example, Rebecca Solnit is drawn to the seemingly empty and wild places of the American West. In her analyses of two landscapes – Yosemite National Park and Nevada Test Site – Solnit uncovers histories of Indian wars and nuclear testing. In seeking to understand how the Yosemite Valley became the iconic view of American wilderness, she uncovers and relates the story of William Savage's genocidal campaign against the Ahwahneechee. In exploring the complexities of the atomic age at Nevada Test Site, Solnit does not neglect to tell the story of the Dann sisters, western Shoshone people whose tribal lands include those behind DOE fences, contaminated by over 900 atomic detonations, as well as those of Utah downwinders affected by fallout. In both criticizing the wilderness narrative and issues of radioactive environmental justice, Solnit's goals intersect with those of Ortiz. While Solnit does not use the terminology of postcolonial studies and no doubt would not describe her book as such, it stands as an excellent example of what a postcolonial western American literature can be at its conciliatory best. When Solnit concludes her book, she remarks about leaving a protest at Nevada Test Site back for her place of residence in San Francisco, "This time I was just going back, because I was already home" (1994: 385); rather than claiming a place, Solnit's sense of home expands and becomes more inclusive. It is the conclusion earned by a resident rather than claimed by a settler, and it is justly earned indeed.

In key ways, Ortiz's view of landscape and his subject position as a colonized indigenous subject share a dynamic of what Homi Bhabha has termed the "third space" of hybridity. This third space "displaces the histories that constitute it, and sets up new structures of authority, new political initiative" (Bhabha 1994: 211). The value of this third space of hybridity is the possibility of a new thought, "a new area of negotiation of meaning and representation" with the potential to break out beyond old essentialist binaries. Ortiz, it must be said, does not position himself as the kind of mixed-blood hybrid figure familiar to readers of Leslie Marmon Silko's *Ceremony*. Yet Ortiz is certainly aware of himself as both of Acoma and of that larger America and the world beyond. As he recalls of his boyhood, it was a time when he considered that "being Aacqumeh was not quite as good as being Mericano," a time he character-izes as before "I learned the language to think and talk about colonialism" (p. 10). The feelings of being between the colonized enclave and the wealthy world beyond, the impact of discrimination and racism, the threats to his sense of self as Acoma, his later alcoholism – these are recognizably the internalized response to a condition of cultural hybridity, a condition which Bhabha makes clear is a violent "splitting" of the self. Yet at the same time the hybrid is of great potential power, for it "disturbs the visibility of the colonial presence and makes the recognition of its authority prob-lematic." The hybrid exposes the "unitary (and essentialist) reference to race, nation or cultural tradition" (Bhabha 1994: 111).

Hybridity as a third space functions in several aspects of Ortiz's poem. As Joni Adamson has argued, Ortiz seeks a "middle place" between nature and culture that is characteristic of Acoma Pueblo ways of working with the land through small-scale agriculture and more generally seeing the natural community as part of rather than opposed to human culture. Thus Ortiz professes an ecology that is a hybrid third, exposing the falsity of wilderness/civilization dualisms so instrumental in colonialist discourse. Furthermore, as we can see from Bruyneel's elaborations on Bhabha's work, Ortiz' writing strains against the temporal and geographical categories that US policy tends to fix upon indigenous nations. Indigenous resistance to such constraint reveals a "'third space of sovereignty' that resides neither simply inside nor outside the American political system but rather exists on these very boundaries, exposing both the practices and the contingencies of American colonial rule" (Bruyneel 2007: xvii). These are postcolonial US literatures, of the borderlands or other marginal and edge-places, Borges' deserts, where lives are conditioned by loss of territory and traditional economies, subaltern positions, forced cultural assimilation, cultural and racial hybrid-ity, places on the other hand often characterized as exotic and oriental, diverse and picturesque.

Into the thirdspace that is more than the sum of its indigenous and Euro-colonial cartographies, Ortiz seeks alliances for liberation. Significantly, as Ortiz discusses historical bases for such alliances, he complicates static notions of racial or ethnic identity. In the Pueblo Revolt of 1680, when Acoma and other pueblos rose against the oppression of the Spanish,

> they were joined in revolt by the *mestizo* and *genizaro*, ancestors of the Chicano people, and the Athapascan-speaking peoples whose descendants are the peoples of the Navajo and Apache nations, and descendants of Africans who had been brought to the New

World as slaves. They were all commonly impoverished. These people rebelled against the oppressive rule of the civil, church, and armed guard of the Spanish colonialist. (p. 347)

Ortiz's recounting of the event underlines the complex hybridization of peoples under colonial rule, and the role of social class as a basis for creating a politics of resistance against the institutions – government, church, military – which enable colonial states. Oppression, and particularly the condition of poverty, joined peoples whose cultural, ethnic, national, and "racial" identifications would otherwise hold them apart. Ortiz contends that even after the reconquest of 1692, the Spanish never again ruled with the kind of complete control and brutality as before the revolt. Subsequently, later in the poem after his examination of the environmental contamination of the region through the uranium industry, Ortiz makes an implicit comparison between the alliance of the revolt in 1680 and the potential for class-based coalition politics in the uranium mines of the Southwest and beyond.

> The American poor and the workers and the white middleclass, who are probably the most ignorant of all U.S. citizens, must understand how they, like Indian people, are forced to serve a national interest, controlled by capitalist vested interests in collusion with U.S. policy makers, which does not serve them. Only when this understanding is attained and decisions are reached and actions taken to overcome economic and political oppression imposed upon all of us will there be no longer a national sacrifice area in the Southwest. Only then will there be no more unnecessary sacrifices of our people and land. (p. 361)

This passage is followed by lines of poetic verse in which Ortiz's feeling of "otherness" departs and he sees horses, "One was a pinto / and the other was red" (p. 362). Horses are iconically related to Indians, but as Alfred Crosby reminds us, are a function of colonization and an example of ecological imperialism; yet these horses are for Ortiz a vision of healing and representative of that thirdspace between nature and culture, neither wild nor domestic. Furthermore, recalling Silko's symbolically hybrid cattle in *Ceremony*, Ortiz more subtly affirms the pinto's undocumented breeding,[6] and the two run "until they vanished / into the folds / of the evening earth / that was the canyon / entering into / the dark near mountain / Srahkaiya" (p. 362). The horses seem symbolic of humanity in its full variety in harmony with landscape.

In his call for a class-based Marxist uprising against capitalist exploitation of poor and middle-class Americans, Ortiz echoes Fanon's Marxist politics and recognizes the need for a critical nationalism in moving toward a decolonized condition. In other words, Ortiz's sense of revolution seems far less radical than that prophesied by Silko in *Almanac of the Dead*, in which "all things European" are swept from the Americas. Indeed in another poem in his collection, "To Change in a Good Way," Ortiz tells a story of the friendship between Pete and Mary, of Laguna Pueblo, and Ida and Bill, an electrician's assistant, who had "come out with Kerr-McGee" from Oklahoma. Mary helps Ida learn to grow a successful garden in the arid country, and, after Bill learns of his brother's death in Vietnam, Pete provides him with an ear of white corn and a cornhusk bundle. Pete admits that he doesn't know all the proper Laguna words and ceremonies, but tells him how to place the materials. "You and Ida are not Indian," Pete says, "but it doesn't make any difference" (p. 314). And Bill carries through, joining pueblo ritual with his own Christian observances. The friendship between the couples recalls Ortiz's memory of his father's work on the railroad, where the laborers were "Indians, Ind-Hispanos, and Blacks, with occasional Okies, and the foremen were always white" (pp. 356–7).

In making connections with hybrid identities and class-based politics, Ortiz again anticipates Bruyneel's description of the postcolonial thirdspace that explodes attempts to lock indigenous peoples into temporal and spatial zones of difference and silence around reservation lands and borders. Expanding the frame further to other borders and borderlands, Edward Soja's conception of thirdspace moves toward a globalized cartography that takes on national borders, reconfiguring the American West as a region on a world stage. Drawing on numerous postcolonial theorists and writers, but chiefly on the work of Henri Lefebvre, Soja theorizes thirdspace as "not deriv[ing] simply from an additive combination of its binary antecedents but rather from a disordering, deconstruction, and tentative reconstitution of their presumed totaliza-tion producing an open alternative that is both similar and strikingly different" (Soja 1996: 61). Soja's postmodern sense of identity, conceived in thirdspace, as a highly dynamic and performative process pushes beyond Ortiz's tendency always to reground himself in Acoma place and oral tradition. Guillermo Gomez-Peña, poet and perform-ance artist of the US–Mexico border, of whom Soja writes, is perhaps more fully an artist of thirdspace, who, in a style different than that of Ortiz, demonstrates how identity itself is de- and re-territorialized as borders are drawn, challenged, redrawn, and transgressed.

Much recent western American literature finds itself in such a dynamic space of hybridity, negotiating forces of globalism with tools of postcolonial critique. Alfredo Véa's *La Maravilla* (1993) and Karen Tei Yamashita's *Tropic of Orange* (1997), set in Phoenix and Los Angeles, respectively, are works of magical realism – a mode, closely associated with postcolonial literatures worldwide. Both have an engagement with colonial history and develop themes of postcoloniality; while Véa's novel is a explora-tion of the richness, anguish, and power of hybrid identity, Yamashita's novel further critiques globalism as yet another manifestation of postcoloniality. Both novels suggest a plasticity of space, through Yaqui peyote ceremonies and magically shifting cartog-raphies. Concerned with "people of the gaps" (Véa, 1993: 221), both end up in affir-mation of the hybrid figure, who in both cases are more than the mere biological sum of their parents' ancestries, but also a function of their family histories of colonization, migration, oppression, survival, alliance, and affiliation.

Though much violence occurred on and around Acoma lands since the Spanish first came in 1540, Ortiz takes care to describe colonization into the US era – after "the West had been won" (p. 348) – as a more pervasive and corrupting process, one based on a cash economy that forced Acoma men to work as laborers. Ortiz writes, "the

Mericano was not called thief or killer; instead he was a missionary, merchant, and businessman, philanthropist, educator, civil servant, and worker" (p. 350). This meant railroad or agricultural work – which made them migrant laborers, weakening their home communities – or, later, in uranium mining and processing – what Churchill and LaDuke term the "radioactive colonization" of indigenous lands. Dispossession, displacement, cultural fragmentation and appropriation, the disruption of traditional farming and pastoral economies, ecological contamination, and environmental justice labor issues: the experience of Acoma and other indigenous nations demonstrates beyond question the importance that postcolonial theory must have to western American literary and cultural studies.

Earlier I made the point that considering the "canonical" tradition of western American literature from the critical standpoint of postcolonialism might prove a thankless enterprise, as such a tradition can be seen as predominantly a settler literature serving the ends of a nationalist and colonial project. In considering texts by Ortiz, Solnit, Véa, Yamashita, and others, we can see multiple literary traditions of the American West that resist a hegemonic view of the West as a consequence of the course of empire, and one could say that to some degree the difference is seeing the American West not as a process but a place – this, of course, is a key idea that Patricia Limerick introduces in *The Legacy of Conquest* (1987: 26–7). What postcolonial readings of western American literature add to Limerick's crucial insight are the means to analyze the ways in which such a place and its inhabitants remain locked in postcolonial relationships and negotiations of power. In this globalized space of shifting borders and hybrid forms, it is tempting to be swept up by the heady energy of global media representations. Postcolonial theory, and writers like Simon Ortiz, help us to remember why terms like home, place, and region, which sometimes seem fusty old concepts, are crucial and contested terrains. Postcolonial theory also models an ambivalence toward globalism that scholars of western American literature must appreciate as it helps us frame our understanding of our regional subject. Globalism is a neocolonial force that, as is always the way in these things, can either disintegrate our project or revitalize it – but cannot help but change it. Most intriguingly, as Rebecca Solnit's *Savage Dreams* demonstrates so effectively, postcolonial theory reframes our project in exciting ways, so that western American literature can bridge nations, moving from regional to global dialogue. This, I believe, will become western literature's highest calling: to play a role in forging connections between peoples, wherever on the globe they live, who live in the tatters of Borges' map of empire.

NOTES

1 In their collection *Reading The Virginian in the New West*, Melody Graulich and Stephen Tatum (along with their contributors) do much to demonstrate the colonial tensions not far beneath the "hopelessly retrograde" surface of Wister's novel (Graulich and Tatum 2003: p. xii). Without question, however, the work reflects elitist, racist, and chauvinistic

attitudes, and is particularly remarkable for its slight and unconvincing representation of Native Americans.

2 Read from a theoretical perspective of postcolonialism, such a tradition is a "settler" literature invested in justifying and naturalizing Anglo-American territorial expansion and colonization. I have painted this "canon" selectively and with extremely broad strokes, of course, and my generalizations are wide open to innumerable exceptions and counter-arguments – the literary traditions of the American West find equally important origins in Helen Hunt Jackson, Sarah Winnemucca Hopkins, and numerous others quite apart from the Turner/Wister tradition. And McCarthy's *Blood Meridian* is hardly a conventional western in its treatment of violence and the presence of indigenous peoples.

3 In their excellent collection *Postcolonial Theory and the United States: Race, Ethnicity, and Literature*, Amritjit Singh and Peter Schmidt describe the "emerging 'borders' paradigm in U.S. studies" (2000: p. xi). Western American literary and cultural studies is in the vanguard of such an emergent paradigm, and I offer a sampling of titles here that break the frame and cross the border in scholarship of the American West: José Aranda's *When We Arrive*; Neil Campbell's *The Cultures of the American New West* and *The Rhizomatic West*; Krista Comer's *Landscapes of the New West* and *Surfer Girls in the New World Order*; Stephanie LeMenager's *Manifest and Other Destinies*; Suan Kollin's *Postwestern Cultures*; José David Saldívar's *Border Matters*; and numerous others whose work in various ways constitutes transnational, global, or hemispheric remappings of the American West.

4 The field's primary organization, the Western Literature Association, has in its annual convention and its journal *Western American Literature* in recent years been welcoming of work in ethnic studies, and indeed has welcomed scholars and writers associated with these fields. Also, recipients of the organization's Distinguished Achievement Award, presented at the annual conference, have over the last twenty years included numerous Native American and Hispanic/Chicano writers. The last four years have honored Sherman Alexie, Patricia Limerick/William Kittredge, Cormac McCarthy, and Luis Valdez.

5 One part of the dialectic between the regional and global is that of environmental literature and place-writing, which has long been an important aspect of western American literature. Such writing certainly can succeed in producing an ethical sense of home, but gets contentious when it makes claim to indigenous status based on the writer's strong connection to place and nature. Leslie Marmon Silko has critiqued this tendency in Gary Snyder's *Turtle Island*, Elizabeth Cook-Lynn has decried it in Wallace Stegner's *Wolf Willow*, and plenty of people have found fault with Edward Abbey's racist eco-romanticism on these grounds. Yet while such critiques are often compelling, they are sometimes merely a canned critique of writers who, with the best of ethical intentions, wish to reconcile with history and form healthy, ethical, and environmentally sustainable connections to their places. A western American postcolonialism that dismissed all such attempts obviously would be counterproductive, for it would provide no achievable vision of decolonization, equality, and sovereignty.

6 Interestingly, in the world of horse-breeding, paints are officially certified by their breeding, by specific bloodlines. Pintos, on the other hand, are determined by color markings without verification of bloodlines.

REFERENCES AND FURTHER READING

Abbey, Edward. (1980). *Good News*. New York: E.P. Dutton.

Adamson, Joni. (2001). *American Indian Literature, Environmental Justice, and Ecocriticism*. Tucson: University of Arizona Press.

Aranda, José F. (2003). *When We Arrive: A New Literary History of Mexican America*. Tucson: University of Arizona Press.

Anzaldúa, Gloria. (1987). *Borderlands/La Frontera: The New Mestiza*. San Francisco: Aunt Lute Books.

Bhabha, Homi K. (1994). *The Location of Culture*. London: Routledge.

Borges, Jorge Luis. (1998). On Exactitude in Science. In *Collected Fictions*, trans. Andrew Hurley. New York: Viking.

Bruyneel, Kevin. (2007). *The Third Space of Sovereignty: The Postcolonial Politics of US–Indigenous Relations*. Minneapolis: University of Minnesota Press.

Campbell, Neil. (2000). *The Cultures of the American New West*. Edinburgh: Edinburgh University Press.

Campbell, Neil. (2008). *The Rhizomatic West: Representing the American West in a Transnational, Global, Media Age*. Lincoln: University of Nebraska Press.

Churchill, Ward, and Winona LaDuke. (1999). Native North America: The Political Economy of Radioactive Colonization. In M. Annette James, ed., *The State of Native America: Genocide, Colonization, and Resistance*, pp. 241–66. Cambridge, MA: South End Press.

Cook-Lynn, Elizabeth. (1996). *Why I Can't Read Wallace Stegner and Other Essays*. Madison: University of Wisconsin Press.

Gómez-Peña, Guillermo. (1996). *The New World Border: Prophecies, Poems, and Loqueras for the End of the Century*. San Francisco: City Lights Books.

Graulich, Melody, and Stephen Tatum. (2003). *Reading* The Virginian *in the New West*. Lincoln: University of Nebraska Press.

Guthrie, A.B. *The Way West*. (1949). Boston: Houghton Mifflin.

Jackson, Helen Hunt. (1995). *A Century of Dishonor: A Sketch of the United States Government's Dealings with Some of the Indian Tribes* [1881]. Norman: University of Oklahoma Press.

Kaplan, Robert. (2005). *Imperial Grunts: The American Military on the Ground*. New York: Random House.

Krupat, Arnold. (1996). *The Turn to the Native: Studies in Criticism and Culture*. Lincoln: University of Nebraska Press.

LeMenager, Stephanie. (2004). *Manifest and Other Destinies: Territorial Fictions of the Nineteenth-Century United States*. Lincoln: University of Nebraska Press.

Limerick, Patricia Nelson. (1987). *The Legacy of Conquest: The Unbroken Past of the American West*. New York: W.W. Norton.

Lopez, Barry. (1992). *The Rediscovery of North America*. New York: Vintage Books.

McCarthy, Cormac. (1992). *Blood Meridian, or Evening Redness in the West* [1985]. New York: Vintage Books.

Ortiz, Simon. (1992). *Fight Back: For the Sake of the People, for the Sake of the Land* [1980]. In *Woven Stone*, pp. 285–365. Tucson: University of Arizona Press.

Rosaldo, Renata. (1989). *Culture and Truth*. Boston: Beacon Books.

Said, Edward. (1979). *Orientalism*. New York: Vintage Books.

Silko, Leslie Marmon. (1981). An Old-Fashioned Indian Attack in Two Parts. In Geary Hobson, ed., *The Remembered Earth*, pp. 195–216. Albuquerque: University of New Mexico Press.

Silko, Leslie Marmon. (1991). *Almanac of the Dead*. New York: Simon & Schuster.

Singh, Amritjit, and Peter Schmidt, eds. (2000). *Postcolonial Theory and the United States: Race, Ethnicity, and Literature*. Jackson: University of Mississippi Press.

Soja, Edward J. (1996) *Thirdspace: Journeys to Los Angeles and Other Real-and-Imagined Spaces*. Oxford: Blackwell.

Solnit, Rebecca. (1994). *Savage Dreams: A Journey into the Hidden Wars of the American West*. San Francisco: Sierra Club Books.

Spivak, Gayatri Chakravorty. (1988). Can the Subaltern Speak? In Cary Nelson and Laurence Grossberg, eds., *Marxism and the Interpretation of Culture*, pp. 271–313. Urbana: University of Illinois Press.

Turner, Frederick Jackson. (1994). The Significance of the Frontier in American History [1893]. In John Mack Faragher, ed., *Rereading Frederick Jackson Turner*, pp. 31–60. New York: Henry Holt & Co.

Véa, Alfredo. (1993). *La Maravilla*. New York: Penguin.

Wister, Owen.(1988). *The Virginian* [1902]. New York: Penguin.

Yamashita, Karen Tei. (1997). *Tropic of Orange*. Minneapolis: Coffee House Press.

16
New West, Urban and Suburban Spaces, Postwest

Krista Comer

> It was likely a foolish business, this going to Oregon, but it was good to think about, like thinking about getting out of old ways and free of old places. Like his pa had said once, telling about coming down the Ohio in a flatboat, there wasn't any place as pretty as the one that lay ahead. (A.B. Guthrie, Jr. *The Way West*, 1949)
>
> I dont know, said John Grady. I dont know where it [my country] is. I dont know what happens to country. (Cormac McCarthy, *All the Pretty Horses*, 1992)

The above epigraph drawn from A.B. Guthrie's novel *The Way West* cogently captures the nexus of associations tied up with nineteenth-century westering which would come to characterize US nationalism in the twentieth century: risk-taking (however seemingly foolish), populism, fresh starts, new ways and places, intrepid travel and mobility, an orientation toward the future and optimism. But of course Guthrie's *The Way West* is not written in the nineteenth century; it is a historical novel published in the immediate period following World War II. One hundred years after colonial territorial disputes in North America are largely settled and national identity formation and its exclusions are established, *The Way West* recounts the classic tale of a journey of settlers traveling from Independence, Missouri, along the Oregon Trail, to disputed British territory where they stake American land claims. Judging from its commercial popularity, eventual translation into film, and critical recognition by the 1950 Pulitzer Prize, *The Way West* resonated broadly with postwar US readers.

Like the majority of immediate postwar narratives produced about the West including, influentially, popular cinematic westerns, *The Way West* did not represent the West through realist convention or style. If contemporaries like John Cheever or, a bit later, John Updike, were writing about the outlier spaces surrounding New York City and Boston in modes that critic Frederick Karl calls suburban realism (Karl 2004), it

A Companion to the Literature and Culture of the American West, First Edition. Edited by Nicolas S. Witschi.
© 2011 Blackwell Publishing Ltd. Published 2011 by Blackwell Publishing Ltd.

would be twenty-five years at least before literary or film westerns began any overt reckoning with the fact that the postwar West was undergoing an enormous economic boom after the lean war years. Historians of the US West like Richard White and Carl Abbott (among many others) have extensively addressed the urbanization and surburbanization of the West's material and cultural landscapes (White 1993; Abbott 2008). All the major wartime industries located in the West retooled themselves toward domestic economies and pent-up consumer demand. Oil and mineral extraction exploded as profit-makers, alongside Cold War-sponsored defense projects and agribusiness. Brisk economic activity created employment and drew new populations to the region in numbers unprecedented since the nineteenth-century migrations. Demand quickly escalated for housing, schools and universities, hospitals, shopping centers, as well as for natural resources like water, always scarce in arid country. With the advent of massive postwar commercial and residential construction, federal dollars flowed to regional treasuries to fund highway and river diversion/reclamation projects able to support the infrastructure of urbanization and suburbanization on a massive scale. Western cities and voter constituencies emerged as players newly powerful on the national political stage. All the while, however, countless Saturday afternoon matinees visualized for moviegoers a nineteenth-century frontier transportation system of train, horse, wagon; not the car or highway system moviegoers used to get themselves to the local theater. The West of literature, cinema, and popular imagination in the 1940s and 1950s remained synonymous with sparsely populated spaces at the edge or frontier of American empire. In fact, this non-presence of the urban should be regarded not as some kind of oversight but as a constitutive feature of postwar western representation. The modern urban constitutes the genre western.

But why the silence surrounding this wholesale reconfiguration of western spaces? And how shall students and critics of western literature and culture understand the ultimate appearance of the urban on the western's imaginative scene? Though fields like history and especially geography have explored urbanism as well as suburbanism in great depth, as topics for western literary studies they have only been sporadically considered (Davis 1992; Campbell forthcoming). If western narratives produced during the nineteenth century were underwritten by movements of people and capital related to nationalist expansion, what I want to explore here are narratives about the West from the postwar period to the twenty-first century and their relation, again, to movements of people and capital and new technologies, but now linked to the emergence of the US as a global power and eventual reigning superpower.

I move through defining periods of transition in western literature and film representations and emphasize relations of narrative and culture to urban, suburban, and rural spaces as well as to ideals of postwar patriotism, Vietnam-era American empire including especially critiques of it, and postnational leanings of the present. The first period concerns the immediate postwar and Cold War years. Scholars have generally understood mid-century film westerns as conversations, across the political spectrum, about Cold War cultural nationalism (Corkin 2004), masculinity (Mitchell 1998), and about film itself as a way of looking at looking. I take up A.B. Guthrie's canonical novel *The Way West* to think toward the emerging urban and suburban Wests and the problem introduced through these social spaces about postwar western nationalist masculinity. To make a larger case across the postwar to postwest period, I draw upon the historian of gender James Gilbert, who argues in *Men in the Middle* that the postwar period marks a new frontier of domesticity as a defining feature of national life (Gilbert 2005). I read *The Way West* as a novel that uses the formula of the Oregon Trail journey to talk about 1950s suburban life, the dramas and satisfactions of the grey-suited professional married man and the patriotic work of his western nuclear family to "keep the world safe for democracy" on the domestic front of a Cold War world.

The subsequent section addresses what critics call the "New West" – generally linked to civil rights and women's liberation narratives and to revisions of western genre conventions occasioned by the global social movements of 1968 and the arrival of poststructural thought (Kowalewski 1996; Comer 1999; Campbell 2000). In this section of the essay the question is: why around 1968 does the urban emerge as an explicit feature of western representation, and on what terms? Surveying a range of writings that articulate their relations to the West by way of emergent gender and nonwhite racial knowledges and imaginations, I show that the breakdown of silence about the urban West issues from a transformative remapping of literary conventions and of social space itself during the civil rights years. Urban space – as a place of longstanding communities for nonwhite western populations and which exposes historical inequalities in the relation of minority groups and also women to the state and its institutions – played a major role in this remapping. Other spaces – such as those of the city, the borderlands, and indigenous tribal lands as well as feminist geographies in which women, gender, and sexuality are deliberate priorities – opened up and became more legible as a consequences of this remapping. Not conforming neatly to the urban, suburban, and rural divides of Anglo-Saxon spatial imaginations (for example is sovereign tribal or reservation space "rural"?), these spaces and the New Western critical modes of analysis needed to articulate them forced a rethinking of the who, what, where, and why of the West. In the matter of who claims or disclaims, the urban, racial, and gender concerns figure significantly.

At the height of the civil rights movement and its massive impact on issues of textuality and representation, on literature and film production, on political policy and everyday life, another turning point simultaneously was under way during the 1970s, much clearer in retrospect than it was at the time: postindustrialism and globalization (Harvey 1990). The final section of this essay puts the West and its postindustrial urban spaces in dialogue with post-civil rights literature and film. The term post-civil rights expresses a political and spatial imagination widely evidenced in cultural productions of the mid-1980s to 9/11 which detaches urban spaces from the regional West and its historical linkages with discourses related to the nation-state as it repositions cities like Los Angeles, Seattle, or Houston in close relation to other global cities and to global capital and labor movements (Comer 2003). Stephen Tatum develops this sense of city-regions as "postregionalism," which describes a system of "strategic interurban commercial and financial centers whose networks of power deterritorialize traditional local,

national, and regional spaces" (Tatum 2007: 12). To illustrate these complex refigura-
tions of western culture and literature toward postnational and postwestern directions
I work from writers associated generally with Generation X. Significantly, it is not only
urban spaces which signify beyond the national to the global. So too do the most
revered or "authentic" of western spaces: those of ranchlands where cowboys make their
lives. Between California urban literary traditions and the border philosophy of Cormac
McCarthy we see postwestern landscapes so completely rewritten that it is unclear
whether or not the genre western can survive this transition even while it has survived
and been retooled to meet so many others.

Historical Fictions, Genre Westerns, the Suburbs

A.B. Guthrie's *The Way West* is a novel that uses the formula of settling Oregon territory to talk about gender formation and its relation to national and global politics
in a world reordered by World War II. The novel's problem has to do with suburbanization, Cold War manhood, and the ties between marriage, respectability, and
keeping the world safe for democracy. Notwithstanding the praise critics offered for
The Way West's historical skill with place names, speech, customs, wagon train gear,
and so on, the *kind* of families traveling westward in Guthrie's wagon trains are nuclear
families. They are not extended families of multiple generations, nor are they clusters
of families from towns moving westward in loosely affiliated groups. Rather, individual families form a collection of disparate and independent social units, mom/dad/
child or children, unknown to one another before the trek, without grandparents,
cousins, maiden aunts, uncles traveling with their own families. Such a social system
with the nuclear family at its center puts us squarely, historically speaking, in the
suburban West.

The text opens upon domestic relations and what we might regard as contented
suburban marriage. The protagonist Lije Evans is a man in large and satisfying agreement with his wife, even as the text takes time to repeatedly reference what a man
wants, should do, should feel, and so on, meaning it is a tale of a man in constant
surveillance of himself about manhood. We might understand this narrative as a
discourse about middle-class masculinity under the regime of the suburb. Is Lije Evans
settling for a domestic joy that falls short of a man's ultimate hopes? Yes is the quiet
answer creating the opening drama, and "Oregon" provides the challenge this man
needs to wrestle himself from suburban complacency.

To understand the power of this particular equation of frontier and rejuvenated
masculinity, it is necessary to understand simultaneously the long and intimate
association between masculine gender formation and frontier culture. The American
West has provided scholars of gender a rather unique opportunity to explore issues
related to masculinity, space, and power because of the notoriously uneven sex ratios
on the developing frontier and the legacies for the West and nation of radically dis-
rupted male/female demographics. For nearly a century men outnumbered women

overwhelmingly, as historians like Susan Johnson have shown (Johnson 2001); frontier culture thus lends itself to studies in masculine homosociality. Literary critic Leslie Fiedler offered a related observation about the frontier in American literature forty years earlier when he famously and controversially formulated homosocial and homoerotic relations between men as unspoken literary themes and argued that representations of the frontier allowed men a recurrent communal retreat from feminized civilization and away from domestication of men by women (Fiedler 1960). The feminist critic Jane Tompkins speaks implicitly to the issues raised by Fiedler of female power and the force of frontier spaces to blunt it. Analyzing the resurgent popularity and aggressiveness of genre westerns at the turn of the twentieth century, Tompkins argues westerns attempted to counter the increasing power of women and women's culture in the public sphere (Tompkins 1993). Although Tompkins does not mark it, the close of the nineteenth-century frontier as eulogized by Frederick Jackson Turner in 1893 should figure as an equally defining moment of transformation in national gender formation. Historian John Gilbert emphasizes Turner's predictions about the relation of the frontier to an evolving national ideal and importantly ties the close of the frontier in 1890 to the year 1950, when, for the first time, the census revealed that the female population outnumbered males. Gilbert sees in this tipping of the scales a new frontier of domesticity "centered on the increasing number and influence of women and the domestic and cultural institutions associated with their lives and needs" (Gilbert 2005: 216). This changed context produces a domino effect of unknowns for men and national manhood.

The Way West opens onto a vague kind of discontent for the novel's protagonist, Lije Evans, and readers find themselves in the middle of Lije's efforts to understand it. His biggest anxiety is not hunger, a lack of property, a sick child, a failed crop, a blight on his farm stock, an Indian attack, or British or other industry encroachment threatening his spread. His anxiety is that "he wanted something more out of life than he had found" (p. 4). But if Lije Evans wants the adventure of Oregon, if he needs it to feel fully like the man he desires from himself, he wants it *with* his wife and teenage son. He's not a man styled on the model of Dick Summers, he's not a mountain man/trail guide/lover of Indian women or carrier-on of the mantle of Leatherstocking or Daniel Boone. He's not John Grady Cole. His wife Rebecca, in the novel's first pages, teases him good-humoredly – "You ain't as young as you were" (p. 4) – when he raises the prospect of them trekking to Oregon. Lije retorts, also good-humoredly, "Nobody is. But I ain't so old, neither. Thirty-five. A man's prime at thirty five" (p. 4). Lije articulates here what might be called an early midlife crisis about purpose and desire of a man in his prime, which again, as does the nuclear family, locates readers in the mid-twentieth century. Mixed into and inseparable from Lije's desire for something more are the text's nationalist ambitions – the drive to "win the country," "make history," settle Oregon and defeat the British, and to hand on a "proud" legacy to "children and their young ones" (pp. 12–13). Indeed, the nationalist discourse of the text produces the terms by which Lije's desires are known and satisfied. Lije comes to double for the nation itself and its challenges. The tale closes on a note of domestic consummation, "Becky, Horrah for Oregon!" (p. 340). A congenial imperial domesticity has been transferred across the continent. Guthrie leaves no doubt that there is much more story left to tell at the end of *Way West*. (And this is not at all the suggestion at the end of McCarthy's border trilogy.)

If a reading of *The Way West* today requires interpretive intervention for it not to seem either quaint or of interest mainly to a western Americana readership, at the moment of its publication it was regarded as serious and important to popular and critical audiences alike. The reason this was so is *not* because the novel "got the Old West right" in terms of a historical realism which corrected distorted popular mythologies, as literary critics of the period like Chatterton (1987) or Milton (1980) argued. Rather, the novel, allegorically, got the suburbs right and the problems they symbolized for national masculinity. The genre western itself can be understood, as Lee Clark Mitchell argues, as a set of problems related to progress, honor, law, and justice in an unjust world, violence, all entangled in masculinity (Mitchell 1998: 3). *The Way West* named a dilemma hardly being conceived in the West in the postwar period and worked it through to a conclusion. What was the educated man of good will (i.e. a Lije Evans) to aspire to if all the big battles were won? If the historic tale of national manhood had required some kind of proving scenario, some epic quest to tackle epic problems that had to be overcome, what was to be the national masculine mission if the future was assured by both postwar economic prosperity and the new powerful place of the US in international politics? Was national masculinity to be tied inevitably to empire, and if the answer to that question was yes, what became of the man for whom empire was an obligation?

New Wests

The signature text announcing the arrival of 1968 and the New West is Joan Didion's first collection of essays *Slouching Toward Bethlehem* (1968). Didion narrates stories of western spaces on the brink of transition from older settled orders to new ones. But if the wife/mother figure of Rebecca of *Way West* manages to hold together her family during the nineteenth-century trek, there is no holding together the New West of the twentieth century, as Didion chronicles it. "The center was not holding" in fact is the famous phrase opening the title essay of Didion's collection (1968: 84). Between Didion's first novel *Run River* (1963) about Sacramento and the New Journalism of the essays in *Slouching Towards Bethlehem*, Didion fills out just what the trouble is. The tell-tale signs of decline in *Run River* come in the form of aerospace engineers, Cadillac dealerships, and country clubs. In a word, for Sacramento the trouble is suburbanization. Old Sacramento loses, after 1950, a communal insularity which produced something like a particular toughness and character linked to frontier history and memories of the Sacramento Valley in the nineteenth century as a "true sea of grass, grass so high a man riding into it could tie it across his saddle" (1968: 172). What Didion mourns is the fracturing of a set of values and an *idea* about the West and about

California. If suburbanization ruins Sacramento, the troubles are starker still in the urban space of nearby San Francisco. Home to an evolving scene on Haight and Ashbury streets of the hippie counterculture, disappearing runaways, LSD and hashish use, and, in the mix of it all, driving the scene, some vague philosophy of human liberation informed, at times, by radical politics, this is a recipe for cultural disaster in Didion's view. The title essay "Slouching Toward Bethlehem" writes the postwar American Dream in utter disarray, the heirs to its privileges are young rebels dangerously under-educated and susceptible to crackpot ideas. At the center of chaos is California as both a New West but also a national dystopia.

If this on-the-scene reporting by Didion at so crucial a social moment would earn her a permanent national reputation for stylistic finesse and intellectual diagnostic power, Didion hardly should be taken as a critical voice who spoke for everyone. Didion articulated her powerful despair from one of the most privileged and authoritative sites in California: that of landed gentry. What imaginative and material lands are represented here but those of the great Central Valley, among the greatest breadbasket agricultural regions of the nation which by definition means a land populated by large communities of migrant field workers? Most laborers in the 1960s were Mexican or Mexican American and likely came into contact with the organizing activities of César Chavez and the United Farm Workers. A cultural landscape of crop-picking and binationalism came to light for the first time in this period in the work of a Central Valley poet like Gary Soto, a Texas novelist like Tomás Rivera, or the playwright Luis Valdez, founder of El Teatro Campesino, a farm workers' traveling theater troupe. An anthology collecting writings about this literary landscape was published recently by Stan Yogi, *Highway 99* (1997).

So Didion called it correctly. The center was not holding. It was pressured from the inside by heroes gone mad (like John Wayne in the classic film *The Searchers*), by powerful women (like Didion), and by its own rebelling suburban youth (middle-class disillusioned hippies). It was pressured at its borders and by those whom it excluded, displaced, and othered. Significantly, however, narratives about the New West and its receding center produced in association with the civil rights movements (a Soto or El Teatro Campesino) did *not* mourn the loss of a center as does Didion or try to reinstate it with different power players. Instead, generally, these narratives embraced the fact the center was not holding as an opening, an opportunity, a reason for hope and for a new social and imaginative geography of "West." Such narratives critics designate today as evidencing a *critical regionalism* (Campbell 2008; Limón 2008; Comer 2010).

No single thesis or theme works to organize the variety of literatures written out of identifications with various civil rights movements and the New West geographical imaginations they developed and deployed. But while no unifying thesis is warranted, it must be remembered that though racial segregation in the West was less official or rigid in its forms than was segregation, especially, in the US Southeast, nonetheless, social custom and informal practice regarding where people of different races were allowed and not allowed conditioned writers' relations to space and to the urban, suburban, and rural divides I have been working on in this essay. Synthetic historical studies show that, overwhelmingly, people of color collected after World War II in urban environments and in racially identified lower-income neighborhoods (Chan et al. 1994). Informal segregation created largely African American communities in places like south Los Angeles and west Oakland, largely Mexican American communities in east Los Angeles, as well as in San Francisco's and other West Coast Chinatowns. Native Americans too, demographically, and notwithstanding reservation populations, were an urban people (Fixico 2000). Urban space allowed sufficient numbers of minorities in a single place to form inter-racial and intra-racial communities and occasional solidarities about practical solutions to shared political problems. In fact the increasing visibility in urban centers of minority populations over the course of the postwar period is an often-cited reason for the infamous large-scale white flight of the period toward the suburbs.

Writing against the pioneer epic told from the vantage point of Anglo-Saxon conquerors, literature of the New West highlighted the relations of the indigenous and colonized to the spaces that existed *prior* to their transformation into "the West." It was thus a literature interested in a different version of history and in how, formally and linguistically, to imagine the past of the vanquished so as to retrieve memory and a different orientation to space and community, and set these differences on a course of collision with contemporary circumstances. The kinds of geographical imaginations at writers' disposal had everything to do with the historical particularity of different groups' interface with US nationalism and the different roles of peoples of color in nation-building (Comer 1999: 34–49). For instance, the literary history of African Americans up to the 1960s and 1970s had been charted mainly through New York City, Chicago, Philadelphia, and parts of the South. The geographical or spatial concerns most evident in this body of work had to do with North/South sectional conflicts, migration patterns, regional economies, politics, and culture. Although a bit of scholarship addressed recognized California writers like Ishmael Reed, Al Young, Ernest Gaines, and Sherley Anne Williams, it did not put them in serious dialogue with western or California spaces and aesthetics. On the whole African American geographical imaginations tended to be enabled by and written through narratives tied to slavery and emancipation, to cultural forms like jazz and blues, all of which, in spatial terms, suggest North/South national designs. It required adjustments of both popular consciousness and scholarly perception to make sense of the western debts and contributions of recognized writers like those mentioned above, or to analyze the work of a poet like Wanda Coleman who was writing explicitly toward southern California of the 1950s – specifically Watts, where she grew up – a world neither western nor African American audiences had yet grappled much with. To make this adjustment and put frontier mythologies in tension with African American literature, "race" westerns, and even hip hop, spaces of the city could not be ignored (Johnson 2001; Allmendinger 2005).

Chicano/a literary production evidenced a claim upon and deep feeling for southwestern spaces – spaces that directly corresponded to lands conquered by the United States in the Mexican–American War of 1846. In the Chicano/a geographic imaginary, this space was renamed "Aztlán," representing the mythic homeland of the Aztec peoples through whom Chicano/a activists located a Mexican American past usable for present political organizing purposes. As an anti-imperialist and civil rights ideology, the myth of Aztlán challenged US political legitimacy in the Southwest. It symbolically took back conquered lands while imaginatively repopulating them with a new, working-class, pagan Catholic, and sometimes feminist *mestizo/a* citizenry. So while the majority population of Mexican Americans lived in urban centers, and while a few writers wrote directly about and out of contemporary urban life, such as Sandra Cisneros (treating Chicago in 1986 in *House on Mango Street*) or John Rechy (writing in 1963, *City of the Night*, about gay male hustling in Los Angeles, New York City, and New Orleans), the principal imaginative world of Chicano/a literature existed upon the terrain of the greater Southwest. Rudolfo Anaya's *Bless Me, Ultima* (1972) laid out what, at the time, was an unknown literary landscape in small-town New Mexico of the World War II years. In this coming-of-age morality tale, the protagonist Antonio weighs the religious farm culture of his mother's family against the wilder *vaquero* (cowboy) side coming through his father and older brothers. In the midst of the two cultures is the mystical Ultima, the *curandera* (healer). *Bless Me, Ultima* experiments with subject matter and language and situates Chicano/a literature at the crossroads of Spanish colonialism, indigenous knowledge, and westerns. Anaya's remapping of this spatial terrain opens the Southwest and reclaims it at the same time; another canonical text in Chicano/a literature, Gloria Anzaldúa's *Borderlands/La Frontera* (1987) will take that opening and resituate readers in the bilingual feminist geographies of the present-day US borderlands with Mexico.

The cultural movements accompanying Asian American civil rights agitations also forwarded group political identity by tying histories of racial oppression to specifically western spaces. Frank Chin, Maxine Hong Kingston, and Amy Tan wrote themselves and their respective communities into national history by blending US western history and spaces, the *Bildungsroman*, and Chinese mythologies. They put places like San Francisco's Chinatown on the cultural map of the nation, tying Chinese Americans to western traditions and cowboy masculinities (and feminist critiques of them), but also to the sixteenth-century Chinese classical epic *Journey to the West*. Japanese internment narratives (like Jeanne Wakatsuki's memoir *Farewell to Manzanar*, 1973) showed the open spaces of western deserts to be less sites of symbolic freedom, as they typically figure in western geographical imaginations, than sites of wartime detention. John Okada's *No-No Boy*, originally published in 1957 but forgotten until Chin and poet Lawson Fusao Inada discovered the novel and sponsored its republication in the 1970s, told about the aftermath of the war for a "no-no boy" from Seattle who must come to terms with his refusals and a country that has dishonored him. Because of the general perception that the West Coast is kind of clearing-house for early Asian immigration and because, into the 1980s, Asian American cultural, political, social, and economic history had been told in general conjunction with the story of western settlement, western American imaginaries centered Asian American letters of the civil rights era even while the "Gold Mountain" mythologies which drew Asians to the Americas rewrote those dominant imaginaries on terms that did not conform to a sense of western movement as meaning continental activity from US eastern locations westward.

American Indian literatures and political agitation also linked themselves to western spaces. In the West, the history of genocide was very effectively evoked. Given that the majority of reservations in the continental US lie west of the Mississippi, the fact of an *un-vanished* people was obvious. But if Asian Americans or Chicano/as struggled to make themselves culturally and nationally visible, American Indians struggled for control over extra-visible discourses of "the Indian." European settlers left a long record of their ambivalent love affair with Indian peoples and their lifeways. American literary traditions evidence this ambivalence from the time of James Fenimore Cooper's *Last of the Mohicans* (1826), through that tale's film adaptations in the twentieth century including the most recent, in 1992. Of course the genre western has long respected the white man who goes native (like Dick Summers in Guthrie's *Way* West) while demonizing the Indian. So the spatial field of the West is toxic for American Indians and the mixed-breed characters living between cultures that typically figure in American Indian literature show that they have been made sick by this history. Writers like N. Scott Momaday (in *House Made of Dawn*, 1968) or Leslie Marmon Silko (in *Ceremony*, 1973) structure their tales as postwar ceremonial healing rituals which can minister to their protagonists' need for cultural revitalization, self-respect, communal hope. If the majority of Indians live in western urban centers in this period, the landscape of Indian literature in the civil rights era most often is that of the reservation (Rice 2005). Tribal lands remind readers of Indian sovereignty and national autonomy. Tribal lands link peoples to sacred memory, ancient knowledge, language, and story even while reservations are represented as desperately poor and, in Silko's *Ceremony*, the sites of new forms of toxicity: uranium extraction.

The geographical imaginations generated by the literatures of 1968 were fueled by urban political unrest, by activities protesting the Vietnam War, and by projects for cultural revitalization and economic opportunity that involved in some cases completing forms of nationalism (for example Aztlán, the sovereign tribe). Unlike the genre film western of the 1945–60s period, these were not allegories, written against suburban backdrops, which worried about the dangers of white complacency. They were not assumed to be narratives whose audiences were the same suburban middle class who consumed genre westerns. And yet even the suburbs would eventually feel pressured as issues related to race and desegregation traveled; no amount of white flight from the city to its outskirts would entirely escape them. Indeed, many white suburbanites had been changed by the civil rights movements, and by women's liberation. The problem with no name (Betty Friedan's phrase for talking about sexism in *The Feminine Mystique*) had been named, in fact. Even in the suburbs. It had *many* names, *many* faces: Didion's treatment of illegal suburban abortion in *Play It as It Lays* (1970), Kingston's refusal to continue traditions of forgetting "no-name women" in *Woman Warrior* (1978), or Anzaldúa's love of borderlands women. Neither could suburbs protect themselves from urban sprawl or the encroachment onto their green spaces of continuing development projects. When a new conservative political bloc gained sufficient momentum to put Ronald Reagan into the White House in 1980, a softening already was underway of the distinguishing divisions between race, urbanism, and suburbanism in the most populous of western states. Identified with California, having worked as an actor in westerns, Reagan was a presence at the helm of global power whose anti-civil rights politics and free market economic philosophies motivated a new generation of Anglo writers to speak out in favor of the environmental protection of western spaces and in favor of a West conceived as multiracial community and not rugged individualist cowboys.

What better set of powerful imaginative and political energies was available for this purpose than that of the geographical imaginations generated by the Chicano/a, American Indian, and Asian American movements and literatures? Defining much of what was "new" about the New West, Anglo writers like Edward Abbey, Ivan Doig, John Nichols, Bill Kittredge, Gretel Ehrlich, Teresa Jordan, Barbara Kingsolver, and Terry Tempest Williams owe much more than is popularly understood to the cultural and aesthetic traditions produced by civil rights writers. That is, after 1970 Anglo literary westerns found a new voice through which to speak about the present because others had found new ways to speak about the past. They had help in this regard, moreover, from the works and legacy of Wallace Stegner – the so-called dean of western literature, a prolific writer, teacher of writers, conservationist, and literary critic who had long urged western writers away from historical fictions. Stegner had been at work for some twenty or more years already to shape a developing discourse about western public history (Comer 1999: 38–49). Many New Western writers would partner with him as powerful spokespeople. Their West favored stable and settled economies over boom-and-bust cycles, a sensitivity to sub-regional ecological variety, and an all-around policy direction that promoted conservation of western natural resources including water and wilderness. In a word, what united Stegner with all of the civil rights writers, was community. The revision of West they all undertook aimed to refigure the region not as a symbol for nationalist rugged individualism but as a community of communities.

Post-Wests

The social formations of community and nation have been fundamentally altered by globalization. The late 1980s and early 1990s saw the heyday of the New Western writers. With the fall of the Berlin Wall in 1989 and the official end of the Cold War, US nationalism went into relative decline as an ideology binding the relation of the regional West to the nation. With the decline of that particular nationalism went the new regionalism of the New West. Urban centers – understood in the civil rights period to represent social forces or civic bodies in dialogue with national politics and economics – assumed more autonomy in the post-Cold War period. To live in a global city like Los Angeles was nearly to be living in a country of its own making, detached from the larger US even if virtually networked into the world's hard drives. As the second largest metropolis in the US, the world's Entertainment Capital as well as its third strongest metropolitan economy, LA captured the imagination of a new genera-tion of young writers who came of age in a world transformed by the civil rights movement, global decolonization, and new information technologies. For them, so-called writers of Generation X like Bret Easton Ellis, Douglas Coupland, Sandra Tsing Loh, and Cynthia Kadohata, to name but a handful, the place/space of Los Angeles presented a frontier or border landscape of the radically changed and sometimes apocalyptic present. Through it they could talk about a world overwhelmed by sign saturation and by a consumer culture which knew no marketing bounds.

The borderlands region of the US and Mexico assumed also something of this primacy as a space productive of thinking about the postwest, most dramatically in the work of Cormac McCarthy which relocates the genre western away from its Monument Valley landscapes toward the borders. McCarthy keeps company with the exhausted heroes of recent postwestern films like *3:10 to Yuma* (2007), *The Three Burials of Melquiades Estrada* (2005), and *Appaloosa* (2008). In LA literature, postwestern film, and in McCarthy's Border trilogy, there is a notable refusal of the optimism associated with genre westerns like *The Way West*. Questions about community, about the attach-ment of people to places or to one another, find very diffuse or find openly dystopic answers. Recent cultural developments suggest the western's exhaustion as a cultural form for the reproduction of national masculinity. The genre western could be said to be like John Grady Cole at the end of *All the Pretty Horses*: vanishing, under erasure.

If among civil rights-inspired writers many differences might be teased out and emphasized, they nonetheless shared a generational worldview in which the largest life-altering public drama of their collective lives centered on the civil rights move-ment and the nation as the proper site of political grievance; the historical memory targeted most often for deconstruction was the classic nation-building pioneer story. That collective history and imperative toward the nation and its deconstruction and reconstruction simply does not obtain for younger writers. Ellis's noir-indebted *Less Than Zero* shows that recounting a Generation X history, even the history of one's own childhood, seems to require Herculean efforts against a numbing exhaustion. The protagonist Clay, arriving in Los Angeles from college in the northeast for the winter holiday, finds nobody home. Nobody ever will come home, in any way that matters for Clay, throughout the tale. The novel's refrain – "people are afraid to merge" – sug-gests some larger impossibility about connection and community, some sense of cultural declension that is worse actually than the gritty details the text portrays (sex, drugs, hustling, snuff films). The repeated phrases "I am just a boy," or "what it comes down to is that I was a boy," frame what is most at issue. Clay's vulnerabilities might be, but then they never are, contained by family or friendship or social purpose. He is abandoned by family and western history itself, a boy of brains and Hollywood's privileges with a father who is in the business. But he has no purpose. His status as a man in a western narrative guarantees him nothing, he is called upon to do nothing, and he expects nothing. The Cold War dilemma of purposeful suburban masculinity has clearly intensified since the end of the Cold War, and an engagement with western narratives offers the dilemma no foothold for masculine recuperation. A sense of orphaning resonates in the pages of *Less Than Zero*, and it takes a more definitive turn in *All the Pretty Horses*.

The earliest pages of this first novel in the McCarthy Border trilogy demonstrate that fate is already sealed for the protagonist John Grady Cole. His home town of 1940s San Angelo is played out; the whole of Texas is played out. "Mexico" beckons as a place where one can still be a cowboy, live one's life with horses, follow that path (in the world of McCarthy) to which a boy like John Grady Cole is born. In this post-Cold War tale, McCarthy actively comments on the changed space of the West and the freedom of men to move in it. Like California, Texas too is a site of ever-increasing globalized economies: ranch culture and other nineteenth-century enterprises are made peripheral and replaced by oil and gas industries, space exploration, agribusiness. One great imaginative terrain of genre westerns – Texas, where everything is bigger than big – is thus growing claustrophobic, constraining. Without "Mexico," there is no place for John Grady Cole to go, nowhere he can ride free of the postwar fence line, no dreamscape on which he might come into the boy/man he must be and is. Without Mexico, his call to masculinity cannot be heard – he becomes a Dick Summers, riding backwards into a nostalgic history.

The text allows a straightforward historical materialist reading of John Grady Cole's dilemma as a worker, wherein oil scouts come to town hunting the big strike and break up large cattle ranches by buying out businesses that no longer pay. In the rupture produced by this forced transformation, as David Holloway shows persuasively, cowboys will be mortally wounded by late modern alienated labor conditions (Holloway 2002). While there is no contradicting this claim, it is not just oil scouts and economic restructuring which figure the massive social transformations and relocations of late modernity. Transformation comes also, as this essay has shown all along, from changing gender formations of the postwar period. The upheaval registered in San Angelo after World War II cannot be understood independently of the flight of the mother from her gendered duties and toward some vague notion of female artistry and desire. The space for the possible realization of this desire is the city, or as close to it, San Antonio, as the mother can easily get. Aspiration toward a nuclear suburban family in this 1940s tale never was. If the text, understanding reader expectations in genre westerns, allows some hardening of the heart to a western mother who loves horses but would sell the ranch, the text makes absolutely clear that the father's legacy to the son is one of utter exhaustion. The father presents no alternative or resource that mediates the mother's remove. He has a choice about the sale of the ranch and he consents. The challenge of the father, *before* his official war-related injury and decline, is that the mother has what he calls "notions" which he has dismissed all along at his own peril. The son inherits the consequences. All of the women whom John Grady Cole, and the narrator, wish to engage seriously are written through this same shattering fact of "notions" or "ideas" gesturing toward some world of desire for women which enters and exits the world of men but does not take its ultimate satisfaction from it. Women want things, they will take steps toward them, and that combination of desire and agency that is linked to men but not finally about them, confuses and ruptures the western's generic bounds. So does the fact that the mother prefers a city landscape because in it she finds openings for herself as an actress. This new order of gender upsets all relations: of space, of inheritance, of bonds between men and women, mothers and fathers and sons. Its ability to unsettle the world is so overpowering in fact that it makes white men, as the father tells the son, like the Comanches of a previous era, "unsafe," "unsure what's going to show up here come daylight" (p. 26).

And hence the cowboy sojourns in "Mexico" – those borderlands of westering imaginations, the place grand hacendados continue on and where it would not be the first time a young Anglo who knows horses but is holding no other aces in his hand might find a señorita with a spread. Mexico, as Alejandra says, is a "Street of Desire," a "Calle de Noche Triste" (p. 253). Mexico is hemispheric Other, romantic and tragic, a space of recourse for a western that's played out. McCarthy asks readers, through Lacey Rawlins's singing about being ill at ease in this border-time, "Will you miss me. Will you miss me when I'm gone?" (p. 37). And the answer produced inside the western genre is a form of mourning, a conceded yes, we will miss you, we already miss you. A sense of longing is produced for a certain kind of manhood, the display of male bodies, the seduction of the ways of the "old waddies" (p. 96) and of loving, as men without women, the open, rough country of bawling cattle and unbroken horses. Here the country doubles, as it does most often in the genre western, as implicitly "woman," there for some kind of taking. The fact of the country's implicit female gendering makes actual women redundant; they are unnecessary since they figure already as eroticized nature (Kolodny 1984). If discourses of "virgin land" implicitly code western country as available to white men, lands south of the border are all the more there for the taking, the site of the primitive, exotic, and real. And this spell of seduction is exactly the one that McCarthy casts but then disallows as the Mexico of *All the Pretty Horses* pushes back, spits out John Grady Cole mercilessly, the Judgment Day upon him and upon the genre western. In a quest that repeats his father's own courtship of the landed lady who loves horses, he fails. He does not become the substitute son of the hacendado with only a female heir. His judgment is bad, his will fails, luck goes against him and he makes his own bad luck. In his defeats he echoes the explorer Cabeza de Vaca, returned to the Spanish king with but his skin and the rags on his back.

But he is an American cowboy, after all, and his return northward ultimately follows the genre demands of the western. All the way, however, those same genre demands are undone. The path of formula westerns requires regeneration through violence in order to restore justice and vindicate (even if far from perfectly) its hero (Slotkin 1975). But McCarthy refuses John Grady Cole this release too. He does *not* kill the captain in order to quiet his own conscience about the fact he has not spoken up against the execution of Blevins. He travels north until he crosses the border. He is a naked teenage boy wet from the river crossing, sitting his horse. This is the single moment in which we see John Grady Cole weep: for his father's death, which he knows to have transpired in his absence, but for all of the additional absences of masculine legacy to which he has returned. He arrives in the Texas of the present on Thanksgiving

Day as some kind of a reconstituted American, but what, McCarthy asks readers, is the nature of this regeneration? What is the fate of the western for imagining it? The concluding conversations with the American judge where the cowboy disclaims "I don't feel justified" (p. 290), finds rhetorical repetition in the final page of the last novel of the trilogy, *Cities of the Plain* (1998), when Billy Parnham declares "I aint nothing." In the first case, the Judge comments that the cowboy is being hard on himself, and the reader may be inclined to agree. But by the end of the trilogy, with all that lies in between, the "specialness" of the cowboy, his exceptionalism and the exceptionalism of the West *as* America, *as* the City on the Hill for the twenty-first century, seems indeed exhausted. At the conclusion of the series, Betty tells Billy Parnham "I know who you are." But this is not conferring exceptional status upon him. Insofar as "country" has centered the love of cowboys for the genre western, insofar as western country has held down the ground as the origin story for US nationalism and empire, *All the Pretty Horses* wedges into that romance a kind of nuclear-powered complication. John Grady Cole breaks with his friend Lacey Rawlins; he breaks with his country, or maybe, the tale suggests, his country has broken with him. In any event, he does not know, as he says, what happens to country. After this kind of catastrophic rupture of land and nation, there are only levels of vanishings, levels of bloody sunsets into which the cowboy can ride.

Moving toward conclusions, if the above close to *All the Pretty Horses* indicates not Old Western or New Western but postwestern cultural landscapes, does that mean that postwestern space is a no man's land, a space beyond dystopia set on the abyss of apocalypse? Is the end of a narrative mode which produces nationalist white masculinity, but also effective critiques of it, an occasion for mourning? Is the western, in fact, over and dead? As critics know well, the history of the western is in part a history of predictions of its death; then instead it survives and adapts. Perhaps westerns will adjust to the postnational moment and some figure from the outside (as did the Italian filmmaker Sergio Leone in his 1968 *Once Upon a Time in the West*) will show everyone else how to imagine it again. My own recent work on surfers as subculturalists and surfing as epistemology was undertaken to explore this transition of western space to the postregional; what I call "girl localism" is one ubiquitous example of western-identified subjectivities and visualities presently being refigured and postnationalized (Comer forthcoming). Others have theorized postwestern space as "rhizomatic third space" (Campbell 2008), a "topography in transition" (Tatum 1998), a blood/land/memory complex (Allen 2002), a "transfrontera contact zone" (Saldívar 1997). All of these frameworks open western spaces onto their edges to show that whatever is deemed outside always also works inside and through the center to unsettle and reorient. Given that the whole postwar to postwest period marks a series of profound transformations in masculinity, how will the above theorizations illuminate gender and its intersections with westerns and with the urban/suburban spaces that predominate in the West?

In considering these questions we should insist that if some of the most accomplished of genre westerns of recent history (like those of McCarthy) write the end of the western, such closures do not mean cultural productions about the West are, inevitably therefore, also over. Indeed McCarthy recently shows himself continuing to work from western borderlands in *No Country for Old Men* (2005) but through narconarrative more than genre western (Tatum). Or take as an example genre fictions that narrate western urban and suburban spaces by emphasizing the conventions of chick lit and chica lit (Mary Castillo, Michelle Serros, Yxta Maya Murray), science fiction (A. Lee Martinez, Rosaura Sáchez, and Beatriz Pita), vampire (Stephanie Meyers, Marta Acosta) and mystery/detective formulas (Sue Grafton, Michael Nava, Walter Mosley). As I noted as the outset, urban spaces have always been constitutive of the western, and suburban spaces underwrote both the sites of production and consumption of mid-century westerns. Gender and race issues have exerted strong pressures on who was willing (or had to) claim or disclaim these spaces. In global popular imaginations about "the West," it is probably still the case that wilderness and rural spaces continue to center what is most defining and prized about the region. Were the field of western literary studies to write toward and deeply explore the urban and suburban as topics we might be surprised what would be found there: no doubt someone is already at work, maybe even a McCarthy producing some feminist genre western about the suburbs.

References and Further Reading

Abbott, Carl. (2008). *How Cities Won the West: Four Centuries of Urban Change in Western North America.* Albuquerque: University of New Mexico Press.

Allen, Chadwick. (2002). *Blood Narrative: Indigenous Identity in American Indian and Maori Literary and Activist Texts.* Durham, NC: Duke University Press.

Allmendinger, Blake. (2005). *Imagining the African American West.* Lincoln: University of Nebraska Press.

Campbell, Neil. (2000) *The Cultures of the American New West.* Edinburgh: University Press of Edinburgh.

Campbell, Neil. (2008). *The Rhizomatic West: Representing the American West in a Transnational, Global, Media Age.* Lincoln: University of Nebraska Press.

Campbell, Neil. (Forthcoming). "The Compass of Possibilities": Re-mapping the Suburbs of Los Angeles in the Writings of D.J. Waldie. *European Journal of American Studies.*

Chan, Sucheng, Douglas Henry Daniels, T. Garcia, and Terry Wilson. (1994). *Peoples of Color in the American West.* Lexington, MA: Heath.

Chatterton, Wayne. (1987). A.B. Guthrie, Jr. In *A Literary History of the American West*, pp. 912–34. Sponsored by the Western Literature Association. Forth Worth: Texas Christian University Press.

Comer, Krista. (1999). *Landscapes of the New West: Gender and Geography in Contemporary Women's Writing.* Chapel Hill: University of North Carolina Press.

Comer, Krista. (2003). Western Literature at Century's End: Sketches in Generation X, Los Angeles, and the Post-Civil Rights Novel. *Pacific Historical Review*, 72/3, 405–13.

Comer, Krista. (2010). Exceptionalisms, Other Wests, Critical Regionalism. *American Literary History.*

Comer, Krista. (Forthcoming). *Surfer Girls in the New World Order.* Durham, NC: Duke University Press.

Corkin, Stanley. (2004). *Cowboys as Cold Warriors: The Western and U.S. History.* Philadelphia: Temple University Press.

Davis, Mike. (1992). *City of Quartz: Excavating the Future in Los Angeles.* New York: Vintage.

Didion, Joan. (1963). *Run River*. New York: Pocket.

Didion, Joan. (1990). *Slouching Toward Bethlehem*. New York: Farrar, Straus & Giroux.

Ellis, Bret Easton. (1984). *Less Than Zero*. New York: Vintage.

Fiedler, Leslie A. (1960). *Love and Death in the American Novel*. Normal, IL: Dalkey Archive Press.

Fixico, Donald L. (2000). *The Urban Indian Experience in America*. Albuquerque: University of New Mexico Press.

Friedan, Betty. (1963). *The Feminine Mystique*. New York: Norton.

Gilbert, James. (2005). *Men in the Middle: Searching for Masculinity in the 1950s*. Chicago: University of Chicago Press.

Guthrie, A.B. (1949). *The Way West*. Boston: Houghton Mifflin.

Harvey, David. (1990). *The Condition of Postmodernity: An Enquiry into the Origins of Cultural Change*. Malden, MA: Blackwell.

Holloway, David. (2002). *The Late Modernism of Cormac McCarthy*. Westport, CT: Greenwood Press.

Johnson. Susan Lee. (2001). *Roaring Camp: The Social World of the California Gold Rush*. New York: Norton.

Kadohata, Cynthia. (1992). *In the Heart of the Valley of Love*. Berkeley: University of California Press.

Karl, Frederick R. (2004). The Fifties and After: An Ambiguous Culture. In Josephine Hendin, ed., *A Concise Companion to Postwar American Literature*, pp. 20–72. Malden, MA: Blackwell.

Kollin, Susan, ed. (2007). *Postwestern Cultures: Literature, Theory, Space*. Lincoln: University of Nebraska Press.

Kolodny, Annette. (1984). *The Land Before Her: Fantasy and Experience of the American Frontiers, 1630–1860*. Chapel Hill: University of North Carolina Press.

Kowalewski, Michael, ed. (1996). *Reading the West: New Essays on the Literature of the American West*. Cambridge: Cambridge University Press.

Limón, José. (2008). Border Literary Histories, Globalization, and Critical Regionalism. *American Literary History*, 20/1–2, 160–82.

McCarthy, Cormac. (1992). *All the Pretty Horses*. New York: Vintage.

McCarthy, Cormac. (1999). *Cities of the Plain*. New York: Vintage.

McCarthy, Cormac. (2007). *No Country for Old Men*. New York: Vintage.

Mitchell, Lee Clark. (1998). *Westerns: Making the Man in Fiction and Film*. Chicago: University of Chicago Press.

Milton, John R. (1980). *The Novel of the American West*. Lincoln: University of Nebraska Press.

Rice, David A. (2005). Witchery, Indigenous Resistance, and Urban Space in Leslie Marmon Silko's *Ceremony*. *Studies in American Indian Literatures*, 17/4 (Winter), 114–43.

Saldívar, José David. (1997). *Border Matters: Remapping American Cultural Studies*. Berkeley: University of California Press.

Slotkin, Richard. (1975). *Regeneration through Violence: The Mythology of the American Frontier, 1600–1860*. Norman: University of Oklahoma Press.

Tatum, Stephen. (1998). Topographies of Transition in Western American Writing. *Western American Literature*, 32, 310–53.

Tatum, Stephen. (2007). Spectrality and the Postregional Interface. In Susan Kollin, ed., *Postwestern Cultures: Literature, Theory, Space*, pp. 3–29. Lincoln: University of Nebraska Press.

Tatum, Stephen. (Forthcoming). "Mercantile Ethics": *No Country for Old Men* and the Narcocorrido. In Sara Spurgeon, ed., *Cormac McCarthy*: All the Pretty Horses, No Country for Old Men, The Road. New York: Continuum.

Tompkins, Jane. (1993). *West of Everything: The Inner Life of Westerns*. New York: Oxford University Press.

Turner, Frederick Jackson. (1986). The Significance of the Frontier in American History [1893]. In *The Frontier in American History*, forward by Wilbur R. Jacobs, pp. 1–38. Tucson: University of Arizona Press.

White, Richard (1993). *"It's Your Misfortune and None of My Own": A New History of the American West*. Norman: University of Oklahoma Press.

Yogi, Stan, Gayle Mak, and Patricia Wakida. (1997). *Highway 99: A Literary Journey Through California's Great Central Valley*. California Council on the Humanities.

Part III
Varieties and Forms

17

What We Talk About When We Talk About Western Art[*]

Brian W. Dippie

Determining what we mean by western art is the first order of business. Western American art has always been defined by its content. Subject matter is primary, artistic treatment secondary, but the two have fused into one. Western art is visually realistic art about Indians and white pioneers – buckskin-clad frontiersmen and soldiers at one time, more commonly cowboys now – and unspoiled landscape. It is overwhelmingly masculine in orientation, though it has extended its coverage in recent years. Artists and especially the museums devoted to showcasing western art (almost all of them located in the West) have, with a desire to remain relevant, sought to expand the genre's boundaries by including art focused on women, children, and ethnic minorities other than American Indians. Diversity is the watchword in keeping with the social history agenda of "New Western History" since the 1980s.

The definition of the West is also obviously important in defining western art. Western art has meant the trans-Mississippi West, a nineteenth-century phenomenon created by the purchase of the Louisiana Territory from France in 1803. The rapid exploration and occupation of the area west of the Mississippi River reinforced the tradition of a frontier line of Anglo-American settlement advancing westward from the oldest English colonies planted on the Atlantic seaboard two centuries before. The "winning of the West" was America's master-narrative, the unfolding of a continental destiny that in crossing the Mississippi assumed the characteristic features enshrined in western art. Process became place, the American West a region stretching to the Pacific Ocean, bounded on the north by the 49th parallel and on the south by the Rio Grande, not because these boundaries made geographical or even historical sense, but because they made cultural sense. The West in western art constitutes a

A Companion to the Literature and Culture of the American West, First Edition. Edited by Nicolas S. Witschi.
© 2011 Blackwell Publishing Ltd. Published 2011 by Blackwell Publishing Ltd.

region defined by culture rather than by topography – a definition summed up in William H. Goetzmann's phrase "the West of the Imagination" (Goetzmann and Goetzmann 2009). It is this West, one way or another, that we are talking about when we talk about western art.

* * *

Through most of the twentieth century western art was appreciated not for its imaginative powers but for its factual value as a documentary record of nineteenth-century western life. The approach was as literal-minded as the art was thought to be. Accuracy was everything. At its best, western art was a mirror of western reality. This assumption was entrenched at the outset by the particular needs of the federal government which, following the purchase of Louisiana Territory, set out under President Thomas Jefferson to explore its new acquisition to the headwaters of the rivers tributary to the Mississippi, and beyond. The celebrated Lewis and Clark expedition in the years 1804 to 1806 traced the Missouri to its source and pressed on to the Pacific Ocean, mapping the northern portion of the American West. Subsequent expeditions led by Zebulon Pike (1806–7) and Stephen H. Long (1819–20) probed the southern reaches of Louisiana Territory. The earliest expeditions anticipated a succession of government-sponsored explorations over the next seventy years. Accompanied by draftsmen and then by photographers, they provided a visual record of the American West. Samuel Seymour (c.1780–1823), Titian Ramsay Peale (1799–1885), John Mix Stanley (1814–72), Richard H. Kern (1821–53), Edward Kern (1823–63), Gustavus Sohon (1825–1903), and others made the exotic familiar. They depicted the landscape and the Native tribes, recording facial features, costumes, customs, and the hunt.

The emphasis on the Indian is a hallmark of western art. Though western art projects an Anglo-American ideology, Indians were essential to the story of white pioneering. They were portrayed either as noble exemplars of natural man or as the wily, savage foe who would have to be conquered in order to secure the West for civilization. Either way the Indian had no role in the future. The future belonged to the descendants of the pioneers. The Indians, the original Americans, were doomed by the universal law of civilized progress; their forests and prairies and the animals they hunted would disappear before the advance of a white population destined to overspread the globe. Savagery and civilization, like wilderness and farms, could not coexist. American Indians were a vanishing race. That fact made them irresistible to artists.

George Catlin (1796–1872) was the best known painter of the Indian in the nineteenth century. A Pennsylvanian trained in the law, he opted for art as his profession and in the 1820s established a reputation as a miniature portrait painter in Philadelphia and New York. But he yearned for more. He wanted an animating purpose in his art, and he found it in 1828 when a visiting delegation of Indians caught his eye. He resolved to become their pictorial historian. They were, he thought, worthy subjects for a lifetime's work. Speed was of the essence; civilization was already

Figure 17.1 George Catlin, *The Author Painting a Chief, at the Base of the Rocky Mountains.* Engraving in George Catlin, *Letters and Notes on the Manners, Customs, and Condition of the North American Indians* (1841), frontispiece. Brian W. Dippie collection, Victoria, BC

encroaching on even their remotest western hunting grounds. He would paint them where they lived, "thus snatching from a hasty oblivion what could be saved for the benefit of posterity, and perpetuating it, as a fair and just monument, to the memory of a truly lofty and noble race" (Dippie 1990: 10). In setting forth his artistic goals, Catlin provided a precedent for later western artists who would also craft mission statements. Western art was never free of ideological assumptions and loftier aspirations.

From 1832 to 1836 Catlin made four trips into Indian country, painting some 500 portraits and scenes of Native life. Blackfeet, Crow, Lakota, Assiniboine, Wichita, Comanche, Kiowa, Chippewa, Dakota – all were added to his "Indian gallery," a private enterprise created, he boasted, without the benefit of patronage, though patronage was ever on his mind and he pressed Congress to purchase his gallery in its entirety. Others before Catlin had painted Indian scenes out west and formed collections of their own. James Otto Lewis (1799–1858) anticipated Catlin in publishing a portfolio of the portraits he made as an observer at treaty councils in the Old Northwest in the mid-1820s, while Peter Rindisbacher (1806–34) had lived on the Red River and the upper Mississippi during his short career as a painter of Indian life, his subjects ranging from buffalo hunts and dances to councils and camp activity. Meanwhile Charles Bird King (1785–1862), on commission from the Indian Office beginning in 1822, had become painter-in-residence in Washington, DC, specializing in portraits of Indian visitors to the nation's capital.

But no one else came close to matching the visionary scope of Catlin's Indian gallery or the zeal with which he pursued his ambition to create a comprehensive pictorial record of Native life in the western hemisphere. A self-promoter and a dreamer, he was the prototypical Indian painter; and though he was unsuccessful in selling his collection at home or, after he moved abroad in 1839, in Europe, it was widely seen on tour in America, Britain, and on the Continent, and through reproductions, notably in Catlin's influential *Letters and Notes on the Manners, Customs, and Condition of the North American Indians* published in London in 1841. Artists who viewed his paintings were inspired to surpass him, since his work seemed either too idealized or too primitive in content and execution. Karl Bodmer (1809–93), a gifted Swiss artist, accompanied his patron Prince Maximilian of Neuwied up the Missouri River in 1833, a year after Catlin, and wintered over near the Mandans. He took advantage of his sustained, close contact with them to produce drawings and watercolors notable for their scientific precision and their deft artistry. From Bodmer's perspective, Catlin was something of a charlatan who over-romanticized the Indians. Rudolph Friederich Kurz (1818–71), another Swiss artist who journeyed up the Missouri in 1846 and resided in Indian Country until 1852, faulted Catlin for not idealizing the Indians enough. In his drawings Kurz rendered the Native men and women he met as variations on Adonis and Aphrodite, dismissing Catlin's figures as "grotesque" and Catlin himself as a "Yankee humbug" (Dippie 1990: 437).

Whatever their judgments on Catlin, a legion of artists were inspired by his example to paint (and later photograph) Indians. Paul Kane (1810–71), a Canadian artist who journeyed to the West Coast and back in the 1840s, formed his own Indian gallery and published an account of his travels, *Wanderings of an Artist among the Indians of North America* (1859), that owed a sizable debt to Catlin's *Letters and Notes*. Charles Deas (1818–67), St. Louis-based, had similar aspirations in the 1840s that were thwarted by a mental breakdown, leaving just a handful of Indian portraits and genre pieces to indicate what might have been. Deas' most compelling painting, *The Death Struggle* (1845), shows an Indian and a trapper locked in mortal combat fatal to them both. It points away from Catlin and Indian galleries to western art's later focus on the violent clash of cultures on a wild frontier. The soldier-artist Seth Eastman (1808–75), trained in topographical drawing but with a taste for figure studies, painted Indian life while stationed on the Mississippi, in Florida, and in Texas. In 1849 he took up residence in Washington to serve as illustrator for Henry R. Schoolcraft's government-funded compilation *Historical and Statistical Information Respecting the History, Condition and Prospects of the Indian Tribes of the United States* (1851–7). Eastman's many Indian-themed paintings in watercolor and oil did not constitute an Indian gallery, perhaps, but the John Mix Stanley (1814–72) collection of 154 paintings based on his travels in Indian Territory, the Southwest, California, Oregon Territory, and across the northern Plains certainly did. Stanley's gallery was exhibited at the Smithsonian Institution through the 1850s before fire destroyed it in 1865, leaving no challenger to Catlin, who finally returned to his native land in 1871.

Catlin had lost his original Indian gallery to creditors years before, but had painted a new collection of Indian pictures in part replicating those in the gallery and adding subjects derived, he claimed, from trips to South America and up the West Coast to Alaska in the 1850s. Until his death in 1872 Catlin clung to the hope of federal patronage. His wish was granted posthumously. Today his Indian Gallery resides in Washington, one of the jewels of the Smithsonian American Art Museum's collection, forming a monument just as he envisioned "to the memory of a truly lofty and noble race." It sits not far from the Smithsonian's National Museum of the American Indian, which constitutes a different sort of monument to a still thriving people.

Alfred Jacob Miller (1810–74), with Catlin and Bodmer the third artist to paint western Indians in the 1830s, is best known today for his unique pictorial record of mountain men at work and play. A Baltimore native, Miller in 1837 accompanied his Scottish patron Sir William Drummond Stewart to the fur trade rendezvous on the Green River and in the span of six months produced about a hundred paintings. His field sketches and finished oils conjured up a sentimental reverie. Amity prevails as Indians and trappers cavort in an unspoiled wilderness, luxuriating in freedom and racing against the imperative of time bound to destroy their earthly paradise. While Indian–white battles would become a staple of western art there would always be a note of regret tingeing even triumphant images of the winning of the West – a sense that progress had eliminated something wonderful.

Carl Wimar (1828–62), a St. Louis painter trained in his native Germany, was a transitional figure in western art. The Indian as Indian might satisfy some, but "pictures of pure savage life, like those by Mr. Catlin, cannot excite our sympathies as strongly as do the representations of beings who belong to our own race," a New York journal observed in 1845 (Clark 2009: 105). Wimar made trips up the Missouri River into Indian country in 1858 and 1859, and painted glowing canvases showing herds of buffalo and the native people he encountered on his travels. Before actually going West he had pictured white women being carried off into captivity, dragoons pursuing fleeing warriors, and wagon trains under attack. Captivity narratives, an established literary form, and pulp fiction had served as his inspiration. Seeing western reality firsthand reined in his fantasies without expunging them from the visual record.

Wimar's most melodramatic subjects anticipated the illustrated papers and magazines of the 1860s–1890s, which were filled with images of Indian-fighting. Even as successive western tribes made their final, futile resistances and yielded to reservation confinement, artists concentrated on the theme of white sacrifice. Pictures showing trappers, cowboys, and soldiers chased by howling Indians or dismounted to make a brave stand against a savage foe fascinated the American public. They confirmed the cost of civilized progress while shifting responsibility from the white interlopers to the Indians who were soon to be dispossessed. Pictures of the western landscape were less ideologically charged, though they carried their own assumptions about owner-ship of the land.

The wilderness – nature in the raw, received directly from God's hand – fascinated American artists for its sublime beauty and as a fit setting for legendary heroes. The expeditionary artists were expected to work in a descriptive mode, rendering what they saw with the scientific precision of the topographical draftsman. Inevitably, they added their own perceptions to the mix, and mountains rose a little higher, canyons plunged a little deeper, and strange rock formations became fantastical in their ren-dering of them. Imagination altered reality – a process already evident in the land-scapes of Catlin, Miller, and even Bodmer, but especially in the work of the major western landscape painters of the nineteenth century. Albert Bierstadt (1830–1902), German-born, made Colorado and the Sierra Nevada his fantasy lands in canvases illuminated by an otherworldly light, while Thomas Moran (1837–1926), English-born, transformed Yellowstone Park and the Grand Canyon into rainbow-hued play-grounds for the imagination. An emotional response by the artist merited an emotional response by the public. The literal was irrelevant.

"The mountains and plains seemed to stimulate man's imagination," Charles M. Russell (1864–1926) wrote. "A man in the States might have been a liar in a small way, but when he comes west he soon takes lessons from the prairies, where ranges a hundred miles away seem within touchin' distance, streams run uphill and Nature appears to lie some herself" (Russell 1996: 191). Such a fabulous landscape was tailor-made for romance, a setting bound to enchant and to astonish. It was a stage for adventure, an American nursery for heroes. Frederic S. Remington (1861–1909) understood all this. Beginning in the mid-1880s he made the winning of the West his master theme. By the 1890s he was at the height of his fame as a prolific illustrator for magazines eager to feed the public's apparently insatiable appetite for things Wild Western. Remington's art was everywhere; to think of the West was to think of his pictures of devil-may-care cowboys, bushy-bearded mountain men, soldiers in blue, and fierce Indians all riding pell-mell across desert and plain. In pen and ink, paint, and, beginning in the mid-1890s, in sculpture he created a gallery of instantly recog-nizable frontier types and planted them in the public's mind. Collectively they con-firmed Frederick Jackson Turner's argument, advanced in 1893, for the lasting effects successive frontiers had in shaping a distinctive American character – self-reliant, independent, and masterful.

Remington is controversial today for what made him popular in his own day: his unblinking approval of American expansion. He loved the rough and tumble of fron-tier life, and anticipated many of the themes that have dominated western art. He pictured gunfights in saloons and in the streets of ramshackle western towns; bucking broncos and cattle stampedes; explorers topping the rise to gaze upon a new-minted land; grizzled trappers in colorful buckskin garb; buffalo hunts and cavalry patrols in deserts shimmering with heat; running fights with the Indians, and desperate stands; wagon trains and stagecoaches under attack; range wars and lone riders silhouetted against sunset skies. It is hard to think of a western cliché that Remington did *not* invent, or at least perpetuate. His influence was simply enormous. A contemporary like the New Jersey artist Charles Schreyvogel (1861–1912), who specialized in theatrical battle pictures replete with plunging horses and blazing guns, was inevitably compared to Remington, to Remington's considerable annoyance. Other artists who did not trespass on his turf found him generous with encouragement and advice: Maynard Dixon (1875–1946), an astute stylist addicted to Arizona's landscape and its native people; Edwin W. Deming (1860–1942), a painter of the Indian more focused on the mystical than the historical; and Carl Rungius (1869–1959), who made overt the strong bond between western and wildlife art.

Charles Russell was another matter. He was Remington's direct contemporary and many of his subjects resembled Remington's. Both men had come West at the beginning of the 1880s, Remington as an upstate New Yorker fresh from a year at Yale's art school, Russell as a restless St. Louis teenager. With his imagination enflamed by thrilling border stories, garish illustrations, the lushly romantic paintings of Carl Wimar, and the well-publicized exploits of master showman Buffalo Bill Cody, he just had to see those far-away mountains and plains for himself. Remington's and Russell's paths diverged at that point.

Apart from a one-year's residence on a sheep ranch in Kansas, Remington would never live in the West; Russell, after 1880, would never live anywhere else. Though

Figure 17.2 Frederic Remington, *Dismounted – The Fourth Troopers Moving the Led Horses*. Engraving, *Century Magazine*, 43 (January 1892), p. 376. Brian W. Dippie collection, Victoria, BC

he traveled widely after 1900, Montana was his home. In 1920 he and his business manager and wife Nancy began wintering in California, and she acquired a lot in Pasadena with the intention of building. But they spent every summer in their cabin on Lake McDonald in Glacier National Park, and still called Great Falls home when he died in 1926. Remington as an artist-correspondent gained a broad exposure to the West, ranging on assignment from Mexico to Canada. The frontier army was his specialty. Russell was a working cowboy from 1882 to 1893, painting on the side. He garnered national attention in 1887 for a watercolor sketch of a starving cow surrounded by wolves, *Waiting for a Chinook*. Depicting the tragic consequences of a severe winter, it marked the end of the glory days of the open-range cattle industry on the northern plains.

Russell's reputation remained local; he was *Montana*'s "cowboy artist." In the same period, Remington's depictions of western life were appearing regularly in such national periodicals as *Harper's Weekly* and *Century Magazine*, assuring a huge audience for his work. Interestingly, Remington's very success imprisoned him in a role he found increasingly constrictive. He wanted to be recognized as an artist, not just an illustrator – a distinction important at the time – and after 1900 made critical acceptance of his painterly, even impressionistic canvases a constant goal. Living in Montana and lacking access to the illustration market, Russell was necessarily an easel painter struggling to make a living from sales of his work. It was his wife who coaxed him to New York in 1903 to knock on the doors of publishers and art galleries. Remington's priorities had so changed by then that he took scant notice of a new, untutored rival whose chief claim to fame was the authenticity derived from experience that he brought to his art. It is possible they met, but Remington was silent on the subject, while Russell limited his comments on Remington to a few discreet criticisms of inaccuracies in his work. Remington and Russell might be the "titans of western art," but they left the titanic struggle over relative merit to their respective champions.

They also left a substantial legacy. Remington, in a thirty-year career, produced over 3,000 works of art on paper and canvas as well as twenty-two sculptures cast in bronze, while Russell over forty years created more than 4,000 works of art and had forty-six subjects cast in bronze. Not only were both men prolific, both saw their work extensively reproduced, broadcasting images far and wide that still, for most people, define the West and the scope of western art. Because of their popularity, Remington and Russell raise all the issues that have dogged the genre. How should their work be evaluated – as art or as document? If it is art, is it simply bad art – anecdotal, contrived, and hopelessly out of date? Does it have any aesthetic merit? If it is document, do aesthetic qualities even matter? What does it document? Should it be judged by its factual content? By its cultural influence? Or by the values it imparts? Why does it still evoke an emotional response when so many critics ignore it or dismiss it?

Certainly Remington's reputation originally rested on the impression that he was a documentary artist, a human camera who "photographed" what he saw. He stood out from his peers because his work was thought to be based on firsthand experience and factually impeccable. Remington was more than happy to accept this judgment when he was attempting to establish himself as the West's foremost pictorial historian. He knew more than the next fellow, the reasoning went, because he had actually scouted with the cavalry in the final phases of the Apache and Sioux wars, rounded up cattle with cowboys, and visited Indian reservations to observe the new realities that were transforming yesterday's warriors into something much less picturesque. Remington boosted the demand for his work by writing up his experiences in articles and amplifying them in short stories that required illustration. In turn, these produced spin-offs like his first book of collected essays, *Pony Tracks* (1895). The title was a stroke of genius, evoking a West "out there" that Remington knew better than any other man alive. Through him, readers could participate vicariously in the closing act of America's great frontier drama, following him on *Crooked Trails* (1898) to a land of *Men with the Bark On* (1900). Collections of his illustrations and portfolios of his paintings reproduced in color hammered home the impression that *his* West was the *real* West, while preserving his art in a form more permanent than periodical publication.

To this day Remington and Russell are often seen as two sides of the same coin. Both showed cowboys and Indians and other familiar western types. But soldiers, a Remington staple, played no role in Russell's art nor, more to the point, did the narrative to which soldiers were central, the winning of the West. In the 1890s Russell did his share of paintings showing Indian–white conflict, adopting Remington's motifs of the pursuit and the desperate stand. But his perspective shifted. In classic Russell art Indians on a promontory in the foreground watch Lewis and Clark, a steamboat, or a wagon train below, contemplating a future beyond their control. His identification is with the Natives, not with the white interlopers invading their land.

Remington and Russell saw the West differently. Remington cheered on progress while Russell lamented change. The body of his art constitutes a sustained elegy. His standard subjects were cowboys at work and play, buffalo hunts, and parties of Indians riding across an open space or surveying what lay before them. The land itself and the wildlife inhabiting it were characters in his art. He preferred things as they used to be before the farmer came along and plowed under the picture and story part of western history. Unabashedly nostalgic, Russell's art has been dismissed as technically unsophisticated. But he had a rare ability to convey movement and project a consistent artistic vision steeped in emotion. His West is as distinctive and enduring as Remington's. Despite different viewpoints, both knew that they were witnesses to the passing of an era in American history.

Looking back on his first trip to Montana in 1881, Remington said, he realized at once that "a heavy feel in the atmosphere" portended transforming change:

> I knew the railroad was coming – I saw men already swarming into the land. I knew the derby hat, the smoking chimneys, the cord-binder, and the thirty-day note were upon us in a resistless surge. I knew the wild riders and the vacant land were about to

Figure 17.3 Charles M. Russell, *The Indian of the Plains as He Was*. First plate in Charles M. Russell, *Pen Sketches* (1899). Brian W. Dippie collection, Victoria, BC

> vanish forever, and the more I considered the subject the bigger the Forever loomed. ... I saw the living, breathing end of three American centuries of smoke and dust and sweat. (Samuels and Samuels 1979: 551)

He was, in short, positioned to observe the closing act of a great drama, the final sweep of civilization across America. Russell arrived in Montana the year before Remington and took an active part in that drama. He relished his role as a working cowboy. It meant youth and freedom to him, and when change inevitably came to the range his sense of loss was intensely personal. As he wrote to an old cowboy friend, "When the nester turned the west grass side down he buried the trails we traveled. But he could not wipe from our memories the life we loved. Man may lose a sweetheart but he don't forget her." Russell's sentiment speaks to the longing for a better time and place, an ideal Old West that lives on "in the harts of her lovers" (Dippie 1994: 7; Russell 1996: p. xix).

In spanning the nineteenth and twentieth centuries, Remington and Russell endowed western art with its retrospective outlook. The West is synonymous with a time as well as a place, and that time is Remington and Russell time. They set the dial to the nineteenth century and it has not moved. Every representative collection of western art features their work, and each has a museum of his own – the Frederic Remington Art Museum in Ogdensburg, New York, and the C.M. Russell Museum in Great Falls, Montana. Technically sophisticated contemporaries like Frank Tenney

Johnson (1874–1939) and William Robinson Leigh (1866–1955) extended their legacy deep into the twentieth century, and a still-thriving school of "cowboy art" has never lost touch with its nineteenth-century origins. The world they paint remains pristine, unscarred by highways and urban clutter, as green as spring beneath an unpolluted sky, and as warm and welcoming as a Thomas Kinkade painting of a house glowing with light on a cold winter's eve. The West in western art occupies the Land Where Time Stood Still. It is a fantasy, rendered with realistic precision. And that is exactly as those who like western art would have it.

By rejecting the imperative of progress, Russell made common cause with those artists who beginning late in the nineteenth century chose Taos, New Mexico, as their home. They achieved national prominence as an artistic community formed around the nucleus of the Taos Society of Artists, established in 1915. If Catlin expounded a creation myth for his Indian Gallery and Remington for his entire body of work on the West, the Taos Society had a founding myth of its own involving a serendipitous accident that combined a spectacular landscape and exotic inhabitants irresistible for artists schooled abroad and in search of a uniquely American inspiration. The pathbreakers were Ernest L. Blumenschein (1874–1960) and Bert G. Phillips (1868–1956) who, following advice proffered by Joseph Henry Sharp (1859–1953) when they were students together in Paris, began a wagon trip from Denver to Mexico with a planned stop in Taos. Their wagon broke down twenty miles short of Taos, and Blumenschein rode on ahead carrying the damaged wheel while Phillips waited with the wagon. What he saw left Blumenschein entranced:

> The beautiful Sangre de Cristo range to my left was quite different in character from the Colorado mountains. Stretching away from the foot of the range was a vast plateau cut by the Rio Grande and by lesser gorges in which were located small villages of flat-roofed adobe houses built around a church and plaza, all fitting into the color scheme of the tawny surroundings. … Then I saw my first Taos Indians, picturesque, colorful, dressed in blankets artistically draped. New Mexico had gripped me … (Dippie 2010: 78)

And so, in proper storybook fashion, the artists discovered Taos.

Painters like Blumenschein, Phillips, Sharp, E.I. Couse (1866–1936), Walter Ufer (1876–1936), and W. Herbert Dunton (1878–1936) were formally trained, but shared a self-taught artist like Charlie Russell's romantic perspective. Indeed, Sharp, Dunton, and another of the Taos painters, Oscar E. Berninghaus (1874–1952), were acquaintances. Like Russell, they were given to commemorating a vanished West. But their master-theme was permanence, not loss; acculturation, not cultural extinction. The clash of Indian and white never gripped them as it did western artists elsewhere. Remington found the Taos aesthetic too decorative for his taste, though he had sympathy for the artists' infatuation with the blending over time of diverse, still vital cultural traditions – Native, Hispanic, and Anglo. After all, he had been drawn to Mexico as an illustrator, and recognized the deep Spanish roots as well as the surface color of life on both sides of the southwestern border. And in his last years he was drawn to Indian themes associated with Taos, including courtship under the romantic cover of darkness.

The Taos artists portrayed a people whose ceremonial life was old when Columbus touched shore in the New World. Change moved at a statelier pace in pueblo land. Sharp, who until 1912 maintained a second studio on the Crow Reservation in Montana, famously explained that he went north because he "realized that Taos would last longer" (Dippie 1982: 288). He harbored Catlin-like ambitions to paint a portrait gallery of old-time Plains Indians, as well as genre scenes among the Crow that paralleled his work in Taos. He was as adept at showing the exterior of firelit tipis glowing like Japanese lanterns as he was at adobe interiors illuminated by hearth fires, a Taos staple associated with Couse whose "fireside reveries" encapsulated the romantic appeal of southwestern art. In Taos, where the old had found a future, modernism established a toehold by the 1920s. Marsden Hartley (1877–1943) and John Marin (1870–1953) both exhibited at the Armory Show in New York in 1913, a landmark event in the history of modernism in America, and both lived in New Mexico for a year, while Georgia O'Keeffe (1887–1986), after regular visits beginning in 1929, made New Mexico her home in 1949. Her paintings of landforms as seamed and human as Alexander Hogue's, strewn with animal bones and desert flowers and the symbols of a venerable Catholic presence, have become, like those of Remington and Russell, a way of envisioning the American West.

* * *

The visual history of the American West does not stop with painting and sculpture, of course. Photography has also played a prominent role. Perhaps 4,500 individuals were active in some aspect of the photographic profession west of the Mississippi River prior to 1866. Most had nothing to do with what we think of as western art, but their numbers are impressive and must be taken into consideration in any reckoning of western imagery. The exchange between art and photography was never a one-way proposition. They learned from one another.

With the invention of photography in 1839, artists immediately recognized its potential usefulness in their work. Some of the earliest western painters used daguerreotype cameras to supplement their field sketches. John Mix Stanley, Carl Wimar, and Albert Bierstadt all took pictures on their western travels in the 1850s, and though none of Stanley's photographs from the Isaac I. Stevens Pacific Railroad Survey in 1853 survive, he claimed success among the Blackfeet. "I made many interesting sketches of their customs," he reported, "and daguerreotypes of their chiefs" (Dippie 1990: 288). Just so were photography and Indian portraiture united in what would prove a long, productive partnership.

Western artists generally were indebted to photography. Indeed, since they were known for their depictions of figures in motion, they were especially indebted to the Californian Eadweard Muybridge (1830–1904) whose stop-action photographs taught them how to portray "animal locomotion" correctly, forever altering the way all artists would depict a running horse. The era of the rocking horse gallop came to an end in the 1880s as the results of Muybridge's camera work infiltrated popular culture. By the 1890s many western artists were more dependent on photographs than field sketches in their studio productions. Remington, for one, was addicted to the Kodak, as he put it. He acquired photographs wherever he traveled, begged contacts to send him more, and recognized that their usefulness to him as an illustrator inhibited him as an artist, retarding his sense of color and anchoring him to the literal. Some of the Taos painters, like E.I. Couse, worked directly from photographs of their models, and Frank Tenney Johnson, known for his bravura brushwork, maintained a photographic reference file of over 4,000 pictures.

Naturally the relationship between art and photography involved a back-and-forth exchange. Photographers emulated artists in their choice of subjects, and often aspired to be considered artists themselves. The work of expeditionary photographers like Timothy O'Sullivan (*c*.1840–82), William Henry Jackson (1843–1942), and Carleton Watkins (1829–1916) had a primarily practical purpose, but each produced photographs that rivaled the landscape tradition in painting, and Watkins' artful views of Yosemite made in the 1860s naturally conjure up comparisons with Bierstadt's. Indian subjects had special appeal to photographers. Charles Bird King painted his Indian sitters in the comfort of Washington, DC, where they were visitors in formal dress attire calling on the president and other influential officials. Photographing delegations of Indian visitors was a natural extension of King's lead. In 1854, an aspiring photographer, Washington Peale from the prominent Philadelphia family of artists and naturalists, urged the government to abandon its practice of having portraits painted of distinguished Indian delegates to Washington and turn instead to photography for a more representative sample of "all grades, ages, sexes." Echoing Catlin, he argued that there was no time to waste in order to preserve "a *complete* record of this once numerous race" now "gradually becoming extinct." The "beautiful art of photography" was the answer (Dippie 1992: 43). Before the decade was out, photographers were filling the role that once belonged to painters. Of course, shooting Indian visitors in the East was equivalent to shooting fish in a barrel.

Catlin for one had always insisted that his portraits of Indians painted in their own country were superior to those painted by artists ensconced in the East. Out West, he was the visitor and they were the hosts, putting them at ease in a setting where the exotic was the familiar. In an era when photographic equipment was cumbersome and producing usable plates under demanding circumstances in the field more than challenging, photographers could not expect to duplicate Catlin's enterprise or supplant expeditionary artists. Indeed, Stanley had differentiated between making sketches of Blackfeet customs – something that called on his artistic skill – and making photographic portraits of tribal dignitaries. Art could convey movement, from galloping horses to charging buffalo (albeit falsely, as Muybridge would show); photography was necessarily static. Only technological changes in the photographic process would permit action pictures. Meanwhile, photography was restricted to landscape, portraiture, and posed groups, thus limiting its impact on western imagery until after the Civil War. When expeditionary photography reached maturity, Custer's wagon train could wend its way through Castle Creek Valley in an 1874 William H. Illingworth (1842–93) stereograph, and by the 1880s cowboys could go about their business in the photographs of L.A. Huffman (1854–1931). But artists still had an advantage – exclusive dominion over color; save when photographers hand-tinted prints, the West of the camera was monochromatic. Perhaps that explains why William Henry Jackson was a painter as well. His splendid photographic views of Yellowstone taken on the Hayden Survey in 1871 offered an attractive introduction to the thermal features and scenery of what would become America's first national park, but his companion Thomas Moran's vibrant watercolors of Yellowstone added the "wonder" to "wonderland."

Photography's reliance on art finds its most familiar western example in the work of photographers in the early twentieth century who set out to make comprehensive pictorial records of old-time Indian culture. Their staged scenes, lovingly composed, invariably pay homage to a hoary conceit. Roland Reed (1864–1934), for example, photographed Indians in Wisconsin, Montana, and the desert Southwest, and in his advertising claimed to have "caught all the truth, all the beauty and all the pathos of the closing epochs of a vanishing race."[1] It has become a convention to note that all of them, and certainly the most famous of the lot, Edward S. Curtis (1868–1952), followed in Catlin's footsteps. From the scope and duration of their respective projects to the personal toll they exacted, Catlin and Curtis make a pair. Forming his original Indian gallery cost Catlin just six years in the 1830s, but promoting and touring it consumed twenty more at the expense of his family and his reputation, while painting and exhibiting a new Indian collection brought him to the end of his days. Curtis sacrificed a promising photographic career and then his marriage to devote his energies to his life's work, a study of the North American Indians published in twenty volumes, each with a photographic portfolio, between 1907 and 1930. His project involved extensive travel to some eighty tribes resulting in an estimated 40,000 photographs, 2,200 of them published in his books. Catlin would have been impressed. That both men were obsessed with preserving a pictorial record of what they deemed vanishing cultures over seventy years apart gives pause about their guiding assumption, but not about their devotion to their art.

Curtis' pictorial aesthetic, with its focus on beauty and its idealization of traditional Native life, has led to the charge that he sacrificed truth to artistry. He may have aspired to be taken seriously as an ethnographer, the argument goes, but he was just another imaginative tourist with an Indian hobby – another Catlin, in short, if the critics of both are to be believed. Perhaps the audacity of their ambition fostered skepticism. Even Russell, who knew Curtis and had his portrait taken by him in Los Angeles in the early 1920s, doubted that any one man could have a thorough knowledge of so many different tribes. But he did not for a moment doubt the intention behind Curtis' enterprise. Like any artist, Curtis had a right to focus on the picture side of Indian life. If he posed his subjects for maximum effect and omitted distracting elements from prints, so what? The most important quality in art, as Remington put it, was imagination. "Without that a fellow is out of luck" (Dippie 2001: 128). On that score, Curtis was fortunate indeed. Whatever controversy surrounds his photographs today, they are stunning works of art.

The visual legacy of the West came alive for audiences when western films achieved mass popularity in the 1920s. Russell counted among his friends such Hollywood luminaries as William S. Hart, Harry Carey, Will Rogers, and Douglas Fairbanks, all of whom owned examples of his art. He watched actors bring the Old West to life for millions of people who would never cross the Mississippi, and while he knew that what appeared on the screen bore scant resemblance to reality, reality was not the issue. "Here's to history and romance," he told Fairbanks, and to "you and your kind … who make folks of history and story bookes live and breath again."[2] Fittingly, Russell's only protégé, Joe De Yong, took the lessons he learned at the master's knee to Hollywood where he served as the historical consultant for such celebrated westerns as *The Plainsman* (1937), *Red River* (1948), and *Shane* (1953). The combination of John Ford, John Wayne, and Monument Valley defined the American West for the world by mid-century, but equally important was the partnership between Ford and Frederic Remington, whose art served as Ford's textbook of choice in composing action scenes and visualizing western types. It is worth noting that the same principle applies to film as to photography: it has become an important source for contemporary western artists, making visual influence once more a busy two-way street.

* * *

When western museums want to reimagine their collections, options are limited. Inclusiveness is the obvious one, adding different artists to represent ethnic and gender diversity and to counteract the dominant white male perspective in traditional western art. Since Indians were always featured in that art, reimagining them turns on letting Indians represent themselves, substituting Native imagery for white imagery of colorful exotics from a vanishing race. To the extent that Indian artists want to tackle stereotypes head on, parody is the obvious ploy. Tonto becomes the trickster and the Lone Ranger his comic foil. Of course any artist can play this game, switching the white hats and the black hats to reinterpret old formulas. Artists from any ethnic minority can address the neglect of their historical experience by adding new subjects to the mix, or by inserting themselves into established conventions, just as women artists have replaced cowboys with cowgirls in myriad bucking horse pictures. Shaking up classic subjects works well by paying homage to tradition while altering it. This is better than banishing old art to dark corners and museum vaults and making the issue not who rides the bucking bronco but whether anyone should.

In the meantime, western art is still its subject matter. It is what western art museums display. A circular definition is appropriate. It conjures up a popular image in western art of Indians circling a wagon train, a fort, or a stalwart band of pioneers. If the last stand symbolizes traditional western art making a last-ditch defense against modernity, the circling Indians can be seen as the noose tightening around tradition's neck. Then what? Will it be time to bring down the curtain on western art, and close the doors of western art museums?

That would be too drastic. Western art forces an often uncomfortable confrontation with the American past. But even if the values of the past seem out of place today, something interesting comes out of an examination of western art: Indians are its common denominator. They are present or implicit in every painting of wilderness landscape. They serve to bridge contradictory perspectives in the Remington and Russell tradition. They are as important to Remington's master-narrative of the winning of the West as they are to Russell's of the losing of the West. It may be fashionable to see both as equally racist, the one overtly, the other covertly – imperialist guff and imperialist nostalgia. But reducing real differences to trendy catchphrases misses the point. The cowboy artist incorporated a buffalo skull – not a steer skull – in his signature because it best symbolized the wrenching change transforming the Old West. If the Indian was at the end of his trail, the cowboy was not far behind. And for those who would instead emphasize cultural continuity and permanence – the Taos artists, for example – Indians were their clinching argument. They were America's tomorrow, not just its yesterday.

What are we talking about when we talk about western art? Indians, mostly. D.H. Lawrence, in an exuberant moment before actually going to America, advised Americans to rediscover a primal earth-knowledge that was their birthright. It coursed through the rituals and beliefs of the First Americans. "Americans must take up life where the Red Indian ... left it off. They must pick up the life-thread where the mysterious Red race let it fall. They must catch the pulse of the life which Cortes and Columbus murdered." "To your tents, O America," he concluded. "Listen to your own, don't listen to Europe."[3] After actually visiting America and residing in Taos, Lawrence conceded that as an Englishman, "My way is my own, old red father; I can't cluster at the drum any more."[3] But could Americans? It is a question at the core of western art. And because it is, western art still has a future rooted in the past.

NOTES

* With gratitude to Raymond Carver. Passages in this essay draw on my earlier essay "Western Art," in *Encyclopedia of the American West*, ed. Charles Phillips and Alan Axelrod (New York: Macmillan Reference USA, 1996).

1 Introduction to *Photographic Art Studies of the North American Indian* (Ortonville, MN: Roland Reed, n.d. [1920s]).

2 C.M. Russell to Douglas Fairbanks, April 27, 1921, private collection.

3 D.H. Lawrence, "America, Listen to Your Own," *New Republic*, 25 (Dec. 15, 1920), 69–70; D.H. Lawrence, "Indians and an Englishman," *Dial*, 74 (Feb. 1923), 152.

REFERENCES AND FURTHER READING

Bruce, Chris, et al. (1990). *Myth of the West*. Seattle: Henry Art Gallery, University of Washington, and Rizzoli, New York. The catalog of an important thematic art exhibition.

Clark, Carol. (2009). *Charles Deas and 1840s America*. Norman: University of Oklahoma Press, with the Denver Art Museum. An interpretive study of an intriguing western artist.

Cowie, Peter. (2004). *John Ford and the American West*. New York: Harry N. Abrams. A consideration of the interplay of imagery between western art and western film.

Dippie, Brian W. (1982). *The Vanishing American: White Attitudes and U.S. Indian Policy*. Lawrence: University Press of Kansas. Examines a pervasive ideology important to western American art.

Dippie, Brian W. (1990). *Catlin and his Contemporaries: The Politics of Patronage*. Lincoln: University of Nebraska Press. An examination of the complex and competitive world of early western art.

Dippie, Brian W. (1992). Photographic Allegories and Indian Destiny. *Montana: The Magazine of Western History*, 42 (Summer): 40–57.

Dippie, Brian W. (1994). *Remington & Russell: The Sid Richardson Collection*. Rev. edn. Austin: University of Texas Press. The catalog of a collection that invites comparison of the two most influential figures in western art.

Dippie, Brian W. (2001). *The Frederic Remington Art Museum Collection*. Ogdensburg, NY: Frederic Remington Art Museum. The catalog of one of the few important western art collections housed outside the interior West.

Dippie, Brian W. (2010). *Crossroads: Desert Caballeros Western Museum*. Wickenburg, AZ: Maricopa County Historical Society, Desert Caballeros Western Museum. The catalog of an impressive, focused western art collection.

Eldredge, Charles C., Julie Schimmel, and William H. Truettner. (1986). *Art in New Mexico, 1900–1945: Paths to Taos and Santa Fe*. Washington, DC: National Museum of American Art, with Abbeville Press, New York. A useful introduction to the southwestern school of western art.

Fleming, Paula Richardson, and Judith Lynn Luskey. (1993). *Grand Endeavors of American Indian Photography*. Washington, DC: Smithsonian Institution Press. One of many books on Indians in photography, but one of the few to consider the photographers who saw their work as art.

Goetzmann, William H., and William N. Goetzmann. (2009). *The West of the Imagination*. 2nd edn. Norman: University of Oklahoma Press. The best overview history of western American art.

Hassrick, Peter H., and Melissa J. Webster. (1996). *Frederic Remington: A Catalogue Raisonné of Paintings, Watercolors and Drawings*. Cody, WY: Buffalo Bill Historical Center. An essential work.

Neff, Emily Ballew. (2006). *The Modern West: American Landscapes, 1890–1950*. New Haven: Yale University Press, with the Museum of Fine Arts, Houston. The catalog of a thematic exhibition introducing important trends in western modernism.

Palmquist, Peter E., and Thomas R. Kailbourn. (2005). *Pioneer Photographers from the Mississippi to the Continental Divide: A Biographical Dictionary, 1839–1865*. Stanford: Stanford University Press. The second of two readable volumes on the early western photographers, both masterpieces of research.

Price, B. Byron, ed. (2007). *Charles M. Russell: A Catalogue Raisonné*. Norman: University of Oklahoma Press. An essential work.

Prown, Jules David, et al. (1992). *Discovered Lands, Invented Pasts: Transforming Visions of the American West*. New Haven: Yale University Press. The catalog of an important thematic exhibition.

Russell, Charles M. (1996). *Trails Plowed Under: Stories of the Old West*. Lincoln: University of Nebraska Press. The classic collection of Russell's yarns first published in 1927.

Samuels, Peggy, and Harold Samuels, eds. (1979). *The Collected Writings of Frederic Remington*. Garden City: Doubleday & Co. A comprehensive anthology of Remington's prose.

Sandweiss, Martha A. (2002). *Print the Legend: Photography and the American West*. New Haven: Yale University Press. A history of western American photography.

Truettner, William H., ed. (1991). *The West as America: Reinterpreting Images of the Frontier, 1820–1920*. Washington, DC: Smithsonian Institution Press for the National Museum of American Art. The catalog of an important thematic exhibition.

18

"All Hat and No Cattle": Romance, Realism, and Late Nineteenth-Century Western American Fiction

Gary Scharnhorst

The blight upon the literature of the West, like that of all provinces, has been its timid-
ity, its childish desire to write for the applause of its masters in the East. ... The West,
reckoning itself an annex of the East, has imitated imitations. (Hamlin Garland, "Literary
Emancipation of the West," 1893)

In his story "The Saving Grace" (1899), Stewart Edward White posed a dilemma faced
by every late nineteenth-century author who presumed to write western American
fiction. An ambitious young literary realist woos an eastern woman devoted to the
"idealistic school of fiction" who demands that he renounce his literary allegiances
and prove his love by writing a romance for her. The spurned realist retreats to a small
town in Wyoming, where he begins a realistic western tale but hits a block when he
portrays his hero "pursued by an avenging band." He has never been pursued on
horseback, so to remain faithful to the tenets of realism he hires a band of cowhands
to chase him on horses while shooting blank cartridges. Unfortunately, another posse,
mistaking the make-believe chase for a real one, joins the pursuit, shoots lead bullets,
and nearly hangs him as an outlaw. The erstwhile realist gets "more realistic experience in ten minutes than he had had in all his previous life." He finally finishes his
"masterpiece" and sends it to his editor, who rejects it as a flight of western fantasy
even though every event in it occurred exactly as depicted. The dismayed realist
rereads his story and concludes that it "was exactly true. Realism could have had no
more accurate exposition of its principles." He submits the story to a rival magazine,
where it is published, and the next day his ex-fiancée hurries to him to rekindle their
love. "When I got to the end" of the tale "and saw the signature," she explains, she
"realized that you had deserted your literary principles just for my sake."

A Companion to the Literature and Culture of the American West, First Edition. Edited by
Nicolas S. Witschi.
© 2011 Blackwell Publishing Ltd. Published 2011 by Blackwell Publishing Ltd.

At the most literal level, White's tale spoofs realism and raises issues of (in)authenticity and imposture in western American fiction. But in a more subtle sense it suggests that at the close of the nineteenth century only a version of western myth would find a sympathetic audience among eastern readers, represented by the fiancée; and that such fiction would inevitably fail the test of realism, expressed in its rejection by the Howells-like editor. The realist was required by the demands of the literary market to compromise aesthetic standards to publish western fiction. I want to explore this idea by reviewing briefly the extent to which the West was commodified for sale in the East and in Europe by the mythmakers and fabulists; then by contending that the "real West" did not sell; and finally by citing a few exceptional realistic western tales of the period that planted the seeds of a western countertradition. Simply put, I ask not *whether* nineteenth-century western American fiction was unrealistic but *why* it was unrealistic.[1]

* * *

The romantic or mythological West was packaged for sale during the nineteenth century: this point is simply incontestable. Bret Harte, for example, understood from the beginning of his career that his success depended upon his popularity in the East, not the West. As he wrote in January 1866, over two years before the founding of the *Overland Monthly*, he expected his first important book to "depend entirely" on its "sale in the East" for its commercial success (Harte 2002: 19). He explained the problem in September 1867: the literary market in California labored under "the old trouble of inadequate supply and demand. We have in fact more writers than readers, more contributors than subscribers" (Harte 1990: 140). By mid-1870, the end of its second year of publication, the *Overland Monthly* – edited by Harte and published in San Francisco – began to circulate as widely in the East as in the states of Nevada, California, and Oregon combined (Taylor 1870). Harte's early western tales were routinely reprinted from the *Overland* in such eastern newspapers as the New York *Evening Post* and the *Hartford Courant* (Scharnhorst 1995: 106). That is, in such comic/pathetic tales as "The Luck of Roaring Camp," "The Outcasts of Poker Flat" (1869), "The Idyl of Red Gulch" (1869), and "Brown of Calaveras" (1870) Harte proved the market for the literary West. However, when he discovered his brand of "local color fading from the West," as Mary Austin observed, "he did what he considered the only safe thing, and carried his young impression away to be worked out untroubled by any newer fact" (Austin 1902: 690). As Howells reminisced, after Harte settled in Great Britain in 1880 he returned "to the semi-mythical California he had half discovered, half created, and wrote Bret Harte over and over again" to the end of his life. It "was the best thing he could do" because the "cockney-syntaxed, Dickens-colored California" of his imagination satisfied "the insatiable English fancy for the wild America no longer to be found on our map" (Howells 1911: 299). During the last years of his life Harte earned more money by selling German translation rights to his stories than he was paid in royalties by his American publishers (Timpe 1965).

Little wonder that Wallace Stegner joked that Harte's popularity "was always greatest in direct proportion to the reader's distance from and ignorance of the mines" (1961: p. x).

The rise of the literary West during the latter third of the nineteenth century was also fueled by the burgeoning popularity of dime novel westerns. All major publishers of these novels were headquartered in New York, and their primitive market studies indicated that the typical reader of westerns "was a young, married man in a manual job who had limited resources and lived in an industrial [that is, an eastern] town" (Bold 1987: 7–8; Jones 1978: 6). According to John G. Cawelti, dime novels were popular escapist fantasies mostly read by males in the eastern US who were suffering a "sense of eroding masculinity" (Cawelti 1976: 211). Most of the writers stabled in these "fiction factories" (for example, Edward S. Ellis and Edward L. Wheeler) were easterners whose "nearest acquaintance with the Great Plains," as Edmund Pearson once put it, "was in White Plains, New York" (1929: 105). According to John Dinan, Gilbert Patten (aka "Wyoming Bill") earned his pseudonym by merely traveling by train once through Wyoming (1983: 12). While these blood-and-thunder tales often featured such real-life westerners as Kit Carson, Joaquin Murietta, and Buffalo Bill Cody, they were fundamentally anti-realistic. As Merle Curti explained, "it was a highly colored picture of the West which hack writers painted for Easterners through the almost endless succession of stories about Texas rangers and cowboys, Nevada miners, California vigilantes, and Montana badmen" (1937: 769). Not until the 1880s were any dime novels written about "cowboys," originally a pejorative term, and even then the cowboy novels rarely contained any cows.

Still, the pulps shaped the impression of the West made on hundreds of thousands of American and European readers. The very first dime novel, Ann S. Stephens' *Malaeska, the Indian Wife of the White Hunter* (1860), sold some 65,000 copies in its first months; and Ellis' *Seth Jones; or The Captives of the Frontier* (1860) sold more than 600,000 copies and was translated into half a dozen languages (Jones 1978: 6, 8). Dime novels became so popular that respectable writers for juveniles, among them Horatio Alger, traveled to the West and penned sensational juvenile tales to compete with them. Alger's popular Pacific series – *The Young Adventurer* (1878), *Joe's Luck* (1878), *The Young Miner* (1879), and *The Young Explorer* (1880) – romanticized the California gold fields in purple prose, sold hundreds of thousands of copies, and remained continuously in print until the 1920s. The device of western travel became so commonplace in boys' books that Edward Stratemeyer (aka Arthur M. Winfield) even exploited it in *The Rover Boys Out West* (1900), and Theodore Roosevelt's histories, particularly *The Winning of the West* (1889–96), were as romantic as the pulps in their bully triumphalism.

Western American fiction appealed at the time no less to European readers. Cooper's *The Pioneers* (1823) was immediately translated into German, Swedish, Spanish, and Danish and earned wide celebrity on the continent. According to Ray Allen Billington, Cooper's European readers regarded him "as a realist who accurately portrayed the frontiersmen and Indians – a judgment that would astound modern readers" (1981:

30–1). Among the last books Franz Schubert read on his deathbed in 1828, in fact, were Cooper's *The Pioneers* and *The Last of the Mohicans* (Deutsch 1946: 819–20). By the late nineteenth century, European publishers no longer needed to pirate Cooper, however. Such authors as Mayne Reid and Karl May met the demand for westerns in the European market. At a time when the *Atlantic Monthly* rarely paid its contributors more than $10 per printed page, Reid never received less than $600 for a pulp he could write in a week (Pearson 1929: 48); and though May never visited the American West, he capitalized on its popularity among German readers between 1875 and his death in 1912 by writing over thirty frontier novels featuring "Old Shatterhand" (a Leatherstocking wannabe) and his loyal Apache sidekick Winnetou (an ersatz Chingachgook). May was a favorite author of both Adolf Hitler and Albert Einstein, and his books remain popular in German-speaking countries. According to Sarah J. Blackstone, his western novels have been translated into twenty languages and read by 300 million people (1986: 6).

Perhaps the best barometer of the market for the commodified West in the late nineteenth century, however, was the "performed West" of lectures, popular melo-drama, and Wild West shows. The performed West was invariably portrayed in exotic terms, represented in ways that appealed to middle-class easterners and Europeans. As early as 1843, P.T. Barnum purported to exhibit "real" Indians at his New York museum, though they were cultural impostors of the type Gerald Vizenor has termed *indians*. Mark Twain delivered his fanciful "Roughing It" lecture dozens of times in the US and England in 1871–2, but never west of Kalamazoo; and Harte delivered his lecture "The Argonauts of '49" hundreds of times in 1872–3, but never west of Omaha. At least a hundred western melodramas and sensational horse operas were produced in the Bowery and on Broadway in New York between 1870 and 1900, including border dramas by Harte, Twain, Dion Boucicault, Clyde Fitch, Joaquin Miller, and Brander Matthews, an average of well over three new theatrical westerns a year for over thirty years. These plays were popular spectacles on stage, featuring live horses and frequent gunplay and such exotic (stereo)types as redshirt miners, primitive Indians, inscrutable Chinese laundrymen, and decayed Spanish aristocrats. These allegories of Manifest Destiny staged a narrative of frontier conquest and affirmed the so-called "triumphalist history" of nineteenth-century America from a colonial point of view familiar to easterners.

Nowhere was this narrative more evident than in the Wild West exhibitions, par-ticularly Buffalo Bill's Wild West, a flamboyant simulacrum of the West. With live animals and cast members such as Sitting Bull, Will Bill Hickok, and Annie Oakley, its celebrated claims to authenticity were rarely challenged. No less a luminary than Mark Twain attended a pair of performances of the Wild West in September 1884 and wrote Cody that "down to its smallest details, the show is genuine" (quoted in Warren 2005: 294–5). The Wild West rarely played west of the Mississippi during its thirty-three years of existence. It was performed on Staten Island during the summer of 1886, for example, with an estimated weekly attendance of 100,000 to 150,000, before it moved to Madison Square Garden that winter and to Earl's Court in London in 1887. The Wild West was staged in Birmingham and Manchester during six months in 1888 and at the Exposition Universelle in Paris in 1889 before commencing a continental tour through southern France, Spain, Italy, Germany, Austria, and Holland. After three and a half years in Europe, Buffalo Bill's Wild West finally returned to the US in October 1892 – whereupon his rival showman Pawnee Bill left with his troupe for Europe. Cody mounted his Wild West and "Congress of Rough Riders of the World" just across the street from the main entrance to the World's Columbian Exposition in Chicago in the summer of 1893 and attracted 6 million attendees. He returned to New York with his Wild West for the 1894 season and, in 1902, embarked on another European tour that lasted four years. In all, as Louis S. Warren notes, the Wild West spent nine years, "almost a third of its life," in Europe (2005: 297). An estimated 50 million people saw Cody in person, more than any other figure in history to that time, and at his death in 1917 he was arguably the most famous celebrity in the world. But he was famous, like Harry Houdini, for the illusions he staged rather than for the realism of his performances.

*   *   *

Consider a corollary to the idea that the West was commodified for sale a century and more ago: it was rarely represented realistically because the "real West" did not sell. Little scholarship has been devoted to this subject, though a case study of the marketing of Mary Austin's western writings illustrates the difficulties her publishers faced. Austin's earliest western fiction was utterly conventional, consisting of such local-color tales as "The Wooing of the Señorita" (1897) and "The Conversion of Ah Lew Sing" (1897). Austin tried to break into the eastern literary market with more realistic western stories, such as "A Shepherd of the Sierras" (1900) and "The Pot of Gold" (1901), though the magazines paid her poorly for them. In July 1902, after reaching an agreement with Austin to issue *The Land of Little Rain*, Bliss Perry of Houghton Mifflin wrote her that the book would appeal "to a comparatively limited number of readers" and, in fact, only about 5,500 copies of the book were sold in 1903 and only 5,825 copies of Austin's *The Basket Woman* the following year. "From the point of view of Houghton Mifflin and other East Coast publishing houses," Karen S. Langlois has explained, "California and its neighboring states in the West were far removed from eastern book distribution centers and accounted for only a minor percentage of book sales" (1988: 32–3, 41). Austin later reminisced about the difficulty in marketing her books. They "were always of the West, which was little known; and always a little in advance of the current notion of it," she allowed. "They were never what is known as 'Westerns'; and they never followed along, one after another" (Austin 1932: 320). As late as 1903, Austin was paid only $8 per printed page for her work in the *Atlantic Monthly* (Fink 1983: 110). In contrast, Owen Wister was paid at least $35 per 1,000 words by *Harper's* – $175 for "Hank's Woman" (1892) and "How Lin McLean Went East" (1892), $300 for "Em'ly" (1893) and "Balaam and Pedro" (1894) (Payne 1985: 164; Samuels 1982: 194). All of the profit was in the mythological

West. At the end of the century, as Sanford E. Marovitz has explained, "Eastern editors and readers wanted to read of a romanticized, often sentimentalized West only vaguely based on truth" (1975: 57).

Under the circumstances, many of the ostensibly "serious" western writers of the period adapted to the realities of the literary market by publishing historical romances that reinforced or promoted the popular mythology of the West. Put another way, rarely were westerns only about the West. From Fenimore Cooper to Gary Cooper, western narratives have functioned as symbolic melodramas, political allegories, or vehicles for social commentary, usually from an eastern point of view with a predictably skewed ethnological and nationalistic focus. Cooper set *The Prairie* (1827) in modern-day Nebraska, a region he never visited, and finished the romance in a hotel room in Paris (France, not Texas), which may begin to explain why he confused prairie, plain, and desert.

To be sure, historical romances sometimes qualified the triumphalist history of the period. One of the few nineteenth-century novels to express outrage about the maltreatment of Indians, Helen Hunt Jackson's *Ramona* (1884), was written in the sentimental-reform tradition of *Uncle Tom's Cabin*. Similarly, Joaquin Miller's play *The Danites* (1880) exploited anti-Mormon prejudices by casting the Latter-Day Saints in the roles of villains, and Harte's "Three Vagabonds of Trinidad" (1900) criticized imperialism and American empire-building after the Spanish–American War. Adolph Bandelier's *The Delight Makers* (1890) takes the genre of historical romance to an extreme; it might be best described as an anthropological fantasy set in prehistoric New Mexico. The son of forty-niners, the Harvard philosopher Josiah Royce recast the land dispute between the Southern Pacific Railroad and California ranchers near Fresno in his romance *The Feud of Oakfield Creek* (1887). Initially subscribing to the conventions of sentimental romance, S. Alice Callahan's *Wynema* (1891) segues into a thinly disguised condemnation of the murder of Sitting Bull and the massacre at Wounded Knee. Other writers depicted the West as an agrarian paradise corrupted by the introduction of barbed wire or as a reenactment of the Civil War, with a southerner (a Virginian or a Texan) defeating a Yankee villain and/or marrying a Yankee ingénue (thus affecting a reconciliation of South and North disguised as a union of West and East) or perhaps even "saving the ranch" (by analogy, a southern plantation without chattel slavery).

More than any other pioneer of the genre, the so-called "sagebrush Kipling" Owen Wister transformed the western into a forum for topical commentary. His story "Em'ly" (1893) was an anti-feminist parable, and his "The Game and the Nation" (1900) allegorized the 1894 Pullman strike to condemn the labor leader Eugene V. Debs. Both stories were later folded into his "colonial romance" (p. ix) *The Virginian* (1902), which concludes with an unapologetic defense of Wyoming ranchers in the Johnson County range war against small farmers in 1892. As early as 1895, in his essay "The Evolution of the Cow-Puncher," Wister argued that the cowboy was the modern heir of the Anglo-Saxon knight errant. His lineage stretched "from the tournament at Camelot to the round-up at Abilene" (p. 604) – a point echoed in the novel when the Virginian is called an "unrewarded knight" (p. 74) after rescuing Molly Wood's stagecoach at South Fork Crossing. His obligatory gunfight with Trampas near the close of the novel is nothing less than a modern version of the medieval joust.

In short, the formulaic western was scarcely grounded in reality. Wister pictured the West through the soft lens of nostalgia. In his preface to *The Virginian*, he referred to "the horseman" or "cowpuncher" as "the last romantic figure upon our soil" (p. x). In Wister's West the best women and men could rise as in the earliest days of the Republic. This theme of moral regeneration, often featuring an eastern dude or tenderfoot, was crucial to popular westerns well into the twentieth century. Yet the Virginian never performs physical labor. He never shoes a horse, drives a cow, ropes a steer, brands a bull, or fixes a fence. *The Virginian* is, like a dime novel, a cowboy novel without any cows. Not surprisingly, given its fairy-tale qualities, it was almost immediately translated into German. It passed through fifteen printings in its first eight months, was the bestselling American novel in 1902, and it was adapted to the stage, where it remained popular for a decade. It has remained continuously in print since its first publication and has sold a total of nearly 2 million copies.

Yet Wister understood the method of the realists and as a literary apprentice he aspired to become one. In his early twenties he wrote a novel, now lost, that he submitted to Howells for his opinion. Howells urged Wister to suppress the story because it contained "hard swearing, hard drinking, too much knowledge of good and evil, and a whole fig tree could not cover the Widow Taylor" (Walker 1960: 361–2). Howells was equally troubled, albeit for different reasons, by Wister's later western writings, which smacked of melodrama. He lamented the "blue-fire" sensationalism Wister was "fond of burning" and the "lingering traits of romanticism" in his first collection of western tales, *Red Men and White* (1895). Such contrivances belonged "with the muted music and other devices of the theatre" (Howells 1895). Predictably, Howells did not review *The Virginian*, if he read it. Henry James certainly read it and, lest there be any remaining doubt that the novel fails the test of realism, his reservations should remove them. He objected to the marriage of the hero and the schoolmarm ("nothing would have induced me to unite him to the little Vermont person"). He thought the Virginian should have died in the climactic gunfight with the villain Trampas ("I wouldn't have let him live & be happy; I should have made him perish in his flower & in some splendid somber way"). And he disapproved of the sentimental ending, which finds the Virginian well on his way to fame and fortune (Bode 1954).

In other words, Wister executed a strategic retreat from realism during the course of his career. He certainly subscribed to the tenets of realism in the diary he kept during his trip to Wyoming in 1891. There he describes how a sadistic rancher blinds his horse by gouging out one of its eyes. Wister's growing realization of the abuse, the staccato dialogue, the realistic detail ("red foam running from the bit," "the sinkhole of blood"), and especially the credibility of his own timid response – this well-known version of the story is worthy of Howells (Wister 1958: 109). Two years later, however, when Wister worked this episode into "Balaam and Pedro," his first story to feature the Virginian, he revised it thoroughly. For several reasons, this version is less impressive than Wister's original diary account. The gory details have been omitted and the focus has shifted from the rancher's sadistic cruelty to the Virginian's heroic response to it. Whereas Wister had merely observed the abuse, Wister reimagined the scene so that his hero exacts revenge for it. However, Wister's friend Theodore Roosevelt objected even to the tepid realism of this revision. "I'm perfectly aware," he wrote Wister,

> Your details really weaken the effect of your story, because they distract the attention from the story as a *whole*, to the details of an offensive and shocking *part*. When you come to publishing it in a volume, throw a veil over what Balaam did to Pedro, leave that to the reader's imagination, and you will greatly strengthen your effect. (Walker 1960: 362)

Wister capitulated. In dedicating *The Virginian* to Roosevelt in 1902, he admitted that he had rewritten one page "because you blamed it" (p. v). In the novel, events are obscured behind a scrim. While it is clear that the Virginian punishes the rancher Balaam, what happens to the horse is virtually unintelligible. Wister's inaction in his original journal account is replaced in this final version of the episode with the Virginian's "sledge-hammer blows of justice" (pp. 192–3). That is, Wister mythologized the western hero as a type of avenging angel who metes out justice. As Larzer Ziff concludes, Wister "produced a literature fit for the followers of Theodore Roosevelt, leaving his realism to smoulder in his journals while his fiction spoke of other things" (1966: 225).

This same retreat from realism is evident in the careers of other western writers of the period. In *The Story of a Country Town* (1883), for example, E.W. Howe anticipated Sinclair Lewis' *Main Street* in its satire of a western border village. The premise was so unpromising, however, that Howe was compelled to self-publish his novel, and it was more a critical than a commercial success. He turned to romance in his subsequent tales *The Mystery of the Locks* (1885) and *The Moonlight Boy* (1886). Richard Watson Gilder, the genteel editor of *Century*, similarly insisted on revisions in Harte's late western stories and reminisced that he "always found Harte quite ready to revise any work" to increase its salability ("Symposium on Bret Harte," 1902). Hamlin Garland began his career as a disciple of Howells in such border fiction as *Main-Travelled Roads* (1891) and *Rose of Dutcher's Coolly* (1895), but he too retreated from realism in response to the demands of the literary market. As he gradually shifted the locale of such novels as *The Eagle's Heart* (1900), *Her Mountain Lover* (1901), and *A Captain of the Gray-Horse Troop* (1902) to the Rocky Mountain West, Garland increasingly veered in the direction of romance. Howells expressed his disappointment with Garland's novel *Cavanagh* (1910) in a private letter to the author: he would have liked "more circumstance and detail" in it. "One day," he added, "I hope you will revert to the temper of your first work, and give us a picture of the wild life you know so well on the lines of *Main-Travelled Roads*" (Howells 1928: II.283). But Garland never reversed course. By the end of his career, he was writing nostalgic autobiographies about his adolescence on the middle border.

Satire enabled some writers to contest the representation of the mythological West. Harte's "Muck-a-Muck" (1865), a parody of Cooper's *The Pioneers*, and Mark Twain's *Roughing It* (1872), a parody of such genteel western narratives as Washington Irving's *A Tour of the Prairies* (1835), set the standard. In *Roughing It*, Twain ridiculed Cooper and Emerson Bennett, frontier melodrama, and all those who insisted on viewing the West through the "mellow moonshine of romance" (p. 149). He wrote the book to debunk the mythological West of ruthless outlaws, noble Indians, and hardy pioneers but, as Robert Edson Lee suggests, "the 'facts' in the book turn out to be less interesting than the subjective interpretation of the facts; reality will be supplanted regularly by romance" (1966: 107). Twain's treatment of the West is at best ambivalent – his West, populated by desperados and confidence men, is as terrifying as it is entertaining. Twain fictionalized many of the specific details of his own experiences in Nevada and California. At the start of chapter 52, a documentary essay on mining, Twain pauses to invite the reader to ignore it: "Since I desire, in this chapter, to say an instructive word or two about the silver mines, the reader may take this fair warning and skip, if he chooses" (p. 376). In his review, Howells referred not to its realism but to its "grotesque exaggeration and broad irony" (Howells 1872: 754). Simply put, *Roughing It* is not a realistic account of life in the West but a tall tale designed to challenge eastern readers' assumptions about the region. Twain's famous essay "Fenimore Cooper's Literary Offenses" (1895) ought also to be read in this context – not as a defense of realism *per se* but as a humorous critique of western romance.

Other writers parodied the popular or pulp western mythology of the period. In his epistolary mock-love story "The Lady from Redhorse" (1891) Ambrose Bierce burlesqued the sentimentality of such tales as Harte's "Brown of Calaveras." Even though Stephen Crane was a self-described Howellsian (Crane 1988: I.63), he travestied the dime novel western in "The Blue Hotel" (1898) and "The Bride Comes to Yellow Sky" (1898) rather than founding a realistic countertradition. In Crane's "A Man and Some Others" (1897), a belligerent Texan is killed by a group of Mexicans. Roosevelt was apparently troubled by this plot reversal as much as he had been by the violence in "Balaam and Pedro." As he wrote Crane, "Some day I want you to write another story of the frontiersman and the Mexican Greaser in which the frontiersman shall come out on top; it is more normal that way!" (Crane 1988: I.249). It was more normal at least in the formulaic western of the period.

No one was more aware of the limited compass of western fiction at the turn of the twentieth century than Frank Norris. "I have great faith in the possibilities" of the West as "a field for fiction," Norris wrote in 1899, but not "the fiction of Bret Harte ... for the country has long since outgrown the 'red shirt' period" (1956: 23). He mercilessly parodied Harte's "The Outcasts of Poker Flat" in "The Hero of Tomato Can" (1897). So far as Norris was concerned, Harte with his precious plots, bathetic endings, artificial dialogue, and failures of verisimilitude epitomized everything that was wrong with western fiction. "We distinctly do not want [the red shirt type] to speak of his local habitation as 'these 'ere diggins's,' or to address us as 'pard' or to speak of death as the passing in of checks," he complained (1956: 1176). Only a few months before his death, Norris condemned "the traducing, falsifying dime-novels which have succeeded only in discrediting our one great chance for distinctive American literature," "the wretched 'Deadwood Dicks' and Buffalo Bills of the yellowback" libraries, and writers like Cooper "who lied and tricked and strutted in Pathfinder and Leather-Stocking series" (1956: 1179). Norris parodied Harte's mining stories in the prospecting chapters in *McTeague* and the cartoon violence of dime novels in the barn dance chapters in *The Octopus* (Hug 1991: 221–2; Witschi 2002: 98). But in truth Norris with his melodramatic excesses had more in common with such romanticists as Cooper than with Howells. He equated Howellsian realism with "the drama of a broken teacup." He claimed instead to be a naturalist of the Zola school, arguing that naturalism was "a form of romanticism, not an inner circle of realism." In a naturalistic tale, "terrible things must happen to the characters" (1956: 1166, 1107), such as the sensational murders of Trina and Maria Macapa in *McTeague* and the reenactment of the Mussel Slough massacre in *The Octopus*.

As a writer of western fiction, Frederic Remington, best known for his western paintings and sculpture, was somewhere north of the dime novel and west of Wister. Between 1887 and 1906 Remington published over a hundred stories and articles and two western novels. But he earned only about a third of what Wister was paid for his magazine work. As his biographers remark, "While the editors were romancing the new boy Wister, they were tightening the screws" on Remington (Samuels and Samuels 1982: 196). The reason is simple: in his writings Remington refused to romanticize the American West, especially as it had been represented in literature and even in some of his own paintings and sculptures. The fissure between his visual art and his writing may be explained in terms of differing markets: Remington earned his living as an artist, selling to eastern patrons who expected cowboys to bust broncos and rope calves. Because he did not depend on his pen for a livelihood, however, Remington was free to depict the western more truthfully in his prose than most writers at the time.

Remington's intentions are evident in his novel *John Ermine of the Yellowstone* (1902), a hybrid *tour de force* and a parody of the conventional westerns popular at the time. In the first chapters, Remington rewrites Harte's "The Luck of Roaring Camp." Whereas Tommy Luck is a mixed-blood boy adopted by white miners, John Ermine is a white boy adopted by Indians. In chapters 5 to 12 Remington parodies Cooper's *The Last of the Mohicans*, *The Pathfinder*, and *The Deerslayer* with John Ermine and his mixed-blood companion Wolf-Voice reenacting the roles of Natty Bumppo and Chingachgook; and in chapters 12 to 14 Remington rewrites the sensational western fiction of Mayne Reid, author of *The Boy Hunters* (1852), *Osceola the Seminole* (1858), and *The Scalp Hunters* (1863).

In the final six chapters of *John Ermine*, however, Remington burlesqued *The Virginian*. Both novels were published in 1902, both are set in Wyoming, and both contain a love story. Like Wister's hero, Ermine falls in love with an eastern woman of higher caste. Much as the Virginian rescues Molly Wood from a runaway stagecoach, Ermine saves Katherine Searles' life after her horse steps in a gopher hole and throws her to the ground. She even permits him to kiss her. But here the comparisons end. Wister's white-bre(a)d hero incarnates the conflict between the natural West and the civilized East, resolves it, marries the heroine, and ends his novel a rich rancher. Remington's hero, a white scout raised by Indians, incarnates the conflict between western or native honesty and eastern or white duplicity, fails to resolve it, is spurned by the anti-heroine, and is killed. *The Virginian* is a romantic, optimistic success story than anticipates a prosperous future for the West, *John Ermine* a tale of decline and failure pervaded by a sense of doom. In the end, both Wister's and Remington's heroes prefer death to dishonor. The difference is that John Ermine actually dies after he has been robbed of his self-respect, forced to become an outlaw, and rejected by the woman he loves. In effect, Remington rewrote the final chapters of *The Virginian* in a way Henry James would have approved. In its recognition of the common purposes of conversion and conquest, of the unspoken alliance between the church and the military in the course of empire, *John Ermine* anticipates such unconventional western novels as Willa Cather's *Death Comes for the Archbishop*. Whereas the open-ended conclusion to *The Virginian* invites a sequel Wister never wrote, Remington reached a narrative dead end in *John Ermine*. Rather than contrive a happy ending according to market pressures and the conventions of the formula western, he subverted those conventions.

* * *

So who were the exceptions? Who were the nineteenth-century western American literary realists? They were women writers who demystified the sensational and masculinized West of the mythmakers. Ironically, their brand of realism reversed the gendered distinction earlier in the century between women writers of sentimental fiction (Hawthorne's "d—-d mob of scribbling women") and the "serious" writers who were men (e.g., Hawthorne). In contrast, during the late nineteenth century the romancers who shaped their western tales according to sentimental convention and sought commercial success were mostly men and the "serious" writers were women.

For example, the Mohawk poet and storyteller E. Pauline Johnson (aka Tekahionwake), Howells' distant cousin, repeatedly insisted on the verisimilitude of many of the protest stories collected in *The Moccasin Maker*. Johnson noted their factual accuracy in several parenthetical asides; for example, an incident in "The Envoy Extraordinary" (1909) "actually occurred on an Ontario farm" (p. 137); and "Mother o' the Men" (1909) was "based upon an actual occurrence" (p. 185). In "A Red Girl's Reasoning" (1893), her best-known story, Johnson depicted a failed inter-racial marriage. The young mixed-blood heroine leaves her white husband when he expresses shame that her parents had never married in the church. If her parents' marriage was illegal because they were married only under Indian law, she asserts, then her own marriage is illegal because it was formalized only by white law. Her reasoning is as impeccable as Johnson's indictment of racial hypocrisy.

Unfortunately, Johnson was unable to earn a living as a writer alone. She was often paid no more than 50 cents per hundred words or $4 per newspaper column (Milz 2004: 129), so she resorted to touring across Canada, the US, and England in stage performances, reciting her less realistic stories and sentimental poems to make money. Much as Remington earned most of his fortune by painting and sculpting the mythological West, freeing him to depict the region more realistically in his prose, Johnson romanticized the West in her public performances. She wore a buckskin dress in the first half of a reading, a Victorian gown in the second – both of them theatrical costumes. Her Aboriginal dress was created specifically for these performances, suggesting "that she was not intending to represent some kind of Mohawk or, for that matter, Aboriginal 'authenticity'" but to "suit the liking of her Canadian, English, and American audiences" by portraying "the popular European stereotype of the 'Indian Princess.'" Her Aboriginal costume was inspired, not by authentic Native dress, but by a picture of Minnehaha in an edition of Longfellow's *Hiawatha* (Milz 2004: 131). Whereas she was a realist in at least some of her fiction, that is, she pandered to European stereotypes of Indians in her public appearances.

Though it was virtually unknown until recently, Drude Krog Janson's *A Saloonkeeper's Daughter* (1887) also deserves to be hailed for its realism. Originally serialized in a Norwegian-language magazine in Minneapolis, it was reprinted in Minneapolis in 1889, though it was not translated into English until 2002. The *roman- à-clef* centers on an immigrant woman's gradual assimilation, her search for a vocation, and the obstacles she must overcome, ending as she spurns marriage to a man she does not love to become a Unitarian minister in the West. Like Edna Pontellier in Kate Chopin's *The Awakening* (1899) a decade later, Janson's heroine Astrid Holm is a type of New Woman who exercises the prerogative of sexual selection. "My body belongs to me," she declares, "and no one else has a right to it" (p. 145). Janson's feminism was no doubt fostered by her friendships with such poets and playwrights as Bjørnstjerne Bjørnson, Knut Hansun, and Henrik Ibsen. The translator Gerald Thorson fairly concludes that the novel may be read "as an authentic story of life in Minneapolis in the late nineteenth century" and that, by "drawing on the realistic and naturalistic trends in Europe and in America," Janson "wrote an American novel that anticipates the works of such writers" as Dreiser (Thorson 2002: pp. ix, x). Kristofer Janson, the author's husband, reformer, and a man of letters in his own right, praised the realism of *A Saloonkeeper's Daughter* in his introduction to the first edition (Thorson 1977: 215); Ørm Øverland similarly alludes to Janson's "devotion to realism" (2002: p. xxv); and Fredrik Chr. Brøgger notes that the novel "is clearly devoted to social mimesis, to representing the life of Minneapolis in a faithful and forthright manner" (2005: 136). Janson's novel antedates Dreiser's *Sister Carrie* by a decade and Ole Rölvaag's immigrant fiction by two generations.

The most unjustly neglected western realist, however, was Mary Hallock Foote. As early as 1898, Charles F. Lummis averred that Foote's fiction was "Western in very truth of scene and 'color' and outlook." As recently as 1951, the literary historian Arthur Hobson Quinn commended Foote: she was "more of a realist than either Harte or Clemens in portraying the life of the mining areas. ... In the history of fiction dealing with the Far West she may claim attention as the first realist of the section" (1951: 645–6). Her characters were not cowboys, Indians, or soldiers, the staples of dime novels, but farmers, miners, and engineers. Her West was racially inclusive, peopled with Cornish miners, Chinese manual laborers, and Mexican kitchen workers. Like Remington, she was also a visual artist, but with a difference: in her illustrations she accurately depicted people and topography. Her realism was both literary and pictorial.

A native New Englander who spent most of her adult life in the West, Foote appropriated Harte's signature material and described the actual business of western mining in her first published sketch, "A California Mining Camp" (1878). Howells accepted for publication in the *Atlantic* her story "In Exile" (1881), a realistic account of the relationship between a California miner and an eastern schoolmarm of the type Harte had sentimentalized in "An Idyl of Red Gulch" Foote's first novel, *The Led-Horse Claim* (1883), described industrial mining in detail – Foote's husband was a hydrologist – and in its review the *Atlantic* called it "an entirely probable story as nature would have told it" ("American Fiction by Women," 1883). The novel recounts a legal dispute between two California mining companies, one of them suspected of tunneling under the claim of the other, the companies in turn represented by a pair of star-crossed lovers. Foote had planned to end the novel the way she thought it "would have ended; the young pair would, in the order of things as they were, never have seen each other again." But, as she later allowed, she "could not get that sort of realism into my stories for I was one of the 'protected' women of that time." Her editor Richard Watson Gilder, the same editor who insisted on revisions in Harte's western fiction, "wouldn't hear of that!" She "had to make a happy ending" (Davidson 1942: 123). Even Foote, it seems, was not immune to market pressures, though she resisted them better than most writers.

But she was never commercially successful. Her most recent biographer notes that, while she was paid $150 by *Century* for "A Story of the Dry Season" (1879), Foote earned a total of only $415 from her writing in 1895. The following year she submitted the manuscript of "Diana of the Ditch Camp" to both the *Century* and the *Atlantic*, asking $500 for it, but it was never published. She sold serial rights to her San Francisco novel *The Prodigal* (1900) to the *Atlantic* for $400, but two years later she was unable to sell any serial rights at all to *The Desert and the Sown* (Miller 2002: 69, 157, 184, 207, 212).

Still, 1902 was a watershed year in western American literary history. *The Virginian* and *John Ermine* were both published, Foote published *The Desert and the Sown* as a book, Austin contracted to write *The Land of Little Rain*, and Andy Adams began to write *The Log of a Cowboy*. The events anticipated the flowering of realism, largely dormant in the late nineteenth-century literary climate, in the fiction of Cather, Rölvaag, and D'Arcy McNickle. This countertradition of western writing, while slow to germinate, anticipates the work of the New Western historians who spurn frontier mythology with its nationalistic, ethnocentric, and sexist associations. When writers finally discovered the "real West," when the "real West" finally attracted an audience, western fiction in general began to pose questions – about environmental destruction, mining and water rights, genocidal wars, the plight of immigrant and indigenous peoples, and the role of women – that the western fabulists had blithely ignored.

NOTE

1 I understand how problematic the terms "realism" or "authenticity" may be. How can a mere text *ever* replicate or recreate "reality"? As Nathaniel Lewis notes, "In literary terms the dime novel is every bit as authentic as the historical narrative, and it makes no sense to say that Zane Grey or Louis L'Amour is less – or more – authentic than Willa Cather or Leslie Silko" (2003: 16). I understand the argument, though I disagree with it. The realists of the late nineteenth century, Howells and Henry James foremost among them, believed they were doing something fundamentally different from the work of such romanticists as Hawthorne and Cooper. Donald Pizer offers a pragmatic solution to the problem: "whatever was being produced in fiction during the 1870s and 1880s that was new, interesting, and roughly similar in a number of ways can be designated as *realism*" (1995: 5). To be sure, the distinction between realism and romance is rarely neat and pretty; rather, the terms should be considered opposing endpoints on a continuum.

REFERENCES AND FURTHER READING

American Fiction by Women. (1883). *Atlantic Monthly*, 52 (July), 119.

Austin, Mary. (1902). Jimville: A Bret Harte Town. *Atlantic Monthly*, 90, 690–4.

Austin, Mary. (1932). *Earth Horizon*. New York: Houghton Mifflin.

Blackstone, Sarah J. (1986). *Buckskins, Bullets, and Business: A History of Buffalo Bill's Wild West*. Westport, CT: Greenwood.

Billington, Ray Allen. (1981). *Land of Savagery, Land of Promise: The European Image of the American Frontier in the Nineteenth Century*. New York: Norton.

Bode, Carl. (1954). Henry James and Owen Wister. *American Literature*, 26 (May), 251–3.

Bold, Christine. (1987). *Selling the Wild West: Popular Western Fiction, 1860 to 1960*. Bloomington: Indiana University Press.

Brøgger, Fredrik Chr. (2005). "Good Lord, They're All the Same": Nature and Sexuality in Drude Krog Janson's *A Saloonkeeper's Daughter*. In Asbjørn Grønstad and Lene Johannessen, eds.,

To Become the Self One Is: A Critical Companion to Drude Krog Janson's "A Saloonkeeper's Daughter," pp. 131–43. Oslo: Novus.

Cawelti, John G. (1976). *Adventure, Mystery, and Romance: Formula Stories as Art and Popular Culture*. Chicago: University of Chicago Press.

Crane, Stephen. (1988). *Correspondence of Stephen Crane*, ed. Stanley Wertheim and Paul Sorrentino, 2 vols. New York: Columbia University Press.

Curti, Merle. (1937). Dime Novels and the American Tradition. *Yale Review*, 26 (Summer), 761–78.

Davidson, Levette Jay. (1942). Letters from Authors. *Colorado Magazine*, 19 (July), 122–6.

Deutsch, Otto Erich. (1946). *Schubert: A Documentary Biography*, trans. Eric Blom. London: Dent & Songs.

Dinan, John. (1983). *The Pulp Western*. San Bernardino, CA: Borgo.

Fink, Augusta. (1983). *I-Mary: A Biography of Mary Austin*. Tucson: University of Arizona Press.

Foote, Mary Hallock. (1883). *The Led-Horse Claim*. Boston: Osgood.

Garland, Hamlin. (1893). Literary Emancipation of the West. *Forum*, 16 (Oct.), 156–66.

Harte, Bret. (1990). *Bret Harte's California: Letters to the Springfield Republican and Christian Register 1866–67*, ed. Gary Scharnhorst. Albuquerque: University of New Mexico Press.

Harte, Bret. (2002). *Selected Letters of Bret Harte*, ed. Gary Scharnhorst. Norman: University of Oklahoma Press.

Howells, W.D. (1872). Recent Literature. *Atlantic Monthly*, 29 (June), 754.

Howells, W.D. (1895). Life and Letters. *Harper's Weekly*, Nov. 30, 1133.

Howells, W.D. (1911). *Literary Friends and Acquaintance*. New York: Harper & Bros.

Howells, W.D. (1928). *Life in Letters of William Dean Howells*, ed. Mildred Howells, 2 vols. Garden City: Doubleday, Doran.

Hug, William J. (1991). *McTeague* as Metafiction? Frank Norris's Parodies of Bret Harte and the Dime Novel. *Western American Literature*, 36 (Nov.), 219–28.

Janson, Drude Krog. (2002). *A Saloonkeeper's Daughter* [1887], trans. Gerald Thorson. Baltimore: Johns Hopkins University Press.

Johnson, E. Pauline. (1987). *The Moccasin Maker* [1913]. Tucson: University of Arizona Press.

Jones, Daryl. (1978). *The Dime Novel Western*. Bowling Green: Bowling Green State University Popular Press.

Langlois, Karen S. (1988). Mary Austin and Houghton Mifflin Co.: A Case Study in the Marketing of a Western Writer. *Western American Literature*, 23 (May), 31–42.

Lee, Robert Edson. (1966). *From West to East: Studies in the Literature of the American West*. Urbana: University of Illinois Press.

Lewis, Nathaniel. (2003). *Unsettling the Literary West: Authenticity and Authorship*. Lincoln: University of Nebraska Press.

Lummis, Charles F. (1898). The New League for Literature and the West. *Land of Sunshine*, 8 (April), 208.

Marovitz, Sanford E. (1975). Romance or Realism? Western Periodical Literature: 1893–1902. *Western American Literature*, 10, 45–58.

Miller, Darlis A. (2002). *Mary Hallock Foote: Author-Illustrator of the American West*. Norman: University of Oklahoma Press.

Milz, Sabine. (2004). "Publica(c)tion": E. Pauline Johnson's Publishing Venues and their Contemporary Significance. *Studies in Canadian Literature*, 29, 127–45.

Norris, Frank. (1956). *The Letters of Frank Norris*, ed. Franklin Walker. San Francisco: Book Club of California.

Norris, Frank. (1986). *Novels and Essays*. New York: Library of America.

Øverland, Ørm. (2002). Introduction. In Drude Krog Janson, *A Saloonkeeper's Daughter*, pp. xi–xxxiv. Baltimore: Johns Hopkins University Press.

Payne, Darwin. (1985). *Owen Wister: Chronicler of the West, Gentleman of the East*. Dallas: Southern Methodist University Press.

Pearson, Edmund. (1929). *Dime Novels*. Boston: Little, Brown.

Pizer, Donald. (1995). Introduction. In *The Cambridge Companion to American Realism and Naturalism*, pp. 1–19. New York: Cambridge University Press.

Quinn, Arthur Hobson. (1951). *The Literature of the American People*. New York: Appleton-Century-Crofts.

Remington, Frederic. (2008). *John Ermine of the Yellowstone* [1902]. Lincoln: University of Nebraska Press.

Samuels, Peggy, and Harold Samuels. (1982). *Frederic Remington: A Biography*. Garden City: Doubleday.

Scharnhorst, Gary. (1995). *Bret Harte: A Bibliography*. Lanham, MD: Scarecrow.

Stegner, Wallace. (1961). Introduction. In Bret Harte, *The Outcasts of Poker Flat and Other Tales*, pp. vii–xvi. New York: Signet.

Symposium on Bret Harte. (1902). *Boston Transcript*, May 10, 18.

T[aylor], B[ayard]. (1870). Through to the Pacific. *New York Tribune*, Aug. 5, 2.

Thorson, Gerald. (1977). Tinsel and Dust: Disenchantment in Two Minneapolis Novels from the 1880s. *Minnesota History*, 45 (Summer), 211–22.

Thorson, Gerald. (2002). Translator's Preface. In Drude Krog Janson, *A Saloonkeeper's Daughter*, pp. ix–x. Baltimore: Johns Hopkins University Press.

Timpe, Eugene F. (1965). Bret Harte's German Public. *Jahrbuch für Amerikanstudien*, 10, 215–20.

Twain, Mark. (1996). *Roughing It* [1872]. New York: Oxford University Press.

Walker, Dale. (1960). Wister, Roosevelt, and James: A Note on the Western. *American Quarterly*, 12 (Fall), 358–66.

Warren, Louis S. (2005). *Buffalo Bill's America: William Cody and the Wild West Show*. New York: Knopf.

White, Stewart Edward. (1904). The Saving Grace [1899]. In *Blazed Trail Stories and Stories of the Wild Life*, pp. 191–221. New York: McClure, Phillips.

Wister, Owen. (1895). The Evolution of the Cow-Puncher. *Harper's*, 91 (Sept.), 602–17.

Wister, Owen. (1958). *Owen Wister Out West: His Letters and Journals*. Chicago: University of Chicago Press.

Wister, Owen. (1979). *The Virginian* [1902]. New York: Signet.

Witschi, Nicolas. (2002). *Traces of Gold: California's Natural Resources and the Claim to Realism in Western American Literature*. Tuscaloosa: University of Alabama Press.

Ziff, Larzer. (1966). *The American 1890s*. New York: Viking.

19

The Coyote Nature of Cowboy Poetry

Barbara Barney Nelson

Classic cowboy poetry is a collective tribute to nature. Just a quick list of images, metaphors, and descriptive details from a few collections includes flies, mosquitoes, cedars, hail, fog, haze, stars, moon, breezes, frost, prickly pear, loco weed, rivers, mountains, passes, canyons, meadow lark, linnet, thistles, screwbean, wild roses, hummingbird, snowflakes, aspen, rattlesnakes, yucca, sage, bear, catfish, lizard, bluebird, drouth, coyote, eagle, bunch grasses, owls, red sumachs, spiders, snipe, ticks, grasshoppers, dew, butterflies, piñon, cottonwoods, mockingbirds, crow, bees, wolf, cumulonimbus, mare's tails, bluebonnets, larkspur, nightshade, blue gramma, raccoons, "3,000 head of box elder bugs" (Charles Potts in Dofflemyer 1994: 110), horned toads, tarantulas, centipedes, sand burrs, side-oats, buffalo, elk, blue herons, deer, antelope, skunks – the list goes on and on. Jim Blasingame in his teacher's guide to cowboy poetry summarizes it beautifully: "The poems often express a spiritual connection to the land, a respect for nature, a love of animals, a reverence for the weather, a love of freedom and an admiration for people of integrity" (n.d.: 5). However, he does not elaborate on respect for nature. I will.

Entire poems are often tributes to some aspect of nature that the poet especially revered or that held special symbolic meaning. S. Omar Barker's "The Silent Master" is a tribute to grass, his "Rangeland Smellin'" to the scent of sage brush, "The Clock of the Cowboy" to the North Star, and many more whose titles are self-explanatory: "Cow Country," "Rain on the Range," "Grand Canyon Cowboy," "Cry, Coyote!," "The Norther," and "The Pecos" (1968: 115, 108, 11, 14, 21, 37, 147, 57, 89). Bruce Kiskaddon's poem "Who Told the Biggest" (1924), is a truth-stretching humorous contest over who has seen the worst weather: rain, flood, blizzards, whirlwinds, cyclones, and lightning (Cannon 1987: 120). Larry Chittendon's "Ode to the Norther"

A Companion to the Literature and Culture of the American West, First Edition. Edited by Nicolas S. Witschi.

celebrates weather because it "makes the heart of oak" (Nelson 1989: 22). Badger
Clark wrote about "The Free Wind," "The Coyote," "Southwestern June," "The
Rains," "God of the Open," "The Buffalo Trail," and "The Smoke-Blue Plains" (1915:
109, 107, 125, 144, 169, 176, 192). Even Curley Fletcher (1931), famous as a writer
of very bawdy poetry and "The Strawberry Roan," also wrote "When Desert Flowers
Bloom" (1986: 11, 38). Leon Flick's "Listen to the Sun Go Down" chronicles the
sounds of evening (Cannon 1990: 18). Howard Norskog's "The Salmon River Breaks"
tries to explain the lure of living in harmony with a particular place (Cannon 1990:
78). Frank Mackie's "Sunrise on the Prairie" (1937; in Nelson 1989: 60), Myrt Wallis'
"Rain in the Night," Sharlot Hall's "Wild Morning Glories," (Bennett 2001: 43, 44),
and Doris Bircham's "Morning Prelude" (Dofflemyer 1994: 10) are just a few of many,
many more. No matter what the subject, the opening lines often describe the surroundings, not as a stage or backdrop but as "place," the main character without whose
influence the story could not happen.

I have argued elsewhere that cowboy poetry comes from a written tradition with
a long history of publication, that the working-class cowboy "sifted" these published
poems, and that considering the poetry folklore and the poet an entertainer has
harmed the poetry and the culture. I have also recapped the history of the cowboy
poetry gatherings and my own involvement (Nelson 2006). I have described the
importance of the polyvocal narrative voice in traditional cowboy poetry and
the insights that Native American criticism can give to this voice. I have argued that
old anonymous poems, like "The Zebra Dun," have much to offer as serious American
literature dealing with race, class, and democratic ideals. The use of "tawny grammar,"
rhyme and meter, and place-based imagery are all serious poetic devices, but literary
criticism simply suffers from East/West academic elitism (Nelson 2000b). Edward
Said (1979) has explained how viewing the "other" through a cultural filter distorts
its reality. I have often argued that literature from the American West suffers from a
similar form of "orientalization" (Nelson 2000a: 17). We rural westerners are imagined as primitive, exotic, a dying culture, and in need of watching by more civilized
eyes. We struggle with identity as though the western US had been – or perhaps still
is – a colony of the eastern US. Over a hundred years ago Kakuzo Okakura in *The
Book of Tea* (1906) summed up the same old problem using words a cowboy might
use but with the direction labels of East/West reversed:

> When will the West [read US East or urban] understand, or try to understand, the East
> [read US West or rural]? We Asiatics [rural westerners] are often appalled by the curious
> web of facts and fancies which has been woven concerning us. ... Why not amuse your-
> selves at our expense? Asia [the rural West] returns the compliment. There would be
> further food for merriment if you were to know all that we have imagined and written
> about you. ... Our writers in the past – the wise men who knew – informed us that
> you had bushy tails somewhere hidden in your garments, and often dined off a fricassee
> of newborn babes! Nay, we had something worse against you: we used to think you the
> most impracticable people on the earth, for you were said to preach what you never
> practiced. (2006: 7–8)

Of course we rural westerners would want to be the owners of those bushy tails. Being the owner of a bushy tail is too high a compliment to pay to some city slicker. We could dismiss this East/West or urban/rural stereotyping as harmless humor if our politics and public policies did not rely on this Orientalized view of the western USA.

Perhaps a glimmer of understanding could begin if the chuckwagon were compared to a tea-room. After the stampede or at the end of a long day, when a cowboy asks, "Whichaway's The Wagon?" (Barker 1968: 9), the closest similar experience I have found is the samurai approaching the tea-room where he can finally remove his sword and rest. According to Okakura, "the tea-room is unimpressive in appearance. It is smaller than the smallest of Japanese houses, while the materials used in its construction are intended to give the suggestion of refined poverty" (2006: 56). Anyone who has ever found the wagon silhouetted against the sunset or its lantern a beacon on a dark night would understand the imagery in this poem loved by tea master Rikiu:

> a solitary cottage stands
> in the waning light
> of an autumn eve.
>
> (qtd. in Okakura 2006: 60)

The best of the old camp cooks could also easily be imagined as tea masters, brewing their perfect liquor in those old black coffee pots. Just as much ritual and symbolism is attached, and as Clark illustrates in "The Old Camp Coffee-Pot," it is able to conjure up the environment associated with its use:

> The solemn challenge of the owl
> The wind song on the piney height,
>   The lilt of rain on canvas roofs,
>   The far-off coyote's hungry howl,
>   And all the campsounds of the night.
> They rise – a thousand things like these –
>   From you, old well of memories.
>
> (1915: 186)

Modern readers interested in Eastern thought or religion will dig for meaning in images of snow, cedars, fog, and wild ducks – but rattlesnakes and centipedes simply bring on a chuckle, smirk, or rolled eyes. According to Dana Gioia, "The term 'Cowboy Poetry' still elicits snickers from literati" (2003: 10).

The rural westerner's respect for nature is as deep as Bashō or Robert Frost, and like theirs, the relationship is usually more like a marriage than a romance. Nature is not just a pretty and friendly face. In one poem about spiders, for instance, the cowboy narrator identifies with one and calls it "the cowboy of the grass, who rides the wind" (Stanley Vestal in Nelson 1989: 94). In another, "The Cowboy's Prayer," the cowboy narrator is bitten by a spider and prays for his life (Fletcher in Cannon 1985: 65–8). Mother Nature seldom returns any sentimentality, is more likely to let a pilgrim die of thirst than provide nurturing, and tends – if at all – to "love like a lioness mother" (Clark 1915: 149).

Kiskaddon captures this yin–yang view of nature in "Rain." His cowboy narrator knows that every living thing depends on rain and he knows he should appreciate it. But – he also lives out in it. His boots and bed are wet, his rope stiffens, his slicker leaks, and both he and his horse are humped up with a bad case of the grumpies. So, yes, all people and animals who depend on grass and water "love" rain, but Kiskaddon (1924) understands the paradox:

> He wants feed and water but let me explain,
> A waddy ain't comf'tble out in the rain.
>
> (Cannon 1987: 97)

This love/hate relationship with weather inspires another of Kiskaddon's narrators to dream of that place with no weather. In "The Cowboy's Dream" the narrator soon realizes that heaven is too good to be true and would not be such a great place to live:

> Such a beautiful range he had never seen,
> Great rivers of purest waters flowed
> Though it never rained and it never snowed.
>   . . .
> Them beautiful rivers, it's sad to think
> There ain't no hosses or cows to drink.
> With all this grass a goin' to seed
> And there ain't no critters to eat the feed.
>
> (Cannon 1987: 38)

Eventually, the dreamer prefers the way the earth actually works: rain and snow and hail, then grass and critters. Kiskaddon's dream of heaven ends with the narrator being kicked out of heaven and wishing "they had let him stay," but he admits that "He didn't repent nor he didn't pray" (Cannon 1987: 39). So his "wishing" was probably idle chatter, like wishing he didn't have to get out of bed and saddle up. Although the narrators of almost all cowboy poetry about bad weather consider moving to "heaven" or at least taking a job in town where "they've got a roof above 'em when the thunder starts to crash / ... They hang on till it's over – then there ain't no need to quit" (Barker 1968: 21).

In classic cowboy poetry, nature almost always displays both "good" and "bad" traits. According to Badger Clark, "a poison spring will sparkle. ... And a worthless rock will glitter" (1915: 72). He says even "the yucca flower daintily swaggers; / At her birth from a cluster of daggers" (1915: 150). When conflicts arise, solutions are seldom black or white either. Laurie Wagner Buyer pauses to admire and speak to a beaver with "a half-chewed willow branch between your artistic paws." The beaver is wreaking havoc with Buyer's irrigation system, so she returns later with a gun to shoot it. But her hands tremble as she watches it "swimming circles in rosy light"

(Dofflemyer 1994: 15). In "Challenging the Trail," Kiskaddon's narrator also feels guilty killing a rattlesnake that gives its rattled warning and then lets the cowboy pass safely. According to the Code of the West, the narrator should repay kindness with kindness, but doesn't. He does feel guilty though:

> He's a pizen bad snake but he give you a brake
> If he did make you draw a quick breath.
> It ain't treatin' him square but you cain't leave him there.
> So you git down and chunk him to death.
>
> (1935: 21–2)

Although Jim Green's narrator in "Bounty Hunter" shows no admiration for the killer of two cougars" (Dofflemyer 1994: 34), most classic cowboy poems do not pass judgment. "Who am I" asks Clark in a poem about outlaws in general, "Who am I that I judge your wars, / Deeds that my daintier soul abhors" (1915: 103). Linda Hasselstrom also takes a very non-judgmental view of killing and death, accepting it as part of life:

> A calf born dead yesterday
> Was found by coyotes in the night
> Only the head and one front foot remains.
> The cat preens in a pile of meadowlark feathers.
> A blue jay is eating baby robins.
> The hens caught a mouse in their corn
> This morning; pecked it to shrieking shreds.
>
> It's spring:
> Time to kill the kittens.
>
> (Dofflemyer 1994: 45)

Wallace McRae's "Reincarnation" makes clear that even human death is just part of the miraculous plan. The narrator humorously finds that his dead friend has actually changed very little after he cycles through dust to dust, becoming a flower that a horse grazes, and then ends up dropped on the ground after passing through the horse (Cannon 1985: 185–6), similar to this classic haiku by Kobayashi Issa (1763–1827):

> thud-thud
> upon the flowers
> drops the horse turd
>
> (Bowers 1996: 62)

The manure from those critters who eat grass and flowers is just another link in nature's chain, a necessary ingredient to replenish real soils in order to grow more real plants, and not something to be ashamed of becoming. Or as "Scar-Face on Nature" says, "What's gone with men? We say they pass; / But nature's got to make the grass. ... We cuss the moth that eats the fur / But he is just a-mindin' *her*" (Linderman 1921: 50–1). Mother Nature needs no condescending help and protection. She is not a dysfunctional co-dependant, she can and will take care of herself and her system, with or without humans.

Most surprisingly, I have found no references to hatred for coyotes or wolves in cowboy poetry. I have found, on the other hand, many poems that admire wolves and coyotes for their music, identify with their projected loneliness, or respect their ability to survive in a hostile world. Although the poets readily admit to mixed feelings toward rain, their feelings toward the coyote are always at least sympathetic if not positive, like these lines found in "The Coyote":

> Slinkin', blinkin', cowardly beast, et up with the mange,
> I can't see what good yer do, out here on the Range.
> Sneakin', peekin' everywhere, with yer ribs all showin',
> Lookin' half starved all the time. There's no way of knowin'
> Why the Good Lawd put you here. Still, we git some fun
> When we chase you with our dogs. Glory! How you run!
> Yappin', snappin', there at night, crazy as a loon
> You set wailin' out yer heart, lookin' at the moon.
> Runnin', sunnin', doglike cunnin', that's you every time,
> Yer the wild dog of the Rangeland, an' that ain't no crime.
> I have faced you, 'bout ter shoot you, it was then I'd see
> Yellow eyes packed full of trouble an' I'd let yer be.
>
> (Mackie 1937: 129)

These words were published ten years before Aldo Leopold's similar and much more famous lines on wolf eyes (1970: 138).

The closest to a negative view of the coyote appears in Eric Sprado's contemporary poem "Our Range." A sheepherder narrator is out checking pastures and runs across a three-toed coyote that he had once trapped. The coyote had subsequently become trap-wise and hard to catch. So,

> We'd been at war ever since,
> With a strange mixture of love and hate,
> I'd sworn to put a hole in him
> For every lamb he ate.

However, during this "magical night" they stare each other down, and the narrator decides not to shoot (Cannon 1990: 144–5). Mary Austin in *The Flock* also argues that sheep and predators have shared the same pastures since time began and relates an incident at El Tejon, during the drought of 1876, when 58,000 head of starving sheep were turned loose in December to die. The staggering flocks slowly disappeared into the bear, cougar, and wolf-infested mountains. The next fall, when rains finally replenished lowland meadows, 53,000 head of healthy sheep trailed themselves back down for the winter (1906: 235). In Austin's mind, sheep were never huddled, helpless masses, too stupid to take care of themselves, and according to Austin, shepherds had no quarrel with predators either:

> It is only against man contrivances, such as a wool tariff or a new ruling of the Forestry Bureau, that the herder becomes loquacious. Wildcats, cougars, coyotes, and bears are merely incidents of the day's work, like putting on stiff boots of a cold morning, [or] running out of garlic. (1906: 176)

Bears, she muses, often stroll harmlessly over sleeping shepherds at night or burn their paws trying to rob frying pans (1906: 186). The grizzly disappeared in California in 1922, hundreds of years after the coming of sheep and shepherds.

Fletcher's narrator in "Chuck-Wagon Blues" assumes a tenderfoot's thinking by claiming to be afraid of nature:

> I'm afraid of a hairy triantula,
> And I don't want no broncos to break.
> I don't like howling coyotes;
> I'm scared of a rattlesnake.
>
> (Fletcher 1986: 19)

In a more serious poem, Fletcher's narrator says almost the opposite:

> I am pining for my old desert homeland,
> Where the moon and the stars shine so bright;
> To again smell the sage and the greasewood,
> While the coyotes howl through the night.
>
> (Fletcher 1986: 38)

Coyote sounds and owl sounds are often paired in the traditional poetry:

> The lonesome owl a-callin',
> The mournful coyote, squawllin'.
>
> (Clark 1915: 69)

And, again by Fletcher,

> The soft wind sways the whispering grass,
> The sun sinks low o'er the Western pass;
> As a coyote mingles his dismal howl,
> With the sad, sweet notes of a lone hoot owl.
>
> (1986: 72)

The sounds are still paired in contemporary poetry, like this from a Utah sheep rancher and herder, Vern Mortensen:

> And the haunting notes of a lone coyote whose
> Evening's hunting howl
> Rose wild and clear in the cold blue night,
> And was answered by the hoot of an owl
>
> (Cannon 1985: 152)

The coyote often seems to represent the wild, bushy-tailed cowboy while the owl represents wisdom, so why the pairing if not for a yin–yang view of the world? And does the meaning change when the coyote is paired with other night birds? E.A. Brinninstool (1926) describes the "yappin' and yelpin' of coyotes or the cry of a nocturnal bird" (Nelson 1989: 17) and contemporary poet Ruth Daniels singles out the dove: "The howl of the coyote vies / With the call of the dove" (Dofflemyer 1994: 25).

Why so much fascination with sound or music? We know that bird "song" is often a territorial warning or mating call, but that doesn't seem to explain the coyote. Is it fear? Is it hunger? Is it laughter (Clark 1915: 128, 154)? To humans the coyote often sounds mournful or lonely. Is it misery? Is it poetry? The coyote's song is more than a descriptive detail of the night. Examples of appreciation for the coyote's music are endless in cowboy poetry. "Dudes" want a radio (Johnson in Cannon 1985: 114), but the cowboy prefers to listen to the sounds of the coming night and finds a saloon a "Funny place for music" (Clark 1915: 115). Instead the music of the coyote is preferred in poem after poem. In, "Ridin'," Clark says,

> Who kin envy kings and czars
> When the coyotes down the valley
> Are a-singin' to the stars.
>
> (1915: 40)

And singing in the night was common to both coyote and cowboy. Trail drivers sang to their cattle to keep both themselves and the critters calm, as in Clark's "A Roundup Lullaby":

> Desert blue and silver in the still moon shine,
> Coyote yappin' lazy on the hill
> Sleepy winks of lightnin' down the far sky line,
> Time for millin' cattle to be still.
> So-o, now, the lightnin's far away,
> The coyote's nothin' skeery;
> He's singin' to his dearie –
> Hee-ya, tammalalleday!
> Settle down, you cattle, till the mornin'.
>
> (1915: 68–9)

Perhaps the most beautiful tribute to the coyote's song was penned by Ernest Thompson Seton in "The Coyote's Song." Seton compares the coyote's song to the barking of prairie dogs, howling winds, frogs, crickets, a Jew's harp, organ, fiddle, flute, "a grand cathedral organ," a calliope, a nightingale, "a vast Aeolian harp," a "wild Wagnerian opera," and a "vocalized tornado." He says the coyote is baritone, soprano, bass, and tenor – in short, an unacknowledged "miracle" (1913: 13–14).

In Laurie Wagner Buyer's contemporary "Haiku from the Mountains" the coyote's song has a timelessness equal to water, stone, and starlight:

> Water rush on stone,
> Coyote calling all alone;
> Starlight spills on me.
>
> (Dofflemyer 1994: 19)

The coyote's song is not a simple atmospheric detail, it's metaphoric meaning changes in almost every poem. Sometimes it represents the rural taste in music, beauty, or art. Sometimes it is nature's siren, reminding the cowboy where his home is located. Sometimes it represents material things that working-class cowboy families have given up. Some days, when regrets come creeping, it is easy to identify with a mangy, persecuted beast who lives in a hole and provides only a meager living for its family. A human listener can come down with a bad case of the high lonesomes or self-pity when a dozen coyotes are obviously having a party or a lone coyote calls and nobody answers. If we learn only one admirable trait from coyote, perhaps it should be humility. Linda Hussa admires the coyote's humility and wonders how it can possibly thrive that way

> While we humans trust in heroes,
> Tell our kids to stand up tall,
> Fight for our beliefs.

She wonders if we could learn "a truth we have not guessed" by paying attention to coyotes (Bennett 2001: 114).

On a good day, the coyote represents a happy singer in the face of poverty and persecution. J. Frank Dobie noticed how Mexican cowboys also identified with and were identified with coyotes. He recalls a summer night in south Texas when he and his family listened to some *vaqueros* play their guitars and sing *corridos* with the coyotes:

High-wailing and long-drawn-out, the notes of native *versos* came over the night air. Perhaps they were about Gregorio Cortez on his little brown horse, perhaps about the young vaquero who did not come back with his comrades from the trail to Kansas, perhaps about the mulberry-blue bull with the goring horns. Whatever the theme, the wild notes seemed to go up to the stars. And as they reached their highest pitch, a chorus of coyote voices joined them. When, at the end of the first ballad, the human voices dimmed into silence, the coyote voices grew higher; then all but one howler ceased. We heard a laugh, and one lusty vaquero yelled out, "*Cantad, amigos!*" – "Sing, friends!" The friends responded with renewed gusto. For a time the antiphonies challenged and cheered each other, now converging, now alternately lapsing. The vaquero singing, on high notes especially, could hardly be distinguished from the coyote singing. (1947: 4–5)

Few appreciate what either hired cowboys or rodent- and rabbit-eating coyotes do for us, but on a beautiful moonlit night neither the cowboys nor the coyotes care much – usually.

Clark's beautiful and lyrical tribute, "The Coyote," probably needs to be quoted here in full to appreciate its onomatopoeic qualities:

> Trailing the last gleam after,
>   In the valleys emptied of light,
> Ripples a whimsical laughter
>   Under the wings of the night.
> Mocking the faded west airily,
> Meeting the little bats merrily,
>   Over the mesas it shrills
>   To the red moon on the hills.
>
> Mournfully rising and waning,
>   Far through the moon-silvered land
> Wails a weird voice of complaining
>   Over the thorns and the sand.
> Out of blue silences eerily.
> On to the black mountains wearily,
>   Till the dim desert is crossed,
>   Wanders the cry, and is lost.
>
> Here by the fire's ruddy streamers,
>   Tired with our hopes and our fears,
> We inarticulate dreamers
>   Hark to the song of our years.
> Up to the brooding divinity
> Far in that sparkling infinity
>   Cry our despair and delight
>   Voice of the Western night!

(1915: 107–8)

Not only does the coyote's song seem to tumble through a medley of emotions, but in the final stanza the "inarticulate" narrator seems to be asking the coyote to speak as a mediator to the "brooding divinity." What kind of humility would ask a mangy creature that lives in a burrow and eats rodents to speak to God on behalf of a poet?

In Barker's "Cry, Coyote!" the coyote seems to offer up a prayer but the gods do not seem to be listening any more:

> Cry, coyote! Cry lonely at dawn
> For days of a past unforgotten but gone;
> For buffalo black on the wide, grassy plains,
> In a land still unfettered by civilized chains.
> Cry shrill for a moonrise undimmed by the glare
> Of cities and highways. Who is there to share
> With a slim little wolf all the longing he wails
> From moon-mystic hilltops and shadowy trails?
> Cry, coyote, gray ghost of the rimrock! Your cry
> Still echoes in hearts where old memories lie.
> Cry, coyote! Cry lonely at dawn
> For open-range freedom now vanished and gone!
>
> (1968: 147)

In a more humorous, contemporary vein, Greg Keeler's coyote heads to Washington, DC, to lobby for more wilderness with coyote still speaking futilely on behalf of the poet. Coyote goes with Dog and Pony who lobby for more dog and pony shows. In private, Dog also lobbies for "pooping in public places" and Pony lobbies for "traps to catch coyotes." Dog ends up working for the Bureau of Land Management and Pony for the Department of the Interior. However, like the cowboy,

> Coyote brought up the rear,
> glumly clanking a leg trap
> behind him down
> the capital steps
>
> (Dofflemyer 1994: 65)

I'm not so sure that a real coyote would lobby for "wilderness" in its modern connotation as much as she would be lobbying to protect her scattered rural neighbors who love to hear her sing because she needs them to stick around and raise more lambs, chickens, and watermelon for her breakfast. Vess Quinlan writes,

> I would offer to stay up
> And guard the melon field;
> Grandfather would say
> I was too small for a shotgun.
> I did not care for shooting;
> I wanted to see
> How a coyote opened a watermelon.
>
> (Dofflemyer 1994: 115)

Real coyotes eat everything from tennis shoes to irrigation pipes. Cowboys are not quite that bad, but I have personally had to carefully insert a spoon past a ring of mold to reach the molasses in the bottom of a jar on a ranch worth millions. Of course, it is only worth millions if someone decides to sell it. Keeping it in operation as "wilderness" is a coyote's job. Baxter Black, who sometimes lists his own occupation as coyote (1983: 114) also wrote a poem called "The Coyote" and refers to its yin–yang split personality similar to the one created in Native American coyote stories:

> ... like all of God's creatures around us
> There's always two sides to the tale.
> I think if the coyote were human
> That most of 'em would be in jail.
>
> ...
>
> You can like and dislike the coyote,
> Many ranchers I know do both
> When he trespasses he will get shot at
> But his song in the night brings a toast.
>
> (1983: 56)

While coyotes ate mostly rabbits and rodents, those that did turn sheep-killer would pick off one at a time with a humane throat bite that killed quickly and cleanly. Coyotes seldom bothered cattle except to clean up the afterbirths during calving season. In contrast, a wolf might kill 400 sheep in one night, ripping and maiming and scattering wool for miles – and eat nothing! Their method of killing was to rush in and cripple, slash, then wait for loss of blood to rush again. Sometimes a kill took hours or days. They often ate from a live animal because they liked their meat hot. Horned cows in a herd could usually protect their calves from wolves, but wolves might kill a freshly weaned yearling steer or heifer every night until none remained. On the other hand, they might simply bite off the teats and bag or rip out the soft reproductive areas and let the animal live in agony. Reasons for hating wolves abound. I expected to find some enlightened tolerance in contemporary poetry, but I thought the old traditional poems, written when wolves actually roamed the country, would absolutely condemn the beast of waste and desolation. And yet I found not a single cowboy poem condemning the wolf!

The closest poem to negative is "Doin' her Best" by Kiskaddon that appeared on a 1955 Los Angeles Union Stock Yards calendar:

> This is a story that's often told,
> A cow with a calf a few days old.
> A couple of wolves a workin' 'round,
> The old cow game and standin' her ground.

But rather than being written to condemn wolves, the poem's purpose is to praise the cow. She stands her ground even though she knows how this tale will end. There are no other cattle close by to hear her bawl and come to her rescue, not even a bluff to watch her back, she "must battle it out on the open ground." Kiskaddon ends the poem lamenting that "When they give rewards and hand out praise" the old cow is simply sent to the "butcher's chute." Eventually both cow and calf become meat, if not for the wolves, for the human. Thus the cow should be honored, not ridiculed.

Kiskaddon also wrote the most beautiful tribute to the wolf I've ever found: "The Gray Wolf" (1924). In the 21-stanza poem, after hearing the wolf howl in the night, the cowboy narrator and his rancher companion find a kill, set a trap, and catch the culprit. However, during skinning, Kiskaddon's narrator begins to admire the wolf's – perhaps cowboy-like – physical prowess:

> He had lived in that beautiful coat of hair,
> Unhampered in race or fight;
> Immune to the desert's heat and glare,
> Or the storms on the coldest night.
>
> Useless, at last, were those padded feet –
> With tendons that never tire;
> On the roughest ledge they were sure and fleet –
> They could race over bog and mire.
>
> And the yellow eyes with their evil gleam,
> That could see by night and day;
> And the deep strong chest that had hurled each scream,
> Or driven his deep-toned bay.
>
> And the cruel head so full – so proud –
> That could plan with such fiendish skill;
> I wondered a creature thus endowed,
> Should only be meant for ill.
>
> We stripped the hide from his body lean –
> I marveled at what I saw;
> The wonderful muscles, long and clean,
> And the powerful neck and jaw.
>
> The great jaw teeth that could crush the bone;
> Or hang at their owner's will;
> They were sharp as the edge of a jagged stone –
> And the fangs that could slash and kill.
>
> The shoulder wide, and the mighty limb,
> That could last through the longest race;
> And yet, with all, he was lithe and trim
> A model of strength and grace.

> (1924: n.p.)

The poem ends with a final benediction: "He had used his gifts as their giver meant." This ode to the wolf was published in the original *Rhymes of the Ranges* in 1924, five years before Arthur H. Carhart and Stanley P. Young published *The Last Stand of the Pack* (1929) in which they built their case for funding legendary government trappers like Big Bill Caywood to track down the last of the killer wolves. However, Kiskaddon's tribute to the wolf is not included in Hal Cannon's new edition of *Rhymes of the Ranges* (1987).

Perhaps because of their poverty and working-class status, the cowboy characters seem to see themselves in wolves: the constant travel, hard and dangerous work, and toned muscles, but also the irrational behavior, the cruelty, and the gluttony. The Code of the West that the old poetry tries to explain, like the codes of all world religions, may be perfect but the people are not. I personally know a cowboy's wife who finally shot and killed her abusive husband. I probably know more divorced ranch couples than those whose marriages have lasted, and maybe some have lasted that shouldn't have. I know cowboy alcoholics, liars, cheaters, pot smokers, and thieves. The animals are not perfect either, not even the horse, as this prose passage from Owen Ulph humorously illustrates:

> More nonsense has been written about the horse than has been written about any topic with the possible exception of religion and Shakespeare. ... The truth is that horses exhibit, in an exaggerated form, many of the worst characteristics of people. They are greedy, envious, spiteful, malicious, slothful, superstitious, and stupid. They are con-genital hysterics and each one is, ominously, a prospective homicide. If horses could talk, they would lie! ... A horse can smell fear. If you're scared, he'll be scared. And if you're scared of him, he'll be scared of you ... [yet] most cowhands become attached to some old horse that has served them well. This testifies only to the sentimentality of the hand and not to the nobility of the animal. ... The days his horse hid in the buckbrush when it was needed in a hurry, the days when it broke into the barn and almost foundered itself on stolen oats, or sneaked into the hay corral ... stepped on the reins and snapped them, rolled over with the saddle and busted the tree, got the bit in its teeth and bolted into the swamp carrying the cowhand with it, shook with him until his innards rattled, swept him under a mahogany limb, or caused him contusions on both knees as it plunged between a pair of close-growing quakers, stumbled with him (once in the middle of the creek), jammed him into the fence smashing a leg and a stirrup, ate his chaps, pulled its picket pin and left him stranded at line camp to hoof it to the ranch packing his gear-days which, at the moment, made the cowhand feel like pawing dust, become, with the mellowing of time, occasions for senile chuck-ling. (1981: 42–51)

They sometimes even named their best horse "Old Coyote" (Pecos Higgins in Nelson 1989: 35). Horses are often the dragons or tricksters of cowboy poetry, rep-resenting the day-to-day solvable problems that give life meaning and self-esteem to humans, but wolves are more of a mystery, a problem that can't be solved. In Clark's poem "The Outlaw," the cowboy narrator can tame the wildest horses and steers, but not himself: For a man is a man but he's partly a beast" and "the one lone beast from west to east / That he can't quite tame is himself" (1915: 61). So instead of poems condemning wolves, the poets' characters identified with the prowling and howling wolves:

> We're the fiercest wolves a-prowlin' and it's
> Just our night for howlin'
> When we're ridin' up the rocky trail from town.
>
> (Clark 1915: 40)

Trails into trouble are always downhill and smooth, but the trail back to the cowboy life is always uphill and rocky. Cas Edwards, in a poem called "Bad Guy" (1944), warns,

> I'm a big, wooly wolf
> With a high-lonesome wail.
> I got nine rows of teeth
> And a barbed-wire tail.
> . . .
> I'm a big wooly wolf
> From the Lone Star State;
> . . .
> And it's my night to howl.
>
> (Nelson 1989: 47)

Cowboy characters in the poems howl at the moon for various reasons, but it often seems to be an attempt to conjure courage:

> I'm mean plum ta the marrer, I'm a holy howlin' terror.
> I'm a he-wolf and it's my night fer to howl
>
> (T.J. McCoy [1921] in Cannon 1985: 19)

In a small side-bar entitled "Warrior Songs," Barry Lopez (1978: 116) reproduces a Sioux "wolf traveling song" collected by Francis Densmore that expresses similar courage-building sentiments:

> A wolf
> I considered myself
>
> But the owls are hooting
> And the night
> I fear.

Lopez explains that a "warrior might also call on wolves in song to come out and eat the flesh of his enemies after a battle, or, by comparing himself to a wolf, warn young men of the dangers that faced them." Warrior songs are very similar to the cowboy poems that use wolves to conjure courage. Perhaps both Indians and cowboy poets speculated that wolves howl in order to drum up their own courage to face the hooves and horns of their prey when hunger forces them into action. Indians, cowboys, and wolves all knew first-hand the force of those hooves and horns. However, Lopez sees the cowboy only as the wolf's enemy (Lopez 1978: 152, 196).

I found no female poets who identified with the wolf, although Sue Wallis' narrator calls herself a coyote bitch in heat, warning, "Do not annoy me, tempt me, or toy with me / I have been lonely too long." Her poem attempts to conjure up "regal wolfish lovers / Strong smart and beautiful" who never appear (Dofflemyer 1994: 143). The poets also sometimes anthropomorphize a sad interpretation and project loneliness into the wolf howl:

> I hear the gray wolf far away:
> "Alo-one!" he says, "Alo-one!
>
> (Clark 1915: 163)

Clark also imagines lonely women as wolves on the prowl:

> During a tempting night in town:
> I went and walked in the city way
>   Down a glitterin' canyon street,
> For the thousand lights looked good and gay
>   And they said life there was sweet.
> So the wimmen laughed while night reeled by
>   And the wine ran red and gold,
> But their laugh was the starved wolf's huntin' cry
>   And their eyes were hard and old.
>
> (Clark 1915: 109–10)

The male poets often warn that happiness is not to be found in the bars and cities and perhaps imagine that even lonely women must conjure their courage with a wolf's howl to face the night.

In one of the old and often recited poems, "The Cowboy's Soliloquy" by Allen McCanless, first published in 1885, but according to Cannon "undoubtedly sung and recited long before that" (1985: 1), the wolf is cast as the cowboy's preacher:

> My ceiling the sky, my carpet the grass,
> My music the lowing of herds as they pass;
> My books are the brooks, my sermons the stones,
> My parson's a wolf on a pulpit of bones.

So what do these wild books, wild sermons, and the wild parson say?

> My books teach me constancy ever to prize,
> My sermon's that small things I should not despise;
> And my parson's remarks from his pulpit of bone,
> Is that "the Lord favors those who look out for their own."
>
> (Cannon 1985: 1)

Looking out for their own was sometimes called stealing. However, within the historical ranching culture, the necessities of life (shelter, water, firewood, and food) were often freely provided to strangers or travelers who were welcome to "steal" them. Cowboys and their families ate meat, often from the same herd they risked their lives to protect. And as old jokes between cattlemen attest, sometimes they ate from a neighbor's herd. As Charlie Russell's paintings illustrate, the old trail drivers had a tolerant attitude toward the "toll" required of their herds. An ode to bison by Fletcher, "The Last of the Thundering Herd," could as easily have been written about cattle:

> A few to fall by the wayside,
> The wolf and the Indian's toll.
>
> (Fletcher 1986: 67)

This tolerance could also be a class issue. The working-class cowboy narrator or trail boss, who did not own the cattle, could afford to feel more sympathetic toward the toll, as the same wages would be paid regardless of profit to the owner.

Mary Austin explained, at about the same time the cattle trail drives ended, that shepherds did not consider predators as thieves but simply animals following their own natural behavior patterns. She sprinkles her writing with constant reminders that under the right circumstances we are all not only animals but thieves: "Times when there is moonlight, watery and cold, a long thin howl detaches itself from any throat and welters on the wind" (1906: 93).

Today calling someone a "cowboy" is often quite similar to calling someone a coyote or a wolf. The stereotype usually includes thievery, reckless disregard for others, sexual promiscuity and deviance, laziness, gluttony for both food and property, or at best a dying breed whose culture has ended. Perhaps a study of cowboy poetry, like the serious study cowboy poets have given to wolf and coyote songs and behavior, can help dispel these stereotypes. Dissertations wait to be written on sense of place, rain, wind and breezes, solitude, spirituality, death, silence, and more. SueEllen Campbell says, "Literary critics are likely to dismiss as trivial or misleading those aspects of texts that are easy to see, the obvious meanings, and consider only what is hidden between and beneath the lines" (Glotfelty and Fromm 1996: 127). For most readers or listeners, the big hat and spurs are too easy to see. To begin to understand, we must read between the lines.

Bruce Kiskaddon, probably the most popular of the classic cowboy poets, wrote his poetry while working as a Hollywood elevator boy. He was not impressed by the stars in their big hats and spurs whose names we have long forgotten and whose bags he carried. He wrote his poems for the people who still lived a coyote's life, warning them in almost every poem to avoid the bright lights and selling their souls. In his poem "Between the Lines" (1924), he lists many hardships: "The buck and the bawl, the sickening fall," the "rough and hard" work, the "shivering nights on guard," the storms and stampedes, blizzards, frostbite, and snow blindness; the loneliness of a line camp, listening to wolves howl, dying cattle moaning, calves wailing, drouth, springs failing, worn-out horses and tattered clothes. Yet he gives "warning" that there is "something" he "could not tell." He says these things

> ... never will reach outsiders,
>   Who were raised in the town's confines;
> But they're here for the hard old riders,
>   Who can read them between the lines.
>
> (Cannon 1987: 17–19)

While Kiskaddon unromantically reports the hardships, poverty, and struggles, he knows that during even the worst of times, his rural audience can "read between the lines" of his poetry. Between those lines and between the lines of almost all traditional cowboy poetry is a deep and sincere love for nature – the "whispering voice of the night wind," an approaching storm, even the wolf.

References and Further Reading

Austin, M. (1906). *The Flock*. Boston: Houghton.

Barker, S.O. (1968). *Rawhide Rhymes: Singing Poems of the Old West*. New York: Doubleday.

Bennett, V., ed. (2001). *Cowgirl Poetry: One Hundred Years of Ridin' and Rhymin'*. Salt Lake City: Gibbs-Smith.

Black, B. (1983). *On the Edge of Common Sense: The Best So Far*. Denver: Coyote Cowboy Co.

Blasingame, J. (n.d.). *They Rhymed with their Boots On: A Teacher's Guide to Cowboy Poetry*. Overland Park, KS: The Writing Conference, Inc.

Bowers, F. (1996). *The Classic Tradition of Haiku: An Anthology*. Mineola, NY: Dover.

Cannon, H., ed. (1985). *Cowboy Poetry: A Gathering*. Salt Lake City: Gibbs M. Smith.

Cannon, H., ed. (1987). *Rhymes of the Ranges: A New Collection of the Poems of Bruce Kiskaddon*. Salt Lake City: Gibbs M. Smith.

Cannon, H., ed. (1990). *New Cowboy Poetry: A Contemporary Gathering*. Salt Lake City: Gibbs M. Smith.

Carhart, A.H., and S.P. Young. (1929). *The Last Stand of the Pack*. New York: J.H. Sears.

Clark, B. (1915). *Sun and Saddle Leather*. Boston: The Gorham Press.

Dobie, J.F. (1947). *The Voice of the Coyote*. Lincoln: University of Nebraska Press.

Dofflemyer, J.C., ed. (1994). *Maverick Western Verse*. Salt Lake City: Gibbs Smith.

Fletcher, C. (1986). *Songs of the Sage: The Poetry of Curley Fletcher*, [1931]. Preface by Hal Canon. Salt Lake City: Gibbs M. Smith.

Gioia, D. (2003). Disappearing Ink: Poetry at the End of Print Culture. *The Hudson Review*, 56/1, 21–49.

Glotfelty, C. and H. Fromm, eds. (1996). *The Ecocriticism Reader: Landmarks in Literary Ecology*. Athens: University of Georgia Press.

Kiskaddon, B. (1924). *Rhymes of the Ranges*. Hollywood: Earl Hoya.

Kiskaddon, B. (1935). *Western Poems*, illustrated by Katherine Field. Los Angeles: Western Livestock Journal.

Kiskaddon, B. (1955). Doin' her best. Los Angeles Union Stock Yards calendar (private collection).

Leopold, A. (1970). *A Sand County Almanac: With Essays on Conservation from Round River* [1949]. New York: Ballantine.

Linderman, F. (1921). *Bunch Grass and Blue Joint*. New York: Charles Scribner's Sons.

Lopez, B.H. (1978). *Of Wolves and Men*. New York, Charles Scribner's Sons.

Mackie, F. (1937). *Spur Jingles*. Dallas: Mathis, Van Nort & Co.

Nelson, B., ed. (1989). *Here's to the Vinegarroon! A Collection of Cowboy Poetry*. Alpine, TX: Territorial Printer.

Nelson, B. (2000a). *The Wild and the Domestic: Animal Representation, Ecocriticism, and Western American Literature*. Reno: University of Nevada Press.

Nelson, B. (2000b). "Every educated feller ain't a plumb greenhorn": Cowboy Poetry's Polyvocal Narrator. *Heritage of the Great Plains*, 33/2, 49–64.

Nelson, B. (2006). Dana Gioia Is Wrong about Cowboy Poetry. *Western American Literature*, 40, 404–22.

Okakura, K. (2006). *The Book of Tea* [1906]. Berkeley: Stone Bridge Press.

Said, E.W. (1979). *Orientalism*. New York: Vintage Books.

Seton, E.T. (1913). *Wild Animals at Home*. New York: Grosset & Dunlap.

Smart, B. (1929). Be a Man. Alpine, TX: Archives of the Big Bend, Sul Ross State University (unpublished manuscript).

Ulph, O. (1981). *The Fiddleback: The Lore of the Line Camp*. Salt Lake City: Dream Garden Press.

20
"The Wind Blew Them Away": Folksinging the West, 1880–1930

David Fenimore

In his essay "John Neuhaus: Wobbly Folklorist," Archie Green recounts the radical West Coast scholar's reaction to Joe Glazer's 1954 recording of Utah labor activist Joe Hill's "The Preacher and the Slave," which censored some of Hill's more controversial verses.[1] Neuhaus told Glazer that

> It's all right for a worker who hears a song and forgets part of it to make a change. He can't help it. But you can read and write, and you know how to find sources. Your change is out of order. (Green 2007: 405)

Although published in the 1912 edition of the International Workers of the World (IWW) songbook, Hill's radical anthem, a clever parody of an 1868 gospel song, achieved an instant reputation as a "folk song," and it was reprinted as such in Carl Sandburg's *American Songbag* (1927). Throughout the Depression thousands of people were singing it in some form from memory, and still do today. Is it a folk song? At first glance, no; it is single-authored, not the product of an anonymous folk tradition, and originated in print rather than collective memory. But why should this make a difference? Composed music which moves in and out of oral tradition by way of sheet music, live performance, radio, or recordings – as did most popular music during this period in the American West – can surely be called music of the folk.

The Romantic definition of folk music would confine it to the pure product of a preliterate community, free of outside influences. But folk music can be studied as a multimedia practice taking place at the intersections of vernacular musical culture with technology, commerce, and politics. In the decades bracketing the turn of the twentieth century the first folklorists generated archival collections, songbooks, and commercial recordings which relocated traditional music far beyond its original

A Companion to the Literature and Culture of the American West, First Edition. Edited by Nicolas S. Witschi.
© 2011 Blackwell Publishing Ltd. Published 2011 by Blackwell Publishing Ltd.

cultures and homelands to be taken up as forms for popular music, and exploited as a fresh set of nationalist symbols. By the 1930s folk-derived popular music served as a soundtrack for both left-wing labor activism and cinematic celebrations of western conquest and settlement. At the same time, folklore studies were shifting from an exclusively literary orientation toward contexts, collisions, and collusions of scholarly and performing cultures.

In the latter days of the 1950s and 1960s folk music revival, the distinction was still made between "folk singers" – those who sang the vernacular music of their community and tended to be diffident and unpolished performers, such as Texas bluesman Lightnin' Hopkins and West Virginia coalminer Hazel Dickens – and "singers of folk songs," those musically educated urban recording artists like Joan Baez and Dave Van Ronk who were more at ease before large crowds and even dared – as Woody Guthrie said dismissively of Burl Ives – to learn some of their songs from books (Cray 2004: 191). To respond to this new class of so-called revivalists, the International Folk Music Council defined "folk music" as

> the product of a musical tradition that has evolved through the process of oral transmission … [and also as] music which has originated with an individual composer and has subsequently been absorbed into the unwritten, living tradition of a community. (Herndon 1980: 4)

This 1954 pronouncement echoed and expanded the traditional paradigm of pioneer American folklorists Francis Child, George Lyman Kittredge, and others who privileged orality over print. Although they were eager to convert the songs they collected into written texts, they drew the line at composed music, especially when it took the form of a personal artistic statement. While a ballad by Joan Baez may reference the oral tradition, it is no longer "folk music" by their definition, since the song is no longer anonymous or primarily situated within its culture of origin but fixed in recorded and sheet music form, and subordinated to an authorial identity. But what about composed and recorded songs which millions of people can sing more or less from memory, altering a word or line here and there? What about Joan Baez, who posts her lyrics on a website in a tacit invitation to reproduce them (Baez 2010)? In media-saturated cultures where orality constantly negotiates with textuality (i.e., in most post-Gutenberg cultures), technology makes more porous the boundary between tradition and individual creativity. When a song enters collective memory and drifts free of written or recorded references, as have for example Guthrie's "This Land is Your Land" and Bob Dylan's "Blowin' in the Wind," then it may be called "folk" music.

Folk music of this wider sort may temporarily take the form of broadsides, printed collections, or handwritten copies – or discs or mp3 files – and in recurrent oral incarnations may be experienced more by means of public performance and electronic broadcasting than through private singing among friends and family, a process William McCarthy calls the supplanting of "the shy tradition" by a "gigantic artificial frame" (McCarthy 1994: 29, 4).

Maud Karpeles (Cecil Sharp's "dear companion" on his early twentieth-century Appalachian collecting trips) refuses to reduce the difference between "folk music" and "art music" to a simple distinction between unwritten and written (Karpeles 1968: 9). Because print and other media penetrated every sizeable settlement in the American West, a useful definition of "folk music" must include compositions simple enough to be easily memorized by ear and performed by an untrained singer, resisting commodification by treating the song as collective rather than private property. Such is Joan Baez's apparent intent, and such was Woody Guthrie's when he wrote in one of his typed and mimeographed songbooks that "anybody caught singing these songs without our permission will be a mighty good friend of our'n" (Guthrie 2009). In this artificial folk community, as in a Quaker meeting, differences diminish between lay listeners and a specialized and trained corps of performers. As Michelle Shocked is said to have said, "music is too important to be left to professionals" (Shocked 2009).

Sean Wilentz and Greil Marcus point out that American folk music never really existed in a purely preliterate oral form, but has always been "snarled" among commercial, political, and academic interests. Their collection *The Rose and the Briar* contains essays on the survival, transformation, and significance of nineteenth-century British folk ballads such as "Barbara Allen" and "Pretty Polly," as well as their modern Western descendants: Marty Robbins' "El Paso," Jan and Dean's "Dead Man's Curve," and Bruce Springsteen's "Nebraska." They argue that the ballad became the "major form through which Americans told each other about themselves and the country they inhabited" and that it has "persisted and even proliferated, not simply as a folksy throwback but as a resource for telling new kinds of stories in old ways" (Wilentz and Marcus 2005: 1–2). If this is true about American folk music as a whole, it must be even more the case in the West. Furthermore, as Kathryn Kalinak points out, all song exists at the intersection of music and text, conveying meaning on multiple levels (Kalinak 2007: 3), so it is unrealistic to separate the study of folk songs of any type from the extra-musical forces that shape them.

Like Edward Curtis dressing up his Indians, many early ethnomusicologists deliberately or inadvertently manufactured their subjects, in some cases suggesting repertoire, smoothing perceived rough edges in performances, and tempering microtonal scales to European standards. Shaping the music even further were nationalist and other ideological agendas, sometimes coded in schemes of classification that blurred regional, tribal, or ethnic identities. John A. Lomax and his son Alan lament "an element of sadness in imprisoning a folk song in type" even as they admit to censoring "unprintable" material, composing composite versions of songs by conflating variant verses, and changing words to fit the regular meters they thought would please their educated middle-class readers (Lomax and Lomax 1994: pp. xxxv, 376n).

In the 1930s, since from the traditional folklorist's point of view Anglo-American folk music was presumed to be unmediated by the capitalistic power structure and thus expressive of an internationalist proletariat culture, the Popular Front of the American Communist Party promoted it as authentic working-class art. Played at

meetings and rallies from California to Maine, folk music became increasingly identified with labor, civil rights, anti-war, and other left-wing movements. Many of the
essays appended to the latest edition of the IWW's *Big Red Songbook* (Green et al.
2007) argue along the same lines that all folk music by its very nature encodes a
rhetoric of resistance. On the other hand, several recent books on the music business
demonstrate that the association of folk music with radical politics derives from the
interaction of an expressive counterculture with socially responsible entrepreneurs
working within the industry. These include Richard Carlin's *Worlds of Sound* (2008)
on the history of the Smithsonian Folkways label, William Kenney's *Recorded Music
in American Life* (1999), and Andre Millard's *America on Record* (2005).

In fact, folk music can as just as easily come to signify imperialism. John Lomax
published the first edition of his cowboy song anthology and D.W. Griffith began
shooting western films in Hollywood the same year that Zane Grey published his first
western romance, *Heritage of the Desert* (1910). Soon the singing-cowboy B-westerns
and more ambitious works by John Ford and his imitators were using folk music of
southeastern US origins to augment plot and setting with a soundtrack designed to
evoke populist nostalgia. Words weren't necessary; just as a strummed nylon-string
guitar conveyed a tinge of border exoticism, the sound of a banjo or harmonica signaled the leading edge of Anglo hegemony. Concurrently the "country and western"
music of performers such as Jimmie Rodgers and the Sons of the Pioneers restored
lyrics to these folk sonorities for highly stylized compositions that saturated the
markets with radio airplay, 78-rpm recordings, and sheet music. The simplicity and
accessibility of this music achieved what might be called a "mock-oral" sound, com-
mercializing Manifest Destiny as a singalong myth that seemed to be the musical
translation of those Turneresque frontier traits of spontaneity, resourcefulness, simplicity, and orality.

John Ford's soundtrack to *Stagecoach* (1939) is listed in the credits as "based on
American folk songs" and, like that of his earlier films, contains mostly tunes of
southern and minstrel origins, as well as a few sentimental popular songs. Twenty-five
years later, he lost his last battle with the studios to use genuine Cheyenne songs in
Cheyenne Autumn (1964) rather than the wall-to-wall orchestrations of Copland-derived
"western" music which ended up being used for all but a few minutes of the film
(Kalinak 2007: 196). Perhaps by the end of his career Ford came to realize that, if
there ever was "pure" folk music in the American West – uncommodified, exclusively
oral, collectively practiced, and anonymously authored – Indian music would most
closely fit the bill.

Native American Music: Pan-Indian Ethnography and Performance Traditions

Can Native American music be called "folk" music? Like the idea of "wilderness," the
category of "folk music" implies adjacent others – such as art music or popular music

– against which it is defined. Before contact, was Native American musical practice even classifiable? Cherokee ethnomusicologist Marcia Herndon argues that Native American music is "neither primitive nor folk music. Rather … it is an aspect of behavior in human society" (Herndon 1980: 6). Despite the problems of generalizing across the many strands of Native American musical traditions,[2] there are significant convergences with the key Romantic criteria of orality, relative isolation, and what McCarthy calls the "conservative restraints … of audience-performer interaction" (McCarthy 1994: 165). It is not surprising, therefore, that it attracted the first generation of scholars and collectors, meaning that a vaster than usual distance yawned between observer and informant. Not much different from Benjamin Franklin, who described Lenape Indian music as "horrid yellings" (Franklin 1961: 132), European-trained ethnographers, under the influence of Social Darwinism, commonly associated Native American music with an earlier stage of civilization. Besides differing conceptions of rhythm, tonality, and harmony, another great barrier to accurate field recording, transcription, and translation was the role played by most Native musical traditions as a ceremonial tool – as a way to heal the sick, establish leadership, or strengthen the community – and not a secular aesthetic and performer-centered experience. Furthermore, many tribes concealed ceremonies or made them off-limits to outsiders, regarding anthropology as another mode of colonialist appropriation.

Despite these and other obstacles, sound recordings of southwestern Indian music were made as early as 1890 by Jesse Fewkes, using a treadle-operated Edison machine (Frisbie 1977: 11). Fewkes seems to have been one of the few nineteenth-century western commentators who attempted to provide a musicological analysis free of comments disparaging its monotony or cacophony. In the early 1900s ethnographers such as Frances Densmore, Franz Boas, and Elsie Clew Parsons spread far and wide over the West to record Native American music in cultural context, a task made all the more urgent because, as they believed, their research subjects would soon vanish. What was in fact vanishing was not the practitioners or their traditions, but the insularity which had heretofore limited western influences. David McAllester provides the lyrics of a Navajo popular song recorded in the 1920s but based on an older traditional form:

> 'E-ne-ya,
> My younger brother,
> My whiskey, have some! Nanya he, ne-he …
>   Navajo Enemyway Skip Dance Song (McAllester 1992: 60)

New attention is being paid to the many ways that Indian musics have been influenced by European culture since contact, and vice versa. In the 1930s the Pueblo peoples of the Southwest were observed singing medieval Spanish ballads (Espinosa 1985: 83–4). Willard Rhodes (1963) records examples of Plains Indian songs whose lyrics were traditionally sung in English, and work is being done on the synthesis of Christian hymns with Native American and Latino musics in the Southwest, in particular on the resemblances between Protestant hymnody and the Pan-Indian peyote songs sung throughout much of the West (Candelaria 2007: 40; McAllester 1992: 55).

Much of this new work looks at the political ramifications of construction and performance of authenticity through music. In *Indian Blues* (2009) John Troutman explains in detail how Indian boarding schools attempted to suppress traditional Native American musical practices while inadvertently providing contexts for the dissemination, evolution, and commercialization of these very practices, which during the early twentieth century became powerful weapons in the struggles of Native peoples to achieve political rights and restore tribal identities, even as they were calculatedly and often ironically fused with European forms to gain audience and advantage.

In much the same way that earlier ethnomusicologists attempted to wedge the non-Western melodies and rhythms they heard into European musical notation, secondary sources subsequently digesting these field notes and academic papers, such as Alan Velie's *American Indian Literature* (1979) attempted to present Native American songs from a formalist point of view as literary works, and in doing so often edited out key elements such as repetition and vocables ("nonsense syllables"). Lately, more emphasis has been placed on not only complete texts in both original languages and English translation, but also fidelity to the actual texts of specific performances and notation of extra-lyrical details. A good example of a song with its full identity restored is the Wintu puberty dance song recorded in the early 1870s and reprinted by Malcolm Margolin in his collection of California Indian traditions:

> Thou art a girl no more
> Thou art a girl no more
> The chief, the chief
> The chief, the chief,
>> Honors thee
> In the dance, in the dance
> In the long and double line
> Of the dance,
>> Dance, dance
>> Dance, dance
>
>   (Margolin 1993: 22)

At present the collections of early recordings held by various libraries and museums across the country are well indexed, many of the old cylinders and discs having been digitized. A wealth of ethnomusicological recordings is also in print and commercially available; the best guide to these is Richard Keeling's pricey but highly regarded *North American Indian Music: A Guide to Published Sources and Selected Recordings* (1997).

La Música de la Gente Chicana: Corridos y
Canciónes en la Frontera

Spanish conquistadors paid little attention to indigenous North American musical traditions, preferring to train native acolytes to perform Western liturgical music in Californio missions and Mexican cathedrals. Chanticleer's 1998 recording of Ignacio de Jerusalem's *Matins para Nuestra Señora de Guadalupe* (1764) re-creates this enforced cross-cultural exchange. Outside of the urban capitals, a more egalitarian musical synthesis was taking place. The chapter on "Ballads and Folksongs" in John O. West's *Mexican-American Folklore* (1988) is a useful general orientation to Chicano/a folk music, including the *corrido*. During the nineteenth and early twentieth centuries this was the most widespread Chicano folk-song type, a heroic ballad descended from the Andalusian troubadour tradition. The Lomaxes reproduce one such *corrido*, collected in northwestern Mexico at the turn of the century. They call it a *tragedia* and, in line with their literary nationalist agenda, extol its "medieval" character (Lomax and Lomax 1994: 368).

As Américo Paredes has shown in *"With his Pistol in his Hand"* (1958), *corridos* such as "The Ballad of Gregorio Cortez" flourished in the hybrid culture of the border-lands.[3] Traditionally sung by traveling entertainers, the *corrido* has been characterized as a sort of "musical newspaper," a mode of oral transmission devoted to spreading news of sensational and revolutionary events (Wald 2001: 5). Before the advent of radio and recording technology, the most popular *corrido* lyrics were often written down for publication. Considered as a body, they add up to a counter-cultural history of forced adaptation to political and economic conditions. Heroes of the traditional *corrido* were usually outlaws who smuggled tequila, *coyotes* who guided fieldworkers across the Rio Grande, or rebels like Pancho Villa who fought the corrupt central government. Antagonists took the shape of soldiers, policemen, or heartlessly efficient Anglo-American immigration officers as in this 1929 *corrido* recorded by Los Hermanos Bañuelos:

> Los güeros son muy maloras, se valen de la ocasión,
> Y a todos los mexicanos, nos tratan sin compasión ...
> Adiós paisanos queridos, ya nos van a deportar
> Pero no somos bandidos, venimos a camellar.
>
> (The whites are very cruel, they take advantage of the situation,
> And they treat all Mexicans without compassion ...
> Goodbye dear countrymen, now they will deport us,
> But we are not bandits, we come to work.)

(Wald 2001: 157)

Wald points out that the *corrido* form was once thought to have died out, whereas what had really happened was that, by mid-century, it had merged with the accordion-heavy *norteño* musical style, based on waltz rhythms imported by German settlers (Wald 2001: 3). Since the 1970s the wildly popular *narcocorrido*, usually recorded in a Los Angeles studio and performed by gaudily dressed superstars, has glorified *coyotes*, drug smugglers, and cocaine cowboys shooting AK-47s at DEA agents from the tinted windows of their SUVs. When Wald traveled through rural Mexico in the 1990s he "found corridos everywhere" (Wald 2001: 4).

Another popular form is worth noting is the *canción*, a more personal and sentimental expression of lost love, disappointment, and nostalgia. Lyrics usually included an easily memorizable refrain, and once recorded *canciónes* were heard over the Spanish-speaking airwaves, their popularity soared. Although the Lomaxes reprint several without identifying them as such, perhaps the first *canción* heard by Anglo listeners was a popular song in *canción* style, "Al pensar en ti," sung by Elvira Rios in John Ford's 1939 film *Stagecoach*.[4] As Kathryn Kalinak points out, the song in this context signifies a double Other, in that its Spanish words are being sung by an Apache character, for whom the pined-for lover represents both her people and her native land, from whom she is exiled as husband of the Mexican stationmaster:

> Al pensar en ti
> Tierra en que nací
> Que nostalgia siente mi corazón
> En mi soledad
> Siento alivio y consuelo en mi dolor.
>
> (When I think of you
> Land where I was born
> Nostalgia fills my heart
> In my loneliness
> I feel relief and solace for my pain.)
>
> (Kalinak 2007: 73)

The forced servitude of Native American women by Spanish settlers is a frequent subject of the *indita*, a kind of folk song found along the borderland between Mexico and New Mexico. Most *inditas* are captivity narratives, told from a female point of view, and typically are sung in Spanish with rhythmic features akin to those of Native American music (Romero 2002: 65). The *alabado*, a religious folk song of Spanish origin, appears in Helen Hunt Jackson's *Ramona* (1884), as the "sunrise hymn sung in all devout Mexican families" (Jackson 1988: 47) serving in the novel as a recurring metaphor for the plantation-like harmony of the Moreno household. In a painstakingly annotated collection of *alabado* lyrics, Thomas Steele (2005) argues that these folk hymns contributed to the social cohesion of disparate ethnic groups in colonial New Mexico. Keith and Rusty McNeil (2001) have recorded a well-known *alabado*, "El Cantico del Alba," in their collection of California Gold Rush songs.

African American Singing Cowboys:
Westward Wandering Minstrels

Although slave songs and spirituals were among the first folklore to be collected in the United States,[5] it took a lot longer for other African American folk musical forms to interest scholars. Sharp and Karpeles ignored the 15 percent of Appalachian citizens who were black, because they were seeking British ballads.[6] John Lomax wrote in his autobiography that he once set up his machine to record a blues song from an African American informant, but it malfunctioned, and the performance was "'gone with the Texas wind'" (Millard 2005: 245). In *The Music of Black Americans: A History*, Eileen Southern briefly looks westward at the musical culture of the 5,000 black men who worked the big cattle drives, naming in passing prominent black cowboy singers like Nat Love ("Deadwood Dick"), Big Jim Simpson of Wyoming, and Blind Sam, who would have performed in the real-life equivalent of one of David Milch's fictional *Deadwood* saloons (Southern 1997: 226–7). But she reproduces none of their repertoire, probably because no one was recording it.

Not until early in the twentieth century, as more African Americans began emigrating to work in the railroad and other industries, did their folkways attract any attention. In the Southwest, where social contact between blacks and Mexicans was tolerated by whites, the guitar was taken up by African American migrants, thereby finding its way eastward into the folk blues and on to recordings. Jazz, rooted in the orality of blues but demanding a higher degree of musical literacy, came west with barrelhouse and stride pianists from New Orleans and Chicago like Ferdinand "Jelly Roll" Morton, who gravitated to urban and affluent communities to find instruments and regular work. Jelly Roll played San Francisco, Los Angeles, and as far northwest as post-Klondike Alaska (Southern 1997: 326).

One important new area of study is the traveling minstrel show. The influence of minstrelsy on country blues, mountain music, and American popular song is well documented, and there is no reason to doubt that westerners would have been humming Stephen Foster's "Carry Me Back to Old Virginny" and W.C. Handy's "St. Louis Blues," whether read from sheet music, remembered from parlor singalongs back home, or learned by ear from itinerant performers. Minstrel influence is even reflected in one of the earliest western romances, *The Virginian*. Beset by Trampas on one side and the unsympathetic Calvinist missionary Dr. MacBride on the other, Wister's protagonist breaks out in several verses of what current scholarship calls, within protective quotation marks, a "coon song": "Jim Crow / dat what de white folks call him" (Wister 1988: 144). This defensive maneuver serves as a marker of the hero's southern upbringing as well as Wister's own racism, but it also highlights the role that traveling minstrel shows played in importing nineteenth-century popular music into the oral traditions of rural western communities.

The travels of minstrel bands are documented in *Ragged But Right* by Lynn Abbott and Doug Seroff (2007). Along with their earlier work, *Out of Sight* (2003), it suggests the broad and lasting impact that blues, ragtime, and jazz had on folk music across the entire continent. Although the surviving itineraries of groups like Rabbit's Foot Minstrels, the Old Plantation Minstrels, and Silas Green from New Orleans for the most part penetrate no further westward than north Texas and "Indian Territory," there are scattered references to performances in Butte, Montana; San Francisco, California; Virginia City, Nevada; New Mexico; and the Pacific Northwest.[7] Allen's New Orleans Minstrels regularly visited Oklahoma and Texas, where they alternated between uncomfortable stays in white towns and royal receptions in predominantly black ones, and were welcomed by the Native American population. According to a 1913 Oklahoma account quoted in an Indiana newspaper, "Allen's Minstrels were 'among the Chocktaw and Apache Indian tribes, and ... heap big show, heap good music ... is the daily comment of these proud but fast disappearing red men" (Abbott 2007: 211).

Some minstrel performers signed with Wild West shows. W.L. Horne's Minstrels joined Young Buffalo's Wild West Show during the 1911–12 season, and minstrel bands traveled with Kit Carson's Buffalo Ranch Wild West Show well into the twentieth century (Abbott 2007: 362). The noted "professor" (trained musician) and pianist Bismark Ferris traveled with Buffalo Bill's Wild West Show performing a 45-minute segment of ragtime and classical music (Abbott 2007: 184). By 1920 Ferris was living in Los Angeles leading a jazz and blues band made up mostly of his children, the Ferris Family Company. In the second decade of the twentieth century, the J.C. Miles Band and Minstrels played a series of shows with the Cole Brothers Circus in California, Nevada, Utah, Colorado, Wyoming, Idaho, Oregon, Montana, and the Dakotas, settling into winter quarters and, for some of them, a permanent home in Riverside, "only a street car ride from Los Angeles" (Abbott 2007: 181).

The Anglo-Celtic Tradition: Text and Triumphalism

These are the songs that came with the Scottish, Irish, Welsh, and English working classes, privately sung and sometimes performed in a tavern or published as broadsides by enterprising printers. In memory or in print, they traveled westward along the emigrant trail. Of the British ballads that Cecil Sharp and Maud Karpeles found preserved among white Appalachian families, the one most often cited by contemporary western sources is "Barbara Allen." But there were others. The episode of *Deadwood* in which Al Swearingen sings "The Unfortunate Rake" – Americans know its tune as "Streets of Laredo" – is one of the more realistic uses of folk music in the HBO series. Such melodramatic ballads of love and death would be familiar to nearly every western ear. On their patterns were created the cowboy ballads that John A. Lomax began collecting in the first years of the twentieth century. Technically speaking these are a relatively small class of "occupational songs," but like Wister and Grey, Lomax regarded the cowboy as a figure of political as well as literary importance. He had been trained to ascribe authorship to some mysterious and anonymous collective tradition, which for him marked a certain kind of irrevocable authenticity. As Benjamin

Filene points out in *Romancing the Folk*, Lomax, who had studied with Child's disciple George Lyman Kittredge, originally insisted on seeing the songs he collected as extensions of, rather than exceptions or challenges to, his teacher's thesis of British folkways encapsulated in American isolation; he even claimed that the cowboy song tradition descended from British yeomanry (Filene 2000: 32–3).

His son and collaborator Alan Lomax revises this racially exclusive reading of western folk song by pointing out in retrospect that "the best of the singers were the black cowboys, who brought their African and Afro-American heritage of hollers and herding songs to the Texas cattle country" (Lomax 1986: pp. xviii–xix). Filene notes this transference of interest on the Lomaxes' part from the folk songs themselves to the singers, who embodied the folk communities which were less accessible to the white middle-class collectors:

> The supposed purity and simplicity of the music had been what attracted the earliest collectors of roots music … But … the Lomaxes added a new source of authenticity – the performers themselves. Purity now was attributed not just to specific songs (e.g., Child ballads) but to the folk figures who sang them. (Filene 2000: 58)

Despite further attempts at revision, the association of the cowboy with Anglo-Celtic folk music is still strong, able into the 1930s to absorb features of other ethnic musics – the Hawaiian slide guitar, blues harmonies and intonations, the accordion, even the saxophone – while still retaining its identity as a rural western oral tradition of white people working the range.

Gradually, however, the myth of folk authorship in western folk music lost currency. The case of "Home on the Range" can serve as an early example of the relationship of text and oral tradition. It appeared without comment, complete with a piano arrangement by music teacher Mary Gresham, in the first edition of John Lomax's *Cowboy Songs and Other Frontier Ballads* (1910). Twenty-three years later, in his opening acknowledgments to *American Ballads and Folk Songs* (1934), Lomax makes the notorious claim that "Home on the Range" was collected in 1909 "from the Negro proprietor of a low drinking and gambling establishment in the slum district of San Antonio" (Lomax and Lomax 1994: p. xii). However, the song, a nationwide hit in 1933, doesn't appear in the book! A half-million-dollar lawsuit established that it had been composed and published in 1873 by a Kansan named Brewster Higley, and although Lomax had changed some verses around, he faced no legal penalty since it was already in the public domain and he had pulled it from *American Ballads* at the last minute while the lawsuit was still in the courts (Porterfield 1996: 528n66).

In fact, by the middle of the century it was becoming clear that many so-called "traditional" cowboy songs had been re-oralized from textual sources. When in 1959 Harry Jackson recorded a variety of material he had learned while working on a Wyoming ranch, folklorist Kenneth Goldstein assumed that it had all been passed down from earlier generations of cowboys. By the time the second edition of the recording was released he had received numerous letters to the effect that this or that song or ballad was attributable to an individual poet and was somewhere or other in print. He appends to his liner notes an admission that

> a rather considerable portion of cowboy songs reported from traditional sources in the 20th century are the work of known cowboy poets, and ... many of these songs started their way into tradition via poetry books, poetry columns in western publications, early recordings, and cowboy song folios. (Goldstein 2007: n.p.)

In fact, a comparison of the transcribed lyrics on the Jackson recording with Lomax's collection reveals many close correspondences, leading to the not improbable conclusion that Jackson and his fellow cowboys learned at least some of their folk songs from a book.

Yet the Romantic myth of the oral tradition was stubborn. Lomax found the whole question of authenticity so nettlesome he pretty much ignored it; according to his biographer, "he showed little interest in keeping track of sources and origins" (Porterfield 1996: 295). Lecturing on cowboy songs in the late 1920s and early 1930s, he would sing them himself; later he would be accompanied by his son Alan, who stood with him on stage to provide musical examples. When the African American musician Huddie "Leadbelly" Ledbetter toured with them, Alan participated as co-performer, joining Leadbelly onstage and glossing his lyrics with folklorish footnotes. Filene discusses the ways in which Lomax and his son Alan used their relationships with informants like Leadbelly to construct their own scholarly authenticity; for example, although Leadbelly was enraptured by Gene Autry's material, the Lomaxes forbade him to perform cowboy songs in public, and furthermore insisted that he wear his convict clothes onstage (Filene 2000: 59).

Despite these shortcomings, the net result of the Lomaxes' work was what Porterfield called "a wave of folksong preservation around the country" (Porterfield 1996: 295) that eventually filled the Archive of American Folksong at the Library of Congress, much of which is available on Smithsonian Folkways records and other "roots music" labels. In addition to their colleagues and correspondents, the Lomaxes inspired audience members at their lectures to gather material. One such was Mr. Owen Wister, who in 1932 attended a Lomax presentation at Bryn Mawr College and subsequently provided the lyrics and music ("in 6/8 time, andante, dwelling at whim on certain unexpected syllables") for a version of "Get Along Little Dogies" he claimed he had heard in 1893 near Brady City, Texas (Lomax and Lomax 1994: 388–9). In fact, Lomax put as much credence in printed and other secondhand sources such as Wister's transcription as he did in the supposedly more authentic informants he tracked down in the field.[8] For example, he collected a song called "Hell in Texas" in broadside form from a Texas saloon proprietor who "had given away more than 100,000 ... copies" and quoted proudly and at length a letter received from a man who had heard his classmates sing it at the Princeton Club in Pittsburgh (1994: 401, 399).

Of course, Wister's imprimatur was a good excuse for Lomax's taking him at his word regarding the provenance of a song. Richard Carlin quotes Smithsonian executive Ralph Rinzler opining that it was the endorsement of Lomax's project by none other than Teddy Roosevelt, along with having studied with Kittredge at Harvard, that persuaded Moe Asch of Folkways Records to pay attention to his cowboy ballads, because "[y]ou couldn't come from the *lumpenproletariat* and stand up and say that this was important stuff" (Carlin 2008: 254–5). Roosevelt's letter, dated August 28, 1910 from Cheyenne, Wyoming, and reprinted in manuscript form in every edition of *Cowboy Songs and Other Frontier Ballads,* calls it "a work emphatically worth doing" to "preserve permanently this unwritten ballad literature" (Lomax 1986: pp. ix–x).

This same kind of authenticity-by-association embodied in the collector's inform-ants, friends, and endorsements rather than coded in the material, served Woody Guthrie's needs in the mid-1930s as he began developing his performing persona. He would "sing some new songs in the old way" (Cray 2004: 132) by splicing his poetry to traditional melodies, but also by cultivating a working-class Oklahoma accent and appearance well after he had relocated to Los Angeles and later to New York City as a professional entertainer and radio host. Although he "never picked anything but a gee-tar" (Cray 2004: 195n), his continual references to hoboing, hopping freights, and living in shacktowns served as a marketing device for his music. His California listeners, many of them displaced Dust Bowl migrants, preferred his folk-derived compositions to the saccharine cowboy music saturating the Los Angeles airwaves, and his New York audiences heard what they thought was a real western character. Everywhere he played, he reinforced the growing connection of folk music to left-wing politics.

What was heard across the dial on Los Angeles radio in the 1930s we might call the first "country and western," but this familiar term needs clarification. Country music *per se* emerged from the folk tradition in the 1920s, with the appearance of a 78-rpm recording of "The Little Old Log Cabin in the Lane" by a genuine mountain-eer, John William "Fiddlin' John" Carson of Georgia (Haslam et al. 1999: 31). His 1923 success ignited a search throughout the South and old Southwest for what the recording companies started to call "old-timey music." The rush to cash in on Carson's success led to some of the first commercial recordings of cowboy music, such as Carl Sprague's 1925 hit version of "When the Work's All Done This Fall" based on a poem published earlier by Montana cowboy D.J. O'Malley, and Jules "The Singing Cowboy" Allen's 1928 recording of Nathan Howard "Jack" Thorpe's 1898 poem "Little Joe the Wrangler." Many of these early recordings are collected on recent CD anthologies such as *When I Was a Cowboy* (1996).

The talent scouts' most famous find, however, wasn't a cowboy. Jimmie Rodgers, a sharp-dressing railroad worker full of vaudeville tunes, scored the first chart-topping country hit, "Blue Yodel," in 1927 and went on to sell millions of records (Kenney 1999: 155). Literally within weeks, recordings by copycat musicians, who either had a repertoire consisting of folk tunes or whose music, like that of Rodgers, was based on folk forms like the blues, blanketed the airwaves from coast to coast. In Texas, eastern-based, mountain-derived music hybridized with cowboy ballads, Mexican music, and, more importantly, the supercharged western imagery broadcast by the film industry, to give birth to what is now known as country and western music. Rodgers moved to Texas and slapped on a ten-gallon hat and the fanciful duds being modeled onscreen by Tom Mix, Ken Maynard, and other cowboy actors. But few if any country and western recordings drew on authentic cowboy music. It was in the 1930s that the "singing cowboy" became a fixture of western film, via Gene Autry and others, working from a songbook of ersatz "western" songs mostly composed by professional songwriters. Thereafter cowboy music would take a different and more humble trail than the Nashville-bound country and western express.

Songs of the Gold Rush – The Epitome of Mock-Orality

While most of the songs of the Gold Rush were likewise composed and professionally performed and therefore not really "folk music," the better-known ones like "My Darling Clementine," "Days of '49," and "Darcy Farrow" have entered the oral tradition and so qualify to be included, even though northern California after 1848 could exemplify the antithesis of the isolated folk community idealized by traditional folklorists. More than anywhere else in the West, California's original cultures, as well as the first-generation Mexican occupiers, were overrun by an epic mass migration of polyglot cultural influences. In one sense, songs about the Gold Rush could be classified as a narrow occupational subgenre, more specialized even than cowboy songs. But more than any collective identity as "forty-niners," the sorts of songs that would have been sung by gold-seekers would reflect their scattered origins among the eastern and southern United States as well as every continent save Antarctica. They would have remembered scraps of familiar lyrics, stray refrains, and verses from popular songs as well as family and regional oral traditions. Euro-Americans would have taken comfort in sentimental songs invoking home, family, and the Victorian cult of domesticity, and laughed at the racist stereotypes peddled by minstrel shows. With money circulating in the camps and nearby population centers such as Sacramento, San Francisco, and, later, Virginia City, entrepreneurs could afford to hire professional entertainers to fulfill the expressive needs of a transient population. Cowboy music enthusiast Teddy Roosevelt lamented this displacement of what he imagined were the pure western oral traditions, observing that "[u]nder modern conditions ... the native ballad is speedily killed by competition with ... what Owen Wister calls the 'ill-smelling saloon cleverness' of the far less interesting compositions of the music-hall singers" (Lomax 1986: pp. ix–x).

Gold Rush lyrics demonstrate a kind of sophisticated humor that indicates the commercial origins of what was formerly thought to be the spontaneous and collective product of folk communities. Music-hall songwriters achieved a kind of mock-orality grafting their witty and topical lyrics on to familiar melodies, a sort of musical palimpsest. The melodies would be familiar enough, and the lyrics were so catchy that the audience would be singing along after a single hearing. One well-known and much-cited mid-twentieth-century collection of Gold Rush songs emphasized above all this parodic nature of the miners' songs. Dwyer and Lingenfelter list in their introduction the most common popular and folk songs of the day that traveled in the emigrants' baggage and were retooled into vehicles for lyrics satirizing the gold-seekers: "Oh! Susanna," "Camptown Races," Old Dan Tucker," and the like (Dwyer and Lingenfelter 1964: 2–3). Their point that the majority of the songs in their list were minstrel songs, their melodies brought to San Francisco and Sacramento by traveling shows, is reinforced by the more recent work cited elsewhere in this article on this widespread influence of this musical form in the West.

As with other musical folk traditions, the more popular and enduring Gold Rush songs – at least, those whose language and subject matter were suited to the middle-class tastes of the reading public – were reprinted in newspapers and periodicals of the day, and anthologized into published collections. Two of these San Francisco publications, *Put's Original California Songster* (1855) and *Johnson's Original Comic Songs* (1858), are cited by the Lomaxes as original sources for several songs in their anthology. Writing in 1964, Dwyer and Lingenfelter admit that they are "more interested in the method of preservation of the gold rush songs than in the manner of their contemporary presentation" (1964: 5). As well as researching these very modes of presentation, there remains the work of further recontextualizing these songs into the wider culture of their time, and in some cases restoring original lyrics and references to bowdlerized or sanitized songs in these and other collections.

There has been some recent effort, notably by musicians Keith and Rusty McNeil (2001), to highlight the lesser-known Gold Rush-era songs that narrate, or purport to narrate, experiences of Chinese, African American, Mexican, and Indian residents and visitors to the mines. They provide recordings, lyrics, and commentary to songs such as "John Chinaman's Appeal," "El Cantico del Alba," and "La Indita." The first of these, though tainted by stereotyping, narrates a somewhat sympathetic account of the difficulties faced by Chinese miners:

> …
> I went to work in an untouched place
> I'm sure I meant no blame, sir,
> But a white man struck me in the face
> And told me to leave his claim sir.
>
> …
> And then I knew not what to do
> I could not get employ
> The Know Nothings would bid me go –
> 'Twas *tu nah mug ahoy.*
>
> (Dwyer and Lingenfelter 1964: 112)

More authoritative, though postdating the Gold Rush, is Marlon Hom's *Songs of Golden Mountain*, which compiles in bilingual form 220 "Chinatown songs" published in 1911 and 1915, addressing concerns of the region's longtime Chinese American residents. This publication follows in the footsteps of recent translations of "wooden barracks" poems, the spontaneous and improvised verse written on the walls of holding cells on Angel Island, where Chinese immigrants to California were quarantined for various lengths of time before being admitted to the United States.

> Ever since I've arrived in Gold Mountain
> Not one day have I dared forget my family.
> My mind is chaotic, like hemp fibers, with constant thought of home.
>
> (Hom 1987: 72)

Bertsolaritza: The Branches of an Ancient Tree

The Basque immigrants who came to the American West from northern Spain and southwestern France brought with them the practice of *bertsolaritza*. This is a form of Basque popular poetry, often competitive and always practiced with audience participation and feedback, in which a singer improvises short verses (*bertsoak*) fitting into traditional metrical patterns, melodies, and rhyme schemes, and ending with a punch line. The subject matter can be suggested by audience members or by a moderator, collectively chosen by the performing *bertsolari*, or some combination of these. Often there is an improvised oral confrontation between two or more *bertsolari*, challenging each performer's memory, poise under pressure, humor, and creative intensity. It can take place in a bar, at a festival, or even in the Basque-language schoolroom. While nowhere near as popular and widespread – or as urbane and topical – as in the Basque provinces of Europe, *bertsolaritza* has been practiced throughout the American West. As chronicled in Joxe Mallea-Olaetxe's *Shooting from the Lip* (2003), it contains a catalog of issues and events connected with Basque immigration, settlement, and *americanuak* culture, including the influence of western movies.

> Alde askora zabaldua da
> gure Arbola Saindua
> esango nuke hurbildu dala
> gaur Euskadi gehientsua
>
> ([The Branches of] our Holy Oak Tree
> have spread to many places.
> I would say that most of Euskadi [the Basque country]
> is very close to [Wyoming] today.)
>
> Ai, Larrañaga, morroi nahi dezu
> nik hauxe nahi dizut kanta
> ikusten denez zuretzako hau
> da oso lurralde xarmanta
> eta zuk berriz oraintxe hartu
> duzu kauboi baten antza

bi pistol ta rifle aundi bat
besterik ez zaitzu falta.

(Ai, Larrañaga, so you want to be hired out.
I will sing you this verse.
Apparently, you think
that this country is very beautiful.
Well, all of a sudden,
you look like a cowboy to me.
Two pistols and a big rifle,
those are the only things you need.)

(Mallea-Olaexte 2003: 231, 232–3)

Due to its traditionally oral character, the most popular and successful *bertsoak* were not recorded in the Basque country until sometime in the late nineteenth century, and in the relatively more rural American Basque communities the earliest compilations date only from the 1920s. As for the rest, like most musical expressions in any predominantly oral tradition, the Basques say, *haizeak eraman ditu* – the wind blew them away. (Mallea-Olaetxe 2003: 43–4).

NOTES

1 One verse softened in Glazer's recording originally went as follows: "Holy Rollers and jumpers come out / And they holler, and they jump, and they shout: / 'Give your money to Jesus,' they say, / 'He will cure all diseases today.'" (Sandburg 1927: 220).

2 In 1954 ethnomusicologist Bruno Nettl analyzed a half-century's worth of records to classify Native American musical traditions into a number of geographical areas, which in the West were the Great Basin, Eskimo-Northwest Coast, Athabascan (Navajo-Apache), Plains-Pueblo, and California-Yuman areas. In 1969, under pressure from specialists in these various tribal cultures, he later modified this taxonomy and urged that his areas be interpreted resiliently, by resisting overarching hypotheses and paying at least as much attention to the specifics of individual traditions.

3 The Cortéz ballad, based on a 1901 border incident, is still recorded on occasion, and Paredes' account of it was loosely adapted for a 1982 made-for-TV film directed by Robert

Young, starring Edward James Olmos in the title role. "Decian los Americanos / 'Si lo vemos que le haremos / Si le entramos por derecho / muy muy poquitos volveremos.'" ("The Americans said / 'If we see him what shall we do to him? / If we face him head on / Very few will return.'") ("El Corrido de Gregorio Cortéz," *c*.1930).

4 Rios sings to the accompaniment of another character strumming a guitar, a Spanish instrument introduced to the borderlands by Mexican *vaqueros*, and in myth if not in reality replacing the more authentically historical fiddle, banjo, and mouth harp as the instrument of choice for an itinerant field hand or cattle driver. The guitar begins to appear in films from the late 1920s and early 1930s being strummed by very un-Mexican singing cowboys like Ken Maynard and Gene Autry, and is quickly adopted by country and western performers.

5 The first published collection of folk music in North America was *Slave Songs of the United States* (1867). In a preface to the modern

edition, Harold Courlander compares its publication to "our first orbital lunar flight" (n.p.) in its early recognition of what the editors called "Lyra Africana" (Allen 1995: p. xxxvii).

6 Sharp was directed by his desire to rediscover British balladry transplanted and existing somehow intact in a kind of time capsule. He aligned and classified his finds according to Child's system of cataloguing British folk song, and insisted on the "folk origins" of the material. But as Jan Harold Brunvand explains, surviving "native American" ballads (in the sense of having originated in the United States) resemble their British ancestors in structure, tone, and type of subject, but are not necessarily direct descendants, and Sharp would have heard African Americans singing them had he paid attention (Brunvand 1998: 326).

7 The Black Patti Troubadours, a minstrel-type show employing black performers (and, as usual, controlled by white producers) played at the turn of the century for mixed audiences in San Francisco, according to contemporary reviews, a "rapid-fire medley of song, story [and] dance with Negro melody, darky fun, the buck dance, the cake walk, stunning specialties and coon shouts, happily interspersed and climaxed by selections from the standard operas" (Abbot and Seroff 2003: 39). Such a mixture of high and low culture was customary fare for the rougher western, where Schubert lieder and operatic arias by trained singers such as Annie Pindell, the "Black Nightingale," rubbed shoulders with folk songs, racial stereotyping, and crowd-pleasing buffoonery (Southern 1997: 247).

8 At first Lomax solicited his material through advertisements and the US mail from various correspondents and only later, as he acquired equipment and funding, in the field from primary sources.

REFERENCES AND FURTHER READING

Abbot, Lynn, and Doug Seroff. (2003). *Out of Sight: The Rise of African American Popular Music, 1889–1895*. Jackson: University Press of Mississippi.

Abbot, Lynn, and Doug Seroff. (2007). *Ragged But Right: Traveling Minstrel Shows, "Coon Songs," and the Dark Pathway to Blues & Jazz*. Jackson: University Press of Mississippi.

Allen, William Francis, with Charles Pickard Ware and Lucy McKim Garrison. (1995). *Slave Songs of the United States* [1867]. New York: Dover.

Baez, Joan. (2010). Lyrics. http://www.joanbaez.com/lyrics.html, accessed March 28, 2010.

The Ballad of Gregorio Cortez. (1982). Dir. Robert M. Young. 104 min. Embassy Pictures.

Brunvand, Jan Harold. (1998). *The Study of American Folklore: An Introduction*, 4th edn. New York: Norton.

Candelaria, Lorenzo, and Daniel Kingman. (2007). *American Music: A Panorama*, 3rd, concise, edn. Belmont, CA: Thompson Schirmer.

Carlin, Richard. (2008). *Worlds of Sound: The Story of Smithsonian Folkways*. New York: Smithsonian Books.

Chanticleer. (1998). *Matins for the Virgin of Guadalupe*. CD. Teldec D123165.

Cray, Ed. (2004). *Ramblin' Man: The Life and Times of Woody Guthrie*. New York: Norton.

Dwyer, Richard A., and Richard E. Lingenfelter. (1964). *The Songs of the Gold Rush*. Berkeley: University of California Press.

Espinosa, Aurelio M. (1985). *The Folklore of Spain in the American Southwest*. Norman: University of Oklahoma Press.

Filene, Benjamin. (2000). *Romancing the Folk: Public Memory and American Roots Music*. Chapel Hill: University of North Carolina Press.

Franklin, Benjamin. (1961). *Benjamin Franklin: The Autobiography and other Writings*. New York: Signet.

Frisbie, Charlotte J. (1977). *Music and Dance Reszearch of Southwestern United States Indians*. Detroit Studies in Musical Research 36. Detroit: Information Coordinators.

Goldstein, Kenneth S. (2007). Liner notes and annotations to Harry Jackson, *The Cowboy: His Songs, Ballads, and Brag Talk* [1959]. CD. Smithsonian Folkways. FH 5723.

Green, Archie, and David Roediger, Franklin Rosemont, and Salvatore Salerno, eds. (2007). *The Big Red Songbook*. Chicago: Charles H. Kerr.

Guthrie, Woody. (2009). *Bound for Glory: The Life and Times of Woody Guthrie.* Museum of Musical Instruments (online exhibit). zhttp://www.themomi.org/museum/Guthrie/index_800.html, accessed Sept. 4, 2009.

Haslam, Gerald, with Alexandra Haslam Russell and Richard Chon. (1999). *Workin' Man Blues: Country Music in California.* Berkeley, CA: Heyday Books.

Herndon, Marcia. (1980). *Native American Music.* Norwood, PA: Norwood Editions.

Hom, Marlon K. (1987). *Songs of Gold Mountain* [Jinshan ge ji]: *Cantonese Rhymes from San Francisco Chinatown.* Berkeley: University of California Press.

Jackson, Helen Hunt. (1988). *Ramona: A Story* [1884]. New York: Signet.

Kalinak, Kathryn. (2007). *How the West Was Sung: Music in the Westerns of John Ford.* Berkeley: University of California Press.

Karpeles, Maud. (1968). The Distinction Between Folk and Popular Music. *Journal of the International Folk Music Council,* 20, 9–12.

Keeling, Richard. (1997). *North American Indian Music: A Guide to Published Sources and Selected Recordings.* Routledge Music Bibliographies. New York: Routledge.

Kenney, William Howland. (1999). *Recorded Music in American Life: The Phonograph and Popular Memory, 1890–1945.* New York: Oxford University Press.

Lomax, John A. (1986). *Cowboy Songs and Other Frontier Ballads* [1910], introd. Alan Lomax. New York: Macmillan.

Lomax, John A. and Alan Lomax. (1994). *American Ballads and Folk Songs* [1934]. New York: Dover.

Mallea-Olaetxe, Joxe. (2003). *Shooting from the Lip:* Bertsolariak Ipar Amerikan, *Improvised Basque Verse-Singing.* Reno, NV: North American Basque Organization.

Margolin, Malcolm, ed. (1993). *The Way We Lived: California Indian Stories, Songs, & Reminiscences,* rev. edn. Berkeley: Heyday Books.

McAllester, David P. (1992). North America/ Native America. In Jeff Todd Titon, ed., *Worlds of Music: An Introduction to the Music of the World's Peoples,* pp. 16–66. New York: Schirmer Books.

McCarthy, William Bernard, ed. (1994). *Jack in Two Worlds.* Chapel Hill: University of North Carolina Press.

McNeil, Keith, and Rusty McNeil. (2001). *California Songs with Historical Narration,* vol. 1: *Nineteenth Century.* CD with songbook and notes. WEM Records.

Millard, Andre. (2005). *America on Record: A History of Recorded Sound,* 2nd edn. New York: Cambridge University Press.

Nettl, Bruno. (1954). *North American Indian Musical Styles.* Memoirs of the American Folklore Society 45. Philadephia.

Nettl, Bruno. (1969). Musical Areas Reconsidered: A Critique of North American Indian Research. In *Essays in Musicology in Honor of Dragan Plamenac on his 70th Birthday,* pp. 181–9. Pittsburgh: University of Pittsburgh Press.

Paredes, Americo. (1958). *"With his Pistol in his Hand": A Border Ballad and its Hero.* Austin: University of Texas Press.

Porterfield, Nolan. (1996). *The Last Cavalier: The Life and Times of John A. Lomax, 1867–1948.* Urbana: University of Illinois Press.

Rhodes, Willard. (1963). North American Indian Music in Transition. *Journal of International Folk Music Council,* 15, 9–14.

Robb, John D. (1980). *Hispanic Folk Music of New Mexico and the Southwest: A Self-Portrait of a People.* Norman: University of Oklahoma.

Romero, Brenda. (2002). The Indita Genre of New Mexico: Gender and Cultural Identification. In Norma Elia Cantú and Olga Najera-Ramirez, eds., *Chicana Traditions: Continuity and Change,* pp. 56–80. Urbana: University of Illinois Press.

Sandburg, Carl. (1990). *American Songbag* [1927]. New York: Mariner Books.

Shocked, Michelle. (2009). http://www.michelle-shocked.com/quotes.htm, accessed Sept. 22, 2009.

Southern, Eileen. (1997). *The Music of Black Americans: A History,* 3rd edn. New York: Norton.

Steele, Thomas J., trans. and ed. (2005). *The Alabados of New Mexico.* Albuquerque: University of New Mexico Press.

Troutman, John W. (2009). *Indian Blues: American Indians and the Politics of Music 1879–1934.* Norman: University of Oklahoma Press.

Velie, Alan R. (1979). *American Indian Literature: An Anthology.* Norman: University of Oklahoma Press.

Wald, Elijah. (2001). *Narcocorrido: A Journey into the Music of Drugs, Guns, and Guerrillas.* New York: HarperCollins.

West, John O. (1988). *Mexican-American Folklore.* Little Rock, AR: August House.

When I Was a Cowboy: Early American Songs of the West. (1996). *Classic Recordings of the 1920's and 30's*, vols. 1 and 2. CD. Yazoo 2022–2023.

Wilentz, Sean, and Greil Marcus, eds. (2005). *The Rose and the Briar: Death, Love and Liberty in the American Ballad.* New York: Norton

Wister, Owen. (1998). *The Virginian: A Horseman of the Plains* [1902]. New York: Oxford University Press.

21
Autobiography

Gioia Woods

Autobiography may seem like the product of an individual's act. It may seem like the evocation of a unitary self, a call to one's memories to pour unimpeded onto the page. The act of self-representation may appear to be a match-making rhetorical process of lining up the dots between the author's name and the first-person pronoun, the "I" he or she purports to be. But nearly half a century of autobiographical criticism has revealed the rich and deceptive complexity of the autobiographical act. We now understand autobiography, or life narrative, to be itself a discursive process, linguistically mediated, capturing more of the self-in-construction than the self already constructed. Autobiography is an act that recapitulates dominant narratives and writes marginalized lives into the historical record. Autobiography lies and brags, makes and deconstructs, normalizes and resists.

Because the genre makes history and conveys cultural information, it is a productive site from which to examine the American West. Western American autobiography composed in and against this region is peculiar because it reveals the complex relationship between the figurative and material conditions of the "frontier," opening up categories like subjectivity, regionalism, history, and colonialism. The American West is shaped by exploration, colonization, and border crossings, as well as by myth, ideology, and desire. Any autobiographical act performed within this geography is a complex tapestry woven in and against shifting understandings of the region itself. An autobiographical subject, in other words, will claim or resist the narrative of western normative identities. Does the life writer, for example, claim the narrative of the cowboy, the colonizer, or the individualist hero? Or does the life writer speak from the border, the road, or the margins? Furthermore, the American West is a region

A Companion to the Literature and Culture of the American West, First Edition. Edited by Nicolas S. Witschi.
© 2011 Blackwell Publishing Ltd. Published 2011 by Blackwell Publishing Ltd.

noted for its ethnic and cultural diversity, migration history, and environmental resources and beauty. How does the life writer negotiate these legacies, these cultural expectations? Surveying the richness of western American autobiography reveals the shifting borders of "region" and "self."

The stories we tell about ourselves in the West often embed nationalist narratives of American exceptionalism and individualism. The formidable scholar of American autobiography James Olney admits that the genre too easily lends itself to nationalist discourse. The French claim that, through Rousseau, autobiography is a French genre; the Germans offer Goethe as proof of the Germanic character of autobiography. Americans, too, claim autobiography as a quintessentially American phenomenon, with Benjamin Franklin as its leading practitioner (Olney 1991: 377). "Autobiography," Jay Parini writes, "could easily be called the essential American genre, a form of writing closely allied to our national self-consciousness" (1999: 11). American identity, Parini explains, is often conflated with the notion of radical equality and individualism; autobiography is the representative genre in a society devoted (in principle) to democracy, in which the individual is valued and representative of a larger body politic. Given the colonial history of the American West, however, how can we claim autobiography as a representative genre? What of those for whom the promise of equality proved empty? Perhaps for those life writers, autobiography is even more the quintessential genre: nowhere in western American literature is the potential to reframe the self, to interrogate dominant knowledges, and to speak from a place of resistance more powerful. The genre serves many voices, and each voice contributes to the meaning of western American identity.

Likewise, nowhere in American national experience is radical individualism and resistance more richly embodied than in the myth and creation of the American West. The west, the story goes, is metonymic of *the* national narrative. But the conflation of region and genre can only get us so far. Frieda Knobloch and others argue that the way we imagine "West" has been bound up in national nostalgia. Such a desire for a pre-modern Platonic space in which social relations are conducted with cowboy diplomacy and the plundering of environmental resources is assumed to be a manifest right sometimes leads scholars to ask the wrong questions. How true to the region, to the dominant narrative, to the author's own biography, is a text? What can it reveal about the "authentic" West? Or the "true" self? These questions produce answers that essentialize both region and subject, deny their complexity, and freeze them in a nostalgic frame of reference. It is no wonder scholars of autobiography have recently argued against these limiting lines of inquiry.

If reading western American autobiography does not provide an experience with the "authentic" West, or the "true" self, it can offer glimpses into how subjects *deploy* authenticity and truth. Instead of asking if life writing reflects an "authentic" West, consider interrogating authenticity itself: Who does authenticity serve, how, and why? When and how has it become productive (politically and otherwise) to resist what is commonly understood as the "authentic" West? How are western American selves constructed and expressed within the pressures of colonization, gender discrimination, racial and ethnic oppression, classist assumptions, and the politics of immigration? Recently, readers and critics of life writing have been urged to imagine an autobiographical self that is not frozen but fluid, a self constructed in relation to multiple factors. Instead of asking if a self is true, a more productive line of inquiry may go something like this: Why would a life writer rely on tropes of truth in constructing a subject? How do western selves wrestle with ideological assumptions embodied in the myths of Manifest Destiny and the "frontier"? How does the autobiographer authorize his or her project? How is identity "performed" in and against socially inscribed norms? How do autobiography's constituent parts – memory, experience, identity, embodiment, and agency – combine to make meaning (Smith and Watson 2001: 15–16)? And, most significantly, what is western about western American autobiography?

Each life narrative answers the former questions differently; it is the latter question that unites autobiographical practice in the West. Although much American literature is characterized by a sense of place, western American literature, and life writing in particular, is marked by a preoccupation with place and the resultant identity issues related to place: rootedness and diaspora, anxiety and nostalgia, migration and nomadism. Clearly, place in western American life writing is not just setting. Often place is a problem to be solved, an entrance to contemplative reflection or a motivation to political action. Just as the experience of living in our body shapes perception, self-understanding, and self-expression, living in places shapes our private and social identities. As autobiography scholar Paul John Eakin explains, identity is relational, continuously shaped in relation to others and to our environment. The story we tell about ourselves is likewise shaped in relation to our environment. "The events of one's life take place, *take place*," insists N. Scott Momaday in *The Names*; "they have meaning in relation to the things around them" (p. 142). Place is not just physical geography, either. "Life narrators," explain Sidonie Smith and Julia Watson, "anchor their narratives in their own temporal, geographical, and cultural milieu" (2001: 9). In other words, life narratives refer discursively to *place*, to the "ground" of lived experience, "even if that ground is comprised in part of cultural myths, dreams, fantasies, and subjective memories" (2001: 9). Of course, as feminist geographers and scholars of the postwest have shown, "western place" is not a stable category, but a zone of shifting boundaries, conflicting desires, and various histories. The western life writer constructs a self that is *subject* to this place; western American identity emerges within physical locations, rhetorical locations, and political locations. Foregrounding the "location" of the West, in fact, may be what is most "western" about western autobiography (Boardman and Woods 2004: 17).

The earliest autobiographical acts in the West pre-date nation and region. Indigenous people west of the Mississippi certainly engaged in self-expression and self-construction; they certainly made meaning about their lives, their communities, and their "western" homes. Arnold Krupat reminds readers of autobiography that these earliest life narratives are beyond our reach because they presented themselves exclusively as oral performances, not as textual objects (1985: 3). These pre-contact autobiographies, according to Hertha Dawn Wong, might be more accurately termed "communo-bio-oratory" to reflect their action and function (1992: 20). A coup tale, vision quest, and naming practice are examples of communo-bio-oratories that recount the life of an individual within a community. Pictorial calendars and graphic representations of war deeds, seasonal events, or spiritual journeys depicted on clothing or dwellings also function to construct identity. But because these autobiographical acts did not conform to structuralist understandings of the life-writing genre – not only did they lack an orderly chronological account of a life from childhood to old age, but they frequently were not accounts of one individual and almost never written down – many scholars assumed indigenous people did not engage in public self-definition. In his seminal work *Native American Autobiography* (1994), Krupat famously argued that studying Native American autobiography can help us understand that what we take to be "natural" – the self – is actually a cultural convention. These autobiographies, whether pictorial, performed, or written, can likewise challenge readers to explore the historically shifting meaning of the West itself.

The earliest written text in which the writer is "subjected" to western place is probably parts of Álvar Núñez Cabeza de Vaca's *La Relación*, first published in Spain in 1542. *La Relación* is often read as an anthropological, historical, or travel narrative; in it Cabeza de Vaca describes his adventures after being shipwrecked off the coast of Florida and his eventual wanderings through Texas and the Southwest. Through the course of the narrative, Cabeza de Vaca describes his encounters with indigenous people and land, his efforts to find riches and food, his enslavement, his life as a trader, and finally his role as a spiritual healer. Cabeza de Vaca performs these various identities by enacting the social scripts available to him, beginning with conquistador, Christian, and European explorer/agent of imperialism. The distinct social and environmental contacts he describes introduce new scripts, and Cabeza de Vaca situates his changing "I" within these contexts. As Cabeza de Vaca and his crew endure shipwreck, loss, enslavement, and near-famine, his rhetorical location shifts. Several scholars have noted that Cabeza de Vaca is transformed by his decade-long series of encounters. In chapter 34, near the narrative's conclusion, he takes pains to distinguish himself from other conquistadors: "we coveted nothing but instead gave away everything that was given to us and kept none of it, while the sole purpose of the others was to steal everything they found, never giving anything to anybody" (1993: 110).

La Relación is an important reference point for readers of western American autobiography not only for its rich detailed description of southwestern environment and its inhabitants, but the way it makes transparent the very apparatus of the autobiographical act. The narrative begins with an address to the Spanish king in which Cabeza de Vaca promises to recall his adventures in the "strange lands." Note the way Cabeza de Vaca acknowledges how memory and language mediate experience, and how they constitute his narrative:

> I can render only this service: to bring to Your Majesty an account of what I learned and saw in the ten years that I wandered lost and naked through many and very strange

lands, noting the location of lands and provinces and the distances between them as well as the sustenance and animals produced in each, and the diverse customs of the many and very barbarous peoples with whom I came into contact and lived, and all the other particulars which I could observe and know. ... I always took great care and diligence to remember the particulars of everything. (1993: 28)

What Cabeza de Vaca offers the king and his readers is an "account," a rhetorical act that assigns meaning to himself and to his travels. He has wandered and mapped, learned what the land had to offer, encountered the Other and survived, and remembered it all. Here memory is used to authorize his narrative – he assures the king of its veracity by underscoring his "great care and diligence." But memory, a primary feature of autobiography, is not a simple recall of past events; it is a reconstruction of experience by a subject, for a subject. And "experience" itself is fraught with complexity – it is already an interpretation of the past within the context of a culturally specific present. This is not to say that Cabeza de Vaca did not "have" experiences; it is to underscore how, in the autobiographical act, experiences are mediated through available discourses. In this case, the "I" Cabeza de Vaca constructs for the king and his readers exists within the discourse common to travel narratives of the era, that is, "migration, conquest, encounter, and transformation" (Smith and Watson 2001: 90). In surveying trends in western American autobiography, *La Relación* provides readers with an important benchmark. Cabeza de Vaca constructed the West as a region of contact and potential transformation, leaving a rhetorical legacy taken up by many future autobiographers.

Many hundreds of years would pass before formal autobiography would be written in and about the West. Other life-writing genres, however, located the experiences of western migrants, entrepreneurs, and settlers. No study of western American autobiography would be complete without an understanding of how letters, journals, and diaries construct selves as subjects of western places. Even in private or familial self-life writing, westerners (or migrants, soon to be westerners) rely upon the language of contact and transformation to make sense of their experiences. Experience, as pointed out earlier, is mediated through available discourse, and this is no less true in a public/political account like *La Relación* than it is in an emigrant journal written for a personal or limited audience. Western emigrants knew themselves as subjects of a particular kind of physical and emotional experience–months on the trail, inclement weather, fear of unfriendly contact with natives, hope for land, gold, or a better life, and stunning dislocation, repetition, and loneliness. Many historians have shown that the experience of overland migration often challenged the performance of gender roles and familial expectations. Emigration and periodic writing about emigration shaped western identities in a "new" social realm. "Everyone lent a helping hand," writes diarist Catherine Haun, and that "might mean anything from building campfires to washing dishes to fighting Indians" (qtd. in Myers 1980: 43). But it is not just changes in the social realm that interests readers of life writing written on western emigration routes; it is the site of storytelling itself: the land.

A storytelling site, according to Smith and Watson, is a "moment in history," a "space in culture," which "perform(s) cultural work" by deeply influencing autobiographical acts (2001: 56). Diarist Helen Carpenter, en route to California in 1857, takes note of wind, weather, and mosquitoes, geographical features in the landscape, the availability of grass and water, and, like most overland diarists, the abundance of trailside graves. Natural and social markers like these often cause the diarist to reflect on the discomfiting prospect of identity transformation. Carpenter, upon waking the morning of July 3, 1857, realizes that she and her family have made camp on a gravesite. "I have mentioned our growing indifference," she writes, "and can but think that what we are obliged to endure each day is robbing us of all sentiment. It is to be hoped that we will not be permanently changed" (Myers 1980: 127). Sites, or locations, work to "coax" the autobiographer to make certain language choices and argue for a specific identity. On the site of an unknown grave, Carpenter fears the loss of a specific sentimental identity; the very next day, in a "beautiful camp beside the river," she notes her tolerance of life on the road by eating something new and improvised, "for on a trip like this one must not be too particular" (Myers 1980: 127–8).

Periodic life writing differs from formal autobiography in important ways: it is written in the "continuous present" without the benefit of historic hindsight (Culley 1998: 220). Unlike autobiography, generally self-consciously constructed so as to make a narrative arc and to accrue meaning through literary conventions like character, plot, and setting, the diurnal nature of a diary forestalls reflection and critical distance. Noted autobiography scholar Philippe Lejeune called for deep research into the forms of periodic life writing, and many scholars of western American culture have responded by collecting, editing, and analyzing western diaries and journals.

Scores of nineteenth-century travel diaries and journals have been collected and published, and beginning in the mid-twentieth century scholars began situating these life narratives within the context of autobiographical theories. Merrill Mates surveyed over 600 diaries in *The Great Platte River Road* (1969), and other historians used emigrant diaries to revise western American history (Schlissel 1982: 11). Pioneering feminist revision work was done by Lillian Schlissel, in her enormously influential study, *Women's Diaries of the Westward Journey*. The nineteenth-century diary, Schlissel explains, "is something like a family history, a souvenir meant to be shared like a Bible, handed down through generations, to be viewed not as an individual's story but as the history of a family's growth" (1982: 10). In other words, according to Schlissel, these diaries were written for an explicit audience with an explicit purpose; they are rhetorical acts.

In her introduction, Schlissel notes that the overland passage was often an agent of transformation for the men who were largely responsible for the decision to head west. Schlissel makes it clear she is recovering women's texts from an overwhelmingly patriarchal history and thus strives to differentiate identity construction based on gender. By comparison, Schlissel concludes that western migration, heroic for men, was likely "anti-mythic" for women, as they were constrained by the domestic sphere, had more contact with illness and death, and more often suffered from dislocation and homesickness. Schlissel tends to assume that women's diaries bring the reader closer to the "human experience" (1982: 15). Due in large part to Schlissel's study and others like it, a significant scholarly movement began. Interest in western women's diaries helped revise the historical record and the ideological assumptions about frontier heroics and Manifest Destiny by recovering life narratives lost to historical record. No less significant, a vibrant debate over the "place" of diurnal writing has energized western American autobiography studies. What happens to diaries that are not "good" stories? Diaries by unreliable narrators? Diaries that reveal sexual violence? Diaries written and revised at the behest of another, more powerful, public figure? Recent work such as *Baby Doe Tabor: The Madwoman in the Cabin*, by Judy Nolte Temple, *The Extraordinary Work of Ordinary Writing: Annie Ray's Diary*, by Jennifer Sinor, *When Montana and I Were Young: A Frontier Childhood*, by Margaret Bell and edited by Mary Clearman Blew, and *Across the Plains: Sarah Royce's Western Narrative*, edited by Jennifer Dawes Adkison, theoretically situate these questions within a feminist, postwestern framework.

Roughly around the time emigrants were traveling overland, indigenous people in the West began to write and publish in the autobiographical genre. Many Native American autobiographers of the late nineteenth and early twentieth centuries construct selves within the pressures of cultural mediation, and their West is figured as a landscape carved by the physical and rhetorical legacies of conquest and colonization. The following examples of Native American life writers exemplify an autobiographical trend: each relies upon the rhetoric of cultural interpretation, ethnography, and authenticity. These autobiographies are heavily mediated by Anglo editors with assimilist assumptions. Problematic as these texts are, they shed light on the body of western American autobiography and its defining dialectic: the relationship between self and place.

Early notable autobiographies by Native Americans in and about the West include Sarah Winnemucca Hopkins' *Life among the Piutes* (1883), Francis LaFlesche's *The Middle Five: Indian Schoolboys of the Omaha Tribe* (1900), and Charles Eastman's *Indian Boyhood* (1902). Hopkins' text, heavily edited by her white benefactor Mrs. Horace G. Mann, begins rather traditionally, with the subject's birthdate. Instead of continuing along this trajectory by naming her ancestry and depicting her early education, however, Hopkins immediately reveals how her life – and her autobiographical act – is situated within a particular western history, the history of Anglo-Native contact: "I was a very small child when the first white people came into our country" (p. 5). Because she and her people were "disappointed" by the results of that contact, Hopkins turned activist, vowing to fight "for my down-trodden race while life lasts" (p. 5). She positions herself within the legacy of contact, and her West is revealed to be destabilized by that very contact. The territory of the Paiute west, which until the mid-nineteenth century included northeastern California and north-central Nevada, rapidly shrank. Hopkins constructs that West as a place where her people, once visible and defined by its landmarks, were forced to become marginal and invisible: the old women, she writes, lamented, "We shall no longer be a happy people, as we now are;

we shall no longer go here and there as of old; we shall no longer build our big fires as a signal to our friends, for we shall always be afraid of being seen by those bad people" (p. 15). The recovery of land becomes Hopkins' central effort as she works to mediate peace between Anglos and Paiutes. Positioned between whom she terms the "inheritor" and the "invader" (p. 207), she appeals to her white audience to act with her to bring justice to the Paiutes. "If they [Paiutes] could have a place, a bit of land … I would teach them habits of industry" (p. 245). Within this appeal is an attempt to mediate between loss of tradition ("a bit of land") and assimilationist rhetoric ("habits of industry").

Hopkins, like Francis LaFlesche and Charles Eastman after her, constructs an ethnographically styled "Indian authenticity" as a means to convince her white readers of Native people's dignity and worth. She spends pages describing Paiute naming ceremonies, migration patterns, and religious beliefs. Francis LaFlesche's *The Middle Five* adopts a different posture toward the West and the project of self-construction. Although also largely dedicated to ethnographic descriptions of the Omaha people – LaFlesche was himself an accomplished ethnographer who recorded dozens of Omaha songs – LaFlesche's authorial position is one of mediator between the "authentic" past of his people and the modern, post-frontier West: "the object of this book," he begins, "is to reveal the true nature … of the Indian boy" (p. xv). This is best accomplished by "dressing up" that boy in his school clothes (Indian education being a primary tool for assimilation) so that he can accurately present "the companions of my own young days to the children of the race that has become possessed of the land of my fathers" (p. xvi). LaFlesche relies upon binary constructions to demonstrate his own efficacy as a bicultural mediator, and like Hopkins positions himself somewhat between what's "wild" and what's "civilized." White people, for example, may understand his country as a wilderness, but he and his fellows "were familiar with every stream, the contour of every hill" (p. xx). Furthermore, his schoolboy friends are known to him by Anglo names and Omaha names, and "normal" spirituality includes native traditions along with Christianity. He constructs himself as both outsider and insider, thus arguing for a new, "authentic" Indian, one who consents to assimilation. Central to the autobiography is an anecdote in which Indian schoolboys at the Mission School are asked who discovered America; without irony, LaFlesche writes that one boy answered "Columbus," "doing credit to their teacher" (p. 99).

Like *The Middle Five*, Charles Eastman's *Indian Boyhood* was written specifically for a young audience. Eastman's autobiographical construction rests upon a familiar trope, one identifying childhood with "Indian savagery" and adulthood with "Anglo civilization." Like LaFlesche, Eastman deploys the language of authenticity to recall a vanished West, one in which an Indian (boy) occupies an idealized role as the noble savage. "What boy would not be an Indian for a while when he thinks of the freest life in the world?" Eastman begins (p. 3). "This life was mine," Eastman assures his readers, complete with "real" game, "real" hunts, "real" medicine dances, and the "real" opportunity to imitate favorite Sioux heroes. The "authentic" and "true" Indian, within Eastman's construction, becomes a character in a national drama. Native people once "dressed up" like Indians; in the age of allotment, they can just as easily "dress up" like Anglos. The West is a stage on which Indian performance is enacted; chapter names underscore the way Eastman establishes a dramatic, ethnographic setting ("An Indian Boy's Training," "A Legend of Devil's Lake," and "Life in the Wood"), from which an Indian actor changes from youth to adult as the setting changes from wilderness to civilization. In the book's final chapter, Eastman himself moves from the sensual impression of life in the wilderness to the verifiable facts of the civilized world. He learns that whites "measure everything ... divide the day into hours"; he receives his first gun, which remakes him "into a new being – the boy had become a man!" (pp. 242, 244). He moves from his "wild life" to his school life, evoking the legacy of Wild West turned domestic space. Through his autobiography, Eastman constructs a self which identifies with "civilizing" efforts. Furthermore, he suggests that his own experience is a model one: as a boy he learned the ways of the wild, and as an adult he – and others – can learn the ways of civilization. The myth of the West has long been codified as a symbol for a national ideology that valued Manifest Destiny and the colonization of native peoples; these autobiographical examples help us identify how the myth was deployed and how it was resisted.

American modernism has long been associated with the metropolitan East and may seem to have no place in a discussion of western American autobiography. However, the American West left its mark on the modern imagination. Iconic western landscapes feature in art by Georgia O'Keeffe, Jackson Pollock, Ansel Adams, and Marsden Hartley. Western American literature also makes use of the physical and mythical west. Regional literature seemed to fall out of favor during the rise of modernism because it was seen as nostalgic, sentimental, and not sufficiently universal enough to take on contemporary themes. Some "regional" writers, however, managed to employ experimental literary techniques while layering their prose with detailed description and "local color." Modernist artists and writers saw, in the West, a landscape and a people that could be used to engage in formal literary experimentation. Literary modernism certainly extends to autobiographical acts in and against the West, and is nowhere more evident than in Mary Austin's 1932 *Earth Horizon*.

Austin experiments with modernist techniques by narrating her autobiography from the first-, second-, and third-person perspective. Other modern autobiographies play with point of view – *The Education of Henry James*, for instance, or the *Autobiography of Alice B. Toklas*. In doing so, James, Stein, and Austin all underscore a central problem in reading autobiography: the seeming simplicity of the "I." There is, many assume, a "then-I" and a "now-I," the narrating subject and the subject being narrated about. But if identity and memory are understood as discursive phenomena, that "I" becomes a good deal more complex. Smith and Watson describe no fewer than four "I"s in autobiography: the historical "I," the narrating "I," the narrated "I," and the ideological "I" (2001: 59). Early in her autobiography Austin differentiates among the "I"s who participate in constructing her life narrative. "I-Mary" is an outside observer, "solid and satisfying," "associated with the pages of books" (pp. 47, 46).

"Mary-by-herself" is timid, an outcast, and unsure of her place within social convention (Graulich 1991: 379). Austin employs the "you" to beckon, coerce, or recognize I-Mary or Mary-by-herself; at other moments she narrates from a conventional autobiographical point of view: "Mary was, as I have suggested, more than ordinarily intelligent about everything but other people" (p. 220).

Aside from the unusual practice of narrating her story from three points of view (and using these narrators to make meaning about the others), Austin's autobiography is innovative in other ways. Austin was a naturist who saw an abundance of primitive signs and symbols in the West. These signs and symbols, terrain and people alike, were often vehicles through which to explore a very modern preoccupation with the subconscious. She especially uses Native American women as embodied examples of the mysteries of art and nature. It is through engagement with these women that she learns her craft, she writes. Cooking was the "sole art which she could happily practice" until "she happened on Indians who could teach her something of the inner meaning of art" (pp. 68, 69). Austin attributes her spiritual revelations to her habit of "putting on the character of an Indian woman" (p. 227). Although Austin was a powerful advocate for Native American civil rights in the Southwest, many of her narrative techniques tend toward essentialism and ideological colonization. Austin becomes "fully herself" by adopting – or exploiting – the ideologies of native cultures.

What makes *Earth Horizon* a western autobiography, in the end, is its deep engagement with place. Language, Austin believed, must accurately reflect and describe the rugged terrain. Like many western life writers before and after her, Austin grapples with the meaning of landscape. She indulges in the desire to touch a simpler land; a wilder, freer, more primitive world – the very world, ironically, that Charles Eastman assures readers Native Americans can leave behind in their efforts to "mature" and assimilate. For Austin, it is the land itself, the wild, primitive West, that is the source of experience, the source of self, the "incalculable blue ring of sky meeting earth" (p. 33), the "earth horizon."

Most western American autobiographies are not as self-consciously modern as Austin's, but many do dwell on the West as a source of self. What makes autobiography western? For the generation of "New Western" life writers, it is finding the right story. That story is developed within the region's history of conquest and colonization. Not surprisingly, two themes emerge: the right story is either the one about the return home to ancestral land, or the discovery of a land outside history from which to rewrite social codes. Historian Elliot West claims that the former story is often deployed by Native American life writers who wish to evoke the fullness of self-recognition that is found in homecoming. For Euro/Anglo American writers, West argues, it is the westward movement away from society and history that imbues their stories with narrative meaning (1995). Although this binary may not suggest a totally accurate frame in which to read contemporary western American life writing – western stories and selves are not solely determined by ethnicity or cultural history – it does point to a significant, even crucial, trend. Western American life writing is about the complexity of making the West home.

The West-as-home became a central theme of life writing in the twentieth century. Contemporary western life writers, especially those whose families had put down roots in western places, attempted to construct the West as a place of family, community, and history. Making the West home, however, meant (and still means) struggling with uncomfortable histories. Mary Clearman Blew, Ivan Doig, and William Kittredge, for example, confront the ideological assumptions of conquest and colonization. Fabiola Cabeza de Baca, N. Scott Momaday, and Leslie Marmon Silko likewise claim home and self within an awareness of the master-narrative. But instead of simply deploying the rhetoric of perpetrator or victim, colonizer or colonized, these life writers question what it means to claim home within the region's fraught history. Issues like longevity, placed-ness, and familiarity with land and community become central. What does it mean to call the West "home"? What are the implications of claiming for oneself the label "westerner"? For most, there is a profound sense of connectedness with land and an open acknowledgment of the troubled relationship between a sense of place and a sense of self. The western American life writer who arguably introduces this line of inquiry to western life writing is Wallace Stegner. In his 1962 memoir *Wolf Willow: A History, a Story, and a Memory of the Last Plains Frontier*, Stegner maps his life as a westerner. The most significant landmark, he discovers, is the frontier mentality that inspired his life-long search for continuity, history, roots, and home (Boardman and Woods 2004: 5). In this mixed-genre memoir, the West becomes the object of the self's search for home. This search, and its elusive end, inform western life writing for generations.

Ivan Doig's *This House of Sky* (1978) is a celebrated memoir that further complicates the theme of the search for home. The narrative Doig constructs of his life, beginning with the death of his mother when he was a child and moving through his high school years, emplots both the desire for home and place and the search for meaning beyond home. Doig's grandparents had come west from Europe, and Doig himself leaves home to find his life's meaning, only to long for the ranchers, sheepherders, laborers, and family adventures of his youth. His father Charlie Doig, a central figure in the memoir, defies the stereotypical western hero (he values community, land, and family) signaling the memoir's place in the "New West." Furthermore, critics have argued that the text is distinctly western because Doig has created a new spatial metaphor to explain the relationship between self and place (Bredahl 1989: 137). This new space is not architectural, but natural, a "house of sky," constructed from fragments of memory and stories told mostly by Doig's father and grandmother. Doig's technique recalls a centuries-old autobiographical tradition: memory is a structure, a built environment to walk into, room by room, story by story, recalling bits of life in each enclosed space. For Doig, memory is "the near-neighborhood of dream," a place offering a casual hospitality, "vast and vaulting," forming the "walls and roof of all life's experiences that my younger self could imagine, a single great house of sky" (p. 106).

Like *House of Sky*, *All But the Waltz* (1991) foregrounds the operation of memory and its special role in the construction of western American identity. Mary Clearman Blew characterizes memory not as a record of events, but as a "superimposition," intimately linked to the story she constructs to make meaning about her western life (p. 11). Memory confuses, it "lights upon a dream as readily as an external event, upon a set of rusty irrigation pipes and a historian's carefully detailed context" (p. 10). Memories are accessed by the narrator within the context of family associations: seeing her father's mud-stained jeans prompts a childhood memory of the teenage Mary; telling her mother she is pregnant opens a narrative space for her mother's childhood story. It is through stories, Blew insists, that the fragments of one's life can be woven together like a scrap quilt. In her essay "The Art of Memoir," Blew explains that "any story depends on its shape"; the shape it takes is like "arranging the scraps that have been passed down" (1992: 7). In *All But the Waltz*, Blew quilts together stories of five generations of her Montana ancestors, trying to discover the "magnet pull of place" (p. 21). The memoir has a decidedly anti-mythic stance; like Doig, Blew is a writer of the New West, one who questions the mythic dimensions of the place she and her ancestors called home. Blew performs a gendered self repeatedly out of place on the western stage. "All I wanted was to be free of the cowboy," Blew writes; she is a woman seeking identity within and against a male-dominated cultural and familial history (p. 54). There were only minor roles for women in the master-narrative of the West. *All But the Waltz*, and indeed much of Blew's work, challenges that patriarchal story in order to make place for women's lives.

Among the life writers who struggle to write against the legacy of the western myth and seek a revised identity for its inhabitants is William Kittredge. Kittredge shares literary terrain with Doig and Blew: his sense of self is informed by the mythic dimensions of the American West, the desire for connection with community and land, the relationship between past and present, and most significantly, the looming significance of western place. More to the point, Kittredge acutely feels the loss of place and struggles to "loop myself into lines of significance" (p. 16). Blew comes to the conclusion that only stories can make the connection between self, place, and past; Kittredge, however, is bereft of stories. His family, he writes, "had lost track of stories like the one that tells us the world is to be cherished as if it exists inside our own skin" (p. 27). However, "without stories ... we do not know who we are, or who we might become" (p. 26). The stories they told themselves did not recall the complex history of the Great Basin, the indigenous lives, the arid climate. The stories his family lived were about property and ownership, blind to the magic inherent in the landscape. Kittredge has "fantasies of connection," but suffers from a severe existential crisis of being out of place (p. 29). The meaning of *experience* is the central trope here. According to Smith and Watson, "experience is already an interpretation of the past and of our place in a culturally and historically mediated present" (2001: 24). Further, experience is discursive, embedded in the language and knowledge produced in and through the places we align ourselves with. The language and knowledge produced by Kittredge's West – the legacy of conquest and colonization – fails to meet his need for connection; he is alienated from place, thus alienated from a sense of self. "Our old pilgrims believed stories in which the West was a promise, a place where decent people could escape the wreckage of failed lives and start over" (p. 236). Although

Kittredge ends his memoir not sure where his ashes should be scattered, still not entirely sure of home, he is decidedly closer to the method of reaching home: "I tell my own stories, and I move a little closer toward feeling at home in the incessant world" (p. 238). The only chance we have as westerners, he believes, is to acknowledge that "we are part of what is sacred ... that is our only chance at paradise" (p. 236). Kittredge self-consciously constructs a self within story. The wrong story, the "old pilgrim" story, reproduces an outmoded identity, one that only distances him from his western home.

By contrast, Fabiola Cabeza de Baca's autobiography is rich with the narrative layers of connections. *We Fed Them Cactus* begins in a paradise. The llano, the high plateau land in northern New Mexico, "lacks nothing for those who enjoy Nature in her full grandeur" (p. 3). Like her Anglo counterparts, Cabeza de Baca writes of the necessity of knowing the "right stories"; it is through stories and traditions that one authenticates western identity. In 1954 Cabeza de Baca published her autobiography, a nostalgic account of Hispanic life on the New Mexican plain just before the land became dominated by Anglos. "The history of the country was imprinted on my mind in early childhood" (p. 51), Cabeza de Baca writes, and it is this intimate knowledge that both authorizes her western identity and opens the door to the multiple discourses that construct self and place. Stories told by community elders populate the book, along with discourses of geography, history, sociology, and psychology. These discourses, writes Tey Diana Rebolledo in the Introduction, "are incorporated into the perspectives of the personal, autobiographical 'I'; personal storytelling binds it all together, yet emphasis remains on the multiplicity of voices telling the stories" (p. xxi). In memoir, a genre of life narrative that is distinguished by the social context of the writer, self-construction is undertaken in relation to the voices and stories of others. Cabeza de Baca's West is a contested landscape where multiple discourses intersect to shape culture, community, and identity. The physicality of the land and its special purpose for Hispanic settlers is a primary theme in the memoir; Cabeza de Baca begins not with ancestry and birth, but with the land: "The llano is a great plateau," colorful, endless, and storied. Cabeza de Baca establishes a Hispanic West in which landmarks are adorned with Spanish names and only Hispanic settlers find it "full of promise and gladness" (p. 3).

Leslie Marmon Silko similarly rewrites the American West and the western American self in *Storyteller* (1981). Like many western American life writers, Silko investigates the complexity of memory, especially competing modes of remembering, as she foregrounds the act of remembering itself. "I remember the stories they used to tell us about places that were meadows full of flowers or about canyons that had wide clear streams. I remember our amazement at these stories ... because the places they spoke about had all changed. ... But I understand now. I will remember this September like they remembered the meadows and streams ... and maybe my grandchildren will also be amazed" (p. 170). Silko's self is relational, that is, it acquires meaning through its association with people past and present, with landscape, and with the stories told about landscape. In *Storyteller* photographs, poems, legends, and short stories are assembled to construct a hybridized identity, one that negotiates discourses from Laguna Pueblo tradition, anthropological knowledge, and family history.

In a similar vein, N. Scott Momaday's memoir *The Names* blends familial and tribal stories in poetry, prose, and visual images, all the while naming significant events that contribute to the construction of his identity. As the title implies, Momaday evokes the power of naming and its centrality to individual and community identity. Like Silko, he reimagines the classic Enlightenment self, the (white) "representative man" who has lived a long public life as a powerful individual. By blending genre and stories, these Native American authors underscore the way self is multiply constructed, relational, and performed within a set of competing cultural norms. These memoirs and others challenge not only traditional notions of western selves but the frontier-dominated ideology of western places.

The American West, as indicated in the introductory discussion above, exerts pressure upon any life writer who constructs identity within or against it. A western American life writer must negotiate self within multiple cultural discourses. The West is both physical and mythic; it is west and north, south and east; desert, mountain, urban, and rural. It is Eden and Atzlán, Gold Mountain and goldfield. A critically useful set of terms exists to describe identity constructed within such a contact zone: border dweller, *mestizo/a*, hybrid, diasporic, migratory, nomadic (Smith and Watson 2001: 145). These "subjects in process" produce a multitude of autobiographical genres in response to the multiple discourse regimes at work. Although many western life narratives easily fit into many genres, it is useful for critics to consider types of autobiography in the West.

The West has long been understood as a landscape with a message; whether it is home or road, it is sublime terrain, sacred space, and "endless" resource. It stands to reason that "ecobiography," a genre of autobiography in which the connection between land and self is fully explored, is well represented. Both Silko's and Momaday's memoirs are aptly described by this category. Other canonical examples include Wallace Stegner's *Wolf Willow*, Edward Abbey's *Desert Solitaire*, and Terry Tempest Williams' *Refuge*. Like many western American life narratives, Stegner's features a hand-drawn map as the frontispiece to underscore the significance of place. "Expose a child to a particular environment," he writes, "and he will perceive in the shapes of that environment until he dies" (p. 21). In ecobiography, the "I" is relational; it is constructed not just within familial or tribal relationships, but within relationship to terrain. A complex doubling of construction occurs here, because the writer responds not only to discourses of knowledge about self, but to discourses of knowledge about the value of the natural world. Often ecobiographies emplot contradictory environmental values: Edward Abbey, passionate defender of wilderness, positions himself as eco-defender against administrative and governmental norms of plunder and resource extraction. For Abbey, wilderness is the necessary antidote to civilization. "Mountains complement desert as desert complements city, as wilderness complements and completes civilization," Abbey insists (p. 148). In wilderness, humans are complete. Abbey constructs wilderness in spiritual terms, as Edenic, and as the Other that shapes his own humanity. On the river, Abbey's "anxieties have vanished, and I feel instead a sense of cradlelike security … a pleasure equivalent to that first entrance – from the outside – into the neck of the womb" (p. 176). Terry Tempest Williams begins her memoir by evoking the "country I come from and how it informs my life" (p. 3). The story of raising lake levels of the Great Salt Lake and the potential destruction of the Bear Migratory Bird Refuge is told simultaneously with the story of her family's struggle with breast cancer. The feminine principle informs Williams' construction of self and land. As her family changes and her landscape changes, Williams finds refuge in change.

In addition to ecobiography, western American life writers engage in a genre called "biomythography." In biomythography, the life writer renegotiates cultural invisibility by calling writing the biography of the mythic self (Smith and Watson 2001: 190). In *Borderlands/La Frontera* (1987) Gloria Anzaldúa embodies Aztec female icons to demonstrate the ability to sustain through transformation. Like Williams' "I," Anzaldúa's "I" is at once political and adaptable. Anzaldúa's contribution to identity studies is significant; in *Borderlands* she names the "new *mestiza*," an identity that bilingually contests borders, religious ideologies, and political narratives. The border between her Texas and Mexico is both geography and mythosphere; at first a source of pain, Anzaldúa claims the border as her figurative and metaphorical dwelling, urging others to do the same.

Like Anzaldúa, Jimmy Santiago Baca claims a mixed or *mestizo* identity in his epic poem *Martín and Meditations on the South Valley* (1986). Baca uses mythical and archetypal symbols and patterns in which to construct his "I." Deeply informed by land, history, and contemporary Chicano culture, Baca confronts the legacies of colonization and detribalization as he rewrites his life away from historical margins and into the western center. Other western American writers use poetry as a vehicle for self-construction in and among cultural discourses, most notably Sherman Alexie in *First Indian on the Moon* and *One Stick Song*.

Related to biomythography is the autobiographical practice that explicitly constructs ethnic identity within a cultural contact zone. Ethnic life writers in the West, often in transit or exile, frequently emplot a desire for a home. Japanese internment memoirs, especially Jeanne Wakatsuki's *Farewell to Manzanar*, exhibit the pressures of negotiating an American nationalist identity and a Japanese cultural identity. In her celebrated memoir *The Woman Warrior* (1975), Maxine Hong Kingston reveals the struggles associated with constructing an ethnic "I." Learning to write in grade school, Kingston had trouble with the first-person pronoun: "I could not understand 'I.' The Chinese 'I' has seven strokes, intricacies. How could an American 'I,' assuredly wearing a hat like the Chinese, have only three strokes, the middle so straight?" (p. 166). Here Kingston reveals the way subjectivity is constructed through the very act of writing, of life writing.

The autobiographical canon begins with the assumption that the genre is a historical record of the representative man, the public or political man. In the second wave of autobiography criticism, we see the emergence of difference. Language about the "self" gives way to a preoccupation with "subjectivity"; concerns with textual truth are replaced with explorations of creative self-construction. Postcolonialism, feminism, linguistics, and psychoanalysis influence readers (and writers) of life narrative to consider how subjects are marginalized and affected by power differentials, how they construct themselves vis-à-vis discursive practices, claim agency, and experience memory. In third-wave autobiography criticism, we assume that writing is a form of invention that creates the self, and that any autobiographical act is performative and creates "dynamic sites for the performance of identities ... identities are not fixed or essentialized ... they are produced and reiterated through cultural norms, and thus remain provisional and unstable" (Smith and Watson 2001: 143). "Self" is no longer a unitary, individual phenomenon, but "historically demarcated and culturally specific" (Smith and Watson 2001: 140). The American West is a complex stage in which to read and write the "I." It is culturally and environmentally diverse and it bears the legacy of multiple ideologies and desires. Autobiographies that emerge from this place are as rich and complex as the social and physical geography, and should be examined as such.

REFERENCES AND FURTHER READING

Abbey, Edward. (1968). *Desert Solitaire: A Season in the Wilderness.* New York: Ballantine.

Adkison, Jennifer Dawes, ed. (2009). *Across the Plains: Sarah Royce's Western Narrative.* Tucson: University of Arizona Press.

Anzaldúa, Gloria. (1987). *Borderlands/La Frontera: The New Mestiza.* San Francisco: Aunt Lute.

Austin, Mary. (1991). *Earth Horizon* [1932]. Afterword by Melody Graulich. Albuquerque: University of New Mexico Press.

Baca, Jimmy Santiago. (1986). *Martín and Meditations from the South Valley.* New York: New Directions.

Blew, Mary Clearman. (1992). *All but the Waltz: A Memoir of Five Generations in the Life of a Montana Family* [1991]. New York: Penguin.

Blew, Mary Clearman. (1992). "The Art of Memoir." In *Bone Deep in Landscape: Writing, Reading, and Place,* pp. 3–8. Norman: University of Oklahoma Press.

Boardman, Kathleen, and Gioia Woods, eds. (2004). *Western Subjects: Autobiographical Writing in the North American West.* Salt Lake City: University of Utah Press.

Bredahl, Carl. (1989). Valuing Surface: The Imagination of Ivan Doig. In *New Ground: Western American Narrative and the Literary Canon,* pp. 135–46. Chapel Hill: University of North Carolina Press.

Cabeza de Vaca, Álvar Núñez (1993). *The Account: Álvar Núñez Cabeza de Vaca's Relación* [1555], ed. José B. Fernández and Martin A. Favata. Houston, TX: Arte Público Press.

Culley, Margo. (1998). Introduction to *A Day at a Time: Diary Literature of American Women, from 1764–1985.* In *Women, Autobiography, Theory: A Reader,* pp. 217–21. Madison: University of Wisconsin Press.

Doig, Ivan. (1978). *This House of Sky: Landscapes of a Western Mind.* New York: Harvest.

Eakin, Paul John. (1999). *How Our Lives Become Stories: Making Selves.* Ithaca, NY: Cornell University Press.

Eastman, Charles A. (1971). *Indian Boyhood* [1902]. New York: Dover.

Gilbert, Fabiola Cabeza de Baca. (1994). *We Fed Them Cactus* [1954], introd. Tey Diana Rebolledo. Albuquerque: University of New Mexico Press.

Graulich, Melody. (1991). Afterword to Mary Austin, *Earth Horizon* [1932]. Albuquerque: University of New Mexico Press.

Hopkins, Sarah Winnemucca. (1994). *Life among the Piutes: Their Wrongs and Claims* [1883]. Reno: University of Nevada Press.

Kingston, Maxine Hong. (1975). *The Woman Warrior: A Girlhood among Ghosts*. New York: Vintage.

Kittredge, William. (1992). *Hole in the Sky: A Memoir*. New York: Vintage.

Knobloch, Frieda. (1996). *The Culture of Wilderness: Agriculture as Colonization in the American West*. Chapel Hill: University of North Carolina Press.

Krupat, Arnold. (1985). *For Those Who Come After*. Berkeley: University of California Press.

Krupat, Arnold, ed. (1994). *Native American Autobiography: An Anthology*. Madison: University of Wisconsin Press.

LaFlesche, Francis. (1963). *The Middle Five: Indian Schoolboys of the Omaha Tribe* [1900]. Madison: University of Wisconsin Press.

Mates, Merrill. (1969). *The Great Platte River Road: The Covered Wagon Mainline via Fort Kearny to Fort Laramie*. Lincoln: Nebraska State Historical Society.

Momaday, N. Scott. (1976). *The Names: A Memoir*. New York: Harper & Row.

Myers, Sandra L. (1980). *Ho for California! Women's Overland Diaries from the Huntington Library*. San Marino, CA: Huntington Library.

Olney, James. (1991). The Autobiography of America. *American Literary History*, 3/2 (Summer), 376–95.

Parini, Jay, ed. (1999). *The Norton Book of American Autobiography*. New York: W.W. Norton.

Schlissel, Lillian. (1982). *Women's Diaries of the Westward Journey*. New York: Schocken Books.

Silko, Leslie Marmon. (1981). *Storyteller*. New York: Little, Brown & Co.

Sinor, Jennifer. (2002). *The Extraordinary Work of Ordinary Writing: Annie Ray's Diary*. Iowa City: University of Iowa Press.

Smith, Sidonie, and Julia Watson. (2001). *Reading Autobiography: A Guide for Interpreting Life Narratives*. Minneapolis: University of Minnesota Press.

Stegner, Wallace. (1990). *Wolf Willow: A History, a Story, and a Memory of the Last Frontier* [1962]. New York: Penguin.

Temple, Judy Nolte. (2009). *Baby Doe Tabor: The Madwoman in the Cabin*. Norman: University of Oklahoma Press.

West, Elliot. (1995). A Narrative History of the West. *Montana: The Magazine of Western History*, 45(3): 64–76.

Williams, Terry Tempest. (1991). *Refuge: An Unnatural History of Family and Place*. New York: Vintage.

Wong, Hertha D. Sweet. (1992). *Sending My Heart Back Across the Years: Tradition and Innovation in Native American Autobiography*. New York: Oxford University Press.

22

Housing the American West: Western Women's Literature, Early Twentieth Century and Beyond

Cathryn Halverson

In her renowned "Little House" series, Laura Ingalls Wilder gives a fictionalized account of her girlhood in a series of little houses across the West. Wilder turns to the home and home practice to explore not only family dynamics, gender roles, and female ambition, but also class, regional, and national identity; race relations; and the challenges of modernity. Her eight novels chart the coming of age of a western girl drawn to male "outdoor" stories that exclude her even as she is groomed for the female "indoor" ones to which she responds with much more ambivalence.

Wilder's sustained attention to domestic life affiliates her with the regional literary tradition of the era in which her historical novels are set. Euro-American women's literature of the West has its roots in letters and journals that document overland journeys away from cherished eastern homes; fictional texts expressing fantasies about ideal homes in the West; and realist accounts of establishing new homes there (Kolodny 1984). *Little House on the Prairie* (1935) thus stands as a Kansan sequel to Caroline Kirkland's Michigan classic, *A New Home, Who'll Follow?* (1839).

Yet Wilder's books are also eminently contemporary, in that western writers throughout the twentieth century probe the meaning of home and the experience of making, escaping, losing, or enduring it. Although the titles of their texts may not announce the subject as openly as hers do, they similarly tell "the sustaining and disturbing story" (Romines 1997: 9) of little houses in the West. A diverse group of women writers found life at home a useful focus for the western stories they would tell. They also found western homes absorbing – and often troubling – in their own right. This is not to say that westerners were more domestic than women of other regions. Rather, it is that they regularly turned to homes to conceptualize distinctly regional experiences, and that homes in their texts often support different kinds of narratives than do those in texts set elsewhere.

A Companion to the Literature and Culture of the American West, First Edition. Edited by Nicolas S. Witschi.

Although it does seek to indicate the trajectory of this extensive literature across the twentieth century, this short essay focuses on a cluster of women's texts, published between 1900 and 1920, that spotlight the problem and promise of "western house-keeping." Some of the most prominent western authors of the time, including Zitkala-Ša, Sui Sin Far, Mary MacLane, Willa Cather, Elinore Pruitt Stewart, and Mary Austin, take up the issue, using homes to articulate ideas about westering, race, class, gender, history, politics, and landscape. As a group, their narratives refract and help establish some of the key themes that endure across a century of women's writing. Reading these diverse texts together shows the resonances between them, suggests the era's range of western literary expression, and helps orient us to the concerns of the decades to come.

Zitkala-Ša

One could argue that twentieth-century western women's literature began with the autobiographical sketches that Zitkala-Ša published – to acclaim – in the *Atlantic Monthly* in January, February, and March of 1900, "Impressions of an Indian Childhood," "The School Days of an Indian Girl," and "An Indian Teacher among Indians." Zitkala-Ša later collected these and other stories and essays in *American Indian Stories* (1921).

Of mixed Dakota and European ancestry, Zitkala-Ša (christened Gertrude Bonnin) was born in 1876 on the Yankton reservation in Dakota Territory. Her early childhood in a pressured but still traditional Native community came to an abrupt end when recruiters persuaded her to depart for a Quaker boarding school in Indiana. In her sketches, Zitkala-Ša uses descriptions of material homes, west and east, to dramatize the trauma of displacement, both her own and that of a whole generation of Native women and men.

In "Impressions of an Indian Childhood," Zitkala-Ša depicts the wigwam her mother constructs as literally letting in the prairie:

> On a bright, clear day, she pulled out the wooden pegs that pinned the skirt of our wigwam to the ground, and rolled the canvas part way up on its frame of slender poles. Then the cool morning breezes swept freely through our dwelling, now and then wafting the perfume of sweet grasses from newly burnt prairie. (Zitkala-Ša 2003: 73)

Their home appears equally open in social ways. Zitkala-Ša portrays Dakota residences as sites of family nurture and education where children learn by imitation; in one memorable scene, when left home alone she somberly prepares and proffers a cup of mud-water "coffee" to an elderly visitor, who just as somberly accepts. They are also readily transformed into public centers. Neighbors and travelers routinely stop by their wigwam, and at a word of invitation, the community's elders "flock" (Zitkala-Ša 2003: 71) to spend evenings there, which they pass telling stories and legends. The child's organic experience of home is potently expressed by her perception of the "great circular horizon of the Dakota prairies" as a "vast wigwam of blue and green" (Zitkala-Ša 2003: 98).

Zitkala-Ša's portrait of idyllic wigwam life makes her following indictment of Native boarding schools, "The School Days of an Indian Girl," all the more searing. As Susan Bernardin and others have shown, the painful contrast between life with her mother and life at school indicts reform movements that sought to eradicate the "savage home" by introducing Native children to Euro-American domestic life. Zitkala-Ša depicts the school she attends as a travesty of a home, run by uncaring adults bent on inculcating their culture at any cost. Like other Native writers of her time, she defamiliarizes Euro-American customs, as when she describes a staircase as "an upward incline of wooden boxes" (Zitkala-Ša 2003: 89). More fundamentally, she exposes the inhumanity of a system that forces Native children to live by the clock and the bell.

Zitkala-Ša records many instances in which she rebels against "the civilizing machine" (Zitkala-Ša 2003: 96), and she goes on to demonstrate her adult agency and success as an orator and teacher. She also reveals, however, her inability as a young adult to locate a satisfactory cultural home of her own, one that incorporates both Native and Euro-American ways. She expresses this lack with images of confinement in "ghastly" (Zitkala-Ša 2003: 105) rooms. We never see her moving, acting, or truly living in these rooms. Instead, she just sits within them, staging herself there at moments of inner crisis. After her first oratory triumph, for example, she recalls, "Leaving the crowd as quickly as possible, I was soon in my room. The rest of the night I sat in an armchair and gazed into the crackling fire … In my mind I saw my mother far away on the Western plains, and she was holding a charge against me" (Zitkala-Ša 2003: 103). Her final sketch is even more emphatic: "Alone in my room, I sat like the petrified Indian woman of whom my mother used to tell me. … alive, in my tomb, I was destitute!" (Zitkala-Ša 2003: 112).

Zitkala-Ša twins her story of cultural dislocation with that of her mother, and she similarly recruits homes to depict her mother's trajectory. Explicitly, she presents a narrative of decline: "First it was a change from the buffalo skin to the white man's canvas that covered our wigwam. Now she had given up her wigwam of slender poles, to live, a foreigner, in a home of clumsy logs" (Zitkala-Ša 2003: 83–4). However, she also reveals that her mother has not, in fact, entirely "given up" the wigwam, but continues to do her cooking in an adjacent "little canvas-covered wigwam" (Zitkala-Ša 2003: 107), combining Euro-American and traditional practice. Zitkala-Ša suggests that, with her different history, her mother may be more adaptable than she: "My mother had never gone to school, and though she meant always to give up her own customs for such of the white man's ways as pleased her, she made only compromises" (Zitkala-Ša 2003: 108).

In her 1911 autobiography, Zitkala-Ša's Ho-Chunk contemporary Angel DeCora (herself a celebrated graduate of Carlisle Indian School and illustrator of Zitkala-Ša's 1901 *Old Indian Legends*), casually suggests that "foreign training" can be reversed:

"My mother, in her childhood, had had a little training in a convent, but when she married my father she gave up all her foreign training and made a good, industrious Indian wife" (DeCora 1911: 279). Neither DeCora nor Zitkala-Ša explore in their texts just how this might be done. That treatment in literature would come later, in contemporary Native texts such as Mary Crow Dog's *Lakota Woman*, which depicts the author's struggle, after marrying a traditional Sioux man, to adjust to living in "not just a one nuclear family place, but rather a settlement for the whole clan, the whole tiyospaye" (Crow Dog 1990: 172). Addressing this issue of reclamation more broadly, twentieth-century Native texts by both women and men frequently include a plot of "homing in" (a term coined by William Bevis), in which Native characters return to home traditions and homelands.

Sui Sin Far

From the open plains of Zitkala-Ša's childhood, the essayist and fiction writer Sui Sin Far takes us to a very different West, that of urban California and Washington. Sui Sin Far leaves largely untold the story of the homes her characters have left behind to focus instead on the new ones they establish in the West. Yet she and Zitkala-Ša have much in common, producing texts at once domestic and political that probe the problem of being at home in the West in the face of steadfast cultural and institutional American racism.

Born Edith Eaton, Sui Sin Far was the daughter of a Chinese mother and British father and the second eldest of thirteen, raised largely in Montreal. Even as a racist society obliged her to see herself as "Chinese," she also recognized that she and her siblings comprised a new and less easily categorized group, "Eurasian."

During her childhood, Sui Sin Far's exposure to other Asians was limited to her family, but her education in Chinese culture accelerated once she moved west. She spent many productive years as a stenographer and journalist in San Francisco, Los Angeles, and most especially Seattle, where, in her own words, she "struck gold, silver, oil, copper, and everything else that luck could strike" (Sui Sin Far 1995: 294). In 1912, she published the book about the "half Chinese" that she had long dreamed of writing, a short story collection entitled *Mrs. Spring Fragrance*. The book exposed her largely white American readership to an often feared minority population within its borders; it also taught them to see their own culture through other eyes.

Many of Sui Sin Far's stories center around the Chinese merchant class in Seattle and San Francisco. Unlike their working-class compatriots, the US government did not prohibit middle-class Chinese men from "importing" their wives, and they thus could have more normative home lives. Through depicting Chinese marriages, families, and domestic life, Sui Sin Far worked to assuage "Yellow Peril" fears of a race composed of inscrutable bachelor laborers, boarding in squalid rooming houses and addicted to opium and gambling. (Ling 1995: 13) Yet while one of her express purposes for writing was to prove "there is no type of white person who cannot find his or her counterpart in some Chinese" (Sui Sin Far 1995: 235), she also shows that the experience of being Chinese in America is a distinctive one.

The book establishes Sui Sin Far as one of the earliest theorists of Asian American identity, and it dramatizes a full range of cultural positions. For the white women in her stories, Sui Sin Far charts the emerging New Woman and probes the modern issue of home versus career, matters about which she could speak from ample personal experience. For her female Chinese characters, however, this kind of struggle does not appear to apply. Instead, the pressing issue for them is the degree of their Americanization.

The eponymous Mrs. Spring Fragrance, a perfect hybrid and perfect housewife, is situated at one end of the spectrum. She speaks English fluently, and she is equally comfortable in traditional Chinese and western clothes. Mrs. Spring Fragrance cooks, studies, travels; gives her husband emotional support; facilitates her neighbors' (literal) affairs. Mirroring the author's own ambition, she also plans to write a book about Americans from the perspective of a Chinese person. Sui Sin Far also, though, features the dark side of acculturation, portraying much more traditional Chinese women who resist American customs and educate their husbands about the limits of how much they will change. In the grimmest of these tales, "The Wisdom of the New," a mother poisons her son rather than see him educated in western ways.

Sui Sin Far's stories of private lives often protest federal racial policies, and her texts of Chinese American families are shadowed by a subtext of homelessness (Chapman: 2008). Mr. Spring Fragrance's brother, for example, is detained on Angel Island; "In the Land of the Free" portrays a couple whose toddler is taken from them by immigration officials. Special targets of Sui Sin Far's satire are those American progressives who, like the officials in Native boarding schools, break up loving homes and proceed to institutionalize the children.

From a different ethnic perspective, contemporary Chicana writers extend Zitkala-Ša's and Sui Sin Far's explorations of mixed identity in America, limning women's efforts to locate home spaces and identities "on the borderlands" of Mexican and Euro-American culture. In her celebrated, multilingual *Borderlands/La Frontera: The New Mestiza* (1987), Gloria Anzaldúa breaks down Mexico and US binaries. She exposes "the border" as a fiction used to police peoples of color, even as she also explores, as a lesbian writer, what she calls "sexual borderlands." Sandra Cisneros' *The House on Mango Street* (1992), set in Chicago but interspersed with journeys to Mexico, expands the range of the "borderlands" to include a midwestern city with Hispanic communities. As in Anzaldúa's memoir, the novel's adolescent protagonist, Esperanza, portrays negotiations of Chicana identity as closely bound up with resisting patriarchal control. The older women in her neighborhood conduct narrow lives of service, but Esperanza dreams of a freer one in her own home: "Not a flat. Not an apartment in back. Not a man's house. Not a daddy's. A house all my own" (Cisneros 1992: 108).

Early protest against the homelessness caused by the United States government also receives fuller expression in a cluster of Japanese American texts recording World War II internment experiences by authors such as Monica Sone, Hisaye Yamamoto,

Yoshiko Uchida, Joy Kogawa, and Jeanne Wakatsuki Houston. A memoir like Wakatsuki Houston's *Farewell to Manzanar* (1973) explores the tensions inherent in setting up housekeeping at a prison site. The girl narrator's growing sense of the desert camp as "home" – in conjunction with her father's unabated anguish of displacement – well captures her inner conflict between identities as Japanese and American. Asian American populations were historically concentrated in rural and urban Pacific Coast areas, and, as Krista Comer suggests, one effect of internment memoirs is to discursively enter Asian American women into those storied landscapes of the interior West from which they are usually excluded (Comer 1999: 210). As such, they complement the way contemporary writers such as Maxine Hong Kingston, Amy Tan, and Wanda Coleman continue to plot a multicultural, urban West.

Mary MacLane

Zitkala-Ša and Sui Sin Far document the experience of losing homes and home territories, and efforts to compensate for them. Mary MacLane, the Butte author of *The Story of Mary MacLane* (1902), presents a different dilemma: her need to escape a home that she experiences as materially comfortable but psychologically oppressive. While this problem has its roots in relative privilege, MacLane portrays it as urgent nevertheless. "Can I be that thing which I am," she demands, "can I be possessed of a peculiar rare genius, and yet drag my life out in obscurity in this uncouth, warped, Montana town!" (MacLane 1993: 17)

MacLane wrote her autobiography on the heels of her high school graduation as a direct bid to leave Butte. She portrays herself as doubly contained, by both the remote mining city and her staid middle-class home. The latter is comprised of "pretty" rooms that her mother "spends her life in the adornment of" (MacLane 1993: 56) – presenting a dismaying model of what her own life might become if she stays in Montana. Distinguishing herself from her mother, MacLane dramatizes her "domesticity with a difference," to use the term that Nicole Tonkovich applies to privileged nineteenth-century writers: she engages in home acts, but each is directed to her satisfaction and testifies to her "genius." "I do a little housework," she confides, "and on the whole am rather fond of it – some parts of it. ... I have gained much of my strength and gracefulness of body from scrubbing the kitchen floor – to say nothing of some fine points of philosophy" (MacLane 1993: 16). Much of this "philosophy" concerns her former English teacher Fannie Corbin – now long gone from Butte – for whom she avows a "man-love, set in the mysterious sensibilities of my woman-nature" (MacLane 1993: 77). MacLane concludes an extended description of her daily fudge habit by asserting, "Though I do ordinary things, when *I* do them they cease to be ordinary" (MacLane 1993: 104).

For all its idiosyncrasy, *The Story of Mary MacLane* is squarely located within a western women's literary tradition of representing locale as both problem and solution. The West appears in such texts as a site of stifling provincialism that is mitigated by inspiring geographies and inspiring racial or ethnic others. MacLane depicts herself as traversing social and geographical space of all kinds. She strikes up stimulating–if fleeting–acquaintances with working-class immigrant women in the neighborhoods of Butte. She is further sustained by excursions into the copper-mining wasteland beyond, which she explicitly figures as an alternative to domestic sites: "Every day the atmosphere of a house becomes unbearable, so every day, I go out to the sand and the barrenness" (MacLane 1993: 19). Unlike Native writers, MacLane presents the plains as an alternative to home and community, claiming terrain emptied of human history as a private arena for solitary reflection and respite.

Willa Cather

Strategies to endure, in MacLane's words, "the atmosphere of a house" figure prominently in some of the era's best-known western women's texts. Jim Burden, the narrator of Willa Cather's *My Ántonia*, gives an account of how he conceptualized his rented college rooms as a site of intellectual discovery rather than banal daily life:

> My bedroom, originally a linen-closet, was unheated and was barely large enough to contain my cot-bed, but it enabled me to call the other room my study. The dresser, and the great walnut wardrobe which held all my clothes, even my hats and shoes, I had pushed out of the way, and I considered them non-existent, as children eliminate incongruous objects when they are playing house. (Cather 1918: 259)

This passage could well serve as a comment upon domestic narratives composed by white westerners, who routinely "eliminate" from their texts "incongruities" of labor, family members, indigenous land claims – and in Cather's case even gender – in order to create more sustaining versions of life at home.

My Ántonia is overdetermined as a domestic text, in that it features homes at every turn. A regular refrain is that of characters trying on others' home lives, as when the Shimerda sisters fantasize about commandeering the abandoned homestead of the Russian couple Peter and Pavel, or their dejected father haunts the orderly household that Jim's grandparents maintain. Most notable are the domestic longings and machinations of Jim himself. We never see him working in a house. Rather, Cather emphasizes his attempts not to *effect* but to *perceive* domesticity in certain ways – as when he views his peaceful indoor routine with his grandmother as a more "adventurous life" than that of "The Swiss Family Robinson" (Cather 1918: 66). For the receptive, Cather suggests, the rugged terrain and multicultural texture of the American West yields new versions of American homes. In the famous Panther Canyon interlude in *The Song of the Lark*, Thea Kronborg recovers from overwork in a "rock-room" that she "took for her own" (Cather 1915: 268) among the ruins of an Anasazi cliff settlement. Alternating nights at the comfortable German ranch house where she boards with days "camping" at the cliffs, Thea strives to imagine a bygone, traditional Native domesticity even as she fiercely resists the gender norms of her own day.

Elinore Pruitt Stewart

Like MacLane and Cather, Elinore Pruitt Stewart also proffers an unsettling account of domestic life in the West. *Letters of a Woman Homesteader* (1914), originally written to a former employer in Denver, Juliet Coney, records Stewart's early years of homesteading near Burnt Fork, Wyoming. Stewart had moved there with her young daughter Jerrine to work as a housekeeper for a local rancher, Clyde Stewart. Within two months she had filed on land adjoining Clyde's; she had also married him. Over a year and a half of correspondence would pass, however, before she disclosed the latter act to Coney. As many scholars have noted, Stewart's text is astonishing for just how much it elides and represses. Even after acknowledging the crucial facts of her marriage and the three sons she soon bore, Stewart continues to present her homesteading as that of "a Woman," to borrow from her book's title, as individual rather than family endeavor. She aggressively shapes her text to support her central claim: that a single woman can do all the work of homesteading herself.

The letters also reflect Stewart's ambivalence about settling down. She confides, "I had not thought I should ever marry again. ... I wanted to just knock about foot-loose and free to see life as a gypsy sees it" (Stewart 1988: 188). The textual choices she makes help her recoup this lost freedom. Her text is highly domestic, but it rarely represents indoor life. Instead, suffused with passages like the following account of a camping trip, it repeatedly depicts domesticity exported outdoors:

> I soon had a roaring fire up against the logs and, cutting away a few branches, let the heat into as snug a bedroom as any one could wish. The pine needles made as soft a carpet as the wealthiest could afford. ... I made our bed and fried our trout. The branches had torn off the bag in which I had my bread, so it was lost in the forest, but who needs bread when they have good, mealy potatoes? ...
>
> I wish you could once sleep on the kind of bed we enjoyed that night. It was both soft and firm, with the clean, spicy smell of the pine. The heat from our big fire came in and we were warm as toast. (Stewart 1988: 31–2)

Stewart's book highlights intrepid Christmas outings spent with strangers far from home. She and a companion prepare massive Christmas dinners that they deliver in a madcap journey to twelve pairs of far-flung shepherds; she leads a group of friends in devising a holiday for Mormon women and children stranded in a hunting cabin by husbands on a drinking binge. She is far briefer, tellingly, in describing a private family Christmas at home.

Mary Austin

While Stewart assays to portray a family endeavor as a solo one, Mary Austin proffers a homesteading narrative without a home. In her autobiography *Earth Horizon* (1932), Austin describes how young homesteaders in southeastern California "were quite content to make of their enforced sojourn on the land a perpetual picnic" (Austin 1991: 199). In accord with this metaphor of outdoor recreation, her family's cabin and any work that may have occurred there never really appear in the text. Austin focuses instead on her experience of wandering the desert and the creative powers unleashed thereby. Her story of recovering from malnutrition by foraging for wild grapes suggests just how redundant the domestic appears in her text. Challenging the preeminence of indoor structures, she presents home as expanding in the desert West – reaching to the "earth horizon."

In the stories and essays that Austin's desert years prepared her to write, collected in *The Land of Little Rain* (1903) and *Lost Borders* (1909), the narrator locates herself everywhere and nowhere. She is privy to all the desert's secrets but has no fixed location of her own – no "place of refuge where she lay by" (Austin 1995: 255), to borrow from her description of one of her characters. Austin is intrigued by the domestic minimalism the desert fosters, an updated version of the life her pioneering forebears led with "no more labored equipment than a wooden pestle and a mortar of Indian make, a tin grater for corn meal, a deep pot and a frying-pan, and *their own intention*" (Austin 1991: 15). She asserts that "prospectors and Indians" need no real shelter. Instead, they are protected by "a kind of a weather shell that remains on the body until death" (Austin 1995: 46). Of "The Pocket-Hunter," an itinerant miner, she enthuses, "The simplicity of his kitchen arrangements was elemental. A pot of beans, a coffee-pot, a frying-pan, a tin to mix bread in – he fed the burros in this when there was need – with these he had been half round our western world and back" (Austin 1995: 43–4). By simply covering her face with her blanket, the Paiute woman Seyavi, the subject of "The Basket Maker," gains the sense of privacy for which middle-class Americans need a whole room. The wandering "Walking Woman" experiences the entire region as her domain, protected by a literal "weather shell," the "fine down all over her face" (Austin 1995: 257) that her outdoor life has engendered, as well as an air of self-possession that wards off sexual predation.

This sense of being at home in the desert at large, however, is complicated by Austin's searing record of "the homesickness of an Indian":

> Oppapago looks on Waban, and Waban on Coso and the Bitter Lake, and the campoodie looks on these three; and more, it sees the beginning of winds along the foot of Coso, the gathering of clouds behind the high ridges, the spring flush, the soft spread of wild almond bloom on the mesa. These first you understand are the Paiute's walls, the other his furnishings. Not the wattled hut is his home, but the land, the winds, the hill front, the stream. These he cannot duplicate at any furbisher's shop as you who live within doors, who if your purse allows may have the same home at Sitka and Samarcand. So

you see how it is that the homesickness of an Indian is often unto death, since he gets no relief from it; neither wind nor weed nor skyline, nor any aspect of the hills of a strange land sufficiently like his own. (Austin 1995: 97)

In her desert texts, Austin does not acknowledge the contradictions inherent in mourning the loss of Native American homes while celebrating the ways white individuals can profit from the same, those who, like the writer herself, are drawn to the alternative the desert offers to "liv[ing] within doors." Envisioning Native inhabitants literally constructing enchanting dwellings for outsiders, Austin gives her readers the following advice: "Take no tent, but if you will, have an Indian build you a wickiup, willows planted in a circle, drawn over to an arch, and bound cunningly with withes, all the leaves on, and chinks to count the stars through" (Austin 1995: 59).

Light Housekeeping

The impulse among white westerners to probe the limits of "light housekeeping" continues throughout the twentieth century. While this theme is especially prominent among the white and the middle class, texts such as *Letters of a Woman Homesteader* or Juanita Harrison's *My Great, Wide, Beautiful World* (1936) demonstrate that it is not exclusive to these groups. Harrison's book records her long journey around the world, eight years of travel in Europe, Asia, and the Middle East that she funded with short-term jobs as a maid or cook. Raised in Mississippi, she claimed California as her own, explaining, "I am glad I chose Calif. for my home before I left as every one know it" (Harrison 1996: 192). Frequently referring to herself as a "European" even while alluding to her African "blood," Harrison asserts a "first-world" identity that depends on her cultural differences from the people she meets in Asia and the Middle East.

By glossing over the work she does in her employers' homes, *My Great, Wide, Beautiful World* buttresses Harrison's containment of her past identity as an African American southern servant in favor of her new incarnation as a Californian/European traveler. Harrison instead accords more sustained narrative attention to the series of private spaces she devises for herself on the road. These range from a rented room complete with flower pots made of "cocnuts shells," "a tin of canned heat for making coca," and "a little pan for stewing eggs frying bacon" to a corner in an Indian railway station where she sleeps under her umbrella on top of her coat. The book concludes with an epilogue set in "the Playgrowns of Waikiki," in which Harrison describes the tent that she erected in the front yard of a Japanese family's home:

I had a 7 × 7 Tent made just as I wanted it I had it that size so I can take up my house and walk. ... it open at each end the same way like what are used on sport shirts instead of laped over or laced up. ... the floor is good but light so I can carry it on my head when I want to move. I have a green linolien on the floor with two small rugs I have a good army cot and a fine matrrews made to order. It is furnished nothing like a home ... it looks like a poch.

Well never in all my life have I slept so wonderful as in my tent ... when the light is out and the door and Windows closed the lights of the street shine through the holes and onto to the Top of my Tent and it looks just like the Stars ... This is my first and only Home. Villa Petit Peep are the name of my Tent as I let my callers sit on a seat in the yard and Peep in so I gave it this True name. (Harrison 1996: 318)

Although anxious that she might miss her life in Europe, she concludes that the multiculturalism of Hawaii in fact extends her travel project: "I have many other things to take its place the Change of going to Chinese gatherns, Japanese, then Hawaiians and when I feel Spanish There are the Potegeise. ... now that I have about finnish my travellers I feel very happy to have choosed this lovely part of the world" (Harrison 1996: 314).

Mona Simpson's *Anywhere But Here* (1987) describes a different kind of home ideal and class aspiration. In *Anywhere But Here*, sets of domestic practices serve as potent symbols of a family's economic and emotional health, and the energy of the text comes from its juxtaposition of deft and dreadful housekeeping. Growing up in Bay City, Wisconsin, Ann Diamond is at once nurtured by her grandmother's careful housekeeping and disoriented by her mother Adele's bizarre practice, which includes mandating an all-meat diet. She and her mother are attracted to a southwestern domestic aesthetic – inspired by the adobe walls, clay tiles, and Mexican "appointments" that distinguish the homes of "Scottsdale and Albuquerque and Bel Air" (Simpson 1987: 4) – but on moving to southern California find themselves powerless to devise a nurturing home for themselves. Longing for the richly textured daily life that they imagine wealth brings, they leave their modest apartments unfurnished and experience their most meaningful "domestic" events in their roomy car. At the book's conclusion, Ann sends her mother money for a down payment on a house, but Adele, true to form, uses it to buy a new car instead.

Marilynne Robinson's *Housekeeping* (1980) similarly narrates a quest for a sustaining but free mode of domesticity, the ability to be at once indoors and outdoors, rooted and on the road. Ruth, the book's narrator, recounts her family's history in northern Idaho. Long before her birth, her pioneering grandfather Edmund Foster was killed when his train plunged into dark, icy Fingerbone Lake, leaving behind him a family of women, the crooked house he built, and a westering impulse that lives on in the individualistic practices that continue to take place there. After the deaths of Ruth's mother and grandmother, her vagrant Aunt Sylvie moved in. "Sylvie talked a great deal about housekeeping," Ruth recalls. "Sylvie believed in stern solvents, and most of all in air. It was for the sake of air that she opened doors and windows, though it was probably through forgetfulness that she left them open" (Robinson 1980: 85). Sylvie's housekeeping is as much a matter of mood setting as utility: "She preferred [the house] sunk in the very element it was meant to exclude. We had crickets in the pantry, squirrels in the eaves, sparrows in the attic" (1980: 99). In a harsh, watery environment marked by drowned parents and vanishing children, abandoned cabins and hobo camps, flimsy clothes and finger food, the text portrays her ways as entirely apt. Sylvie seems less to be asserting individual preference than following the dictates of Foster family nature – or perhaps even of Fingerbone nature. She and Ruth eventually give up the house for a life of transience, but continue to dream of it forever after.

"So Big and So Free"?

Harrison's early history as an underpaid domestic worker in the US reminds us that the flip side of fascination with a liberating domesticity is the experience of an oppressive one, and this, too, is amply represented in twentieth-century western women's writing. Many texts highlight the dangers of rural, patriarchal households and the strategies of endurance and resistance they prompt, including renowned contemporary memoirs by Teresa Jordan, Mary Clearman Blew, and Terry Tempest Williams.

Mari Sandoz's *Old Jules* (1935) is a pathbreaking text in this regard, an exploration of frontier life that presents western heroism and western brutality as two sides of the same coin. A biography of the author's father Jules and his mighty efforts to tame the Nebraska frontier, it is also a record of the systematic abuse this pioneer inflicted on his wives and children. In *The Wind* (1925), a novel of gothic texture set in west Texas, Dorothy Scarborough also represents the home as a site of terror. Letty, the young Virginian protagonist, is intent on making a new life for herself in Sweetwater County. However, the physical and social isolation of the place – along with its relentless wind – brings about murder and madness. B.M. Bower's *Lonesome Land* (1912), an early western, tells another story of an eastern transplant to the West. Instead of the expansive life she anticipated in Montana, "so big and so free" (Bower 1997: 2), Val Peyson finds herself wed to an alcoholic and confined to a house.

Mourning Dove's *Cogewea, The Half-Blood* (1927) reworks the conventions of formula westerns, not only in gendered but also in racial ways. Her mixed-race heroine lives on a ranch on the Flathead reservation in Montana but dreams of a professional life in the East; the girl's ambition mirrors that of the Okanogan/Colville author herself, who labored over the book in a tent at night after putting in long days as a migrant laborer. Cogewea finally escapes a rapacious white suitor, and the book concludes with her eminently apt betrothal to her friend Jim. She also, however, shuts down her professional, literary, and geographical ambition, resigning herself to remaining within the "corral" of local identity and aspiration.

Its comic texture notwithstanding, Jean Stafford's *The Mountain Lion* ends on an even grimmer note. The novel portrays the consequences of its adolescent heroine Molly's move from suburban southern California to a cattle ranch in the Rockies. Even as she satirizes the highly feminized domestic landscape of Molly's childhood, Stafford suggests its appeal:

[O]ut West you would not find such falderal as Miss Runyon went in for. Miss Runyon lived next to the Wash in a little white house with green shutters and begonia in all the windows and Molly had loved it before Grandpa called it "a devil of a note." The flower garden came straight down to the road and standing among the beds of phlox and bachelor's buttons and oxalis were all sorts of curious creatures: a huge green frog, three brownies, a duck and four ducklings, two bluebirds as big as cats, a little Dutch girl in a sunbonnet, and a totem pole. There was a sign over the front door of the house which said "Dew Drop Inn." Next to the house was a doghouse built exactly like Dew Drop Inn and over its door was a sign that said "Dun Rovin." (Stafford 1993: 8–9)

Miniature, eccentric, women-run homes are everywhere in *The Mountain Lion*. Molly, though, is destined to go "out west" and live as an uneasy guest in her Uncle Claude's cavernous ranch house. Confronted with its "big, bare rooms" (Stafford 1993: 97) and a macho ethos that values hunting and breeding over language and writing (Rosowski 1996), Molly annexes small private spaces. She retreats to the bathroom and, more positively, locates "an ideal glade for her study" (Stafford 1993: 206), a stand of chokecherry trees surrounding a large, flat rock. But just when she seems most at home in the mountains, exploring their expansive terrain on her own, Molly is shot by her near-sighted brother when he mistakes her for the area's last remaining mountain lion. The book concludes with the pronouncement made by Magdalene, the ranch's African American cook: " 'Lord Jesus. The pore little old piece of white trash' " (Stafford 1993: 231). Magdalene's words underscore the fact that racial privilege does not always protect women in the West.

The Mountain Lion dramatizes the distinct problems women face in a region long associated with masculinity. Comer reminds us that open landscape coded as white, public, and male, remains the signature of the American West:

> Because western space, throughout American history, usually has connoted outdoor or wild spaces rather than domestic or indoor spaces, it predominantly signals *public* space. Far less suggestive of "home on the range" than of the range itself and the expansive possibilities invoked thereby, the dominant spatial field ... emplots normative western spaces in "open," "free," uncontained terms. (Comer 1999: 27)

"Western housekeeping" can seem like a paradox. If the West is synonymous with open space, than how can the homes within it matter? Such seeming contradiction may lie behind the surprising claim with which Nina Baym concluded her plenary lecture at the Western American Literature Association's 2008 conference, "The Many Wests of American Women's Writing, 1833–1928": that once women (presumably white and middle-class) had established homes in the West, the West as such no longer existed. Their homemaking standardized the region, making it indistinguishable from anywhere else.

This essay, I hope, has suggested otherwise. Writers do not erase but in fact construct the West in narratives that probe the implications of domestic acts. Proffering their own versions of western scripts of freedom, individualism, cultural encounter, racial conflict, landscape, and violence, they bring into their regional purview both the West's celebrated "open spaces" and its less recognized indoor ones too.

REFERENCES AND FURTHER READING

Anzaldúa, Gloria. (1987). *Borderlands/La Frontera: The New Mestiza*. San Francisco: Aunt Lute Books.

Austin, Mary. (1991). *Earth Horizon: An Autobiography*. Afterword by Melody Graulich. Albuquerque: University of New Mexico Press.

Austin, Mary. (1995). *Stories from the Country of Lost Borders*, ed. Marjorie Pryse. New Brunswick: Rutgers University Press.

Bernardin, Susan. (1997). The Lessons of a Sentimental Education: Zitkala-Ša's Autobiographical Narratives. *Western American Literature*, 32/3, 212–38.

Bevis, William. (1987). Native American Novels: Homing in. In Brian Swann and Arnold Krupat, eds., *Recovering the Word: Essays on Native American Literature*, pp. 580–620. Berkeley: University of California Press.

Bower, B.M. (1997). *Lonesome Land*, introd. Pam Houston. Lincoln: University of Nebraska Press.

Cather, Willa. (1915). *The Song of the Lark*. Boston: Houghton Mifflin.

Cather, Willa. (1918). *My Ántonia*. Boston: Houghton Mifflin.

Chapman, Mary. (2008). A "Revolution in Ink": Sui Sin Far and Chinese Reform Discourse. *American Quarterly*, 60/4, 975–1001.

Cisneros, Sandra. (1992). *The House on Mango Street*. London: Bloomsbury.

Comer, Krista. (1999). *Landscapes of the New West: Gender and Geography in Contemporary Women's Writing*. Chapel Hill: University of North Carolina.

Crow Dog, Mary, and Richard Erdoes. (1991). *Lakota Woman*. New York: HarperPerennial.

DeCora, Angel. (1911). An Autobiography. In *The Red Man*, pp. 279–85. Carlisle, PA: Carlisle Indian Press.

Harrison, Juanita. (1996). *My Great, Wide, Beautiful World*, introd. Adele Logan Alexander. New York: G.K. Hall & Co.

Houston, Jeanne Wakatsuki, and James D. Houston. (1973). *Farewell to Manzanar: A True Story of Japanese American Experience During and After the World War II Internment*. Boston: Houghton Mifflin.

Kolodny, Annette. (1984). *The Land Before Her: Fantasy and Experience of the American Frontiers, 1630–1860*. Chapel Hill: University of North Carolina Press.

Ling, Amy. (1995). Introduction. In Sui Sin Far, *Mrs. Spring Fragrance and Other Writings*. Urbana: University of Illinois Press.

MacLane, Mary. (1993). *Tender Darkness: A Mary MacLane Anthology*, ed. Elisabeth Pruitt. Belmont, CA: Abernathy & Brown.

Robinson, Marilynne, (1980). *Housekeeping*. New York: Picador.

Romines, Ann. (1997). *Constructing the Little House: Gender, Culture, and Laura Ingalls Wilder*. Amherst: University of Massachusetts Press.

Rosowski, Susan J. (1996). Molly's Truth Telling, or Jean Stafford Rewrites the Western. In Michael Kowalewski, ed., *Reading the West: New Essays on the Literature of the American West*, pp. 157–76. Cambridge: Cambridge University Press.

Simpson, Mona. (1987). *Anywhere But Here*. New York: Alfred A. Knopf.

Stafford, Jean. (1993). *The Mountain Lion*. Austin: University of Texas Press.

Stewart, Elinore Pruitt. (1988). *Letters of a Woman Homesteader*, foreword Gretel Ehrlich. Lincoln: University of Nebraska Press.

Sui Sin Far [Edith Maude Eaton]. (1995). *Mrs. Spring Fragrance and Other Writings*, ed. Amy Ling and Annette White-Parks. Urbana: University of Illinois Press.

Tonkovich, Nicole. (1997). *Domesticity with a Difference: The Nonfiction of Catharine Beecher, Sarah J. Hale, Fanny Fern, and Margaret Fuller*. Jackson: University Press of Mississippi.

Zitkala-Ša [Gertrude Simmons Bonnin]. (2003). *American Indian Stories, Legends, and Other Writings*, ed., introd., and notes Cathy N. Davidson and Ada Norris. New York: Penguin Books.

23

The Apple Doesn't Fall Far from the Tree: Western American Literature and Environmental Literary Criticism

Hal Crimmel

Critics of western American literature have always been sensitive to questions of place and the human relationship to nature, while the more recent advent of ecocriticism has more specifically addressed those concerns. This essay seeks to explore the roots of the relationship between western American literature and ecocriticism, and trace the ongoing evolution of the interrelationship between the two.

Our first step is to attempt a definition of western literature. Though the task is complicated by the tremendous expansion of its horizons over the years, the standard definition of western American literature is still relevant: all literature written about places west of the 100th meridian, the oft-cited line beyond which agriculture is impossible without irrigation. This standard definition also encompasses topics traditionally considered "western" such as those dealing with open spaces, ranching, mining, agriculture, and wild lands – in short, the elements of the "Old" West. Or, as Kathleen A. Boardman describes it, "Traditionally the West has represented the frontier, the self-reliant white male hero, the myth of virgin land and the fresh start, the safety valve for illiterates and misfits, the last gasp of the American Dream and the backwater of the American mainstream" (1997: 45).

Four decades ago, this definition seemed unproblematic. Even if the canon of western American literature and history was in fact more diverse than mainstream definitions reflected, the wave of poststructuralist-driven criticism that would open the canon and its criticism was still some distance away, though the ideas had certainly been lapping at the coasts for some time. Allen Ginsberg's poem "Howl," for example, was performed in 1955 in San Francisco. But its anti-capitalist agenda and explicit descriptions of homosexual behavior were not topics that mainstream America was ready to accept as American, let alone "western." The space of the West was still

A Companion to the Literature and Culture of the American West, First Edition. Edited by Nicolas S. Witschi.
© 2011 Blackwell Publishing Ltd. Published 2011 by Blackwell Publishing Ltd.

reserved for the icon of the cowboy (heterosexual, of course), livestock, and wide-open spaces.

A tally of the gender distribution of authors and a consideration of the types of articles published in *Western American Literature*, the flagship journal of western American literary criticism, from its first issue in 1966 through 1968, reflects a publication dominated by males on "Old" West topics. During this three-year period, *Western American Literature* published 140 editorials, essays, and book reviews by men, and 7 by women. Contrast that with the near 1:1 ratio of men to women in the journal's offerings over the last three years. And in its first decade the scholarly focus of *Western American Literature* was weighted heavily toward such figures as Willa Cather, Jack London, Larry McMurtry, or Frank Norris. Titles of articles frequently included such keywords as "Wilderness," "Frontier," "Mountain Man," "Cowboy," "Indian," "Pioneer," and other terms closely tied to the mythology of the "Old" West. Such essays, which often explore individual relationships to place and/or the natural world, reveal a latent ecocritical focus that would take another thirty years to fully emerge.

Today's readers of *Western American Literature* are as likely to encounter essays on these familiar, now canonical figures, and encounter title keywords similar to those found forty years ago, as they are to encounter essays on "Translating Nature," "Culture Tectonics," "Place and Gender," "Figuring the Wild," or "The Cliff Dwellers and New Historicism," essays clearly influenced by the trends in critical theory that have figured prominently in scholarship over the last three decades. As such, *Western American Literature*'s topical and theoretical horizons have become much wider and more complex than four decades ago. As Susan Rosowski wrote back in 1997:

> Whereas writing of the Old West proceeded from assumptions of opposition – West versus East, settlement versus wilderness, civilization versus savagery – writing of the New Wests proceeds from assumptions of both: inside and outside, the individual in community. Once the modernist's lament that the center cannot hold has given way to an acknowledgement of multiple centers, the aim is no longer to resolve difference but instead to find points of convergence. (1997: 222)

This literature and criticism of the New West has expanded the critical canon. As the scholarship of western literature began to focus on previously marginalized issues ranging from race and ethnicity to queer studies, as evidenced in texts by Greta Gaard, Joni Adamson, Alex Hunt, Krista Comer, or Susan Kollin, for instance, it was able to move off the ranch and out of the rural West to polyglot cities like Los Angeles or Phoenix – and then back again. Consider the discussions generated by *Brokeback Mountain*, for example, and how this "western" advanced topics Louis L'Amour or Zane Grey wouldn't have touched with the proverbial ten-foot pole.

Within this decentering movement one focus of western American literature and its criticism has remained: an abiding interest in the relationships between humans and nature, and the places they inhabit. In *The Practice of the Wild*, Gary Snyder declared that "bioregionalism is the entry of place into the dialectic of history. Also we might say there are 'classes' which have so far been overlooked – the animals, rivers, rocks, and grasses – now entering history" (1990: 44). Animals, rivers, rocks and grasses have always been present in literature, but the history of literary criticism suggests these were rarely considered to be more than elements of setting or tropes to advance some other theme. However, western American literature critics and ecocritics discussing western writers such as Dan Philippon, Don Scheese, Barney Nelson, Glen Love, and Nicolas Witschi for instance, have consistently demonstrated that these "classes," and the human relationship to them, could be an important critical focus of scholarship. In so doing, these critics and others helped legitimize how "stories with trees in them"[1] and the ensuing critical consideration could figure prominently as an interpretive tradition, one that invited examinations of how human relationships to the natural world were in fact not at the margins, but at the thematic core of so many texts.

Thus it is not surprising that one branch of ecocriticism's headwaters is found in western American literature and its attendant scholarship. This story is well documented elsewhere, but ecocriticism, as "the study of the relationship between literature and the physical environment" (Glotfelty 2001: p. xviii) didn't gain widespread attention until the early 1990s, with the establishment in 1992 of ASLE (Association for the Study of Literature and Environment) at a meeting of the Western American Literature conference. This was followed in 1993 by the establishment of the journal *ISLE* (*Interdisciplinary Studies in Literature and Environment*), and finally in 1995 with the inaugural ASLE conference at Colorado State University. Next year, Cheryll Glotfelty and Harold Fromm published *The Ecocriticism Reader: Landmarks in Literary Ecology*, which effectively introduced the term "ecocriticism" to a broader scholarly audience, despite the fact that William Rueckert had coined it in 1978. The historical roots of ecocriticism extend much further, but as Lawrence Buell notes, "The quest for an inception point can trap one in an infinite regress" (2005: 13).[2] Ecocriticism's contemporary prominence is easier to trace. A group of individuals affiliated with western American literature was able to define ecocriticism in a way that struck a chord with readers disillusioned with, shall we say, the excesses of poststructuralist literary criticism, which to some, at least, resulted in a practice that left literature barren and devoid of meaning. As poststructuralist critics successfully trawled the canon to illustrate how texts lacked meaning, they left in their wake disillusioned readers who, despite the indeterminacy of language, wanted connection. Where did some of these critics turn? To the same spaces American authors and their protagonists repeatedly turned: to nature.

In 1996, when ecocriticism itself was just beginning to carve a course for itself, newly minted ecocritics began to trace the origins of their intellectual concerns back to such seminal works in American and British literary studies as Henry Nash Smith's *Virgin Land* (1950), Leo Marx's *The Machine in the Garden* (1964), Roderick Nash's *Wilderness and the American Mind* (1967), Raymond Williams' *The Country and the City*

(1973), Joseph Meeker's *The Comedy of Survival* (1974), and Annette Kolodny's *The Lay of the Land* (1975) (Heise 2006: 505).

These early ecocritics discovered they were not alone in their interests. Personally speaking, these texts were invigorating for me as a graduate student in the early 1990s. Coming across *Wilderness and the American Mind*, for example, seemed an oasis in what seemed my graduate program's forced march through the endless desert of continental theorists. Yet here was a book that, in addition to being highly readable, engaged themes in literature ignored by other critical approaches. Ursula Heise has suggested that "Like feminism and critical race studies, ecocriticism started with a critical reconceptualization of modernist notions of human psychological identity and political subjecthood" (2006: 506). But it seems ironic to describe ecocriticism's origins this way. As a graduate student wanting to combine outdoor interests with the study of literature that evinced a connection to nature, I doubt my interest in what would come to be called ecocriticism had much to do with "a critical reconceptualization of modernist notions of human psychological identity" (Heise 2006: 506) – or it at least wasn't filtered through language that seemed to contradict the clarity I sought. Ecocriticism seemed to me, at least, a way to legitimize the study of the intersection of people and nature in literature.

Finding the Western Literature Association and a group of people who shared my burgeoning interest in place, wilderness, nature, and our relationship to it enabled the pursuit of this interest within the context of an established field of study. Perhaps this is merely an anecdotal explanation of the connection between western American literature and ecocriticism. But I suspect many whose interest in ecocriticism was kindled in the early 1990s have a similar story to tell about how and where their own interest in environmental literature found professional legitimacy, because they were not finding it from the MLA, the ALA, or the CCCC, or any other literary organization at the time.

Still, in 1996, ecocriticism was relatively theoretically naive. Its focus was fairly narrow, concerned with nature writing, or wilderness encounters, and so forth. It had not yet broadly questioned the social or cultural contexts that shaped these traditions, our attitudes toward "nature" or "wilderness," or even the very concepts themselves. In this respect, it mirrored the origins of western American literature's scholarship which, as noted above, had a narrow canonical and critical horizon. Today, as John Tallmadge writes in the foreword to *Teaching North American Environmental Literature*, "The environmental view has become a mode of omnibus critique, on a par, I would argue, with feminism, gender, race, culture, ethnicity and even deconstruction in the challenge it mounts to dominant modes of thought, discourse, and social relations" (2008: 3).

Ecocriticism, then, firmly validated the study of literature and the production of criticism connected to the natural world, including "locating vestiges of nature within cities and/or exposing crimes of eco-injustice against society's marginal groups" (Buell 2005: 24). By questioning its assumptions and seeking out its many blind spots, ecocriticism slowly added a self-reflective component, thanks to the work of Michael

Bennett, Karla Armbruster, Kathleen Wallace, and Michael Cohen, among others. As Ursula Heise has noted, "Like other areas of cultural theory, ecocriticism saw its initial assumptions questioned for what they had socially excluded, historically erased, and textually forgotten" (2006: 507); this process diversified the field to the extent that defining its relationship with western American literature and criticism is today more challenging than it once was. Ecocriticism has grown into a broad, mature field that makes precise definitions elusive. Currently ecocriticism focuses on nature writing, bioregionalism, urban nature, the idea of wilderness and nature, and the wild. At the same time it questions these very concepts. It also explores environmental justice, ecofeminism, and race-, class-, and gender-related issues, and the way we interpret landscape, among others. Ecocriticism has validated the process of "narrative scholarship," whereby a critic combines library research with what Don Scheese calls "foot notes" (2002: 10) – that is, the process of including field observations and personal reflections generated by hands-on experience – to create a fresh and, some would argue, more holistic form of literary criticism. In sum, it may be difficult today to wrestle ecocriticism into a concise definition, but the expansion of the field's critical biodiversity has helped to ensure its continuing vitality. And that is a good thing.

Western writers, like ecocritics, realize that celebrating the West and its landscapes is not enough any more; one has to engage the story behind the scenery. As I remind my students, for instance, Utah has some of the most spectacular and diverse wild lands in the nation: deep canyons on the Green and Colorado rivers, serpentine slickrock canyons, remote mesas, avalanche-prone mountain ranges rising above 12,000 feet, rare species of fish, plants, and animals. There are priceless ancestral puebloan sites. In short, the state is rich in geologic formations, fossils, wildlife, and viewscapes. Yet, like so many other western states, Utah also has just about every imaginable environmental problem: devastating urban air pollution that ranks among the worst in the nation, habitat fragmentation wrought by off-road vehicle use, urban and suburban sprawl, Superfund sites, including uranium mine tailings that leach into the Colorado River at Moab, contaminating the drinking water of more than 10 million downstream users in Las Vegas, Phoenix, and southern California. Dams on the Green and other tributary streams have wreaked havoc with riparian flora and fauna. One water project proposal after another seeks to divert or use water from the already over-allocated Colorado system. Utah stores nuclear waste and chemical weapons upwind of 2 million people. Energy development in the form of coal mining and oil and gas drilling on otherwise wilderness-quality lands scars and impacts these places for centuries. There's more, but you get the idea. Utah is a place of great beauty but it is also home to a litany of environmental problems.

For some westerners, the "Old" West stock-raising and extraction industry culture still lives on. For urban westerners those sunny skies are often obscured by "red air" days when pollution limits exceed federal EPA standards. There are chain-link fences and big-box retailers and parking lots and fast-food chains, and violent crime. All are not unusual in twenty-first-century urban America. But they have little to do on a daily basis with cowboys, wide-open spaces, stock-raising cultures, or any of the associated mythologies present in those pickup truck advertisements that look like they've all been filmed in Montana. Perhaps as a result, prominent contemporary western writers' work has as much to do with industrial civilization as with the dominant metaphors of the Old West. Writers such as Terry Tempest Williams, Rick Bass, Barry Lopez, Rebecca Solnit, Gloria Anzaldúa, and Leslie Marmon Silko, among many others, temper an affinity for western places with a sense of loss. Williams, for example, in her classic *Refuge: An Unnatural History of Family and Place* (1992), is an example of a contemporary work that combines a lyrical celebration of nature with an acute awareness of the damage industrial civilization – specifically nuclear testing – has wrought on human health. *Refuge* offers a look at the devastating effects of the technological sublime while juxtaposing them with the magic of migratory birds in the Bear River Migratory Bird Refuge north of Salt Lake City. Given the nature of the contemporary West, then, with its peculiar mix of the pristine and the polluted, it's not surprising that western American literature and its attendant scholarship find themselves closely intertwined with the concerns of ecocriticism.

Examining three representative texts in the western American literary canon can help illustrate how the ecocritical apple has not fallen far from the western American literature tree. Willa Cather's *My Ántonia*, Edward Abbey's *Desert Solitaire*, and Leslie Marmon Silko's *Ceremony* provide a look at representative texts evincing both "western" and ecocritically relevant themes, and they trace the trajectory from pioneer-themed "Old West" literature to that addressing racial and social injustice west of the 100th meridian.

Cather's *My Ántonia*, published in 1918, chronicles the settlement of the Nebraska prairie, and the shift from the wild grasslands that characterized the region prior to European settlement to the domesticated agrarian landscape present today. The novel's themes are quintessentially western, including those of the pioneer struggle to subdue wild lands, coping with isolation wrought by the process of settlement, and, among others, regret over the loss of the once wild prairie. I'd like here, however, to focus on the theme of struggling to accept and understand an unfamiliar landscape, an effort documented in the diaries and journals of explorers, trappers, pioneers, and other early settlers. The root of this struggle as found in western American literature usually has to do with the disorienting effects of aridity on those accustomed to a damp green climate full of trees. Doris Grumbach's foreword to the novel notes that in "no other book has Cather invoked the mystic nature of man's relation to the soil to timelessly as in *My Ántonia*" (1988: p. xxiv). But as Jim Burden, Cather's narrator, inadvertently reveals, the "timeless" relation is one of misperception. Jim says, "Trees were so rare in that country, and they had to make such a hard fight to grow, that we used to feel anxious about them, and visit them as if they were persons. It must have been the scarcity of detail in that tawny landscape that made detail so precious" (p. 21).

Jim's reaction, as a Virginia native, is the classic response of the easterner to the more arid regions of the country. He perceives the prairie as a place where "scarcity of detail" is a defining characteristic. Jim defines detail through trees, as he is not yet able to see the particulars found in the subtle contours of the land and the great diversity of native plants, for instance. As Tom Lynch, drawing on the work of Jay Arthur, notes in regard to dominant American landscape aesthetics, "the new place is always a flawed version of England. And the more the new landscape deviates from England, the more flawed it will seem" (2008: 31). *My Ántonia* is set in fictional Red Cloud, Nebraska (Cather renamed it "Black Hawk" for the novel) just west of the 98th meridian. Though the country is not as arid as far western Nebraska, to the eyes of the novel's Virginia-born narrator it is still a land of "scarcity."

Cather's characters' interest in land reflects that abiding central concern of western American literature with one's relationship to place. This is also a central concern of ecocriticism, which has helped us consider how culturally bound our perceptions of landscape are, and how those perceptions influence readings of this novel and others. "The aesthetic denigration of grasslands," notes John Price, "has helped entrench these negative opinions, validating efforts to convert prairie into forest or field" (2008: 142). Price discusses how influential authors, including Dickens and Cooper, viewed the prairie as "blank" or "barren" (2008: 142), which has contributed to the persistence of such attitudes today. So if western American literature and its attendant criticism helped validate, for instance, the role of landscape in shaping a sense of place, ecocriticism offered a path to provide more critical self-examination of how attitudes toward a particular landscape resulted in negative impacts to the ecological health of those places. Cather's *My Ántonia*, then, is an excellent example of a "western" text where ecocriticism's fresh approach can point to the centrality of environmental issues, with the novel's apparent celebration of the settling of the grasslands. The pioneer, much celebrated in literature, demands a reformulation when consideration is given to the effects of the plow on native grasslands. Citing a quotation found in *One Man's Montana*, Edward Abbey critiques the idea of the pioneer in *Desert Solitaire*: "In my book a pioneer is a man who comes to virgin country, traps off all the fur, kills off all the wild meat, cuts down all the trees, grazes off all the grass, plows the roots up and strings ten million miles of wire. A pioneer destroys things and calls it civilization" (Abbey 1971: 208).

With this troubling reconsideration of the much-celebrated pioneer in mind, Cather's imagery of an abandoned plow "left standing in the field" (p. 156) seems less a nostalgic symbol of a bygone era and even less a symbol of a "heroic" era, and rather an instrument of ecological devastation.[3] Cather writes, "Magnified across the distance by the horizontal light, it stood out against the sun, was exactly contained within the circle of the disk; the handles, the tongue, the share – black against the molted red. There it was, heroic in size, a picture writing on the sun" (p. 156). This central symbol of the novel has many interpretations, of course, one of which is the promise of regeneration. But the regeneration seems less of an ecological and more of an intellectual sort. Book III of the novel, which emphasizes Jim's return to the prairie through the "world of ideas" (p. 165), follows a few pages after the symbol of the plow appears, and in this book Jim regenerates his past through the lens of time. But he's still too close to the era of settlement to consider the ecological effects of the sod-busting era or to clearly articulate how the plow has irrevocably diminished the wild prairie.

Edward Abbey's *Desert Solitaire*, on the other hand, published in 1968, is a celebration of the desert and an attack against those who would destroy it. Based on Abbey's work as a park ranger in what is now Arches National Park near Moab, Utah, the book is important for its attempt to help reconfigure the nation's attitudes toward its arid lands. As a Pennsylvania native, the prejudices of Abbey's well-watered upbringing have not entirely disappeared: the cover of the original edition of *Desert Solitaire* contains the caption "A celebration of the beauty of living in a harsh and hostile land." Here Abbey seems to be reflecting the notion that "the word *drought* configures normal weather patterns as abnormal and even as immoral, as something to be struggled against and endured rather than as something to be adapted to" (Lynch 2008: 33–4), in that the desert is a place perceived to be "harsh and hostile." Yet, in his chapter "Water" Abbey clearly feels that "there is no shortage of water in the desert but exactly the right amount, a perfect ratio of water to rock, or water to sand (p. 159), in contrast to the tourist from Ohio who things the region would be good country "'if only you had some water'" (p. 141).

Desert Solitaire celebrates "Old West" individuals who make a living from ranching or from extraction industries such as uranium prospecting. Abbey writes of the "free and friendly" atmosphere of a Moab tavern that is filled with "prospectors, miners, geologists, cowboys, truckdrivers and sheepherders" (p. 49), in contrast to that of white-collar bars with their "sad, sour gloom ... where nervous men in tight collars brood over their drinks" (pp. 49–50). This "Old West" bar-room scene and Abbey's reflections on why these individuals are "happy" and "self-confident" (p. 50) leads, ironically, into his polemic against industrial tourism, which as a function of industrial society, is indirectly enabled by those prospecting for the precious metals and fuels upon which his twentieth-century civilization is built. In any case, *Desert Solitaire* celebrates stereotypical western traits such as self-reliance, solitary work in the out-of-doors, and an appreciation for wide-open, unpeopled spaces. With its "western" themes and ferocious environmental awareness it's not surprising that this book (along with many of Abbey's other works) is considered a core text for western American literature scholars and for ecocritics. What I am getting at here is that in the post-war era, with an ever-increasing industrial civilization, literature produced in the American West about the American West exhibits an increasingly acute sense of ecological concern, in contrast to a book like *My Ántonia*. Whether it is because of the vast dam projects proposed for the Colorado system, nuclear testing, the growth of the interstate system, or numerous other reasons, western writers address their growing concerns with these issues. Abbey, for instance, in his chapter "Down the River," floats Glen Canyon on the Colorado for one last time, railing at the short-sighted development schemes that will flood this canyon for his lifetime, at least. Though it took the literary-critical establishment decades to validate environmental issues as a vital theme, western literary critics by necessity needed to address the environmental thought found in Abbey's work and that of other like-minded writers.

Much as literary critics managed to overcome their attitudes about the validity of ecologically related themes as a "valid" field of study, western writers continued to work to overcome the prejudice toward arid lands as something to be despised, conquered, or both, and to replace it with an acceptance, if not reverence, for these places. Leslie Marmon Silko's *Ceremony*, published in 1977, traces the main character Tayo's recovery from cultural alienation brought on by racism the horrors of World War II, and a sense that his home, the Laguna Pueblo reservation, is just "goddamn dried-up country" (p. 55). Tayo is able to reestablish a connection with place that connects him to the sweep of ceremonial time, with its traditions, rituals, and sense of belonging. Whereas *Desert Solitaire* was the work of a newcomer to arid lands, Ceremony represents the work of an indigenous writer (who perhaps, in Willa Cather's day, may have been unable to get her work published). Silko's work both points to the racist attitude toward Indians that pervades the West (and the rest of America) and opens readers' eyes to the adaptive possibilities of living in an arid region. If Tayo and his people have been taught that their land is worthless because it seems devoid of water, the novel explores how that perception can be reversed. As the canon of western American literature has expanded to encompass writers of Hispanic, Asian, and Native American descent, ecocriticism's foci have shifted as well.

In *Ceremony*, for instance, Silko writes of the need for Tayo to reestablish an intimate connection with the land. If Tayo is a proxy for his people, his ability to make this connection suggests the possibility that the tribe as a whole can do the same. But such deep relationships with land that are on a par with intimate interpersonal relationships can seem incomprehensible to the non-Native reader. Silko's personification of the land is reflective of Indian beliefs, but it is also a helpful trope. Tayo makes love to Ts'eh, one of his spiritual mentors, next to a spring; he "couldn't feel where her body ended and the sand began" (p. 222), in a suggestion that intimate physical connection with place is a necessary component of being human. His relationship with place is sharply contrasted with that of the "white" world, where ranchers fence in the sacred mountain Tse'pina, and seek to track and kill the same ethereal mountain lion that Tayo describes as "becoming what you are with each breath, your substance changing with the earth and sky" (p. 196). Tayo sees reservation land as a place where his people's stories are intertwined, a place where stories provide spiritual sustenance, in contrast to white ranchers who want to imprison the land and destroy its native creatures, and in contrast to a government that wants to use the earth for destruction. Silko writes:

> The gray stone was streaked with powdery yellow uranium, bright and alive as pollen; veins of sooty black formed lines with the yellow, making mountain ranges and rivers across the stone. But they had taken these beautiful rocks from deep within the earth and they had laid them in a monstrous design, realizing destruction on a scale only *they* could have dreamed. (p. 246)

Here the symbolism of yellow, a color sacred to the Laguna Pueblo for its connections to corn pollen, the very stuff of life, has been corrupted in the quest for uranium ore needed to make nuclear weapons, the most lethal tool for worldwide human destruction. In the United States, uranium comes primarily from deposits of carnotite. Carnotite, a bright yellowish mineral, is found in large concentrations on the Colorado Plateau, including on the lands belonging to the Navajo Nation and to the Laguna Pueblo tribe. The world's largest open uranium mine, which operated from 1953 to 1982, is found on the Laguna Pueblo reservation (Quandelacy 2010: para. 1). During the years of the mine's operation, the social effects on the tribe were profound, if not disastrous. "During the time of the mines, alcohol and drug abuse surfaced, along with spouse and child abuse. [And] the peak production years of the mines were also peak years for suicides and dropout rates" (Quandelacy 2010: para. 32). For the Laguna Pueblo, mining was a deeply offensive act that violated their sense of the earth as a source of sustenance, not destruction. Whether measured by kilotons of explosive power or by the radiation sickness experienced by Laguna Pueblo mine workers, or by the rash of social ills that coincided with mining operations, the excavation of carnotite proved to be deadly in more ways than one. Even today the ill effects continue for many Indians living on and around the Colorado Plateau, giving rise to the term "nuclear racism." There are an estimated 1,100 uranium tailings piles on the Navajo Nation alone, and many Navajos live in dwellings close to tailings that emit radiation in excess of federal limits. Hundreds of other Navajos who worked in the mines are dying or have died of radiation-related cancers (Schneider 1993).

Thus as the canon of western literature has expanded to include texts written by previously marginalized peoples, literary critics such as Mei Mei Evans, Joni Adamson, and Rachel Stein, among others, have become attuned to environmental justice issues implicit in texts like Silko's. Ecocriticism has enabled and empowered critics who wish to explore, for instance, the Laguna Pueblo worldview, with its intimate relationship to nature. It has also made it possible to explore how the nuclear West left in its wake indigenous communities devastated both spiritually and physically by uranium mining and nuclear testing while practicing literary criticism.

Finally, western American literature written in the last decade illustrates the increasing awareness of the paradox between the West's dramatic natural landscapes and the diminished – if not contaminated – nature of these places. Ellen Meloy's *The Last Cheater's Waltz: Beauty and Violence in the Desert Southwest* (1999) is one such work. Meloy, an accomplished nonfiction writer and, before her death, a resident of the Colorado Plateau, sets out to try and reconcile the "inscrutable tension" found between the West's open spaces and the darker stories they contain. Her task is to come to terms with the notion that "In this abundant space and isolation, the energy lords extract their bounty of natural resources, and the curators of mass destruction once mined their egregious weapons and reckless acts" (p. 7). The thematic thread of the nuclear West, then, stretches from Abbey's *Desert Solitaire*, to Silko's *Ceremony*, and through Williams' *Refuge*, to Meloy's *The Last Cheater's Waltz*. Her book, perhaps more than any of the others, reflects an obsession with the sense that the place she calls home is literally contaminated with uranium mines but also morally contaminated by the mines' connection to the development and testing of the atomic bomb. She writes: "At Trinity I had discovered that my own neighborhood might be wired to the vortex of apocalyptic horror" (p. 100). As a "western" writer she is deeply interested in those themes we began this essay with: questions of place and the human relationship to nature. As an ecocritically relevant text, *The Last Cheater's Waltz* goes beyond a neo-Romantic celebration of open spaces and the human relationship to nature; in fact it goes so far as to deconstruct that relationship, illustrating the troubling contemporary relationship of people to place in the American West. The contemporary convergence of western American literature with ecocriticism, I suggest, is manifest in a work such as this.

Accordingly, western American literature and ecocriticism are in many respects inseparable. Environmental consciousness – whether in the shape of the preservationist thought articulated by John Muir so many years ago, or simply in a foregrounding of the human relationship to place – is at the heart of the western American literary tradition. As more writers, critics, and citizens become aware of the countless environmental challenges facing us in the American West and around the globe, the relationship between ecocriticism and western American literature, which teaches us how to better understand the places we inhabit and the people we encounter there, will continue to have a lasting, meaningful relationship.

Notes

1 "Stories with trees in them" refers to a sentence from the rejection letter Norman Maclean received from a publisher who objected to the prominent place the natural world played in his classic novella *A River Runs Through It*.

2 The ecocritical impulse had been gathering momentum for two decades, at least; some would say for centuries. (See Buell 2005: 13–14). In his *A Century of Early Ecocriticism* (2001), David Mazel has collected essays stretching back to 1864 that reflect early ecocritical thought, even if it was not known as such at the time. But the late 1980s and

1990s was "a time when environmentalism itself began to undergo profound changes: the realization of the global nature of our most pressing ecological problems, the long-overdue concern with environmental justice and environmental racism" as well as a reconsideration of terms such as nature, wilderness, or environment, notes Mazel (2001: 17); these concerns helped propel ecocriticism forward as a critical approach.

3 In Iowa, for instance, notes John Price, "less than one-tenth of one percent of native habitat remains" (2008: 139).

References and Further Reading

Abbey, Edward. (1971). *Desert Solitaire: A Season in the Wilderness* [1968]. New York: Ballantine Books.

Adamson, Joni. (2001). *American Indian Literature, Environmental Justice, and Ecocriticism: The Middle Place*. Tucson: University of Arizona Press.

Adamson, Joni, Mei Mei Evans, and Rachel Stein, eds. (2002). *The Environmental Justice Reader:*

Politics, Poetics, and Pedagogy. Tucson: University of Arizona Press.

Armbruster, Karla, and Kathleen R. Wallace. (2001). *Beyond Nature Writing: Expanding the Boundaries of Ecocriticism*. Charlottesville: University Press of Virginia.

Bennett, Michael. (2001). From Wide Open Spaces to Metropolitan Space: The Urban Challenge to

Ecocriticism. *Interdisciplinary Studies in Literature and Environment*, 8/1, 31–52.

Bennett, Michael, and David W. Teague, eds. (2009). *The Nature of Cities: Ecocriticism and Urban Environments*. Tucson: University of Arizona Press.

Boardman, Kathleen A. (1997). Western American Literature and the Canon. In Thomas J. Lyon, ed., *Updating the Literary West*, pp. 44–70. Fort Worth: Texas Christian University Press.

Buell, Lawrence. (1995). *The Environmental Imagination: Thoreau, Nature Writing, and the Formation of American Culture*. Cambridge, MA: Harvard University Press.

Buell, Lawrence. (2005). *The Future of Environmental Criticism: Environmental Crisis and Literary Imagination*. Oxford: Blackwell Publishing.

Buell, Lawrence. (2009). Foreword. In Alan C. Braddock and Christoph Irmscher, eds., *A Keener Perception: Ecocritical Studies in American Art History*. Tuscaloosa: University of Alabama Press.

Cahalan, James M. (2001). *Edward Abbey: A Life*. Tucson: University of Arizona Press.

Campbell, SueEllen. (1997). Connecting the Countery. In Thomas J. Lyon, ed., *Updating the Literary West*, pp. 3–13. Fort Worth: Texas Christian University Press.

Cather, Willa. (1988). *My Ántonia* [1918]. Boston: Houghton Mifflin.

Christensen, Laird, and Hal Crimmel, eds. (2008). *Teaching about Place: Learning from the Land*. Reno: University of Nevada Press.

Christensen, Laird, Mark C. Long, and Fred Waage, eds. (2008). *Teaching North American Environmental Literature*. New York: MLA.

Cohen, Michael. (2004). Blues in the Green: Ecocriticism Under Critique. *Environmental History*, 9/1, 9–36.

Comer, Krista. (1999). *Landscapes of the New West: Gender and Geography in Contemporary Women's Writing*. Chapel Hill: University of North Carolina Press.

Ecocriticism (1999). Special issue of *New Literary History*, 30/3, 505–716.

Gaard, Greta. (2004). Toward a Queer Ecofeminism. In Rachel Stein, ed., *New Perspectives on Environmental Justice: Gender, Sexuality, and Activism*, pp. 21–44. Piscataway, NJ: Rutgers University Press.

Garrard, Greg. (2004). *Ecocriticism: The New Critical Idiom*. Oxford: Routledge.

Glotfelty, Cheryll. (1996). Introduction. In Cheryll Glotfelty and Harold Fromm, eds., *The Ecocriticism Reader: Landmarks in Literary Ecology*, pp. xv–xxxvii. Athens: University of Georgia Press.

Glotfelty, Cheryll. (2001). Literary Bashing, Test Site Nevada. In Karla Armbruster and Kathleen R. Wallace, eds., *Beyond Nature Writing: Expanding the Boundaries of Ecocriticism*, pp. 233–47. Charlottesville: University Press of Virginia.

Grumbach, Doris. (1988). Foreword. In Willa Cather, *My Ántonia*. Boston: Houghton Mifflin.

Heise, Ursula K. (2006). The Hitchhiker's Guide to Ecocriticism. *PMLA*, 121/2, 503–16.

Hunt, Alex. (2009). *The Geographical Imagination of Annie Proulx: Rethinking Regionalism*. Lanham, MD: Lexington Books.

Kollin, Susan, ed. (2007). *Postwestern Cultures: Literature, Theory, Space*. Lincoln: University of Nebraska Press.

Kowaleweski, Michael, ed. (1996). *Reading the West: New Essays on the Literature of the American West*. Cambridge: Cambridge University Press.

Limerick, Patricia Nelson, Andrew Cornell, and Sharon K. Collinge, eds. (2009). *Remedies for a New West: Healing Landscapes, Histories, and Cultures*. Tucson: University of Arizona Press.

Love, Glen. (1990). Revaluing Nature: Toward an Ecological Criticism. *Western American Literature*, 25/3 (Nov.), 201–15.

Lynch, Tom. (2008). *Xerophilia: Ecocritical Explorations in Southwestern Literature*. Lubbock: Texas Tech University Press.

Lyon, Thomas J. (1997a). What Is Happening in the West Today, and What It Might Mean. In *Updating the Literary West*, pp. 961–3. Fort Worth: Texas Christian University Press.

Lyon, Thomas J., ed. (1997b). *Updating the Literary West*. Fort Worth: Texas Christian University Press.

Mazel, David. (2001). Introduction. In David Mazel, ed., *A Century of Early Ecocriticism*, pp. 1–19. Athens: University of Georgia Press.

Meloy, Ellen. (1999). *The Last Cheater's Waltz: Beauty and Violence in the Desert Southwest*. Tucson: University of Arizona Press.

Meyers, Jeffrey. (2005). *Converging Stories: Race, Ecology, and Environmental Justice in American Literature*. Athens: University of Georgia Press.

Muir, John. (1988). *My First Summer in the Sierra.* San Francisco: Sierra Club Books.

Murphy, Patrick D. (2009). *Ecocritical Explorations in Literary and Cultural Studies: Fences, Boundaries and Fields.* Lanham, MD: Lexington Books.

Nelson, Barney. (2000). *The Wild and the Domestic: Animal Representation, Ecocriticism, and Western American Literature.* Reno: University of Nevada Press.

Phillipon, Daniel J. (2005). *Conserving Words: How American Nature Writers Shaped the Environmental Movement.* Athens: University of Georgia Press.

Price, John. (2008). Idiot Out Wandering Around: A Few Words about Teaching Place in the Heartland. In Laird Christensen and Hal Crimmel, eds., *Teaching about Place: Learning from the Land*, pp. 139–53. Reno: University of Nevada Press.

Quandelacy, Talia. (2010). Nuclear Racism: Uranium Mining on the Laguna and Navajo Reservations. *The Interdisciplinary Journal of Health, Ethics and Policy.* TuftScope. June 6, 2010. http://s3.amazonaws.com/tuftscope_articles/documents/52/6.0_Nuclear_Racism_Uranium_Mining_on_the_Laguna.pdf.

Rosowski, Susan J. (1997). New Wests. In Thomas J. Lyon, ed., *Updating the Literary West*, pp. 217–22. Fort Worth: Texas Christian University Press.

Scheese, Don. (2002). *Nature Writing: The Pastoral Impulse in America* [1995]. New York: Routledge.

Schneider, Keith. (1993). A Valley of Death for the Navajo Uranium Miners. *The New York Times*, online, May 3, 1993.

Silko, Leslie Marmon. (1977). *Ceremony.* New York: Penguin.

Slovic, Scott, ed. (2001). *Getting Over the Color Green: Contemporary Environmental Literature of the Southwest.* Tucson: University of Arizona Press.

Snyder, Gary. (1990). *The Practice of the Wild* [Originally published by North Point Press, San Francisco, 1990]. Shoemaker Hoard.

Tallmadge, John. (2008). Foreword. In Laird Christensen, Mark C. Long, and Fred Waage, eds., *Teaching North American Environmental Literature*, pp. 1–5. New York: MLA.

Taylor, J. Golden, and Thomas J. Lyon.(1987). *A Literary History of the American West.* Fort Worth: Texas Christian University Press.

Witschi, Nicolas S. (2001). *Traces of Gold: California's Natural Resources and the Claim to Realism in Western American Literature.* Tuscaloosa: University of Alabama Press.

24
Detective Fiction

Nicolas S. Witschi

In 1902, Mark Twain published a short little book called *A Double-Barrelled Detective Story*. This whimsical but uneven novel tells the story of Archy Stillman, a young man who is charged by his mother with seeking out and psychologically tormenting his long-absent father, an abusive man who had years earlier stripped his mother naked and tied her to a tree before disappearing from their lives. Endowed with an absurdly powerful sense of smell, Stillman pursues his task ·(literally, following the scent) through several western mining regions, ultimately arriving in a California gold camp. A case of mistaken identity drives the plot, for Stillman winds up tormenting not his father but a cousin of his father's. Meanwhile, a seemingly unconnected parallel story about the murder of an abusive miner in that same California camp ultimately provides the key to both narratives – the murdered miner proves to have been none other than Stillman's father. In order to appear less freakish, Stillman pretends that the information he learns through his nose is actually the result of keen observation and reasoning. In so doing, he acts as detective and solves the murder, thereby also resolving his own need for revenge. But the most salient feature of this satire is the detective figure whom Stillman bests in working out the details of the murder: Sherlock Holmes, who had come to California's mining country to meet with a nephew of his.

Not nearly as compelling as *Pudd'nhead Wilson* (1894), Twain's more famous novel of crime, detection, and mistaken identity, *A Double-Barrelled Detective Story* nevertheless offers a glimpse into a moment of cultural and literary history that proves particularly useful in gauging the incipient popularity of an important twentieth-century genre, the detective novel. As a number of commentators have pointed out, Twain's satirical treatment of Sherlock Holmes certainly attests to the international popularity of the latter figure, a literary icon known for his formidable intellect. In Twain's hands,

A Companion to the Literature and Culture of the American West, First Edition. Edited by Nicolas S. Witschi.
© 2011 Blackwell Publishing Ltd. Published 2011 by Blackwell Publishing Ltd.

though, Holmes becomes an inept and supercilious bumbler, a detective who misses or ignores obvious clues in favor of theories supported by his more abstruse and presumably scientific methods. As one admirer in camp puts it (while talking to another character named "Ham Sandwich"), Holmes brings "'*scientific* work. Intellect – just pure intellect'" to a case, while "'Archy is all right, and it don't become anybody to belittle *him*, I can tell you. But his gift is only eyesight, sharp as an owl's, as near as I can make it out just a grand natural animal talent, no more, no less, and prime as far as it goes, but no intellect in it'" (p. 103). When Holmes's methods fail to produce a murderer, though, it falls to Archy to identify the killer. That he does so not with "eyesight, sharp as an owl's" but with his nose represents an ironic twist on empirical observation that only furthers Twain's satirical assault on the literary conventions of detection.

Indeed, it is the textual nature of detective fiction that ultimately receives the sharpest rebuke. For one, Twain's rather tortured structure mirrors that of Arthur Conan Doyle's first Sherlock Holmes novel, *A Study in Scarlet* (1887), which was also constructed around two seemingly unrelated plots (one set in the American West) that converge only at the very end, hence "double-barrelled." And the preciousness of literary language as a whole is skewered in the still puzzling but oft-cited description of a sunny California morning:

> It was a crisp and spicy morning in early October. The lilacs and laburnums, lit with the glory-fires of autumn, hung burning and flashing in the upper air, a fairy bridge provided by kind Nature for the wingless wild things that have their homes in the tree-tops and would visit together; the larch and the pomegranate flung their purple and yellow flames in brilliant broad splashes along the slanting sweep of the woodland; the sensuous fragrance of innumerable deciduous flowers rose upon the swooning atmosphere; far in the empty sky a solitary oesophagus slept upon motionless wing. (pp. 53–4)

With his strange adjectives and incongruous nouns, Twain anticipates the criticism of British detective fiction that arises frequently in American crime-writing circles, namely that it is far too contrived in plotting and precious in diction to satisfy as a literature that is focused on the brutality of homicide and the ostensibly pragmatic discovery of truth. In short, Twain's little book testifies to the fact that, in 1902, the mystery novel was already making broad cultural inroads, already known and, whether admired or despised, already influential. That it is set in one of the American West's most iconic landscapes, a gold camp in California, alludes to a further signpost in the history of the genre: the importance of the American West in the evolution of the form, both in its beginnings in the nineteenth century and in its rise to maturity over the course of the twentieth century. Which is to say, as will be demonstrated below, at almost every acknowledged point of significance in its history, the detective novel in the United States relies vitally on the American West – as subject, as topos, or even simply as setting – to aid in the process of evolution or reinvention.

After Edgar Allan Poe's genre-inaugurating tales of ratiocination, the first American detective stories were chiefly adventure narratives set in the American West. Allan Pinkerton, whose detective organization had chased after Jesse James and Butch Cassidy and had worked to suppress miners' attempts to organize (in both the East and the West), published a series of sensational but ostensibly autobiographical accounts of his exploits. In books such as *The Expressman and the Detective* (1874), *The Molly Maguires and the Detectives* (1877), and *Bank-Robbers and the Detectives* (1883), Pinkerton, or more precisely his ghost writers, borrowed heavily from the conventions of dime novel westerns and adventure tales in chronicling his and his company's exploits (Denning 1987: 118–48; Klein 1994: 133–54; Panek 2006: 133–4). The connection is a telling one, for in the study of adventure narratives and their various constitutive sub-genres, it has become something of a commonplace to observe that the distinctly American detective story is by and large a genre western transposed into an urban environment, that the cynical and disillusioned gumshoe is but a twentieth-century gunslinger in a cheap suit and a fedora. More to the point, the relationship between western vigilante and detective has become traditionally viewed as progressive, the former leading into and becoming the latter. This perspective was perhaps best articulated by Henry Nash Smith, who offered that "the Western hero had become a self-reliant two-gun man who behaved in almost exactly the same fashion whether he were outlaw or peace officer. Eventually he was transformed into a detective and ceased in any significant sense to be Western" (1971: 119). Leslie Fiedler would reinforce this point by observing that "the private eye is not the dandy turned sleuth; he is the cowboy adapted to life on the city streets" (1966: 476). But as Cynthia Hamilton (1987) and Marcus Klein (1994) have affirmed, the two genres, and hence their respective literary figures, in large part evolved coevally and in often overlapping ways. Thus can a former Pinkerton operative and ranch worker named Charlie Siringo offer a memoir entitled *A Cowboy Detective* (1912), a linguistic construction that seeks to modify an established profession, "detective," with the relatively newer popular cultural category of "cowboy." To be sure, cowboys as a class existed well before the first decade of the twentieth century. But as David Hamilton Murdoch points out when challenging the idea that "the cowboy was replaced by the detective," detective fiction was a common feature of the popular literary marketplace well before the ascent of the mythic cowboy figure (2001: 61). Thus, while not a novel but rather a chronicle of cases worked and adventures lived through, Siringo's book nevertheless attests to the simultaneous rise to mythic status of both ideas.

It would fall to another Pinkerton operative turned writer, however, to truly inaugurate the twentieth-century American detective novel, and he would do so primarily by drawing on material from the American West. In 1923 Dashiell Hammett began to publish short stories in *Black Mask*, a pulp magazine that was the standard bearer for sensational tales of crime, adventure, and detection (see Nolan 1985). His detective was a rather unheroic type, a short and dumpy investigator with the Continental Detective Agency known simply as the Continental Op, and his stories about this otherwise unnamed detective feature a darkly comic tone and a cynical outlook. As

Leonard Cassuto observes, the Op represents the beginnings of the hard-boiled detective who relies as much on intuition and feeling as he does on reason (2009: 14), a move away from the "scientific" mode of pure reasoning satirized by Twain. Hammett's first novel, *Red Harvest* (1929), brings together four loosely connected Op stories from *Black Mask* that relate the Op's investigation of the murder of a newspaper editor. Fueled by outrage, the Op goes beyond his initial charge by deciding to clean up the thoroughly corrupt Montana mining town of Personville (which the Op as narrator tells us is pronounced by the local cynics as "Poisonville"). Best understood as a novel that thematically explores the alienating impact of the modern urbanscape on culture and society (Marling 1995: 108–9), *Red Harvest* also offers a number of meditations on the figurative connection between humans and the more familiar "natural" landscapes of the American West as well. Foremost among such meditations lies the double meaning of the title, which refers simultaneously to the extensive copper ore-mining operations to be found in the novel's loosely fictional version of Anaconda, Montana, and the human bloodshed that mars the town. In this manner, Hammett enters into the conversation about the American West not simply by way of the lone figure of retributive justice represented by the Op but also by assessing the human cost associated with the ways in which the landscapes of the West had come to be valued (Witschi 2002: 155–7).

In 1930, Hammett's *The Maltese Falcon* introduced readers to Sam Spade, a San Francisco-based private investigator with an ambitious, practical streak that at times trumps his equally well-developed morality. On the one hand, Spade investigates the murder of his longtime business partner, Miles Archer, in order to ensure that justice is properly served; on the other hand, he is certainly quick to erase Archer's name from their shared office door, thus establishing himself at the very beginning as a singular entity, a lone man in charge. Moreover, his participation in the labyrinthine search for the book's eponymous object is motivated to a great extent by his desire to keep secret the fact that that he had been having an affair with Archer's wife. Not surprisingly, Hammett explores over the course of the novel a number of such ambiguities or contradictions, particularly those frequently associated with modernity. For one, questions of loyalty and honor abound as Spade seek retribution for Archer's death while clearly benefiting from the same. And questions of value, which were of paramount importance in a nation just beginning to come to terms with the stock market crash of 1929, are explicitly at issue in the matter of the falcon itself, a statuette encrusted with gold and jewels that is at the center of the plot but which is never actually seen, an absent signifier. Perhaps most importantly, matters of gender and representation are questioned not only through the character of Brigid O'Shaughnessy – a complexly conniving lover/antagonist – but also by the figures of the distinctly effeminate Joel Cairo and Caspar Gutman's henchman Wilmer, referred to daringly as a "gunsel" (contrary to popular assumption, this term does not mean "hired gun" but rather derives from a Yiddish word for "gosling" and refers derisively to the young, homosexual partner of an older man). Through representations such as these, Hammett inaugurates not only the tradition of the tough-talking, callous, and hyper-individualistic detective, he also locates that figure within a range of at times contrasting, at times complementary alternative figurations of identity. Altogether, Hammett's minimalist, often fragmentary and distractingly plotted novel epitomizes the "modernization of the American detective story" (Naremore 1998: 63).

With a modernist cynicism that is tempered by a Romantic sensibility much more fully invested in the ostensibly "high art" qualities of fiction, Raymond Chandler rightly stands as the next key innovator in the history of the detective novel in the United States. As was the case with Hammett, Chandler also began his career by publishing stories in *Black Mask* and, also like Hammett, he used his fiction to plumb the darker ambiguities and uncertainties of modern life. Leonard Cassuto summarizes the case in his analysis of Chandler's first novel, published in 1939: "A grimy story involving pornography, drugs, and a particularly nasty hired killer in the employ of organized crime, *The Big Sleep* also offers none of the clean, cathartic redemption that typically ended pre-hard-boiled detective stories" (2009: 82). In contrast to his predecessor, though, Chandler much more deeply examines the extent to which his characters are affected by and integrate their lives into the spaces they occupy. Avid readers greatly enjoy tracking Chandler's detective, Philip Marlowe, as he moves almost Leopold Bloom-like through a recognizable landscape in which the names are but thinly disguised versions of their real-life analogues. For example, Chandler uses Bay City instead of Santa Monica, Little Fawn Lake instead of Big Bear Lake, Poodle Springs instead of Palm Springs, and Esmerelda instead of La Jolla (the former is Spanish for "emerald" while the latter is thought by some to be a Spanish corruption of a Native American place name, while others believe it to be a misspelling of the Spanish word for jewel, "la joya"). More particularly, though, in all of these places an honorable yet cynical Marlowe finds corruption, decay, and above all a great many characters who either tether their lives to a moribund ideal or, more frequently, embody a sadness born of a distinctly western American alienation. Through the juxtaposition of urbanization with the nature-based industries that typically defined the West (see Witschi 2002: 139–66), Chandler describes such elements of California society as the overdetermined stultification of wealth and power derived from the oil industry (e.g., *The Big Sleep*); the erasure of identity as literalized in and around a high mountain reservoir (*The Lady in the Lake* [1943]); and the changing economic and (to a lesser degree, to be sure) racial demographics of Los Angeles' various neighborhoods (e.g., *Farewell, My Lovely* [1940] and *The Long Goodbye* [1953]).

There is certainly nothing exclusively "western" about such matters, since detective fiction in the hard-boiled mode was emerging not just in California but in New York City and other places around the country as well (see especially McCann 2000; Marling 1995: 39–92). However, the widely recognized signposts in the development of this specific sub-genre of detective fiction are predominantly those represented by Hammett and Chandler. Evidence of the American West's vital role in the development of the genre may be seen in the quasi-cowboy figure who investigates crime, the self-employed loner. While the Continental Op was usually inclined to working by his own set of rules, he was nevertheless in the employ of a large, impersonal corporation. On the other hand, the next generation of literary detectives, such as Sam Spade and Philip Marlowe, work for themselves and presume to live by their own moral code. In being so represented, these characters exemplify the highly individualistic masculinity at the heart of the cowboy–detective analogy. Finally, as a locus overwhelmingly determined by the relation of its people to its often spectacular spaces, the West lends to the detective novel one of its central conceits, namely the extent to which the detectives' movements figuratively define their identities in relation to their spaces. Referring to the relationship of high modernism to both popular and mass-produced forms of cultural expression, James Naremore observes in his chapter on the literary and cultural antecedents to film noir that, in the twentieth century, "the streets at night were transformed into the privileged mise-en-scène of the masculine unconscious" (Naremore 1998: 44). And it is from Chandler himself, in "The Simple Art of Murder," that we learn that when it comes to defining the detective, it all hangs on the assumption that "down these mean streets must go a man who is himself not mean" (p. 59).

Chandler offers this organizing metaphor in what might well be viewed as a manifesto for the modern American detective novel, his 1944 essay for *The Atlantic Monthly* entitled "The Simple Art of Murder." In defining his hero as "the best man in his world and a good enough man for any world," he continues:

> He is a relatively poor man, or he would not be a detective at all. He is a common man or he could not go among common people; he has a sense of character, or he would not know his job. ... [H]e is a lonely man and his pride is that you will treat him as a proud man or be very sorry you ever saw him. He talks as the man of his age talks – that is, with rude wit, a lively sense of the grotesque, a disgust for sham, and a contempt for pettiness. (p. 59)

Chandler presents his criteria for a proper detective or mystery story – a work of "art" that includes messy crime, realistic dialogue, and above all a moral but individualistic hero – at the conclusion of an extensive reading of the Arthur Conan Doyle/Dorothy Sayers tradition. As had Mark Twain several decades earlier, Chandler derides the precious language and implausibly constructed plots of a mostly British genre, with its "its heavy crust of English gentility and American pseudo-gentility" (p. 57), "murders scented with magnolia" (p. 58), and clever plotting that amounts to little more than a game of "spillikins in the parlor" (p. 59). Preferring instead something akin to a pragmatics of crime and detection, Chandler advocates a fiction that has the artistic merit of literary realism, gives "murder back to the kind of people who commit if for reasons" (p. 58), and employs an intensely masculine detective figure who will restore order while operating out of some inherent code of propriety. Cassuto rightly observes that "Chandler's mythic archetype ... comes to stand for a raft of male characters that he doesn't particularly resemble, perpetuating a stereotype. Hard-boiled masculinity is something of a made-up idea to begin with, but depending on Chandler and his early peers to represent it means relying on an extreme made-up version"

(2009: 192–3). But as an oft-cited manifesto Chandler's essay has very much proven to have supplied the kind of measure which subsequent practitioners of the form have butted up against in one manner or another.

One very explicitly rendered echo of Chandler's "best man in his world" ethos is Lew Archer, the detective in a series of southern California-based mysteries by Kenneth Millar, who published under the pseudonym of Ross Macdonald. In a run of eighteen wonderfully literary and complexly structured novels that appeared from 1949 through the 1970s, Archer surveys the state of American "civilization" at its far western edge – mostly Los Angeles and a stand-in for Santa Barbara called Santa Teresa – and often finds it lacking (see Speir 1984). What drives this survey is Archer's capacity as "an everyman of sympathy" (Cassuto 2009: 162); as a character in *The Galton Case* (1959) says of him, Archer has "'a reputation for tempering the wind to the shorn lamb'" (p. 225). Thus, Macdonald most frequently shows his detective helping families to excavate and perhaps rectify the memory of events and relationships rendered traumatic through murder and misunderstanding in equal parts. Moreover, he frequently places Archer's cases in settings that figuratively point to another set of important relationships, namely the ecological or environmental. Thus, in a novel such as *The Underground Man* (1971), Macdonald has Archer move quite directly not only across a landscape set ablaze by a late summer forest fire but also through California's various social and racial strata. In one chapter, for example, Archer travels from a wealthy family's mansion under threat of fire in the hills, past streets in the valleys below where "Black and Chicano children stood beside the road and watched us go by as if we were a procession of foreign dignitaries," right to the doorstep of a servant who works in that mansion (p. 52). But the solution to a Lew Archer mystery is never merely a matter of exposing the hypocrisy of the rich or of protecting the interests of the vulnerable. Through a first-person narration that, stylistically, frequently suggests an intermixing of internal emotional states with external physicality, Macdonald presents a detective who in bridging with psychological insight the many social strata he crosses, finds both corruption and good-heartedness at every stopping point. Ultimately, Archer's adventures suggest that hope is to be had if there is a willingness to recognize and nurture a relationship rather than exploit it, whether it is ecological or familial in nature.

Another author who definitely sees herself as the inheritor of a tradition is Sue Grafton, whose alphabet series (*"A" is for Alibi* [1982], *"B" is for Burglar* [1985], and as of this writing up through *"U" is for Undertow* [2009]) features the investigative work of Kinsey Millhone. It has been widely observed that Grafton's character shares the same initials as Kenneth Millar, Ross Macdonald's given name. More directly, however, and just as frequently noted, is the fact that Grafton announces her debt to Macdonald by setting her novels just north of Los Angeles in the same Santa Teresa in which Lew Archer works. Of course, Grafton's most significant departure from the Chandler/Macdonald model may be found in her depiction of the professional detective as a woman. As Charles J. Rzepka, among others, has noted, "Grafton takes many of the standard features of the masculine hard-boiled hero – detachment, toughness, cynicism – and gives them a personal history that distinguishes her detective heroine ... from her masculine precursors" (Rzepka 2005: 242; see also Cassuto 2009: 188–95). But Millhone is still very much a character cut from a mold similar to that of Chandler's ideal private eye – a twice-divorced, heterosexual freelancer who earns her money mostly by investigating insurance fraud, she is cynical about the world yet has a moral bearing that is best described as idealistic: usually she will take cases out of some implicit social obligation, to right a wrong. In Grafton's first novel the pattern is set, for instance, by the fact that when offered money to investigate a murder that had ostensibly been settled long ago but which still has the hint of a wrongful conviction about it, Millhone replies, "I don't want to be paid to rehash old business" (*Alibi*, p. 6). The key, of course, is that she will rehash that business, just not with profit as the primary motive.

Grafton depicts Millhone rather conventionally when it comes to the use of natural settings in the search for balance or order. In this respect, Grafton's work is very much of a piece with western American literature's frequent emphasis on the restorative potential that may be found in natural spaces. Described as a reluctant but persistent runner, Millhone frequently seeks a measure of solace by jogging through the more natural spaces of the various California landscapes she works in. In one particularly telling instance in *"A" is for Alibi*, for example, she goes for a run in Los Angeles along a route that takes her "across to San Vicente at Twenty-sixth Street. Once I got in the wide grassy divider, I could feel myself hit stride" (pp. 179–80). As brief as it is, the finding of a moment's balance while on a grassy strip in the middle of a busy asphalt thoroughfare is emblematic of how Grafton frames Kinsey Millhone's encounters with the outdoors; wherever and whenever she can find them, these brief touches with the green world afford her a moment of orderly stability. Granted, the peace is just that, momentary, and Grafton ensures that the fleeting quality of this moment is confirmed by the fact that Millhone must literally run for her life along a beach at the end of this same novel. But the point remains: Kinsey Millhone is a seeker of restorative order.

The principal means by which Millhone seeks to re-establish order in her world is, surprisingly enough, through paperwork. Grafton depicts her organizing the narrative of each investigation visually – for herself, not for the readers – with index cards tacked to a bulletin board or taped to the wall. Thus does Kinsey Millhone render explicit the connection between detection and narration: discover how the story goes and you will have found the solution to the mystery. Millhone is also repeatedly shown reading files, preparing documents, and typing up reports for her own files and for her occasional employers. And by implication, each novel ends with the filing of such a report with the readers. In almost all of the books in the series, an Epilogue to the narrative concludes with the words "Respectfully submitted, Kinsey Millhone." Should the reader infer that the text of the novel itself is one of the reports that Millhone is described as typing up over the course of the story? Again, at the beginning of the series on the first page of *"A" is for Alibi*, Grafton indicates that the account that is to follow, a sort of flashback, is specifically intended to provide the emotional context for fully understanding the otherwise unseen report: "I've already given a statement to the police, which I initialed page by page and then signed. I filled out a similar report for the office files. The language in both documents is neutral, the terminology oblique, and neither says quite enough" (p. 1). Thus, Millhone's concluding reports exist in the world of the story, but the novels' readers are granted access to a far different narrative, the one that ostensibly allows for understanding and sympathy to temper the facts of the crime being investigated. This point is further reinforced by the high degree of interiority that characterizes the first-person narration used throughout the series. In any case, Grafton's final report-like conclusions have the effect of establishing at least a partial sense of order where at the beginning there was none. Indeed, these endings never render a complete or satisfying restoration – Millhone is always worrying in these epilogues about the long-term effects on herself and on her clients of the traumatic events they have just endured together.

The woman detective has in recent decades been the subject of reinvention by a number of authors and for a number of regions, not only in Grafton's fiction but also in novels by Sara Paretsky, Patricia Cornwell, and Barbara Neely. The American West, though, has fostered a particularly strong collection of detective series that expand the genre's intersecting interests in gender, region, and racial identity. Distinctly tough women appear in Marcia Muller's Sharon McCone mysteries, which detail the adventures of an employee of the All Souls Legal Co-operative in San Francisco, and in Dana Stabenow's Kate Shugak mysteries, which are set in Alaska and feature a part-Native, part-white detective. Paula Woods and Katherine V. Forrest push ever further against the inherited conventions of the genre by writing about women in the employ of the Los Angeles Police Department whose identities are not commonly found in detective fiction: Woods' Charlotte Justice is African American while Forrest's Kate Delafield is a lesbian. Laurie King's Kate Martinelli novels follow an inspector with the San Francisco police who is also a lesbian, while Lucha Corpi's novels follow the investigations of her Chicana detective Gloria Damasco. And Nevada Barr's Anna Pigeon mysteries, fully half of which are set in the West, chronicle the often gender-based insecurities and uncertainties of a National Park Service law enforcement officer who finds herself solving murders in such settings as Yosemite, Rocky Mountain, and Mesa Verde national parks. Altogether, this burgeoning of detective fiction testifies to the possibilities for stretching the genre in ways that provide for much more than just locating "the best man in his world."

The reconfiguration of the detective genre in the American West, to be sure, has hardly been restricted to the question of how it handles gender; as the examples of Corpi, Stabenow, and Woods would attest, the region's complex mix of cultures, races, and ethnicities has prompted an equally compelling set of reinventions. One writer who has rendered the contact zone that is the desert Southwest with keen insight and sensitivity is Tony Hillerman, whose mysteries involve the investigations of not one but two officers with the Navajo Tribal Police, Lieutenant Joe Leaphorn and Officer Jim Chee. Although criticized at times for being a non-Native presuming to write about Native issues and people, Hillerman has for the most part been favorably received for his sensitivity to both the ambitions of and the daily difficulties faced by the Navajo in the modern world. In his memoir *Seldom Disappointed*, Hillerman describes the source of his relationship with Native Americans as "eight grades in an Indian school, Indian playmates, growing up knowing that the us of the us-and-them formula put us hardscrabble rural folks, Indians and whites, in the same category" (2001: 251). This formulation effectively sets aside, without erasing, ethnicity and race in favor of shared economic and cultural determinants. This is the very approach his fiction takes to representing the West – his is a landscape deep with history, a place in which the construction of identity is not an isolated or isolating experience but rather shared.

To communicate what his texts seek to accomplish and what one should broadly understand about the contemporary Southwest, Hillerman offers a powerful metaphor in the map that Joe Leaphorn uses in his investigations. A wall-sized, corkboard-mounted reproduction of "a common 'Indian Country' map published by the Auto Club of Southern California and popular for its large scale and its accurate detail" (*Skinwalkers*, p. 19), Leaphorn's map not only makes possible the search for patterns and order but also records a powerful array of cross-cultural and historical information:

> It was decorated in a hundred places with colored pins, each color representing its own sort of crime. It was inscribed in a hundred places with notes written in Leaphorn's cryptic shorthand. The notes reminded Leaphorn of information he'd accumulated in a lifetime of living on the reservation and half a lifetime of working it as a cop. The tiny *q* west of Three Turkey Ruins meant quicksand in Tse Des Zygee Wash. The *r* beside the road to Ojleto on the Utah border (and beside dozens of other such roads) recalled spots where rainstorms made passage doubtful. The *c*'s linked with family initials marked sites of summer sheep camps along the mountain slopes. Myriad such reminders freckled the map. *W*'s marked places where witchcraft incidents had been reported. *B*'s marked the homes of bootleggers.
>
> The notes were permanent, but the pins came and went with the ebb and flow of misbehavior. Blue ones marked places where cattle had been stolen. ... Gaudy rashes of scarlet, red, and pink ones (the colors Leaphorn attached to alcohol-related crimes) spread and subsided inside the reservation with the fate of bootleggers. They made a permanent rosy blotch around reservation border towns and lined the entrance highways. Markers for rapes, violent assaults, family mayhem, and other, less damaging, violent losses of control tended to follow and mingle with the red. A few pins, mostly on the reservation's margins, marked such white-man crimes as burglary, vandalism, and robbery. (*Skinwalkers*, pp. 20–1)

And homicides are marked by brown pins with white centers. Leaphorn uses this visual organization of information, which is strikingly similar to the index-card narrative that Grafton describes Kinsey Millhone as using, in his efforts to grasp the underlying patterns of life (and crime) in the region. Unlike Millhone's index cards, though, the map is not merely specific to one case or another. Rather, it represents a bridging of cultures in which the meshing of knowledge includes both the "accurate detail" of an Anglo-European pathways map and the equally important local and historical knowledge of washed-out arroyos and the demographic distribution of people.

Jim Chee's knowledge of the region is somewhat more aligned with an orientation that is best described as spiritual, less focused on quantifiable pattern, and thus his outlook offers a useful complement to Leaphorn's map (though he too is a policeman ultimately interested in order). A typical Chee moment regarding the landscape has him driving across it and pausing to reflect upon a particularly impressive vista:

> On the vast, rolling prairie that led away from the highway toward the black shape of Ship Rock every clump of sagebrush, every juniper, every snakeweed, every hummock of bunch grass cast its long blue shadow – an infinity of lines of darkness undulating across the glowing landscape. Beautiful. Chee's spirit lifted. (*Coyote Waits*, p. 92)

In this manner Hillerman renders the landscape as a palimpsest of information drawn not only from multiple cultural sources but also from the ineffable understanding that comes from having a direct experience of a region. But with the accumulated layers of jurisdiction represented by the Navajo people, the Tribal Police, the FBI, the Bureau of Indian Affairs, and the academic historians, anthropologists, and archeologists who crop up in every novel, Hillerman resists the all-too-familiar urge to render the desert Southwest as some sort of spiritually or socially exceptional haven characterized by simple and stunning beauty. The history of western conquest is never far from Hillerman's representations, which means that more significantly than the map, "Hillerman uses crimes as a metaphor for crime – small for large – and has created detectives whose main purpose is not solving the lesser crimes but, constantly pointing out the larger ones and revealing how they continue to victimize" (Templeton 1999: 39). Thus, while the construction of identity in Hillerman's Southwest is a shared experience of community, his is certainly not a simple fantasy of harmony and peace.

Critics and aficionados alike have hailed Walter Mosley's Easy Rawlins novels as the return of the Chandlerian hero. More to the point, the Los Angeles-based Rawlins represents a further adaptation and renewal of the form, most significantly in the fact that Mosley's detective is African American, and consequently here too the tensions of inter-community contact are frequently the subject of representation. Only quite recently has a genuine critical discussion emerged regarding the presence of African Americans in a region and history most familiarly (though incorrectly) associated with white settlers at odds with Natives and Hispanics (think Little Big Horn and The Alamo). Thus, while Mosley's novels are themselves not, strictly speaking, historiography, they do bring into the genre a number of historical contexts and events only hinted at in others. By placing Rawlins in situations that test his ability to identify variously as a man, an African American, a laborer, a homeowner, a detective, and a community or family member, Mosley effectively tracks the history of how the postwar experience of African Americans in the urban West differed significantly from that of the types of people represented, for instance, in Chandler and Macdonald (see Gruesser 1999). Beginning with *Devil in a Blue Dress* (1990), Rawlins may be found attempting to enter the postwar middle class that was forming during the defense industry boom of the late 1940s, struggling with the social implications of the Red Scare of the 1950s, and helping to maintain his community both by taking a position as a plant manager at a junior high school and by adopting a Hispanic boy and a biracial girl whom he'd found abandoned over the course of his investigations. A prequel to the series, *Gone Fishin'* (1997), dramatizes the social and economic forces that spurred the significant migration to southern California in the years immediately surrounding World War II (see Taylor 1998: 268). And while Ross Macdonald may hint at racial tension in something like *The Underground Man*, a novel such as Mosley's *Little Scarlet* (2004), set in the immediate aftermath of the Watts riots of 1965, does not chronicle a white observer's perception of the difficulty faced by non-white populations but instead explores those communities' traumas much more directly. Rawlins' attempts to be the best man in his world are certainly made more difficult by the environment of hate he is frequently depicted as living in the midst of, but in general Mosley depicts him as a moral figure who serves as a model for successful community-building.

A particular focus on community, historical patterns, or a combination of the two is also a prominent thematic feature of recent Chicano detective fiction (see especially Rodriguez 2005). In addition to Lucha Corpi's explorations of post-Chicano identity already alluded to above, the genre in its western American form has also been greatly enlivened by Rudolfo Anaya and Michael Nava. In a quartet of novels that figuratively take their investigator, Sonny Baca, through an entire cycle of seasons (*Zia Summer* [1995], *Rio Grande Fall* [1996], *Shaman Winter* [1999], and *Jemez Spring* [2005]), Anaya explores the ways that myth and genre intersect with the deep history of Nuevo Mexicanos as it exists within the more recently dominant cultures surrounding and at times subsuming it. In *Zia Summer*, Anaya employs the reappearance of green leaves on an ancient tree thought to be long dead as a concluding metaphor for the re-emergence of a feeling for community and cultural complexity among Alburquerque's (*sic*) Chicano population. And in Nava's Henry Rios novels, questions of cultural and ethnic identity come face to face with that other dominant strain of detective fiction, gender. Rios is an openly gay lawyer in San Francisco, and Nava uses his stories to document the ravages of AIDS as well as the deleterious effects that assumptions about both masculinity and racial and ethnic identity can have.

Finally, one ostensibly "western" writer of detective fiction worth considering for the questions he raises about the possible connections between region, authorial identity, and genre form, is Martin Cruz Smith. A Pennsylvania-born writer wishing to distinguish his name in the marketplace, he adopted at the start of his career as his middle name the surname of his Pueblo Indian maternal grandmother. The author of a number of pseudonymously published genre westerns and adventure novels

(Mengel 2009: 94, 99), Smith has also written a dramatic novel set in the American West, *Stallion Gate* (1986), which tells the story of the part-Native American soldier assigned as a personal bodyguard to J. Robert Oppenheimer during the building of the first atomic weapon at Los Alamos, New Mexico. Such details – his history as a genre writer and his choice of name – simply demonstrate that Smith knows the West and has at times turned to it for material. Once recognized, though, traces such as these become clearly evident in Smith's most significant literary production, his series of hard-boiled novels about Arkady Renko, a Russian police inspector in Moscow. Nothing about the setting in these novels, beginning with *Gorky Park* (1981), is specifically western American (although Alaska is featured briefly as a location in the second Renko novel, *Polar Star*). Nevertheless, Renko is very much the "best man in his world," a skilled but flawed investigator who has a keener moral sense than do any of his contemporaries. With a Mosley-like approach to historical narrative, Smith imagines the historical processes that drove the Soviet Union, that led to its dissolution, and that characterized the emergence of a more capitalist Russia as an economic power. This is not to say that Smith should be viewed unambiguously as a western American writer. But his example does show that things "western," from genre codes to authorial identity, may be a part of almost any detective novel. That is, the genre can be very much "western" without initially seeming so.

Conventionally, the detective novel has been identified as a largely conservative form (see especially Porter 1981), and to a certain extent this assessment is easily warranted. For one, from its earliest incarnations the genre has been about the discovery and nullification of forces that threaten to upend social or civil order, about re-narrating events so that they serve to restore the status quo. But as critics such as McCann, Hamilton, Cassuto, and Rzepka, among others, have made quite plain, the form has also allowed for writers from Hammett to Chester Himes to Sarah Paretsky, not to mention Grafton and Nava and Mosley, to diagnose and explore the myriad ways in which a society imposes order, in the process also exposing the fissures wherein power may be exercised by the ostensibly disenfranchised. In the right hands, the detective novel is less a genre focused on the (re)establishment of order than it is about asking questions about the limits of order and about asserting alternative possibilities. Just as the mature phase of the American detective novel had its early genesis in Pinkerton narratives about lawmen and outlaws on the western frontier, so too with successive generations or waves does the West as topos lead the way as the American detective novel grows. Even a stalwart East Coast-based detective, Robert B. Parker's Spenser from Boston, heads West in one of Parker's later novels, *Potshot* (2001), a knowing, self-aware nod to the regional affinities that have so frequently defined the genre. And perhaps most recently, the American West as a region has once again led to new explorations in the genre with Naomi Hirahara's novels about a Japanese survivor of Hiroshima who works as a gardener in Los Angeles and also happens to investigate crime. In short, the American detective novel rarely fails to return to the West for renewal and reinvention.

REFERENCES AND FURTHER READING

Anaya, Rudolfo. (1995). *Zia Summer*. New York: Warner Books.

Anaya, Rudolfo. (1996). *Rio Grande Fall*. New York: Warner Books.

Anaya, Rudolfo. (1999). *Shaman Winter*. New York: Warner Books.

Anaya, Rudolfo. (2005). *Jemez Spring*. Albuquerque: University of New Mexico Press.

Barr, Nevada. (2003). *Track of the Cat* [1993]. New York: Berkley Books.

Barr, Nevada. (2005). *High Country* [2004]. New York: Berkley Books.

Browne, Ray B. (2004). *Murder on the Reservation: American Indian Crime Fiction: Aims and Achievements*. Madison: University of Wisconsin Press.

Cassuto, Leonard. (2009). *Hard-Boiled Sentimentality: The Secret History of American Crime Stories*. New York: Columbia University Press.

Chandler, Raymond. (1944). The Simple Art of Murder. *Atlantic Monthly*, Dec., 53–9.

Chandler, Raymond. (1988). *The Big Sleep* [1939]. New York: Vintage.

Corpi, Lucha. (1995). *Cactus Blood*. Houston: Arte Publico Press.

Denning, Michael. (1987). *Mechanic Accents: Dime Novels and Working-Class Culture in America*. London: Verso.

Fiedler, Leslie. (1960). *Love and Death in the American Novel*. New York: Criterion.

Fischer-Hornung, Dorothea, and Monika Mueller, eds. (2004). *Sleuthing Ethnicity: The Detective in Multiethnic Crime Fiction*. Madison, NJ: Fairleigh Dickinson University Press.

Gosselin, Adrienne Johnson, ed. (1999). *Multicultural Detective Fiction: Murder from the "Other" Side*. New York: Garland.

Grafton, Sue. (2005). *"F" Is for Fugitive* [1989]. New York: St. Martin's.

Grafton, Sue. (2008). *"A" Is for Alibi* [1982]. New York: St. Martin's.

Gruesser, John Cullen. (1999). An Un-Easy Relationship: Walter Mosley's Signifyin(g) Detective and the Black Community. In Adrienne Johnson Gosselin, ed., *Multicultural Detective Fiction: Murder from the "Other" Side*, pp. 235–55. New York: Garland.

Hamilton, Cynthia S. (1987). *Western and Hard-Boiled Detective Fiction in America: From High Noon to Midnight*. Iowa City: University of Iowa Press.

Hammett, Dashiell. (1999). *Red Harvest* [1929]. In *Complete Novels*, pp. 1–187. New York: Library of America.

Hammett, Dashiell. (1999). *The Maltese Falcon* [1930]. In *Complete Novels*, pp. 387–585. New York: Library of America.

Hillerman, Tony. (2001). *Seldom Disappointed: A Memoir*. New York: HarperCollins.

Hillerman, Tony. (2002). *Skinwalkers* [1986]. New York: HarperTorch.

Hillerman, Tony. (2009). *Coyote Waits* [1990]. New York: Harper.

Klein, Marcus. (1994). *Easterns, Westerns, and Private Eyes: American Matters, 1870–1900*. Madison: University of Wisconsin Press.

Libretti, Tim. (1999). Lucha Corpi and the Politics of Detective Fiction. In Adrienne Johnson Gosselin, ed., *Multicultural Detective Fiction: Murder from the "Other" Side*, pp. 61–81. New York: Garland.

Macdonald, Ross [Kenneth Millar]. (1996). *The Underground Man* [1971]. New York: Vintage.

Marling, William. (1995). *The American Roman Noir: Hammett, Cain, and Chandler*. Athens: University of Georgia Press.

McCann, Sean. (2000). *Gumshoe America: Hard-Boiled Crime Fiction and the Rise and Fall of New Deal*. Durham, NC: Duke University Press.

Mengel, Bradley. (2009). *Serial Vigilantes of Paperback Fiction: An Encyclopedia from Able Team to Z-Comm*. Jefferson, NC: McFarland.

Mosley, Walter. (1990). *Devil in a Blue Dress*. New York: Norton.

Mosley, Walter. (1997). *Gone Fishin'*. Baltimore: Black Classic Press.

Mosley, Walter. (2004). *Little Scarlet*. New York: Warner Vision Books.

Murdoch, David Hamilton. (2001). *The American West: The Invention of a Myth*. Reno: University of Nevada Press.

Naremore, James. (1998). *More Than Night: Film Noir in its Contexts*. Berkeley: University of California Press.

Nava, Michael. (1986). *The Little Death*. Boston: Alyson Publications.

Nava, Michael. (1996). *The Death of Friends*. New York: G.P. Putnam's.

Nolan, William. (1985). *The Black Mask Boys: Masters in the Hard-Boiled School of Detective Fiction*. New York: William Morrow.

Panek, LeRoy. (2006). *The Origins of the American Detective Story*. Jefferson, NC: McFarland.

Parker, Robert B. (2001). *Potshot*. New York: Berkley Books.

Porter, Dennis. (1981). *The Pursuit of Crime: Art and Ideology in Detective Fiction*. New Haven: Yale University Press.

Rodriquez, Ralph E. (2005). *Brown Gumshoes: Detective Fiction and the Search for Chicana/o Identity*. Austin: University of Texas Press.

Rzepka, Charles J. (2005). *Detective Fiction*. Cambridge: Polity.

Siringo, Charles A. (1912). *A Cowboy Detective, a True Story of Twenty-Two Years with a World-Famous Detective Agency*. Chicago: W.B. Conkey.

Smith, Henry Nash. (1971). *Virgin Land; the American West as Symbol and Myth* [1950]. Cambridge, MA: Harvard University Press.

Smith, Martin Cruz. (1981). *Gorky Park*. New York: Random House.

Smith, Martin Cruz. (1989). *Polar Star*. New York: Random House.

Smith, Martin Cruz. (1986). *Stallion Gate*. New York: Random House.

Sotelo, Susan Baker. (2005). *Chicano Detective Fiction: A Critical Study of Five Novelists*. Jefferson, NC: McFarland.

Speir, Jerry. (1984). The Ultimate Seacoast: Ross Macdonald's California. In David Fine, ed., *Los Angeles in Fiction*, pp. 133–44. Albuquerque: University of New Mexico Press.

Taylor, Quintard. (1998). *In Search of the Racial Frontier: African Americans in the American West, 1528–1990*. New York: Norton.

Templeton, Wayne. (1999). Xojo and Homicide: The Postcolonial Mysteries of Tony Hillerman. In Adrienne Johnson Gosselin, ed. *Multicultural Detective Fiction: Murder from the "Other" Side*, pp. 37–59. New York: Garland.

Twain, Mark. (1902). *A Double-Barrelled Detective Story*. New York: Harper & Brothers. Repr. in Mark Twain, *The Stolen White Elephant and Other Detective Stories*. The Oxford Mark Twain. New York: Oxford University Press, 1996.

Witschi, Nicolas. (2002). *Traces of Gold: California's Natural Resources and the Claim to Realism in Western American Literature*. Tuscaloosa: University of Alabama Press.

25

The American Western Film

Corey K. Creekmur

Remembering the Western

The film western, once a ubiquitous vehicle for representing the past in American popular culture, must now be approached as itself a historical artifact rather than a vital movie genre.[1] Writing in the early 1950s, the French critic André Bazin could confidently assert that "the Western is the only genre whose origins are almost identical with those of the cinema itself and which is as alive as ever after almost half a century of uninterrupted success" (Bazin 2005a: 140). Indeed, as Bazin suggested, some of the earliest motion pictures featured "western" subjects: the Edison Company's 1894 Kinetoscope films *Sioux Ghost Dance, Bucking Broncho*, and *Annie Oakley*, for instance, each depict members of William F. "Buffalo Bill" Cody's Wild West show, some of whom, like Cody himself, could claim authentic links to the actual frontier history they now performed for urban audiences. For decades thereafter, the expectation that the American film industry would supply westerns to eager audiences was regularly met, and thus largely taken for granted. As soon as the initial novelty of moving pictures wore off and the movies secured a lasting place in mass culture, westerns were a basic ingredient in any standard film program: by 1910 about one out of every five films released in the United States was a western, and in 1911 firms like the American Film Manufacturing Company offered exhibitors two of its popular "Flying A cowboy pictures" each week (Altman 1999: 37) while Essanay, according to its trade advertisements the "indisputable originators of cowboy films," also offered "thrilling stories of early days in western America" every week (Abel 2006: 69). (At the same time, trade journals also warned that the vogue for western films was probably coming to an end, perhaps the first of many premature announcements of the

A Companion to the Literature and Culture of the American West, First Edition. Edited by Nicolas S. Witschi.
© 2011 Blackwell Publishing Ltd. Published 2011 by Blackwell Publishing Ltd.

genre's demise.) As a fully industrialized studio system developed in Hollywood in the next decade and moved toward standardized feature film production, the western continued to appear with the efficiency of any well-manufactured product, but it also began to achieve unique significance as the essential contribution to the consolidation of a dominant form of popular cinema soon viewed worldwide as distinctively American. (Indeed, Bazin's [2005a] essay celebrating the genre's persistence was written to preface a study entitled *Le Western ou le cinéma américain par excellence.*) After American manufacturers effectively challenged an attempt by the powerful French production company Pathé-Frères to dominate the market with "authentic" westerns made by its American branch, the genre's increased popularity became deeply inter-twined with what appeared to be its quintessential Americanness. By the end of the first decade of the twentieth century, the western was intricately associated with the discourse of Americanization, which itself began to impart a national identity to the country's rapidly expanding popular cinema.

However, by the late 1950s the "uninterrupted success" of the western, which Bazin seemed to assume should continue indefinitely, had began to crumble along with the Hollywood studio system itself, and the number of westerns produced in the United States sharply and steadily declined, until in the twenty-first century the genre barely survives as a viable commercial or creative option, much less as a set of familiar nar-rative tropes and icons once shared by millions of moviegoers. As a narrative form that often took it upon itself to offer elegiac accounts of late nineteenth-century American history for early twentieth-century audiences, the western now seems either an object of wistful nostalgia for a "simpler time" when the genre thrived (such as the 1950s, the last decade of the genre's centrality), or as an antiquated form justifi-ably left behind by current sensibilities. In *Horizons West* (1969), one of the first major studies of the western, Jim Kitses echoed Bazin's early assurance when he claimed that "It is only because the western has been everywhere before us for so long that it 'works.'" Due to this persistence, "over the years a highly sophisticated sub-language of the cinema has been created that is intuitively understood by the audience" (Kitses 1969: 21). Although western films are still produced from time to time, any contem-porary example now functions in isolation from that once-assumed context, in which the rules of the genre were "intuitively understood"; given their current scarcity, recent westerns simply cannot draw upon the shared cultural knowledge once readily available to even the genre's most humble examples, which were fully imbued with the accumulated significance provided by its popularity. To choose a single example, contemporary audiences can no longer be assumed to recognize, as earlier audiences clearly did, what it means when a cowboy reveals his poker hand to contain "aces and eights," the "dead man's hand" that announces the fate of characters in countless westerns. The absence of westerns from contemporary movie (and television) screens not only signals a shift in the genre's popularity, but perhaps the loss of a shared language with which Americans once narrated their history.

What, then, *was* the western? Our growing distance from not only the historical era represented in westerns – roughly between 1865 and 1890, or the end of the Civil

War and the official closing of the frontier – but especially from the regular production and consumption of such representations, has also allowed for a distortion as well
as a forgetting of the genre in both popular memory and scholarly accounts. Recent
audiences who have seen few westerns other than the outrageous parody *Blazing
Saddles* (Mel Brooks, 1974) or the revisionist *Unforgiven* (Clint Eastwood, 1992), are
in a poor position to understand how fully both films rely upon familiarity with the
long history of the genre that precedes them. But even more dedicated fans of
the genre acquainted with established classics such as *High Noon* (Fred Zinnemann,
1952), *Shane* (George Stevens, 1953), or *The Magnificent Seven* (John Sturges, 1960)
– films generally more popular with audiences than critics – may easily misrecognize
how such "defining" westerns differed from more typical examples playing in theaters
when they first appeared. For example, the most commercially successful western in
1953 (among approximately fifty releases), was the now largely forgotten *The Charge
at Feather River*, one of almost a dozen westerns to appear that year in the novelty of
3-D. Removed from a context in which its images and actions were shared with many
other westerns, *Shane* may no longer strike audiences as a self-conscious intensification
of familiar tropes (what Bazin decried as a decadent "superwestern" perhaps marking
the genre's collapse), but as a typical, "classic" example. To some extent this distortion
– or, more accurately, this *narrowing* – of the western was authorized by the genre's
first critics, who reasonably attempted to come to grips with a staggeringly vast body
of films by distinguishing a canon of the western's key works and major *auteurs*. The
critical recognition of Hollywood directors such as John Ford, Howard Hawks,
Anthony Mann, and Budd Boetticher, and of their key westerns, including *Stagecoach*
(Ford, 1939), *Red River* (Hawks, 1948), *The Naked Spur* (Mann, 1953), and *The Tall
T* (Boetticher, 1957), sought to legitimate serious treatment of the genre by isolating
its greatest artists and their masterpieces from an overwhelming number of average,
"generic" examples. Yet while praise of any Hollywood western once entailed a bold
critical gesture – even John Ford was not awarded any of his five Oscars for one of his
westerns – this evaluation of the prolific genre has had the lingering effect of obscur-
ing its actual range and diversity. The following account of what was once a common
narrative form will therefore simultaneously address the American western as a historical phenomenon which produced a large body of films and as a critical category
built upon a set of assumptions that significantly delimited that body, emphasizing
the way in which the characterization of the large genre through a few select examples
has often curtailed our full understanding of the western, at least until the expansive
work of recent scholars.

What was the western? At its best, the western has been acclaimed as an ideal
representation of American values, character, and exceptionalism, providing a modern
mythology for a nation without an ancient past by instilling frontier history with
greater symbolic resonance than a relatively brief period in American history might
otherwise engender. The western thus not only glowingly recalls a key period in
American history, but in effect summarizes America as a whole and being American
as a national identity. (According to the evidence of the box office, the settling of

the frontier, rather than the infrequently represented American Revolution, is the true American national epic.) In its best examples, the western as a narrative genre also exhibits a classical formal rigor: Bazin famously described Ford's *Stagecoach* as "like a wheel, so perfectly made that it remains in equilibrium on its axis in any position" (Bazin 2005b: 149). For the astute American cultural critic Robert Warshow, writing in 1954, the western was "an art form for connoisseurs, where the spectator derives his pleasure from the appreciation of minor variations within the working out of a pre-established order" (Warshow 2001: 116). While the film western was preceded by popular frontier stories in other media, the core elements of the genre, rooted in visceral images rather than abstract words, and in decisive action rather than sophisticated ideas, seemed to find their perfect expression in the fundamental "motion pictures" that defined cinema itself. In its frequent celebration, through location shooting, of the awe-inspiring western American landscape (most famously, in John Ford's recurrent depictions of Monument Valley) the film western even aligns itself with the pictorial tradition of the sublime. For its fans and critics, the form of the western is elegant, and its meanings are elemental and profound, despite its common dismissal as an escapist boy's genre: as Warshow summarized, in its "apparent simplicity" the genre gave "the figure of the Westerner an apparent moral clarity which corresponds to the clarity of his physical image against his bare landscape; initially, at any rate, the Western movie presents itself as being without mystery, its whole universe comprehended in what we see on the screen" (Warshow 2001: 109).

What *else* was the western? At its worst, the western has also been denounced as an artifact of and implicit justification for brutal conquest and genocide by "superior," "civilized" Anglo-Saxon and Christian hegemony. By often treating Native Americans as indiscriminate "savages," the western provides one of American popular culture's most shameful defenses of racist misrepresentation and mistreatment, relying on broad stereotypes of undifferentiated "Injuns" so pervasive that they have not yet been fully undone in popular culture. And if the western is relentlessly racist, it is equally sexist, the Hollywood genre most devoted to the unrepentant celebration of assertive patriarchy, physical dominance, and masculine violence. Presumably made by, for, and about (implicitly heterosexual) men, the western seems to have largely ignored the female audience (and characters) otherwise crucial to the success of the cinema as a mass medium. For many of the genre's later critics, the western, especially after World War II, also regularly functioned as a displaced allegory of Cold War politics and the tensions of the civil rights era (with Indians often taking the place on screen of otherwise unrepresented African Americans, additional evidence of the genre's racism); although this indirect engagement with current events perhaps allowed for some subtle critique in the genre's rare "liberal" variations, on the whole, the western has been deemed politically conservative or even reactionary, tacitly offering its traditional frontier heroes as models to be emulated by later American leaders in matters of both national and international policy. Moreover, simply as a generic narrative form, for many viewers (obviously not Warshow's connoisseurs) the western is numbingly repetitive, tediously conventional, and childishly simplistic in its Manichean opposition of "good guys" and "bad guys": if you've seen one, such viewers insist, you've seen them all.

One way to acknowledge the actual diversity and complexity of the body of western films might be to admit that all of these views are valid, and many films could reinforce these apparently contradictory evaluations. Almost simultaneously, the genre still offers even contemporary viewers moments of great beauty and rich meaning alongside laughable clichés and offensive representations: John Ford's *The Searchers* (1956), a modest success upon release and eventually the focus of intense critical analysis, is by no means the only western that might impress and distress contemporary audiences in almost equal measure. However, as suggested earlier, even these opposed positions tend to be based upon a limited and thus misleading set of films extricated from a vast collection of actual examples. Compelling studies of masculinity in the western (by Tompkins [1992] and Mitchell [1996]), for example, rely on a very small number of compelling examples to support their claims, which might be challenged by full engagement with the frequent but rarely considered westerns produced throughout the genre's history to focus on female characters and tailored to feature female stars: the presumption that the western relies exclusively on masculine heroics can only be maintained if one ignores *Belle Starr* (1941), *Frontier Gal* (1945), *Cattle Queen* (1951), or *Westward the Women* (1953), among many other westerns that announced their focus on female characters through their titles alone. Recently, historians of the western (including Richard Abel, Scott Simmon, Andrew Brodie Smith, Peter Stanfield, and Nanna Verhoeff) have expanded the previously limited horizon for understanding this once central form of American culture by recovering neglected films or historical contexts that disallow limited views of only the "greatest" westerns and their directors. In the compact survey that follows, the more diverse landscape of the western explored by recent scholarship – which more fully engages with silent cinema, the B-western, and the persistent role of women throughout the genre – will thus be emphasized alongside more familiar accounts.

Inventing the Western

In addition to reducing the western to a small set of examples, critical attention to the film western has often isolated movies from the rich multi-media context preceding or surrounding their production and consumption. To take a single representative example, David Belasco's extremely popular stage melodrama *The Girl of the Golden West* was produced in 1905 and adapted into Giacomo Puccini's opera (the first set in the United States) *La fanciulla del West* in 1910. A "novelization" of the play was published in 1911, and film versions of the story were produced in 1915 (by Cecil B. DeMille), 1923, 1930, and 1938 (as an operetta), creating a web of revisions, remakes, and versions in multiple media that in fact characterizes the western's popular dissemination. Thus early film westerns were anticipated by and drew upon frontier melodramas, Wild West shows and rodeos, dime novels, and popular fiction, including Owen Wister's bestselling novel *The Virginian* (1902) and the enormously popular stories of Zane Grey such as *Riders of the Purple Sage* (1912); the American West was also represented by a rapidly expanding visual culture of popular illustrations, photography, and paintings, increasingly disseminated to a mass audience through technologies of mass reproduction such as lithography. Later, the film western would compete for an audience but also benefit from tie-ins with western pulp magazines and comic books (inheriting the market from dime novels), radio and television programs, and the commercial category of "country and western" music, which received a boost in the 1930s from the arrival of the singing cowboy as a central figure in Hollywood B-westerns. Historians of both the American West and the western have not entirely neglected such common interactions, however: many have emphasized the suggestive coincidence of Fredrick Jackson Turner's influential address "The Significance of the Frontier in American History" and the appearance of Buffalo Bill Cody's Wild West show, which both took place alongside the World's Columbian Exposition in Chicago in 1893. Thomas A. Edison had also intended to unveil his Kinetoscope at that event, but the new motion picture device was not quite ready: however, shortly after the fair shut down, as noted earlier, Edison filmed members of Cody's troupe and other western subjects, inaugurating what would soon be the regular translation of the American West into movies, providing Turner's officially closed frontier with its imaginative reopening and expansion.

Despite precedents for the western in other media, film historians have recently emphasized that the often casual, seemingly obvious identification of the western in early cinema is the result of a retrospective understanding. Edwin S. Porter's *The Great Train Robbery* (1903), made for the Edison Company, has often been identified as the first film western, but scholars have demonstrated that at the time the category of the western was not fully in place, and thus not used to describe Porter's film when it first appeared. As Rick Altman emphasizes, it took a while before "a growing production of 'Wild West films', Western chase films', 'Western comedies', 'Western melodramas', 'Western romances', and 'Western epics', solidified into a genre called simply the 'Western'" (Altman 1999: 36). Through extensive archival research, Nanna Verhoeff has also suggested that "the West" was a frequent topic for early films before the label of "the western" was available to corral them, a significant historical recognition that reinforces her important claim "that any genre definition is subject to an inevitable, yet problematic, anachronism" (Verhoeff 2006: 114).

In addition to the early instability (or flexibility) of the category itself, the eventual focus of the western narrative around a set of key plots and conflicts – influentially summarized by Jim Kitses as a set of "shifting antinomies" such as wilderness vs. civilization (Kitses 1969: 11) – also does not accurately identify the concerns of this early period. The later sense of the western as almost exclusively a narrative of white, masculine conflict and conquest especially did not define or dominate early films, as recent historians have found: most notably, the silent western was, unlike the western of later periods, especially devoted to sympathetic "Indian" stories, often drawing upon the influential models of James Fenimore Cooper's "Leatherstocking" novels, Henry Wadsworth Longfellow's narrative poetry, or the enduring myth of the "Indian princess" embodied by the figure of Pocahontas. "Indian films" (as they were most often known) relied upon the tropes of the "noble savage" and the "vanishing race" to support dignified images of Native Americans, although such images safely isolated admirable Indians in films from the actual Native Americans recently confined to reservations. Among many others, D.W. Griffith, then establishing his career at the American Biograph Company, produced numerous "Indian films," beginning with *The Redman and the Child* (1908) and including an adaptation of Helen Hunt Jackson's popular novel *Ramona* (1910). Deeply influenced by Cooper, and often set in that author's pastoral forest landscapes, the consistently negative view of the Indian as savage in Griffith's (and others') films would largely emerge with the shift of production to California and films like *The Battle of Elderbush Gulch* (1913), which corresponded with a broad narrative and spatial shift to stories of the Plains Wars that presented undifferentiated hordes of Sioux, Comanche, Cheyenne, or Apache warriors which solidified the limited sense of the genre that persists to this day. The silent cinema is also unusual in retrospect for the frequent participation of Native American filmmakers and performers in crafting their own images: the Winnebago James Young Deer produced perhaps sixty films (most now lost), including *White Fawn's Devotion* (1910), often featuring his wife, Lillian St. Cyr, who appeared as Princess Redwing. A cycle of feature films including *Strongheart* (1914), *Braveheart* (1925), and *Redskin* (1929), often featuring white actors in "red face," also looked at the problems facing contemporary Native Americans: it would be decades before another regular cycle of films centered around and expressed sympathy for Indians when, in the civil rights era, the concerns of Native Americans were raised again, perhaps only as a means to allegorically address African American inequality.

In addition to greater participation by Native Americans, women also played a now largely forgotten role as stars, audiences, and sometimes creators of early westerns. Richard Abel has drawn attention to early trade journal reviews of "westerns in which 'cowboy girls' perform heroic feats in stories of their own" (Abel 1999: 171). These action-packed films featuring "cowboy girls" (a term soon replaced by "cowgirl") drew on rowdy female characters such as the cross-dressing Calamity Jane in earlier dime novels, as well as the heroines of popular adventure stories. Among other early cowgirl stars, Louise Lester was featured between 1912 and 1914 in a dozen "Calamity Anne" films directed by Alan Dwan (a director of westerns throughout his long career) for the American Film Company, and Marie Walcamp played Tempest Cody in nine "Spur and Saddle" films for Universal in 1919. As early as 1917, in her film *49-17*, screenwriter and director Ruth Ann Baldwin cleverly parodied the genre: early, gentle parodies of the western could also be found in the popular novels of the prolific Bertha Muzzie Bower (who published with her gender obscured as B.M. Bower), many of which were adapted into films. Arguably, the most important silent cowgirl was Texas Guinan, promoted as "the female Bill Hart," who starred in a number of westerns, such as *The Gun Woman* (Frank Borzage, 1918), produced by her own companies.

Tomboyish cowgirls would remain popular in westerns in later decades as well, although critics and audiences have subsequently neglected her presence, treating the more conventional opposition of the proper eastern woman and the shady dancehall girl in other films as paradigmatic rather than in fact just two of the genre's options for female characters.

The Western in Hollywood

As the production of popular films was streamlined by a factory-like studio system centered in Hollywood, California (which allowed for much more authentic locations than earlier films), the western became a staple of American popular entertainment, with some early production companies, such as producer Thomas Ince's influential Bison westerns, devoted almost exclusively to the genre. By legend, the first feature film made in Hollywood was a western, Cecil B. DeMille's debut *The Squaw Man* (1914), his first of three eventual versions of the once well-known 1905 stage melodrama. The development of the western also reinforced the early development of cinema's emerging star system, and together the popular genre and the audience's fascination with "picture personalities" elevated Gilbert M. Anderson, a co-founder of the Essanay Studio, to worldwide fame as "Broncho Billy," the screen's first cowboy star whose intriguingly ambiguous persona as a "good badman" across hundreds of films would arguably influence some of the genre's later key figures ranging from William S. Hart to Clint Eastwood. Supported by an even more fully elaborated star system and publicity apparatus (including movie fan magazines), later silent films featuring major cowboy stars like William S. Hart and Tom Mix successfully carried the narrative film from compact one- and two-reelers to more elaborate feature-length stories. Hart and Mix, in fact, effectively marked the contours of the silent feature western, stretching from the grim realism of Hart's Christian morality tales to the amazing stunts – often with his horse Tony – and increasingly flamboyant costumes that made Mix a wildly popular "jazz age" cowboy. By the 1920s, many film studios were producing series westerns featuring such stars as Buck Jones, Hoot Gibson, Tim McCoy, and Ken Maynard (all sharing the screen with their equally famous horses). The regular production of series westerns provided audiences with reliable, action-driven entertainment before the silent period came to a close with a few more ambitious western "epics": *The Covered Wagon* (James Cruze, 1923), *The Iron Horse* (John Ford, 1924), and William S. Hart's final film, *Tumbleweeds* (King Baggot, 1925) all staked out claims for the genre's important function in narrating American history – especially the ideology of "Manifest Destiny" enacted through westward expansion – and the American character embodied in the heroic cowboy.

"With the coming of sound to the Western in 1929," Scott Simmon claims, "the genre goes schizophrenic" (Simmon 2003: 99), splitting itself into a limited number of prestigious films featuring major stars and large budgets, and hundreds of quickly produced low-budget B-films, which found their most popular icon in the singing cowboy (already a radio star) Gene Autry. Until recently, critics have neglected both strands of the 1930s western, including prestigious early sound westerns such as *The Virginian* (Victor Fleming, 1929) starring Gary Cooper in his first talkie, *Billy the Kid* (King Vidor, 1930), the ambitious commercial failure *The Big Trail* (Raoul Walsh, 1930), starring John Wayne and produced in an early widescreen format, and the female-centered *Cimarron* (Wesley Ruggles, 1931), despite the latter's Best Picture Academy Award. Aside from their adjustment to the new demands of sound (made more difficult by the location shooting that had become a highlight of westerns), these early sound films provide evidence of the genre's desire to satisfy various audiences, including the women who, filmmakers continued to assume, demanded the romantic plots that balanced the action central to such films. Even more neglected by critics until recently have been the hundreds of formulaic B-films (created to fill the approximately hour-long B-slot with a longer A-film on a full program) produced by "Poverty Row" studios like Republic and Monogram. As Simmon has pointed out, early sound westerns were "comfortable propounding ideas about American historical and political life" (Simmon 1999: 103), whereas, as he and Peter Stanfield (2002) have both demonstrated, many B-westerns were set in the present (which included cars, airplanes, and radio, among other modern technologies) and, in spite of their dismissal as a frivolous diversion for boys and unsophisticated rural audiences, often took up concerns of direct significance to their viewers, including the conservation issues highlighted by the Dust Bowl droughts of the period. Critics attuned only to the often more conventional gender politics of later A-westerns have also neglected convincing evidence that B-westerns, often written by female screenwriters, were appealing to women. B-westerns frequently built upon the already successful radio and recording careers of their stars, who typically played versions of themselves (thus Gene Autry played "radio star" Gene Autry in most of his films). Often highly self-reflexive (with frequent stories about the filming of westerns by small studios), and sometimes slightly surreal, B-westerns typically rely upon performative traditions abandoned by mainstream cinema (including vaudeville and minstrel traditions), and have therefore been misleadingly judged by standards irrelevant to their main audiences. The B-western also (unlike most major westerns of the period) found regular roles for feisty cowgirls, usually depicted as a cowboy's capable companions rather than romantic partners. If the sexuality of the western, already muted by Hollywood's Production Code, was especially chaste in the B-western, the removal of female characters from romantic plots offered possibilities rarely available in more prominent westerns.

Too often in earlier critical evaluations, the Hollywood western is seen to have only achieved noteworthy status at the end of the decade via John Ford's *Stagecoach* (1939), the director's first sound western, which rescued John Wayne from a decade of low-budget programmers after the failure of *The Big Trail*: while *Stagecoach* indeed established Ford and Wayne as among the most important figures in the history of the genre, its steadily accumulated prestige – and especially its odd location as the starting point for the genre – has too often obscured the long history of hundreds of interesting westerns that precede and surround it. Nevertheless, *Stagecoach* and other successful westerns from major studios with big stars – such as *Dodge City* (Michael Curtiz, 1939), an elaborate color film starring Errol Flynn which was in fact the year's most successful western – encouraged the increased production of more westerns by the major Hollywood studios, a pace which would reduce somewhat during the war years, but which increased after the war, leading to the era, following the prolific 1920s, of the genre's most consistent and widespread popularity. In this period, some of the genre's key directors, such as Anthony Mann, Budd Boetticher, and Howard Hawks emerged, and leading men such as Gary Cooper and John Wayne returned to indelible cowboy roles after stints as film soldiers, while actors such as James Stewart and Henry Fonda became increasingly associated with the genre. The western also took full advantage of the aesthetic possibilities offered by the increased availability of color cinematography, with Ford's *She Wore a Yellow Ribbon* (1949) winning an Oscar for its stunning images; the "gimmick" of widescreen formats like CinemaScope, in part developed to counter the competition of television, also found the western's reliance on landscape to justify the sweeping vistas of films like *Broken Lance* (Edward Dmytryk, 1954) and *River of No Return* (Otto Preminger, 1954).

In addition to the regular output of solid exercises in the genre, or forays into more expensive color and widescreen films, the western was increasingly used to explore more serious social and psychological topics: the "adult" western, which signaled an increased tendency to explore the sexuality and psychology (often related) of the western, included notable examples such as the Freudian and film noir-influenced *Pursued* (Raoul Walsh, 1947), starring a haunted Robert Mitchum, *Duel in the Sun* (King Vidor, 1946), producer David O. Selznick's lustful and hyperbolic blending of the women's melodrama and the western, and serious mediations on the ethics of western violence such as *The Ox-Bow Incident* (William A. Wellman, 1943) and *The Gunfighter* (Henry King, 1950). Returning to concerns last fully explored in the 1920s, a cycle of "liberal" Indian films, including *Broken Arrow* (Delmer Daves, 1950), *Devil's Doorway* (Anthony Mann, 1950), and *Apache* (Robert Aldrich, 1954), argued for racial tolerance in an era otherwise preoccupied with fears of Communism and black–white relations in America.

By the late 1950s and early 1960s, the critical reevaluation of the American cinema in terms of the *auteur* theory, which identified some directors as artists whose creative vision defined the (otherwise collaborative) works they made within the constraints of the studio system, established John Ford as one of America's great artists, not for his prestigious, Oscar-winning films, but for his westerns, including an impressive series of post-World War II films, including *My Darling Clementine* (1946), *Fort Apache* (1948), *She Wore a Yellow Ribbon* (1949), *Rio Grande* (1950) (the latter three known as Ford's unofficial "Cavalry Trilogy"), and *The Searchers* (1956), which has slowly emerged as Ford's masterpiece, a conflicted meditation on the racism and sexual fears that drove western expansion (and popular narratives). Two of Ford's later films, *The Man Who Shot Liberty Valance* (1962) and *Cheyenne Autumn* (1964), are now viewed as, respectively, an ambivalent elegy for the genre and a mild apology for the mistreatment of Native Americans. In many ways, the process that simultaneously led to the identification of Ford as an artist and his westerns as his greatest work is at the core of the critical legitimation of popular Hollywood cinema, and allowed other directors and films to be equally valued.

The identification of *auteurs* among the regular directors of Hollywood westerns was thus especially crucial in drawing attention to the significant contributions of Anthony Mann and Budd Boetticher to the genre. Mann's series of films starring James Stewart including *Winchester '73* (1950), *Bend of the River* (1952), *The Naked Spur* (1953), *The Far Country* (1954), and *The Man from Laramie* (1955), as well as the grim *Man of the West* (1958) starring Gary Cooper, are now viewed as among the genre's greatest achievements, in part for their staging of gripping narratives of revenge and redemption against western spaces that both test and define Mann's characters. Boetticher's series of westerns starring Randolph Scott – *Seven Men from Now* (1956), *The Tall T* (1957), *Buchanan Rides Alone* (1958), *Westbound* (1959), *Ride Lonesome* (1959), and *Comanche Station* (1960) – are also highly regarded for their taut, concentrated narratives that seem to reduce the western to its core elements.

But the critical consensus that has celebrated such films and filmmakers as demonstrating that the western is an essentially masculine genre also deflects attention from the persistence with which filmmakers throughout the 1950s made westerns that featured female characters and stars: while the baroque *Johnny Guitar* (Nicholas Ray, 1954), starring Joan Crawford, has achieved cult status, the regular association of Hollywood veteran Barbara Stanwyck (who had played cowgirl *Annie Oakley* in 1935) with the genre in such films as *The Furies* (Anthony Mann, 1950), *Cattle Queen of Montana* (Allan Dwan, 1954), and *Forty Guns* (Samuel Fuller, 1957), among others, implies that the genre was more accommodating of female stars than is often assumed. Many independent films, including the growing number of films openly defined as "exploitation" moves for distribution to drive-in and "grind house" theaters, produced as the Hollywood studio system lost its dominance, also emphasized western women, including the prolific producer-director Roger Corman's earliest films such as *The Oklahoma Woman* (1956) starring Peggie Castle as an outlaw queen, and *Gunslinger* (1956), starring Beverly Garland as a female sheriff. Inevitably, the rise of a "mainstream" pornographic cinema also produced films that drew upon western iconography, alongside avant-garde work such as Andy Warhol's *Lonesome Cowboys* (1968), which perhaps suggested the genre's range as well as its inevitable decadence.

Revision and Elegy

Designated by various critics of the genre as "twilight" or "elegiac" westerns, the films of Sam Peckinpah and Clint Eastwood appear to represent the last regular association between American directors (and in Eastwood's case, a major star) and the western. The other key figure in this period is the Italian Sergio Leone, whose extremely influential, highly stylized "spaghetti westerns," including the trilogy – *A Fistful of Dollars* (1964), *For a Few Dollars More* (1965), and *The Good, the Bad, and the Ugly* (1966) – that carried Eastwood to international stardom as "the man with no name," are certainly the most significant non-American contributions to the genre. If Peckinpah's *Ride the High Country* (1962), starring former cowboy stars Joel McCrea and Randolph Scott, offered a graceful farewell to the classic western, *The Wild Bunch* (1969), which also featured aging actors with previous credits in the genre, was an apocalyptic vision of the western. Both infamous and influential for its elaborate "blood ballets" filmed in slow-motion, the film fully embraced the violence at the heart of the genre but muted under the Hollywood Production Code, which had just given way to the new ratings system before the release of the film. *The Wild Bunch* was commonly viewed as a "Vietnam western," and unleashed a new savagery in representations of the West that seemed appropriate for the current context. Westerns, once derided for opposing heroes and villains simply through their white and black hats, now depicted bloodthirsty anti-heroes – including George Armstrong Custer in *Little Big Man* (Arthur Penn, 1970) – and psychotic gunfighters as more terrifying figures than uncivilized Indians. Such films generally suggested that the romantic, heroic model of the western was not longer viable and could only be invoked as a tradition to be comically undermined – in parodies such as *Cat Ballou* (Elliot Silverstein, 1965) – or boldly denounced.

The declining status of the western as a commercial Hollywood product seemed to be summed up by the disastrous failure of *Heaven's Gate* (Michael Cimino, 1980), an ambitious tale of class conflict in the West that virtually destroyed United Artists, its venerable production company. The success of later westerns such as *Silverado* (Lawrence Kasdan, 1980), *Dances with Wolves* (Kevin Costner, 1990), and *Tombstone* (George P. Cosmatos, 1993) has not encouraged a full-scale revival of the genre; less commercially successful films such as *Wyatt Earp* (Lawrence Kasdan, 1994), *All the Pretty Horses* (Billy Bob Thornton, 2000), and *Open Range* (Kevin Costner, 2003) offer little additional encouragement to producers to continue to finance what has become an increasingly risky genre.

Following the impact of Peckinpah and Leone, only Clint Eastwood has been regularly associated with the western, as both star and director, even though the genre now in fact only represents a small portion of his long career: following the ambitious *The Outlaw Josey Wales* (1976), and the most modest *Pale Rider* (1985), Eastwood's *Unforgiven* (1992) seemed to have been designed to be his (and even the genre's) final statement, a grim meditation on and perhaps apology for the violence at the heart of the genre. The film and Eastwood, as director, both won Academy Awards, a late affirmation of the genre that had been more popular and lucrative than honored by the Hollywood industry. Nevertheless, the fact that Eastwood has not returned to the genre with which he remains associated in almost two decades itself suggests the end of an era in the genre's history.

The Western's Endurance

Critics (if not audiences) have also appreciated some of the more radical revisions of the genre, including the surreal *Dead Man* (Jim Jarmusch, 1995) and the gender-bending *The Ballad of Little Jo* (Maggie Greenwald, 1993), amazingly the first sound western directed by a woman. Perhaps the most surprisingly successful western in recent years was *Brokeback Mountain* (Ang Lee, 2005), both celebrated and derided as a "gay western," a designation that was viewed as either an audacious conjunction or full acknowledgment of a "tradition" of male eroticism that has often marked the genre. Such examples continue to demonstrate that the borders of the genre, as always, are flexible rather than tightly controlled, even as the genre's popularity wanes.

While the Hollywood western has often been pronounced dead (since at least 1911!), and the regular production of westerns is clearly past, recent examples such as *3:10 to Yuma* (James Mangold, 2007, a remake of Delmer Daves' 1957 film), *The Assassination of Jesse James by the Coward Robert Ford* (Andrew Dominik, 2007), and *Appaloosa* (Ed Harris, 2008) were all modest hits, suggesting continued interest in the genre (along with popular, though now equally rare, television westerns). When, just before his untimely death in 1958, Bazin expressed his hope that the western "will remain the western we hope our grandchildren will still be allowed to know" (Bazin 2005b: 157), he suggested the genre's stubborn continuity while hinting at the risk of its increased obscurity. While, following in his critical footsteps, the genre remains of ongoing interest to film scholars and a dedicated group of aging fans, there's little denying that such films can no longer draw upon the familiar settings, actions, and characters that for decades resonated throughout American popular culture and much of the world. Nevertheless, the western remains a defining aspect of American popular culture, and any serious attempt to understand that culture must confront this once pervasive and persistently resonant genre.

NOTE

1 References in this essay to "the western" or "westerns" will generally and exclusively indicate American films, even though the essay otherwise insists that western movies must be appreciated within a cultural context that included examples of the genre across popular media, including theater, music, fiction, radio, comics, and television, among other formats.

REFERENCES AND FURTHER READING

Abel, Richard. (1999). *The Red Rooster Scare: Making Cinema American, 1900–1910*. Berkeley: University of California Press. An important historical study of the "Americanization" of cinema, with the western playing a key role.

Abel, Richard. (2006). *Americanizing the Movies and "Movie-Mad" Audiences, 1910–1914*. Berkeley: University of California Press. A rich historical study of the development of the western as an American film genre.

Altman, Rick. (1999). *Film/Genre*. London: British Film Institute. A major study of the concept of genre, with significant attention to the western.

Bazin, André. (2005a). The Western: or the American Film Par Excellence [1971]. In *What is Cinema?* trans. Hugh Gray, vol. 2, pp. 140–8. Berkeley: University of California Press. This and the following entry are two key essays on the genre from a major film critic and theorist.

Bazin, André. (2005b). The Evolution of the Western [1971]. In *What is Cinema?* trans. Hugh Gray, vol. 2, pp. 149–57. Berkeley: University of California Press.

Buscombe, Edward, and Roberta E. Pearson, eds. (1998). *Back in the Saddle Again: New Essays on the Western*. London: British Film Institute. A collection of essays providing new directions for study of the genre.

Cameron, Ian, and Douglas Pye, eds. (1996). *The Book of Westerns*. New York: Continuum. A strong collection of essays on familiar and less familiar films.

Coyne, Michael. (2007). *The Crowded Prairie: American National Identity in the Hollywood Western*. New York: I.B. Tauris. An analysis of the western as political allegory.

Kitses, Jim. (1969). *Horizons West*. Bloomington: Indiana University Press. New edn., published as *Horizons West: Directing the Western from John Ford to Clint Eastwood*. London: British Film Institute, 2004. A groundbreaking study of the genre and its key directors, significantly expanded after thirty years.

Kitses, Jim, and Gregg Rickman, eds. (1998). *The Western Reader*. New York: Liveright. A collection of key and original essays.

Lusted, David. (2003). *The Western*. Harlow: Pearson Longman. A wide-ranging, comprehensive overview.

Mitchell, Lee Clark. (1996). *Westerns: Making the Man in Fiction and Film*. Chicago: University of Chicago Press. A study of the genre's representation of masculinity.

Simmon, Scott. (2003). *The Invention of the Western Film: A Cultural History of the Genre's First Half-Century*. Cambridge: Cambridge University Press. An innovative approach to the genre's history, especially its first decades.

Slotkin, Richard. (1992). *Gunfighter Nation: The Myth of the Frontier in Twentieth-Century America*. New York: Atheneum. A major study of the western as an allegory for twentieth-century American politics.

Smith, Andrew Brodie. (2003). *Shooting Cowboys and Indians: Silent Western Films, American Culture, and the Birth of Hollywood*. Boulder: University Press of Colorado. An informative study of the neglected silent western.

Stanfield, Peter. (2002). *Horse Opera: The Strange History of the 1930s Singing Cowboy*. Urbana: University of Illinois Press. One of the few critical assessments of the neglected B-western.

Tompkins, Jane. (1992). *West of Everything: The Inner Life of Westerns*. New York: Oxford University Press. The most significant feminist approach to the western.

Verhoeff, Nanna. (2006). *The West in Early Cinema: After the Beginning*. Amsterdam: Amsterdam University Press. An innovative historical and theoretical study of the representation of the West in early cinema.

Walker, Janet, ed. (2001). *Westerns: Films through History*. New York: Routledge/American Film Institute. Essays on the genre's complex relation to history.

Warshow, Robert. (2001). Movie Chronicle: The Westerner. In *The Immediate Experience*, rev. edn., pp. 105–24. Cambridge, MA: Harvard University Press. An influential early essay by a major cultural critic.

Wright, Will. (1975). *Sixguns and Society: A Structural Study of the Western*. Berkeley: University of California Press. An important early semiotic study of the genre.

26
Post-Western Cinema

Neil Campbell

Dead Westerns

In 1996, Lee Clark Mitchell called the last chapter of his book *Westerns*, "Last Rites," commenting that almost at their inception in 1913 producer Thomas Ince stated to cowboy actor William S. Hart that westerns "were on their way out" (Mitchell 1996: 257). In 1998 Jim Kitses opened his introduction to *The Western Reader* with a single statement: "Someone is always trying to bury the Western," going on to claim that if all these proclamations of ending had headstones, they would "overflow even Tombstone's cemetery" (Kitses and Rickman 1998: 15). Most recently, in 2006 Alex Cox, British director of "punk" westerns *Straight to Hell* and *Walker*, wrote that, "this genre … has, to all intents and purposes, died."

> The genre, which had once been a celebration of traditional American values of self-reliance and individuality, had forked. Its reactionary tendency – the films of Burt Kennedy and [John] Wayne – had hit a brick wall. Its revolutionary tendency was postmodern, respecting neither genre nor linear narrative: the cowboy version of punk. Hollywood was wasting money on the former, and afraid of the latter. (Cox 2006: n.p.)

Cox's "forked" explanation reduces the western to binary streams, "reactionary" and "revolutionary," failing to recognize that far from being dead these generic negotiations signify its reinvention and survivance (its "living on" in new or altered forms). In between Cox's binaries westerns survived as they always had, traveling across generic boundaries, poaching and borrowing from many different earlier traditions,

A Companion to the Literature and Culture of the American West, First Edition. Edited by Nicolas S. Witschi.

whilst contributing to the innovation of the genre. As this chapter will argue, the "dead" genre refuses to remain dead and the "last rites" are premature, for the western is constantly "resuscitated" as Vera Dika points out, "arising, occurring, or continuing *after death*"; a genre returning and haunting American and global cultures in various forms (Dika 2003: 215). In fact, as André Bazin pointed out some years ago, the western's "roots continue to spread under the Hollywood humus and one is amazed to see green and robust suckers spring up in the midst of the seductive but sterile hybrids that some would replace them by" (Bazin 2005: 152). Thus, from under America's ground of being, its "humus," emerges the haunting presence of the western, endlessly transfigured *posthumously* (after its *pronounced* death, from beyond the earth of its "critical" burial).

According to Thomas Schatz, "The significance and impact of the Western as America's foundation ritual have been articulated most clearly and effectively in the cinema," projecting "a formalized vision of the nation's infinite possibilities and limitless vistas ... serving to 'naturalize' the policies of westward expansion and Manifest Destiny" and thus present a purified form of the national narrative (Schatz 1981: 46–7). However, the western has in fact shown a remarkable "impurity," over-spilling its boundaries, becoming mobile and "rhizomatic"; "a principle of contamination, a law of impurity, a parasitical economy ... a sort of participation without belonging – a taking part in without being part of, without having membership in a set" (Derrida 1980: 59).

Elsewhere, Derrida asks: "What are we doing when, to practice a 'genre,' we quote a genre, represent it, stage it, expose its *generic law*, analyze it practically? Are we still practicing the genre? Does the work still belong to the genre it re-cites?" Derrida suggests generic forms like the western do not have to destroy their precursors in order to function critically, since the generic process "interrupts the very belonging [to a genre] of which it is a necessary condition" (Derrida 1991: 259). From within the genre, as the post-western I am defining here, form folds outward whilst maintaining a vital connecting tissue to its "inside," allowing relation, reflection, *and* critical interaction simultaneously.

Michel de Certeau's *The Writing of History* offers an interesting commentary on the process I am charting, arguing that history constructs a usable past by asserting "progress" and presenting a stable "story" where much is "forgotten" or lost through the "management" of "'scenarios' capable of organizing practices into a currently intelligible discourse" (De Certeau 1988: 6). These "scenarios" parallel cinematic representations of the western past, of the "pure" national narrative and its mythic origin story (its "cosmogenesis"). However,

> whatever this new understanding of the past holds to be irrelevant – shards created by the selection of materials, remainders left aside by an explication – comes back, despite everything, on the edges of discourse or in the rifts and crannies: "resistances," "survivals," or delays discreetly perturb the pretty order of a line of "progress" or a system of interpretation ... Therein they symbolize the return of the repressed ... a return of what,

at a given moment, has *become* unthinkable in order for a new identity to *become* think-able. (1988: 4)

For the West these "shards [... and] remainders" return from the "edges of discourse" in different ways, one of which, I would argue, is via the "rifts and crannies" of post-westerns that *inherit* and *perform* histories and identities whilst commenting critically upon the social weight and ideological assumptions embedded within them. Mitchell argues that "The *West* is stable, the *Western* labile" (Mitchell 1996: 5) – fixing the landscape of the West as forever constant whilst the genre itself is likely to metamor-phose: "the image of a man with a gun, sitting astride a horse, silhouetted against an empty landscape" (1996: 264). What he ignores, however, is the genre's capacity to respond to a changing social, economic, and cultural landscape and *still* be a western, still examine both the types of anxieties his book analyzes as well as "anxieties yet unimagined" (1996: 264).

The post-western exists precisely because of its complex, unstable relations with the cinematic past, an inheritance of tropes endorsing settlement against the odds, establishing roots in the New World, transforming the earth from wilderness to garden, taming land from "savage" populations, expressing a renewing masculinity as the source of these actions, and (often reluctantly) domesticating the feminine within this new western world. However, we must recognize the "radical and neces-sary heterogeneity of an inheritance," for as Derrida reminds us, "An inheritance is never gathered together, it is never one with itself. Its presumed unity, if there is one, can consist only in the injunction to reaffirm by choosing" (Derrida 2006: 18). Examining this inheritance with its "presumed unity" and generic "purity" is crucial to the post-western, for as Derrida remarks, the critical process means

> one must filter, sift, criticize, one must sort out several different possibles that inhabit the same injunction. And inhabit it in a contradictory fashion around a secret. If the readability of a legacy were given, natural, transparent, univocal, if it did not call for and at the same time defy interpretation, we would never have anything to inherit from it ... One always inherits from a secret – which says "read me, will you ever be able to do so?" (Derrida 2006: 18)

Such an "unreadable" inheritance cannot be unified or mythic except (in typically contrary Derridean terms) by "dividing itself, tearing itself apart, differing/deferring itself, by speaking at the same time several times – and in several voices" (2006: 18). Such is the inheritance of western cultural history played out in the fictional "injunc-tions" of post-western cinema; dialogic and heteroglossic – "speaking at the same time several times – and in several voices," folding around its many "secrets" buried in the past, exhumed into the present and projecting into the future as both debts and burdens obsessively repeated, worked through, and challenged.

Post-westerns reflect upon these inherited tropes, interrogate their *afterlife*, and delve into their persistence through a process that begins from a premise of investigative doubt, suspicion, and uncanniness. That is, the presumed home (the geography of established western hope) is unsettled by the examination of salient fragments *un-earthed* to question its cohesion, closure, and solidity. Through layers of representational "humus," post-westerns assert an archeological probing into foundations forgotten, repressed, or built over. Recalling de Certeau's shards and remainders, modern westerns reveal nature as their source: relics, fragments, and remains born out of geographical or historical ruins as if from cultural memory. Consider, for example, *Bad Day at Black Rock, Bring Me the Head of Alfredo Garcia, Lone Star,* or *Silver City,* where something surges *back* and *into* the world again – the dead return (like the genre itself, as we have noted) – and the apparently smooth surface of myth, memory, and history is ruptured.

One could argue that the thrust of classical western cinema was towards the validation and settlement of what remained when the action ceased; after the showdown, after the hero exited the scene; after the last battle; after the burial of the dead; after the domestic is established; after the expulsion of evil, and the storm has passed. Simultaneously, it was concerned with the *afterlife* of violent action, with, as I said above, establishing settlement, community, and home through resolution of difference and the proclamation of unanimity. However, post-westerns return to the mythic "scene" concerned with *the remains of what remains* from the action the western represented; its dark inheritance and ghostly consequences. It is fascinated by the *afterlife* of the classic western's *afterlife*, traced in the fragility of cultural haunting and postmortem investigations; with the unsettled and un-homely.

Derrida says, in Ken McMullen's 1983 film *Ghost Dance,* "The cinema is the art of ghosts, a battle of phantoms, it's the art of letting ghosts come back," an art that is far from regressive since, as he argues, "I believe ghosts are part of the future and that the modern technology of images like cinematography ... enhances the power of ghosts and their ability to haunt us" (MacMullen 2006). We must "learn to live with ghosts ... To live otherwise and better ... more justly. But *with them* ... [as] a politics of memory, of inheritance, and of generations" (Derrida 2006: pp. xvii–xviii). To live justly means to show responsibility to all those "beyond ... the living present," that is "those who *are not there,* of those no longer or who are not yet *present and living*" (Derrida 2006: p. xviii). Given the history of the American West, its expansionism and legacy of conquest, we might see post-westerns as sites where such "justice" is traced, back into the past and forward to the future, existing *in between* in order to be responsible to both. The stress on "beyond" in Derrida's discussion reminds us of the significance of the term "post" as that which has a distinct responsibility for carrying us *beyond* the concerns only of the present and the past, creating instead "a spectral moment ... that no longer belongs to time," "furtive and untimely," "questioning ... asking ourselves about this instant" (Derrida 2006: p. xix). Post-western cinematic memories reinvoke the past, bringing back ghosts of the West as living and lived, contested, spectral *inheritances* engaging the viewer in learning to live with justice and responsibility. But in one regard, as Derrida understood, the notion of speaking with ghosts is something scholars find hard to admit, preferring instead to work on the solid ground of oppositions like "what is present and what is not" (Derrida 2006: 12). Yet "beyond this opposition" exist "theatrical fiction, literature and speculation," the very fields often dismissed by western historians, but which, if we are "mad enough," might "*unlock* the possibility of such an address [with ghosts]," something "more actual than what is so blithely called a living presence," something that through our active engagement with it, has the power to *move* us, *affect* us intellectually and emotionally, to think differently and better (Derrida 2006: 13).

"The 'Western' in Quotes"

The opening and closing of the Coen brothers' *The Big Lebowski* (1998) represents "theatrical fiction, literature and speculation" "mad enough" to embody many of the attributes of the post-western. Whilst emphasizing the iconography of the western's regionalist form through its images, expectations, and generic parameters it becomes simultaneously a kind of conduit into another, less contained or settled, cinematic experience. The Sons of the Pioneers' "Tumbling Tumbleweeds" on the soundtrack accompanies the visual trope of tumbleweed blowing across a western desert scene, providing a reassuring cliché of "west-ness" as the narrator, Sam Elliott (The Stranger), in his western drawl, tells us that "way out West, there was this feller, feller I want to tell you about, feller by the name of Jeff Lebowski." The Stranger is, as one critic put it, "a sort of Ghost of Cowboys Past," carrying traces of the mythic West into the present, focusing the audience's attention upon the spectral relations of past and present (Merkin 1998: 98). Based on this opening sequence, as Tyree and Walters write, "Plainly, this is a Western" (2007: 38). As we literally follow the tumbleweed's reassuring path it takes us suddenly beyond our expectations, over a ridge, and into a less familiar landscape, looking down onto Los Angeles' neon sprawl. The relative security of Mitchell's mantra "The *West* is stable, the *Western* labile" is shockingly troubled by this moment, requiring the audience to reconsider the iconic familiarity of western tropes now undone by the garishly unfamiliar modern West of an urban cityscape. This is the uncanny effect of so many post-westerns. The deliberate jarring of expectations is a common feature, from *Lonely are the Brave*'s horse on the highway to *Down in the Valley*'s use of the San Fernando Valley (see Campbell 2009).

As a microcosm of the post-western effect, this projects its audience from "roots" in the familiar landscape of historical "pastness" and its position, in Susan Kollin's words, as a "pre-lapsarian, pre-social, and pre-modern space of … established forms," along new "routes" of "presentness" bound up with images and values of the mythic and real past it both embraces and eschews (Kollin 2007: p. xiii). As we watch, one text folds into another, deframing its iconographies, being both *of* the Western whilst also *more than*, engaging in Derrida's "participation without belonging," a ghosting where one form haunts the other. So, as Tyree and Walters *return* (as the uncanny effect demands we all do) to their statement "Plainly, this is a Western," they are forced to concede:

Hmm. Not a Western, then. Yet we're still following that tumbleweed, along a bridge over a freeway, down a street, past a burrito stand and onto the beach itself. Tumbleweed on a beach? What kind of a movie is this anyway? (2007: 38)

Their dilemma is crucial, expressing the inherent strange familiarity of post-westerns, jarring the reader into a space of reflection, a critical dialogue with the form, its assumptions and histories.

Dude (Jeff Lebowski) says to The Stranger later in the film, "Well, I dig your style too, man. Got a whole cowboy thing goin'." The "cowboy thing," the film's "west-ness," is ever present, though "post" in the sense of coming after and going beyond the traditional western whilst engaging with and commenting on its deeply haunting assumptions and values. Indeed, as so often, as Richard Slotkin's work demonstrates, westerns reflect beyond themselves to contemporary themes and issues – just as with *The Big Lebowski*, since "this here story I'm about to unfold," says The Stranger, "took place in the early '90s – just about the time of our conflict with Sad'm and the I-raqis."

Even as The Stranger attempts to "unfold" (his word used twice in the sequence and recalling Derrida's folded genre) the story of the Dude and his world, he admits "there was a lot about the Dude that didn't make a whole lot of sense. And a lot about where he lived, likewise." As a consequence of this "senselessness" the narrative is soon broken, interrupted by his very attempt to articulate it: "Well, I lost my train of thought here. But ... aw, hell. I've done introduced it enough." The Stranger, as narrator, cannot reduce the tale to a linear form or to a set of simple meanings; instead all he has is what the Dude and his "place" (the West) represent; mystery, ambiguity, instability, and layered complexity. But through its representation, through the need to tell the story, The Stranger speaks for us all: "But then again, maybe that's why I found the place so darned interestin'."

Theorizing the Post-Western

The problem of the meaning of the prefix "post" is critical to this discussion of what I am calling "post-western" cinema, for contained within the debates surrounding it much is revealed about the relationships of the western to its "past," "present," and "future." Commenting on the use of "post" in postcolonialism, Stuart Hall argues for it as a continuum, as "not only 'after' but 'going beyond' the colonial, as post-mod-ernism is both 'going beyond' and coming 'after' modernism, and post-structuralism both follows chronologically and achieves its theoretical gains 'on the back of' struc-turalism" (Hall 1996: 253). A similar logic can be usefully employed to discuss the relations and tensions between the western and its "post" forms as both "going beyond and after" its earlier "classic" structures and themes. To borrow the phrasing Hall uses, "It is because the relations which characterised the 'colonial' [*read* classic western] are no longer in the same place and relative position, that we are able not simply to oppose them but to critique, to deconstruct and try to 'go beyond' them" (1996: 254).

The "post" never just means the "past" as in the term "post-western," but rather "a process of disengagement" from the system it is in tension with, in the full knowledge that it is "probably inescapable" from that system as well (1996: 246). Thus westerns and post-westerns "never operated in a purely binary way" but always interact, overlap and interrelate, as argued earlier, in complex dialogical ways.

The term "postwestern" (*sic*) within western studies has a related history, beginning with Virginia Scharff in 1994 calling for "a postwestern history" "to question the stability of our most cherished historical categories of analysis" recognizing both "the weight of the western frame" and seeing the need to treat it with a certain skepticism, or in her words, to be "alert, edgy and restless" and to "burst the boundaries of region" (Scharff 1999: 167). This debate continued in works by Kerwin Lee Klein and Frieda Knobloch in 1996, and is best summarized in Susan Kollin's collection *Postwestern Cultures* (2007) as "an emerging critical approach" working "against a narrowly conceived regionalism" and with a distinct awareness of how the West has been seen as a "predetermined entity with static borders and boundaries" and calls for a determined approach based on the "critical reassessment of those very restrictions, whether they be theoretical, geographical, or political" (Kollin 2007: p. xi). She explains very clearly how the problem manifests itself:

> in dominant national discourse, the American West has been imagined and celebrated largely for its status as "pre" – for its position as a pre-lapsarian, pre-social, and pre-modern space ... so that like the very spaces of an idealized western geography, some literary and cultural scholarship about the region has adopted a pre- or even anti-theoretical stance, as if regional studies could offer a similar retreat or refuge from a dehumanizing culture. (Kollin 2007: p. xiii)

Similarly, classic westerns reproduced this sense of "retreat or refuge" in a "pre-modern" community governed by specific values and ideologies. In *Cinema 2*, Deleuze coined the term "neo-western" to define films critiquing this sense of "pre-" by not "addressing a people, which is *presupposed already there*, but of contributing to the invention of a people" (Deleuze 2000: 217). He argued that classical Hollywood asserted a unanimous "people" in its dominant genres, such as westerns, where communities were built and settled through the struggles of individuals in and against the wilderness. *My Darling Clementine* (1946) might stand as the perfect example of a Cold War western engaged in both "writing history" as ultimately orderly and resolved whilst also embodying the needs of a postwar, ideologically defined community: European, white, male, entrepreneurial, and imperial. As Corkin puts it, such films provide "a conceptual bridge between frontier mythology and Cold War imperatives," endorsing "a triumphal moment when a compendium of quintessentially American traditions took hold" (Corkin 2004: 23, 21).

For Deleuze the neo-western anticipated the "break-up" of such visions since "the American people ... could no longer believe themselves to be either the melting-pot of peoples or the seed of a people to come" (Deleuze 2000: 216). The ideological frameworks "presupposed already there" were under scrutiny in neo-westerns and this "modern political cinema," as Deleuze called it, developed in a post-1945 climate of increased social and political movements, was built on the fragmentation and questioning of "unanimity"; rejecting *one* "people," asserting "several peoples, an infinity of peoples," and refuting "tyrannical unity." The role of the "author/director" is, wrote Deleuze, about "destroying myths from the inside," to show "the raw drive and social violence underneath the myth," producing "[n]ot the myth of a past people, but the story-telling of the people to come ... to create itself as a foreign language in a dominant language" (2000: 217, 216, 220, 217, 219, 223). This latter phrase refers to the "minor" as an emergent, complicating, and potentially radical alternative "voice" that rises up *within* an established form, from the mythical "inside" framework. Thus precisely because of the "major" voice of the classic western in American culture there emerged through generic twists and mutations, "minor" languages utilizing its tropes and iconographies for new and different ends.

Developing Deleuze's ideas traces how the "neo" relates to the post-western, further interrogating versions of "unanimity" and its values, unbuckling the "presupposed already there" from a more nuanced and layered approach to social and cultural constructions of the West. Indeed, at the very heart of the neo-western is a determined examination of the western genre itself from "inside," placing, in the words of director Jim Jarmusch "the 'Western' in quotes" (Jarmusch 2005: 78). This approach challenges the separation of modern and classic forms of the western, suggesting rather a discontinuous but dialogical relationship between them whereby themes, tropes, and issues interrelate and infuse each other. Remember, the "post" in post-western has a self-conscious reference to and echo of the word "posthumous" and therefore of the specific meaning of something – in this case a film genre – that continues to "live on" beyond its "death" generating a spectral inheritance within the present. Post-westerns are, as we discussed earlier, always already an elaborate afterimage – persisting even after the visual or cultural stimulus causing it has ceased to exist.

Bad Day at Black Rock: "A politics of memory, of inheritance, and of generations"

> I'd say Westerns are one form that will remain ... They represent something almost mystical to many people. Perhaps it has something to do with the myths of how our nation was built. (Sturges, qtd. in Cherry 1969: 9)

An early example of the post-western is John Sturges' *Bad Day at Black Rock* (1954), whose comment above demonstrates his awareness of the genre's significance and its visceral relationship with the American people as "almost mystical," connecting them elegiacally to their past. Yet the film was not a mainstream western but a continuation from an earlier film, *The Walking Hills* (1949), a "rugged outdoor adventure" of the modern West, whose relative success "served as [Sturges'] passport from eager apprentice to respected studio hand ... at MGM" where he would make *Bad Day at Black Rock* (Lovell 2008: 49).

The film's post-western credentials emerge immediately as we watch the arrival of a train in a bleak desert landscape, an image familiar to a number of classic westerns (such as *High Noon* and *The Man Who Shot Liberty Valance*), and yet here, as the scene unfolds, it is the isolated, enclosed and ruined space we note. As Christopher Woodward reminds us, "When we contemplate ruins, we contemplate our own future" alongside "that strange sense of displacement which occurs when we find that, living, we cannot fill the footprints of the dead" (Woodward 2002: 2, 5). *Bad Day at Black Rock* confronts us with both spatial and moral "ruins" within a post-war western landscape, and in so doing confronts its audience (the "living") with both the "footprints of the dead" and with the haunting that "secretly unhinges it," as Derrida puts it (2006: p. xviii). At Black Rock's heart is a very specific ruin, the murdered Japanese farmer Komoko's homestead, epitomizing the past's dark secret in its scattered remains and buried violence. But also, as a post-western, it *comes after* and *goes beyond* classical westerns, confronting the apparent "death" and ruin of the most traditional genre whilst signaling its reinvention as a relevant, political form. Primarily, the film comments upon racism, xenophobia, and an inward-looking imperialism that, as its local tyrant, Reno Smith explains, is totally bound up with the West as territory and idea:

> I don't know. People are always looking for something in this part of the West. To the historian, it's the "Old West." To the book writers, it's the "Wild West." To the businessmen, it's the "Undeveloped West." They all say we're backward and poor, and I guess we are. We don't even have enough water. But this place, to us, is our West. I just wish they'd leave us alone.

Recalling Woodward's words, the shooting script for the film begins with a significant description of the town as ruined space:

> ... abandoned, in an extreme state of dilapidation. The structure is blistered by the resolute sun, the roof is weather-warped. Dry rot and mildew wage a relentless battle against the foundation ... floorboards twisted by time, termites and the elements ... From the overhang is appended a rectangular panel on which, in flaky paint, the town is identified: Black Rock.

Even the wires holding this panel are lopsided, "cocking the sign irregularly," clearly linking this cultural landscape with the surrounding natural one, itself damaged: "The morning sun lays over this wasteland of the American Southwest, a gigantic yellow bruise from which heat waves like bloodshot arteries spread themselves over the poisoned sky." The language of disease and pollution suggests the Southwest's association with military testing and the nuclear industry. Indeed, the shadow of the war hangs over the film in many ways, directly through ex-soldier Macreedy (Spencer Tracy) and his quest for Japanese settler Komoko, but also in Smith's discussion of the draft, as well as the more "absent" reminders of the military-industrial complex of the Southwest and of the internment camp Manzanar close by.

With the precision Sergio Leone would later bring to *Once Upon a Time in the West*, Sturges' *mise-en-scène* establishes a critical geometry the film will constantly utilize and develop, revealing a concern for more than place, signifying a fundamental metaphysical collapse of structure and an impending breakdown of settlement in an allegorical landscape of loss (a "settled melancholy," Doc Velie calls it). After all, contrary to the idealized western image – and as Sturges fully intended – this is a settlement with no families, women, or children – a community of the living dead.

As this opening demonstrates, mythic assumptions about the West are compromised by contrary forces of decay, disintegration, and misuse portraying not a land of promise but a ruined, poisoned junkyard where historical complexity has been replaced by myths of distorted patriotism. The familiar, "homely" landscape of westerns veers towards the unfamiliar and "unhomely" in the uncanny conditions of Black Rock, or as Vidler writes, "its power lies no longer in the model of unity but in the intimation of the fragmentary, the morselated, the broken" (Vidler 1999: 70) – in other words, in its ruins.

The town and its people are in their death throes, "twisted by time" and living vicariously on their mythic cowboy past, tottering on some momentous threshold between life and death.

> The town and the terrain surrounding it have, if nothing else, the quality of inertia and immutability – nothing moves, not even an insect; nothing breathes, not even the wind. Town and terrain seem to be trapped, caught and held forever in the sullen, abrasive earth.

This establishes the film's discursive and ideological terrain of "inertia and immutability" where everything seems trapped, contained, and deathly, symbolizing the postwar world of containment and suspicion, a McCarthyite culture of repressed anger and paranoia played out as western exceptionalism, traditional values, and masculine power. The West as America is under scrutiny in what Millard Kaufman, the screenwriter, called a "protest film" at the heart of which was "its indictment of racism in the golden west" (2008: 71). The mythic land of opportunity is reconsidered here as the breeding ground for abhorrent values "trapped, caught and held" by the inwardness of *un*critical regionalism and emphasized through Sturges' geometrical set-ups, complex architectural enclosure, and intense angularity of space and light. Human beings have created a grid of containment – noted in the early sequences of the film – to control and manage their lives against the penetrative "outside"; anchoring their static community against the more unpredictable, dynamic, and natural landscape of the West *and* the threatening differences of the world beyond it. Black Rock is a sterile, deathly grid of white masculinity defined by patriarchal values, xenophobia, violence, racism and misogyny, seeing the outside world as defined exclusively by "do-gooders, trouble makers, [and] freaks," as Reno Smith puts it.

It is the film's geometry once again that emphasizes this grid: the intersection of rail and town, the hotel lobby with its stairs, windows, and doors straining at the cinematic frame, the jail's dark, elaborate framings, and the contrasting hierarchies of vision. Dana Polan in his DVD commentary refers to the town's "circumscribed geography" whereby characters return repeatedly to the same places like pieces on a grid-like chess board. Sturges himself, quoted in 1963, referred to "the story of men who want freedom, opposed by men determined that they don't. It could be called a gigantic chess game" (Anon. 1963: 18).

The actual film begins with CinemaScope's rendition of the desert Southwest pierced by the onrushing Streamliner Express followed by a shot of the train head-on as if the audience were on a collision course with all it represents here: modernity, the forces of history and memory, the "otherness" of the urban West (of Los Angeles or Phoenix), and what it carries within, John J. Macreedy. Significantly, he arrives from the future (the modern city), bringing with him the past (the war, the memory of Komoko) to challenge the world established and "set" in Black Rock – "the presupposed already there." The final shot of the sequence shows the slow arrival of the train at the curious desert crossing of "The dismal ur-town of Black Rock" (Kaufman 2008: 78); literally a few scattered buildings set against the immensity of the mountains behind. The framing draws our attention to the intersection, the crossing of railroad and community, past and present, *roots* and *routes*, and crucially the intervention in this by the train and the stranger soon to arrive; "big-shouldered, a granite-like wedge of a man with calm, *piercing* eyes" (as the script describes Macreedy). This announces the film as one of *crossings*, or what Stephen Tatum has termed "topographies of transition," where liminal junctions and thresholds are flirted with and challenged, "a zone of verging and merging ... recognized by the presence of *paradox*: familiar antitheses and differences ... kneaded together and revealed," often "critiquing masculinist, imperializing desires for mastery and which provides the ground for a genuine community to emerge" (Tatum 1998: 317, 318).

As Macreedy *pierces* the forebodingly named Black Rock, like a granite wedge, he enters *and* opens a space defined by Tatum as archetypally "western": "a construct resulting from the intersection of geography with geology, with social and economic forces – and with human desires as these have materialized over time and have been expressed in cultural artefacts" (Tatum 1998: 315). The central figure of *crossing*, Macreedy, is a *transitional* man, who emerges from the train to great consternation, since it has not stopped there in four years: "The *secure ritual* of the train passing through, never stopping, has somehow, for some unknown reason, been *violated*," claims the draft shooting script. The disruptive, piercing presence of the outsider *violates* the enclosed, inward-looking western town with its secretive and buried past encrypted in the stories or silences it has inherited and constructed about itself and its history. Amid the surprised looks of the local people, the conductor comments, "Man, they look woebegone and far away," and when Macreedy retorts he's only staying twenty-four hours, continues, "In a place like this it could be a lifetime." Macreedy is the violating outsider from the future bringing back fragments of the past and provoking repressed memories of this western town which will, over the course of these traumatic twenty-four hours, unravel a lifetime of active forgetting and cultural and historical evasion. His is a kind of western "postmemory" borne back by the survivor of trauma into the world of the "living" – a "very particular form of memory precisely because its connection to its object or source is mediated not through recollection but through an imaginative investment and creation" (Hirsch 1997: 22). Thus, Macreedy carries the memory of Komoko's son Joe back into Black Rock mediated by the soldier's death now invested with heroism and racism, inadvertently to provoke the buried memories of another death and silence, surrounding the first Komoko. This action, in turn, questions those established narratives of the West embedded deep in Black Rock's cowboy culture.

To emphasize Macreedy's role as a violating, disruptive, *transitional* force, he is appropriately marked (or *crossed*) by paradox, conveying a "stately ... granite-like" appearance *and* a profound disability, an arm with the "lifeless rigidity of paralysis" and "eyes ... of a man who has lately lived in somber familiarity with pain." He brings a bodily "irregularity" or disjunction into the geometric space and psychology of Black Rock, confronting its version of cultural, social, and racial sameness with *difference* (one-armed, urban, taciturn, self-possessed, reluctant). As I have said, Macreedy comes from the future in order to challenge the past – he *disjoints* time – arriving out of the dust of the desert floor, a ghostly presence dressed in black and white, somber, granite-like, and stoic he haunts the screen, drifting into and out of its spaces with the "ghost of a grin" (as the script puts it), constantly tracked and watched by others, who have never "heard of him, no John J. Macreedy, no listing, no record, no information, nothing." This ghostly sense is matched by the film's effects where, as the script puts it, "the wind howls like a lost ghost on the soundtrack, but not a leaf or blade of grass stirs" and where repeatedly we observe spectral reflections of characters in and through windows.

Macreedy is a "revenant" back from the dead (of war), "a nothing, a nobody" come to "collect" the "unpaid symbolic debt" of the man who allowed him to continue to live – Komoko's son (Žižek 1992: 23). He carries the *debt* into the film, a debt of honor from the world of war and history outside; an exchange of his life for the memory of the Japanese American who saved him in Italy. But significantly, it is a *posthumous* gesture, symbolized by the medal Macreedy carries back from war to give to the (now dead) father of the recently dead soldier-son. The dead and their debts are not to be forgotten in the "golden West" as the revenant Macreedy ironically searches out the other ghost (*or* ghost of the Other), Komoko, creating an endlessly spectral quality to the film.

This is, however, a town of absence and silence. Everything is blocked, one-directional, and contained within the town and its own enclosed system governed by Reno Smith. Telephone lines are "busy" or cut, telegrams intercepted or not sent, and letters returned throughout the film. Macreedy is the sole disturbing factor, an uncanny "message" from *outside*, "sent" into their world, the carrier of a bundle of "dead letters" (returned, address unknown); the ghostly unread words to, and of, the dead (both

Komokos). Macreedy's task is to reopen and to reconnect this static western town to its past and to the world beyond, to give "voice" to the memories of the dead, and in so doing to return a repressed history back to Black Rock's mythic rituals of enclosure. Of course, to Smith, all Macreedy carries is contamination from the dreaded "outside": "This guy's like a carrier of small pox. Since he arrived, there's been a fever in this town, an infection. And it's spreading." For Smith, the violent bigot, time and history bring only infection to his bleached-out, dusty world of whiteness and patriarchal nostalgia; a cowboy culture of hunting, bar fights, misogyny, intimidation, and gun play. Like Komoko in his immediate past, Smith refutes, denies, and blocks all *outside* messages that appear threatening or challenging.

When Macreedy says the town acts like it's "sitting on a keg," Smith claims the "suspicion of strangers" is a "hangover from the Old West." Indeed one might argue that much of the power of the film, as a post-western, is its deconstruction of the "hangover" of western mythologies, such as the mythic cowboy, now turned ever inward and blinkered, calcified in Smith's sidekicks Coley (Ernest Borgnine) and Hector (Lee Marvin). This sentiment is famously inscribed in Smith's vision, quoted earlier, of a West best "left alone" by businessmen, historians, and writers, ideally untouched by the outside.

In Black Rock cowboys have become as static as the town, hanging around in hotel lobbies and bars, strangely out of time, like Hector, referred to in the script as "like an unkempt monument," bullying ("hectoring") Macreedy and seen playing ritualistically with his gun and holster as if remembering his heritage now only as performance. Doc Velie (Walter Brennan) comments on the mythic West telling of how he sold men land for gold prospecting, then for farming, and then buried them when they failed at both. The frontier dream is here compressed ironically into Doc's dual role as both "notary" and "mortician" – authenticating and certifying legal deeds and signatures on the one hand whilst signing off the dead on the other.

As a man of the dead, Doc understands the town's own ruined, ghostly condition perfectly: "Four years ago something terrible happened here. We did nothing about it. Nothing. The whole town fell into a sort of settled melancholy, and the people in it closed their eyes and held their tongues and failed the test with a whimper." His assessment reminds us again of the film's interest in history and memory, both that of Komoko and of the West itself, and suggesting the connection between the two. It is as though the perversion of "west-ness" into an inward-looking distortion of an original dream finds its perfect expression in the murder of Komoko and the cover-up of his "place" within it.

Of course, at the heart of the film and the object of Macreedy's search is the scene of death, Komoko's homestead at Adobe Flat, where standing "in the wreckage" we are again confronted by the ruins that opened the film, now more excessive and terminal:

> The remains of an iron bed. The burned-out shell of a pick-up truck. Part of a stove. A morass of bottles, all sizes and shapes, some of them broken ... He touches the burned

out frame of a picture. The frame falls to the ground, leaving an un-scorched square
on the surface of the wall ... Suddenly he halts, arrested by something among the rubble,
the rottenness and the ashes.

In the fragments and traces of absence before him amid the cruel geometry of death,
Macreedy sees wild flowers growing on the desert floor, a sign of life, of memory – the
posthumous, emerging from the grave of the lynched Komoko. This ultimately redemptive scene suggests the faint hope present in the film, a hope Macreedy carries back
to the town, like the flowers in his pocket, to confront Smith:

> All that land lying fallow. Could be put to some use. Like a graveyard. (*Smith opens his
> mouth to speak but Macreedy goes on*) Something's buried out there. (*He takes the wild flowers
> from his pocket, holding them in front of Smith*). See these wild flowers? That means a grave.
> I've seen it overseas. I figure it isn't a man's grave or someone would have marked it.
> Sort of a mystery, isn't it?

Out of death comes life. Out of a genuine confrontation with history and memory
comes realization. As Macreedy says to Pete just before he confesses to the lynching,
"You're as dead as Komoko, only you don't know it!"

But the town has blocked its past, repressed the difference Komoko represents, and
erased his existence from the West, and yet it is his absent presence, his ghostliness,
that haunts the film and the lives of the living in Black Rock. The film as we watch
and rewatch it, think and rethink it, "lives on" and comes back *posthumously*, affecting
us with a kind of spectral signature altering our perceptions and challenging our
assumptions. Macreedy's role in this haunting, emphasizing the film's focal interest
in memory, cultural silence and the need for the past to be confronted and not
repressed, is summarized near the climax:

> You'd like me to die quickly ... without me wasting too much of your time, or quietly
> so I won't embarrass you too much, or even thankfully so your memory of me won't be
> too unpleasant.

Macreedy refuses to join the dead or the silent. Indeed, out of the ruins of Black
Rock and Komoko's death, Sturges' post-western allegory is not without hope, for as
Walter Benjamin wrote, "Allegories are, in the realm of thoughts, what ruins are in
the realm of things" (Benjamin 1998: 178). In J.B. Jackson's words, echoing Benjamin,
"ruins provide the incentive for restoration ... There has to be an interim of death or
rejection before there can be renewal and reform. The old order has to die before
there can be a born-again landscape ... redeeming what has been neglected" (Jackson
1980: 102).

Interestingly, Doc, at the end of the film, after Smith's death, wants the medal
Macreedy has brought for Komoko (the symbolic artefact representing the debt of the
dead son, his Father, and the guilty West): "Well, we need it, I guess. It's something
we can maybe build on. This town is wrecked, just as bad as if it was bombed out.

Maybe it can *come back*. ..." The town – now both western enclosure *and* postwar world – can "come back" from its own "death," its self-inflicted "wreckage," its physical and allegorical ruins, and begin again, have a "second chance" (as Doc says), *posthumously*; to live better, incorporating what the medal, its recipient and carrier represent, a different vision of the West as multicultural, open to its history and memory, and globalized. Tellingly, in the final shots of the film, reversing those of the opening, people and families appear again as if to assert the possibility of "transition" toward "genuine community," as Tatum called it. As Macreedy says finally, "Some towns come back. Some don't. It depends on the people." This tentatively suggests Deleuze's neo-westerns, rejecting the "presupposed already there" and proposing instead the "seeds of a people to come" emerging from the ruins of mythic "unanimity" and "tyranny" to assert a more complex and varied sense of community and history.

Simultaneously too, as I have proposed throughout this case study, the dead genre of the western could *come back* as a more complex history of the region confronting its ruins and, at least, attempting to "fill the footprints of the dead." As Castricano puts it, following Derrida: "To learn to live with ghosts is to rethink ourselves through the dead or, rather, through the return of the dead (in us) and thus through haunting" (Castricano 2001: 19). As Derrida writes, "Only from the other and by death" do we learn to live, "from the other at the edge of life," and "this *being-with* spectres would also be, not only but also, a *politics* of memory, of inheritance, and of generations" (Derrida 2006: pp. xvii, xviii). It is with this profound thought that *Bad Day at Black Rock,* as an early example of the post-western, reminds us that both generically and thematically, as Derrida has written, "the posthumous is already here ... [for it] inhabits the work" dialogically, demanding of its audience a more critically complex understanding of the interplay of history, region and representation, so that we might learn to live better and more justly (Derrida 1996: 10–11).

REFERENCES AND FURTHER READING

Anon. (1963). Sturges' Basic Approach Brings Story of Gallantry to Screen. *Motion Picture Herald*, May 29, 17–18.

Bad Day at Black Rock. Script. http://www.weeklyscript.com/Bad%20Day%20At%20Black%20Rock.txt, accessed June 3, 2008.

Bazin, A. (2005). The Evolution of the Western [1971]. In *What Is Cinema?* trans. Hugh Gray, vol. 2. Berkeley: University of California Press.

Benjamin, W. (1998) *The Origin of German Tragic Drama*. London: Verso.

Campbell, N. (2009) Post-Western Cinema: *Down in the Valley. Journal of the West*, 4/1 (Winter), 8–14.

Castricano, J. (2001). *Cryptomimesis: The Gothic and Jacques Derrida's Ghost Writing*. Montreal: McGill-Queens University Press.

Cherry, R. (1969). Capsule of John Sturges: He Would Rather Do It Himself. *Action*, Nov–Dec, 9–11.

Corkin, S. (2004). *Cowboys as Cold War Warriors: The Western and US History*. Philadelphia: Temple University Press.

Cox, A. (2006). A Bullet in the Back. *Guardian*, Friday, May 5. http://www.guardian.co.uk/film/2006/may/05/3, accessed June 22, 2009.

De Certeau, M. (1988). *The Writing of History*. New York: Columbia University Press.

Deleuze, G. (2000). *Cinema 2* [1989]. London: Athlone Press.

Derrida, J. (1980). The Law of Genre. *Critical Inquiry*, 7 (Autumn), 55–81.

Derrida, J. (1991). Living On / Borderlines. In P. Kamuf, ed., *A Derrida Reader: Between the Blinds*. Hemel Hempstead: Harvester Wheatsheaf.

Derrida, J. (1996). In Ernst Behler, The Contemporary and the Posthumous: Roundtable Discussion. *Surfaces*, 4/102 (v.1.0 A – 07/08/1996), 1–42, http://www.pum.umontreal.ca/revues/surfaces/vol6/behler.html. Accessed June 22, 2009.

Derrida, J. (2006). *Specters of Marx* [1994]. London: Routledge.

Dika, V. (2003). *Recycled Culture in Contemporary Art and Film: The Uses of Nostalgia*. Cambridge: Cambridge University Press.

Hall, S. (1996). "When Was the Post-Colonial?" Thinking at the Limit. In I. Chambers and L. Curti, eds., *The Postcolonial Question*. London: Routledge.

Hirsch, M. (1997). *Family Frames: Photography, Narrative and Postmemory*. Cambridge, MA: Harvard University Press.

Jackson, J.B. (1980). *The Necessity for Ruins*. Amherst: University of Massachusetts Press.

Jarmusch, J. (2005). *Ghost Dancer*. Uncut DVD, Nov.–Dec.

Kaufman, M. (2008). A Vehicle for Tracy: The Road to Black Rock. *The Hopkins Review*, 1/1, 70–88.

Kaufman, M. (2008). Script for *Bad Day at Black Rock* held at the Margaret Herrick Library in Los Angeles.

Kitses, J., and G. Rickman, eds. (1998). *The Western Reader*. New York: Limelight Editions.

Klein, K. Lee. (1996). Reclaiming the "F" Word: Or Being and Becoming Postwestern. *The Pacific Historical Review*, 65/2, 179–215.

Kollin, S., ed. (2007). *Postwestern Cultures: Literature, Theory, Space*. Lincoln: University of Nebraska Press.

Knobloch, F. (1996). *The Culture of Wilderness: Agriculture as Colonization in the American West*. Chapel Hill: University of North Carolina Press.

Lovell, G. (2008). *Escape Artist: The Life and Films of John Sturges*. Madison: University of Wisconsin Press.

McMullen, Ken. (2006). *Ghost Dance*. Classic World Art Cinema DVD.

Merkin, D. (1998). Smart Alecks. *New Yorker*, March 23, 2.

Mitchell, L. Clark. (1996). *Westerns: Making the Man in Fiction and Film*. Chicago: University of Chicago Press.

Polan, D. (2005). DVD Commentary on *Bad Day at Black Rock*. Warner Brothers.

Robertson, W. Preston. (1998). *The Big Lebowski: The Making of a Coen Brothers Film*. New York: Norton.

Scharff, V. (1999). Mobility, Women, and the West. In V.J. Matsumoto and B. Allmendinger, eds., *Over the Edge: Remapping the American West*, pp. 160–71. Berkeley: University of California Press.

Schatz, T. (1981). *Hollywood Genres: Formulas, Filmmaking and the Studio System*. New York: Random House.

Slotkin, R. (1993). *Gunfighter Nation: The Myth of the Frontier in the Twentieth Century*. New York: HarperPerennial.

Solnit, R. (2003). *River of Shadows: Eadweard Muybridge and the Technological West*. New York: Penguin.

Streamas, J. (2003). "Patriotic Drunk": To be Yellow, Brave, and Disappeared in *Bad Day at Black Rock*. *American Studies*, 44, 1/2 (Spring/ Summer), 99–119.

Tatum, S. (1998). Topographies of Transition in Western American Literature. *Western American Literature*, 5/32 (Feb), 310–52.

Tyree, J.M. and B. Walters. (2007). *The Big Lebowski*. London: British Film Institute.

Vidler, A. (1999). *The Architectural Uncanny*. Cambridge, MA: The MIT Press.

Woodward, C. (2002). *In Ruins*. London: Verso.

Žižek, S. (1992). *Looking Awry: An Introduction to Jacques Lacan through Popular Culture*. Cambridge, MA: MIT Press.

Part IV
Issues, Themes, Case Studies

27
America Unscripted:
Performing the Wild West

Jefferson D. Slagle

The exhibition is full of human interest, and it is a story of human accomplishment illustrated by those to whose efforts the outcome is due, and it presents in a series of living and active tableaux scenes which historians have pictured to us; around which novelists have woven many a fascinating romance. The actors in the everyday scenes have studied no part and have no manufactured "business" to rehearse, but have simply and effectively for our amusement and enlightenment lived over scenes which they have under other circumstances and conditions been compelled to enact. From the first scene to the end of the performance there does not appear before the audience a single individual who is aught less than he there shows himself to be. (*Chicago Herald*, September 24, 1893)

Buffalo Bill was real. Everything he did was real. In fact this is one time that the man may be greater than the legend itself. ... If this isn't the way it happened, perhaps it's the way it should have happened. (Koury 2003)

When Buffalo Bill's Wild West traveled to Italy in 1890, the exhibition initially received the same plaudits for its historical accuracy and educational value that it had garnered in its previous sixteen years of travels. In Rome, however, the media and the public turned on Cody's show. In response to a challenge issued to Cody's riders by Prince Sermonta, the American cowboys rode a herd of wild Italian horses in ten minutes. Cody, in turn, challenged a group of Italian horsemen to ride his American broncos; when the Italians succeeded, Cody refused to pay the winners on the grounds that they had taken longer than the ten minutes his frontiersmen needed to ride the prince's animals. The Roman media vilified Cody and ridiculed the purported "authenticity" of the Wild West, declaring that the show was a farce, that the "wild" animals

A Companion to the Literature and Culture of the American West, First Edition. Edited by Nicolas S. Witschi.

and Indians who ostensibly enacted historical events were in fact merely play-actors, and poor ones at that. In the midst of the uproar, a reporter from Florence's *Il Corriere Italiano* penned this apology for Cody's show:

> It is only natural that in a ring of restricted size the life that is lived on the immense American plains may be reproduced only in miniature; it is therefore an imitation, more than an exact reproduction.
>
> Buffalo Bill ... cannot offer us the marvelous spectacles of the plains.
>
> It is natural! Colonel Cody cannot load, with American advertising, on his ship ... a piece of America; neither can he make the Mississippi run in our arenas; neither raise the Rocky Mountains, nor plant virgin forests inhabited by birds of paradise; neither scatter high grasses hiding rattlesnakes, nor entwine tremendous boa constrictors among colossal plants.
>
> The advertising, for those of us who are not Americans, has been excessive: on the other hand, so have some people's expectations of the show.
>
> It seems to me that going to Buffalo Bill, as many have gone, with the sole purpose of gaining an idea of the apparel imagined so many times while reading romances and travelogues, one must not feel any greater disillusionment than that which might be felt attending one of the exhibitions of the Senegalese or of any other unknown or little-known people. (Translation mine)

The *Corriere*'s analysis of the obstacles and presumptions of Buffalo Bill's Wild West hints at a number of questions that are essential to understanding the reasons why Americans found the show thoroughly authentic while some foreign observers, viewing the show from a perspective outside of Americans' desire for affirmations of national self-identity, derided it as an "awkward caricature" (*Corriere*). To resolve this split requires answering a number of questions sparked by the *Corriere*: What were the sources and criteria of authenticity in postbellum America? How did Cody and his cohorts seek to reinforce or alter those criteria? Why did so many people on both sides of the Atlantic ignore the Wild West's clear status as artistic performance and receive it as history, accepting the show on its own terms? To answer these questions is to understand "authenticity" in the era of the disappearing frontier, as well as the promotion and reception of Buffalo Bill's Wild West in America.

Buffalo Bill's Wild West was a traveling exhibition, an arena performance comprised of a series of western vignettes executed by "real westerners"; between 1883 and 1913, the Wild West crisscrossed the US and traversed the Atlantic to perform for ten seasons in England and on the Continent. Remarkably democratic in its appeal, the show's audiences consisted of all classes of society, including street urchins, businessmen, schoolboys, presidents, and Queen Victoria. The exhibition was held inside an open canvas arena that was moved from place to place with the show and was adaptable to the varied locations (fairgrounds, fields, etc.) which were booked for Wild West performances; the performance space averaged 166 feet by 347 feet and varied by up to 50 feet in either dimension. Within this space, audiences witnessed what promoters billed as "Life-Like, Vivid, and Thrilling Pictures of Western Life" (1885 program): sharpshooting and lassoing exhibitions; burro, horse, and foot races; bronco riding; a re-enactment of Custer's Last Stand; a Pony Express ride; a dramatization of a historical duel between Buffalo Bill and the Cheyenne Yellow Hair; and an Indian attack on the Deadwood stagecoach. The Wild West claimed that many of the performers in these vignettes had been participants in the historical events they re-enacted in the arena – they, were, its promoters insisted, not actors. Before the formal performances of the Wild West in each city, performers marched through town in a grand parade, and they were also available for visits at the Wild West encampment before and after performances. The Wild West was conceived of as a coherent whole, all of these parts contributing to its often cited educational (or nationally interpella-tive) function. Its pastiche form coincided nicely with the episodic nature of popular conceptions of frontier history, both writing and reinforcing that history as a series of often unrelated conflicts enacted in a mythic frontier space.

There are several ways in which Wild West performance could conceivably be understood as authentic or "real": it could occur in the same location as the events it represents, a geographic authenticity; it could transport performers and believers to the moment of time at which these events occurred, a temporal authenticity; it could reproduce precisely the same actions that transpired historically, a narrative authenticity; and it could utilize the actual participants in those events, a corporeal authenticity. All of these elements, of course, are necessary to produce a "real" event, and even the *Corriere*'s apology recognizes the impossibility of geographic authenticity in a traveling show and seems to take for granted the unattainability of temporal authenticity, a construction which its author never even seems to consider a significant part of the Wild West's function. Indeed, what is perhaps most startling about the Wild West's claim of authenticity, as critic Joy Kasson argues, is that "against all evidence of stagecraft, promoters and observers alike clung to their sense that Buffalo Bill was a historical personage and that the experience of viewing his spectacles offered a 'lifelike' glimpse of the American West" (2000: 621). Though they may have noted the chronological distance between past events and present representation, most viewers did not view this rupture as a motive to doubt the show's historicity or realism.

If American audiences disregarded the first two models of authenticity, then, nar-rative and corporeal authenticity were made to bear the burden of the show's rhetoric of "reality," to efface its shortcomings by constructing a hyperreality that would mask the Wild West's conspicuous showmanship. The Wild West's traveling character, the impracticability of time travel, and the constrained nature of the exhibition's arena in comparison to the broad panorama of western landscapes were obvious differences from the history the Wild West claimed to display. The Wild West, then, relied on the last two categories, narrative and corporeal authenticities, to do the work of all four; the authentic bodies of its performers both mimicked and instantiated a popular history of the West in order to authenticate the show's place, space, and time: to make it "real." These performers, demonstrating what they had done "out there" in the

West, infused the arena's empty space with authenticity as they inscribed on that space the experience of events that they themselves had lived. These bodies, actually "there," brought western place to the arena's space and to the narratives enacted within it. They broke down barriers of time and space, ritually recreating the mythic time of American frontier conflict by demonstrating the continued existence of those events in the bodies that lived them.

Performing History in the Wild West

Walter Benjamin argues that "even the most perfect reproduction of a work of art is lacking in one element: its presence in time and space, its unique existence at the place where it happens to be. This unique existence of the work of art determined the history to which it was subject throughout the time of its existence" (1968: 220); even a perfect reproduction is still a reproduction. History, however, particularly popular history, operates in multiple valences, and can be regarded as simultaneously both "real" and "fake." Superficially, a historical re-enactment is not history itself, but under certain circumstances it can be perceived as such, despite the lack of Benjamin's "presence in time and space" that would seem to be the hallmark of a historical event. Historian Hayden White argues that history and fiction share more commonalities than are often recognized. History, he asserts, is "accessible only by way of language; our experience of history is indistinguishable from our discourse about it" (1999: 1). In other words, history exists only as narrative ordered by the historian. This is not, of course, to say that the past does not exist until it is seized upon by the writer of history, but rather that, as White says,

> the events, persons, structures, and processes of the past can be taken as objects of study by any and all of the disciplines of human and social sciences, and indeed, even by many of the physical sciences. To be sure, it is only insofar as they *are* past or are effectively so treated that such entities can be studied historically; but it is not their pastness that makes them historical. They become historical only in the extent to which they are represented as subjects of a specifically historical kind of writing. (1999: 2)

History is an *approach* to the past, not the past itself – other academic disciplines may also study the "events, persons, structures, and processes of the past," but their approaches to that material will be grounded in their particular disciplines.

Of course, this differs from the popular perception that history is "the past," and it is in the gap between these definitions that Buffalo Bill's Wild West constructed itself as authentic. The phrase "The Raw Material of America" was coined by Cody and his publicists to promote the Wild West as historical re-enactment by real westerners performing themselves; the Wild West was, by their order, never to be referred to as a "show." This exhibition of historical events saw itself as closer to an embodied history book than a staged play, and deliberately disavowed many of the traditional conventions of the stage drama in order to liberate itself from the inherited cultural associations of the dramatic performance, associations which would link the Wild West to a tradition of performance art, rather than history, and thus threaten the show's aura of authenticity. Though its status as a show is clear to observers who benefit from the perspective provided by temporal distance, its reliance on the events of the past – and its resonance with postbellum historical narratives – marked it as historical to audiences of its day.

Richard Slotkin argues that Cody's achievement – and the genius of the Wild West – was the structuring of the "various conventions and media" that already represented the West "around a coherent set of plot formulas drawn from a literary mythology whose structure and language were (by 1870) well developed and widely recognized" (1992: 71). The narrative of the Wild West, in fact, is identical to what historian William Deverell calls the "great narrative of the American West":

> We all know about this West, the West of little houses and prairies, good and bad guys, Conestogas, and lusty days of yesteryear. This image is one that, as one writer put it, casts the West as "America's primordial sandbox." This is the mega-narrative, the super-narrative of many names, one equally as good as another: the legend of national fulfill-ment, the saga of cowboys and Indians, the hardy pioneer epic. ... It is what so many people, adults and schoolkids alike, still think and believe when they imagine the West: that it is somehow different from the rest of the country and its history is different from the rest of the country's history, that it is marked by adjectives like rugged, brave, and true more than any other time or any other place in all the American past. (1996: 32)

The "mega-narrative" outlined here by Deverell serves to locate the creation of American identity in the mythical West and to locate that West as America, or inscribe western identity as American identity. Deverell's model also shares thematic and structural commonalities with the Wild West, which should not surprise us since the Wild West is one of the most influential forces in creating this narrative. As a writer for the Columbus (Ohio) *Dispatch* wrote in 1893, "'Buffalo Bill,' or Colonel William F. Cody, statesman, orator, Indian scout, trapper, and herder, has gained more distinction as a historian than any other living man" ("Buffalo Bill's Show"). The characters, spaces, and ideals of Deverell's description are the substances from which Cody and his associates assembled the Wild West.

Structurally, Deverell's mega-narrative is episodic in nature – it does not maintain a single sustained narrative thread, but rather relies on its overarching ideals and themes to link together scenes that otherwise have little to do with each other. This is precisely the form of the discourse exhibited in the Wild West. The incidents depicted in the arena can be organized into several broad, loosely related categories. The first of these consisted of re-enactments of specific historical events such as "The Battle of the Little Big Horn, Showing with Historical Accuracy the scene of Custer's Last Charge," which ostensibly included several Native performers who had partici-pated in that battle, and a "Representation of the duel between Buffalo Bill and the Sioux Chief, Yellow Hand," in which Cody sought to avenge Custer's defeat. The second category included re-enactments of "typical" frontier events – incidents widely perceived as components of a mythologized popular western history. The "Attack on Settlers' Cabin by Indians" and "Stage Coach Attacked by Indians" were typical of this type of performance. The third grouping comprised demonstrations of frontier "skills," including horse racing, "Bucking Ponies," and shooting exhibitions. There is, of course, a certain amount of overlap among these forms, as in the use of the Deadwood stagecoach, made famous by dozens of dime novels, for the Indian attack scene. According to the 1884 program, "When [Cody] learned that [the stage] had been attacked and abandoned and was lying neglected on the plains, he organized a party, and, starting on the trail, rescued and brought the vehicle into camp" for use in the Wild West. The stage thus became a specific authenticating object for the ostensibly typical or representative sketch.

These events, and their lack of cohesive structure, were cast not as the product of an author's creative genius, but rather as a transcription of history. This perceived lack of script and of cohesive plot set the Wild West apart as a genre separate from, if related to, the drama, and thus petitioned audience and reviewer to adopt alternative viewing strategies and critical apparatuses appropriate to witnessing history, rather than consuming fiction. Nearly without exception, American audiences accepted these apparatuses, and understood the Wild West as history. Journalist and editor Brick Pomeroy's newspaper account, included in the 1885 Wild West program that provided textual interpretation for the exhibition's audiences, is a typical, if eloquent, statement of this position:

> [Cody] has brought together material for what he correctly terms a Wild West Exhibition. I should call it the Wild West Reality. The idea is not merely to take in money from those who witness a very lively exhibition, but to give people in the East a correct representation of life on the plains, and the incidental life of the hardy, brave, intelligent pioneers, who are the first to blaze the way to the future homes and greatness of America. He ... wishes to present as many facts as possible to the public, so that those who will, can see actual pictures of life in the West, brought to the East for the inspection and education of the public.
>
> "Buffalo Bill" has brought the Wild West to the doors of the East. There is more of real life, of genuine interest, of positive education in this startling exhibition, than I have ever before seen, and it is so true to nature and life as it really is with those who are smoothing the way for millions to follow. All of this imaginary Romeo and Juliet business sinks to utter insignificance in comparison to the drama of existence as is here so well enacted, and all the operas in the world appear like pretty playthings for emasculated children by the side of the setting of reality. ... I wish every person east of the Missouri river could only see this true graphic picture of wild western life; they would know more and think better of the genuine men of the West.

Echoing much of what the Wild West troupe has said about itself, Pomeroy recycles the language of American frontier progress in the image of pioneer bodies laying the groundwork for America and the frontiersmen "smoothing the way." He accepts without question the exhibition's claim to represent "as many facts as possible," its "setting of reality," and its performers' genuine western essence. The evidence of the Wild West's authenticity is visible as "actual pictures of life" performed for audiences' scrutiny. The "material" he cites consists primarily of the bodies of Wild West performers whose historicity is informed by texts like Pomeroy's. Pomeroy also implicitly analogizes photography (motion pictures not yet having been invented) and the Wild West's vignettes; historian Martha Sandweiss argues that "even in the nineteenth century, [western] photographs plucked the mystic chords of memory and stirred the imagination of Americans curious about the social and geographical landscape of the nation's new west" (2002: 14). The effects of photography were precisely the aims of the Wild West: to evoke the nostalgic social imaginings to which Sandweiss refers; to answer those imaginings with an accurate, even scientific, representation of frontier conditions; and to fix perceptions of those conditions in particular images and moments through a "graphic picture." Pomeroy contrasts the authenticity of photographic representation with the imaginary, insignificant, emasculated, infantilized stage drama represented by Shakespeare and opera. The explicit contrasts between these forms are reinforced by further set of binaries that the comparison evokes: England/America, old/new, dead/living, art/history, high/low culture, and fake/real. In each of these oppositions, the Wild West is associated with the positive component of the pairing, as viewed through postbellum American eyes.

But if the Wild West reflected popular notions of the West, it also helped to create those notions. It both reflected a particular version of American historiography and performatively instantiated that historiography, in effect bringing into being the very historical discourse whereby its authenticity would be adjudicated. That is, as these bodies perform the particular histories of their lives on the frontier, they also bring into historical being a particular version of the West – a physical performance that, in gender and performance theorist Judith Butler's terms, "constitutes as an effect the very subject it appears to express" (1991: 24). To be sure, performance and performativity do not necessarily coincide in all cases, but one consequence of the cultural expectation of western authenticity is that western performance must instantiate the popular western history and identity it claims merely to present. White argues that "history must be written before it can be read (or, for that matter, before it can be spoken, sung, danced, acted, or even filmed)" (1999: 2), and Buffalo Bill's Wild West was a significant participant in the writing, speaking, singing, dancing, and acting of popular western history. Wild Westers performed themselves, their own "authentic" identities, and by so doing brought into being models of how westerners looked and behaved, what westerners did, and how the "West was won." Wild West performance, then, constituted a frontier history that it appeared to simply express or reflect, and the incidents performed by Wild Westers became history via the act of performance.

In fact, the Wild West's performance of signature events in the sacred American drama of westward expansion evoked the foundational moments of American myth, ritually transporting its viewers to the sacred time and place of national identity formation. Slotkin calls the Wild West arena "a mythic space in which past and present, fiction and reality, could co-exist: space in which history, translated into myth, was re-enacted as ritual" (1992: 69). One promotional piece, in fact, adopts the rhetoric of religiosity in its description of the exhibition, calling it the Wild West "revelation." The bodies of "contemporaneous participants" returned the exhibition to the originary moments of American frontier history, the nation's closest approximation of an official theology (1898 Courier Book). The Wild West evoked a ritual time of American history that has much in common with Mircea Eliade's description of religious rite:

> one re-enacts fabulous, exalting, significant events, one again witnesses the creative deeds of the Supernaturals; one ceases to exist in the everyday world and enters a transfigured, auroral world impregnated with the Supernaturals' presence. What is involved is not a commemoration of mythic events but a reiteration of them. The protagonists of the myth are made present, one becomes their contemporary. This also implies that one is no longer living in chronological time, but in the primordial Time, the time when the event *first took place*. (1981: 19)

Eliade roots ritual re-enactment in three elements: the monumentality of the events re-enacted, the perceived proximity of the individuals who lived in the mythic time of these events, and the impression that the time of those individuals is identical with the time of the ritual's participants. In the Wild West, events were monumental because they served as the origins of an American identity rooted in the frontier experience; the originary individuals were, in fact, in the arena; and their continued life signified that their time was indeed identical with the time of the witnessing audience, despite the imminent threat of the disappearing frontier.

One Wild West program referred to the showground as a "moving canvas world, which has been seen in almost every city or town of importance in Europe and North America." If the arena was a traveling world unto itself, then the laws that governed that world could differ from those outside – the laws of Wild West time and space, in fact, are malleable, allowing its audiences to be transported to another place and time through the mythogenic and historiographical performance they witness. The performance that occurred inside the arena was merely the most highly regimented portion of the larger performance of westernness that continued outside. Wild West audiences experienced this ritual time on a daily (and sometimes twice-daily) schedule, participating in the compulsive "re-acting" of the originary time of American history, witnessing "the spectacle" of western acts, "meeting with" authentic westerners and "relearning the lesson" of American frontier experience *illo tempore* as those westerners re-created it. The Wild West claimed to reflect "the *absolute truth*, because it narrated a *sacred history*" (Eliade 1981: 23), the nationally sacred historical truth of American frontier expansion. Thus, the Wild West was perceived as overcoming the boundaries of space and time, relocating its performance in the mythic period and geography of frontier conflict through the prophetic, authentic bodies of its performers.

The Wild West Body

If the Wild West served as a performative history, the bodies that performed that history were paramount in assuring its authenticity. The bodies of Wild West performers are nearly always emphasized over the space in which they act; the primary function of a mythically empty space, whether in the wide-open West or in the confined blank of the Wild West arena, is to focus attention on the action that can occur there. In the view of Cody and his associates, the authentic West necessarily accompanied them on their tours, for it was embedded in their performing bodies. As Cody said, the Wild West was "reality itself" and the performers "appear just as they are; nothing more, nothing less" (qtd. in Reddin 1999: 61). Unlike Cody in his early stage career, when, as Joy Kasson argues, he "played the part of a real frontiersman playing the part of an actor playing the part of a frontiersman" (2000: 24), Wild West performers ostensibly "played" themselves. Wild West participants were thus viewed not as actors, but as re-enactors, and visits to the Wild West encampment assured visitors that the performers would not, because they could not, break character. The events the Wild West displayed were generally authenticated in one of two ways: as re-creation or representation of historical moments, or by the use of performers connected to such events. The use of "authentic" performers reinforced the historicity of the re-enactments, and the reliance on historical events coded the performers as authentic westerners – a circular, self-reinforcing system of authentication.

Buffalo Bill's fight with the Cheyenne Yellow Hand (sometimes referred to as Yellow Hair) provides us with an example of how this authentication functions. Cody anticipated the performance possibilities of his 1876 confrontation with Yellow Hand and understood the potential historical significance of that event in post-Custer America. He dressed up for his battle, co-authored the news report of the event, starred in *The Red Right Hand; Or, Buffalo Bill's First Scalp for Custer* – the stage version of the story – and played himself in the Wild West re-enactment of the event (Kasson 2000: 36–7). This incident is intersected by interrelated discourses of authentication, and Cody's understanding of the actual event as a performance. As Kasson notes, Cody "report[ed] that it took place in front of a cheering audience of soldiers," and he collected artifacts from the incident, including Yellow Hand's scalp, for later use in *Red Right Hand* and the Wild West (2000: 36). The use of these artifacts would authenticate the Wild West re-enactment of the incident. This interrelation of history, performance, and artifact draws attention to the ways in which the Wild West both reflects and participates in popular frontier history, as well as to the role of authentic bodies in that history. In this case, the West for which Cody's body stands in is constituted by his performance, a circular authentication that permits Cody to both assert a version of western history and then claim that history is accurate because he performed it; his body stands at the center of this system of authentication to guarantee both the original performance and the accuracy of the reproduction.

Bill's body was constantly fetishized as a stand-in for the West – Wild West programs invariably depict him as their primary aesthetic, or authentic, object, and his presence in the physical and symbolic center of the arena continually reinforced the historicity of the exhibition by reminding the audience of the layers of frontier experience inscribed on his body. Kasson, in fact, claims that "the most valuable asset of the Wild West was the body of its star" (2000: 268), and his body remained a valuable property even as the popularity of the Wild West diminished. In contradistinction to Kasson's description of Cody's convoluted early stage career, the invariable and intense attention to Buffalo Bill's body during the Wild West period echoes Jean Baudrillard's description of the icon: it is "[a] perfect simulacr[um], forever radiant with [its] own fascination" (1994: 5); it is Cody playing Buffalo Bill playing Cody. The attention to Buffalo Bill's body derives from a desire to make the body authenticate the show, or to enforce the body's capacity to stand in for and conceal the hyperreality of the frontier that both body and show represented. Buffalo Bill protected his own iconography by cultivating his status as authentic; after a brief stint as Custer, Cody did not perform roles other than himself, and others did not play him until his late films. He was, in other words, purely himself; as the demands of western authenticity required, his body was precisely what it appeared to be. Richard Dyer's argument that "stars are involved in making themselves into commodities; they are both labour and the thing that labour produces" bears an additional burden in Cody's case (1986: 6): he is not only labor and its product, but also authentic and what authenticity produces, history and what history produces. The corporeal construction named Buffalo Bill is an overdetermined system of authentication that produces a hyperreal version of the frontier self and of American history.

As the most exemplary of frontiersmen, Cody's biography was viewed as identical with the history of postbellum American expansion, and his body was the signifier of the national effects of that experience. While much of Cody's perceived authenticity was due to his fame as a hero of dime novels and stage dramas, these experiences and their fictional overtones were largely disavowed in order to emphasize Cody's frontier body. Cody's 1883 program had already begun, in fact, to structure his claim to authenticity in these terms: "Thus it will be seen that notwithstanding it may sometimes be thought his fame rests upon the pen of romancer and novelist, had they never been attracted to him (and they were solely by his sterling worth), W. Cody would none the less have been a character in American history." The emphasis here is on visual perception – Cody's authenticity "will be seen" by the audience that gazes upon his body; the authors who have textualized his biography have provided an introduction to Cody, but one that is necessarily deficient and duplicitous because of its textual status. Textual representations of Buffalo Bill provide merely a preliminary knowledge of this character, just as his textual publicity lays the groundwork for a national celebrity grounded in physical performance. The 1883 program biography calls Cody "the representative man of the frontiersman of the past," "a child of the plains, who was raised there, and familiar with the country previous to railroads," "insensibly inured to the hardships and dangers of primitive existence," and "possessed of those qualities that afterward enabled him to hold positions of trust and without his knowing or intending it." In other words, Cody's fame is based in personal experience, and is a product of that experience, rather than of "intent" or even recognition – Cody, of all things, the reluctant celebrity! The biography continues: "Buffalo Bill *par excellence* is exemplar of the strong and unique traits that characterize *a true American frontiersman*. ... The principal incidents and episodes have additional interest from having been identified with [his] life." Cody, then, is not merely authentic but is exemplary, and his body structures and informs the meaning of the western medium he invented.

Kasson and Slotkin list Cody's occupations as ox-team driver, messenger for the outfit that would operate the Pony Express, wagon-train participant, prospector, trapper, hunter, Indian and outlaw fighter, civilian army scout and guide, hotelier, railroad and real-estate speculator, buffalo hunter, cattle rancher, development advocate, farmer, teamster, drover, "Civil War soldier in a Jayhawk regiment," and posseman; he was also linked to "horse races, buffalo-shooting contests, and hunting excursions" in which he exhibited frontier skills for a variety of publics (Kasson 2000: 11–13). This long list of occupations and skills maps Cody's life, and the construction of the character of Buffalo Bill, nearly seamlessly onto Deverell's "mega-narrative" (1996: 32). His participation in virtually all of the various frontiers that constitute this mega-narrative inscribed on his body the representative experiences of those frontiers, enabling him to authenticate re-creations of those experiences and making the body of Buffalo Bill an experientially overdetermined stand-in for the frontier, and thus for America. Bill's Body became the text on which the frontier could be read and interpreted. Thus, an 1898 promotional piece "JUST WHAT IT IS" ends with the declaration that "[M]any spasmodic, ephemeral efforts to imitate [the Wild West] have been made, but all lacking in their LEADERS the service, association and universal recognition that renders the fame and standing of Buffalo Bill's Wild West imperishable" (Wild West Courier Book). The exhibition's appeal, even its implied immortality, are a result of Cody's service, association, and recognition – in other words, the presence of his body, imbued with that authenticity, in the arena.

The 1910 program's "Valedictory" statement, Cody's farewell to the public, alludes to this connection, saying:

> Few remain of the great leaders in war and peace, many of whom "came out of the West," – the West of the old pioneer days, – the "Wild West," with which all my life has been so closely interwoven.
>
> From early boyhood to these whitening years, I have tried to play my part in the great drama of our national life. ...
>
> It has been my privilege to be an eye-witness of the opening, and marvelous development, of the Far West, from an uncharted battle-ground of roaming tribes of hostile Indians to its transformation into the greatest agricultural, mining and industrial field of achievement, on the face of the habitable globe.

Cody "interweaves" his own life with the imaginative life of American national history, claiming that the American frontier experience and his own experience are identical. That experience is coded as a "drama," echoing the Wild West's performance and Cody's earlier stage career. He again evokes these forms with his invocation of "eye-witnessing," the same function he has asked his audiences to perform for decades. And he invokes the tribal past and industrial future of America, implicitly locating himself at the center of this transition as the individual responsible for effecting it. The cost of this evolution, though, is the possibility of others like him. The 1898 Courier book includes a statement from "a leading journalist" that Cody is "decidedly the most unique character of the century, the one connecting link that holds together the wild, rough frontier past, with all its glories of physical manhood, and the almost too intensely refined present of mental manhood, machine action and emasculating commercialism." Cody unites in his body the past and future of a nation that, after Congressional closure of the frontier in 1890, lacks such bodies.

It may be this absence of contemporary equals to these frontier bodies that motivates the 1898 Courier book to state:

> It has been well said that there often arises a man who makes the world think, but how few have made the world stare. Among the latter Buffalo Bill is so pre-eminent that those who visit his great, realistic, life-endowed reflex of heroic and romantic history and universal equitation wish for a dozen pair of eyes to drink in all its lessons and enchantments.

This passage renders the primary attraction of the Wild West in spectatorial terms. Cody has "made the world stare" – specifically, they have stared at him as the signifier of western history. Cody's authentic body is the subject of the gaze that desires "a dozen pair of eyes" to "drink in" his nationally signifying body. This body is marked by its pre-eminence, even among the other authentic western bodies of the Wild West.

Perceptions of Cody's authentic body were not shaped wholly by his historicity, but also by its evident capacity for western masculine action. The 1885 program includes a piece by "Curtis Guild, proprietor and editor of the conservative *Commercial Bulletin*, Boston" that demonstrates the degree to which the physical capability of Cody's body served as a primary locus of attention:

> Never was a finer picture of American manhood presented than when Buffalo Bill stepped out to show the capabilities of the Western teamster's whip. Tall beyond the lot of ordinary mortals, straight as an arrow, not an ounce of useless flesh upon his limbs, but every muscle firm, and hard as the sinews of a stag, with the frank, kindly eye of a devoted friend and a natural courtly grace of manner which would become a marshal of France, Buffalo Bill is from spurs to sombrero one of the finest types of manhood this continent has ever produced.

Cody here demonstrates the "capabilities" of the whip, but by extension his own capability. His body exceeds those of other humans in its size, shape, utility, strength, and "grace," a reminder that western authenticity includes elements of the corporeally exceptional, even the superlative. This authentic body provides meaning to the exhibition and concrete demonstration of American history, becoming the most significant signifier of that history. No wonder the inside cover of the 1898 Courier Book contains this statement from Cody, under the title "Col. Cody's Only Card":

TO THE PUBLIC:

Once and for all, and all rumors and reports to the contrary notwithstanding, I beg to most positively assure my comrades, friends, patrons, and the press, that wherever and whenever my "Wild West and Congress of Rough Riders of the World" is billed to appear, there will I be with it also. That I not only personally direct it as a whole and every production connected therewith, but invariably appear at each and every afternoon and evening performance, conscientiously fulfilling every advertised promise made in my name. My place has always been at the front; I have not been accustomed to loiter at the rear.

The implicit message of this statement is that audiences attend the Wild West to view the body of Buffalo Bill, which serves as a synecdoche for the West. The final sentence of the piece emphasizes Cody's frontier character, which is often derived from his martial experiences in the West: he has "been accustomed" to the front both militarily and at the syntactical and physical form of his own Buffalo Bill's Wild West. His body "appears" in each of its performances and "directs" the exhibition as it provides historiographical meaning to the events represented therein.

Perhaps nowhere is the significance of Buffalo Bill's body clearer than in the Wild West's publicity posters, most of which feature Cody. In an often reprinted 1889 poster advertising the Wild West's arrival in France, Cody's face appears superimposed on the side of a running buffalo; the caption reads "Je viens," or "I am coming." The first person singular is notable here – Cody says "I am coming," not "We are coming." This utterance melds his identity with that of the iconic animal of the American West to symbolically fuse the two words of his own sobriquet; in this poster Buffalo Bill becomes Buffalo/Bill. Indeed, the two images are remarkably similar: facing in the same direction, both with woolly beards, the arcing outline of Cody's hat echoing the upsweep and decline of the buffalo's back. Cody is the West just as the buffalo is the West, natives of that soil who belong there, who emblematize frontier freedom, strength, and nostalgic loss. When Cody says, "Je viens," all of this is bound up in the "je" indicated: the land, animal, wildness, action, and iconic face are all represented in Cody. His visage stands in for all that the bodies of buffalo and Bill have experienced, for the American frontier West.

The suggestion of this relationship becomes overt in an 1890 illustration of Buffalo Bill by Alick P.F. Ritchie. In this illustration, Cody's bust is outlined in rope, and the lasso loop of that rope forms the brim of his ten-gallon hat. The crown of his hat is a tepee, while his shoulders and the neckline of his shirt are made of spears, a rifle, and a tomahawk. His flesh is similarly constituted of the apparatus of the West: his

Figure 27.1   Poster for Buffalo Bill's Wild West, London 1890. Library of Congress, Prints & Photographs Division, LC-USZ62-53793

jaw line is a quiver of arrows; his beard a buffalo head; his moustache a pair of snow-shoes; his nose a sword, pistol, and axe; his ear the head of a horse; his eyebrows gun belts; and his orbital bones stirrups, a belt, and a knife. The outline of his face is done in beadwork, and his forehead is bordered by a bow. In this illustration, the verbal rhetoric that makes Cody and the West equivalent finds its most explicit visual expression. The West is literally written on the body of Buffalo Bill; the land, frontier history, and flesh of William F. Cody are collapsed into the popular construction of Buffalo Bill.

Cody's own Wild West was not the only entity to recognize the historical as well as the financial power of his body, as his late-career stints with the less popular and successful Wild Wests of Pawnee Bill, Sells-Floto, and the Miller Brothers demonstrate. Each of these shows emphasizes his corporeal presence as authenticating force; they effectively bought authenticity in the form of Cody's body. In 1914, when Cody performed with the Sells-Floto Circus, his is the only segment in which no action is described: "Before you appears Buffalo Bill himself, famous scout, Indian fighter, civilization builder, one of America's Best Beloved Citizens – the friend of presidents, famous generals, princes and kings – and a man who has carried the United States flag to every city of consequence in Europe." Cody performed no action in the Sells-Floto arena: he simply rode out into the ring to be seen. The mere presence of his body was sufficient to signify the American frontier experience; his body has symbolically subsumed this history, becoming an icon of frontier America. By 1903, in fact, Cody needed no other authentication – at least on his program cover. This cover features a bust of Cody, isolated, without even text to interpret his significance. His body is all.

The *Corriere*, lacking the American cultural context necessary to read authentic bodies, rooted authenticity in geography, or the presence of landscape, and the absence of that exclusively American geography made the aesthetic and ethnological appreciation of costumes the primary, indeed the only, value imparted by the Wild West. For Americans, on the other hand, those costumes and the bodies that inhabited them were precisely the crux of the Wild West's ability to literally embody the mythical American history that those performers brought into existence. These performing bodies were the ingredient the exhibition provided to authenticate the veracity of American history – it was their presence that ratified the idea of America and gave the Wild West both its significance to live audiences and its influence, though sometimes unrecognized, over the western form in subsequent decades.

Historian Mike Koury's statement at the beginning of this essay, part of a commentary on the Wild West that accompanies clips of the exhibition itself, demonstrates the temporal staying power of this authentication – even in the face of evidence to the contrary. Koury notes the gap between the Wild West and history, the supplement that the show provides to the events of the past, but closes that fissure by referencing Cody's authentic body:

> to him it was always an exhibition – an exhibition of the great things he'd seen and the things he'd done – oh, maybe they were a little grander when he retold them, but he did them – he was there in person, and it makes all the difference in the world. ... So you see the material that Bill used in the Wild West show actually came from real life – while perhaps embellished, he really was there, he really did do it. ... But all these were real and Buffalo Bill was real and it made the difference in this Wild West show because Buffalo Bill had been there and he had done it.

Even in this twentieth-century historical commentary, the real is associated with the authentic body of Cody himself, and the events of the past are subject to revision by performance historiography: "If this isn't the way it happened, perhaps it's the way it should have happened." Cody's body serves to perform a history that is, paradoxically, more credible than the historical events that actually transpired. His body, icon of western historical experience, possessed the ability to write history; his having "been there" and "done it" renders any production in which he participates authentic. The performing body thus became the story of the West and the purpose of the western, and the Wild West provided the corporeal-historical model for others to imitate.

442   *Jefferson D. Slagle*

REFERENCES AND FURTHER READING

Baudrillard, Jean. (1994). *Simulacra and Simulation*, trans Sheila Faria Glaser [1981]. Ann Arbor: University of Michigan Press.

Benjamin, Walter. (1968). *Illuminations*, trans. Harry Zohn [1955]. New York: Schocken.

"Buffalo Bill." *Il Corriere Italiano* (March 18, 1890). Florence, Italy. William F. Cody, comp. 1890 scrapbook, roll #2/c.1. Buffalo Bill Historical Center, Cody, Wyoming.

"Buffalo Bill's Show. Many Unique Features Faithfully Portraying the Western Life of Pioneers – Beginning Wednesday." (April 21, 1893). *Columbus Dispatch* [Ohio]. William F. Cody, comp. 1893 scrapbook. MS6 Series IX box 8. Buffalo Bill Historical Center, Cody, Wyoming.

Buffalo Bill's Wild West 1883 program. MS6 Series VI:A 1/2. Buffalo Bill Historical Center, Cody, Wyoming.

Buffalo Bill's Wild West 1884 program. MS6 Series VI:A 1/3. Buffalo Bill Historical Center, Cody, Wyoming.

Buffalo Bill's Wild West 1885 program. MS6 Series VI:A 1/4. Buffalo Bill Historical Center, Cody, Wyoming.

Buffalo Bill's Wild West 1898 Courier Book. Ser. VI:A 1/15. Buffalo Bill Historical Center, Cody, Wyoming.

Buffalo Bill's Wild West 1903 program. MS6 Series VI:A microfilm roll #2. Buffalo Bill Historical Center, Cody, Wyoming.

Buffalo Bill's Wild West program [*c.*1906/7]. MS6 Series VI:A microfilm roll #2. Buffalo Bill Historical Center, Cody, Wyoming.

Buffalo Bill's Wild West 1910 program. MS6 Series VI:A microfilm roll #2. Buffalo Bill Historical Center, Cody, Wyoming.

Butler, Judith. (1991). Imitation and Gender Insubordination. In Diana Fuss, ed., *Inside/Out:*
Lesbian Theories, Gay Theories, pp. 13–31. New York: Routledge.

Deverell, William. (1996). Fighting Words: The Significance of the American West in the History of the United States. In Clyde A. Milner II, ed., *A New Significance: Re-envisioning the History of the American West*, pp. 29–55. New York: Oxford University Press.

Dyer, Richard. (1986). *Heavenly Bodies: Film Stars and Society*. New York: St. Martins.

Eliade, Mircea. (1960). *Myths, Dreams, and Mysteries; The Encounter between Contemporary Faiths and Archaic Realities*, trans. Philip Mairet. London: Harvill.

Eliade, Mircea. (1981). *Myth and Reality* [1963], trans. Willard R. Trask. New York: Harper & Row.

Kasson, Joy S. (2000). *Buffalo Bill's Wild West: Celebrity, Memory, and Popular History*. New York: Hill & Wang.

Koury, Mike, dir., prod., perf. (2003). *Buffalo Bill's Wild West Show*. 1987 DVD. Johnstown, CO: Old Army Press.

Reddin, Paul. (1999). *Wild West Shows*. Urbana: University of Illinois.

Sandweiss, Martha. (2002). *Print the Legend: Photography and the American West*. New Haven: Yale University Press.

Sells-Floto Circus 1914 program. MS6 microfilm roll #2. Buffalo Bill Historical Center, Cody, Wyoming.

Slotkin, Richard. (1992). *Gunfighter Nation: The Myth of the Frontier in Twentieth-Century America*. New York: Harper.

Warren, Louis S. (2005) *Buffalo Bill's America: William Cody and the Wild West Show*. New York: Knopf.

White, Hayden. (1999). *Figural Realism*. Baltimore: Johns Hopkins University Press.

28

Revising Public Memory in the American West: Native American Performance in the *Ramona Outdoor Play*

Karen E. Ramirez

Introduction

Public memory rooted in western American places provides a rich artery for western American narrative study. Public memory is a shared, communal understanding about the past, generally situated by a place or a localized event, which impacts how a public also understands its present and future (see Bodnar 1992: 15). As Edward S. Casey explains, public memory "always occurs in some particular place" (2004: 32) and is "both attached to a past (typically an originating event of some sort) *and* acts to ensure a future of further remembering of that same event" (2004: 17). Public memory is expressed and maintained through historically based community performances, such as the *Ramona Outdoor Play*, which is the longest-running outdoor community performance in the US and the primary focus of this chapter. Public memories also take many other forms, including community festivals centered on a past event or experience, such as the annual Pioneer Day celebrations held every July across Utah (Farmer 2008: 371); living history experiences, like those held at Fort Laramie, Wyoming, as discussed in John D. Dorst's book *Looking West*; interpretive programs at national monuments and national historic sites, like those at the Little Bighorn battlefield, as discussed in Michael A. Elliot's studies, and those at Devils Tower, as discussed by Dorst. Not surprisingly, many expressions of public memory in the American West are Anglocentric, originating in Anglo-American nationalist narratives of progress, adventure, freedom, and independence tied to western places – narratives about becoming "native" to western places, in part, through the removal of, or denial of, Native people.

A Companion to the Literature and Culture of the American West, First Edition. Edited by Nicolas S. Witschi.

The *Ramona Outdoor Play* serves as a site of western American public memory on several levels. To begin, the play enacts the story of Helen Hunt Jackson's 1884 novel *Ramona*, and in closely following Jackson's novel it reflects a localized public remembering of southern California's colonialist history (*c*.1850s) and its impact on the Native Californian and Californio populations. Although Jackson wrote *Ramona* as an anti-imperialist reform novel in defense of the Native Californians' claim to their ancestral lands, she framed her critique with regionalist description of the declining Californio rancho lifestyle and with a sentimentalist love story, and the novel's main claim to popularity lay in its nostalgic treatment of the Californio era and its romantic plot (see Ramirez 2006: 18–34 on *Ramona*'s regionalism and sentimentalism). Soon after publication, the Ramona story tapped into an existing tourist interest in what Carey McWilliams calls the Californio "fantasy heritage" (1949: 35), and Ramona-related sites sprang up across the region, leading the Hemet-San Jacinto Chamber of Commerce to start the *Ramona Pageant* in 1923 (see DeLyser 2005: chs. 2 and 8). Thus, as one of many Ramona-inspired tourist locations, the play reflects a second public memory of a romanticized Californio past. The *Ramona Pageant*, which was renamed the *Ramona Outdoor Play* in 2003, is staged in a huge outdoor amphitheater called the Ramona Bowl. It is a community production, involving an all-volunteer cast of about 400 community members with a production and support team of another nearly 300 community members (Anderson, pers. comm. 2009). In being staged as a community pageant, the play reflects the goals of early twentieth-century American pageantry and thus a third level of public memory: unifying a community by publicly re-enacting local history. Finally, in being a defining event in Hemet since 1923 (except for brief interruptions during the Depression and World War II), it reflects the memories and traditions of the communities formed through the play itself (see Matson 2006 for examples of the play creating its own community).

In sum, as a site of public memory, as I illustrate below, the *Ramona Outdoor Play* predominantly has reflected a nationalist narrative that reinforces Anglo-American ideals of progress and expansion – both through the story it tells of Native American removal and through the play's genesis in public pageantry and tourism. Additionally, until the early 1990s, the Elder Blessing scene (the play's Native American-focused music and dance scene) provided a venue for "playing Indian" (to borrow Philip J. Deloria's term), or an occasion for Anglo-Americans to act out a spectacle of the exotic, "vanished" Indian, which only reinforced the play's dominant nationalist narrative.

Yet public memory constantly evolves by engaging competing ideas of what is important to be remembered (or forgotten) and whose version of the past to authorize (see Bodnar 1992: 13–14). As such, sites of public memory invite studying the ongoing interplay and dialogue between dominant, Anglocentric narratives about the past that are associated with western places, and silenced or repressed narratives about the same western places. One provocation for such interplay of place-based narratives arises when Native American peoples assert culturally distinct understandings of place within or alongside established, Anglocentric public memories of those same places.

For instance, Michael A. Elliott's discussion of the public commemoration of a new Indian memorial at the Battle of the Little Bighorn national monument in 2003 considers one such interplay, which he discusses as the "aggregation" of competing nationalisms (Elliott 2006: 1010). By analyzing Russell Means's speech at the National Park Service dedication ceremony, in which Means both defended American Indian resistance of colonialist aggression at the Battle of the Little Bighorn and expressed contemporary American Indian pride in being Americans who "put 'American' before our ethnicity" (2006: 989), Elliott elegantly argues that such "conscious acts of allegiance to multiple nation-states" creates "a position so thoroughly charged with national interpellation that these allegiances can be turned against one another or coexist in a discomfiting, but unironic, tandem" (2006: 992). For Elliott, one expression of nationalism does not negate another; they exist as a living juxtaposition of organic narratives about the place of the Battle of the Little Bighorn. Elliot writes that "what happened at the Little Bighorn in 2003 is not only shaped by what occurred there in 1988, 1976, 1926, and so on; rather, the contemporary memorialization of the Little Bighorn produces meaning for its participants through its relationship to these earlier acts of memorialization. ... The result is not a hybrid form of nationalism. ... Rather, it is a matrix of political emotion that is thoroughly saturated by nationalism" (2006: 1010). Here is the dynamism and significance of public memory at "play."

It is precisely this sort of "discomfiting, but unironic, tandem" of an American nationalist narrative and a Native American autoethnographic narrative that I witness emerging through the recent participation of Native American performers in the *Ramona Outdoor Play*. The *Ramona Outdoor Play* annually re-enacts a story based on one moment in the history of the Native Californians who continue to live in the Hemet and San Jacinto area, particularly on the nearby federally recognized reservation for the Soboba Band of Luiseño Indians and the Cahuilla reservation. A wider diaspora of Native peoples also live in the region, partly the result of twentieth-century relocation to the Los Angeles area. Beginning in 1995 the play's artistic director, Dennis Anderson, and the Native American Advisory Committee, made up of representatives from the local Soboba and Cahuilla reservations along with Native Americans already performing in the play, began revising the play to encourage local Native residents to have a greater say in its performance. Since then, particularly the Elder Blessing scene has been expanded and revised to showcase local Native American volunteer performers. In the discussion that follows, I consider how these changes create a dialogue between the play's nationalist narrative and a narrative of local Native American cultural expression. The participation of Native American volunteer performers is a form of Indigenous self-expression that exists in tension with the encompassing *Ramona Outdoor Play*, thereby calling attention to the multiple perspectives through which to approach this performance. For while the Elder Blessing scene can be appreciated as the Native American participants' expression of cultural existence, it can also be interpreted, or re-contained, through existing narratives that the play has a record of forwarding.

The *Ramona Outdoor Play* as a Nationalist Narrative

With a few exceptions, the *Ramona Outdoor Play* is quite true to Jackson's 1884 novel. Set in southern California in the 1850s, soon after the Treaty of Guadalupe Hidalgo granted California to the United States, the novel tells the story of Ramona Ortegña, a half-Indian, half-Anglo orphan, who is raised by the Señora Moreno as a Californio. The señora is a domineering matriarch who runs the Moreno rancho although her son, Felipe, is nominally in charge. It is at the rancho that Ramona (unaware of her lineage) and Alessandro, the son of the nearby Temecula Indians' chief (to use Jackson's language), meet and fall in love despite the cultural, racial, and economic barriers that divide the Native Californians and Californios. Although Señora Moreno forbids Ramona to wed Alessandro (because Ramona was raised Californio), after Ramona discovers her true heritage, she leaves the rancho to join the Temecula band of Luiseño Indians, who have been displaced from their village by incoming American settlers. After Ramona and Alessandro leave the rancho, the novel becomes closely based on historical events (see Ramirez 2006: 14–15 on Jackson's sources). Ramona and Alessandro suffer one misfortune after another – they are repeatedly removed from their homes, their first child dies, Alessandro goes crazy, and finally he is murdered after taking an Anglo rancher's horse in a moment of insanity. At the end of the novel, after Alessandro's murder, Felipe finds Ramona and her second child at a Cahuilla village in the San Jacinto Mountains, takes them back to the rancho, and ultimately moves with them to Mexico, where Ramona marries Felipe.

The *Ramona Outdoor Play* carries forward the central paradox of Jackson's novel between its reform message, in defense of Native Californians remaining on their ancestral lands, and its nationalist implications, in confirmation of the American colonization of those very lands. Simply by retelling the Ramona story, the play keeps alive Jackson's call for legal justice for all Native Americans and her particular scorn of nineteenth-century Californian Natives' removal, which she also opposed through local actions, such as hiring a law firm to defend the Soboba land claim in 1883 (Robinson 1998). Additionally, by performing this historically based story in the area where descendants of these Californian Natives continue to live, the play necessarily makes Jackson's message and efforts all the more pertinent.

However, the play predominantly functions as an American nationalist narrative or one that, as Donald Pease writes, may be described "as having constituted literary forms wherein official national fantasies were transmitted to a 'national people' that they aspired simultaneously to consolidate and represent" (1997: 4).[1] The *Ramona Outdoor Play* renders the national fantasies of expansion, progress, and distinctiveness, in part, through the tragic story it tells of conquest. The Ramona story does present the historical experience of both the Californio rancho occupants and the southern Californian Natives being evicted in the face of an American physical and legal invasion of their ancestral lands (see Ramirez 2006: 19–23 and 29–33). Yet, in offering no alternatives apart from removal, in the end, Ramona, Alessandro, and the other

Natives and Californios who populate the novel become absent presences in the history that is told; they are there in order to be removed and sympathetically, even patriotically remembered. Ironically, the recognition of injustice against the victims of America's colonialist past (including Native Americans) can serve as a consolidating nationalist factor through what Kenneth E. Foote refers to as "oblique means of confronting the past" (2003: 324). Paying tribute to martyrs who embody values of heroism and sacrifice actually reinforces, for the American public, a set of civic, communitarian values (Foote 2003: 334).

The *Ramona Outdoor Play* also embodies nationalist fantasies through its connection to both early twentieth-century American pageantry and southern California's early twentieth-century Ramona-land tourist boom. As the original title, *Ramona Pageant*, suggests, the play reflects elements of American pageantry, which had its heyday at the turn of the twentieth century. Pageantry began as a Progressive Era art form, and pageant organizers deliberately sought to generate community consolidation and social reform through performance. In American pageantry, the *text* was community consolidation and the *audience* was the community members who themselves were enacting the performance. As Naima Prevots explains, American pageants were large-scale, "secular community ritual(s)," involving anywhere from 200 to 5,000 community members (1990: 9, 3). By bringing varied community members together (rich and poor, recent immigrants and long-time residents, men and women) to stage a community performance, pageant producers very specifically hoped to "provide a way of breaking down social, cultural, and economic barriers" (Prevots 1990: 2). Pageants typically shared some local history and they were often performed outdoors in a setting that would stand as a physical symbol of the communal history being commemorated and staged (Prevots 1990: 4). Performing local history was a tool to create community consolidation, for "history could be made into a dramatic public ritual through which the residents of a town, by acting out the right version of their past, could bring about some kind of future social and political transformation" (Glassberg 1990: 4). The stories deemed "right" to enact in this format reinforced dominant Anglo-American economic and ethnic power dynamics on a local level, thereby producing a local version of a national story. While the Ramona story is more overtly critical of Anglo-American colonialism than most pageant texts, expansion has long been a national fantasy tinged with remorse. The *Ramona Outdoor Play* reaffirms the "American" ideals of justice and human equality by mourning past injustice, while still reinforcing expansionist ideals of progress and movement.

The *Ramona Outdoor Play* also has roots in the consumerist goal of tourism. Jackson's novel contributed to an already-existing Anglo commodification of southern California's Spanish past (Kropp 2006: 19–46) and led to a Ramona-centered tourist industry that proliferated in southern California between 1885 and the mid-twentieth century (DeLyser 2005: p. xii). Visitors to southern California searched for the "real" Ramona and visited "real" venues that Jackson references in her novel, and as DeLyser documents, this led people to experience and remember California through *Ramona*'s story (2005: pp. xii–xv and 180–8). Thus, the novel helped solidify a public memory focused on a heroic Californio past that denied brutality toward Native Californians during the Californio mission and secularization eras (see Jackson and Castillo 1995: 80–6, 96–7), and looked past American injustice toward Native Americans, past and present. Essentially, the novel fueled an extended experience of imperialist nostalgia in which generations of Anglo-American visitors and residents of California could presume their own innocence in the despoliation of pre-existing cultures and landscapes through the nostalgic incorporation of remnants of those cultures and landscapes (see Ramirez 2006: 39–48).

While the *Ramona Pageant* was sponsored by the Hemet-San Jacinto Chamber of Commerce to attract tourists to the San Jacinto valley, it was written and directed by the well-established outdoor dramatist Garnet Holme, who encouraged creating an outdoor performance staged by local performers (Brigandi 1991: 36, 43), and who actively brought divergent populations together through the performance. As one early participant recalled, Holme would "get the Kiwanians working with the Rotarians, and the disc and dry farmers working with the irrigating farmers" (Pullen 1973: 164, 238, qtd. in Brigandi 1991: 48). Holme scripted the Ramona story around three distinct "eras" of Ramona and Alessandro's lives: first at the Moreno rancho, secondly at a Luiseño village, and finally on the run into the San Jacinto Mountains to escape advancing American settlers. Each era is highlighted by a spectacular element of dance, music, or motion: a Californio fiesta celebrating Felipe's return to health, a Native Elder Blessing of Ramona and Alessandro's first child, and a dramatic horseback posse chase for Alessandro's murderer. Neither the blessing scene nor the posse chase is strictly original to the novel.

These spectacular scenes emphasize colonialist understandings of the Californios, Natives, and Anglo-American settlers respectively. The Californio fiesta is light-hearted and colorful, featuring paired dancing that encompasses the entire main amphitheater "stage" along with a series of cameo dance performances. The Native American blessing scene is moving and spiritualistic, featuring a spoken blessing by "Mara," an elderly Native in the village, followed by dancing and drumming, and concluding with a sung blessing performed from the top of the amphitheater bowl, during which dozens of children, dubbed the "Rock Indians," appear with arms upraised across the hill of the amphitheater. As the Elder Blessing scene concludes, the "Americanos" on horseback descend from the top of the amphitheater, riding past the Indian children, who remain with their arms upraised. The posse chase, which occurs near the end of the play, is fast-paced and forceful, featuring a set of riders on horseback who race up the side of the amphitheater while shooting guns and yelling.

"Playing Indian" in the *Ramona Outdoor Play*

Given the Ramona story's benevolent but tragic presentation of American Indians, it is unsurprising that for generations, from 1923 through the late 1990s, the play provided an occasion for non-Indians to dress as Indians and act out widely recognized signifiers of Indianness. The central roles of Ramona and Alessandro were most often played by non-Native actors (see Elkin 2007: 88–100), and the Elder Blessing scene, which until 1995 was called the Christening scene, provided many opportunities for local residents to play Indian roles (see Elkin 2007: 114–15 on the name change). In spite of a history of some Native American participation, this extended experience of play-acting as Indian further secured the *Ramona Outdoor Play* as an Anglo-American nationalist narrative and also established a public memory of "Indian" experience within the play itself.

There has long been some interest in including and representing Californian Natives and wider Native American culture in the play, particularly in the Christening/ Elder Blessing scene. From the outset, some Californian Natives participated in the play, perhaps the most notable example being Mariana Costo, a member of the Rincon band of Luiseño Indians who married into a Cahuilla family, and who played Mara off and on from 1923 until 1962.[2] Mrs. Costo's longevity in the play suggests that the play became for her an important form of self-expression and that she was a valued and integral part of the production. The Ramona Bowl Museum Library houses correspondence between Mrs. Costo and the Chamber of Commerce indicating that, in spite of the volunteer nature of the production, they provided transportation for Mrs. Costo from San Diego to Hemet, beginning in 1925 (Hemet-San Jacinto; Brigandi, pers. comm. 2007).[3] Mrs. Costo offered a local Native legitimacy within the play by acting in the main "Indian" role outside of the leads and, as the Chamber of Commerce's letter to Mrs. Costo indicated, by translating her spoken blessing "into the Indian" (Hemet-San Jacinto). The letter's lack of clear reference to *which* "Indian" language Mrs. Costo would speak suggests the potential tokenism of her "authenticity."

Mrs. Costo's involvement could not fundamentally alter the overarching focus of the Christening scene on signifiers of Indian "Otherness." For instance, in the 1920s and 1930s the Christening scene featured individuals wearing little clothing and painted faces performing basic circle dances. By 1937, the Indian dances were performed by a "local non-Indian group that had done the scene for some years" and who demanded pay (Pullen 1973: 305). This unprecedented request to pay local performers was rejected by the play's director, Victor Jory, who instead turned to young Native men at the nearby Sherman Institute to perform in the Christening scene (Pullen 1973: 306). The Sherman Institute, which opened in 1892 in Perris and moved in 1902 to Riverside, served as one of the last non-reservation Indian boarding schools built in the United States; it continues today as a boarding school for Native American youth from California and elsewhere, called Sherman Indian High School (Mushrush). By the late 1930s, during a period when Californian Natives were integrated into public schools, the Sherman Institute primarily housed youth from distant tribes, including those from the Southwest, Pacific Northwest, and Plains (Mushrush). Incorporating the Sherman students in the Christening/Elder Blessing scene was the first of many instances in which the play visibly included the region's Native American diaspora. The 1938 performance program even showcased the Sherman participants' varied tribal backgrounds, listing them by name and tribal affiliation.

According to a local 1938 newspaper article, Victor Jory included the Sherman students "principally because of the increased authenticity and artistry that can be brought to the play by the presentation of genuine Indian dancers," a particular incongruity when juxtaposed with the Sherman Institute's function as an assimilation-ist school and thus the implied and imposed physical and emotional distance between the students and their Native traditions ("Sherman Indians"). When placed on display for an existing public memory of "Indians," the dancers' "authenticity and artistry" is revealed as primarily "authentic" to a narrative of "Indians" as exoticized and rec-ognizably distinct. The Sherman students comprised a recognized group of Native Americans whose presence in the region reinforced an Anglo-American ideal of accul-turation and whose prepared performances easily facilitated Anglo-American ideas of the Indian. Of course, by turning to the Sherman students, the play also effectively discounted and silenced the Californian Natives living on nearby reservations. Notable changes brought by these "Native" dancers included the introduction of eagle and hoop dances, two southwestern dance styles that remained long after the Sherman dancers stopped participating in 1941, becoming an example of how the play creates and maintains its own public memory of "Indian" expression. To this day, hoop dancing is included in the Elder Blessing scene, an element which has been performed since 1996 by Terry Goedell (Yakima).

By far, the vast majority of participants in the Christening/Elder Blessing scene were non-Natives up until the 1990s. For generations, the play offered a venue for the nationalistic performance of American identity through Indian representation that Philip J. Deloria discusses as "playing Indian." Deloria considers the "persistent tradi-tion" of non-Indians dressing and role-playing as Indians (from the Boston Tea Party, to the Indian-inspired woodcraft activities of Boy Scouts and Camp Fire Girls, to New Age devotees of Indian spiritualism), demonstrating that "playing Indian" has long been used to connect to "a deep, authentic, aboriginal Americanness" (Deloria 1998: 7, 183). Since play-acting as an Indian serves a *need* for the actor, and the demonstration of the Indian "Other" reflects the *desire* of the actor, "playing Indian" serves as a site for studying American identities (see Deloria 1998: 1–9). Americans have disguised themselves as imagined Indians in order to express national visions of strength, resist-ance, and a close connection to the land, even while simultaneously supporting policies to destroy and/or assimilate Native peoples and the land itself (Deloria 1998: 191).

The power drawn from "playing Indian" depends on a set of widely recognized signifiers of Indianness, determined by the nationalistic motivations, that can be assumed and removed. Program pictures of the Christening scene from the early 1950s through the 1980s generally show such signifiers of Indianness (mainly from Plains and southwestern tribal traditions), including wigs of long black hair, feathers, fringed buckskin shirts and/or loincloths, drums, eagle and hoop dance regalia, and poses that communicate solemnity, such as standing with one's arms crossed or with one's arms raised in a "V" above the head.

The Christening/Elder Blessing scene centers on Mara's blessing of Ramona and Alessandro's child, which connects the child both to the Native community and to

Figure 28.1 Christening scene, *Ramona Pageant*, *c*.1950s. Indians (Pageant) Folder. Courtesy of the Ramona Bowl Museum Library, Hemet, CA

their physical environment. The link between Natives and the natural environment becomes visually manifested in the scene's conclusion, when the "Rock Indians" emerge across the entire face of the outdoor amphitheater in one of the emotional highlights of the play. Thus, performing as an Indian in the *Ramona Pageant* (as it was then called), offered local residents an opportunity to enact, even if temporarily, a potent experience of being Natively connected to the physical place they inhabited. As Deloria points out, role-playing as an Indian "was powerful, for it not only made meanings, it made them *real*. The donning of Indian clothes moved ideas from brains to bodies, from the realm of abstraction to the physical world of concrete experience" (1998: 184). Yet this concrete experience of Indianness also remained non-threatening to one's normative self; the costume would be removed, ultimately revealing and reinforcing the "whiteness" of the actors underneath.

The association between performing as an Indian in the play and experiencing a connection to the natural environment was perhaps most evident when, starting in the 1950s, the Christening scene began featuring the local Boy Scout troops' Order of the Arrow members, whose participation in the "Indian" dances and songs in the play dovetailed with their Boy Scouting "woodcraft" activities (Brigandi, pers. comm.

2007).[4] (Figure 28.1 is from this era.) In making the opportunity to "be" an Indian in the *Ramona Pageant* a component of the boys' scouting experience, this era of the play's history closely reflects a local manifestation of the national ideal that positioned Indians as "close to nature" and offered young men the chance to enact and appropriate an "Indian" relationship to the natural order through a performance of these recognized Indian signifiers.

Recent Evolution of the Elder Blessing Scene

The play clearly held an entrenched public memory of romanticizing and commodifying Indians by the mid-1990s, when artistic director Dennis Anderson and the Native American Advisory Committee began revising the Elder Blessing scene to "include [the] artistic input and knowledge of Indian traditions and customs" (Native American Advisory Committee [1997?]). The attention given to this scene over the past fifteen years demonstrates both the vitality of public memory and Deloria's observation that "[e]ven as Indian play has been an invasion of the realities of native people, it has been an intercultural meeting ground upon which Indians and non-Indians have created new identities, not only for white Americans, but for Indians themselves" (1998: 187). Since 1995, several significant changes have been made to the Elder Blessing scene as a result of the combined vision of the play's staff, the Native American Advisory Committee, and several of the play's actors. The scene was moved from "the mesa," a small upper terrace in the outdoor amphitheater, down to the main stage, and expanded from seven to about sixteen minutes; the actors began presenting the sung and spoken blessings in Cahuilla (though the spoken blessing has currently reverted back to English); and the scene began featuring a volunteer group of Native American dancers and musicians, most of whom live locally, though not all are members of local Native tribes. The Elder Blessing scene now combines intertribal pow-wow-style drumming and dancing with Native music and dance from the area – namely, permitted Cahuilla bird songs and dances that are part of a creation song cycle relating emergence and migration stories of the Cahuilla people (Apodaca 1999: 4).

Though the scene changes somewhat from year to year, typically the performance begins on the main stage with the Bird songs, which are accompanied by gourd rattles, followed by Mara's blessing of the child (which occurs on the mesa and involves all the performers on both stages as they collectively call to the four directions). Since 2008, a brief memorial for community members who have passed follows Mara's blessing. The scene then features a drumming circle and a series of intertribal dances, including men's grass dances, women's fancy shawl dances, men's traditional dances, and hoop dances. At the conclusion of this song and dance component, a soloist sings a blessing from the top of the amphitheater while the "Rock Indians" jump up, and then the singers and dancers exit the stage through a choreographed exit, accompanied by rattles.

Figure 28.2 Cahuilla bird singing in Elder Blessing scene, *Ramona Outdoor Play*, Hemet, CA. Personal photograph by author, April 25, 2009

The timing of the changes to the Elder Blessing scene no doubt reflects the broad cultural and political shifts in the United States over the past quarter-century toward a cultural ethic of multiculturalism (see Elliott 2007: 4–6) and toward some political recognition of tribal sovereignty (see Wilkins and Lomawaima 2001: 249–63), including the 1987 Supreme Court victory for the Cabazon Indians of southern California which spearheaded the rise of Native economic enterprise and an associated rise in some Native tribes' economic and political influence (see Wilkinson 2005: 329–51). Five tribally run casinos are located within approximately thirty miles of the Ramona Bowl, the closest being the Soboba Casino, which is a regular sponsor of the *Ramona Outdoor Play*. Certainly increased public recognition of Native Americans' physical, political, and economic presence has impacted the meaning of Natives in Anglocentric public memory at the *Ramona Outdoor Play* and well beyond.

Witnessing Native American Performance in the Elder Blessing Scene

However, to consider the Native American participation in the *Ramona Outdoor Play* as catering to cultural, political, and economic exigencies overlooks the Native American performers' active involvement in instituting changes that reflect their own individual or collective presentation of Native culture. Jacqueline Shea Murphy, in her discussion of Native American dances performed "on stage" (as opposed to a specifically ceremonial setting) provocatively suggests that stage dances "really aren't about the non-Native viewers watching; they are about the performers' actions, and their representations of themselves, their peoples and their histories – and about viewer's roles as witnesses and participants in *their* representation" (2002: 17). In interviewing Elder Blessing scene participants, I repeatedly heard resonances of precisely this experience of cultural self- and community-rendering. For instance, members of the Red Tail Spirit Singers and Dancers, the primary group participating in the Elder Blessing scene for the past several years, mentioned that the play "gives us an opportunity to represent ourselves" (pers. comm. 2009), provides a way to "teach the kids their songs," and that in participating in the play "we are demonstrating something that belongs to us" (pers. comm. 2007). In 2008, the Elder Blessing scene participants added a brief memorial of the performers' elders and parents who had recently passed away (Anderson pers. comm. 2009), indicating how the scene functions on a interpersonal level as a community narrative of memorialization and healing and how the participants may reinterpret and culturally designate the meaning of "elder blessing." While celebrating lost relatives could seem out of place within the existing narrative of the *Ramona Outdoor Play*, and could furthermore be seen as perpetuating established simulations of Native Americans as ritualistic, such interpretations only focus on an audience perception of the celebration, negating the cultural, communal public memory at the heart of many Native beliefs and traditions. The reclaiming of "elder blessing" within the existing and loaded narrative of the Elder Blessing scene demonstrates what Elliott refers to as the "aggregation" of competing meanings held in "discomfiting, but unironic, tandem" (2007: 1010) and exemplifies the dynamism of public memory, or that evolution of what gets publicly remembered and by which "public."

In making this scene their own, the Native American participants certainly demonstrate agency in constructing a narrative of representation within the *Ramona Outdoor Play* (see also Elkin 2007: 103–19). The view of what should be represented in the Elder Blessing scene, however, varies within the diverse Native American communities of the Hemet-San Jacinto area. Some see a regression in the scene away from a sharing of Cahuilla and Luiseño culture and language toward the flashier appeal of the pow-wow-style dance and drum elements (Luiseño Language Class Attendees, pers. comm.). For others, featuring some pow-wow-style regalia and dance is itself a conscious expression of empowerment. As artistic director Dennis Anderson explained, "the vast majority of Native American local dancers and performers do not want to re-create 1850 California in terms of regalia or dances. They do not want to be seen as victims but as triumphant with the colorful regalia and spectacle" (pers. comm. 2006). These debates, in part, indicate that the Elder Blessing scene functions as a type of autoethnographic narrative, or one "in which people undertake to describe themselves in ways that engage with representations others have made of them" (Pratt 1991: 2). In this case, the contemporary Elder Blessing scene necessarily exists in dialogue with the *Ramona Outdoor Play*'s history of "playing Indian" and the expectations and representations that history produced.

As an autoethnographic narrative, the Elder Blessing scene may function in a transformative way, as an example of what Mary Lawlor discusses as "cultural self-representation" that works toward "correcting narratives that have gained ascendancy through historiographies and images orchestrated from Euro-American perspectives" (2006: 6). For instance, by incorporating some contemporary Cahuilla bird singing, the scene defies the play's narrative of Californian Natives' dispersal and disappearance. Furthermore, by working with a prominent nationalist narrative in creating Indigenous expressions, the scene demonstrates a resistance or push-back to that nationalist narrative. Simon Ortiz describes this idea of "resistance" thus: "the indigenous peoples of the Americas have taken the languages of the colonialists and used them for their own purposes. ... [I]t is the way that Indian people have creatively responded to forced colonization. And this response has been one of resistance; there is no clearer word for it than resistance" (1981b: 10). Such a resistance must take place in the colonialist language; yet the resistance transcends the colonialist language, never being controlled by it.

Since the Elder Blessing scene is housed within the nationalist narrative of the *Ramona Outdoor Play*, though, the agency and empowerment produced through the scene remain in tension with the potential for re-containment into a dominant narrative that denies or overlooks the participants' cultural expressions. This possibility was made painfully obvious to me when I first saw the play in 2000. During the presentation of the Cahuilla bird songs and dance, a person sitting behind me commented (loudly), "What are they doing up there? Is that dancing? If this is the first dancing in the country, the Spanish sure improved on it." The speaker reacted to an unfamiliar Native American cultural production with a familiar narrative of "Indians" as "primitive" and thus worthy of being "improved upon" (or "tamed" as part of the "wild" West) – a narrative that interprets Native American experience solely for its meaning for a non-Native population.

Beyond ignorance and racism, there are other ways that the "resistance" generated by the Elder Blessing scene may be re-policed through discourses that deny or overlook Native American agency. For instance, if Native American participation is approached as an instance of equal treatment, then this involvement becomes assimilated into a national fantasy of unity through the inclusion of diversity. This modern American nationalist narrative of "different but equal" often works to flatten difference and uniqueness by emphasizing "equality," thereby regulating diverse expressions according to a controlling narrative of American fairness. John D. Dorst elucidates this idea of reincorporating Native American cultural expression into a narrative of balance in his discussion of intersecting public memories at Devils Tower national monument.[5] As Dorst explains, recently this national monument experienced an "explosion of narratives" (1999: 206) created by the increased visibility of Native Plains tribes' experience of the tower as a sacred site, Bear Lodge, and the increased use of the tower by rock climbers – two experiences of place that conflict with each other and with the long-standing "management of this Monument as a visual commodity" (1999: 198). The National Park Service's response to this "explosion of narratives," a management plan that seeks to "balance" the spiritual interests of Natives and recreational interests of rock climbers through a voluntary ban on climbing in June (during the Sundance ceremony), refocuses attention on how the National Park Service accommodates conflicting interests. Far from inviting discussion of questions about "cultural ownership and control, about reappropriation, about rights of access and use" (1999: 208), the conflict gets redirected into a display of an equalizing management of competing uses of the national monument. Likewise, at the *Ramona Outdoor Play*, a similar process occurs when attention turns to comparisons between the Elder Blessing and the Fiesta scenes, for instance in terms of the length of time accorded to the two scenes or the impression created by the scenes' spectacle. Such debates reflect an interest in, or I would argue the guise of, the idea of equal treatment of minorities, rather than recognizing or valuing Indigenous experience itself.[6]

Interpreting the self- and community-rendering in the Elder Blessing scene in terms of its "authenticity" can further police Native American participation. The inclusion of Indigenous performance in the play raises many questions about authenticity. To what extent should the scene be "accurate" with regard to local Soboba and Cahuilla cultures, and would accuracy mean reflecting aspects of those tribal cultures from the 1850s or today? What aspects of cultural expression are appropriate to share in this venue? Is the pow-wow-style drumming and dancing a pandering to audience expectation or the legacy of *Ramona Outdoor Play* Indians, or is it a chance for the diaspora of Native Americans in the area to maintain and share their evolving cultures? While these questions will no doubt be a part of ongoing local debates amongst the diverse Native American populations impacted by the *Ramona Outdoor Play* and the play's staff, a critical approach that focuses on "authenticity" imposes a limiting interpretive framework because the critic inevitably assumes a referent (Indianness, or playing Indian, for instance) through which to judge the experience being viewed, thereby reinforcing the referent narrative, not necessarily the emerging Native expression (see Bernardin 2004).

In contrast, Michael F. Brown suggests in *Who Owns Native Culture?* that critics recognize the "relational nature" of Indigenous "expressive life" in order to "promote respectful treatment of native cultures and indigenous forms of self-expression within mass societies" (2003: 10). Part of this respectful treatment, it seems to me, involves acknowledging the complexity, variety, and contestedness of Indigenous representation as it is expressed literally *within* a non-Indigenous narrative. The recent evolution of the Elder Blessing scene reveals the tension and negotiation emerging in the interplay between dominant, nationalist narratives and existing or emerging Native American narratives. In choosing to "perform" Native identity within the *Ramona Outdoor Play*, the performance remains always in conversation with the nationalist narrative of the play and the possibilities for re-containment. But though the dominant narrative houses this Indigenous practice, it may fail to dominate. For the individual participants, and through them for a wider group and public memory, the play exists also as a venue to practice what is needed now and what is important now. The scene both responds to the dominant narrative and provides for resistive cultural expression at once; these two experiences cannot be pulled apart without doing a disservice to the complexity of this cultural expression.

Conclusion

The shift in the *Ramona Outdoor Play*'s Elder Blessing scene from a scene of "playing Indian" into a scene of Native American self- and community-representation has started conversations and debates. In 2009 I asked Charlene Ryan (Soboba tribal member), the founder and former director of the Soboba Cultural Center, whether she would like the play to continue, given its long history of objectifying and misrepresenting the Soboba and Cahuilla people. She indicated that "it would be a tragedy" to lose the play because it "is a story about the events that took place." For Charlene, there are too few vehicles for discussing the Soboba people and their history, and she sees this conversation as vital, even if in an imperfect venue. So while she concedes that "there may be issues with" the play, she sees it is a medium for sharing and learning public memory.[7]

The *Ramona Outdoor Play*, with roots both in Jackson's historically based, anti-imperialist reform novel and in the nationalist narrative of American expansion that Jackson's novel paradoxically helped promote, provides a particularly complicated and rich site for considering an evolving public memory of Native American experience in southern California. The play demonstrates how Native experience has been deployed to imagine non-Indigenous peoples as "natives" of the region, while its historical story of Native oppression simultaneously offers a foundation for ongoing expressions of Native American resistance and renewal.

But as a narrative of Anglocentric public memory the *Ramona Outdoor Play* is far from unique. Across the American West are harbored numerous narratives that have been written onto the landscape and subsequently into public memory, many of which repress and silence various people (including Native Americans). Jared Farmer's recent study of how Mount Timpanogos (near Provo, Utah) developed into a cultural landmark, through the paradoxical combination of forgetting the area's indigenous Utes and remembering a "fake Indian legend" about the Utes (2008: 4), also speaks to "how place-stories and storied places created by colonizers are persistently haunted by the colonized" (2008: 16). Furthermore, like my analysis of "playing Indian" in the *Ramona Outdoor Play*, Farmer's study reveals the dynamism of public memories that have long *mis*represented Indigenous populations and yet may be revised by contemporary Native people. Farmer concludes by discussing a 1997 orchestral and choral composition by Kurt Bestor, thematically inspired by the Legend of Timpanogos, for which Terry Tempest Williams wrote the libretto. Working with a Ute tribal elder and a tribal linguist, Williams incorporated permitted Ute language and perspectives into her libretto and urged that the concert program include "'The Real Story of Timpanogos,' as related by tribal elder Ethel Grant" (2008: 375). Farmer indicates that this "'real story' would appear to be a modern hybrid," thereby recognizing the inefficacy of seeking an "authentic" Native legend for this landmark (2008: 375, 378). Instead, as my discussion of integrating Indigenous expression into the *Ramona Outdoor Play*'s Elder Blessing scene also reveals, the greater significance of incorporating a Ute-centered understanding of Timpanogos into this musical production lies in witnessing alternative narratives about the place and in the potential conversations thus generated.

Conversation necessarily involves recognition, acknowledgment, a voicing. What echoes from the past are heard and remembered? What do these echoes come to mean? How do they help a public understand itself in a local place? I am reminded of Simon Ortiz's prose poem in *from Sand Creek*, "[r]epression works like shadow, clouding memory and sometimes even to blind, and when it is on a national scale, it is just not good" (1981a: 14). The unclouding of memory occurs through recognition and "resistance," a process that Ortiz's own *from Sand Creek* embodies, and one that also may be experienced through the incremental revision of Anglocentric public memory through local debates and conversations. Studying expressions of public memory rooted in western American places and how they exist in dialogue with alternative ways of occupying and narrating those places can expose and challenge the power structures embedded in the dominant narratives. This interplay of narratives of place creates moments of disruption to the established public memory that can offer fresh understanding of the places and the memories they hold.

NOTES

1 Pease borrows Jacqueline Rose's idea of "fantasy" as the "psychic glue" that binds together a state's or nation's subjects (Pease 1997: 3, 14). Rose describes "fantasy" as "the unconscious dreams of nations," which is not "antagonistic to social reality; it is its precondition or psychic glue" (Rose 1996: 3).

2 Mrs. Costo went under the name of "Mrs. Isadore Costo" in the *Ramona Pageant* programs. Phil Brigandi (pers. comm. 2009) informed me of Mrs. Costo's first name. Information on her tribal affiliation is drawn from the 1970 *Daily Enterprise* article "Isadore Costo," which covers Mrs. Costo's death. Matson discusses Mrs. Costo, but incorrectly refers to her as "Isadore Costo," a Cahuilla

Indian (Matson 2006: 198). Isadore was her husband's name, and he was Cahuilla.

3 Phil Brigandi, southern Californian historian and Ramona Bowl historian, shared many insights into Mrs. Costo's importance to the *Ramona Pageant*. Brigandi's extensive knowledge about the *Ramona Outdoor Play* and his eagerness to share his knowledge were instrumental in my exploration of the play.

4 The Order of the Arrow, the Boy Scouts' national honor society, began in 1915 and was approved as part of the scouting program in 1934 ("OA Basics"). Deloria explains how this organization turned scouting "back toward the Indianness" (Deloria 1998: 126) earlier promoted by Ernest Thompson

Seton's Woodcraft Indians organization (1998: 96).

5 Though Dorst doesn't use the term "public memory," his subject matter, the "discourse of looking," is one expression of public memory since public memory involves the collective process of organizing "visual experience" (Dorst 1999: 96).

6 In both 2007 and 2009 Dennis Anderson mentioned this comparison between the scenes as a common concern amongst audience members and Ramona Bowl board members. In 2010 the Elder Blessing scene was reduced by five

minutes to respond to a perceived imbalance between the scenes (Anderson, pers. comm. 2010). I greatly appreciate Anderson's availability for repeated interviews and his clarity in sharing details about the performance.

7 Charlene Ryan's welcome at the Soboba Cultural Center and her openness in sharing her wisdom about Soboba history, culture, and contemporary experiences greatly expanded my understanding of Soboba and the multiplicity of responses to the *Ramona Outdoor Play* in the Soboba community.

REFERENCES AND FURTHER READING

Personal Communications

Anderson, Dennis. Email to the author. May 2, 2006.

Anderson, Dennis. Personal interview. May 3, 2007.

Anderson, Dennis. Personal interview. April 24, 2009.

Anderson, Dennis. Telephone interview. May 17, 2010.

Brigandi, Phil. Personal interview. May 3, 2007.

Brigandi, Phil. Personal interview. April 25, 2009.

Luiseño Language Class Attendees. Private conversation. Cham-Mix Poki' (Soboba Cultural Center). San Jacinto, CA. May 3, 2007.

Red Tail Spirit Singers and Dancers. Personal interview. May 5, 2007.

Red Tail Spirit Singers and Dancers. Personal interview. April 25, 2009.

Ryan, Charlene. Personal interview. April 24, 2009.

Performances

Performance program. (1938). Cast, in order of their appearance. *Ramona Outdoor Play of Early California*, at Ramona Bowl Museum Library, Hemet, CA.

The Ramona Pageant. (2000). Adapt. Garnet Holme. By Helen Hunt Jackson. Dir. Dennis Anderson. Ramona Bowl Amphitheater, Hemet, CA. May 13.

The Ramona Outdoor Play. (2009). Adapt. Garnet Holme. By Helen Hunt Jackson. Dir. Dennis Anderson. Ramona Bowl Amphitheater, Hemet, CA. April 25.

Other Sources

Apodaca, Paul. (1999). Cahuilla Bird Songs (with Luke Madrigal). *California Chronicles*, 2/2, n.p. [*MasterFILE Premier*. Accessed online April 6, 2010.]

Bernardin, Susan. (2004). The Authenticity Game: "Getting Real" in Contemporary American Indian Literature. In William R. Handley and Nathaniel Lewis, eds., *True West: Authenticity and the American West*, pp. 155–78. Lincoln: University of Nebraska Press.

Bodnar, John. (1992). *Remaking America: Public Memory, Commemoration, and Patriotism in the Twentieth Century*. Princeton: Princeton University Press.

Brigandi, Phil. (1991). *Garnet Holme: California's Pageant Master*. Hemet: Ramona Pageant Association.

Brown, Michael F. (2003). *Who Owns Native Culture?* Cambridge, MA: Harvard University Press.

Casey, Edward S. (2004). Public Memory in Place and Time. In Kendall R. Phillips, ed., *Framing Public Memory*, pp. 17–44. Tuscaloosa: University of Alabama Press.

Deloria, Philip J. (1998). *Playing Indian*. New Haven: Yale University Press.

DeLyser, Dydia. (2005). *Ramona Memories: Tourism and the Shaping of Southern California*. Minneapolis: University of Minnesota Press.

Dorst, John D. (1999). *Looking West*. Philadelphia: University of Pennsylvania Press.

Elkin, Courtney Carmel. (2007). Clashes of Cultural Memory in Popular Festival Performance in Southern California: 1910s–Present. Dissertation. University of California, Los Angeles. [*Dissertations & Theses: A&I, ProQuest*. Accessed online Feb. 2, 2010.]

Elliott, Michael A. (2006). Indian Patriots on Last Stand Hill. *American Quarterly*, 58/4, 987–1015. [*Project Muse*. Accessed online Jan. 15, 2009.]

Elliott, Michael A. (2007). *Custerology: The Enduring Legacy of the Indian Wars and George Armstrong Custer*. Chicago: University of Chicago Press.

Farmer, Jared. (2008). *On Zion's Mount: Mormons, Indians, and the American Landscape*. Cambridge, MA: Harvard University Press.

Foote, Kenneth E. (2003). *Shadowed Ground: America's Landscapes of Violence and Tragedy*, rev. edn. Austin: University of Texas Press.

Glassberg, David. (1990). *American Historical Pageantry: The Uses of Tradition in the Early Tewentieth Century*. Chapel Hill: University of North Carolina Press.

Hemet-San Jacinto. Chamber of Commerce. Letter to Mrs. I.A. Costo. April 20, 1925. Local Indians Folder. Hemet, CA: Ramona Bowl Museum Library.

"Isadore Costo Dies in Escondido." *Daily Enterprise*, June 25, 1970, C-3. Local Indians Folder. Hemet, CA: Ramona Bowl Museum Library.

Jackson, Helen Hunt. (2005). *Ramona* [1884]. New York: Modern Library.

Jackson, Robert H., and Edward D. Castillo. (1995). *Indians, Franciscans, and Spanish Colonization: The Impact of the Mission System on California Indians*. Albuquerque: University of New Mexico Press.

Kropp, Phoebe S. (2006). *California Vieja: Culture and Memory in a Modern American Place*. Berkeley: University of California Press.

Lawlor, Mary. (2006). *Public Native America: Tribal Self-Representations in Casinos, Museums, and Powwows*. New Brunswick, NJ: Rutgers University Press.

Matson, Barb Ann. (2006). Performing Identity, Staging Injustice: California's "Ramona"

Festival as Ritual. Dissertation. University of Colorado at Boulder. [*Dissertations & Theses @ University of Colorado System, ProQuest*. Accessed online May 9, 2007.]

McWilliams, Carey. (1949). *North from Mexico: The Spanish Speaking People of the United States*. Philadelphia: Lippincott.

Murphy, Jacqueline Shea. (2002). Policing Authenticity: Native American Dance and the "Western" Stage. *Discourses in Dance*, 1/2, 5–28. [*Rapid: COD*. Accessed online April 15, 2010.]

Mushrush, Stephanie. (2009). Sherman Indian High School History. *Sherman Indian Museum*, Sept. 15, 2009. [Accessed online Feb. 23, 2010.]

Native American Advisory Committee. [1997?] Native American Advisory Committee Folder. Hemet, CA: Ramona Bowl Museum Library.

"OA Basics." (2009). Order of the Arrow: Scouting's National Honor Society. *Order of the Arrow*. Order of the Arrow. Boy Scouts of America. Oct. 15. [Accessed online March 7, 2010.]

Ortiz, Simon J. (1981a). *from Sand Creek*. Tuscon: University of Arizona Press.

Ortiz, Simon J. (1981b). Towards a National Indian Literature: Cultural Authenticity in Nationalism. *MELUS*, 8/2, 7–12. [*MLA International Bibliography*. Accessed online Aug. 5, 2009.]

Pease, Donald E. (1997). National Narratives, Postnational Narration. *Modern Fiction Studies*, 43/1, 1–23. [*Project Muse*. Accessed online Feb. 14, 2010.]

Pratt, Mary Louise. (1991). Arts of the Contact Zone. *Profession*, 91, 33–40. [*MLA International Bibliography*. Accessed online July 17, 2009.]

Prevots, Naima. (1990). *American Pageantry: A Movement for Art and Democracy*. Ann Arbor: UMI Research Press.

Pullen, William Augustus. (1973). The Ramona Pageant: A Historical and Analytical Study. Dissertation. University of Southern California. [*Dissertations & Theses: A&I, ProQuest*. Accessed online Jan. 10, 2010.]

Ramirez, Karen E. (2006). *Reading Helen Hunt Jackson's "Ramona"*. Boise: Boise State University Western Writers Series.

Robinson, John W. (1998). Ordeal of the Sobobas. *Dogtown Territorial Quarterly*, 35, n.p.

Rose, Jacqueline. (1996). *States of Fantasy*. Oxford: Clarendon Press.

"Sherman Indians to Dance in Play." *Gazette* [Beaumont, CA]. April 7, 1938. Sherman Institute Folder. Hemet, CA: Ramona Bowl Museum Library.

Wilkins, David E., and K. Tsianina Lomawaima. (2001). *Uneven Ground: American Indian Sovereignty and Federal Law*. Norman: University of Oklahoma Press.

Wilkinson, Charles. (2005). *Blood Struggle: The Rise of Modern Indian Nations*. New York: Norton.

29

Omnimedia Marketing: The Case of *The Lone Ranger*

Chadwick Allen

Boys! Get My Official Picture Rings!
Girls! Wear Lucky Lone Ranger Bracelets!

> (Advertisement for "Swell Premiums,"
> back cover of Lone Ranger Ice Cream Cones *Comics*)

Omnimedia marketing? Of westerns? The concept of a coordinated advertising campaign networked through *all* media would seem most applicable to business practices
or commercial entertainment launched in the late twentieth and early twenty-first
centuries (what we have come to think of as the era of "new" communications technologies) and thus decades after conventional print, film, and television westerns
peaked in popularity.

An obvious example of omnimedia marketing is the phenomenal promotion of *Star
Wars* – that epic space western set "a long time ago in a galaxy far, far away" – across
four decades. First released in the US in 1977, the film quickly circulated the globe,
its enormous popularity due in no small part to aggressive marketing organized by
its distributor, 20th Century Fox, and extensive franchising negotiated by its creator,
George Lucas. Conceived well in advance of its release, the marketing for *Star Wars*
began with an image and with a text that were remarkable less for their novelty than
for the uncanny familiarity of their key icons and basic plot. In dramatic poster art,
a young warrior brandished a shining saber (of neon light). In the screenplay's adaptation as a paperback novel, this untested hero, bearing a prophetic name (Skywalker),
quested after his true (Jedi) identity and led a motley crew of (intergalactic and multi-
form) friends into a (cosmic) battle of good (federation) versus evil (empire). Once

A Companion to the Literature and Culture of the American West, First Edition. Edited by
Nicolas S. Witschi.
© 2011 Blackwell Publishing Ltd. Published 2011 by Blackwell Publishing Ltd.

released, a steady promotional stream propelled the film's popularity through its initial theater run into the next several years and into several sequels.

While aspects of this marketing were typical, others seemed strikingly innovative. Additional novels were published, as were books for children and a series of comic books. An animated cartoon series ran on Saturday morning television, and interactive games could be played at video arcades; there was even an aural adaptation for National Public Radio to reach older demographics. An array of licensing agreements produced toys, action figures, trading cards, lunch boxes, school notebooks, Halloween costumes, and much more, as well as tie-ins with the menus at fast food restaurant chains. Every possible consumable, collectible, or performable iteration of *Star Wars* became available to eager fans. Significantly, these multiple promotions did more than simply advertise a fixed product: they actively developed and even expanded the film's plotlines, characters, settings, and themes beyond the limits of their two-hour textual origin.

From the beginning, *Star Wars* appears to have been conceived as a broadly appealing, highly lucrative brand rather than as a one-off, single-medium product. During the several-year period between the release of the original film and its first sequel, the owners of that brand maintained its visibility and accentuated its profitability by continuing to collaborate with commercial sponsors and multiple manufacturers. These processes of franchising and saturation marketing were repeated during the periods of build-up and follow-up for each sequel, over time creating what is known as the Star Wars Expanded Universe: officially licensed *Star Wars* materials that fall outside the central texts of the six feature films.[1]

Although Lucas, 20th Century Fox, and their promotional machines may appear to have originated such techniques, the basic strategies for omnimedia marketing – and for expanding the sellable "universe" of a particular brand – were developed decades earlier, and westerns played a significant role. The 2010 death of Fess Parker, the genial actor best known for playing the role of Davy Crockett, "king of the wild frontier," has brought renewed attention, for instance, to the broad-based, highly diversified marketing that was tied to popular western media products in the mid- and late 1950s. The Disney Corporation's *Davy Crockett* television series ran for only five episodes in 1954 and 1955, but it was wildly popular with young viewers, and it created a "frenzy" over Crockett-themed merchandise: everything from coloring books to pajamas, but especially the handsome frontiersman's signature coonskin cap. By the end of the series' short run, the Crockett brand was reported to have been marketed through more than 3,000 different products.[2]

The history of the omnimedia marketing of westerns, however, pre-dates even the broad distribution of television into American homes that propelled *Davy Crockett* and other series into extensive franchising. Indeed, listeners to the radio adaptation of *Star Wars* likely recalled that in the 1930s, 1940s, and early 1950s, an era dominated not by television but by radio as a popular home-based medium for drama, the products of several radio genres were successfully branded and profitably franchised across multiple media.[3] Prominent among these were formulaic stories of mystery, adventure, and crime-solving set in the historical and contemporary American West, featuring both mythic frontier heroes and real-life celebrity cowboys. In fact, riding on the heels of the Great Depression, the producers of radio westerns helped pioneer the marketing, promotion, and franchise practices we now call omnimedia. These radio station owners and holders of radio program copyrights, their staffs of writers, and the commercial sponsors and manufacturers with whom they collaborated – first locally, then regionally, and eventually nationally – understood how the popular western brand could function as an organizing principle across all available forms of media and across all available networks for marketing and distribution. More than two decades before Disney introduced television viewers to *Davy Crockett*, these radio producers developed techniques to encourage listeners to identify strongly with particular western brands and to consume franchised western products regularly and in multiple forms.

Similar to the *Star Wars* films in the 1970s, 1980s, 1990s, and early 2000s, and similar to the *Davy Crockett* miniseries in the mid-1950s, the radio westerns that proved most adaptable and most profitable for omnimedia marketing in the 1930s, 1940s, and early 1950s were those whose uncanny familiarity could be commercialized into *distinct brands* (and thus exploited as exclusive property) but whose trademarked signs could be promoted as enduring *public icons* of a significant era or ideal. In other words, those best suited for omnimedia marketing were those that could be made to marry some form of merchandisable novelty (the aura of a celebrity's real or imagined lifestyle, the symbolic power of a character's light saber or coonskin cap) to popular and pervasive ideologies. In the case of westerns, such ideologies typically revolved around assertions of the western hero's or performer's uniquely American character and assertions of the western region's centrality to the nation's unique destiny and historical exception.

The promotional strategies developed for a number of well-known radio westerns exemplify this type of branding and the early practices of omnimedia marketing: *Red Ryder* (1942–51) and *Hopalong Cassidy* (1950–2), for instance, or *Gene Autry's Melody Ranch* (1940–56) and *The Roy Rogers Show* (1944–55).[4] All of these 1940s and early 1950s ventures into franchising and coordinated, multi-level advertising, however, owed a substantial debt to the producers and commercial sponsors of *The Lone Ranger*. This western originated as a radio drama in the early 1930s; its immediate and unprecedented popularity, especially with juvenile and adolescent listeners, led its producers to quickly develop their initial product into a profitable brand suitable for exploitation across a wide range of merchandise and all available media. No other promotional team of its era was as widely successful at integrating multiple media formats around a western brand as early – or for as long.

As a case study, then, this chapter investigates how The Lone Ranger, Inc., owners of *The Lone Ranger* radio program, transformed what had been originally conceived as a single-medium product into an iconic American brand suitable for omnimedia marketing, and did so almost immediately after its initial creation for the aural medium. In the 1930s, the corporation expanded its product into additional media and collaborated with manufacturers to produce a range of inexpensive "must have" Lone Ranger promotions and merchandise. These strategies worked to amplify the pleasurable effects of the original program by extending the highly individualized and participatory nature of radio listening to other forms of consumption, especially for younger audiences. Moreover, in this era of Depression and recovery, these strategies helped to link the consumption of goods identified with the Lone Ranger's "wholesome" and "patriotic" western brand to powerful ideologies of America's moral innocence, physical bounty, and economic success.

Through the years of World War II and into the height of the brand's popularity during the era of the Cold War in the mid- and late 1950s (the same era in which Disney's *Davy Crockett* and other television westerns proved so profitable), The Lone Ranger, Inc., successfully linked the consumption of goods identified with its brand to increasingly dominant, future-oriented ideologies of US moral, economic, and military leadership on the global stage. This level of popularity and profitability did not last, however, and attempts to revive the Lone Ranger brand in the late 1970s and early 1980s era of *Star Wars* were largely unsuccessful. By the end of the twentieth century, the brand was most visible as a locus for nostalgia: the masked hero was featured at conventions devoted to comics or other forms of popular culture, in magazines devoted to "classic" westerns, and, most notably, on internet websites devoted to the auction of increasingly rare memorabilia or to personal tributes offered by aging fans. Whether the Lone Ranger brand will continue to fade into nostalgic longing for another era, or whether its owners will be able to link the trademarked icons of their nineteenth-century hero to the new technologies and populist ideologies emerging in the early twenty-first century – in ways that will be compelling to large audiences and profitable for a wide range of manufacturers and sponsors – remains to be seen.

Return with us now to those thrilling days of *marketing* yesteryear ...[5]

The Lone Ranger, Inc.

Although it is most remembered today as a popular 1950s television series starring Clayton Moore as the Masked Rider of the Plains and Jay Silverheels as his faithful Indian companion, Tonto, *The Lone Ranger* began its long life as a western serial on radio. Debuting on station WXYZ in Detroit, Michigan, on February 2, 1933, by 1934 *The Lone Ranger* could be heard nationally three evenings a week, first on the Mutual Radio Network and then on NBC Blue, which later became ABC.[6] Between 1933 and its final live broadcast on September 3, 1954, the radio series aired over 3,300 original half-hour episodes of frontier crime-solving and six-gun adventure, set to the stirring music of the Finale from *The William Tell Overture* and punctuated by the hero's trademark cry, "Hi-Yo, Silver! Away!" After a full year of repeats, *The Lone Ranger* aired its final program in September 1955. During these nearly twenty-three years of regular radio broadcasts and for several years after, *The Lone Ranger*'s owners, producers, and commercial sponsors worked to apply what had quickly become an iconic brand – the mysterious hero's white horse, black eye-mask, and silver bullets, especially – to products made for every available medium and genre.[7] And they kept a tight rein on those business entities with whom they collaborated, insuring that every one of these literally hundreds of different products maintained the quintessentially American image of their hero and supported the "clean," "wholesome," and "patriotic" values endorsed as his trademark. This level of moral and ideological oversight became even more important to the copyright holders during the years of US involvement in World War II and the first decade of the Cold War.

In fact, The Lone Ranger, Inc.'s assertion of its role as an arbiter of American values was codified in an official Creed, written by the principal writer of the radio series, Fran Striker, but always voiced on air (or signed in print) by the Lone Ranger himself:

> I believe that to have a friend, a man must be one. That all men are created equal and that everyone has within himself the power to make this a better world. That God put the firewood there but that every man must gather and light it himself. In being prepared physically, mentally and morally to fight when necessary for that which is right. That a man should make the most of what equipment he has. That "This government, of the people, by the people and for the people" shall live always. That men should live by the rule of what is best for the greatest number. That sooner or later … somewhere … somehow … we must settle with the world and make payment for what we have taken. That all things change but truth, and that truth alone, lives on forever. In my Creator, my country, my fellow man. (*The Lone Ranger*)

Similar to the hero's defining black mask, white horse, silver bullets, Indian companion, and trademark call, both the Creed itself and various distillations of its main tenets became central to the omnimedia marketing of the Lone Ranger brand and franchised products.

Between 1933 and 1958, the year of its twenty-fifth anniversary, at least sixteen major iterations of *The Lone Ranger* were produced in multiple media. Several continued into the next decades:

1   The original radio series, aired regularly three evenings a week from February 1933 through September 1955.
2   Live performances of the Lone Ranger and Tonto (and the horse Silver), appearing regularly at circuses, state fairs, rodeos, and civic fundraising events, beginning in 1933 and continuing throughout the period.[8]
3   Clubs and organizations for juvenile and adolescent fans, beginning with the Lone Ranger Safety Club in 1935, plus the Lone Ranger Deputies, the Lone Ranger Junior Deputies, and the Lone Ranger Peace Patrol, and, during World War II, the Victory Lone Ranger Safety Club, the Lone Ranger Victory Corps, and the Lone Ranger National Defenders.
4   Fifteen Lone Ranger titles in the Big Little Books series, published by Whitman between 1935 and 1968.

5   Eighteen Lone Ranger novels, published by Grosset and Dunlap between 1936 and 1956.

6   Eight issues of *The Lone Ranger Magazine*, published April–November 1937.

7   A daily newspaper comic strip series, distributed by King Features between 1938 and 1971.

8   A fifteen-part film serial, *The Lone Ranger*, released by Republic Studios in 1938, then re-edited and released in 1940 as the feature film *Hi-Yo Silver!*

9   A fifteen-part film serial sequel, *The Lone Ranger Rides Again*, released by Republic Studios in 1939.

10 A number of one-off Lone Ranger comic books, published irregularly by Dell Comics in its Large Feature, Feature Book, and Four Color series, between 1939 and 1947.

11 A comic book series, *The Lone Ranger*, published regularly by Dell between 1948 and 1962.

12 A television series, *The Lone Ranger*, aired on the ABC network between 1949 and 1957, plus many years in syndicated re-runs.

13 A second comic book series, *The Lone Ranger's Companion Tonto*, published regularly by Dell between 1951 and 1959.

14 A third comic book series, *The Lone Ranger's Famous Horse Hi-Yo Silver!*, published regularly by Dell between 1952 and 1960.

15 A feature film, *The Lone Ranger*, released by Warner Brothers in 1956.

16 A second feature film, *The Lone Ranger and the Lost City of Gold*, released by United Artists in 1958.

Many of these major iterations of the Lone Ranger brand were multi-part series produced over a number of years, and elements of their media-specific plots had to be integrated into the ongoing narrative of the original program on radio. For instance, when Republic Studios decided that the Lone Ranger and Tonto should not appear on screen riding nearly identical white horses, as they did on the airwaves, the writers of the radio series quickly developed a storyline in which Tonto's first mount, White Feller, injures his leg and has to be replaced by another horse from the majestic herd at Wild Horse Valley.[9] Scout soon entered the radio serial and, by the time the television series was in production a decade later, Tonto's paint pony had become an essential element of both the Lone Ranger narrative and the Lone Ranger brand.

In addition, The Lone Ranger, Inc., collaborated with its commercial sponsors to produce a variety of inexpensive mail-order premiums, asking young fans to "Simply send 25¢ and the words 'The Sugar-Toasted Oat and Wheat Cereal' from a Sugar Jets boxtop" in order to receive a prized icon of the series, such as a "bang gun" or silver bullet. Such collaborations produced, as well, a range of giveaways and other series tie-ins, including mini-comic books and pasteboard black masks, and, for the Lone Ranger clubs and organizations, letters of admission, official charters, manuals, "secret" folders and portfolios, club newspapers and newsletters, and pin-back badges. The Lone Ranger, Inc., contracted with several publishing houses to produce Lone Ranger

books in multiple formats suitable for juvenile and adolescent readers, and it negotiated licensing agreements to manufacture a wide assortment of Lone Ranger merchandise for both children and adults. Moreover, the corporation sought out, fostered, and
at times created all manner of "objective" journalism about its successful brand and
expanding franchise. Together, these products created a highly commercialized vision
of a supposedly rustic – and as yet economically undeveloped – frontier West.

Marketing a Masked Rider

The year 1938 provides a suggestive snapshot of the extent and diversity of Lone
Ranger omnimedia marketing practices during the first decade of the brand. The radio
program, based in Detroit but airing coast to coast, was in its fifth season. The Lone
Ranger Safety Club, organized through the radio program's many regional commercial
sponsors, was now in its third year and reported over a million members. The daily
newspaper comic strip series appeared in local newspapers across the US, and Republic
Studios, based in Hollywood, released the first version of the Lone Ranger and Tonto
made for the silver screen. At least five full-length books were published with Lone
Ranger titles. Grosset and Dunlap, based in New York, released *The Lone Ranger and
the Mystery Ranch* in its Lone Ranger novel series, written by Fran Striker and illustrated by Paul Laune, as well as a children's adaptation of the Republic serial, *The
Lone Ranger and the Texas Renegades*, written by Striker and illustrated by Ted Horn.[10]
Whitman, based in Racine, Wisconsin, released *The Lone Ranger and the Menace of
Murder Valley* in its Big Little Book series, written by Buck Wilson and illustrated
by Robert R. Weisman.[11] The prolific Striker saw two other Lone Ranger titles published in 1938. The large-format *Heigh-Yo Silver! A Story of the Lone Ranger*, illustrated
by Weisman, was published by New York-based Dell and then reprinted, also in 1938,
in a standard format by the Los Angeles-based Bantam Books as *The Lone Ranger and
the Secret of Thunder Mountain*. Dell also published Striker's *The Lone Ranger and the
Lost Valley* as part of its Fast-Action Story Book series for younger readers.

   In addition to the title in its Big Little Book series, in 1938 Whitman published
the interactive *Hi-Yo Silver! The Lone Ranger Paint Book*, illustrated by Horn. Chappell
& Co., based in New York, published sheet music for "Hi-Yo, Silver! The Lone
Ranger's Song," written by Vaughn De Leath and Jack Erickson. Parker Brothers,
Inc., based in Salem, Massachusetts, released an elaborate Lone Ranger board game
and a smaller-scale Lone Ranger card game. The *1938–9 Sears Catalogue* advertised
both a "Lone Ranger Outfit" and a "Lone Ranger Guitar." A wide range of other Lone
Ranger merchandise could be purchased as well, including gum cards, ice cream cones,
belts, sailor hats, a "picture printing set," first aid kits, a "silver bullet" pencil sharp-
ener, pencil boxes, a tie rack, a target and gun set, and a wrist watch. There was even
a boxed set of specialty soaps molded into the forms of the Lone Ranger, Silver, and
Tonto so that the western adventure could continue during a young fan's bath. Popular
entertainment and family magazines celebrated the series, including *Good Housekeeping*,

which featured an article in November 1938 written by Lee Powell, star of the Republic serial, titled "I Am the Lone Ranger."

The *Good Housekeeping* article was but one of the many media products on which The Lone Ranger, Inc., collaborated with Republic Studios in order to promote their mutual financial interests. Republic developed an elaborate, large-format press book designed to sell the fifteen-part serial to local theater owners as well as to help those theater owners advertise the film in their lobbies and on their printed schedules, in the pages of their local newspapers, and in the shop windows of local businesses. Not surprisingly, the fourteen-page press book begins by extolling the marketing prowess of the Lone Ranger brand. Bold headlines assert, "A Ready-Made Audience Of Over Seventeen Million Radio Listeners! 'Lone Ranger' Fans From Coast To Coast Spell Box-Office For Exhibitors!" and "Lone Ranger Safety Club Boasting Over One And One-Half Million Members Means Money In The Box-Office – And Assures Exhibitors Of Child Patronage" (pp. 1–2). After a chapter-by-chapter synopsis (pp. 3–4), the book describes key tie-ins to other Lone Ranger products, such as the Big Little Book series and Lone Ranger shirts, and provides compelling examples of "Smash Advertising For Smash Business!" (pp. 5–8).

Next, the press book offers theater owners four pages of strategic "Lone Ranger Publicity" designed to build anticipation and then sustain interest in the serial's fifteen-week run. Several of these brief articles are formatted for inclusion in programs; others are set in columns for newspapers. Meant to appeal broadly, some articles are marked specifically as "biographical features" of individual actors or as film "reviews." Headlines range from "Silver Proved Tough Casting" to "Full-Blooded Cherokee Indian Seen In New Republic Chapter-Thriller" to "Styles Created For New Serial" and "Players Risk All to Bring Film Thrills" to "Serial Production Calls For Real Expert Writers" and "Story of New Serial Packs Great Wallop." Film stills or actors' publicity photos accompany several of the articles, and each article is formatted so that theater owners can insert the name of their theater as well as the date of the first serial installment (pp. 9–12). The press book concludes with samples of Lone Ranger lobby cards, posters, and banners.[12]

Thus, in 1938 both children and adults could listen to *The Lone Ranger* radio program three evenings a week, read *The Lone Ranger* daily comic strip in their local newspaper, watch the Republic serial at their local theater over a series of fifteen weeks, and read multiple book-length Lone Ranger stories. They could gather round the kitchen table to play *The Lone Ranger* board game, or gather round the piano to play and sing "The Lone Ranger's Song": "Hors-es come and hors-es go, But there is one that you all know, Peo-ple greet him with ac-claim, Sil-ver is his name!" Fans could purchase a range of Lone Ranger-themed merchandise and read about celebrity personalities associated with Lone Ranger productions in their local newspapers and in popular national periodicals. If they lived in Detroit, in December 1938 they could visit the Lone Ranger Toy Village on the ninth floor of Kern's department store.[13] Such diverse manifestations of the Lone Ranger brand did more than build consumer excitement and sustain consumer loyalty. They systematically tied the wholesome and patriotic "American" values of the Lone Ranger brand to the activity of continuous consumption.

This account does not include the regular advertising, giveaways, and mail-in premiums proffered by the commercial sponsors of the radio program, often in conjunction with the Lone Ranger Safety Club. By 1938, The Lone Ranger, Inc., was well aware of the potential for both increased advertising revenue to support the radio program and increased sales revenue from specific Lone Ranger merchandise if the multiple forms of its brand were integrated into a single omnimedia marketing campaign. Following the unprecedented success of the Republic serial, the corporation created an elaborate kit for its sales team to further promote the radio series and its various tie-ins to additional stations and sponsors around the country. This sales kit included the substantial document titled "Details of Procedure in Handling the Exploitation of the Program for Maximum Retail Results" and "The Lone Ranger Merchandising Exploitation Publicity Supplement," as well as samples of promotional journalism, advertising, Safety Club materials, giveaways, and premiums.

One of the featured giveaways is an inexpensive Lone Ranger eye-mask on which radio stations can print their call numbers and companies can print their logos. The kit describes the mask as "A Give-Away That 'Cleans House' for Retailers and Door-to-Door Salesmen" and offers testimonials of businesses distributing "350,000 In One Day." The promotion ends, "Don't Overlook This Sales 'HYPO' – Place Your Order Promptly. The Lone Ranger mask giveaway brings trade."[14] In the 1940s and 1950s, as the popularity of *The Lone Ranger* went from national to international, the owners developed even more diverse, pervasive, and complex strategies to propel their brand and its particular vision of continuous consumption as a frontier value.

Serials, Grains, and Gold: Words from our Sponsors

The early commercial sponsors of *The Lone Ranger* radio program were regional bakeries, makers of "wholesome" products suitable for the series' primary audience of children and families, as well as for the Lone Ranger character's image as a clean, healthy, patriotic American. These bakeries produced the appropriately named Silvercup Bread, one of the first sponsors of the serial, as well as Merita Bread, Bond Bread, and Butter-Nut Bread (all of which were eventually acquired by the American Bakeries Company). In 1941, General Mills, maker of popular prepared breakfast cereals Cheerios (called Cheeri-oats until 1945), Kix, Wheaties, and Trix, among others, became a principal sponsor of the nationally broadcast radio show and, at the end of the decade, of the nationally broadcast television series.

From the mid-1930s until 1941, the regional sponsors encouraged listeners of the radio program – or their mothers – to purchase their baked goods by including Lone Ranger images and slogans in their regular print advertising. A 1938 Butter-Nut Bread advertisement, for instance, promotes the Lone Ranger character as "The Modern Robin Hood" and the radio program as "America's Most Famous Radio Serial

– Clean, Thrilling Entertainment for the Entire Family" with "Adventures of the Exciting Frontier Days!" The advertisement ends, however, with a specific sales pitch to children: "Remind Mother to Order Butter-Nut Bread [and] Dolly Madison Cakes."[15] A 1940 advertisement for Merita Bread links the wholesome frontier masculinity of the Lone Ranger character to the nutritional promises (and, in this instance, the specific gender promises) of their product: "HI-YO SILVER Boyhood's *by-word* builds manliness."[16] Lone Ranger images and slogans appeared as well on the printed wrappers for the bakeries' loaves of sliced bread. Inside the wrappers, the bakeries inserted mail-in coupons for Lone Ranger premiums, including autographed picture and photo cards of Lone Ranger characters and WXYZ actors, pin-back buttons, printed covers for school books, and membership kits, charters, and metal badges for the Lone Ranger Safety Club.

One of most interesting early premiums, which encouraged careful listening to the radio program but also allowed the voice behind its mysterious hero to take a short vacation from his thrice-weekly live performances, was the "Lone Ranger Hunt Map" sponsored by the Gordon Baking Company. The front side of the premium features a large advertisement for the company's Silvercup Bread ("The World's Finest") and an explanation for the map:

Where's The Lone Ranger?

What has happened to the masked rider of the plains? Has he been kidnapped by the gangs of rustlers known to be lurking in the territory where he was last seen? Where is Silver, the great, white horse? Is he with his master, the Lone Ranger? There are many outlaws who would want the Lone Ranger out of the way so they could carry on their work unhindered by this rider of justice.

Does Tonto Know?

The Lone Ranger's Faithful Indian scout has always known the plans of the masked man. Does he know where the Lone Ranger has disappeared to? Or is the Lone Ranger on a secret mission – too dangerous for even Tonto to know about? But maybe Tonto knows more than he pretends. Maybe he is part of the Lone Ranger's mysterious disappearance.

Listen For Clues On The Lone Ranger Program

Clues will turn up on this hunt. Listen every Monday, Wednesday and Friday evening over Station WXYZ, WOR, or WGN. Follow the progress of this great hunt with your map that Tonto and Cactus Pete have made. Listen for the clues and check them on your map.

The reverse side features "Tonto's Map of South West Texas" as "Explained by Cactus Pete" (a recurrent character). During a special series of episodes in which the Lone Ranger is "missing," fans listened for clues from Tonto and other characters, tracing the story action on their colorful maps, trying to fix the hero's location among depictions of mountains, woods, range land, creeks, Indian villages, and Mexican and Anglo settlements on either side of the Rio Grande.[17]

The bakeries inserted an assortment of inexpensive but exciting "must have" Lone Ranger giveaways inside their bread wrappers as well. Two of the more elaborate of these were small booklets, broken up into multiple installments, that provided back story for the ongoing Lone Ranger radio narrative. *How the Lone Ranger Captured Silver* was distributed in seven installments, while *The Life of Tonto* was distributed in eleven.[18] Each week, the bakeries included in their bread wrappers a new chapter of the story, which consisted of a single, three- by six-inch sheet of thin paper printed on both sides. After collecting all seven or eleven of the installment chapters, plus the booklet's illustrated cover, fans were encouraged to punch the holes marked on each chapter sheet and to complete the assembly of their booklets by binding the sheets and cover together with string, twine, yarn, or another fastener.[19] After the initial multiple-week promotion in bread wrappers, the booklets were redesigned as weekly installments in the bakeries' or other sponsors' regular advertising in newspapers.

Innovative marketing strategies such as the mail-in premium "Hunt Map" and the giveaway booklets broken into installment chapters proved highly successful. In January 1940, *Radio Guide*, a precursor to *TV Guide*, published a feature article with the main title "Hi-Yo Silver and Gold." The secondary title spells out the financial implications of Lone Ranger omnimedia marketing even more overtly: "'The Lone Ranger' becomes young America's favorite legend and a breadmaker's gold mine." After summarizing the development of the character and the program, the article states, "The wide appeal of the Lone Ranger for children is not – any more than was the character's creation – a matter of guesswork" (Chase 1940: 13). Already in 1940, the beginning of the radio serial's seventh season, the author notes that "In all, sixty-four different manufacturers of children's clothing and novelties and games have been licensed to use the magic name of the Lone Ranger," and he estimates that "receipts for the past year [are] well above $400,000." He concludes, "The fact remains that the Lone Ranger is important both as an industry and as a legend" (Chase 1940: 13). In less than a decade after the Great Depression, the licensed Lone Ranger character had become an icon of the American nation's treasured values of "frontier" independence and freedom, while the trademarked Lone Ranger brand had become symbolic of American capitalism's triumphant renewal.

When General Mills became a principal sponsor of the series, it included images of the Masked Rider in its own print advertising and on the bright pasteboards of its cereal boxes. Similar to the regional bakeries, General Mills offered giveaways that provided new listeners and viewers with essential back story to the ongoing radio and television narratives. In 1954, for example, two mini-comics could be found inside specially marked packages of Cheerios: *The Lone Ranger and the Story of Silver* and *The Lone Ranger, His Mask, and How He Met Tonto*. On the cereal boxes themselves, General Mills offered punch-out masks of Lone Ranger characters, as well as coupons for various mail-in premiums. The latter included everything from an official Lone

Ranger Kit (a silver bullet *and* a black eye-mask) to a Six-Shooter Ring ("Wear Your Shootin' Iron Right On Your Finger!"), a Hike-O-Meter, a "hand-beaded" Tonto Belt, and plastic cowboy and Indian figures.

Many of the most successful premiums were attached to the several Lone Ranger clubs and organizations, which promoted the brand's "wholesome" values of safety, lawfulness, patriotism, and good citizenship. Membership involved sending away for various letters and certificates of admission, pledge cards, codes of honor, and club charters, but also more elaborate premiums, such as the *Lone Ranger Deputy Secret Folder* and *The Lone Ranger National Defenders Secret Portfolio*. These materials actively instructed members to identify with the brand, to see themselves as the Lone Ranger's "Deputies," "Chief Scouts," and "Silver Bullet Defenders." But they also repeatedly instructed members both to consume and promote the sponsor's products. An early Safety Club giveaway pamphlet, for instance, sponsored by Franz Bakery of Portland, Oregon, instructed members in how to demonstrate their club loyalty through specific consumption:

"BE LOYAL" ... says *the* LONE RANGER

Always remember that it helps to carry on this great SAFETY CAMPAIGN when you order and eat ... Franz' Butter-Nut[,] The GOOD Bread! Always get Franz' Bread when you go to the grocer's for mother. Ask her and her friends to use it, too. Tell them how we are ALL working together in the interests of SAFETY. They'll be glad to cooperate, and will be mighty happy that you asked them to use Franz' ... for they'll agree that it's **mighty** good bread![20]

In 1943, the year the radio program celebrated its tenth anniversary and two years after General Mills had become a principal sponsor, the Lone Ranger Safety Club reported 4,400,000 members, a large and loyal consumer force that could be mobilized to encourage parents, friends, and neighbors to purchase miles of sliced bread and mountains of prepared cereals.[21]

For the fifteenth anniversary of the radio program in 1948, General Mills developed an elaborate Lone Ranger Frontier Town, which it advertised as "An Exact Likeness Of The Wide-Open, Wild And Woolly Western Town Made Famous By the Lone Ranger And Tonto!" For 10 cents and a Cheerios box top, fans could send in for one of four town "sections," each a large map that, when put together, created a three-and-a-half by four-and-a-half foot "ground plan" for the Frontier Town and surrounding countryside. After sending in four dimes and four box tops to receive all four quadrants of the map, fans still had to purchase nine additional, differently marked boxes of Cheerios in order to collect all seventy-one models created for the town and its environs printed on the back pasteboards. Once punched out and folded together ("No scissors or glue needed!"), the three-dimensional, scale models of Frontier Town buildings, bridges, forts, wagons, mines, and Indian villages could be arranged and rearranged on the large map as fans listened to *The Lone Ranger*. Similar to promotions for the Hunt Map a decade earlier, advertisements for the elaborate Frontier Town claimed that it would help bring the frontier West and its wholesome American values into listeners' living rooms:

> So real that when you build your Lone Ranger Frontier Town complete, you can follow the action of the Lone Ranger programs, *right in your own home*! When the Lone Ranger rides in from the Sawtooth Mountains, over the Red Valley Desert and up to Sheriff Taylor's office … When the Lone Ranger meets Tonto at Lone Pine Railroad Bridge, you can trace practically every step … almost "be right there with them" in their dangerous and exciting adventures![22]

As an additional tie-in, the city of Cheyenne, Wyoming, declared itself "Lone Ranger Frontier Town" – for a day – and the Cheyenne mayor hosted an official fifteenth-anniversary celebration that featured live appearances by the Masked Man himself. Not surprisingly, the events were widely reported. Photographs of the Lone Ranger and Silver swarmed by fans, many behind their own iconic masks, appeared around the nation in the pages of newspapers and popular magazines.[23]

General Mills' collaboration with The Lone Ranger, Inc., was so successful that in November 1949, soon after the television series began in September, the company published a full-page advertisement in *The Saturday Evening Post* titled "How the Lone Ranger Rounds Up Jobs," in which the masked hero is revealed as a premier capitalist salesman.[24] In a striking anachronism, the advertisement features a half-page photograph of Clayton Moore as the nineteenth-century Lone Ranger, astride the majestic Silver, offering directions to a contemporary motorist. "General Mills, Inc." is painted on the door panel of the car, and the photograph is captioned:

> Who's Behind That Mask? None other than the Lone Ranger, symbol of fair play out where men are men. He breathes the spirit of frontier adventure to the 12 million fans who enjoy his radio and television programs (sponsored in the Southeast by the American Bakeries Co., bakers of Merita Bread and Cakes, and in the rest of the nation by General Mills). But this handsome horseman is more than an entertainer. Like his friend, above – William H. Barry, one of our 723 grocery products salesmen – he's a "crack salesman" of General Mills products. And like *all* crack salesmen, the Lone Ranger creates better jobs – for a lot of people.

The brief text below the caption describes General Mills as an employer and highlights its increased sales and workforce. Although the article reveals that General Mills' economic success story began much earlier than its association with the Lone Ranger in 1941, the photograph and caption link contemporary and, importantly, *future* economic success to the iconic power of the Masked Rider. General Mills also featured The Lone Ranger, Inc., in several glowing articles published in its company newsletter, the *Millwheel*, such as "Lone Ranger Honored As 'National Institution'" in 1955 and "Here's TV's Top Cereal Salesman" in 1957.

When the second feature film, *The Lone Ranger and the Lost City of Gold*, was being promoted to theater owners for its release in 1958, the year of the twenty-fifth anniversary, General Mills made even larger claims for the power of its long-running collaboration with the Lone Ranger brand and several Lone Ranger franchises:

* 61,000 people watch "The Lone Ranger" every week on 82 ABC-TV network stations (sponsored by General Mills, Inc.) and on 76 CBS-TV network stations sponsored by General Mills, Inc.-Nestles. Also 4 CBC stations in Canada.
* 90,000 consumers reached through store displays carrying General Mills products and thru newspaper and magazine ads.
* 50,000 cereal boxes of Wheaties, Cheerios and other General Mills cereals have carried Lone Ranger promotions consisting of cutouts on the outside of the package plus mail-in offers of Lone Ranger plastic figurines.
* More than 6000 supermarkets and grocery stores in 40 states display the giant Lone Ranger spectacular standees, window cards, insert cards and other promotional material.
* 1000 General Mills fieldmen are out working on the 25th Lone Ranger Silver Anniversary with which this picture is identified. They will work with you.
* Live shots of the Lone Ranger and Tonto are featured on the Cheerios and Wheaties commercials.[25]

Like the mythic western frontier they promoted, these marketing collaborations with The Lone Ranger, Inc., appeared endlessly profitable and expansive. The build-up to the twenty-fifth anniversary and the release of the second feature film, however, marked the height of an impressive – but soon to end – omnimedia era for the Lone Ranger brand.

Branding National Iconicity

Fifteen years earlier, when *The Lone Ranger* radio program celebrated its tenth anniversary in 1943, the Masked Man and his trademark western values were available on the "wireless" airwaves, in the panels of comic strips, and on the pages of comic books not only around the country but also across many parts of the globe. As the United States entered World War II, those who controlled the Lone Ranger brand shifted the emphasis of their licensed images and slogans from broad-based consumerism to more focused wartime ideologies. In all versions of the franchise, ideas of American freedom, self-reliance, capitalism, militarism, patriotism, and heroic citizenship were spotlighted to even greater degrees. The Lone Ranger clubs and organizations actively instructed their members to "help Uncle Sam" with the war effort at home, while General Mills offered new premiums such as "The Lone Ranger War Album of Victory Battles," "The Lone Ranger Black Out Kit," and "The Lone Ranger Danger-Warning Siren." Eventually, the federal government itself enlisted the Lone Ranger's assistance in promoting the sale of US War Bonds.

The assertion of the Masked Mystery Rider of the Plains as an icon of distinctly American values, perseverance, and leadership during a time of national and global crisis is summed up in an article titled "Hi-Yo Silver! Lochinvar of Radioland Rides Into Hearts of Circus-Goers!," published in the August 1943 issue of *Movie-Radio Guide*.[26] The specific event of the article's title was the Lone Ranger's much-anticipated appearance with the Olympia Circus. One of the article's purposes is to report the enormous draw of these live performances:

> When after ten years on the airlanes the Lone Ranger was booked as the top attraction with the Olympia Circus in Chicago and Detroit, five hundred thousand of the twelve million persons who listen three times every week (Monday, Wednesday and Friday at 7:30 p.m. EWT) to his broadcasts over 129 stations of the Blue Network turned out to see him in person. Disappointed were close to a hundred thousand more who were turned away from the ticket-stands of the packed stadiums in both cities. (Anon. 1943: 63)

The article does more, however, than simply report these successes or advertise the ongoing radio program. In an era of competing American icons, both at home on the domestic front and on the frontlines of the war effort abroad, it aims for nothing less than to secure the prime ideological status of The Lone Ranger, Inc.'s western brand.

The article begins by situating the Lone Ranger character and the Lone Ranger brand within a global symbolic economy:

> "Hi-Yo Silver, Awa-a-ay!" That clarion call of America's "Lone Ranger" girdles the globe via radio, movies, cartoon strips in 156 newspapers and comic books, as well as on many articles of merchandise that bear his name. Before the war millions of newspaper readers in Belgrade, Paris and Manila followed eagerly the exploits of the Ranger. Over in England his was the radio voice that brought the colorful West of the New World to listeners. Out in the Libyan desert, "Hi- Yo Silver" was the battle-cry of a British tank corps as the firing began. (1943: 16)

Having established the Lone Ranger as a world icon for esteemed US values, the article continues by asserting the Lone Ranger's links to various kinds of wholesome celebrity status:

> In far-off Australia, General MacArthur's small son never misses a "Lone Ranger" broadcast or movie if he can help it. And that goes for Helen Hayes' whole family in New York and Shirley Temple in Hollywood. To American soldiers in lonely outposts, it brings the radio in the living-room at home a little nearer. (1943: 63)

Next, the article asserts the unique appeal of the Lone Ranger to all US citizens, especially in this time of war, instability, and global crisis:

> Certainly no single figure on radio or screen has so captured the hearts and imagination of Americans as the Lone Ranger. To cliff-dwellers in the steel canyons of great cities,

he stands for the romantic, adventure-filled West, described in stories they have read about the country that lies over the rim of their world, the places they dream of seeing one day. To the real westerner, who has wandered far from his native diggin's, the call of the Ranger and the beat of Silver's hoofs conjures a vivid background of ragged peaks that hood themselves in purple splendor at sunset. To every American, the radio and screen dramas of the "Lone Ranger," founded as they are on the law of right living and plain justice, spell something of the spirit that makes America – the spirit and way of life Americans are fighting to keep alive in a war-torn world. (1943: 63)

The article goes on to list several recent honors bestowed on *The Lone Ranger* radio program, including special recognition from the National Safety Council "for distinguished service to safety" and an award from the New Jersey branch of the National Federation of Press Women for the best children's program on the "airlanes," because of the "valuable influence it has exerted in subtly instilling into youthful listeners' minds the principles of good citizenship, courage and high ideals" (1943: 63). Predictably, the article ends by reiterating the Lone Ranger Creed:

But in the final analysis, it takes more than box-tops, excellent breakfast cereals, or even a man and his horse to make a radio and screen character the hero of boys and girls the world over. In the Lone Ranger's case, we believe that his creed of living has much to do with his fabulous popularity, especially in this last stronghold of freedom that is America. Here it is: […] (1943: 63)

As always, the Creed is signed "The Lone Ranger," followed by a listing of the air times for the radio program in various parts of the country.

Even in the midst of world war, The Lone Ranger, Inc., which undoubtedly produced the basic elements of this "anonymous" article (if not its verbatim script), developed strategies to insinuate its iconic brand into the emotional, psychological, and ideological fabric of the nation and its wartime allies. During this difficult time, the corporation not only maintained but enhanced the profitability of its brand by further abstracting its version of the frontier West from a highly commercialized into a highly militarized ideology. Importantly, that ideology centered on a set of values that could be promoted as distinctly American and enduringly under threat – and thus in constant need of renewal through ongoing consumption.

Renewing a Legend, Reviving a Brand

After original programming for the radio and television series ended and the two feature films completed their original theater runs in the mid- and late 1950s, *The Lone Ranger* remained visible in multiple forms in the US and abroad, although the peak of the brand's popularity had clearly passed. The major iterations of the franchise quickly became associated with nostalgia for childhoods lived in another age. Older fans could still enjoy the daily newspaper comic strip series until 1971, and they could listen to individual episodes of the radio show released on long-playing vinyl records in the 1960s and 1970s. Gold Key issued a scaled-down Lone Ranger comic book series in 1964–9, 1972, and 1974–7, while the CBS television network aired a Lone Ranger animated cartoon series aimed at younger viewers in 1966–9, and the Boys' and Girls' March of Comics series of giveaway mini-comics, distributed in department stores and small businesses, ran a number of Lone Ranger titles into the early 1970s. New Lone Ranger juvenile books were published, and new Lone Ranger toys, games, action figures, and models were developed and retailed. Perhaps most significantly, Pinnacle Books, based in Los Angeles, reprinted the first eight Lone Ranger novels from the Grosset and Dunlap series in inexpensive paperback editions between 1975 and 1979.

The reprinted novels were part of a buildup to the production and promotion of the first major iteration of the brand in over two decades, the feature film *The Legend of The Lone Ranger*, released in 1981 by the Wrather Corporation/Lone Ranger Television, which had purchased *The Lone Range*r property – and control of its brand – from The Lone Ranger, Inc., in 1954. The film's production disappointed older fans and generated a great deal of unwanted controversy, while the film itself received largely negative reviews and a weak return at the box office.[27] In addition to the paperback reprints, to help promote the new film and in an effort to revive the Lone Ranger brand, Wrather authorized a new animated cartoon series, produced by Filmation, that ran from 1980 to 1982, and a new daily comic strip series, distributed by New York Times Special Features, that ran from 1981 to 1984. General Mills did its part by creating a "Lone Ranger Deputy Kit" as a mail-in premium from Cheerios. Included were an Official Lone Ranger Deputy Certificate, an Official Lone Ranger Deputy badge, a black eye-mask, and a large poster signed "Good luck always, The Lone Ranger and Tonto." Ballatine Books published a novelization of the film's screen-play, written by Gary McCarthy, while Random House published *The Legend of the Lone Ranger Storybook*, adapted for younger readers by Larry Weinberg, *The Lone Ranger Pop-Up Book*, illustrated by Ken Barr and engineered by Ib Penick, and *The Lone Ranger Rocking Book*, illustrated by Tom Beecham. MCA Records released *The Legend of the Lone Ranger* soundtrack.

As The Lone Ranger, Inc., had done in the past, Wrather negotiated licensing agreements for the production of retail merchandise tied to its new Lone Ranger film. Milton Bradley produced a new board game, while the Gabriel Corporation produced a new series of action figures. There were new holster sets, gun sets, rifle and target sets, and bow-and-arrow sets; writing tablets, desk sets, and bulletin boards; school bags and lunch boxes; stickers and party sets; inflatable TV chairs and punching bags; suspenders, printed T-shirts, Underoos underwear, and Lone Ranger sneakers. None, however, could compete with the profitability of Lone Ranger tie-ins from decades past. There was no ongoing, popular series, in any medium, with which to establish reciprocal relationships: the series promoting specific products in its plotlines and commercial advertising, the products promoting the regular series and the larger brand. The new retail items may have appealed to children enamored of cowboys and Indians or guns and horses, and to collectors of memorabilia, but they were unsuccessful in attracting sizeable audiences for the new film, and they had relatively little impact on attempts to expand or even maintain the market for the Lone Ranger brand.

Since the early 1980s, episodes from *The Lone Ranger* radio program have been released in cassette, CD, and MP3 formats and streamed over the internet. *The Lone Ranger* film serials, television series, feature films, and animated cartoons have been released on VHS and DVD. There has been relatively little new, authorized production, however, in any format. Pure Imagination Publishing released a largely ignored one-off Lone Ranger comic book in 1993. The better-known Topps Comics marketed a more successful four-part Lone Ranger comic book series in 1994, in an updated graphic style and with a compelling, genre-crossing story. In 1995, the Topps series was repackaged as a Lone Ranger Graphic Album. Several scripts for Lone Ranger feature films were shopped around Hollywood in the 1990s, though none was produced.[28] In 2003, the WB network aired a made-for-television Lone Ranger film (meant to serve as the pilot for a new Lone Ranger television series), which received embarrassing reviews and quickly fell into obscurity. Thus far in the new century, the most successful iteration of the brand has been a Lone Ranger comic book series produced by Dynamite Comics, which debuted in 2007. As this chapter is being written in 2009 and 2010, the popular Dynamite series, with its bold style, muscular characters, and dark vision of the frontier West, remains ongoing. And there are rumors in industry trade magazines and on internet blogs that the Disney Corporation has plans to produce a new Lone Ranger feature film, supported by significant star power, in the near future.

In the final decades of the twentieth century and in the initial decade of the twenty-first, *The Lone Ranger* has been most pervasive not as a vibrant force in broadcast, publication, retail, or ideological marketing, but rather as a more ghostly presence on the internet. On a given day, the auction site eBay lists between 800 and 1,000 items of Lone Ranger memorabilia up for bid. Lone Ranger nostalgia sites and Clayton Moore tribute sites offer versions of Lone Ranger history (some more accurate than others) and pages of Lone Ranger trivia, plus access to publicity photos, film and television clips, and audio excerpts. In the absence of ongoing, large-scale Lone Ranger production, the most salient function of these internet sites is neither marketing nor promotion. Instead, they provide a space for fans to collectively consume – and to collectively produce – positive, often utopian images of the eras associated with the major Lone Ranger series. The sites provide an opportunity to remember – or imagine – the world of a 1930s, 1940s, or 1950s childhood through the lens of the hero's trademark eye-mask, to conceive those worlds within the terms of his trademark Creed: more wholesome than the present, more selfless and self-reliant, more patriotic. No longer a profitable brand for marketing myths of the nation's collective adolescence on its western frontiers, *The Lone Ranger* remains a catalyst for another kind of mythmaking, for a more intimate style of heroic legend.

NOTES

1   The Star Wars Expanded Universe thus does not include, for instance, parodies of the films, characters, or storylines, or unauthorized celebratory texts and images created by fans.

2   Richard Severo, "Fess Parker, Who as Davy Crockett Set Off Coonskin Cap Craze, Dies at 85." See also Charles McGrath, "An Enemy of Raccoons but a Friend to Marketers," and the anonymous "Back Then: 1955: Davy Crockett, King of the Retail Frontier."

3   As the first home-based electronic medium available in the United States, "wireless" radio was the first truly pervasive medium through which drama could be consumed regularly by large audiences – relaxing in individual living rooms while linked together across a large geographic region and, eventually, across the nation as a whole. Although early television was available in limited areas of the United States in the 1930s, wider access to television did not begin until after the end of World War II, with an early boom in sales of television sets in 1948 and 1949, precisely when *The Lone Ranger* television series was developed.

4   *Red Ryder* starred Reed Hadley (1942–4), Carlton KaDell (1945), and Brooke Temple (1946–51) as the eponymous hero. This western series originated not on radio, however, but in a popular newspaper comic strip, beginning in 1938. *Hopalong Cassidy* starred William Boyd. The Hopalong Cassidy character originated in a series of twenty-eight novels written by Clarence E. Mulford, published between 1907 and 1941; he was made especially famous through his appearance in a series of sixty-six films, also starring William Boyd, released between 1935 and 1948. The long and diverse career of Gene Autry, "The Singing Cowboy," who first became famous through his music recordings and work in films, and eventually through his work on television, included starring on radio in *Gene Autry's Melody Ranch*. (Autry's horse, Champion, starred in his own radio series, *The Adventures of Champion*, in 1949 and 1950.) Similarly, the long and diverse career of Roy Rogers, the "King of the Cowboys,"

included music, film, and television, as well as starring on radio in *The Roy Rogers Show*.

5   The opening narration for *The Lone Ranger* radio show included these lines: "With his faithful Indian companion, Tonto, the daring and resourceful Masked Rider of the Plains led the fight for law and order in the early western United States. Nowhere in the pages of History can one find a greater champion of Justice. Return with us now to those thrilling days of yesteryear. ..."

6   Several popular histories of the Lone Ranger phenomenon have been published, including David Rothel's *Who Was That Masked Man? The Story of the Lone Ranger* (1976, rev. edn. 1981), Dave Holland's *From Out of the Past: A Pictorial History of the Lone Ranger* (1988), and James Van Hise's *Who Was That Masked Man? The Story of the Lone Ranger* (1990). There are also published guides to Lone Ranger collectibles, such as Lee Felbinger's *Collector's Reference and Value Guide to The Lone Ranger* (1998). My accounts of Lone Ranger history draw from these sources as well as from my own primary and secondary research. For literary and cultural interpretations of the Lone Ranger, see my "Hero With Two Faces: The Lone Ranger as Treaty Discourse" (1996), "Sight in the Sound: Seeing and Being Seen in *The Lone Ranger* Radio Show" (2007), and "Tonto on Vacation, or How To Be an Indian Lawyer" (2009).

7   The owner of station WXYZ in Detroit and the president of The Lone Ranger, Inc., during most of the radio era was George Washington Trendle. Prior to his work in radio, Trendle had been a part owner of the Kunsky-Trendle chain of silent film palaces. With the advent of talking films, in 1930 Trendle and his partner sold their theaters and purchased Detroit's radio station WGHP, which they renamed WXYZ so that they could advertise as "the Last Word in Radio." Trendle sold The Lone Ranger, Inc. to Jack Wrather in 1954.

8   The Lone Ranger's first live appearance occurred after only six months of radio broadcasts, July 30, 1933, at the Belle Isle

children's circus in Detroit. In a now famous incident in Lone Ranger lore, an unexpected 10,000 children and adults showed up for the advertised event, overwhelming park security. Fortunately, the Masked Man was there to help keep order. In November 1933 The Lone Ranger was also adapted as a stage play for Detroit's Fisher Theater.

9   Republic Studios thought it would be too difficult for theater audiences to distinguish two riders on white horses in the black and white film, especially in long shots.

10   The title page includes this line: "Story and Illustrations Based on Republic's Serial 'The Lone Ranger.'"

11   Buck Wilson was a pen name for the prolific pulp writer Gaylord Dubois.

12   An even more elaborate press book was developed for Republic's sequel in 1939.

13   Kern's department store advertisement from *The Detroit News*, Dec. 15, 1938, reprinted in Felbinger 1998: 22.

14   The Lone Ranger sales kit was described and scanned for the internet auction site eBay, July 26, 2001. The anonymous seller stated that he received the kit from the grandson of someone who worked for station WXYZ in Detroit in the 1930s.

15   Butter-Nut Bread advertisement reprinted in Felbinger 1998: 21.

16   Merita Bread advertisement reprinted in Felbinger 1998: 139.

17   Holland dates the hunt map to 1937 and explains that the actor who played the Lone Ranger at that time, Earle Graser, was on vacation during the special series of episodes in which the masked hero is searched for but does not actually speak (Holland 1988: 113). The radio show was not recorded until 1938. Felbinger dates the hunt map to 1941, which suggests the premium may have been used more than once (1998: 136). Earle Graser died suddenly on April 8, 1941; after a "transition" series of episodes, he was replaced by Brace Beemer, the best-known voice of the Lone Ranger on radio.

18   *How the Lone Ranger Captured Silver* was written by David Arnsan, "One of His Greatest Admirers," and distributed by Bond Bread in 1934 and by Silvercup Bread and Merita Bread in 1936. Although attributed

to the Lone Ranger, *The Life of Tonto* was actually written by Fran Striker and distributed by Merita Bread (and likely by other bakeries as well) in 1940.

19   My personal copy of *How the Lone Ranger Captured Silver*, which I purchased on the internet, appears to have been much loved by its original owner. It also appears to have been used for target practice. The cover image of the famous white stallion has been shot through with a BB gun.

20   *The Story of the Lone Ranger* (Anon. n.d.).

21   "Hi-Yo Silver! Lochinvar of Radioland Rides into Hearts of Circus-Goers!" (Anon. 1943).

22   Advertisement reprinted in Holland 1988: 366 and Felbinger 1998: 129. Image of complete Frontier Town in Holland 1988: 436 and Felbinger 1998: 127.

23   See, for example, "The Lone Ranger Campaigns for Good Citizens," *Look*, 13/13 (21 June), 13–14, 17 (Anon. 1949).

24   The advertisement appeared in other magazines as well, including the back cover of the *This Week* magazine from the *Oregon Sunday Journal* for Oct. 30, 1949.

25   "General Mills Gigantic Point-Of-Sale Promotion!" Press book for *The Lone Ranger and the Lost City of Gold*, 1958.

26   "Lochinvar" is the title of a poem about a young knight of the same name, written by Sir Walter Scott and originally published in 1808 as part of Scott's long narrative poem *Marmion*. For many years the poem was a staple of the US school curriculum; in 1943, the knight Lochinvar, who came "out of the west," and his amazing steed would have been recognized by many readers.

27   The controversy surrounding the production of the 1981 feature film focused largely on the treatment of Clayton Moore, the actor who played the Lone Ranger in the television series and in the two earlier feature films, and who continued to make regular public appearances in character – and in costume – into the 1970s. The Wrather corporation, who owned the trademark, used a restraining order to bar Moore from appearing in public in the Lone Ranger's distinctive eye-mask during the film's production and run. The order was lifted in 1984. For Moore's own

account of the episode, see his memoir, *I Was That Masked Man*, written with Frank Thompson (1996).

28 I was able to purchase an unpublished 1997 Lone Ranger screenplay written by Steven Maeda on the internet.

REFERENCES AND FURTHER READING

Allen, C. (1996). Hero with Two Faces: The Lone Ranger as Treaty Discourse. *American Literature*, 68/3, 609–38.

Allen, C. (2007). Sight in the Sound: Seeing and Being Seen in *The Lone Ranger* Radio Show. *Western American Literature*, 42/2, 117–40.

Allen, C. (2009). Tonto on Vacation, or How To Be an Indian Lawyer. *Canadian Review of American Studies*, 39/2, 139–61.

Anon. (n.d.). *The Story of the Lone Ranger*. Franz's Lone Ranger Safety Club. Portland, OR: Franz Bakery. Pamphlet. Los Angeles: Autry Research Library, Autry National Center.

Anon. (1943). Hi-Yo Silver! Lochinvar of Radioland Rides into Hearts of Circus-Goers! *Movie-Radio Guide*, 13/6, 16, 63.

Anon. (1949). The Lone Ranger Campaigns for Good Citizens. *Look*, 13/13, June 21, 13–14, 17.

Anon. (2010). Back Then: 1955: Davy Crockett, King of the Retail Frontier. *New York Times Reprints*, accessed online March 19.

Chase, F. (1940). Hi-Yo Silver and Gold. *Radio Guide*, 9/13, 12–13.

Felbinger, L.J. (1998). *Collector's Reference and Value Guide to The Lone Ranger*. Paducah, KY: Collector Books.

Holland, D. (1988). *From Out of the Past: A Pictorial History of the Lone Ranger*. Granada Hills, CA: Holland House.

McGrath, C. (2010). An Enemy of Raccoons but a Friend of Marketers. *New York Times*, accessed online March 22.

Moore, C. (1996). *I Was That Masked Man*, with F. Thompson. Dallas: Taylor.

Rothel, D. (1976). *Who Was That Masked Man? The Story of the Lone Ranger*. South Brunswick, NJ: Barnes. Rev. edn. San Diego, CA: Barnes, 1981.

Severo, R. (2010). Fess Parker, who as Davy Crockett Set Off Coonskin Cap Craze, Dies at 85. *New York Times*, accessed online March 19.

Van Hise, J. (1990). *Who Was That Masked Man? The Story of the Lone Ranger*. Las Vegas: Pioneer Books.

30

The Nuclear Southwest

Audrey Goodman

The history of the nuclear Southwest, which began at New Mexico's Los Alamos National Laboratory and continues to be concentrated in the deserts of New Mexico, Colorado, Utah, and Nevada, recapitulates and intensifies dominant patterns in western American history. In the study that has most powerfully defined these patterns for scholars from the late twentieth century into the current era, *The Legacy of Conquest* (1987), Patricia Limerick observes that "the American West has been particularly close to the power of the atom, in ways that followed directly in the established themes of Western history" (Limerick 1987: 159). While Limerick's historical work led to many revisionary studies of the western United States, it has been the work of novelists, poets, nonfiction writers, and photographers to articulate new understandings of the Southwest's unevenly visible nuclear history.

The first theme that connects atomic and western histories is the Anglo-European fantasy that the West contains ample and uninhabited open spaces ready to be discovered. The decision to build the first nuclear weapons laboratory in the New Mexican desert seems to repeat this imperial pattern of the American West's Anglo-European conquest. To build Los Alamos, the US government first seized land from the Pueblos of San Ildefonso and Santa Clara and from the heirs of a land grant originally held by Ramón Vigil, then imported a scientific elite and effectively divided local communities according to race and class. The isolation of the desert locations selected for the development and testing of atomic bombs allowed scientists to feel they were at the frontier of both new territory and new knowledge. However, the planning and controlled operation of all territory used for atomic weapons development and testing also produced a culture of secrecy in the decades the followed, as well as conflict with surrounding communities. Historian Jake Kosek recently

A Companion to the Literature and Culture of the American West, First Edition. Edited by Nicolas S. Witschi.

characterized "iridescent" Los Alamos as "many things to many people," including "the epicenter of U.S. nation building" and the means of earning a living for many local residents, the place "where the most horrific instruments of mass destruction are produced" and "the site of one of the most successful collaborations of brilliant minds in the history of the nation" (Kosek 2006: 229). He and other historians of the nuclear Southwest's city of origin now emphasize the inextricable link between creative (and primarily masculine) ambition and universal destruction, seeking through retrospective analysis to understand the legacy of Los Alamos' deep and irreconcilable contradictions.

A second theme that connects western and nuclear histories is the recurrence of boom-and-bust cycles, a pattern that perpetuated migration and the optimism of newcomers, as well as the marginality of immigrant and native laborers. Historians have compared the frenzy to find uranium on the Colorado Plateau in the 1950s to the Gold Rush a century before; this time, though "[s]ome prospectors got rich," many more got sick from radiation (Riebsame 1997: 132). The economic boom created by federal investment in the nuclear weapons program during World War II and the early years of the Cold War lured a new kind of prospector, the highly paid scientist, to laboratories at Los Alamos and Livermore, California, as well as to the Hanford Engineer Works in Washington and the Nevada Test Site, to name just the major projects developed by the Atomic Energy Commission (AEC); meanwhile, people living near and working in uranium mines and test sites rarely benefited from this federal investment and were often exposed to contamination without notification of their risk. At Laguna, for instance, a community that had long suffered from high unemployment suddenly found ample work at the Jackpile-Paguate uranium mine, but the prosperity lasted only until the mine was closed and abandoned – less than thirty years, the span of a single generation. The Atomic Age also saw the emergence of nuclear tourism. The AEC publicized a schedule of selected detonations in 1957 so that tourists could plan their excursions accordingly (Miller 1986: 240–1). Visitors watched nuclear explosions as if they were movies, and Las Vegas hotels held pageants to crown "Miss Atomic Bomb." However, the horror movies inspired by atomic testing, including *Them!* (1954), a Warner Brothers film about giant mutant ants set in New Mexico, and the real and darkly comic treatments of nuclear holocaust released in 1964, Sidney Lumet's *Fail-Safe* and Stanley Kubrick's *Dr. Strangelove*, began to reveal fears that the nuclear project could damage the natural world in unpredictable ways.[1] It would take several decades and the end of the Cold War for activists and artists to realize these dangers fully and to articulate them for a national audience.

The third theme is what Limerick calls "the unforeseen, maddening, and persistent side effects" of the conquest of nature: the production of waste – in this case, of bodies, water, and lands. Between 1951 and 1963, 126 atomic bombs were detonated above ground at the Nevada Test Site, about fifty miles northwest of Las Vegas (Hevly and Findlay 1998: 5); other bombs were exploded underground in western Colorado and above ground near Fallon, Nevada (Riebsame 1997: 133). Fallout from just one group of bombs dropped at the Nevada site, the Plumbbomb series, spread from the Pacific Northwest to New England (Solnit 1994: 19). People injured by radioactive fallout began to protest through bringing lawsuits against the government. Ranchers whose sheep died or gave birth to deformed lambs brought their case to Federal District Court twice, first in the late 1950s and again in the 1980s. They lost the first time, and the Supreme Court denied their appeal the second.[2] Between 1963 and 1988, the tests continued underground. Because of these tests and the dispersal of fallout, the US is "the most nuclear-bombed country in the world" and a major source of global contamination (Kosek 2006: 263). Although some of the territory used to develop the nuclear program was already claimed by the government, many areas designated for testing and dumping, including Nevada's Yucca Mountain and New Mexico's Carlsbad Caverns, had long been settled by people native to the region. Of the uranium reserves in the United States, two-thirds are found on Indian lands, and "80 to 90 percent of the mining and milling that has taken place in the last fifty years has been on or adjacent to reservations."[3] Valerie Kuletz has traced how "two land-scapes – Indian and nuclear – meet at nearly every point of the nuclear cycle, from uranium mining to weapons testing to the disposal of nuclear waste" (Kuletz 1998: 12). Whereas the US government has viewed these landscapes as expendable and easily sacrificed, indigenous people understand them as sacred geographies. Abandoned uranium mines pose disproportionately great and long-lasting danger to the Southwest's Navajo, Hopi, Pueblo, Ute, Southern Paiute, Goshute, Shoshone, and Apache peoples, to the extent that Kuletz and others refer to the policies of the AEC as "internal colonialism." Much of the country's nuclear contamination continues to be concentrated on tribal lands, and the ongoing effort by Congress to secure a license from the Nuclear Regulatory Commission to dispose of nuclear waste at Yucca Mountain, Nevada, on Western Shoshone land explicitly identifies Indian lands and people as nuclear targets.

From its origin, marked by the successful detonation of the first bomb on July 16, 1945, at the Trinity Site near Alamogordo, New Mexico, to the end of nuclear testing in 1994, the Atomic Age compressed and exaggerated the patterns that we now understand to define the region's particular history of conquest, economic development, and environmental change. Its early stage produced fascinating first-hand documents of scientific experimentation, descriptions of everyday life in atomic cities, and arresting images of the equipment required to make, house, and detonate atomic bombs. To gain access to the thinking of atomic scientists and the experience of leading the Manhattan Project, one can read lectures and letters by J. Robert Oppenheimer, General Leslie Groves' memoir *Now It Can Be Told* (1962), and Richard Rhodes' definitive history, *The Making of the Atomic Bomb* (1986). To learn of domestic routines at Los Alamos and nearby Otowi Bridge, one can consult the composite memoir *Standing By and Making Do: Women of Los Alamos* (Wilson and Serber 1988), the oral history *Children of Lost Alamos* (Mason 1995), Peggy Pond Church's recollections of *The House at Otowi Bridge* (1960), or Frank Waters' novel *The Woman at Otowi Crossing* (1966). Photographs from the Manhattan Project, such as those collected by

Rachel Fermi and Esther Samra in *Picturing the Bomb* (1995) and by Michael Light in *100 Suns* (2003), document the "gadget" itself, the base camp, and the first detonation at Trinity, as well as the variety of mushroom clouds that came to define an atomic bomb in the public imagination. Documentary films, including *The Atomic Café* (1982) and *The Plutonium Circus* (1995), reflect on the attitudes of the Cold War and the experience of testing and assembling weapons. These documents prove that the pathbreaking discoveries of atomic scientists inspire awe about the creative process, interest in the domestic and institutional arrangements that support advanced research, and fascination about the apparently inescapable link between death and beauty.

More recently, however, written and photographic responses to the nuclear Southwest have struggled to reconcile the excitement of discovery, the rhetoric of opportunity, and the pride at surpassing nature's limits evident in the early texts with knowledge of the suffering and destruction that has followed. If an elite group of international scientists produced, deployed, and named atomic weapons, a much more diverse group of historians, indigenous people, photographers, feminists, and environmental writers have worked together to tell the "understories" of atomic development. Cultural historians, including Carl Abbott, Peter Hales, Bryan Taylor, and Hugh Gusterson, have performed extensive studies of the social and political geographies of towns organized to support the laboratories and test sites, focusing on the way city planning and architecture reinforced the government's official mechanisms of control. Building on his earlier analysis of America's nuclear culture from the dawn of the Atomic Age through the Cold War in *By the Bomb's Early Light* (1985), Paul Boyer's *Fallout* (1998) explores the "intense and continuing impact" of the nuclear arms race on the American consciousness through official and public responses to occasions like the anniversary of Hiroshima, Ronald Reagan's nuclear initiatives, and the controversy over the Enola Gray exhibit. These studies provide useful analyses of the significance of the nuclear Southwest within the broader contexts of federal investment, regional politics, and the culture of the Cold War.

The remainder of this essay will examine a limited but representative group of literary and photographic texts that challenge the nuclear Southwest's master-narrative from a variety of perspectives. While these texts all share a commitment to expose the environmental dangers of nuclear testing, they also reveal competing conceptions of the land's cultural and social meanings and projections about what the future will hold. I first consider the Hispano and Native American writers Rudolfo Anaya, Leslie Marmon Silko, and Simon J. Ortiz, whose fiction and poetry belie the notion that the Southwest had ever been empty territory. The Atomic Age threatened their sacred places, their homelands, and their communities, and they resisted these threats with renewed assertions of cultural identity. The photographers of the self-styled "Atomic Photography Guild," including Peter Goin, Carole Gallagher, and Patrick Nagatani, produced images that test the aesthetic and spiritual legacies of regional landscapes against devastating evidence of ruin. The second section of this essay explores how their visual studies articulate the environmental and human consequences of the bust that followed the Atomic Age's boom. Finally, I turn to the ecological and spiritual journeys narrated by contemporary feminist writers Terry Tempest Williams and Ellen Meloy. In *Refuge* and *The Last Cheater's Waltz*, Williams and Meloy experiment with new forms for telling stories of the region's contaminated landscapes. By combining natural, cultural, and personal histories, these ecofeminist works show how the nuclear Southwest is both a real place that poses serious environmental and human threats *and* a culture "created by a whole body of ideas, struggles, and representations" (Campbell 2000: 5).

Native Stories of the Atomic Age

Beginning in the late 1960s, native southwestern writers Rudolfo Anaya, Leslie Silko, and Simon Ortiz spoke out against the US military presence and its nuclear legacy on behalf of their culture and their homelands in novels, stories, and poems. Environmental activist Edward Abbey had already set his early novel *Fire on the Mountain* (1962) at White Sands Missile Range to show the intensifying conflict between the US military-industrial complex and the wilderness. The "Rocks" section of Abbey's memoir *Desert Solitaire* (1968) then used the parable of Billy-Joe Husk, son of a uranium miner, to explore connections between the nightmare of nuclear annihilation and the potentially redemptive visions caused by the poisonous Jimson weed plant.[4] However, while Abbey declared a fierce and protective love for the desert in these works, he wrote from the position of a solitary outsider. For the region's Hispano and Native American writers, the nuclear industry threatened not just the desert but their entire culture, whose identity still depends on a reciprocal relation with the land. The Southwest's Native writers produced the first collective articulations of resistance to the industry and introduced the tropes that now define the literature of the Atomic Age: scenes of encounter with contaminated landscapes, a narrative quest for historical truth and new knowledge, and an imagined restoration of Native lands within communal or tribal contexts.

In *Bless Me, Ultima*, Anaya's novel first published in 1972, an atomic detonation initially emerges only indirectly as a rumor, but eventually it infiltrates the novel's entire figuration of environmental and religious evil. At the start, as the inhabitants of the New Mexican village of Guadalupe debate the truth of an atomic bomb said to be released nearby, they reveal more about their own beliefs than about the effects of the blast. Antonio Márez, Anaya's young protagonist, discusses the controversy with his father. Having heard from the village's devout Catholic women that the bomb represents a human desire to know all, he wants to know why the people he loved were killed and why evil exists. Antonio's father views the cause of destruction as disrespect for nature, blaming the way rich rancheros "sucked the earth dry with their deep wells" and overgrazed the land (Anaya 1999: 201). The winds blew harder as punishment, Antonio's father believes. "It is not manly to blame our mistakes on the bomb, or any other thing." he declares. "It is we who misuse the earth and must pay for our sins" (p. 202).

The dreams and visions which interrupt Anaya's magical realist novel, along with the presence of Ultima (Antonio's aunt and a powerful *curandera*) and the legend of the golden carp, introduce alternate temporalities and symbolic meanings which exceed traditional and rational ways of knowing. So does the final veiled appearance of the bomb, in the form of a puzzling tempest of black rocks that fall suddenly on the Agua Negra ranch. In Héctor Calderón's analysis, this event "cannot be explained by magical causality." The episode "is strategically placed … to mark the passing of an innocent age with Ultima's death and the coming nuclear age" (Calderón 2004: 53). Such intimation of nuclear consciousness in a work dominated by magical thought returns at the end of the novel, when Antonio runs from his uncle's house to his own to try to save Ultima, whom he knows to be in danger. He also runs, he recalls, "to preserve those moments when beauty mingled with sadness and flowed through my soul like the stream of time. … I felt light, like the wind, as my even strides carried me homeward" (Anaya 1999: 272). This wind, a figure for the inarticulate knowledge of nature and history, also may contain invisible fallout; in the narrative's penultimate moment, Antonio opens his body both to the sadness of impending loss and to the landscape's nuclear future.

Although *Bless Me, Ultima* resists the spectacle of detonation and the explicit dangers of fallout, its association of nuclear testing with evil and the unknown anticipates a literary pattern that Anaya extends in his story "Devil Deer" (2006). Set in the Jemez Mountains at the edge of the Los Alamos National Laboratory, the story contrasts the pueblo's traditional rituals, which include hunting in the mountains in autumn, telling stories of hunts from long ago, and preparing the meat that will sustain them through the winter, with the secret operations of Los Alamos' scientific community. The area the people call "Black Ridge" spans both pueblo and government land, but in between is a chain-link fence, a symbol of the artificial border imposed by the government and feared by the people. Before the story's protagonist Cruz sets out to hunt there, he has a nightmare that a misshapen black bear, the deformed embodiment of a stone fetish he usually carries with him, walks toward him on two feet like a man and warns him to stay away. When Cruz questions the meaning of the dream during his hunt, it seems that he can hear the mountain's dying breath and concludes that the bear meant to warn him that "[t]he earth was dying." He spots a deer on government land and pursues it until he finds a hole in the fence, steps across, and prepares to shoot. The buck, however, behaves strangely, not responding to Cruz's fire, as does the mountain, which seems full of ominous sounds. Cruz speculates that the sounds could be coming from "Accelerators. Plutonium. Atom smashers." He cannot be sure, and declares, "I only know I want my brother to return to the pueblo with me. Feed my family. Venison steaks with fried potatoes and onions" (Anaya 2006: 136). Close scrutiny of the deer reveals hair growing on its antlers, "a green bile seep[ing] from the holes the bullets had made," and strangely white, blind eyes (p. 137). At this point Cruz realizes that behind "the ridge lay Los Alamos, the laboratories, and nobody knew what in the hell went on there. But whatever it was, it was seeping into the earth, seeping into the animals of the forest," an unknown and pervasive threat (p. 137). The story ends with Cruz's return to the pueblo, "devil deer" in hand, and with the question of whether he can ever recover from his encounter with the contaminated landscape. Anaya writes, "The medicine men would perform a cleansing ceremony; they would pray for Cruz. But did they have enough good medicine to wash away the evil the young man had touched?" (p. 139). The story does not answer this question, leaving the challenge to fight back for the land to resonate into the future.

Silko writes more explicitly about the effects of the bomb on Laguna land and people in the novel *Ceremony* (published in 1977) and the essay "Interior and Exterior Landscapes" (1998). The Jackpile Mine destroyed land where people used to cultivate gardens and orchards, and after the miners dug out the uranium they abandoned the site, leaving behind deep pits, barbed wire fences, stripped shacks, and dead cattle; *Ceremony* confronts the challenge of re-storying this ravaged territory. It tells of the quest of Tayo, a young mixed-blood man who returns to the pueblo from serving as a soldier in World War II with nightmares about the Japanese men he refused to kill, his cousin and fellow soldier Rocky who died, and his uncle Josiah, whom he imagines he killed, to recover his connection with his homeland. Silko enacts a series of rituals to heal Tayo's trauma and the disintegration of the Laguna people. By figuring Tayo's alienation through his hollow body and reinforcing the alienation through his uncontrollable flashbacks of bodies destroyed by human and atomic warfare, Silko locates a major source of her protagonist's deterritorialization in the development and detonation of the first nuclear weapons. Modern warfare may lie outside the Pueblo imagination, seeming "monstrous" in its inhumanity, but nuclear warfare lies beyond any human comprehension, Silko suggests. Attributable only to the worst witchery, the sudden transformation of humans into shadows (as occurred in Hiroshima and Nagasaki) can be reversed by neither traditional healing methods nor western medicine.[5]

The novel shows that it is essential for Tayo to understand the boundary that divides Pueblo and white consciousness in order to reconstruct both individual and tribal identities. Whereas at the veterans' hospital Tayo feels like a mere "outline" of a body, after he leaves the Navajo healer Betonie he begins to feel whole. Rather than riding in a truck, he wants "to walk until he recognized himself again" and notices how sounds like the buzz of grasshoppers and the crackle of dead sunflower stalks surround him (Silko 2006: 143). Unlike his friends Harley, Emo, and Leroy, who saw and could not forget the overwhelming and alienating sensations of being in cities and fighting with weapons, Tayo learns to replace his own recent memories with the more powerful feelings of re-immersion in his homeland. Gradually, as he realizes the deceit of the white people who told him lies, claimed his cattle, and stole his land, Tayo discovers that he can sing again and feels that "the instant of the dawn was an event in which a single moment gathered all things together" (p. 169). By the time he returns to take care of his uncle's cattle, he is certain that despite his losses, "nothing was lost; all was retained between the sky and the earth, and within himself" (p. 204). Because of this internal and hard-won conviction, Tayo can look at the mountain side, feel its motion from within, and know that "the world was alive" (p. 205).

The conclusion to *Ceremony* has been read by some critics "as an allegorical call to practice vigilance for destructive ecological actions" and by others "as a human rights watch for nuclear weapons in the service of aggressive wars and global capitalism" (Teuton 2008: 140). In fact, these interpretations are connected. While standing on the abandoned mine, Tayo finally connects the warfare in Japan with its technological origins in his desert homeland just 100 miles from Los Alamos and 300 miles from the Trinity site. He realizes that all humans can be understood as "united by a circle of death" that spans 12,000 miles (Silko 2006: 228), and at this point he finally grasps the urgency of resisting such a conception of his home as contaminated with the lived experience of his body, the sacred stories he knows, and his imagination of a future when the people and the land will again be integrated.

Ortiz writes *Fight Back: For the Sake of the Land, for the Sake of the People* out of a similar resolution to confront the legacy of the uranium industry, mobilize a community of workers and readers, and preserve his Ácoma pueblo homeland. First published in 1980, the collection alternates prayers for survival with testimony of the people employed by the Kerr-McGee mine near Ácoma who suffered discrimination and injury; it thus seeks to remember those who were sacrificed for an industry that in Ortiz's view was only interested in profit. It begins with a "Mid-America Prayer" that locates the reader "within and among all things" and all life, thus placing the perspective of the entire work at the center of a spiral that connects individuals, cultures, lands, sky, and belief. The "Prayer" unites speaker and reader in a declaration of responsibility for pursuing "hope, courage, peace, / strength, vision, unity and continuance" (Ortiz 1992: 290). It proceeds to link the poet's own recollections of his family and his experiences as a young man with the stories of fellow workers like Lacey, a Navajo man killed while operating the "Primary Crusher" that pulverized ore, and Bill and Ida, a uranium worker and his wife whose son died after stepping on an "American" mine. Through these recollections and stories, Ortiz articulates the sorrow and rage that lead him to call for a common struggle to preserve and protect Indian lands against capitalist and nuclear oppression, not just for the people native to the Southwest but for "all people of this nation" (p. 360).

It is due in great part to the aesthetic and rhetorical power of these literary texts that literary, feminist, and environmental historians have made the rights of indigenous people central to their studies of the nuclear Southwest. For example, Rebecca Solnit's *Savage Dreams: A Journey into the Landscape Wars of the American West* (1994) chronicles the author's personal history as a protester at the Nevada Test Site and integrates this experience with extensive research into the area's Native histories. By situating the legacy of nuclear development within the contexts of the American environmental imagination and indigenous struggles for sovereignty, Solnit shows how the nuclear West exemplifies the fight over the ownership and meaning of western lands. Linda Helstern also advocates Native perspectives in her introduction to a special issue of *Southwestern American Literature* on "the Atomic Southwest" when she cites Louis Owens' 1994 novel *Bone Game* to illustrate "the overlap between Native geography and nuclear geography" (Helstern 2008: 9). Other critics foreground the effects of nuclear development on New Mexico's Pueblo and Spanish-speaking communities.[6] Because writers native to the Southwest translated the discourse of protest so effectively into narratives that integrate indigenous and traditional Anglo-European literary forms, they demonstrate how individual and communal struggles to reclaim the land can function as models for coming to terms with the social and environmental costs of the nuclear industry.

Images and Activism: The Atomic Photographers' Guild

From the early years of Ronald Reagan's presidency through the demise of the Cold War and into our current era of global environmental awareness, the "nuclear menace" has taken diverse academic, artistic, and mass cultural forms. The damage wrought by testing at the Nevada Test Site produced especially strong protests against the US nuclear program by photographers and writers for whom the "New West" meant the altered landscapes created by urbanization and the desert's militarization. In 1986, Robert Del Tredici organized the Atomic Photographers' Guild with the premise that everyone faces the threat posed by nuclear fallout and with the commitment to reveal the destruction left in the wake of the nuclear boom. Peter Goin and Carole Gallagher were among the international Guild's original members; they pursued a strategy of "progressive, documentary realism" in order to restore nuclear objects to the public imagination (Taylor 2000: 56). Other members experimented with strategies of pastiche and reconstruction to involve viewers and make them question the process of looking at nuclear landscapes. Taken together, these aesthetic approaches confront the difficulty of displaying an environmental threat that is pervasive but rarely visible.

Peter Goin's *Nuclear Landscapes* (1991) documents artifacts and lands damaged by nuclear testing, from Frenchman Flat in Nevada to the Bikini Atoll islands. He focuses on the "relics, ruins, and structures emblematic of the nuclear age," such as the buildings and vehicles that nuclear blasts turned into warped debris, aiming to "elevate the objects within the photographs to iconic significance" (Goin 1991: p. xxii). Especially powerful are portraits of the seemingly abandoned desert at Trinity or the Nevada Test Site, bounded by a metal chain-link fence but otherwise unpoliced and unnoticed. These images seem to be invitations to look down at the desert itself: unevenly covered with scrub grass and cacti, scarred by dirt paths and roads, gouged by tires, the ground seems wasted and eerily luminous by turns. Although a site's official markers sometimes appear, like the cenotaph at Trinity or the crumbling observation tower at the Nevada site, viewers would probably not detect their exhausted purpose without captions or the surrounding text. In his introduction Goin writes of the profoundly unsettling feeling of entering these "secluded" and contaminated landscapes. The opposite of a refuge or oasis, it seems to render the witness "alien" and to undermine the power of human senses, which cannot detect radiation's danger.

Goin explains that the "subliminal sense of foreboding is an important element in the landscape" (Goin 1991: p. xx), as is the fear of knowing just how much human suffering the nuclear tests caused. While his photographs enclose the sites by documenting their fences and framing them, they also reveal how nuclear fear cannot be contained. By positioning viewers in the foreground or elevating them in the air, they suggest that we are already surrounded by environmental danger; if we want to witness the extent of the desert's destruction, we must put ourselves at risk. Richard Misrach's ambitious photographs of the nuclear Southwest in *Bravo 20* (1990) further dramatize the landscape's potent mixture of beauty and fear by alternating close-ups of dead animals and graffiti with surveys of empty bombing ranges and aircraft hangars. Misrach's images deliberately shock the viewer with their obvious grandeur and undeniable violence; they question the cultural myths of conquest and wilderness and show the region's desert landscapes to be "terrifying, surreal, dreamlike" (Campbell 2000: 60). Both Goin's and Misrach's photographs need to be read through the contexts of the landscape's many and conflicting cultural histories, from its interpretation as sublime nature by Europeans and Anglo-Americans to its significance as sacred space for Native Americans, its removal from public access through designation as a military zone, and its political re-emergence as contaminated territory. Neither sequential nor coherent, such multiple contexts complicate the relation between seeing and knowing the nuclear landscape.

In *American Ground Zero* (1993), Gallagher reveals the human costs of nuclear testing by documenting the breakdown of irradiated bodies. Her mixed-media project probes the fragile surfaces of people and communities affected by radiation released from the Nevada Test Site, documenting the experiences of survivors in black-and-white portraits and first-person testimonials. Throughout the book, the bodies and voices of veterans and survivors speak for the dead and for the ruined land. While any one of Gallagher's subjects might be capable of telling his or her own story, the sequence of stories in the book works to connect individual testimonials into a complex narrative of suffering and partial redemption. Gallagher's exposure of radiation's hidden histories thus continues the work of anti-nuclear activists by making her viewers see directly the human and natural damage of what Mike Davis has called "an atomic plague" and a "secret holocaust" (Davis 2002).

A third significant work by a member of the Atomic Photographers' Guild is Patrick Nagatani's *Nuclear Enchantment* (Nagatani and Janis 1991), a collection of photographs that explore the sacrifice of Native American lands through juxtaposing myths and practices of everyday life with signs of nuclear danger and contamination. The title indicates the book's central subject: the deadly magic of the Atomic Age. With the discoveries of nuclear physics, "the mysterious and invisible all-seeing, all-destroying 'rays' which had fascinated people for millennia" suddenly became concrete and real (Janis, in Nagatani and Janis 1991: 10). Nagatani makes such invisible "rays" material in a photograph like "Contaminated Radioactive Sediment, Mortandad Canyon, Los Alamos National Laboratory, New Mexico, 1990." Without the title, the image could be mistaken for a peaceful winter landscape, as large flakes of snow seem to be falling from a dark sky onto the canyon's pine trees, bushes, and rocks; with it, the image reveals the way contamination has invaded this natural scene and made it uninhabitable. Rather than documenting existing sites and people, Nagatani creates visual effects to present his own perspective on both the persistent fascination of nuclear power and the strange ways that people have learned to live with it. He conducts extensive research on nuclear policies, the history of mining and testing, and storage sites to prepare for photographing. Then he engages actors or family members to play the role of tourists and sets them either directly in a nuclear environment or separately, to be pasted onto cardboard and positioned in the photographic set later. A photograph of "Radium Springs, New Mexico, 1989" depicts a family and their dog just after bathing, the bodies strangely green from exposure. In "The Evening News, Native American Pueblo Dwelling, New Mexico, 1990," a composition of obviously pasted figures gathers around a Scrabble game, the board covered with words drawn from a nuclear vocabulary, while another figure gazes at a television set reporting on a Waste Isolation Pilot Plant in Carlsbad, New Mexico. In these typical images, Nagatani shows how the government's nuclear program has invaded the bodies, domestic spaces, leisure time, and imagination of the people who live in the Southwest.

The work of members of the Atomic Photographers' Guild functioned as forms of protest that supported the thousands of anti-nuclear activists who were arrested at the Nevada Test Site and provided critical models for new kinds of interdisciplinary and collaborative histories. As witnesses, photographers now can only observe the Atomic Age's legacy of destruction rather than the moment of its creation. This exemplifies our current position as citizens of a natural world polluted by those who came before – and still compromised by our own patterns of use and limited powers of protection. Yet these photographers also cultivate new ways of looking at nuclear landscapes that challenge the myths of the region's past and reconfigure our conception of beauty as a realm where aesthetics and history are entwined. As writers and critics of the nuclear Southwest continue to recognize, "beauty still exists and beauty may still be redemptive" (Tatum 2006: 141), even if we never again recover the illusion of the desert as open space, untouched wilderness, refuge, or economic opportunity.

Feminist and Ecological Narratives

Gendered language characterized the Atomic Age from the start. Scientists at Los Alamos "called the prototype tested in New Mexico 'Robert's [Oppenheimer's] baby'; the bomb dropped on Hiroshima was named 'Little Boy'" (Gusterson 2004: 161). A message describing the successful birth of a boy baby meant a positive outcome for the test of a hydrogen bomb. Such language extended to technical terms, too, figuring the generative mechanisms that hold the bombs as "cradles" and the shells that hold ICBMs as "cribs." However, although male scientists used tropes of birth and nurture, female protestors have long challenged the association of weapons with creation and sought to reclaim the southwestern desert for future generations. "War was a men's issue, but contamination became a women's issue" (Solnit 1994: 96). Some of the first protests against nuclear testing focused on the dangers radiation posed for children, prompting many women to write letters of opposition to President Eisenhower in 1957, organize the Women's Strike for Peace in 1962, and lead anti-nuclear movements in the 1980s. Along with Solnit, Terry Tempest Williams and Ellen Meloy have been important figures in extending critiques of nuclear iconology through the 1990s in feminist and ecological directions. Each of these writers begins with the experience of her female body and then proceeds to investigate the way physical contact with contaminated places produces complex, embodied understandings of nuclear history, ecology, and spirituality.

Williams explains in the Prologue to her memoir *Refuge* that the Great Salt Lake "is a landscape so surreal one can never know what it is for certain" and that she is "telling this story in an attempt to heal myself, to confront what I do not know, to create a path for myself with the idea that 'memory is the only way home'" (Williams 1992: 3–4). For this writer, "the natural and familial history of place with all its secrets are bound up with the land," and to uncover these secrets she must tell the land's stories (Campbell 2000: 56). When she realizes that her mother's cancer was probably caused by contamination from nuclear fallout, she seeks correspondences between human, ecological, and social systems. A Mormon and a naturalist, Williams loves her native landscape and wants to make it right again. She describes repeated journeys into the Great Salt Lake and the Bear River Bird Refuge, where she observes how a flood has disturbed the birds' patterns of nesting and migration and discovers a dead swan, and each time she returns from these sites of natural disaster she contemplates the delayed fallout from nuclear testing: the irrevocable losses of her family and her Mormon faith. Mixing representations of suffering with observations of natural beauty, Williams tries to reorder the desert's spiritual geography and reclaim its healing power by rendering its inner life.

Ellen Meloy similarly begins her memoir of "beauty and violence in the desert Southwest" with an account of her sudden alienation from the Utah desert she loves and claims as her homeland. Meloy felt that she had "lost all frames of reference" and perhaps "forgotten the point of consciousness" (Meloy 1999: 3–4), and she knows that her journey back must involve rituals of contact: "To reinhabit my own body I had to traverse, again and again, the desert's cruel and beautiful skin" (1999: 8). Organized around enclosed spaces that the narrative seeks to unbound and surfaces that it seeks to penetrate, *The Last Cheater's Waltz* emphasizes how the shock of sensation keeps breaking apart the coherent story the author hoped to tell and opens the possibility for gaining access to historical truth. Such narrative encounters with the physical evidence of nuclear testing constitute an important practice of what Stephen Tatum has called "forensic aesthetics" because they seek beauty and justice in the face of visible human and environmental destruction. In these scenes, the text functions as both an ecological quest and an investigation of how to narrate the collective trauma of nuclear contamination through the embodied female subject (Tatum 2006: 140).

The interconnected quest for immersion in her adopted homeland and for the origins of the Atomic Age culminates at the Trinity site, where Meloy examines the "obelisk-shaped cenotaph" at ground zero and wants "to lie down on the seam, linking the imprint of destruction with the landscape that surrounds it," hoping that by rupturing the surface of both landscape and human body she will evoke emotion that "leads to meaning, then understanding" (Meloy 1999: 36). Although this understanding is far from certain, the abandonment of the old myths of conquest, prosperity, and redemption makes its emergence possible. Meloy proposes, "[t]he sterilization of landscape allows its reinvention; only at zero can there be a beginning, a blank slate to fill, even if the story that fills it – an apocalypse – itself becomes nothing again, in an instant" (1999: 20). This is an apt description of the ongoing process of writing about the ruins of the Atomic Age.

Conclusion

"We're extremely fortunate / not to know precisely / the kind of world we live in," writes the Nobel Prize-winning Polish poet Wisława Szymborska. To know our world precisely, "One would have / to live a long, long time"; "Rise above the flesh"; "transcend time"; and "one might as well bid farewell / to incidents and details" (Szymborska 2000: 258). Such absolute knowledge, she suggests, would contradict the human limits of mortality, the experience of the body, our sense of place in history, and the texture of everyday life. The photography and literature of the nuclear Southwest similarly explore the necessity of being immersed in the world in order to discover the limits of knowledge. Rather than claiming discovery, as the original atomic scientists did, photographers and writers now confront uncertainty by returning to test sites and articulate the necessity of restoring contaminated places. Like Szymborska's poetry, which was written in response to wartime destruction in Europe, the art of the nuclear Southwest tests the boundaries between knowing and unknowing, past events and present experience, human body and natural environment.

Photographers and writers in the post-nuclear era continue to look back and revise the histories of major sites in the nuclear Southwest, but they also imagine the future that we will all inhabit. As Limerick explains, "Our fortunes, as well as our misfortunes are intertwined" (Limerick 1992: 168). While such a complex and open-ended project of historical revision often involves exposing painful truths, the challenge of reconfiguring the past within ecological and spiritual frameworks can also produce new understandings of the networks that connect people and places, the boundaries that separate realms of knowledge, and the significance of lived and sacred spaces. If "the meaning of the American landscape [lies] in its future rather than its past," as Solnit proclaims, then artists must continue to look ahead and embrace the Southwest's mixture of destruction and beauty, "the process of improvisation," and the exhilaration of uncertainty (Solnit 1994: 182–3). In the tension between the necessity of exposing facts that have long been suppressed and the desire to find forms of experience that can transform those facts into new knowledge of the future lies the poetics of the post-nuclear Southwest.

NOTES

1   For discussions of these films as ecological critiques and complex responses to the Cold War and the Cuban Missile Crisis, see "Western Ecological Films" (Lawrence 2006) and *"Dr. Strangelove*: Stanley Kubrick Presents the Apocalypse," in *Fallout* (Boyer 1998: 95–102).

2   Although "downwinders" in Utah did win a ruling that the federal government had been negligent in warning local residents and "unreasonably placed" them "at risk of injury" in the 1984 case *Irene Allen v. United States*, the 1987 Tenth Circuit Court of Appeals in Denver reversed the ruling, arguing that the federal government had the right to pursue any activities vital to national security. In 1988, atomic veterans who had been exposed directly to contamination during nuclear tests finally received some recognition and compensation through a directive by Congress, and in 1990 the Radiation

Exposure Act was passed, apologizing for the exposure and providing some compensation for damages. For details of these cases, see Keith Schneider, Foreword to *American Ground Zero* (Gallagher 1993: pp. xv–xix).

3   See Jace Weaver's introduction to Thorpe 1996: 47.

4   For a full discussion of Abbey's texts, see "The New Atomic Wilderness" (Hunt 2008).

5   Akira Lippit explores how *hibakusha* "absorbed and *were absorbed* by the invisible radiation" of the atomic bombs, vanishing until nothing but their negatives remained. See ch. 4 of *Atomic Light* (Lippit 2005: 81–103).

6   Consult, for example, Sara Spurgeon's discussion of Martin Cruz Smith's novel *Stallion Gate* (1986) in "Mimesis and the Bomb" (Spurgeon 2008) and her analysis of Ana Castillo's 1993 novel *So Far from God* (Spurgeon 2005).

REFERENCES AND FURTHER READING

Anaya, Rudolfo. (1999). *Bless Me, Ultima* [1972]. New York: Warner Books.

Anaya, Rudolfo. (2006). Devil Deer. In *The Man Who Could Fly and Other Stories*, pp. 132–9. Norman: University of Oklahoma Press.

Boyer, Paul. (1985). *By the Bomb's Early Light: American Thought and Culture at the Dawn of the Atomic Age*. New York: Pantheon.

Boyer, Paul. (1998) *Fallout: A Historian Reflects on America's Half-Century Encounter with Nuclear Weapons*. Columbus: Ohio State University Press.

Calderón, Héctor. (2004). *Narratives of Greater Mexico: Essays on Chicano Literary History, Genre, & Borders*. Austin: University of Texas Press.

Campbell, Neil. (2000). *The Cultures of the American New West*. Edinburgh: Edinburgh University Press.

Castillo, Ana. (1993). *So Far From God*. New York: Penguin Books.

Church, Peggy Pond. (1998). *The House at Otowi Bridge* [1960]. Albuquerque: University of New Mexico Press.

Conant, Jennet. (2005). *109 East Palace: Robert Oppenheimer and the Secret City of Los Alamos*. New York: Simon & Schuster.

Davis, Mike. (2002). *Dead Cities and Other Tales*. New York: New Press.

Fermi, Rachel, and Esther Samra. (1995). *Picturing the Bomb: Photographs from the Secret World of the Manhattan Project*. New York: Harry Abrams.

Fisher, Phyllis. (1985). *Los Alamos Experience*. New York: Japan Publications.

Gallagher, Carole. (1993). *American Ground Zero*. Cambridge, MA: MIT Press.

Goin, Peter. (1991). *Nuclear Landscapes*. Baltimore: Johns Hopkins University Press.

Groves, Leslie R. (1962). *Now It Can Be Told: The Story of the Manhattan Project*. New York: Harper.

Gusterson, Hugh. (2004). *People of the Bomb: Portraits of America's Nuclear Complex*. Minneapolis: University of Minnesota Press.

Hales, Peter Bacon. (1997). *Atomic Spaces: Living on the Manhattan Project*. Urbana: University of Illinois Press.

Helstern, Linda Lizut. (2008). The Atomic Southwest: Guest Editor's Introduction. *Southwestern American Literature*, 34/1, 9–14.

Hevly, Bruce, and John M. Findlay, eds. (1998). *The Atomic West*. Seattle: University of Washington Press.

Hunt, Alex. (2008). The New Atomic Wilderness: Ed Abbey's Post-Apocalyptic Southwest. *Southwestern American Literature*, 34/1, 41–53.

Kelly, Cynthia C., ed. (2004). *Remembering the Manhattan Project: Perspectives on the Making of the Bomb and its Legacy*. Hacksensack, NJ: World Scientific.

Kosek, Jake. (2006). *Understories: The Political Life of Forests in Northern New Mexico*. Durham, NC: Duke University Press.

Kuletz, Valerie. (1998). *The Tainted Desert: Environmental Ruin in the American West*. New York: Routledge.

Lawrence, John Shelton. (2006). Western Ecological Films: The Subgenre with No Name. In Deborah A. Carmichael, ed., *The Landscape of Hollywood Westerns*, pp. 19–49. Salt Lake City: University of Utah Press.

Light, Michael. (2003). *100 Suns*. New York: Knopf.

Limerick, Patricia Nelson. (1987). *The Legacy of Conquest: The Unbroken Past of the American West*. New York: W.W. Norton

Limerick, Patricia Nelson. (1992). The Significance of Hanford in American History. In David H. Stratton, ed., *Washington Comes of Age: The State in the National Experience*, pp. 153–71. Pullman: Washington State University Press.

Lippit, Akira Mizuta. (2005). *Atomic Light (Shadow Optics)*. Minneapolis: University of Minnesota Press.

Loader, Jayne, Kevin Rafferty, and Pierce Rafferty, dir. (1982). *The Atomic Café*. Archives Project.

Mason, Katrina R., ed. (1995). *Children of Los Alamos: An Oral History of the Town Where the Atomic Age Began*. New York: Twayne.

Matsunaga, Kyoko. Resisting and Surviving Apocalypse: Simon J. Ortiz's (Post) Colonial Nuclear Narrative. *Southwestern American Literature*, 34/1, 15–27.

Meloy, Ellen. (1999). *The Last Cheater's Waltz: Beauty and Violence in the Desert Southwest*. Tucson: University of Arizona Press.

Miller, Richard L. (1986). *Under the Cloud: The Decades of Nuclear Testing*. New York: Free Press.

Misrach, Richard. (1990). *Bravo 20: The Bombing of the American West*. Baltimore: Johns Hopkins University Press.

Nagatani, Patrick, and Eugenia Parry Janis. (1991). *Nuclear Enchantment*. Albuquerque: University of New Mexico Press.

Ortiz, Simon J. (1992). *Fight Back: For the Sake of the People, for the Sake of the Land* [1980]. In *Woven Stone*, pp. 285–365. Tucson: University of Arizona Press.

Ratliff, George, dir. (1995). *The Plutonium Circus*. Wildcatter Productions.

Rhodes, Richard. (1986). *The Making of the Atomic Bomb*. New York: Simon & Schuster.

Riebsame, W.E., ed. (1997). The Ugly West. In *Atlas of the New West: Portrait of a Changing Region*, pp. 132–41. New York: W.W. Norton.

Silko, Leslie Marmon. (2006). *Ceremony* [1977]. New York: Penguin Books.

Silko, Leslie Marmon. (1998). Interior and Exterior Landscapes. In Simon J. Ortiz, ed., *Speaking for the Generations*, pp. 2–24. Tucson: University of Arizona Press.

Solnit, Rebecca. (1994). *Savage Dreams: A Journey into the Landscape Wars of the American West*. Berkeley: University of California Press.

Spurgeon, Sara L. (2005). *Exploding the Western: Myths of Empire on the Postmodern Frontier*. College Station: Texas A&M University Press.

Spurgeon, Sara L. (2008). Mimesis and the Bomb: Race, Masculinity, and (de)Colonial Identities in Martin Cruz Smith's *Stallion Gate*. *Southwestern American Literature*, 34/1, 29–40.

Szymborska, Wisława. (2000). *Poems New and Collected*, trans. Stanisław Barańczak and Clare Cavanaugh. New York: Harcourt.

Tatum, Stephen. (2006). Spectral Beauty and Forensic Aesthetics in *the West*. *Western American Literature*, 41/2, 123–45.

Taylor, Bryan. (2000). Nuclear Pictures and Metapictures. In Larry J. Reynolds and Gordon Hutner, eds., *National Imaginaries, American Identities: The Cultural Work of American*

Iconography, pp. 52–82. Princeton: Princeton University Press.

Teuton, Sean Kicummah. (2008). *Red Land, Red Power: Grounding Knowledge in the American Indian Novel*. Durham, NC: Duke University Press.

Thorpe, Grace. (1996). Our Homes Are Not Dumps: Creating Nuclear-Free Zones. In Jace Weaver, ed., *Defending Mother Earth: Native American Perspectives on Environmental Justice*, pp. 47–58. Maryknoll, NY: Orbis Books.

Waters, Frank. (1966). *The Woman at Otowi Crossing*. Denver: Swallow Books.

Williams, Terry Tempest. (1992). *Refuge: An Unnatural History of Family and Place* [1911]. New York: Vintage Books.

Wilson, Jane, and Charlotte Serber, eds. (1988). *Standing By and Making Do: Women of Wartime Los Alamos*. Los Alamos: Los Alamos Historical Society.

31

Ranging over Stegner's Arid West: Mobility as Adaptive Strategy

Bonney MacDonald

In an open country everyone is a traveler. (Wallace Stegner)

Contemporary mobility theory – advanced most recently by John Urry, and borrowing from Georg Simmel and Heidegger – suggests new ways of thinking about place-making in the West. Investigating such multiple forms of mobility as exchange, consumerism, transnationalism, and tourism, as well as cultural geography and theories of place, Urry suggests that place-making is not always about being what Wallace Stegner called a "sticker" (Stegner 1992: p. xxii); in fact it can be defined by and dependent on movement and connected to what human geographer Nigel Thrift called "movement-spaces" (Thrift 2004: 582). Looking to multiple mobilities, Urry examines the "significance of mobility infrastructures" and turns to a recent translation of Simmel to discuss the performative and transitory process by which humans create space and place.

Places, like those who make them, are "not fixed and unchanging but depend upon what gets bodily performed within them" (Urry 2007: 269). A place is reached, after all, because a person leaves a former location and arrives at a new one. There is, Urry claims, an "exceptional human achievement that is involved in creating a path that links two particular places" (2007: 20). Or, to use Simmel's terms, it is "only by visibly impressing the path into the surface of the earth that the places were objectively connected." Dwelling and place-making depend on motion across physical space.

Through an inquiry into place and motion, this essay asserts two potentially opposite claims: (1) that *place* matters, that we should settle into particular geographies, and (2) that the *transience* and movement that have characterized western life may, in fact, be an ideal form of adaptation to arid lands. Wallace Stegner, known for his laments over a boom-and-bust, transient West, marshaled "an environmentalism

A Companion to the Literature and Culture of the American West, First Edition. Edited by Nicolas S. Witschi.

[that] came from his abiding hope that Americans might eventually learn to live well
... in their places on the land" (LaDow 2002: 275–6). In search of a geography of
hope, Stegner quotes Wendell Berry's observation that "if you don't know *where* you
are you don't know *who* you are." And, throughout much of the West, many people
are west of the 100th meridian, in the land of little rain. As Stegner insists in
"Thoughts on a Dry Land," the West was defined by aridity and its two main consequences: space and mobility.

Seeing the West: Aridity, Scale, and Color

For Stegner, the West has been defined by and has even encouraged transience; and
it's been transience with a price, producing ghost towns and temporary settlements,
hardly conducive to stable, thriving communities – what Gretel Ehrlich called "metal
knots on flat land" (Ehrlich 1985: 4). Newcomers to the West have long underesti-
mated western aridity, not just because they wanted to defy it for their own self-
interest, but also because they *couldn't really see it*. From the 1789 Northwest Ordinance
to the 1862 Homestead Act, the 1936 Taylor Grazing Act and modern ranchettes,
western space has been misperceived, mismapped, and misused.

The West is hard to *see*, in part, simply because of the size of it all – the *scale*. We
have to "learn to see all over again," and this "westernizing" of perceptions can take
a while. Stegner recalls picking up his Aunt Min at the Salt Lake City airport after
she had flown in from Iowa. They drove past Mount Nebo and the Wasatch, and she
didn't so much as notice. Later, as Stegner turned the car east and faced the "towering,
level front of the ... Plateau," he asked, "'How do you like that, Aunt Min?'" Like
"any Westerner," he recalls, "I liked to impress Iowans, and the easiest way to do it
is with size. She blinked [and said], 'That's nice. It reminds me of the river bluffs in
the county park at Fort Dodge.'" As Stegner remarks, "She couldn't even see it. She
had no experience, no scale by which to judge an unbroken mountain wall more than
a mile high" (Stegner 1992: 52).

As William Fox notes in *The Void, the Grid, and the Sign: Traversing the Great Basin*,
the desert West is "so large that we can't get our minds around it just by looking at
it" (Fox 2000: 11). Moreover, the lack of "verticals" on the surface – trees, windmills,
buildings – makes it all foreground and horizon with "no middle ground" by which
to triangulate or gain depth perspective (Fox 2000: 55): "It lacks the natural features
of built structures that allow us to focus on that part of the landscape where normally
our vision, hence our imagination, spends most of its time" (Fox 2000: 53). And in
that wide-open space, cognitive and cultural habits fail. Without "markers ... it is
harder for us to build ... a context for our lives" (Fox 2000: 29). We can't easily mark
where we are. And, if Wendell Berry is right, we therefore have difficulty knowing *who*
we are. In fact, Fox extends the point, suggesting that, without vertical markers, it's
not only hard to see where you *are*, but hard to remember where you *were*. And memory,
as Stegner insisted, is what makes a place a place. Not merely a geographical location,

a "place" is made only by "slow accrual" of births, lives, and deaths. A *place* comes about because stories and memories emerge from experience on that land. The fact that "Daniel Boone killed a bear at a certain spot ... did not make it a place." It accrued this status, however, when Boone and others *"remembered* the spot as Bear Run, and [others] ... called their settlement by it" (Stegner 1992: 201–2). For a place to become a place, events must be "remembered in history, ballads, yarns, legends, or monuments" (Stegner 1992: 201–2). And in the arid West, where markers are few and memories are hard to fasten to particular spots, the accumulation may take a long time.

Our resulting inability to remember the land's details also makes it easy to make mistakes out there. For Fox, misperceptions of arid land lead to a geographical ignorance by which land can too easily be mapped, mined, and seized for private gain. In fact, even contemporary intellectuals have a hard time getting the West right. Baudrillard's 1986 *America*, in fact, "confuses the western slopes with ... the Rockies, a seven-hundred mile blunder that has him describe water flowing off the mountains in Colorado and into San Francisco Bay" (Fox 2000: 9). But a twentieth-century French intellectual's mistake comes in for less criticism than do earlier perceptual blunders. Our inability truly to see the arid West has not only led us to project onto that blank space our fantasies of nature, but it has also led us to place a grid over that void in an effort to understand and control it. The rectilinear grid generated "misplaced trust" in our mapping powers, and brought out the worst in a culture. Maps, Fox claims, constitute a "cartographic imperative" that directly correlates to "the doctrine of Manifest Destiny, which in [the nineteenth century] held that the land was ours for the taking, [and] that America's purpose was to use the land so we could infinitely people it" (Fox 2000: 62). Maps and the grids they depend on "exercise authority over space by applying a ruler to it in all senses of the word":

> A map is nothing less than a tightly controlled abstraction of the worlds ... which we are deeply conditioned ... to accept on faith as an accurate representation of reality. The question always remains however: under whose control and to what purpose? As an artificial extension of our egocentric triangulation of the world, the grid is automatically suspect. (Fox 2000: 129–30)

For Fox, Fremont's maps and those that followed underwrote a massive power-grab of western lands.

Stegner levels his own harsh critique at previous misperceptions of the West. Those errors, however, follow less from the West's disorienting open spaces than from what makes those lands wide open in the first place – aridity: "more than anything else, [aridity] gives the Western landscape its character." From the "dry clarity of the air," to the "brilliance" of light, the erosion of soil and the "mobile animals of the dry grasslands," a "shortage of water" has shaped the West (Stegner 1992: 46). And the "consequences of [that] aridity multiply by a kind of domino effect" because, in our inability to perceive the West, and in our "attempt to compensate for nature's lacks, we have remade whole sections of the western landscape" (Stegner 1992: 47). In our mapping, mining, plowing, and irrigating of arid lands, we "have acted upon the western landscape with the force of a geological agent" (Stegner 1992: 47).

In this account, the good guys are hard to tell from the bad. The denial of aridity as well as the over-mapped, over-engineered projects that sought to claim, settle, and "oversell the West as the Garden of the World" have a complicated history. He finds it "hard to tell the boosters from the suckers [because t]hey may be the same people." Stegner knows that mistakes happened, charts the dire consequences, and recognizes that the blunders remain part of the rough and still unfinished story:

> True or false … it has all gone into the hopper and influenced our understanding and response. … The … mapping of great areas of the West was not completed for decades after real exploration had ended; and the trial and error … by which we began to be an oasis civilization was forced upon us by country and climate, but against the most mule-headed resistance and unwillingness to understand, accept and change. (Stegner 1992: 49)

Just as open land and scale – created and magnified by aridity – led to long-term misperceptions of the West, so too did the seeming absence of color lead to mistakes. Color is hard to see in the desert West because we don't get the contrast that comes with greener climates. If western spaces lack the distinction between foreground and background, the same holds true with respect to the color spectrum. Those desert browns, beiges, sage greens, and stark whites constitute, as Fox notes, "a spectrum of color so narrow that [newcomers] just couldn't see the sagebrush, shadescale" and other "chromatic subtleties of the land" (Fox 2000: 12). You have to "get over the color green," as Stegner famously put it, stop "associating beauty with gardens and lawns" (1992: 54), and start seeing new and distinct shades of brown, gray, sand, and sage.

Western Mobility: Character and Community

Moreover, such misperceptions of the West create habits of thought, culture, and settlement that result in a transient West – in settlers thinking that they can force or trick a land into yielding vast crops, rose gardens, instant gold, or plentiful water. When these schemes fail, the dreamers pick up and move to the next place. As Stegner's "myth-deflating autobiographical novel" illustrates, the West is strewn with the wreckage of dreams gone sour" (LaDow 2002: 274). Modeled on Stegner's father, Bo Mason, of *The Big Rock Candy Mountain*, may have been a "good story-teller, a hearty drinker and a ribald companion" (Stegner 1991: 29); but he was also a western man "born with the itch in his bones … telling stories of men who had gone over the hills to some new place and found a land of Canaan, made their pile [and] got to be big men in the communities they fathered" (Stegner 1991: 83). And that fictional father searched a lifetime, dragging family in his wake, always looking for "some Big Rock Candy Mountain where life was effortless and rich and unrestricted and full of adventure and action, where something could be had for nothing" (Stegner 1991: 83). Bo left a family without a feeling of home, and he created – like other transient seekers in that early West – an American landscape sorely lacking in community, sorely lacking in what Stegner calls "stickers." "Deeply lived in places," as Stegner laments, "are exceptions rather than the rule in the West." A "recognizable culture" in the West, one to "match the scenery," must come from the "stickers" – not those who pillage and run but ... those who settle and love the life they have made and the place they have made it in" (Stegner 1992: p. xxvii).

The legacy? The interior, arid West, as Stegner writes, was "largely a civilization in motion, driven by dreams." Recalling Margaret Mead's quip that the West was just an "overnight camp," Stegner finds that the arid West has "space" instead of "place" (1992: 72), that the interior West is "not a place but a way, a trail to the Promised Land ... [filled less with] settlements than way stations" (1992: 70). And those trails or "ways" that do last, which do become towns, emerge less as a social unit or community than as a random arrangement of buildings, "lost and self-sufficient, scruffy and indispensable." Town roads lead into "wide emptiness" through a "fringe of service stations, taverns, a motel or two," pass a few "commercial buildings," and then disappear "into more wide emptiness" (Stegner 1992: 74). Mobility, here, is a "curse." When "Charles Dickens, in the Mississippi Valley, met a full-sized dwelling house coming down the road at a round trot, he was looking at the American people head on" (Stegner 1992: 71, 72). Westerners are on the move and potentially without a sense of place. In Kittredge's *Owning It All*, a roughneck, working on Wyoming oilrigs, set up his life in this way:

[He] ran his big-tired diesel Ford pickup down to Ogden and hauled back about three-thousand dollars worth of motel furniture from a wholesale outlet, everything but a TV, and set up housekeeping in the sagebrush around a fire ring. He lived there like a crowned king of the imagination until October, when the rains commenced. He left the stuff sitting, and headed back to winter in Texas ... [E]verything on rubber, and open roads. (Kittredge 1987: 111–12)

Looking back on his childhood, Stegner laments that he was "born on wheels" (1992: 3) and tries to understand the harsh realities of western mobility, both through his childhood experience and the character of his restless father. Early on, Stegner lived and breathed "characteristic western migratoriness," spending his "first five years [in] ... constant motion" (1992: 4) and living in more than twenty houses between the ages of 12 and 20 (1992: 15). If his mother was associated with "place," or at least with trying to make a place and a home, and with family albums in the attic and a backyard worn with the years of play and life, his father "believed only in movement" (1992: 33).

Space and aridity produce mobility; and that mobility shapes a culture, a family and, in *Big Rock Candy Mountain*, the characters of Bo Mason and his son, Bruce. After entering law school, and shortly after his brother's death, Bruce struggles to understand the scope, history, and meaning of his troubled family, especially Bo. In the wake of Chet's death, Bruce sees that, in the Mason family, "everything got off on the wrong foot" (Stegner, 1991: 436). He considers that, in trying to understand himself and his family, it's almost impossible to know "[w]here to begin" – with himself, his father, grandfather? "[W]here did the evil come in?" (1991: 436). Once again, it's hard to tell the good guys from the bad, and blame becomes hard to assign because "any person is an exercise in genealogy. A man is not a static organism ... [but] movement, motion, a continuum. There is no beginning to him. He runs through his ancestors" (1991: 436). So, just for starters, Bruce begins with his father's "observable characteristics" (1991: 436).

Bo Mason sought "quick wealth" but was hemmed in by a "streak of penuriousness ... a kind of Dutch caution" (1991: 437). He was a "self-centered and dominating egotist" who ruled over his family with his will but who remained "completely dependent on his wife" (1991: 437). But his traits and even his do not even "scratch[] the surface" because "everything has a history that goes back [to] ... a vanishing point" (1991: 437). Bo left home at 14; he "worked in the woods on the railroad and as a big league ball player" (1991: 438). That history – and more – produced a man with an "evil temper ... egotism and physical energy" whose penchant for chasing pipe-dreams, wearing down his wife, and humiliating his son left a legacy.

After Bo dies – first killing his mistress in a cheap hotel lobby and then shooting himself – Bruce resumes his accounting of his father. Sitting in "judgment," he finds Bo "guilty of violence, brutality, [and] willfulness ... inconsiderate of others[, and] obtuse about their wishes" (1991: 560). Dragging the family from one failure-ridden spot to another, from one boom-and-bust scheme to the next Big Break, Bo all the while "chafed against domestic restraints, ruled by violence ... [and] forced his wife and children to live a life they despised and hated. ... He wore out his wife and broke her heart, he destroyed one son and turned the other against him" (1991: 560).

With his Klondike scheme, his managing of a rundown lunchroom in Washington state, his land rush in Saskatchewan, his liquor running in Utah and his work in a Reno gambling joint, Bo Mason, like Stegner's father, wrecked lives. Moreover, as the Introduction to *Where the Bluebird Sings to the Lemonade Springs* makes clear, Bo Mason's life story constitutes Stegner's "first and most heartfelt commentary on Western opti-mism and enterprise and the common man's dream of something for nothing. ... [The] vagrant's vision of beatitude [and a Big Rock Candy Mountain where all is well] summarized his unquenchable hope as it summarizes the indigenous optimism of the West. ... What lures many people to the West has always been, and still is, mirage" (Stegner 1992: p. xxi).

Western Mobility Reconsidered

Despite this critique of western transience, Stegner does not claim that "western hopefulness is a cynical joke" (Stegner 1992: p. xxii); indeed, he tries "to give hope the last word" (LaDow 2002: 278). More particularly, the mobility and transience that marked both Stegner's father and Bo Mason come up for re-evaluation. Given Stegner's harsh portrait of his own father and of Bo, and given his attendant critique of a boom-and-bust culture that led hoboes and settlers, miners and ranchers, and wives and children out to a West that would become used and abused, Stegner is right: we do need to "amend" our enthusiasms about the wide-open West. It's a fragile environment that has too often been taken to the bank – over-grazed, over-built, over-mined, and over-mythologized. And it lacks community and a sense of place because of those mistakes. And yet Stegner's complaints about the transience that kept us from settling into and caring for western lands and communities constitute only part of his account. In fact, the opening paragraphs to *Where the Bluebird Sings* are worth quoting at length because they articulate Stegner's heartfelt faith in the still-present promise of the West:

> Once I said in print that the remaining western wilderness is the geography of hope, and ... that the West at large is hope's native home, the youngest and freshest of America's regions, magnificently endowed and with the chance to become something unprecedented and unmatched in the world.
>
> [N]othing would gratify me more than to see [the West become] both prosperous and environmentally healthy. Whenever I return to the Rocky Mountain states where I am most at home ... the smell of distance excites me, the largeness and the clarity take the scales from my eyes, and I respond as unthinkingly as a salmon that swims past a rivermouth and tastes the waters of its birth. (Stegner 1992: p. xv)

This hope is not based merely on nostalgia or the emotional rush of witnessing the sublime landscape of the West. Instead, Stegner's hope for a culture to match western lands is in part underwritten by the consequences of western aridity and transience. Indeed even Stegner's land ethic is rarely straightforward, revealing him to be a some-time enthusiastic and sometime "unlikely and reluctant environmentalist" (LaDow 2002: 274). Both *Where the Bluebird Sings* and *Big Rock Candy Mountain* offer an argument not often associated with Stegner's environmental ethic: they both suggest that a reasonable strategy in an arid land is in fact some form of transience – some form of continuing movement and adaptation. In this reconsideration, movement and mobility aren't just symptoms of a placeless people, but, in certain forms, the real beginnings of a character and "civilization to match the scenery."

Picking up on Stegner's and DeVoto's, as well as Paul Starrs' claims about eastern misperceptions of western land, consider for a moment whether some of our well-intentioned models of place – commitment to community in place, staying put, becoming a "sticker" – are themselves not truly fitted to the West and are, perhaps, remnants of previous eastern misperceptions. Wonder if staying in place – and denouncing the transience and mobility so associated with boom-and-bust life in the West – is good for communities but not always good for the land? We have deemed late nineteenth- and twentieth-century transience as indicative of an empty and greedy culture afflicted by placelessness and as symptomatic of a boom-and-bust economy that ravaged an innocent landscape and gutted native cultures. And we have reacted against that extractive, abusive model by reassessing our role on the land, by assessing our part in its decline, and by hunkering down and becoming "stickers." But sometimes even the best environmental and cultural intentions can be built on misperceptions.

Over the past twenty years, Americans have thought a lot about *place*. They've tried to counter the effects of a people on the move with a renewed attention to the local, to the regional. In much of the New Western history from the 1990s, in ecocriticism and in Douglas Reichert Powell's more recent vision of New Critical regionalism, they've been assessing the costs of their national greed and mobility; and, for the good of the land and their culture, they have searched for a new land ethic and a new approach to their places, trying to frame what Michael Malone calls a "genuine regionalism" (Malone 1991: 100). Despite the good intentions, and frequently good results, however, one can't help but wonder if part of this model isn't inspired as much by Thoreau's verdant New England as by the topography of the arid West. Some American notions of place – in particular, the dismissal of transience and mobility – are quite possibly still bound up in eastern models of place where staying put in one spot can yield good crops and a good life because water, shade, and plentiful plant life offer food, shelter and stability for the long term.

However, if Stegner, in his introduction to *Where the Bluebird Sings to the Lemonade Springs*, feels compelled to "amend [his] enthusiasm" for the West's redemptive myth of open land and hope with the sobering realities of the environmental and cultural damage, he also – albeit less explicitly – amends this critique of mobility with models of adaptation that *require* mobility, motion, and transience. In other words, Stegner's rejection of transience isn't as complete as it seems. Within his critique of western mobility dwells the following message: mobility, temporary settlements, and continual movement over land may, in fact, be the best way to adapt to an arid West. Mobility and transience still hold a limited promise for Stegner and remain an essential, although seldom noticed, part of Stegner's vision of a "civilization to match the scenery" (Stegner 1992: p. xv).

To begin with, in an autobiographical essay, Stegner admits to himself that he "had [his] father's restless blood in [him], and the habit of moving" (1992: 19). And, in *Big Rock Candy Mountain*, much of Bo lives on in his son. In fact, what makes this novel not only a critique and an epic of the West, but also a heartfelt portrait laced with forgiveness and understanding of those same excesses, is Bruce's ultimate acceptance of his father's traits in himself. By the end, Bruce recognizes and even embraces mobility, transience, and life on the road. They become, for him, a source of identity and, ultimately, his home.

The pivotal recognition-scene begins when Bruce, after his first year in law school in Minnesota, comes back West for his brother's funeral. His mother and father are now living in Tahoe and his father helps run a gambling joint outside of Reno. En route, Bruce cannot bring himself to say or even think that he's returning "home" because – at the beginning stage of his reflections and coming revelation – he doesn't yet know where or even what home would be. He is going back, "[b]ut going home where? Where do I belong in this?" He proceeds to list and question, as he drives across the "continental sprawling hugeness of America" (Stegner 1991: 457), all the particular regions or places that *might* be home: Reno? He's never "been in Reno more than six hours" (1991: 458). Salt Lake City, where the Masons settled for a time while Bo ran liquor, isn't sufficient either. Maybe it's Minnesota, he thinks, because his mother came from there. Or perhaps "some Pennsylvania valley" from which a "great or great-great grandfather ... started moving rootless around the continent" (1991: 458). Or perhaps Great Forks, North Dakota, where he was born "behind a bar in a cheap hotel" (1991: 459). "Or maybe," he thinks, he has "never been home" (1991: 458). And if home "isn't where your family comes from, and isn't where you were born," maybe it's "where you spent your childhood" (1991: 459). But with an itinerant childhood and a family that never stopped moving, these working definitions fall short and Bruce lets "himself envy people who had all those things" that spoke of a solid home "under one roof" – memories packed into baseball mitts in the basement and photo albums in the living room near a well-worn sofa (1991: 459). He longs, in this unfolding fantasy of place, to be like those who can "know always ... that there was one place to which you belonged and to which you would return ... to know and love a single place" (1991: 460), rich in childhood and family recollections: "I wish ... that I were going home to a place where all the associations of twenty-two years were collected together. I wish I could go out in the back yard and see the mounded ruins of caves I dug when I was eight" (1991: 460).

Bruce's discontent over his own rootless past leads him to see the problem as extended into a larger picture in which his own lack of a coherent history becomes America's problem writ large. Stegner, as his biography of DeVoto illustrates, tends toward "[h]istory by synecdoche" – or, as Beth LaDow describes it, "the illumination of whole areas and periods through concentration upon one brief time, one single-sequence, a ... representative character" (LaDow 2002: 240). The whole nation – here in the 1930s, but living out a legacy from a boom-and-bust past – has "been footloose too long." These "were the things that not only his family but thousands of Americans had missed. ... Heaven had been just over the next range for too many generations" (Stegner 1991: 460).

As the scene builds towards epiphany, Bruce realizes that he's more like his father than he'd thought – more like Bo Mason, who "can't stand to be still for a minute" (Stegner 1991: 448). Bruce concedes that he "had a notion," after all, " where home would turn out to be, for himself, as for his father: over the next range, on the Big Rock Candy Mountain, that place of impossible loveliness that had pulled the whole nation westward" (1991: 460–1). With the beginnings of this admission, Bruce – in near-echoes of Whitman's celebration of land and names in the 1855 *Preface* – plays with town and place names and uses them to see, celebrate, and "place" a growing sense of identity. "[I]ntoxicating himself on names" (Stegner, 1991: 458), he makes up limericks for the little Plains towns he drives through: "A Jesus from Grand Forks,

No Dak / Went hunting his home with a Kodak. / There were plenty of mansions / And suburban expansions / But no home, either No. Dak or So. Dak." Bruce's plays on town and place names here echoes Stegner's intense interest in the Adamic process by which American places received – or inspired – their names. In "George Stewart and the American Land," Stegner records his interest in Stewart's *Names on the Land*, which considers "how we went about putting our marks on the unnamed continent, and in doing so both added ourselves to the continent and added the continent to ourselves" (Stegner 1992: 157). Names that emerged from the European presence in North America are still young enough to be "traceable, or at least guessable" (1992: 167). The histories are still accessible in those places. And, with the history still accessible – with the attempts at "civilization building" (1992: 176) still readable – the beginnings of the story of a place are accessible. Place names help us do this looking back to origins and remind us that "nothing is comprehended, much less possessed, until it has been given a name" (1992: 168).

The wordplay on place names continues as Bruce drives through Minnesota, dreaming up a limerick about "A maiden from Alibert Lea / Though her knee had been bit by a flea. / She lifted her skirt / To see what had hurt , / But it wasn't a flea, it was me" (Stegner 1991: 458–9). With the pluck of a Dean Moriarty, Bruce is soon "bounc[ing] into the streets of Faribault talking to himself." Taking in the street life, he sees a young man "squiring up two dressed-up girls" and the "earnestness" of the man's attempt to be "scrupulously impartial, to offer an arm to each, to keep his head turning on a metronome swing from one to the other made Bruce laugh." Town and place become a little poem: "There were two pretty maidens from Faribault / Who agreed they would willingly share a beau / But one beau to a pair / Was no better than fair. / It was worse than not fair, it was taibault" (1991: 458).

The miles and open spaces roll by as Bruce crosses the plains, and, from his car, he adds local signs to the mix of rhymed land and words:

> "We love our children. Please drive slow."
>   We're also proud of our hybrid corn.
> "Registered Rest Rooms. Road maps free. Snappy
>   service – Just toot your horn"
> Ma's Home Cooking and Herb's Good Eats, …
>   Rotary every Thursday noon,
> And the wind of a hurrying car ahead blowing the
>   flat green-tumbleweed.
>
>   (Stegner 1991: 463)

An echo of Whitman's endless lists of American places, rivers, and people and Kerouac's celebration of local billboards and diners as Sal and Dean traverse the bulge of the continent, Bruce's own list signals the beginning of his embrace of the road, and his acceptance of the road as home.

With these tributes to life seen through a Ford windshield, Bruce slowly lets go his longing for home as a fixed, regional place and starts to feel at home in the driver's seat. Despite all the torment of wishing for a stable home place, "he felt good" and "settl[ed,] his bare arm gingerly on the hot door [as he] opened his mouth to sing" (Stegner 1991: 460). As Bruce begins his own "Song of the Open Road" and advances to a new definition of home, he watches "the straight road running clean and white westward." The "sky to the West was a clear blue ... clean and pure and empty, as if there were nothing beyond, or everything." He starts here – under a western sky and with an open horizon in his vision – to understand "the itch to see the unknown world." Like Bo, he admits, he "could easily enough have been a chaser of rainbows." And he finds it "easy to see why men moved westward as inevitably as the roulette-ball of a sun rolled that way. ... There were so many chances, such lovely possibilities" (Stegner 1991: 461).

Seeing his father in himself and feeling, as a result, the pull of the continent's horizon, Bruce articulates a new and evolving definition of home. All right, "I'll take it, he said. I love it, whatever good that does. Even if I don't know *where* home is, I know *when* I *feel* at home" (Stegner 1991: 463; emphasis on "where" and "when" added). Born of his road journey, Bruce's home in the West begins to be less bound to location and more to time; in an echo of Frederick Jackson Turner, his evolving West has less to do with place than process. By shifting a definition of a home in the West from "where" to "when," Bruce finds, for the first time, a feeling of home: he pulls in to the "next service station ... and felt it even stronger, the feeling of belonging, of being in a well-worn and familiar groove" (1991: 463). Giving in simultaneously to his family's migratory past and his own undefined future, and relegating his sense of belonging less to place than to motion and time, Bruce gives in: "Anything beyond the Missouri was close to home, at least. He was a westerner, whatever that was. ... [T]he minute the grass got sparser and the air dryer and the service stations less grandiose and the towns rattier ... [h]e knew [h]e belonged" (1991: 463–4).

Bruce surrenders to the relief brought on by his realization that his home is in his movement – that his "place," literally, is in motion. The recognition and "feeling came on him like sun after an overcast day, and in pure contentment he limbered his knees and slouched deeper against the Ford's lefthand door" (Stegner 1991: 464). Bruce's point of reference and support is now a means of motion, literally a vehicle; and his surrender to the migratory life it spins out – his surrender, really, to the life of his father and the life of a still-beckoning continent – puts him back on the road and brings him home for the first time. With the reddening sun highlighting Bruce's revelation as steadily as it illuminated Cather's prairie plow, the sky's last light intensifies and Bruce – an American wanderer desperate for a sense of place – finally arrives home:

> At sunset he was still wheeling across the plains toward Chamberlain, the sun fiery through the dust and the wide wings of the west going red to saffron to green as he watched, and the horizon ahead of him vast and empty and beckoning like an open gate. At ten o'clock he was still driving, and at twelve. As long as the road ran west he didn't

want to stop, because that was where he was going, west beyond the Dakotas toward home. (Stegner 1991: 464)

Stegner's language finely tunes a young man's definition of home. Here, the traveler does not *arrive* home. That is, he does not arrive at a set location or place, complete with front porch, yard, and memories. He also does not arrive at a final, complete or certain destination, but is merely oriented *toward* home. Like Emerson's seeker in "Experience," or many a traveler in American road stories, Bruce is home when he is seeking, when he is en route, when he is enacting connections and paths on and over the land. His western home is not contained either by location or certainty, but is found on the road – on the created path that connects one space with another. Here, dwelling and place-making on the one hand and travel and motion on the other work together. Place-making, for Bruce, is not about staying put but involves, as Heidegger claims of dwelling, connecting "near and remote locales" (Heidegger 1993: 359). To dwell, as Urry writes, is "always to be moving and sensing, both within and beyond" (Urry 2007: 31). Even bridges, as Urry notes, do not connect banks that already exist as banks. They are not places yet. The stream banks, Urry argues, "only emerge as a consequence of a bridge." Or, as Heidegger puts it: the bridge "brings stream and bank and land into each other's neighborhood" (Heidegger 1993: 354). Similarly, roads – the built pathways on the earth over which we travel – enact or "gather" a connection between places (Heidegger 1993: 354). Time on these roads, and time in motion, *becomes* Bruce's route to finding home, his means of place-making.

Moreover, like a Jamesian, pragmatic truth, Stegner's emerging model of place is ever in the making, always on the move. Thus, in "Thoughts on a Dry Land," Stegner praises the migratory lives described in Karl Kranzel's *The Great Plains in Transition*. These men "had to develop the same mobility that marked the buffalo, antelope, wolves, coyotes, and horse Indians in that country. They go as far for a swim or for shopping as an antelope will go for a drink, and for very similar reasons. They often go hundreds of miles to farm":

> [T]he suitcase farmer ... spends the winter in some town or city ... but ... in early Spring hitches his trailer-home to his pickup and takes off for the West. ... There he plants his wheat ... living through the summer in his trailer and driving forty or fifty miles for his supplies and entertainment. In the fall, he harvests his crop, does his fall plowing, hitches up his trailer again, and returns to [some distant town]. (Stegner 1992: 51)

This account of mobility as a "sensible adaptation" is not a pillaging of resources or an undermining of placed communities, but a nomadic and adaptive strategy that suits a dry environment. Aridity, after all, is a "difficult fact of life for Americans to accept, and an even more difficult one for them to adapt to" (Stegner 1992: p. xvii). One of these days, we have to "accept the limitations imposed by aridity," Stegner writes; and mobility and even the isolation it brings may be a smart move towards that end.

At Home on the Range:
Mobility as a Modern, Adaptive Strategy

The modern individual is, above all else, a mobile human being. (Sennett 1994: 255)

Casting a new light on Kittredge's oilrig worker with all of his scattered motel furniture, Stegner reminds us that open space and aridity naturally create mobility. We should not overdo it, of course, but neither can or should we reject it entirely – mobility and transience needn't be "placed" out of the West. As long as aridity reigns west of the 100th meridian, process, movement and transience will be a part of *place*. In his essays, and in the final quarter of *Big Rock Candy Mountain*, Stegner puts *mobility* back into a *sense of place* in the West. Or, better said, by putting place into motion, he suggests that true adaptation to an arid, even desert, West includes not only nesting or "stick[ing]" (Stegner 1992: p. xxii) to one place, but also movement and ranging over that land.

The transient West and the restless life it prompted may be a cliché or frontier legacy that Americans would like to move past. Hoboes and train-riders, road-novels and drifter-heroes can seem like popular types from a previous era, and even seem like obstacles to a life committed to place, community, and environmental stability. But before they dismiss these Dean Moriarty fantasies – even these Bo Masons – as romantic enactments of a false consciousness, or as nostalgic players in an earlier time, they might consider the arid, western places that prompted these enactments. With aridity as its geographically and culturally determining trait, the West can inspire an embrace of mobility and an acceptance of the road. Through Bruce's discovery of home as on the road in the West, Stegner revises and enlarges his vision of a "civilization to match the scenery" by including movement and motion in his epic account of western place; in so doing, he suggests that movement and ranging may, in fact, be a suitable form of adaptation in an arid West. In these closing chapters of Stegner's autobiographical epic, Bruce Mason puts place into motion and finds himself – to recall a cliché – at home on the range.

Moreover these scenes suggest a viability and necessity generated by a "will to connection," or what Georg Simmel calls the "miracle of the road" (Simmel 1997: 171). A true "civilization to match the scenery," then, reveals that nomadic movement and ranging over land constitutes a legitimate adaptation to the environment. Indeed, Tim Cresswell's *On the Move* proposes that cultural studies, anthropology, and sociology, as well as architecture, provide useful ways of seeing mobility as "socially produced motion" that operates within "fields of power and meaning" (Cresswell 2006: 10). The social construction and enactment of mobility peak in our own age as a result of the fluidity accrued from capital, trade, tourism, and exchange. Cresswell locates the roots of this modern – or postmodern – practice, however, in earlier times, as well.

In an intriguing linkage that leads to a connection between mobility and early modern notions of freedom, Cresswell turns to the early seventeenth century to note William Harvey's revolutionary theories on the flow of blood through the body. He further suggests that Galileo's not unrelated claim that the "natural state of things was movement with rest being a mere accident" continues the life of an idea. This emerging world, for Galileo and Harvey, was an "infinite, restless entanglement of persistent movement" and motion (Cresswell 2006: 14). An early modern idea of mobility as freedom, however, emerges more pointedly with Hobbes, who "borrowed from Galileo's new science to place relentless movement at the heart of a philosophy of human life that equated movement with liberty" and who consciously echoed Harvey: "Now vital movement is the movement of the blood," Hobbes writes, "perpetually circulating (as has been shown ... by Doctor Harvey) in the veins and arteries." Thus, Hobbes claims that "Liberty signifieth (properly) the absence of Opposition; (by Opposition, I mean externall Impediments of movement)" (qtd. in Cresswell 2006: 14). Mobility further streams into our modern and postmodern worlds, of course, in the form of migration, colonial empires; as Appadurai notes, migration is "at the heart of the modern" (Cresswell 2006: 19).

Mobility and placedness become, for Cresswell, ideologically produced and producing "moral geographies." In his critique of our dependence on placedness as a measure of cultural maturity and stability, he turns to figures who come under fire for marginalizing the importance of mobility and privileging the supposedly innate urge to find a stable place. In contrast to urban architects and landscape critics such as Robert Venturi, Denise Scott Brown, Bernard Tschumi, and J.B. Jackson – all of whom see buildings and landscape through the lens of motion – Yi-Fu Tuan becomes associated with a "sedentarist metaphysics," which sees "place, home and roots ... as a fundamental human need":

> As place is an essentially moral concept, mobility and movement [in Tuan], insofar as they undermine attachment and commitment, are antithetical to moral worlds. By implication, mobility appears to involve a number of absences – the absence of commitment and attachment and involvement – a lack of significance. Places marked by an abundance of mobility become *placeless*. (Cresswell 2006: 31)

More recently, anthropologists James Clifford and Marc Auge offer progress beyond the place vs. mobility model in their very terminology. Replacing "roots" with "routes," Clifford writes: "If we rethink culture ... in terms of travel then the organic, naturalizing bias of the term culture – seen as a rooted body that grows, lives, dies, etc., – is questioned. Constructed and disputed historicities, sites of displacement, interference, and interaction, come more sharply into view" (Clifford 1992: 101). As travel increases and migrations grow, cultures are no longer exclusively placed or "anchored since time immemorial in the permanence of an intact soil" (Auge 1995: 44).

If "[m]obile lives need nomad thought to make a new kind of sense" (Clifford 1992: 44), Stegner's American West – anchored as our understanding of it has been in place, soil, and landscape – offers a glimpse into place-appropriate nomadism. These mobilities, embraced by Bruce at the end of Stegner's epic novel, allow and advocate a mobility prompted by aridity and open space and echoing not a nostalgic frontier past but a migratory, contemporary western experience.

REFERENCES

Appadurai, Arjun. (1996). *Modernity at Large*. Minneapolis: University of Minnesota Press.

Auge, Marc. (1995). *Non-Places: Introduction to an Anthropology of Supermodernity*. London: Verso.

Camp, Jennie A. (2007). Angling for Repose: Demythologizing the American West in Wallace Stegner's *The Big Rock Candy Mountain*. *South Dakota Review*, 74/2, 19–39.

Clifford, James. (1992). Traveling Cultures. In Lawrence Grossberg, Cary Nelson, and Paula Treichler, eds., *Cultural Studies*, pp. 96–111. London: Routledge.

Cresswell, Tim. (2006). *On the Move: Mobility in the Modern Western World*. London: Routledge.

DeVoto, Bernard. (1952). *The Course of Empire*. Boston: Houghton Mifflin.

Ehrlich, Gretel. (1985). *The Solace of Open Spaces*. New York: Penguin Books.

Etulain, Richard. (1996). *Re-Imagining the Modern American West: A Century of Fiction, History and Art*. Tucson: University of Arizona Press.

Fox, William L. (2000). *The Void, the Grid and the Sign: Traversing the Great Basin*. Reno: University of Nevada Press.

Hanson, Ralph E. (2001). The Smell of Distance: Wallace Stegner's Definition of Western Non-Fiction. *Social Science Journal*, 38/4, 557–65.

Heidegger, Martin. (1993). *Basic Writings*, ed. D. Farrell Krell. London: Routledge.

Hobbes, Thomas. (1839). *The English Works of Thomas Hobbes of Malmesbury*. London: J. Bohn.

James, William. (1975). *Pragmatism and The Meaning of Truth*. Cambridge, MA: Harvard University Press.

Kerouac, Jack. (2002). *On the Road*. New York: Penguin Books.

Kittredge, William. (1987). *Owning It All*. St. Paul: Graywolf Press.

LaDow, Beth. (2002). Geography of Hope Revisited. *Reviews in American History*, 30/2, 273–8.

Malone, Michael. (1991).The "New Western History," an Assessment. In Patricia Nelson Limerick, Clyde A. Milner II, and Charles E. Rankin, eds., *Trails: Toward a New Western History*. Lawrence: University Press of Kansas.

Packer, Nancy Huddleston. (2009). Wallace Stegner: A Passionate and Committed Heart. *Sewanee Review*, 117/2, 208–22.

Sennett, Richard. (1994). *Flesh and Stone: The Body and the City in Western Civilization*. New York: W.W. Norton.

Simmel, G. (1990). *The Philosophy of Money*. London: Routledge.

Simmel, G. (1997). *Simmel on Culture*, ed. D. Frisby and M. Featherston. London: Sage.

Starrs, Paul. (2000). *Let the Cowboy Ride: Cattle Ranching in the American West*. Baltimore: Johns Hopkins University Press.

Stegner, Wallace. (1991). *The Big Rock Candy Mountain*. New York: Penguin Books.

Stegner, Wallace. (1992). *Where the Bluebird Sings to the Lemonade Springs: Living and Writing in the American West*. New York: Penguin Books.

Stegner, Wallace, and Page Stegner. (1999). *Marking the Sparrow's Fall*. New York: Holt Paperbacks.

Thrift, Nigel. (2004). Movement-Space: The Changing Domain of Thinking Resulting from the Development of New Kinds of Spatial Awareness. *Economy and Society*, 33, 582–604.

Tuan, Yi-Fu. (1977). *Space and Place: The Perspective of Experience*. Minneapolis: University of Minnesota Press.

Urry, John. (2007). *Mobilities*. Cambridge: Polity.

Webb, Walter Prescott. (1931). *The Great Plains*. New York: Grosset & Dunlap.

32

The Global West:
Temporality, Spatial Politics,
and Literary Production

Susan Kollin

> a central concern … is how to think differently about the American West, to decentral-
> ize and dislocate the ways it has so often been considered, even among so-called revision-
> ist writers and scholars, so that we might see westness as part of a larger system of
> discourse, beyond the national imaginary, pointing in many directions at once. (Campbell
> 2008: 41)

At a time when scholars of American literature and culture are recasting their research
through new frameworks provided by globalization in the form of transnational,
hemispheric, and postnational American studies, the field of US regional criticism has
also undergone a significant remapping. In the case of western American literary
studies, US borderlands scholars have offered productive means of reconceptualizing
the region, moving away from notions of the American West as a bounded or static
entity toward an understanding of the space as an ever-shifting and contested geography shaped by various flows and movements across the US–Mexican border. Scholars
of Asian American literature and culture have likewise offered useful models for
refiguring the region by focusing on the travels of human labor, capital, and culture
across the Pacific Rim as well as the various barriers and exclusions to such movements. In examining the complexities of these larger transnational attachments as
well as the cultures of the diaspora and the politics of the borderlands, such scholars
have helped disrupt the Turnerian model that once dominated western American
scholarship and that positioned the region as a frontier zone whose meanings emerge
from a narrowly focused Euro-American experience.[1]

In a similar way, the insights of ecocriticism and transnational environmental
movements have also complicated notions of regions and other local terrain as bounded

A Companion to the Literature and Culture of the American West, First Edition. Edited by
Nicolas S. Witschi.
© 2011 Blackwell Publishing Ltd. Published 2011 by Blackwell Publishing Ltd.

space, with factors such as global climate change, struggles over land use, species extinction, and concerns about toxic landscapes decidedly ignoring the borders of local spaces as defined by human populations. As ecocritics and activists have long noted, none of us escapes the impact of global ecological developments; all local spaces and communities are intimately tied to the events that take place elsewhere. Thus, in recent years, a significant body of literature has emerged that examines the relation between local communities in the American West and larger global environmental developments, from the novels of Karen Tei Yamashita and Ana Castillo, to the fiction of Leslie Marmon Silko and Ruth Ozeki.[2]

Given these challenges, scholars of western American literature have likewise begun locating new routes of inquiry for conceptualizing the region, and in doing so have placed the US West back at the center of national and world maps. As a popular construct in the dominant national imagination, the American West has typically functioned as a meaningful geography precisely because it was somehow positioned off the map. Figured as a marginal zone situated far from the national center, the West was imagined as unmapped terrain, an empty land awaiting the arrival of intrepid American Adams and Eves, never mind that it was already occupied by Native Americans and that it was also the site of other nations' national desires. Alongside this spatial discourse, a temporal logic also emerged that positioned the region as a land outside time, a terrain that somehow escapes historical changes. Within this logic, the region came to hold significance as anti-modern space, a prelapsarian landscape that offers a refuge from the turmoil and conflict located in the hyperdeveloped centers of the nation and the rest of the world. As a result, cultural production about the region was often shaped by anxieties concerning threats to those edenic spaces and the seemingly inevitable loss of the region's wildness.

Such tropes of space and time necessarily require the erasure of different histories and understandings of the land, a point driven home in studies of multiculturalism and globalization. As such criticism indicates, competing dreams and ideas about the region have produced a space whose meanings and identity shift depending on the location of the observer. In theorizing notions of place for a global era, Philip Joseph points to how American literary regionalism has often functioned "at the center of a public conversation on locality that has become all but closed to the modern realities of transcultural movements and multicentered subjectivity" (2006: 10). Throughout history, however, the American West has been understood by competing populations and through different geographical imaginaries. As "Gold Mountain," "El Norte," "Russian America," "the frontier," or simply home, the many Wests came into existence precisely because the terrain attracted the attention of diverse populations across the nation and the globe.[3] Far from being a land located outside history or a space of retreat opposed to the forces of hyperdevelopment, the American West might be better understood as the very product of a larger history and culture of modernization that is transnational and global in scope.

A recognition of these multiply inflected Wests requires critics to reassess previous assumptions shaping regional studies. Neil Campbell argues, for instance, that the concept of a bounded, contained region must be abandoned in favor of a "multifaceted, evolving discursive formation constantly spilling out, reforming, splitting, and connecting" (2008: 22). While he concedes that there indeed exists a "'mappable,' gridded West defined by state and national borders that one could label as region," the vision by itself is ultimately "too narrow and restrictive, excluding vital aspects of all that exceeded such contained definitions" (2008: 41). As Campbell explains, the American West "has never been simply a geographical region contained by traditions and customs; it is instead a complex construction, an architecture, designed and built by the intersection of discourses from many interested parties, refracted through time, space, and nations" (2008: 42). Indeed, for many critics region itself is best understood as a symptom of larger national and global forces and flows of power. Hsuan Hsu argues along these lines, suggesting that critics treat regional literature less as a genre than as a discourse, what he calls the "*imagining* of a local community that at least *appears* to be distinct from external forces" (Hsu 2009: 219, my emphasis). For Hsu, regional spaces may be understood as sites of struggle that emerge out of "discrepancies in culture, wealth, or power between regional settings and metropolitan centers: the word 'region' after all, derives from the Latin *regere* ('to rule'), and denotes a spatial unit of control" (2009: 219).

Such discrepancies about the meaning of place have captured the interest of critics studying the fate of the local in the wake of globalization. Critic Anna Lowenhaupt Tsing describes such contact as "friction," an interaction that involves "awkward, unequal, unstable, and creative qualities of interconnection across difference" (2005: 1, 4). Elaborating on the possibilities entailed in the metaphor, she explains:

> a study of global connections shows the grip of encounter: friction. A wheel turns because of its encounter with the surface of the road; spinning in the air goes nowhere. Rubbing two sticks together produces heat and light; one stick is just a stick. As a metaphorical image, friction reminds us that heterogeneous and unequal encounters can lead to new arrangements of culture and power. (2005: 5)

For Tsing, the outcome of global encounters of difference and diversity may have dual or competing results that cannot be determined in advance. Such encounters may prove to be either "compromising or empowering" for local populations. As she explains, friction "is not a synonym for resistance. Hegemony is made as well as unmade with friction" (2005: 6).

James Welch's historical novel *The Heartsong of Charging Elk* provides a literary exploration of the "friction" that occurs as his young Oglala Sioux protagonist confronts national and global forces that bring changes to his community in the Black Hills. While Welch's narrative employs tropes of space and time that have been central to the logics of western American regionalism, it does so for decidedly different purposes. In Welch's text, temporality is at the center of debates concerning contact between the "New World" and the "Old World," as ideas of modern identity – based on an imagined divide between savagery and civilization, superstition and the

Enlightenment – become the battleground for the narrative's European and Native American characters. Spatial politics also play an important role in the text, as Welch's exploration of a global West indicates how local spaces themselves may be radically shaped by events and belief systems arising elsewhere. In his trans-Atlantic travels with the Wild West show, the protagonist Charging Elk undergoes a complicated and diverse quest for identity, and in the process highlights how populations, as Stephen Tatum has argued, may "simultaneously occupy multiple spaces – such as the local and the global" and how they may "possess multiple geographic imaginations" (2004: 462). Such understandings of time and space complicate popular constructions of the region and its narrative forms. Rather than serving as a space of retreat – a marginal terrain safely ensconced outside history – the American West in Welch's novel is fully located within a broader history of nation-building, imperialism as well as the global flows of populations, products, and ideas. As the protagonist himself experiences vexing problems as well as new possibilities because of these developments, the novel offers new maps for understanding and writing regional, national, and global spaces as well as the complex interaction between such entities.

Unbounded Regionalism and the Shifting Meanings of Home

Published in 2000, *The Heartsong of Charging Elk* opens in the late nineteenth century during a time of tremendous change for tribal peoples across the United States. Set in an era when American Indians faced forced relocation and confinement on reservation lands, the novel traces Charging Elk's experiences with Buffalo Bill's Wild West show and his subsequent travels to Europe, where he "plays Indian" to fascinated audiences. In Welch's novel, the main character ends up becoming stranded in a Marseilles hospital where he is recovering from injuries incurred on the job. There he is abandoned by the show after its members come to believe he has died of influenza. At first, Charging Elk is overwhelmed by nineteenth-century French society and tries to figure out ways of returning home to the Black Hills. The character's encounters with various aspects of French culture are indeed full of conflict and misunderstandings as he faces illness, poverty, sexual assault, and several years of imprisonment. Charging Elk eventually gains his freedom and learns the language and customs of the country. He meets Nathalie, a young woman from a provincial farm, with whom he falls in love; he ultimately chooses not to return to the reservation, but to instead make a new home for himself in France.

In many ways, Welch's novel may be read as a postwestern text that disrupts the codes and conventions of the classic western by reversing the geographical movement that propels the genre and its characters from east to west in favor of a journey from the Black Hills across the Atlantic to Europe. The novel likewise replaces the Anglo hero with an American Indian, a figure who is liberated from his role as the antagonist of national progress and Euro-American civilization, and who is no longer confined merely to experiences of dispossession and defeat. Instead, Welch's protagonist has access to mobility and adventures while managing to claim a full humanity for himself in his newly chosen home. In the process, Welch's narrative recasts the solitary individualism of the American Adam often populating the western and whose experiences, as R.W.B. Lewis writes, "emancipated from history, happily bereft of ancestry ... of family and race ... standing alone, self-reliant, and self-propelling," ultimately prove to be unhealthy models of identity (1995: 5). Welch's narrative unfolds in a slow, methodic manner, focusing less on the fast-paced action so central to the genre in order to dwell on the rich inner life of the main character. In moving beyond the popular western in his narrative, Welch likewise critiques other philosophical traditions that have shaped the imagined Indian in American culture. Through the main character's encounters with various populations and institutions across France, the novel examines the underside of the European Enlightenment, laying bare its false universalisms concerning truth, liberty, and what it means to be human, all of which had important consequences for how American Indians were historically represented and understood at home and abroad.

By focusing on the travels of Charging Elk outside tribal lands, Welch's novel also complicates aspects of contemporary American Indian fiction, especially those surrounding place and identity. P. Jane Hafen highlights the entanglements shaping both landscape and Indian identity in order to elucidate what is stake for Native American authors in the writing of place. She explains:

> the literature of indigenous peoples in regard to place or region has an imperative more compelling than any other American literatures. As original inhabitants of this continent and with a history of dispossession and removal and government-sanctioned attempts at cultural assimilation, contemporary American Indian writers have a unique perspective and responsibility. (Hafen 2003: 154)

Welch's decision to imagine the story of a fictional Indian character positioned in France, far away from his tribal community, actually came out of experiences he had during various book tours where he met French descendants of American Indians who had performed with the Wild West show in Europe and decided to stay behind, experiences that were also reported in autobiographical works by writers such as Luther Standing Bear and Nicholas Black Elk.[4] Giorgio Mariani notes how Welch's novel operates "against the grain of a critical tradition that sees American Indian novels as 'homing in'" by positioning the main character outside his local community in the American West where he must engage in redefinitions of home itself (2006: 218).[5] Mariani suggests that the novel explores the conflicts Indian characters face when global forces require them to move "beyond tradition" and locate new opportunities for finding "positive energies that, even at times of crisis, can carry us over to a further shore – across the Atlantic, across cultures, across language, across hearts" (2006: 218).

Charging Elk's travels outside the American West and his struggles to make a life for himself in France, however, do not entirely ignore the importance and meaning of place. Where he is located still matters here, as the character's displacement from tribal lands raises questions about the fate of Native populations in the wake of US nation-building and globalization. Indeed, as the editors of *Literary Landscapes: From Modernism to Postmodernism* have argued, issues of place and character – the question of "how they are where they are" – necessarily encourage us to consider what is "cultural and political" (De Lange et al. 2008: p. xiii). Initially in the novel, Charging Elk cannot imagine making a life for himself in France. While he is recuperating in the hospital, he panics at the thought of being left behind in Europe, far from his home and community. "To die here alone! What would happen to his *nagi*, his spirit? How would it find its way to the other side, to the real world beyond this one[?]" (p. 23). Charging Elk fears the possible cultural and spiritual death he would face if he were to remain in Marseilles. "His own *nagi* would run restless over the land here, far from his people, far from the real world. He could not stay here, waiting to die. He would not wait. With the help of Wakan Tanka, he would find his way home" (p. 23).

Charging Elk's attempts to return home are complicated, however, by bureaucratic red tape; he is officially reported dead in a case of mistaken identity after another Indian from the Wild West show named Featherman succumbs to the flu and dies in the same hospital.[6] As the months and years go by and Charging Elk faces a number of conflicts that prevent his homecoming, he slowly begins to realize that a return to life on the land he left may no longer be possible. Back home as a young man, Charging Elk had refused to cooperate with the US government's policies regarding tribal peoples. Rather than stay on the reservation or agree to be schooled far away from his home and his family, Charging Elk chose instead to relocate to a place in the badlands called the "Stronghold" where he and his friends lived by "hunting game, exploring, learning and continuing the old ways with the help of two old medicine people" (p. 14). Tribal belonging is thus complicated early in the text as the community itself is divided over how to best respond to the changes imposed by the US government. Charging Elk recalls that he and his friends "had laughed and mocked those Indians collecting their meager commodities, their spoiled meat, learning to worship the white man's god, learning to talk the strange tongue" (p. 20). While they resist the spatial confinement and forced assimilation that other members of his family and community reluctantly accepted, even life in the Stronghold provides only limited escape for Charging Elk and others after it creates deep rifts within the tribe. "[T]he white men, soldiers and settlers alike, were afraid of the Stronghold. The Indians out there were considered bad Indians, even by their own people who had settled at the agency and the surrounding communities" (p. 14).

Early in the novel, Welch thus foregrounds the problems that arise between place and identity for his Native American character, a complication that, Hsuan Hsu argues, often shapes the work of ethnic regionalists. According to Hsu, "regionalism should be understood not only in terms of social and economic geography, but also as a means of imposing and exploiting differential relationships to mobility," relationships that often involve metropolitan domination over peripheral spaces, an imbalance between the city and the countryside (2009: 237). As he explains:

being rooted in place can be experienced as either privilege or constraint, either a mode of agrarian independence or an inability to change one's circumstances. ... regions can function, for some readers and characters, as terrains that embody and expand the scope of American identity. ... They can also, however, serve as sites of captivity or foreclosure ... as sites where racially differentiated groups are allowed to work but prevented from dwelling, included as bodies but excluded as landowners, citizens, or social equals. (2009: 237)

While reservation life is not an appealing choice for Charging Elk and his friends, a retreat to the Stronghold likewise provides only limited options. "There was nothing left at home. The American bosses were making the *ikce wicasa* plant potatoes and corn. What kind of life was that ... ?" (p. 29). When Buffalo Bill's Wild West show recruits new Indian performers near his home, Charging Elk finds a possible alternative.

[H]e remembered the day Buffalo Bill's scouts came to Pine Ridge to select the young Oglalas who would go away and tour with the Wild West show. ... They were very excited because the show would take them to a land beyond a big water. It was the favored land to the east where the white men came from. They had never seen Indians and they would treat the Indians like important chiefs. (p. 32)

Charging Elk and his friends are lured by the thrill of traveling across the Atlantic to an unknown land, by the promise of having more autonomy than was available through life on the reservation, and by the realization that the salary they could earn as performers in the show would be large enough to share with their families who were struggling to survive back home (p. 33).

Upon arriving in Europe, Charging Elk and the other performers initially experience a modernist "shock of the new" in their encounters with a different culture, an entity that appears to them as strange and perplexing. Welch writes:

He saw the women in their strange dresses with the big butts. Then he saw an omnibus go by, with its two levels of passengers, and he remembered that he and some of the other Indians had ridden in such a wagon before, when the interpreters took them on the rare tour ... sometimes they would all wave, or whoop, at a pretty woman or cart full of meat. ... the young Indians enjoyed the spectacle of themselves reflected in the astonished eyes of the French people. (p. 22)

In Welch's novel, encounters with difference operate both ways. As the Indians gaze at the French and the French likewise eye the Indian performers or *Peaux-Rouges* ("red skins") as they were called, both groups become fascinated by their contact with the exotic other.[7] Furthermore, because these encounters appear through the perspective of Charging Elk and his friends, the novel helps provincialize French culture by providing descriptions of its various strange customs and defamiliarizing social practices.

At one point, Charging Elk recalls a story his friend back home had told him about a Wild West performance that had been given for the queen of England and how her husband the prince "had ridden in the show's stagecoach while the Indians chased it around the arena. Then all the white chiefs wanted to be chased by the Indians. They may have been important bosses in their lands but they were like children who wanted the Indians to chase them" (p. 32). Postcolonial critics have pointed to the ways imperialist stories of multicultural contact often present these encounters within a temporal logic that figures the non-European participant as cast out of time. Johannes Fabian uses the concept of chronopolitics to describe a denial of coevalness or coexistence that features the non-European as belonging outside history, as a child in relation to the European adult, or as a primitive, savage person instead of a civilized and modern being (1983: 31–2). In the story Charging Elk recalls, such temporal politics are critiqued as Europeans become childlike in their encounters with the Indians, who in turn prove to be the more worldly and experienced adults. Here Welch gestures toward a different understanding of temporality and identity; rather than featuring contact between a so-called Old World and New World with one side somehow always belated, the novel recasts the encounter. As critic Brigitte Georgi-Findlay argues, the cross-cultural meeting operates on new terms, as an interaction "between Old (Native) America and Old Europe," with each entity having a long history as well as well-established cultural traditions (2007: 105).

In his book, *Provincializing Europe*, postcolonial critic Dipesh Chakrabarty builds on Fabian's account in assessing how European ideas of time often operated alongside imperialist projects. While European Enlightenment thought advanced universalist notions of truth, reason, and the human, Chakrabarty argues that the European colonizer of the nineteenth century effectively "preached this Enlightenment humanism at the colonized and at the same time denied it in practice" (2000: 4). They did so largely by employing an "ideology of progress" which announced that the Other hadn't properly entered historical time yet (2000: 7). As a result, "inhabitants of the colonies ... were assigned a place 'elsewhere' in the 'first in Europe and then elsewhere' structure of time" (2000: 8). Colonized peoples were thus consigned "to an imaginary waiting room of history" that suggested all human populations were "headed for the same destination," while contending that "some people were to arrive earlier than others." For Chakrabarty, "that was what historicist consciousness was: a recommendation to the colonized to wait" (2000: 8).

In Welch's novel, Charging Elk is indeed consigned to the fate of waiting. The bureaucratic mistake that lists him as deceased relegates him to a state of non-existence and non-belonging. He is officially left waiting the return of his own humanity and citizenship, which has vanished with the stroke of French bureaucrat's pen. When he is imprisoned for killing an assailant, Charging Elk's status as a US citizen is debated by the French authorities, who belatedly decide he is a member of a separate Indian nation, a status that allows him to be reclassified as a political prisoner whereby he is pardoned and released (p. 361). With its convoluted and intricate sense of justice, the French system of law proves to be less than rational or enlightened in its dealings with Charging Elk. As if to draw further attention to the anachronisms of the French system of justice, the jail where Charging Elk is first held after his escape from the Marseilles hospital is described by one character as "right out of the Inquisition," while the prison where Charging Elk serves out his sentence was built in the medieval period to serve as a "Crusader fortress" (p. 344).

Global Affinities and Transnational Spaces

Through Charging Elk's experiences in Marseilles, Welch recasts the relations between margins and centers as well as between the metropolis and the provinces. Marseilles – the port city where he first resides – appears as a multicultural crossroads, a meeting ground where one can order "bouillabaisse or couscous for lunch" because of the imperial flows that bring to the city different populations of laborers and commercial products from all over the world (p. 95). Yet even with these diverse exchanges, the city is still home to ethnocentric and xenophobic characters who at times show a lack of worldliness and appreciation for cultural difference. Charging Elk is thus marginalized at various moments by some of the French characters as an innocent "child of nature," a pre-modern savage who seemingly does not share the same place in time and history as they do.

As he moves through the streets of Marseilles, however, Charging Elk eventually finds he has much in common with the colonial populations that also reside there. He discovers that in the city's slums live the new groups of immigrants from "the Barbary States and the Levant," Arab populations that always work the "worst jobs in the soap and hemp factories, the abattoirs and tanneries" (p. 84). Charging Elk later chooses to live in their neighborhood because he realizes that the Arab immigrants "were closer to his own than any of the others he had come across since he left Pine Ridge" (p. 190). He likewise forges alliances with other marginalized people in the city, from the working-class prostitute Marie to her friend Breteuil, who is outcast as a member of a sexual minority and who later devises a complicated scheme whereby he drugs and sexually assaults Charging Elk. In featuring a series of successful and unsuccessful allegiances, Welch's novel foregrounds the damaging effects of the politics of difference and how the creation of otherness – whether it involves sexual minorities, the working class, or members of colonized nations – produces its own irrational and violent blowback.

Furthermore, rather than only beginning with his journey to a new land, Charging Elk's experiences of displacement originate in prior global developments that shaped his life even before he joined the Wild West show on its travels across the United States and Europe. His arrival on the other side of the Atlantic places him on a circuit where Enlightenment beliefs about American Indians as primitive Others were initially developed and disseminated globally in a flow of ideas that also affected his early life in South Dakota. Ulla Haselstein argues that his travels to France "takes Charging Elk into the heart of whiteness" where ideas about the Noble Savage were first devised and at a time where a new version of "primitivist otherness" was emerging (2007: 236). The nineteenth-century fascination with the primitive, in fact, helped propel many Europeans to the American West, the romantic and celebrated land of wild Indians and wild nature that became a favorite setting for a number of writers and painters across the Atlantic. This cult of the primitive likewise helped make Buffalo Bill's Wild West show the huge success that it was.

From 1883 to 1916, the Wild West show experienced a tremendous popular reception, drawing millions of people to its performances across the United States and Europe. As Robert Rydell and Rob Kroes argue in their study *Buffalo Bill in Bologna*, the show became a major player in the "Americanization of the world," as US mass cultural forms like the show were exported globally where they helped define American national presence around the world (Rydell and Kroes 2005: 2). Both at home and abroad, the Wild West show staged interpretations of American history, with a particular focus on regional re-enactments of conflict between white settlers and American Indians on the so-called "frontier." In addition to its international travels, the Wild West show had a global dimension in the content of its performances. By the turn of the century, for instance, the show's Congress of Rough Riders of the World featured US cowboys and American Indians alongside representatives from other horse cultures across the globe, including Hungarians, Turks, North Africans, Mexicans, Russians, German, French, and Japanese (Kasson 2000: 4; Moos 2005: 152, 154). As Paul Redding argues, these performances pitted the international league of horsemen in a "race between races," with the logic of Social Darwinism ensuring that the US cowboy usually won the event (1999: 128).

Dan Moos argues that, as "the American West became an integral part of official culture, helping to delineate U.S. national identity during the late nineteenth and early twentieth centuries, Buffalo Bill's Wild West manifested the vision so necessary to a nation striving for greater political power internationally and great social cohesion internally" (2005: 155). Ironically, even as such national unity rested on continually defeating Native Americans and other national threats on staged battlefields, the show also enabled Charging Elk and his real-life counterparts to escape the very confinements of reservation and boarding-school life that were needed to ensure such internal national cohesion. While Moos points to the irony of a "subjugated people play[ing] hyperstylized images of themselves," he argues that many of the Indian performers accepted certain aspects of William Cody's visions of Native American identity "for practical and political purposes" (Moos 2005: 150). He contends that the show enabled its Indian participants to present themselves as "potential Americans" for national and international crowds (2005: 150). Likewise, Cody's relationship with the show's Native American performers was complicated, for even as he presented them as villains in his historical re-enactments, Cody looked after them in other ways, taking care, for instance, to ensure that his employees had equal rights and pay across the board (2005: 158).

Such complex power dynamics likewise shape Charging Elk's experiences throughout the novel. While Charging Elk is cast as a belated Other who seems to occupy a different place on an imagined historical timeline, the narrative provides a number of instances where these assumptions are effectively overturned. Charging Elk's early life had been shaped by a culture where dreams and visions carry powerful weight, and in the novel Welch shows how the European characters likewise abide by similar forms of knowledge that were supposedly banished by Enlightenment rationality, science, and logic.

At one point, Charging Elk recalls stories told to him about a virgin giving birth to a holy man, while a Catholic friend of his receives powerful visions from the Virgin Mary. In another instance, he adopts aspects of modern Enlightenment subjectivity as an autonomous, self-possessed individual when he lavishly spends money on himself rather than buy Christmas presents for the French family with whom he lives. In this case, the outcome of his transformation into an Enlightenment subject proves to be less than desirable, as Welch describes the shame Charging Elk feels in putting his own needs above those of others through acts of individualism that the character believes make him savage rather than civilized. Charging Elk reflects on the ways he had once been taught by his family "to share with others, whether it was the pain of the loss of a child or husband or an abundance of meat and berries. Somewhere along the way, he had lost that desire to share, replaced by an attention only to himself and his own desires" (p. 243). Charging Elk's stay in France does not have a fully civilizing effect on his identity and character, but instead makes him regress at times to less humane forms of behavior.

Identity, Place, and Globalization

The realization that multiple and shifting factors influence identity underpins the larger politics at play in Welch's novel, as the narrative offers insights about the challenges Charging Elk faces in becoming worldly and cosmopolitan while also maintaining an indigenous identity that is philosophically, spiritually, and ethically connected to tribal traditions rooted in another land. In this context, Andrea Opitz points to the ways Welch offers a complicated account of identity formation for American Indians. "Left behind like a ghost," she argues, "*Charging Elk* exposes how the 'Indian' is repeatedly produced as vanishing, quite literally, at the end of the show" (2006: 99). As a way of countering narratives about Vanishing Indians or essentialized understandings of self, Welch's novel "conceptualizes cultural identity as becoming – an identity that is performed and conceived in relation to the fragmented memories, histories of his own culture, the representation of him as 'exotic' ... and legal and political regulations" (Opitz 2006: 99). Ultimately the main character survives because he is amenable to change and adaptation in forging a new sense of social belonging; at the same time, his worldview remains fundamentally linked to the beliefs of his tribe. In that sense, the character opts for what James Donahue calls a "middle ground" (2006: 70), a realization that "separation from his homeland need not mean the loss of his identity" (2006: 58). By the end of his novel, Welch has recast American

Indian identity as fluid and adaptable in the context of national and global pressures, thus undermining Eurocentric attitudes about temporality and race, as well as about historicism and western American regionalism.

In reconceptualizing regionalism, identity, and narrative, James Welch contributes to a larger project of understanding of Native American identities in a global context. Brigitte Georgi-Findlay notes that *The Heartsong of Charging Elk* fits into a recent trend in Native American fiction that includes Leslie Marmon Silko's *Gardens in the Dunes* (1999) and Louise Erdrich's *The Master Butcher's Singing Club* (2003) and that has "opened perspectives on global networks and responsibilities" which offer new indigenous "visions of a connectedness that transcends geographic and cultural boundaries" (Georgi-Findlay 2007: 90). Cherokee-German author Thomas King, who grew up in California and now makes his home in Canada, is likewise known for adopting similar transnational frameworks in his writings. King has spent his literary career crossing national boundaries, not only as a working author and academic, but also in the imaginative worlds he has constructed in novels such as *Medicine River* (1989), *Green Grass, Running Water* (1993), and *Truth and Bright Water* (1999). Arguing that the national border – in his case, the 49th parallel – is a "figment of someone else's imagination," King has produced narratives whose indigenous characters move back and forth between the US and Canada and whose identities do not rely on rigid spatial delineations (King 2003: 102).

In making sense of a globalized West, it is useful to consider borders and boundaries as both fiction and fact, as a line imposed by someone else but also a demarcation that nevertheless carries great power. As Shari M. Huhndorf contends, Native American scholarship and writing offer important challenges to the ways postnational frameworks have been produced precisely because of the historical determinations of those borders and boundaries. As the founding moment in US history, the "colonization of Native America exposes U.S. identity, from its origins to the present, as constituted through conquest, the imposition of political control, and the appropriation of indigenous lands," she writes. "Contained by neither geographical region nor time period, this ongoing process cannot be marginalized; it implicates all non-indigenous peoples in that conquest" (2009: 16). Any study of a global or transnational West must thus attend to the violence that has gone into making such lines on the map as well as the efforts of many contemporary Native American writers who critique the limits that these boundaries and borders often pose for themselves and their work.

NOTES

1 For a representative sample of this work, see Gilroy 1993; Lowe 1996; Saldivar 1997; Rowe 2000; Lim et al. 2006; Anzaldúa 2007; Levander and Levine 2007; and Shukla and Tinsman 2007. For an overview of the limita-

tions of Frederick Jackson Turner's frontier model, see Tatum 2004.

2 See, for instance, Yamashita's *Tropic of Orange*; Castillo's *So Far From God*; and Ozeki's *All Over Creation*.

3   For a useful overview of the multiple spatial identities that comprise the American West, see Wrobel and Steiner 1997.
4   These events are described in Ferguson 2006: 36.
5   Ulla Haselstein notes how Welch had faced criticism for his treatment of place and time as well as his rearticulation of "homing in" as a strategy for Native American authors. As she explains, several scholars have "denigrated the novel as a corroboration of the theory of the 'Vanishing American'" (2007: 226). For more on Welch and the "homing in" strategy in Native American literature, see Lee Schweninger 2003.

6   Suzanne Ferguson notes that Welch worked closely with sources from the period; in the case of Indian performers with the Wild West show, some did die in the flu epidemic in 1889–90 in Marseilles and Spain. One man named Featherman died of smallpox, and Welch notes that he saw Featherman's dead certificate during a research trip to France (Ferguson 2000: 38).
7   For a related discussion of viewing politics and the project of returning the gaze, see Bernardin et al. 2003.

References and Further Reading

Anzaldúa, Gloria. (2007). *Borderlands/La Frontera: The New Mestiza*. San Francisco: Aunt Lute.

Bernardin, Susan, Lisa MacFarlane, Nicole Tonkovich, and Melody Graulich. (2003). *Trading Gazes: Euro-American Women Photographers and Native North Americans, 1880–1940*. New Brunswick: Rutgers University Press.

Campbell, Neil. (2008). *The Rhizomatic West: Representing the American West in a Transnational, Global, Media Age*. Lincoln: University of Nebraska Press.

Castillo, Ana. (2005). *So Far From God: A Novel*. New York: W.W. Norton.

Chakrabarty, Dipesh. (2000). *Provincializing Europe: Postcolonial Thought and Historical Difference*. Princeton: Princeton University Press.

De Lange, Attie, Gail Fincham, Jeremy Hawthorn, and Jakob Lothe. (2008). Introduction. In Attie De Lang, Gail Fincham, Jeremy Hawthorn, and Jakob Lothe, eds., *Literary Landscapes: From Modernism to Postmodernism*, pp. xi–xxiv. New York: Palgrave Macmillan.

Donahue, James J. (2006). "A World Away from his People": James Welch's *The Heartsong of Charging Elk* and the Indian Historical Novel. *Studies in American Indian Literatures: The Journal of the Association for the Study of American Indian Literatures*, 18/2 (Summer), 54–82.

Fabian, Johannes. (1983). *Time and the Other: How Anthropology Makes its Object*. New York: Columbia University Press.

Ferguson, Suzanne. (2006). Europe and the Quest for Home in James Welch's *The Heartsong of Charging Elk* and Leslie Marmon Silko's *Gardens in the Dunes*. *Studies in American Indian Literatures: The Journal of the Association for the Study of American Indian Literatures*, 18/2 (Summer), 34–53.

Georgi-Findlay, Brigitte. (2007). Transatlantic Crossings: New Directions in the Contemporary Native American Novel. In Elvira Pulitano, ed., *Transatlantic Voices: Interpretations of North American Literatures*, pp. 89–107. Lincoln: University of Nebraska Press.

Gilroy, Paul. (1993). *The Black Atlantic: Modernity and Double Consciousness*. Cambridge, MA: Harvard University Press.

Hafen, P. Jane. (2003). Indigenous People and Place. In Charles L. Crow, ed., *A Companion to the Regional Literatures of America*, pp. 154–70. Oxford: Blackwell.

Haselstein, Ulla. (2007). Double Translation: James Welch's *The Heartsong of Charging Elk*. In Elvira Pulitano, ed., *Transatlantic Voices: Interpretations of North American Literatures*, pp. 225–48. Lincoln: University of Nebraska Press.

Hsu, Hsuan. (2009). New Regionalisms: Literature and Uneven Development. In John T. Matthews, ed., *A Companion to the Modern American Novel, 1900–1950*, pp. 218–39. Oxford: Blackwell.

Huhndorf, Shari M. (2009). *Mapping the Americas: The Transnational Politics of Contemporary Native Culture*. Ithaca, NY: Cornell University Press.

Joseph, Philip. (2006). *American Literary Regionalism in a Global Age*. Baton Rouge: Louisiana State University Pres.

Kasson, Joy. (2000). *Buffalo Bill's Wild West: Celebrity, Memory and Popular History*. New York: Hill & Wang.

King, Thomas. (2003). *The Truth About Stories: A Native Narrative*. Toronto: Anansi Press.

Levander, Caroline F., and Robert S. Levine, eds. (2007). *Hemispheric American Studies*. New Brunswick: Rutgers University Press.

Lewis, R.W.B. (1995). *The American Adam: Innocence, Tragedy, and Tradition in the Nineteenth Century*. Chicago: University of Chicago Press.

Lim, Shirley, John Gamber, Stephen Sohn, and Gina Valentino, eds. (2006). *Transnational Asian American Literature: Sites and Transits*. Philadelphia: Temple University Press.

Lowe, Lisa. (1996). *Immigrant Acts: On Asian American Cultural Politics*. Durham, NC: Duke University Press.

Mariani, Giorgio. (2006). Rewriting the Captivity Narrative: James Welch's *The Heartsong of Charging Elk*. In Massimo Bacigalupo and Gregory Dowling, eds., *Ambassadors: American Studies in a Changing World*, pp. 214–19. Genoa, Italy: AISNA – Associazione Italiana di Studi.

Moos, Dan. (2005). *Outside America: Race, Ethnicity, and the Role of the American West in National Belonging*. Hanover: Dartmouth College Press.

Opitz, Andrea. (2006). "The Primitive Has Escaped Control": Narrating the Nation in *The Heartsong of Charging Elk*. Studies in American Indian Literatures: The Journal of the Association for the Study of American Indian Literatures, 18/3 (Fall), 98–106.

Ozeki, Ruth. (2004). *All Over Creation*. New York: Penguin.

Redding, Paul. (1999). *Wild West Shows*. Urbana: University of Illinois Press.

Rowe, John Carlos. (2000). *Post-Nationalist American Studies*. Berkeley: University of California Press.

Rydell, Robert, and Rob Kroes. (2005). *Buffalo Bill in Bologna: The Americanization of the World, 1869–1922*. Chicago: University of Chicago Press.

Saldivar, Jose David. (1997). *Border Matters: Remapping American Cultural Studies*. Berkeley: University of California Press.

Schweninger, Lee. (2003). Claiming Europe: Native American Literary Responses to the Old World. *American Indian Culture and Research Journal*, 27/2, 61–76.

Shukla, Sandhya, and Heidi Tinsman, eds. (2007). *Imagining Our Americas: Toward a Transnational Frame*. Durham, NC: Duke University Press.

Silko, Leslie Marmon. (1992). *Almanac of the Dead*. New York: Penguin.

Tatum, Stephen. (2004). Postfrontier Horizons. *MFS: Modern Fiction Studies*, 50/2, 460–8.

Tsing, Anna Lowenhaupt. (2005). *Friction: An Ethnography of Global Connection*. Princeton: Princeton University Press.

Welch, James. (2000). *The Heartsong of Charging Elk*. New York: Anchor.

Wrobel, David M., and Michael C. Steiner, eds. (1997). *The Many Wests: Place, Culture, and Regional Identity*. Lawrence: University Press of Kansas.

Yamashita, Karen. (1997). *Tropic of Orange*. Minneapolis: Coffee House Press.

33

Tumbling Dice: The Problem of Las Vegas

Stephen Tatum and Nathaniel Lewis

Rocks Off: The Problem of Development

A society that unthinkingly privileges the present, real time, to the detriment of past and future, also privileges accidents. (Paul Virilio, *The Original Accident*, 23)

"The problem of the West is nothing less than the problem of American development" (Turner 1992a: 205). With these words Frederick Jackson Turner opened his *Atlantic Monthly* essay of 1896, "The Problem of the West." Applied to Las Vegas in the early twenty-first century, the words sound prophetic, as the city over the past decade has fallen victim to the boom-and-bust cycle of the globalized world economy, an uncanny repetition of the uneven economic development plaguing the American West in Turner's era. For years regarded as one of the fastest-growing urban areas in the United States, Las Vegas evokes images of its constantly evolving built environment: casino-hotels, neon skylines, and urban sprawl, all epitomizing the relatively unregulated development of urban and suburban space in the post-1945 American West. Although by "development" Turner here primarily connotes economic growth through continuing material or physical expansion, his strategic use of this word at the end of the modernizing nineteenth century nevertheless also introduces some of the "problems" faced by historians, critics, and cultural producers studying the region's evolution into a postmodern, postindustrial society.

"The Problem of the West" represents a popular-press sequel to Turner's 1893 historiographical essay "The Significance of the Frontier in American History" (Turner

A Companion to the Literature and Culture of the American West, First Edition. Edited by Nicolas S. Witschi.

1992b), which argued that the essential features of both American democracy and the American character were produced by a westward-moving settler culture's frontier experience. Turner's repeated use of the word "development" in "The Problem of the West" further discloses the imprint of Darwinian theory: a phrase like "stages of development" connotes the evolutionary adaptations a settler culture was forced to make on its way West, its pre-existing "social conditions" continually modified by the "transforming influences of free land," with the result that the West – considered as a "social form" rather than geographical site – evolved from savagery to civilization:

> The West, at bottom, is a form of society rather than an area. It is the term applied to the region whose social conditions result from the application of older institutions and ideas to the transforming influences of free land. ... The wilderness disappears, the "West" proper passes on to a new frontier, and, in the former area, a new society has emerged from this contact with the backwoods. Gradually this society loses its primitive conditions, and assimilates itself to the type of the older social conditions of the East; but it bears within it enduring and distinguishing survivals of its frontier experience. Decade after decade, West after West, this rebirth of American society has gone on, has left its traces behind it, and has reacted on the East. (Turner 1992a: 205)

Turner was neither the first nor the last public intellectual to equate the regional West's historical fortunes with those of the nation. But what remains interesting over a century later is how "the significance" of the frontier gets transformed in his thinking into "the problem" of the West, in at least two dimensions. First, according to the US Census Bureau in 1890, the "frontier" as a category useful for registering a certain (low) level of population density was officially closed. Without the existence of the frontier, given Turner's logic, what would be the fate in a more urban, industrial United States of American democratic ideals it supposedly spawned? By 1896 American democratic ideals were to Turner's mind already troubled by the lingering economic turmoil that followed the 1893 Panic. Thus in his analysis, the deflation in agricultural prices throughout the 1890s and the steep plunge in the silver market after the 1893 repeal of the Sherman Silver Purchase Act had transformed a specifically "western problem" into a "social problem on the national scale."

More subtly embedded in Turner's notion of "development" is the second dimension of the "problem" posed by the West, one associated with understanding or interpreting historical "stages of development." However much one might identify economic, social, and political "forces" at work in history and, in the end, attribute "significance" or meaning, there remains in Turner's discourse an underlying, somewhat somber, realization that things inexorably change and accidents inevitably happen – that contingency often rules rather than the perceived patterns fostered by particular "forces." By Turner's own logic, the West constitutes not only "a form of society" and to some degree a geographical "section" or region of the country; it also defines a *temporal* condition, one supremely transformative, as transitory and ephemeral as is the Las Vegas Strip's spectacular "development" throughout the twentieth century. Turner's "West" reveals the very condition of temporal flux, with the ceaseless mobility of its settler culture westward imaged as a horizontal movement across the "page" of the western landscape – an image that anticipates what a century later Dave Hickey would describe, albeit on a smaller scale, as "the horizontal drift" or "long lateral blend of Vegas iconography" (1997: 22).

Conceptually speaking, such a West can never be identical with or fully present to itself in any one place or moment, for it is always in process, always emerging and evolving until – as Turner notes at the opening of his 1893 "Significance" essay – it is "closed." On the one hand, as he says in a well-known passage from his first important essay, "The Significance of History" (1891), "the aim of history ... is to know the elements of the present by understanding what came into the present from the past. For the present is simply the developing past, the past the undeveloped present" (Turner 1994: 19). Turner hungered, as Patricia Nelson Limerick writes, "for ideas that would hold the fragmented world together," believing that the historian's intellect "could diagram the working parts of human history and then show how the parts fit together" (2001: 158). From this perspective, Turner emerges as an early structuralist thinker, theorizing a grammar and syntax for the nation's "development," its forms of desire as well as of society. Notwithstanding Turner's seeming clarity of conviction in such statements, however, the fact is – as he acknowledges elsewhere in his work – that there remains no guarantee that the present will acknowledge, much less understand, the imprint of the past on its contours. Indeed, there remains nothing simple or transparent about the way any surviving "traces" of the past enter into and become visible in the present. So on the other hand, even as his archeological metaphors argue for a settler society's perennial rebirth at each stage of frontier "development," his assigning of origins and his celebration of originality – these gestures are always already haunted by foregone conclusions and by the subterranean "traces" of history's serial losses, its repeated extinctions.

Turner's "West" thus paradoxically centers both on its own originality (he uses the word "new" twenty-seven times in "The Problem of the West") and its repeatability ("Decade after decade, West after West"). Any repetition and any remembering – any replication of a past event, object, or thing – by definition can never be exactly identical or at one with itself, its origin. Writing around the time of Las Vegas' own beginning, "the problem of the West" for Turner is not only an economic and political problem that serves to equate the regional with the national identity. The phrase also signifies the problem of history itself – of how to witness, understand, and then represent its "stages of development." A generation before Turner, Henry David Thoreau summarized a national mythology when he wrote in his essay "Walking" that "we go westward as into the future" (2001: 235); but as we can see in Turner's discourse's disjunctive tonal registers and logical contradictions, Thoreau's "westward" directive, even when idealized in the form of the then-called "virgin land," gets composed of and informed by what we might call, following Paul Virilio, the "accidents" of the past. For these serve both to qualify faith in any master-narrative of progress and development through clearly defined "stages" and to become later the subject of our mourning and melancholia.

In the context of Las Vegas and its "development" over the past century – especially the transformations of its built environment over the past few decades through a series of architectural and marketing makeovers inaugurated by spectacular building implosions – there remains something haunting about revisiting Turner and the legacy of his thinking about the West. Conceptualized as a geophysical place overdetermined by history's indeterminacy, bound by a paradox of repetition and originality, and subject to the ongoing incompleteness or unevenness about the past's relation to the present, his "West" returns to us with a melancholy splendor from over a century ago. His essays published during the early years of Las Vegas' transformation from an isolated desert valley with a few ranches into an incorporated railroad town resemble a palimpsest, a complex verbal artifact whose exposed layers provide clues for anyone considering not only Turner's but also our present era's "problem of the West." With Turner's writings in mind, in short, when we retrace "the problem of the West" in the context of Las Vegas' "development," what must be acknowledged, for starters, is that an emergent, dominant structure of feeling about the West gets organized and sustained by a dialectical tension best defined, as Hickey remarks about the phenomenological experience of the Las Vegas Strip, as a "sleek frisson of anxiety and promise" (1997: 23).

On one level, it is a dominant structure of feeling whose "frisson" not only emanates from the seductive power of Las Vegas' "sleek," stimulating neon surfaces, but also one that, in our contemporary risk society signified by the prevalence of gambling, relays an intensified culture of consumption's primary anxiety about either proletarianization or moral decline. On another level, to anticipate Robert Venturi et al. writing on the Las Vegas Strip's built environment in the early 1970s, this dominant structure of feeling's "frisson of anxiety and promise" is grounded by the fact of *obsolescence*, apparent both in the fabric of historical narratives about western "development" and the cognitive maps of the Las Vegas built environment, itself repeatedly rebuilt and transformed over the past century, its past "traces" seemingly erased through a repetitive process that William L. Fox believes illustrates a fundamental "desire for immortality" (2005: p. xii). For a generation or more now, cultural historians have attempted to refute Turner's perceived nationalist positivism by identifying how the achievement of a distinctively American democratic polity and character was enabled not so much by the existence of free land on the western frontiers as by the violence of conquest. Still, perhaps that undeniable violence, rather than a cause helping revise our understanding of the "problem of the West," is itself an elusive symptom. Perhaps there is also something darker at work, for as Freud pointed out during Turner's era, the past is never totally erased or buried. It is repressed, only for its "traces" to return in uncanny fashion through the primary mechanism of repetition compulsion.

Of all these things – of all these "problems" of/with the West associated with history and with its representation or understanding – Las Vegas is the symbol. Or perhaps, thinking here of Melville's white whale, its "embodiment," rather than "symbol," for such a word suggests the history of any place as corporeal, as a material incarnation of the spectacle under the sign of the commodity and, simultaneously, as an elusive, spectral presence. We must account for how this *frisson* accruing from the dialectical movement between anxiety and promise has shaped the cultural production and meaning of Las Vegas in a variety of media and genres throughout the history of its development. *The systolic movement out*: accelerated speed and the promissory note of beauty tendered by a neo-Baroque aesthetic of excess; the fluid sprawl of the Strip south and west from Fremont Street; the promise communicated across Las Vegas' vast space by the billboards and neon signs and the post-Venturi architecture of themed environments, its Luxor Hotel casino's vertical white light registering a latter-day, secular and technological desert version of William Bradford's image of the Plymouth Colony as a "shining city on the hill." And, too, *the diastolic rhythm of return, of repetition and the retracing of pathways*: obsolescence and Virilio's "accident" encrypted in the city's corporeal presence, its sedimented remains on display at the Neon Boneyard and Moulin Rouge; in the spectral images of casinos imploding on YouTube videos or recycled in Hollywood movies; in the exploitation of workers in a service economy that periodically surfaces in the *mise-en-scène* of such popular television shows as *CSI: Crime Scene Investigation*; in the detritus of the Atomic West surrounding its Las Vegas epicenter, its imagined past scenario of environmental apocalypse uncannily repeated in future projections of Las Vegas as a ghost town when the Colorado River more or less runs dry.

For a century Las Vegas has reinvented itself for each new age of settlement and tourism – each new stage of capitalism's development – always moving forward, transforming itself, in Fox's words, both "as our desires shift ground in relation to other entertainments" and also in response to the gaming economy's expansion beyond Nevada's borders to include riverboat gambling, Indian casinos, and virtual gambling on the internet (Fox 2005: p. xiii). But, like Turner's westward-moving frontier, it always repeats itself. Amidst its "institutionalized indulgence," its investment in the spectacle's intensity of the moment, Las Vegas is also built upon the sepulchers of its and the region's past, as if Vegas Vic were Walter Benjamin's Angel of History, his foreshortened form now repositioned as part of "the Fremont Street experience" in our illuminated, digitalized present, even as his iconic cowboy face conjures up the nation's mythological western past. Where some might see, like Turner, a chain of events, history's separate currents composed and synthesized into a single wave, *this* "development" our Vegas Vic unceasingly sees – as does Hunter Thompson writing in Las Vegas about the end of the American Dream only fourscore years after Turner noted the frontier's closing – as a single catastrophe that keeps piling wreckage upon wreckage in front of his cowboy boots.

Casino Boogie: The Problem of Representation

Las Vegas space is so different from the docile spaces for which our analytical and conceptual tools were evolved that we need new concepts and theories to handle it. (Venturi et al., *Learning from Las Vegas*, 1972)

Through all of its transformations and reinventions over the past century – which, from one perspective, illustrate what Turner called "this perennial rebirth, this fluidity of American life, this expansion westward with new opportunities" (Turner 1992b: 2) – Las Vegas typically has been regarded by artists and cultural critics as expressing in purest form, for better or worse, the new aesthetic and democratic social order spawned by consumer capitalism and its associated technological developments. Just as Turner saw "the problem of the West" as in fact the problem of American development, "Las Vegas is a wonderful lens through which to view America," argues Dave Hickey, in part because it represents "the wellspring of our indigenous visual culture" (1997: 23). Hickey for one describes how the city "stretches out into the night like a neon garden, supine in its worldly innocence, the pure virus of American culture denatured, literally, in the petri dish of the desert – virgin territory" (1997: 175).

With phrases like "neon garden," "worldly innocence," and "pure virus," along with the implicit, gendered imagery of the odalisque reclining female nude ("stretches out"; "supine"; "virgin"), Hickey's phrasing on one level represents Las Vegas as a paradoxical space. In keeping with a host of other cultural critics who have written about the city since the landmark 1972 publication of Robert Venturi et al.'s *Learning from Las Vegas*, Hickey's Las Vegas blurs the boundaries between technology and culture, sexuality and innocence, purity and contamination. But on another level, his imagery here of the petri dish and the garden/desert binary effectively blurs the boundary between the secular and the sacred – as does architectural historian Reyner Banham when he concludes that indeed "it is in Las Vegas that one comes nearest to seeing gross matter transformed into ethereal substance by the power of light" (1975: 62). The result is that, to Hickey's way of seeing, Las Vegas's storied, neon cityscape epitomizes a kind of heavenly city or walled oasis in the desert, an illuminated, spatial urban utopia inoculated against both history's entropic forces and the environing dominant culture's puritanical repression of what he elsewhere labels "our own theatricality, instability, insincerity, and excess." Even as he recognizes how the city's commodified spectacle is grounded on the anxious intensities associated with risk, he nevertheless argues for its overriding *frisson* of possibility – its redemptive "promise." Thus, "the Saturnalia of Vegas and the redemptive rituals of [a] Siegfried and Roy recall a less class-ridden sense of American possibilities," illustrating to his mind the utopian possibilities of a truly democratic commercial or vernacular art (1975: 180).

Hickey's and Banham's by now familiar focus on Las Vegas' distinctive neon signs and its sprawling commercial strip highlights another familiar theme: how Las Vegas marks the transition to the reign of the sign, the image, or the simulacrum in relation to the new highway and automobile culture emerging after World War II. For Jean Baudrillard, for example, one only has "to see Las Vegas, sublime Las Vegas, rise in its entirety from the desert at nightfall bathed in phosphorescent lights, and return to the desert when the sun rises, after exhausting its intense, superficial energy all night long, still more intense in the first light of dawn, to understand the secret of the desert and the signs to be found there: a spellbinding discontinuity, an all-enveloping radiation" (1988: 127). What he calls "the power of the desert form," which is linked in his discourse to the analogous power of gambling, "is the erasure of traces in the deserts, of the signified of signs in the cities" (1988: 125). In Baudrillard's lexicon this is a way to describe how the hyperreal – the speeded-up circulation of signs or copies without origins – produces the so-called "desert of the real," whose towns "have about them something of the mirage, which may vanish at any instant" (1988: 125). From this alternative critical perspective, if Las Vegas can be said arguably to represent a spatial utopia, it should be regarded as a degenerate rather than the redemptive one Hickey describes. Degenerate because the Strip's seductive array of illuminated utopian fantasies, rather than providing for the possibility of cultural critique, instead – like the impact of the Mojave desert which surrounds Las Vegas – "supplies a prophylactic barrier against reality" (Rugoff, qtd. in Fox 2005: 4). For Baudrillard, its cityscape's particular merger of technological wizardry and endless capital accumulation promotes the intensities associated with the urban spectacle as a commodity, in the process reproducing not history *per se* but rather a succession of historical "styles," as well as an uncritical aesthetic sensibility on the part of its leisured consumers (see Harvey 2000: 166–8).

We have then, broadly speaking, two apparently conflicting cultural and critical responses to Las Vegas: one which embraces the city's utopian, liberating "promise," and the other which focuses on its dystopian, cynical erasures – its "anxiety." Yet within this thematic binary it remains fascinating how many writers, filmmakers, photographers, and artists through the years have considered the ways in which Las Vegas' "formlessness and tastelessness" (Banham's words) mark what might be termed a Turnerian "problem in development" both thematically and formally. The thematic problem – the utopian promise/dystopian anxiety paradox – may be understood as interpretive: How do we make sense of Las Vegas, its signs, meanings, and portents? What can we learn from Las Vegas? Or, what can it teach us? This problem is best articulated in *Learning from Las Vegas*, which seeks, as a result of its authors' exposure to the Las Vegas Strip, "to question how we look at things." The formal problem is the problem of representation: How best to depict and recode Las Vegas' development, its accelerated transformations of the built environment? What sign system, what aesthetic, best represents the city's seductive paradoxes, best accounts for the phenomenological experience of the Strip and Glitter Gulch? The point is that Las Vegas represents not only where it all comes together as a space of the spectacle created by late capitalism. As a paradoxical, largely neo-Baroque space of desire, it also realizes a western version of Foucault's heterotopia, a simultaneously mythic and real space of complexity and contradiction. Thus, even as it manifests the hyper-real/global network of flows and the seeming erasure of history, it also inspires revisionist historiography and innovative cultural productions about local and regional places.

When centered on Las Vegas, such interpretation and representation inevitably involve spatiality, the interplay of mobility and stasis, of the order and disorder created by the intersection of the built environment and the desert landscape, of the past and present. Roads create a network of directional markings upon the desert, a grid of movement and flow from which to read the proliferating cultural signs for meaning. As Venturi et al. write: "A city is a set of intertwined activities that form a pattern on the land. The Las Vegas Strip is not a chaotic sprawl but a set of activities whose pattern, as with other cities, depends on the technology of movement and communication and the economic value of land" (1972: 76). We will return to the "economic value of land" in the last section of this essay, for it remains a perennial complication for western "development," but for the moment let us consider this interplay of pattern, technology, movement, and land, which is to say *a spatial dynamic both exaggeratedly natural and culturally constructed*. In *Diamonds Are Forever*, for example, Ian Fleming offers a relatively early representation of "the ghastly glitter of The Strip" (2003: 132). Literalizing (or unintentionally parodying) the University of Chicago notion of "urban ecology" still influential in the 1950s, Fleming describes James Bond's first encounter with the Strip as seductively organic: "The desert on both sides of the road, which had been empty except for occasional hoardings advertising the hotels, was beginning to sprout gas stations and motels. ... The great six-lane highway stretched on through a forest of multi-colored signs and frontages until it lost itself downtown in a dancing lake of heat waves" (2003: 130–1). Fleming's imagery deliberately confuses the realms of nature and culture (gas stations "sprout" like plants; a sign "forest"), producing through Bond's eyes a largely ironic vision of Las Vegas as an attractive/repulsive "jungle of neon" (2003: 157), in which each tourist is reduced to a "customer-mouse in the central gambling trap" – what Fleming calls "a new school of functional architecture" (2003: 135). Evoking both an illusory jungle and a desert paradise, Las Vegas emerges here as an intentionally designed environment based on desire, in which no one is surprised by sin and every one is as dazed and confused as the highway which loses itself in a mirage of heat waves. Bond's cognitive dissonance upon his entry into Las Vegas anticipates by nearly two decades the definitive postmodern cognitive dissonance Fredric Jameson endures while navigating Los Angeles' Bonaventure Hotel.

Even as creative, critical, and popular responses to Las Vegas inevitably focus on the spatial dynamics of the Las Vegas built environment in relation to speed and temporality (as in Fleming's scene, so many prose works about Las Vegas begin with the driving experience), they also subtly and almost compulsively invoke the notion of historical transformation so central to the problem of development. This is hyperbolically true of the Strip's architectural "reproductions" of Venice, Rome, Paris, and the Wild West, for even as absurdly unrealistic simulacra of empire they nevertheless theorize a response to the past. Despite the charge by some that Las Vegas is a postmodern city with "no memory" (see Bruce Begout's *Zeropolis* [2003]), the "pattern upon the land" in Las Vegas inevitably tells a story of historic change: from desert to city, from Sin City to family playground, from the Strip to sprawl. At every moment, the surrounding desert – in concert with the spooling literary, cinematic, and televisual Las Vegas images that saturate our mediascape – reminds us of the past, reminds us of the problem of development, even as its vacant, undeveloped plots seem to promise or threaten future construction. That is, the paradoxes we saw in Frederick Jackson Turner's historicism *become* the abiding spectacle of Las Vegas. Consider how Tom Wolfe, writing in 1964, describes Bugsy Siegel's Flamingo aesthetic as "sweeping Las Vegas like gold fever." He writes: "And there were builders of the West equal to the opportunity. All over Las Vegas the incredible electric pastels were repeated. Overnight the Baroque Modern forms made Las Vegas one of the few architecturally unified cities of the world – the style was Late American Rich – and without the bother and bad humor of a City Council ordinance" (1995: 9). Wolfe contradicts himself by design, conjoining history's grand, hard-fought mythic West ("gold fever," "builders of the West") with the echo of the Turnerian West's claim of newness and freedom ("overnight," "without … ordinance"). Wolfe's allusion to the Baroque aesthetic is even more perceptive, for no style has ever produced such an effective combination of cultural restrictions (crowd control) and formal liberties (crowd inducements); no style has so thoroughly capitalized on the relationship between religious lyricism and vulgar spectacle.

Still, we would argue that the neo-Baroque Las Vegas style of representation ultimately belongs to Benjamin's *Trauerspiel*, that of allegories and ruins, in which "history has merged into setting" rather than being lost like Fleming's highway in the mirage of heatwaves. For even in Fleming's novel it makes perfect sense that the villain of *Diamonds are Forever*, Seraffimo Spang, has converted a dilapidated mining camp outside of Las Vegas, "a whole ghost town way out on Highway 95," into a re-creation of the Old West, a self-indulgent pleasure palace: "wooden sidewalks, a fancy saloon, clapboard hotel … even the old railroad station." James Bond is told by his driver that "way back in '05 or thereabouts, this dump – Spectreville it's called seeing how it's right alongside the Spectre range – was a rarin' silver camp" (2003: 148). The invocation of 1905 – the year of the SPLA&SL railroad's completion, of the frenzied auction of the Clark Las Vegas townsites, and of the Colorado/Salton Sea flood which led to the construction of the Hoover Dam – is no accident. The name "Spectreville" amounts to an inside joke, a spectral linking of the desert (Spectre Mountain), the region's iconographic frontier past, and the hyperreal present (Spectre as the organizational front for Bond's enemies).

Or consider another familiar example: the moment in *Bugsy* (1991) when Warren Beatty, standing alone in the late desert sun, has his epiphany. The year is 1945 and Beatty, playing Bugsy Siegel, is driving back to Los Angeles at high speed after a disappointing visit to the seedy cow town that was Las Vegas at the time. As his car speeds along he suddenly stops, walks into the desert, and experiences revelation. It is in many ways a hyperreal moment of cinematic confection, as Beatty concocts a Hollywood moment of western mythmaking notable primarily for its self-conscious artificiality. Viewers never forget that they are watching Warren Beatty making a movie, and that is central to the pleasure of the scene. We watch Beatty from our perch in the present as he re-creates an invented historical past, and then we watch him as actor, staring at the desert's apparent nothingness, peering into the future and envisioning the Flamingo, the Strip, banking on our own compulsive addictions to risk and entertainment to make the vision of the future come to fruition. If he is reading a landscape, he is also inventing a place and a time, and we can see the inchoate Las Vegas in his eyes. The hyperreality of the scene reverses Baudrillard's observation, for here the physical desert is the mirage, about to be swept away by the inevitable development of the hyperreal Strip that comes to constitute the real.

Bugsy Siegel is the closest thing in the Las Vegas story to a transcendental signified, for the legend of his desert epiphany amounts to a creation myth, being both the author/god's originating act and the apple-bite of prescient knowledge. In Michael Herr's telling of this foundational myth, Siegel "pulled off of Highway 91 and pointed towards the emptiness and said, decreed, fatally *insisted*, that right there in the middle of what looked just like nowhere to everyone else, he would build his fabulous Flamingo Hotel" (1986: 142). We can almost hear Siegel thunder into the void, "let there be light," and there was light, and it was neon. Siegel was the city's "practical father," in Herr's words, and "in his desert rapture he dreamed up everything we mean when we say Las Vegas" (1986: 143). Thus the dissemination of our own speaking about Las Vegas is grounded in the Siegel logos, or truth. Or, in Ian Fleming's more modest phrase, Siegel "saw the possibilities." But then, the death of Siegel and the later implosion of some of the early landmarks of the Strip – the Sands, the Stardust, the Desert Inn – symbolically register a loss of certainty about the very meaning of those "possibilities." Certainly by the mid-1960s, as Continental poststructuralism as practiced by Derrida and Barthes began its investigation of the culture of signs, many of the nation's major writers and critics were pondering the elusive epistemology of Las Vegas. And for a decade or so, from roughly 1964 through 1972, a surprising number of them – including, among others, Tom Wolfe, Joan Didion, Hunter Thompson, Robert Venturi, and Reyner Banham – agreed that Las Vegas was a major text, a jumble of signs and speed, of desires and decay. But they rarely agreed on the ultimate meaning, or even the existence of meaning.

"Almost everyone notes that there is no 'time' in Las Vegas, no night and no day and no past and no future," Joan Didion wrote in 1967; "neither is there any logical sense of where one is. One is standing on a highway in the middle of a vast hostile desert looking at an 80-foot sign that blinks STARDUST or CAESARS PALACE. Yes, but what does that explain? This geographical implausibility reinforces the sense that what happens there has no connection with 'real' life" (1995: 171–2). While this kind of postmodern riff on cognitive dissonance echoes Fleming and anticipates Jameson, at about the same moment Tom Wolfe raises the ante, so to speak, in remarking on the Strip's distinctive neon signage: "Las Vegas' sign makers work so far beyond the frontiers of conventional studio art that they have no names themselves for the forms they create" (1995: 6). Paradoxically, the emergent Las Vegas style is beyond the "frontiers" of conventional theory and practice, and yet such a style is nevertheless emblematic in Wolfe's eyes, America writ large: "Las Vegas takes what in other American towns is but a quixotic inflammation of the senses ... and magnifies it, foliates it, embellishes it into an institution" (1995: 5). As is the case, in the end, for

Didion, when she observes that "Las Vegas is the most extreme and allegorical of American settlements."

Las Vegas is simultaneously beyond the frontier, *sui generis*, and yet the most representative American settlement, and in *this* paradox we are returned to Turner's definition of "problem of the West." Las Vegas enacts the Turnerian repetition of historical patterns of the West, accelerating at high speed beyond the boundaries of the past cultural myths and artistic conventions seemingly into the future, all the while reproducing and ultimately reinscribing those very boundaries, myths, and conventions. Michael Herr intuits this paradox when he recognizes that visitors to Las Vegas "pronounced it fabulous, and inimitable, and never stopped to ask why it was, and has always been, that almost everybody who comes here for the first time has the feeling that they've been here before. And not just before, but all along" (1986: 140). Ross Macdonald had suggested something similar in his 1966 detective novel, *Black Money*. Undoing Fleming's and Hickey's imagistic conflation of the natural and the cultural, Macdonald's narrator-character Lew Archer remarks of Fremont Street that "the jostling neon colors of its signs made the few stars in the narrow sky look pale and embarrassed" (1966: 175). At the same moment that Joan Didion gazes in wonder at the recently constructed neon signs, Lew Archer has seen it all before. Following a lead in Las Vegas, he makes his way upstairs to the office of the casino boss, stopping at "the creative end of the money factory," the craps table, to watch "a girl in a low-backed gown fling herself and the dice around" (1966: 176). Later, emerging from the office, Archer makes his way out: "The man with the wide shoulders and narrow head was waiting to accompany me downstairs. The girl … was at one of the crap tables with a different escort. Everything that happened in Vegas seemed to be a repetition of something that had happened before" (1966: 180).

Macdonald's noir-inflected vagueness ("something") is marvelously precise, capturing the paradox of a place hurtling into possibility, with every new throw of the dice, while yet endlessly repeating the past (both the characters and the odds remain static). For their part, discussing the signs and pop architectures of the Strip, Venturi and Scott Brown identify in Las Vegas "a new but old direction in architecture," and their choice of the word "direction" (as opposed to "style" or "form") conveys their insistence on movement and development. But again, the aesthetic direction they chart itself is paradoxical, one oscillating between past commercial art conventions and more recent applications (the Pop Art influence). For them, due to the road's and the automobile's domineering presence, both space and time have to be reimagined. What the "inclusive architecture" of Las Vegas teaches is how, "in combination," the buildings and parking lots and signs "embrace continuity *and* discontinuity, going *and* stopping, clarity *and* ambiguity, cooperation *and* competition, the community *and* rugged individualism" (Venturi et al. 2000: 20). Deploying repetition and development, contradiction and reason, this sentence formally typifies both the sprawl and the order they perceive in the city. Though often labeled postmodernist, their theorized readings of Las Vegas ultimately reject such a simple formulation, in part because their embrace of popular culture remains situated squarely (as it were) in high culture (2000: 161), but more importantly because their approach itself, which they term "revolutionary," is opposed to the "progressive" and "utopian" modern architecture that would "change the existing environment rather than enhance what is there." Thus Venturi and Scott Brown are intent on "learning from the existing landscape," which is a way of saying that they are, as was Turner before them, reading the present, recalling the past, and thinking into the ways in which the past comes into the present. But if in unexpected ways Venturi et al. share their intellectual project with Frederick Jackson Turner, they do not share Turner's underlying pathos about the closing of the frontier. For Venturi and Scott Brown see the instability or contradictory juxtaposition of parts in the Las Vegas built environment's palimpsest as constituting an essential "development" of democratic ideals. History in this case is not a "problem" but rather a complex yet pleasurable scene of instruction.

The gift of Robert Venturi and Denise Scott Brown is not that they cracked the Las Vegas code but that, in rejecting the predictable, puritanical dismissals of Las Vegas, they saw the possibilities. The gerund of their book's title suggests process – of a being in a present defined, as the representations of Bugsy Siegel suggest, as a being haunted by the past while imagining a future. The familiar academic dismissals of Las Vegas strike the same chords today that they did in 1972. Venturi and Scott Brown emphasize that they are not questioning "Las Vegas's values": "the morality of commercial advertising, gambling interests, and the competitive instinct is not at issue here, although, indeed, we believe it should be in the architect's broader, *synthetic* tasks" (2000: 6). To this we would add serious concerns about the environmental sustainability of the region's sprawl, as well as the troubling reproduction of capitalist consumer-culture as a hyperreal. But dismissals of Las Vegas themselves tend to reproduce abstractions that abrade on one another, as if we have learned nothing – they are solutions that never acknowledge the problem(s) of Las Vegas.

Shine a Light: The Problem of Place

> The more deeply one ventures into the superficial space of the Strip, the more it appears to be symptomatic of our current cultural condition. Las Vegas illuminates the ephemerality that is our "reality." ... The bright lights of the Strip stage a virtual potlatch of meaning. Instead of communicating meaning, which can be read at a distance, proliferating signs immerse us in a superficial flux that never ends. (Mark Taylor, *Hiding*, 1997)

Excerpted from the conclusion to his "Ground Zero" chapter, Mark Taylor's comment reminds us of how Las Vegas' developmental stages over the past century have long been regarded, both by cultural critics and by artists working in a diversity of genres and media, as being "symptomatic" of our cultural condition. Writing in the period between the assassinations of Robert Kennedy, Jr., and Martin Luther King and the 1972 presidential election and subsequent Watergate scandal, for example, Hunter

Thompson's persona in *Fear and Loathing in Las Vegas* locates the "main nerve" of the American Dream in the Horatio Alger-like history of the Circus Hotel casino owner, a man who as a kid dreamed of running away to join the circus and who now "has his *own* circus, and a license to steal, too" (1998: 191). In Douglas Coupland's 1995 novel *Microserfs*, a character argues that mega-themed resorts such as the Las Vegas MGM Grand (at the time of its opening the hotel with the largest number of rooms in the world), represents "the Detroit of the postindustrial economy" (1995: 337). We are always, so it seems, "learning from Las Vegas," but Coupland's character claims that Las Vegas raises a different "problem of the West" than that outlined by Frederick Jackson Turner at the turn of the twentieth century, let alone Robert Venturi and his architectural colleagues in the late twentieth century. For Taylor's explicit contrast here between the Strip's signs, which can be read for meaning and orientation in space, and its "proliferating signs [which] immerse us in a superficial flux" highlights the crucial transformation in "our cultural condition" since the moment of Venturi, Scott Brown, and Izenour's *Learning from Las Vegas*.

For Venturi et al., monumental neon signage provides orientation, direction, and – yes – meaning within the Strip's commercial transformation of the West's vast spaces in relation to automobile speeds. But beginning with the entrance of entrepreneur Steve Wynn onto the scene and the construction between the 1980s and the end of the century of such themed mega-hotel casino resorts as the Mirage, the Bellagio, and Mandalay Bay, the Strip was transformed yet again. As Robert Venturi and Denise Scott Brown described this transformation in 1996, nearly a quarter-century after their influential *Learning from Las Vegas* was published, it was a transition from commercial strip and urban sprawl to boulevard and Disneyland-type scenography; from electric to electronic; from neon to pixel signage; from pop culture kitsch to gentrification and upscale taste in dining, entertainment, and shopping (McMorrough 2009: 142). Indeed, both the Strip and Fremont Street emerged as largely *pedestrian* promenades, dominated by an endless array of electronic screens and digital displays (rather than neon *per se*). The Strip's newer hotel casino signage typically featured short video sequences relying on computer or television displays; the so-called "Fremont Street Experience" was created by an overhead, constantly changing, computer-animated electronic skin or surface. No longer looking through an automobile windshield and passively observing the Strip's or Fremont Street's cinemascape unwind, participant-spectators are now immersed in what Hunter Thompson had earlier called "the circus." And thus as reality itself becomes dematerialized, its substance or forms occluded by pulsing and flickering light displays, its stable meaning sacrificed (hence "potlatch") by means of the technological sublime's electronic, simulated fire, Taylor argues that the kind of faith in the signifier–signified relationship displayed by Venturi et al. has become misplaced.

Certainly this extended attention to surfaces ("the superficial space of the Strip") and to the intensities of the moment ("the superficial flux") underlined by imagery of illumination suggests that the Las Vegas built environment not only blurs the boundary between so-called high and low or popular art, but also that between the zones of art or culture and commerce. Along with the erosion of boundaries highlighted by most commentators – some with *Learning from Las Vegas* in mind – who find Las Vegas illustrative of a postmodern, populist aesthetic, the more recent transformation of Las Vegas into an interactive pedestrian promenade with simulated attractions also dissolves the boundary between the real and the virtual. On the one hand, we would argue that such boundary dissolution and the accompanying cognitive dissonance it produces have accompanied Las Vegas' development since its origins in 1905. On the other hand, such boundary dissolution in Las Vegas' more recent development, where the real and the virtual have become interchangeable, identifies an emergent "problem of the West": this is the fate of place or of regional identity as a result of what Coupland's character labels our "postindustrial society."

As William Fox notes, driving on I-15 across the desert – with its extremes of heat and cold; its unfamiliar vegetation and seemingly open vast space – "was a disorienting experience, and thus one quickly romanticized as an adventure into the exotic" (2005: 3). For Fox, Las Vegas' existence as "a place in the sun," an oasis seemingly divorced from the constraints imposed by its physical environment, fostered a series of global architectural fantasies on the Strip that remarkably swerved the Strip's spectacle away from its initial desert- or western-themed branding (for example, the Frontier; the Sahara). Still, it's not so much the "placelessness" occasioned by the simulated movie set appearance of Las Vegas' built environment that needs to be emphasized here. Rather, we believe it important to recognize how the accumulating imagery of flow or flux and circulation – whether attached to the speed of automobiles (by Venturi or Fox) or of electric signs and video displays (by Taylor) – diagnose both the presence and the consequences of a globalizing world system's economic restructuring both of Las Vegas and of the regional, and national landscapes. From this perspective, Las Vegas represents not only what Didion calls an "allegorical American settlement," but also is symptomatic of how, in a networked global economy enabled by advanced communication technologies, there results a "separation between functional flows [of people, technology, and capital] and historically determined places as two disjointed spheres of human experience. People live in places, power rules through flows" (Castells 1989: 349).

As the example of the Venetian Hotel casino in Macau as well as Las Vegas suggests – global, macroeconomic forces, striving to integrate manufacturing production, commercial trade, and speculative investments with new technological paradigms (such as animatronics and robotics) – are redrawing and in the process determining the contour lines of local, regional, and national maps. For one thing, global flows of capital investment and visual imagery (think feature-film landscapes and Travel Channel television specials) collapse the older binaries of global/local or metropolitan center/regional periphery associated with the colonialism of Turner's era. As the spectacular rise of the convention and tourism/entertainment industry suggests, the local or regional "exotic" difference – crucial features of what are now called "branding" or marketing strategies – are rearticulated with transnational markets. One result of visual and verbal "branding" – think of the slogan "What Happens in Vegas Stays in

Vegas"; of the iconic "Welcome to Las Vegas" sign on the Strip – is this: the local or regional must now be understood less as a specific geographical locale and more as a product of visual and verbal discourse, a cultural imaginary produced by the intersection of media imagery, transnational capital, and the voluntary and forced travel of peoples to a particular locale as a result of consumer desire.

If we are asked to think of the local and regional not as particular places, nor as Turner's form of society, but rather as discursive, imagined constructs produced by the flows of capital investment – human populations, technology, and media imagery – along *non*-isomorphic paths, then it is no longer feasible to demand or expect a one-to-one or isomorphic relation between a local or regional culture and its particular topography. Epitomized by Cirque du Soleil's dominant presence on the Strip, in the increasingly postindustrial environment ruled by global flows of data, electronic technologies, and imagery, local or regional cultural economies are deterritorialized, unmoored from specific physical places. The difference now is that if once upon a time traveling across the desert to reach Las Vegas effectively divorced one from the reality of place, now the theme-park spectacle of "Las Vegas" simply exaggerates or intensifies what is our everyday virtualized "desert of the real." Further, following cultural geographer Edward Soja's work, new geographies of power emerge as a result of the globalizing world system's continuous restructuring of the economic landscape as a space of flows in tension with the space of places. Between the national and global scale, for instance, there exists "supra-state regionalism" as represented by such entities as the European Union. Between the national and local or regional economic scales, however, there exists a new geography of power Soja calls the "city-region states," whose intrusion in the transnational geographies of flows creates less a sense of regional identity as much as "a global network of local places" (Soja 1989: 157–89; Sassen 2000: 226). From this perspective, postindustrial Las Vegas represents one of the emergent and powerful "city-region states," a nodal point on the transnational economic grid in the American West along with Salt Lake City, the San Francisco Bay area, Los Angeles, and Mexico City.

Such networked "city regions" are not only linked by the tourist grid of flows (Los Angeles and Hollywood linked with Las Vegas and the Zion, Bryce Canyon, and Grand Canyon National Parks circuit). They are also linked by technological developments associated with the military, aerospace, and entertainment industries, located physically in the American West, and economically with manufacturing zones in Asia. Both the advanced digital effects technology associated with cinema and computer online gaming and the animatronics associated with theme parks and the entertainment industry in California and Nevada compose a postregional grid linking Palmdale, California, with Area 51 in southern Nevada; the Bay Area's Pixar and Industrial Light and southern California's Walt Disney Corporation with Harrah's Entertainment Corporation in Las Vegas; and, of course, as has been the case since the Strip's initial development and expansion during and after World War II, Hollywood-style celebrity culture and Las Vegas showrooms. The transformation of the traditional geopolitical space defining the regional into "a global network of local places" registers how critics need to rethink (and reorganize) the spatial hierarchies usually taken for granted, such as local < national < global. With all the global flows of people, images, technology, and capital coming together in local places like Las Vegas, the spatial hierarchies directing critical cultural analysis need to be reframed: local > national > global.

In the context of such social, political, and economic transformations which ask us to re-evaluate the lure of the local, so to speak, what are the consequences for critical thinking about the local or regional cultural economy? If, as Soja argues, it is still entirely possible for a local or regional cultural economy to function amidst the circuits of global flows, what are this emergent cultural economy's major features? What themes, forms, images, and rhetorical figures begin to define what we might call a postregional cultural style, one that nevertheless bears the traces of an older regional iconography and mythology about so-called "western" places with their specific histories? As Krista Comer asks, in the process of answering such questions triggered by any "post" critical impulse, "Can a critical field that began by way of an oppositional identity and an ethics of place retain that ethics as on important genealogy while evolving beyond it?" (Comer forthcoming: 2–3).

For starters, we might well consider how the emerging discursive terrain of an emergent, deterritorialized postregional cultural imaginary materializes as a particular *interface* between geographical or topographical environments, finance protocols, and emergent types and divisions of labor. And as the non-isomorphic paths of people, capital, and images surpass fixed geopolitical boundaries, we should be alert to how – in novels like Coupland's *Microserfs* and in television shows like *CSI: Crime Scene Investigation* – postregional economies of representation focus on how embodied "laboring populations" are brought "into the lower-class sectors and spaces of relatively wealthy societies" based on traffic in data, information, and investment capital (Appadurai 1996: 37). Defining the (post)region in our globalizing world-system through the particular flow of laboring bodies as they interface with the spaces of relatively wealthy societies directs our attention to the Las Vegas "city state region" interface of commerce, tourist, and entertainment zones, university research and development, and suburban corporate campuses. In considering Las Vegas as such a "city state region," what comes to the foreground is that interface between embodied human (and animal) bodies and computer and digital technology and robotics. In short, the new "problem of the West" is the technological prosthesis between humans and machines. And though the ghosts of Howard Hughes and Frank Sinatra and even Navajo skinwalkers may well haunt our moment's cybernetic developments, this particular interface further manifests spectrality as theme, metaphor, and principle through cultural productions stressing the flickering images and languages pulsing on the surfaces of electronic screens, monitors, and displays of computers, on cellular devices, and other miniaturized technologies and programmed machines and virtual environments powered by electricity generated from the West's coal and water sources.

We might call this interface the emergent postregional western dream of "becoming electronic," which of course starkly contrasts with the perennial western American cultural dream of "becoming authentic" by reverting to the aboriginal or animal primitive on Turner's westward-moving frontier lines of settlement. With this kind of interface and this version of the spectral in mind, perhaps the forensic lab detailed in *CSI*, or the computerized slot machines in Nevada casinos that return to gamblers paper receipts with universal bar codes rather than actual coins, most compellingly illustrate another way to approach rather than leave Las Vegas.

REFERENCES AND FURTHER READING

Appadurai, Arjun. (1996). *Modernity at Large.* Minneapolis: University of Minnesota Press.

Banham, Reyner. (1975). *Age of the Masters: A Personal View of Modern Architecture.* London: Architectural Press.

Baudrillard, Jean (1988). *America*, trans. Chris Turner. London: Verso.

Begout, Bruce. (2003). *Zeropolis: The Experience of Las Vegas.* London: Reaktion.

Campbell, Neil. (2000). *The Cultures of the New American West.* Edinburgh: Edinburgh University Press.

Castells, Manuel. (1989). *The Informational City: Information, Technology, Economic Restructuring, and the Urban-Regional Process.* Oxford: Blackwell.

Comer, Krista. (Forthcoming). *Exceptionalism, Other Wests, Critical Regionalism. American Literary History.* Available online through Oxford University Press: Advance Access, published Aug. 24, 2010, doi:10.1093/alh/ajq043.

Coupland, Douglas. (1995). *Microserfs.* New York: HarperCollins.

Didion, Joan. (1995). Marrying Absurd. In Mike Tronnes, ed., *Literary Las Vegas: The Best Writing about America's Most Fabulous City*, pp. 170–4. New York: Henry Holt.

Dunne, John Gregory. (1974). *Vegas: A Memoir of a Dark Season.* New York: Random House.

Fleming, Ian. (2003). *Diamonds Are Forever* [1956]. New York: Penguin.

Fox, William L. (2005). *In the Desert of Desire: Las Vegas and the Culture of Spectacle.* Reno: University of Nevada Press.

Harvey, David. (2000). *Spaces of Hope.* Berkeley: University of California Press.

Herr, Michael. (1986). *The Big Room.* New York: Summit Books.

Hickey, Dave. (1997). *Air Guitar: Essays on Art and Democracy.* Los Angeles: Art issues Press.

Limerick, Patricia Nelson. (2001). *Something in the Soil: Legacies and Reckonings in the New West.* New York: W.W. Norton.

Macdonald, Ross. (1966). *Black Money.* New York: Knopf.

McMorrough, John. (2009). On Billboards and Other Signs Around (*Learning from*) Las Vegas. In Aron Vinegar and Michael J. Golec, eds., *Relearning from Las Vegas* [1996], pp. 129–46. Minneapolis: University of Minnesota Press.

Sassen, Saskia. (2000). Spatialities and Temporalities of the Global: Elements for a Theorization. *Public Culture*, 12, 215–32.

Soja, Edward. (1989). *Postmodern Geographies: The Reassertion of Space in Critical Social Theory.* London: Verso.

Taylor, Mark. (1997). *Hiding.* Chicago: University of Chicago Press.

Thompson, Hunter. (1998). *Fear and Loathing in Las Vegas: A Savage Journey to the Heart of the American Dream* [1971]. New York: Vintage.

Thoreau, Henry David. (2001). Walking [1862]. In *Collected Essays and Poems*, ed. Elizabeth Hall Witherell. New York: Library of America.

Turner, Frederick Jackson. (1992a). The Problem of the West [1896]. In *The Frontier in American History* [1920], pp. 205–21. Tucson: University of Arizona Press.

Turner, Frederick Jackson. (1992b). The Significance of the Frontier in American History [1893]. In *The Frontier in American History* [1920], pp. 1–38. Tucson: University of Arizona Press.

Turner, Frederick Jackson. (1994). The Significance of History [1891]. In John Mack Farragher, ed., *Rereading Frederick Jackson Turner: "The Significance of the Frontier in American History" and Other Essays.* New York: Henry Holt.

Venturi, Robert, Denise Scott Brown, and Steven Izenour. (2000). *Learning from Las Vegas* [1972]. Cambridge, MA: MIT Press.

Virilio, Paul. (2007). *The Original Accident*, trans. Julie Rose. Malden, MA: Polity Press.

Wolfe, Tom. (1995). Las Vegas (What?) Las Vegas (Can't hear you! Too noisy) Las Vegas!!!! In Mike Tronnes, ed., *Literary Las Vegas: The Best Writing about America's Most Fabulous City*, pp. 1–24. New York: Henry Holt.

Index

A Companion to the Literature and Culture of the American West, First Edition. Edited by
Nicolas S. Witschi.
© 2011 Blackwell Publishing Ltd. Published 2011 by Blackwell Publishing Ltd.